Turning Points

De Gruyter Contemporary Social Sciences

—

Volume 37

Turning Points

Challenges for Western Democracies
in the 21st Century

Edited by
Holger Janusch, Witold Mucha, Julia Schwanholz,
Alexander Reichwein and Daniel Lorberg

DE GRUYTER

The printing of this publication was subsidized by the Faculty of Social Sciences at the University of Duisburg-Essen.

ISBN 978-3-11-163103-5
e-ISBN (PDF) 978-3-11-127290-0
e-ISBN (EPUB) 978-3-11-127294-8
ISSN 2747-5689
e-ISSN 2747-5697

Library of Congress Control Number: 2023944089

Bibliographic information published by the Deutsche Nationalbibliothek
The Deutsche Nationalbibliothek lists this publication in the Deutsche Nationalbibliografie; detailed bibliographic data are available on the internet at http://dnb.dnb.de.

www.degruyter.com

Preface

This edited volume is the result of the conference entitled *Turning Points in Democracies. Challenges and Opportunities for the EU and the U.S.* in Wuppertal in March 2022, hosted by the NGO Publik e.V. and organized by the editors of this volume.

The conference took place during the last third of the COVID-19 pandemic under strict infection control measures. At that time, many of the participants, if not all, had not attended such an event live and not only digitally for over 2 years. Before the pandemic, it was normal for scientists to go to such events frequently. But since the beginning of the pandemic, many things were no longer normal. Now that more than a year has passed since the conference, the pandemic is officially over. The old normal had given way to a new normal and this now again to a new one, or is it simply the old normal again? Was the COVID-19 pandemic actually a turning point, and if so, for what? We can ask the same about many events that challenge the normal. The Russian war on Ukraine, Brexit, the Trump presidency, climate change, digitalization and now AI make us wonder if the world will be the same afterwards. Which events are or will become turning points and how can this concept be understood and made scientifically fruitful? To explore these questions, political scientists as well as economists and historians have come together in Wuppertal to discuss the concept and meaning of turning points and have brought together their reflections and insights in this anthology. We hope you enjoy reading this book and that it will provide you with one or the other turning point in your thoughts.

We would like to thank all participants for enriching the workshop and also all authors for their contributions that made this anthology possible. In addition, we thank all the helpers of Publik e.V. for the great conference realization in the beautiful "Alte Glaserei" in Wuppertal. Last but not least, we are grateful and happy for the interest of De Gruyter in this anthology and the possibility to publish it in the Contemporary Social Sciences series.

Julia Schwanholz, Berlin 2023
Holger Janusch, Berlin 2023
Witold Mucha, Düsseldorf 2023
Daniel Lorberg, Berlin 2023
Alexander Reichwein, Gießen / Frankfurt, 2023

https://doi.org/10.1515/9783111272900-202

About the Editors

Holger Janusch is a Professor of International Relations with a special focus on US foreign and security policy at the Department of the Intelligence Services at the Federal University of Applied Sciences for Public Administration, Berlin, Germany. Previously, he worked as an Associate Professor at the Rheinische Friedrich Wilhelms University in Bonn, Germany and as a guest professor at the Andrássy University in Budapest, Hungary. He also was a visiting scholar at the Johns Hopkins University in Washington, DC. His research focus is on power in IR theory, international negotiations, and US foreign and trade policy.

Witold Mucha is an interim Professor of Political Economy with a special focus on the international political economy of the Global South at the Institute of Social Sciences at the Heinrich-Heine University in Düsseldorf , Germany. Previously, he worked as researcher at the Institute for Advanced Studies in the Humanities (KWI) and the Institute for Development and Peace (INEF) at the University of Duisburg-Essen, Germany. He also was a visiting scholar at the Centre for Advanced Internet Studies (CAIS) at the Ruhr University in Bochum, Germany, and the School of Political Science and International Studies (POLSIS) at the University of Queensland in Brisbane, Australia. Before joining academia he has been engaged in development cooperation in Latin America and Sub-Saharan Africa. His research focus is on international relations and peace and conflict studies.

Julia Schwanholz is a Political Scientist and Senior Lecturer at the University of Duisburg-Essen, Germany. Her expertise lies in parliaments, democracy, and public policy research with an emphasis on digital transformation. She represented interim professorships for democracy research as well as comparative politics and ethics in politics at several German Universities. She has held research assignments in Australia (University of Melbourne; Monash University, Melbourne; Queensland University of Technology, Brisbane), in France (Sciences Po, Paris), in the Netherlands (University of Groningen), in Sweden (Lund University), and in Germany at the Alexander von Humboldt Institute for Internet and Society (HIIG, Berlin).

Alexander Reichwein is a Senior Lecturer in International Relations and PostDoc Researcher at the Department of Political Science at the Justus-Liebig-University in Gießen, Germany. He is also a co-speaker of the research section Norms and Changes in Global Politics at the Giessen Graduate Centre for Social Sciences, Business, Economics and Law (GGS). Amongst others, he was Guest Lecturer and Research Fellow at the Department of Political Science at the University of Copenhagen, Denmark. Alex is doing research on the Intellectual History of the Discipline (I)nternational (R)elations and on the European 20th Century theoretical traditions in IR, on the Varieties of Realism in IR and in Foreign Policy Analysis, and on Humanitarian Interventions and the Responsibility to Protect with a focus on the misuse of norms by states. Alex holds a PhD in Political Science from the Goethe-University Frankfurt with a thesis on Hans J Morgenthau's liberal and normative Realism (2014).

Daniel Lorberg is a Professor of Economics and Business Administration at the Department of Social Security Administration at the Federal University of Applied Sciences for Public Administration in Berlin, Germany. Previously, he spent two decades as a science manager and consultant. Among other positions, he was general director and director of economics and social sciences at Solar Decathlon Europe, the largest international sustainability competition, lecturer and management director at the Institute of Political Science at the University of Wuppertal, Germany, and founding

https://doi.org/10.1515/9783111272900-203

manager of the IST University of Management. He is an author and editor of various publications in the field of economics and politics and has been a lecturer and visiting scholar at many universities in Germany and around the world, including the United States, China, South Africa, and Hungary. His research focuses on change and stability in the relationships between business, government, and society.

Contents

Holger Janusch, Witold Mucha, Julia Schwanholz, Daniel Lorberg
and Alexander Reichwein

Introduction: Turning Points, Typology, and Puzzles

At the beginning of the 21st century, liberal democracies are facing both old and new challenges and threats causing fragmentation, instability, and fear. Economic crises such as global financial crises and the Covid-19 pandemic have threatened the welfare and social cohesion of democracies. In some cases, these crises have caused increasing polarisation in societies and disenchantment with politics, undermining the legitimacy and functioning of democracies. As a result, and facilitated by other events such as migration, populism, and nationalism are gaining ground in democracies, threating their liberal norms, policy making, and institutions. The consequences of rising populism are not limited to domestic challenges for democracies. Right-wing populism has hampered international cooperation among democracies and undermined international institutions. For instance, Brexit endangered the painstaking European integration process that has been taking place since the end of World War II. Also, the Trump presidency led to the United States withdrawing from international commitments and treaties such as the Paris Agreement on Climate Change and the nuclear deal with Iran.

Further, autocratic states, especially revisionist great powers, increasingly challenge the liberal world order. Russia's invasion of Ukraine poses serious threats not only to the stability of a young consolidating democracy, but to the peaceful European security architecture. In addition, the economic, military, and technological rise of China is causing growing tensions and rivalry in the Indo-Pacific region, whether it is about the status of Taiwan, territorial disputes in the South China Sea, or unfair trade practices. Thereby, China questions basic principles and norms of the existing liberal world order. As a consequence of these domestic and international challenges, international institutions such as the United Nations and World Trade Organisation have decreased legitimacy and are pressured to reform and transform, with no tangible solution in sight. If these problems are not enough, on

Holger Janusch, Federal University of Applied Sciences for Public Administration, Faculty of Intelligence Services
Witold Mucha, Heinrich-Heine University Düsseldorf, Institute of Social Sciences
Julia Schwanholz, University of Duisburg-Essen, Department of Political Science
Daniel Lorberg, Federal University of Applied Sciences for Public Administration, Faculty of Social Security Administration
Alexander Reichwein, Justus-Liebig University Giessen, Department of Political Science

https://doi.org/10.1515/9783111272900-001

top democracies are confronted with fundamental challenges such as digitalisation, demographic change, and climate change. All these cross-cutting issues and mega trends put pressure on democratic societies toward costly transformation processes. Moreover, they are not only transforming societies and the global economy but are also deepening social inequalities and instigating possible old and new challenges and threats within democracies.

In public discourse and academia, these developments and challenges are often referred to as *turning points*. For instance, the reoccurrence of war in Europe is argued to be a turning point for the European security architecture. China's rise may be a breaking point for the liberal world order. Brexit is called a critical juncture for European integration. Migration may lead toward a tipping point for the social cohesion of democracies by facilitating polarisation and right-wing populism. Studies in political science, including comparative politics, political economy, public policy, and international relations have investigated turning points such as major crises, conflicts and wars, revolutions and transformations, or radical changes domestically and at the international level. However, the definition and conceptualisation of turning points as a key term in political science has been surprisingly neglected. While major concepts such as *conflict* (Nye 2017a), *crisis* (Phillips and Rimkunas 1978), *power* (Baldwin 2016; Barnett and Duvall 2005; Lukes 2021; Nye 2017b), and *norms* (Deitelhoff and Zimmermann 2020; Finnemore and Sikkink 1998; Mende, Heller and Reichwein 2022) have been intensively studied and discussed by political scientists, a comprehensive discussion of turning points and its consequences is lacking so far. Scientists often talk about and analyse turning points without defining them precisely (e.g., Moravcsik 1998). An exception is given by historical institutionalism (Capoccia and Kelemen 2007; Capoccia 2015; Sydow et al. 2015), which accordingly defines *critical junctures*. While historical institutionalism, however, focuses exclusively on turning points as *institutional change*, studies about politics and policies with a broader scope and over a longer time horizon have largely gone under the radar. Another exception is research on social norms and the related discussion of tipping points, although the conceptual focus is rather on the cycle of norms (Finnemore and Sikkink 1998; Panke and Peterson 2016).

Addressing this research gap is of great importance: First, it helps scholars clarify their research subject and assess the extent of change in domestic policies, politics, and polity. Second, it allows researchers to analytically grasp the tectonic changes liberal democracies and the international system have been and are still facing at the onset of the 21st century. Third, a proper conceptual understanding can be enriching not only for theoretical debates but also for empirical studies and practical advice. To better understand current trends and challenges in democracies and in global politics, we need conceptual clarity about the diversity and ambivalence of key concepts. By bringing together an interdisciplinary reflection on the concept of turning points with case study analyses, this edited volume aims to fill this research gap. Therefore, it makes both a theoretical and an empirical contribution to better understand and explain the upcoming and recent turning points for and within Western democracies and beyond.

1 Typology of turning points

We distinguish four types of "turning points" (in a broader sense) – turning point, tipping point, critical juncture, and breaking point – based on three criteria: the direction of a path, the direction of gravitational forces, and the nexus of agency and uncertainty.

The **path direction** refers to whether a path is stable and persistent and has a clear, steady direction in which it runs, or whether it is rather volatile and has unpredictable swings (cf. Sydow et al. 2015). Depending on the preferred theory, research field, or empirical focus, a path can be different things, for example, the stability of institutions, the popularity of a political party, the economic development of a state, the willingness of a government to use force in a conflict, or the contestation and diffusion of a norm.

The **direction of gravitational forces** describes forces pushing a path in a specific direction and making it more difficult to steer the path in a new direction. A gravitational force could be, for example, societal pressure to comply with a norm or economies of scale in production. The idea of gravitational forces relates to the concept of path dependencies, i.e., self-reinforcing mechanisms that make it harder to leave an existing path over time (Capoccia and Kelemen 2007; Mahoney 2000; Sydow et al. 2015). Path dependencies are one form of gravitational force, but not the only one. While path dependencies become stronger over time, other forces may exist independently of the path or change beyond a specific threshold, for example, the ability of nature to regenerate after pollution.

The **agency-uncertainty nexus** describes whether periods of agency and uncertainty exist and how they relate to each other. The nexus is located in the agent-structure debate (Franke and Roos 2010; Ruggie 1998; Wendt 1987). In this debate, the central question is whether human beings and their organisations can purposely reproduce and transform a society or social relationships structure the interactions between actors and constrain the options of agents. Periods of agency describe times in which agents have more control over structure. Structure loses its constraining effect, leaving agents with more options to act. In times of structure, actors have fewer options for action because the structure constrains their behaviour. The distinction made here is about the relative shifting of forces – either in favour of agency or in favour of structure as a determinant (or constraining power of change).

Times of uncertainty are periods in which it is harder for agents to anticipate the direction of a path. At times outside a period of uncertainty, agents are better able to predict the direction of a path, either because they have more control or because the structure constrains their options. However, uncertainty describes a situation in which agents are confronted with a lack or ambiguity of information. As a result, they cannot adequately describe or explain current and past situations or accurately predict future events or outcomes. There are different sources of uncertainty that can be addressed with different forms of learning. For example, agents can solve the problem of incomplete information by collecting more information. On the other hand, when confronted with the problem of an overflow of information due to cognitive limitations, agents can use a heuristic. Then, to address different interpretations about norms, agents can try to build up shared identities for better understanding (Rathbun 2007; cf. Iida 1993).

Based on these three criteria, we can now define *different types* of turning points. It is important to stress that turning points can only be understood in terms of time. They cannot be captured at a single point in time, but only if the time before, during, and after the turning point is taken into consideration. The three criteria can then be used to highlight the important defining features of the types of turning points. Let us start with turning points as commonly understood and used in everyday language.

Turning point: A turning point describes a point in time at which a substantial or radical change in direction from an old to a new persistent path happens. Here, the key aspect is *path direction* (see Figure 1). Path does not necessarily describe a positive or negative trend but could also be a constant. The path is also not necessarily consolidated by some kind of self-reinforcing mechanism or driving force but could simply have been constant since some point in time, without any forces determining it. However, what is important is that the paths are steadily and persistently heading in one direction before and after the turning point; that is, the two paths are not volatile with unpredictable swings. Without stable paths heading in different directions before and after a certain point in time, the term "turning point" would lose its deeper meaning. It would then make more sense to just speak of change. Good examples include a revolution that leads to new political institutions, a previously successful election campaign that results in steady losses among voters after a scandal, or a decisive battle in a war that ends the military advance of an attacking military and turns the tide in favour of the defender.

Tipping point: In contrast to a turning point, a tipping point does not describe a turn of a path. Rather the opposite, it is characterized by the fact that a

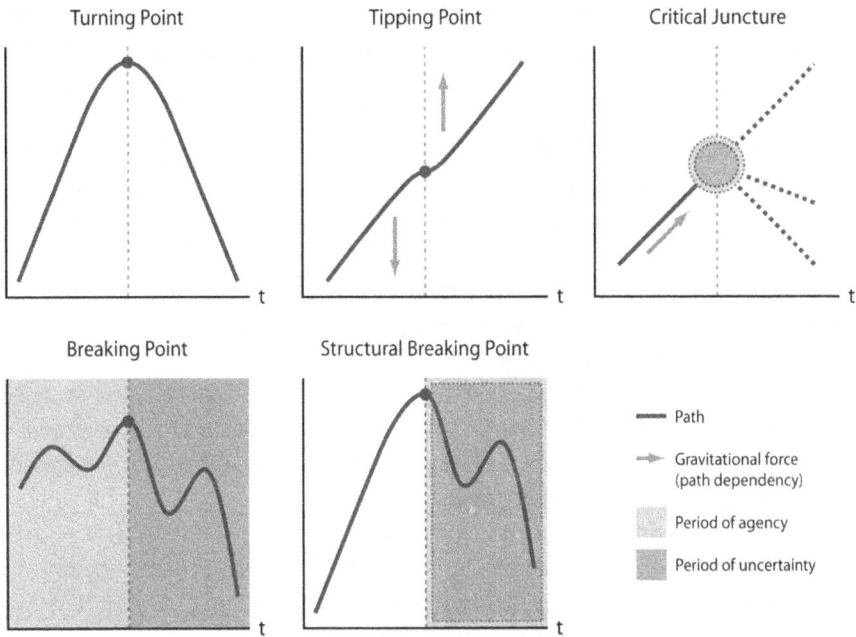

Figure 1: Typology of turning points.

path goes in one direction before and after the tipping point. What turns is not the path direction but the *direction of a gravitational force* (see Figure 1). That is, a tipping point describes a steady path or trend, but at a certain point the forces acting for or against the trend reverse. Gladwell (2001: 12) defines a tipping point as *"the moment of critical mass, the threshold, the boiling point."* It is the inversion of a gravitational force. It is important to note that a tipping point is not only a weakening of a gravitational force, but always its reversal. For example, nature has a tipping point where it loses its ability to regenerate itself after pollution and then tends to self-destruct (Lenton et al. 2008). Another example is societal pressure when it comes to norm compliance. In the beginning, people must fight societal pressure to spread a new norm. But at some point, when the norm is more widely accepted, societal pressure begins to shift in favour of spreading the norm.

Critical juncture: In historical institutionalism, scholars speak of a critical juncture instead of a turning point. Capoccia and Kelemen (2007: 348) define *"critical junctures as relatively short periods of time during which there is a substantially heightened probability that agents' choices will affect the outcome of interest."* Critical junctures are closely linked to the idea of *path dependency*, which describes a process according to which institutions that once implemented constraint increasingly affect the future choices of agents (Sydow et al. 2015). While critical junctures can mark the end of an old path (dependency) and the beginning of a new one, they do not necessarily imply a turn in path direction; they merely hold the heightened probability for it. Instead, the key to understanding critical junctures is the nexus of agency and uncertainty. Critical junctures are a period of uncertainty during which a former path dependency (structure) loses its constraining effect. At the same time, actors gain control and agency. Thus, the periods of agency and uncertainty overlap during critical junctures (see Figure 1). In contrast to a tipping point, a critical juncture may result in a new path direction and path dependency; however, the path dependency is not necessarily the reversal of the previous one. For example, when norms and rules in a political system lose their constraining effect, spaces open for political actors to overthrow the old system and create a new one. Another example is technological innovation, which opens the possibility for producers and consumers to overcome the settled technology. However, in both cases, old path dependencies may prevail, leaving the path as it previously was.

Breaking point: While turning points, tipping points, and critical junctures are all related to a steady path (even if in different ways), breaking points are not. That is, whether a stable path heading in a clear direction exists is not important in the definition of a breaking point. Instead, a breaking point describes the point in time at which a substantial (not necessarily absolute) loss of control, influence, or impact occurs relatively abruptly, i.e., agents lose their ability to act and influence events or determine a path. For instance, in psychology, Kimble (1996: 100) defines the term as *"the degree of tension or stress at which something breaks."* Accordingly, in the period before the breaking point, there is a period of control for agents, which ends at the breaking point, initiating a period of new uncertainty (see Figure 1). A good example is a driver who loses control of his car during a snowstorm. What "turns" is not the direction of the path, but the agent's ability to control outcomes, leading to a new period of uncertainty. For example, an insurrection marks a breaking point for the establishment because the establishment loses control over law making, leading to a period in which it is uncertain who makes the law and how.

While the above definition of breaking points describes an agent's loss of control, a breaking point may also describe a point in time when structures abruptly lose their constraining effect on agents. In this case, agents suddenly gain control. We define this kind of event as a **structural breaking point**. As in the case of a critical juncture, the times of agency and uncertainty are then not separate periods but exist simultaneously (see Figure 1). Let us take the example of the insurrection again. When the establishment loses control, the breaking of established institutions allows other actors to create new ones. The insurrection is thus not only a loss of control over the rules of the game but also a gain in agency to shape new rules of the game.

Table 1: Typology of turning points.

Type	Path direction	Direction of gravitational force	Agency-uncertainty nexus
Turning point	Substantial turn from an old persistent path to a new one		
Tipping point	Steady path in one direction	Inversion of gravitational force	
Critical juncture	Heightened probability of a substantial turn from an old persistent path to a new one	Path dependencies	Overlapping periods of heightened control and uncertainty
Breaking point	Path under control of agents that is lost		End of a period of control, start of a new period of uncertainty
Structural breaking point	Path under structural constraint that is lost		Overlapping periods of heightened control and uncertainty

While the different types of turning points have been presented as distinct types, they are often related to each other or appear as hybrid (see Table 1). For example, a critical juncture is by definition related to the understanding of turning points and structural breaking points. Critical junctures imply the possibility of a turning point and structural breaking points initiate the beginning of critical junctures. The other types can also appear as hybrid in theory and empirics. For example, a tipping point may be the result of a breaking point. In this case, the loss of control causes the inversion of gravitational force. In general, describing phenomena of change as having certain characteristics of turning points can only happen in retrospect.

The definitions are applicable to all social contexts, whether we are dealing with institutions, conflicts, negotiations, or discourses. To evaluate whether an event or period can be classified as a turning point, scholars must first clarify the perspective from which they are analysing the period and the context. The same event can be a turning point, a tipping point, a breaking point, or just a simple change when it is viewed from different perspectives and in consideration of different contexts. For example, the Russian invasion in Ukraine may turn out to be a turning point for the European security order, a breaking point for Russian foreign policy, or a tipping point for German foreign policy toward Russia. Events are often called turning points when researchers perceive their historical relevance and impact. However, what is of historical relevance and impact also depends on the perspective and context. If the electoral success of a right-wing populist party is only relevant for the affected nation and irrelevant for democracies worldwide, it may be a turning point from a national perspective. However, if it pushes a new trend internationally, it could also be a turning point from a global perspective. Whether an event is a turning point can only be understood when reflecting in a transparent manner on the perspective and context.

While the proposed typology clarifies the differences between a turning point, tipping point, critical juncture, and breaking point, it leaves open the threshold at which a change can be considered a turning point. If too many (major) changes are classified as turning points, the term becomes inflationary and loses its meaning. Against this backdrop, three aspects are posited as central to identifying a turning point and distinguishing it from simple changes. (1) the angle (degree) of changing path direction, (2) the time span, (3) and the (historical) relevance and impact. While we do not want to give strict criteria for these three dimensions, scholars should reflect on and address them when specifically dealing with turning points and their variants.

First, not every change in the direction of a path is a turning point. At what angle is a redirection of a path large enough to be called a turning point? If a newly elected populist party slightly restricts civil liberties, is it fair to already speak of a turning point for a democracy? To identify turning points, scholars must discuss the angle or degree of change; in other words, how much does a new path diverge from the previous one? While it may be difficult to determine or measure a specific degree, a change should be substantial or radical; otherwise, all changes meet the definitional criteria of turning points. However, whether we talk about a turning point or just change may also depend on the durability of the path before and after the events in question. For example, if a constitution has not changed at all for over a century, a minor change that leads to more and more incremental changes may constitute a turning point.

Second, a turning point refers to a specific or episodic point in time rather than a longer period. However, a turning point does not have to be a single event but can extend over a short time span. What counts as long or brief is not fixed, though, as it depends on the subject under investigation and the duration of the old and new paths. For example, a scandal of a presidential frontrunner during a political campaign could constitute a turning point for the upcoming election. In contrast, a military coup may take a longer period of time but still represents a turning point in relation to the previous long existence of democratic institutions. And when dealing with the rise and fall of empires over centuries, a decade may be a brief time in comparison.

Third, turning points can only be identified as such when they have historical relevance or an impact on the research object under investigation. In the political context, the term is often used by scholars and in the public discourse to describe major historical events or periods of time that have a substantial and long-term impact. In a purely definitional sense, however, this is not necessarily the case. We still argue that an event or period of time should have a historical impact to count as turning point. Otherwise, the term loses its deeper semantic meaning. However, what counts as a substantial impact depends on the research object under investigation. In the analysis of a specific election, a political scandal can have a substantial impact, and it would make sense to speak of a turning point. Yet for the stability of a democratic institution, such events may be irrelevant.

In light of this, scholars need to be transparent and rigid when it comes to their understanding of turning points. Even when it is difficult to define an exact threshold for an angle of changing path direction, a time span, or a historical impact, scholars should problematize and discuss these aspects in a transparent manner to prevent an inflationary use of the term. A parsimonious use of the term seems to be the wisest approach to assess if the research object can be classified as a turning point or not to avoid criticisms of confirmation or selection bias.

2 Outline of the book

The volume is divided into six parts that discuss turning points from various empirical and theoretically inspired perspectives. The first part deals with possible turning points that can be seen as pushing back globalisation. In the **first chapter**, Stefan Schirm analyses how global and European economic liberalisation and governance influenced the interests and perceptions of British voters and thus contributed to the Brexit vote. Inspired by critical junctures in historical institutionalism, he sees a turning point in the substantial domestic economic repercussions, which contribute to a change of ideational interpretations and material circumstances in the society. Schirm argues that the traditional liberal international economic order and globalisation have led to socioeconomic divisions and increased support for nationally oriented economic policies in Western societies. In the **second chapter**, Oliver Schwarz uses the theoretical approach of differentiated integration to better understand the crucial changes brought about by Brexit. According to the author, the institutional dilemma has not ended with the Trade and Cooperation Agreement. Therefore, flexibility will be part of the evolving post-Brexit international relationships. In the **third chapter**, Holger Janusch and Daniel Lorberg discuss whether Trump's questioning of American democracy contributes to a hegemonic crisis and a possible turning point in the prevailing state and world order. By proposing a neo-Gramscian definition of turning points and structural breaking points, they explain the growing crises of hegemony within the United States and the wider liberal world order. They conclude that hegemonic crisis marks a time when the power relations are up for debate, which opens the door for a charismatic leader such as President Trump. In the **fourth chapter**, Holger Janusch and Daniel Lorberg identify the Trump presidency as a critical juncture for U.S. trade policy, as it led to a radical shift from a belief in free trade to managed trade. Based on liberal intergovernmentalism, they define a critical juncture as a period of great confusion about public and societal group interests and beliefs that enables policymakers to question and abandon existing path dependencies.

The second part of the volume examines Western interventionism and revisionist great powers as challenges for the existing world order. In the **fifth chapter**, Hubert Zimmermann defines a post-interventionist world order and explains the turning points in debates over interventions as a result of the interplay of domestic and international shifts from a neoclassical realist perspective. According to him, military interventions were among the most conspicuous and contested phenomena of global politics in the decades following the end of the Cold War. However, eventually the "age of liberal interventionism" came to an end in the 2010s. In the **sixth chapter**, Witold Mucha analyses whether China's One Belt and One Road Initiative and the Asian Infrastructure Investment Bank mark a turning point. Referring to the critical juncture concept and Strange's notion of structural power, he discusses to what extent China's international economic investments and institutions have contributed permanently to China's geo-economic rise and thereby to the alteration of global economic governance. In the **seventh chapter**, John Callahan refers to historical concepts of what a turning point in the rise or fall of a great power looks like. With a focus on Paul Kennedy's work, he argues that the Russian invasion of Ukraine and failure to quickly defeat Ukraine has encapsulated several turning points and created the conditions for a complete turnaround in the post 9–11 paths of great powers.

The third part analyses norms and practices as characteristics for social change as turning points. In the **eighth chapter**, Julia Herrmann offers a constructivist analysis of feminist foreign policy. By applying the norm life cycle model, she assesses the tipping point a norm must exceed to diffuse successfully on the international stage. The steady path direction of feminist norms in foreign policy and the motion of gravitational forces are considered potential key indicators for such a tipping point. In the **ninth chapter**, Lars Berger reflects on the circularity of realism and the missed opportunity of using the Arab Spring as a turning point. He argues that policies inspired by realist thinking contributed to the circularity of authoritarianism and insecurity. To break this cycle, Berger argues for facilitating a transition to free(er) media and a free civil society, which will strengthen transparent and accountable political authorities and thus reduce the likelihood of negative security surprises that realism fears. In the **tenth chapter**, Susanne Fischer analyses if and how digital innovations challenged intelligence professionals' routinized practices of data collection. With recourse to Bourdieu, she defines the breakthrough of emerging practices as a type of turning point. Fischer demonstrates how German intelligence services, supported by the U.S. National Intelligence Service, reached a digital breakthrough, leading to new practices of data collection.

The fourth part of this volume focuses on turning points in long-established policies and possible ways out of "frozen" policies. In the **eleventh chapter**, Julia Rakers examines how migration and integration have been discussed in the German Bundestag after 2015. She argues that the 2015 migration situation, based on increased attention, could have the potential to be a turning point for the way a topic is addressed and can be utilized by societal groups to facilitate change. Empirically, she finds that migration politics in Germany from 2013 to 2017 may indeed be a special policy field characterized by a more positive parliamentary debate compared to a rather negative public opinion. In the **twelfth chapter**, Benjamin Ewert discusses the trajectories from health care to public health under the conditions of the Covid-19 pandemic in German health policy. The author applies two turning point conceptions: theoretical insights on critical junctures and Peter Hall's approach to policy paradigms and social learning. His findings show that Covid-19 does not represent an immediate turning point in German health policy but might spur paradigmatic policy change in the long run. In the **thirteenth chapter**, Maximilian Schiffers and Sandra Plümer discuss the hurdled path of lobbying transparency in Europe and Germany's position at the end of the Merkel era when Germany finally introduced a lobbying register. Applying the punctuated equilibrium theory, the authors examine a variety of policy documents using process tracing and qualitative content analysis. Their results show that a breakthrough involved the combination of three mechanisms: A dethematisation of the policy issue, a growing network favouring stricter transparency regulations, and increasing public validation of the issue through a buildup of scandals, leading to a waived refusal to put the issue on the parliamentary agenda.

The fifth part deals with issues of leadership and market in times of economic and social crises. In the **fourteenth chapter**, Joscha Abels, Hans-Jürgen Bieling, and Sarah Kassem reconstruct the way toward European high-tech capitalism by means of the EU digitalisation strategy after the Covid-19 pandemic. Based on regulation theory, extended by a neo-Gramscian crisis conception, the authors characterize recent developments as so-called second-order change, not yet translated into a new paradigm but fundamentally altering policy instruments. According to Abels, Bieling, and Kassem, the Covid-19 pandemic has opened the political and discursive space to break with the previous fiscal consolidation agenda and served as a catalyst for a more interventionist high-tech agenda. In the **fifteenth chapter**, Nils Goldschmidt and Mark McAdam deal with institutional change by looking at the historical introduction of the Social Market Economy in Germany using the theoretical perspective of historical institutionalism. The authors argue that uncertainty and crisis are merely signals for necessary reforms to make the economic order suitable for contemporary problems. They conclude that the importance of inflection points as well as the ideational level lead to a specific tension: whereas crisis can lead to abrupt institutional changes, many ideational underpinnings typically only change slowly and gradually.

The sixth and final part of the volume reflects uncertainty and turning points from an epistemological perspective. In the **sixteenth chapter**, Rogelio Madrueño provides a systematic analysis, based on bibliometric techniques, of more than 6,800 publications from the Web of Science over the last four decades. He argues that it is possible to identify the presence of turning points and uncertainties in contemporary world politics by focusing on the academic analysis of global threats and risks through the detection of citation bursts from bibliometric analysis. Furthermore, his findings indicate that researchers play a supporting role in the creation of hegemonic discourses. Also, the promotion of discursive practices relies on the role of scholars located in the global North. In the **seventeenth chapter**, Nora Schrader-Rashidkhan discusses uncertainty as a political challenge to Western democracies. She focuses on the question of whether there is something qualitatively new about some of the vividly discussed challenges. The author adopts a systematisation of threats to develop an argument about core characteristics and to distinguish emergent turning points. Thereby, she identifies qualitative differences within current political challenges and assesses their inherent "turning point potential."

References

Baldwin, David A. 2016. *Power and International Relations: A Conceptual Approach*. Princeton: Princeton University Press.

Barnett, Michael, and Raymond Duvall. 2005. Power in International Politics. *International Organization* 59(1). 39–75.

Capoccia, Giovanni. 2015. "Critical Junctures and Institutional Change." In *Advances in Comparative-Historical Analysis*, edited by James Mahoney and Kathleen A. Thelen, 147–79. Cambridge: Cambridge University Press.

Capoccia, Giovanni, and R. Daniel Kelemen. 2007. The Study of Critical Junctures: Theory, Narrative, and Counterfactuals in Historical Institutionalism. *World Politics* 59(3). 341–369.

Deitelhoff, Nicole, and Lisbeth Zimmermann. 2020. Things We Lost in the Fire: How Different Types of Contestation Affect the Robustness of International Norms. *International Studies Review* 22(1), 51–76.

Finnemore, Martha, and Kathryn Sikkink. 1998. International Norm Dynamics and Political Change. *International Organization* 52(4). 887–917.

Franke, Ulrich, and Ulrich Roos. 2010. Actor, structure, process: Transcending the state person-hood debate by means of a pragmatist ontological model for international relations theory. *Review of International Studies* 36(4), 1057–77.

Gladwell, Malcolm. 2001. *The Tipping Point: How Little Things Can Make a Big Difference*. New York: Little, Brown and Company.

Iida, Keisuke. 1993. "Analytic Uncertainty and International Cooperation: Theory and Application to International Economic Policy Coordination." *International Studies Quarterly* 37(4). 431–57.

Kimble, Gregory A. 1996. *Psychology: The Hope of a Science*. Cambridge: MIT Press.

Lenton, Timothy M., Hermann Held, Elmar Kriegler, Jim W. Hall, Wolfgang Lucht, Stefan Rahmstorf, and Hans Joachim Schellnhuber. 2008. Tipping Elements in the Earth's Climate System. *Proceedings of the National Academy of Sciences of the United States of America* 105(6). 1786–1793.

Lukes, Steven. 2021. *Power: A Radical View*. Third edition. London: Red Globe Press.

Mahoney, James. 2000. Path Dependence in Historical Sociology. *Theory and Society* 29(4). 507–548.

Mende, Janne, Regina Heller, and Alexander Reichwein (guest editors). 2022. Special Issue Transcending a Western Bias. Towards a Decolonised and Entangled Perspective in Norms Research. *European Review of International Studies* 9(3), 339–522.

Moravcsik, Andrew. 1998. *The Choice for Europe: Social Purpose and State Power from Messina to Maastricht*. Ithaca, N.Y.: Cornell University Press.

Nye, Joseph S. Jr. 2017a. *Understanding Global Conflict and Cooperation: An Introduction to Theory and History*. Boston: Pearson.

Nye, Joseph. 2017b. Soft power: The Origins and Political Progress of a Concept. *Palgrave Commununications* 3(17008).

Panke, Diana, and Ulrich Petersohn. 2016. "Norm Challenges and Norm Death: The Inexplicable?" *Cooperation and Conflict* 51(1). 3–19.

Phillips, Warren, and Richard Rimkunas. 1978. The Concept of Crisis in International Politics. *Journal of Peace Research* 15(3). 259–272.

Rathbun, Brian C. 2007. Uncertain About Uncertainty: Understanding the Multiple Meanings of a Crucial Concept in International Relations Theory. *International Studies Quarterly* 51(3). 533–557.

Ruggie, John G. 2006. *Constructing the World Polity: Essays on International Institutionalization*. London: Routledge.

Sydow, Georg, Georg Schreyögg, and Jochen Koch. 2009. "Organizational Path Dependence: Opening the Black Box." *Academy of Management Review* 34(4). 689–709.

Wendt, Alexander E. 1987. The Agent-Structure Problem in International Relations Theory. *International Organization* 41(3). 335–370.

I **Pushing Back Globalisation? Brexit and Trump**

Stefan A. Schirm

The impact of globalization and Europeanization on the societal foundations of Brexit

Abstract: How and why did a society's ideas and interests concerning international economic integration shape politicians' nation-centered policy (NCP) preferences? Which form of critical junctures and turning points contributed to strengthening demands for NCP? I argue that the traditional LIO, globalization and economic regionalization had two core adverse effects on large segments of Western societies, which triggered socioeconomic divisions and rising support for NCP. First, the liberalization of finance and trade in the framework of international organizations like the WTO and EU contributed to economic losses and gains that increased inequality of income distribution. This has alienated voters that materially lost or only gained little and de-legitimized international integration in the eyes of voters who grew ideationally discontent with inequality. Second, the increasing powers of seemingly opaque and non-accountable multilateral bureaucracies and rules have left many voters with the impression of heteronomy and loss of control. These effects of international economic integration have prompted some parties and politicians to grasp discontent and advocate a more nation-centered course, especially in liberal market economies with weak compensation for economic inequality, such as in the United Kingdom. Following the Societal Approach, these arguments will be examined regarding UK's Brexit decision.

Keywords: Brexit, Globalisation, United Kingdom, European Union, Societal Approach, Domestic Politics, Turning Points

1 Introduction and puzzle

In the past decade, international economic integration has been challenged in many countries around the world by nation-centered policies.[1] An increasing em-

---

1 This chapter is a revised and shortened version of Schirm, Stefan A. (2022) Globalisation, divided societies and nation-centred economic policies in America and Britain, in: European Review of International Studies 9(2): 240–269. A previous version of this chapter was presented at the workshop "Turning Points in Democracies. Challenges and Opportunities for the European

---

Stefan A. Schirm, Ruhr University Bochum, stefan.schirm@rub.de

https://doi.org/10.1515/9783111272900-002

phasis on national sovereignty and domestic groups weakened liberal international and regional orders, which had been promoting multilateral economic governance and cross-border liberalizations (Colgan/Keohane 2017; Etzioni 2018; Ikenberry 2018; Schirm 2019a). The most visible examples for this trend are the decision of the majority of the British electorate to leave the European Union (EU) and the election of Donald Trump, whose foreign economic policy weakened the US commitment to multilateral rules (Schirm 2022). With the Brexit referendum in 2016 and the election of Boris Johnson in 2019, the United Kingdom embarked on ending its membership in the world's economically most integrated multilateral organization, the EU. Donald Trump started a trade war with China, withdrew from the Trans-Pacific Partnership (TPP), renegotiated the North American Free Trade Agreement (NAFTA) into the United States-Mexico-Canada Agreement, and weakened the World Trade Organization (WTO). Other countries like Poland, Italy, Greece, Brazil, and India have also been governed by political parties that opposed liberal internationalism and advocated for stronger national self-determination and the privileging of specific domestic groups and voters. These instances share the common ground of challenging the Liberal International Economic Order (LIO) and of striving for more Nation-Centered foreign economic Policies (NCP). NCP is defined as a policy that seeks to strengthen national sovereignty to the detriment of multilateral rules and international organizations and aims at privileging certain domestic interests and ideas (Schirm 2022: 243). This chapter addresses the question on the reasons for increasing NCP, especially concerning the United Kingdom as a country that formerly spearheaded the LIO. Why has the United Kingdom turned away from its long-standing commitment to regional multilateral rules and economic integration by leaving the EU?

Considering the focus of this edited volume, the chapter is focused on investigating the domestic sources for voters' preferences and the possible critical junctures and turning points that help in explaining the societal demands for Brexit. The key questions are: How and why did a society's ideas and interests concerning international economic integration shape politicians' nation-centered policy preferences? Which form of critical junctures and turning points contributed to strengthening societal demands for nation-centered policy? I argue that the traditional LIO, globalization and economic regionalization have had two core adverse effects on large segments of Western societies, which triggered socioeconomic divisions and rising support for NCP. First, the liberalization of finance and trade in the framework of international organizations like the WTO and EU contributed to

Union and the United States," Wuppertal, Germany, March 31/April 1, 2022. I am grateful for the valuable comments of Holger Janusch and of the participants of the workshop.

economic losses in many countries and to rising inequality of income distribution. This challenge has alienated voters that materially lost or only gained little from globalization and de-legitimized international economic integration in the eyes of voters who grew ideationally discontent with rising inequality. Second, the increasing powers of seemingly opaque and non-accountable transnational bureaucracies and multilateral rules have left many voters with the impression of heteronomy and a loss of control. These effects of international economic integration have prompted some parties and politicians to grasp societal discontent and direct economic policy toward a more nation-centered course, especially in majority voting systems and liberal market economies with weak compensation for economic inequality, such as in the United Kingdom and the United States.

Thus, while Brexit was often analyzed as a turning point and critical juncture for other areas like European integration, the global economy, or British politics (Bulmer/Quaglia 2018; Nölke 2017; Zimmermann 2019), *this chapter investigates the question of how the institutionalization of global and European economic liberalization and governance influenced the interests and ideas of British voters and possibly contributed to the Brexit* vote in the referendum 2016 and the election of Boris Johnson on a pro-Brexit campaign ("get Brexit done") in 2019.

2 The societal approach, critical junctures, and turning points

The analysis of the questions raised above will employ the societal approach to governmental preference formation and complements it with a conceptualization of international critical junctures and domestic turning points. The societal approach contends that domestic value-based ideas, material interests, and national institutions crucially shape governmental preferences (Schirm 2020). The historical institutionalist concept of critical junctures analyzes international or national phases of institutional flux and crises and the lasting impact of choices made during those phases, while the concept of exogenous shocks addresses the role of crises as mechanisms of (domestic) change (Capoccia/Kelemen 2007; Widmaier et al. 2007; for a typology on turning points see the introduction to this edited volume). The following presents the societal approach and several elements of critical junctures and turning points as drivers of change.

The Societal Approach. To address the question on how a society's ideas and interests regarding international economic integration shaped politicians' nation-centered policy preferences, theories of International Political Economy (IPE), which offer a bottom-up explanation for governmental preferences seem appropriate. While some domestic politics approaches to IPE have centered on the role of material interests (Milner 1997; Lake 2009), others concentrated on domestic institutions (Fioretos 2011) and ideas (Goldstein/Keohane 1993; Schmidt 2017). Still other theories like the liberal theory of International Relations (IR) (Moravcsik 1997) and Comparative Political Economy theories (Hall 1997) consider all three dimensions, but neither focuses on the topics of IPE nor the conditions for the relative significance of each domestic variable for governmental preferences. The latter perspective is at the center of the societal approach to governmental preference formation, which I developed in the context of the above-mentioned domestic politics theories of IPE and IR (Schirm 2011, 2013, 2016, 2019b, 2020; van Loon 2021).

Besides the concept of societal *alignments* (see below), the novel contributions of the societal approach include the consideration of actors' circumstances *and* interpretation, and especially the conceptualization of specific conditions under which each of the three variables' ideas, institutions, and interests matters and plausibly prevails in shaping government politicians' positions. Several studies have employed the societal approach to explaining the variation of governmental preferences over time and in cross-country comparisons concerning trade policy, investment cooperation, global economic governance, the Eurozone, and the global financial crisis (for instance, Novak 2020; Harnisch 2018; Kassim et.al 2020; Mahrenbach 2019; Franke 2020; Schirm 2011, 2013, 2018, 2016, 2022; van Loon 2018; Su 2022). These studies demonstrate the strengths of the approach in explaining under which conditions societal ideas and interests matter and how they interact by competing or reinforcing each other in influencing governmental preferences. In addition, the studies show the limitations of the approach, which does not consider the direct influence of international organizations on governmental preferences and the complete theoretical range of ideas, interests and institutions.

The societal approach seems especially adequate for the analysis of the puzzle at stake because it conceptualizes conditions for the prevalence of competing societal ideas and material interests as well as for the relevance of "alignments" between *reinforcing* ideas and interests. Its basic assumption is that governments wish to remain in office and that opposition parties aim to win. Therefore, government and opposition politicians tend to be responsive to societal demands in democratic political systems. Weak responsiveness would, in turn, lead to electoral defeat. This chapter conceptually refines and empirically investigates how certain ideas and interests can converge, overlap, mutually reinforce each other, work in parallel (politically *de facto* align), and compete with different alignments of other converging ideas and interests in informing governmental preferences. Additionally, this chapter investigates general societal interests through material indicators (circumstances) and opinion polls (interpretation), and evidences sectoral interests through changes in competitiveness (circumstances) as well as positions of business associations (interpretation). Therefore, by looking conceptually and empirically at the structural circumstances and their interpretation (through opinion polls and statements), the societal approach includes both the material and interpretative dimensions of preference formation.

Interests are defined here as material considerations of voters (general societal interests) and of economic sectors (sectoral interests) whose cost-benefit calculations can change according to circumstances, such as economic crises, income distribution, competitiveness, and new global, regional as well as national regulations. Interests can diverge, for example, regarding the desire for protection from competition versus the demand for liberalization. *Ideas* are defined as value-based expectations of voters concerning appropriate governmental positions. Societal ideas express themselves as attitudes that are empirically evidenced in public opinion polls and statements. With regard to the topic of this chapter, relevant societal ideas refer to the appropriate role of the government via-à-vis international economic integration, particularly concerning international organizations, the (dis)advantages of international trade, and income distribution. Societal ideas and interests interact with one another and can mutually constitute, support, or oppose one another. The analytical separation serves the purpose of identifying their *sui generis* characteristics. Indicators for the independent variables "value-based ideas" and "material interests" may overlap in their meaning. For instance, "distribution" has a material dimension (income), but may also concern an idea (equality), whereas "national self-determination" can be an idea (autonomy) and an interest (national jurisdiction). Thus, ideas and interests can overlap and constitute each other conceptually and empirically.

Conceptualization of de facto alignments between ideas and interests. Given the plurality of ideas and interests in societies, ideational expectations may encounter material interests, which demand similar policies from the government, while different ideational expectations may go hand in hand with other material interests, leading to a competition of diverging societal demands that both rest on ideas and interests. This argument implies that the preferences of the government and politicians striving for governmental office can be informed by *de facto* alignments of converging and mutually supportive ideas and interests that prevail over other alignments of ideas and interests that favor a different course (Schirm 2022: 246). Which of the competing alignments of ideas and interests prevails, plausibly depends, first, on voters' and sectors' support (due to concern and issue salience) and, second, on ideas and interests in one camp reinforcing each other (due to similarity or complementary of the policy demands). The policy change is thus conceived as induced by an ascending alignment prevailing over the established alignment.

The societal approach, in its complete version, also includes domestic *institutions* as an independent variable for the explanation of governmental preferences (Schirm 2016, 2020). Domestic institutions are defined as formal regulations, which structure domestic political (e.g., voting system) and socioeconomic (e.g., welfare state) coordination. Governments' preferences toward international economic integration are informed by the consideration of how international rules will affect domestic regulations that shape domestic sectors' competitive situations. In addition to these material efficiency calculations, governmental preferences also tend to be consistent with long-term domestic institutional settings due to their path-dependent ideational legitimacy. Besides, institutions represent the codification of previously existing sets of ideas and interests and can influence current societal ideas and interests (Schirm 2020: 403–406). The domestic institutions possibly relevant for the turn to NCP by many voters and interest groups can be political and economical in nature. First, it seems plausible that majority voting systems allow for policy change induced by voter disaffection faster than more proportional electoral systems. Second, Liberal Market Economies (LME) as defined by the Varieties of Capitalism theory (Hall/Soskice 2001), such as the United Kingdom possess smaller welfare provisions than Coordinated Market Economies (CME), such as Germany. Therefore, material compensation for those disadvantaged by free trade is smaller in LMEs, which plausibly contributes to a stronger opposition against economic liberalism.

As mentioned above, this chapter's aims are twofold. First, with the societal approach it focuses on the reasons for the increasing strength of the ideational-material alignment that supports NCP. Second, the analysis will employ facets of "critical junctures" and "turning points" to shed additional light on the growth of the pro-NCP alignment in the decade leading up to the Brexit referendum in 2016. However, since no generally accepted definition of (domestic) turning points and (international) critical junctures exists, this chapter proceeds through "analytic eclecticism" (Sil/Katzenstein 2010) inspired by conceptual elements borrowed from Widmaier et al (2007: 749) who look at "turning points for policy change" and from Capoccia and Kelemen (2007: 341–342) who stated that "path dependence is a crucial causal mechanism for historical institutionalists, and critical junctures constitute the starting point for many path-dependent processes," *In recourse to critical junctures and turning points, I argue that international institutional changes started a path-dependent process of accelerated globalization, which ultimately contributed to domestic costs such as economic losses, inequality, and perceived heteronomy, which raised societal opposition to LIO* (see Table 1). Hence, domestic political change (turning points) may follow from international institutional changes (critical junctures). This argument refers to institutional developments, such as European integration (leading to economic liberalization and member states' transfer of national competencies), the liberalization of financial markets (contributing to the magnitude of the global financial crisis in 2008), and China's accession to the WTO (leading to a surge of Chinese imports).

Consequently, turning points are defined here following the societal approach as *considerable shifts of societal value-based ideas and material interests, which influence the strength of ideational-material alignments and thus lead to a policy change*. Thus, turning points are conceived as domestic shifts of ideas and interests, which can lead to a policy change. Following the societal approach, ideas and interests can be evidenced by looking at material circumstances and their interpretation, for instance, through opinion polls and statements. Although this chapter is a theory-guided, qualitative empirical analysis, it draws upon some core claims of the constructivist-institutionalist literature, for instance, through the inclusion of *interpretation* in addition to material structures (Schmidt 2017; Widmaier et al. 2007: 748). Thus, the interpretation of the meaning of critical events to voters and politicians is considered in addition to their material-structural dimension. Conclusively, a turning point is conceived here as a substantial shift in the strength of domestic ideational-material alignments. This shift, in turn, can lead to a policy change. Regarding the reasons for the increasing power of the domestic alignment that demanded more NCP, plausible causes refer to the domestic socioeconomic consequences of international and European economic integration and policy-making. Hence, it is argued here that the turning points for voter's policy demands can be found in substantial domestic economic repercussions of exogenous incidents and influences, which path-dependent follow from the international institutionalization of globalization and Europeanization (see Table 1). Turning points can occur at the level of *economic* circumstances and their interpretation concerning incomes, jobs, inequality, and recession as well as at the level of *political* circumstances and their interpretation concerning representation, control, and self-determination.

As regards critical junctures, I argue that the shifts in domestic societal demands were influenced by prior changes in international institutional settings that represent critical junctures. In a period of institutional flux between the 1970s and 1990s, governments decided to internationally liberalize trade and finance and institutionalize this liberalization, for instance, through the WTO, International Monetary Fund (IMF), and EU. Broadly speaking, the neo-Keynesian consensus of the post-war decades was substituted by a trend toward neoliberal de-regulation nationally (Thatcher in the United Kingdom, "riguer" in France, Reaganomics in the United States, etc.), regionally (Single European Act, Maastricht Treaty etc. in Europe, NAFTA in North America), and internationally (founding of the WTO, accession of emerging markets to the WTO, IMF's Washington consensus, etc.). The international institutional anchoring of de-regulation and liberalization had path-dependent consequences, for instance, the accession of China to the WTO, which accelerated global competition as well as the increasing size and volatility of capital flows, which shaped the magnitude of the global financial crisis in 2008. Thus, the disaffection with the LIO due to job losses, inequality, and perceived heteronomy in the United Kingdom may follow from the path-dependent consequences of the decision to institutionalize globalization and liberalization on the international and European levels.

Table 1: Eclectic adaptation of elements of critical junctions and turning points to explain the Brexit puzzle.

International institutional critical juncture (starting neoliberal path dependence)	>	Domestic effects of international institutional path dependence	>	Turning point of domestic societal demands	>	Government preference, policy change
Institutionalization of liberalization/ globalization: founding of WTO, China's WTO accession, liberalization of financial markets	>	Economic crises & losses, social inequality in the UK; perceived loss of control	>	Discontent with LIO, ascending ideational-material alignment favoring the nation-centered economic policy	>	Majority votes for pro-Brexit policy in 2016 and 2019

Source: Author's compilation 2022.

3 Globalization, Europeanization, and the societal foundations of Brexit

Brexit is a fascinating case for examining the path-dependent effects of international institutional critical junctures (institutionalization of economic liberalization), domestic turning points for societal demands, and the question of how societal ideas and material interests partly compete and reinforce each other in *de facto alignments*. Both the Remain-camp that favoured a continuation of UK's membership in the EU and the Leave-camp that advocated ending it rested on ideational and material considerations. Thus, the competition for influence on governmental preferences through the result of the referendum concerning the British EU membership in 2016 and the parliamentary election in 2019 included ideas and interests on both sides. Both ideational-material *alignments* were composed of several groups and issues. Broadly speaking, the Remain camp encompassed large parts of the financial industry, a majority of the urban voters, the well-off and highly educated, and strongly (Liberal Democrat) to ambivalent (Labor, Tories) also political parties. The Leave camp was predominantly supported in smaller cities and rural areas, by middle to low-income and education segments of the electorate, in the Midlands, Northern and Southeast England (Colantone/Stanig 2018; Goodhart 2017; Hobolt 2016).

The referendum in June 2016 was the culmination of a long process of domestic controversies over the political and economic costs and benefits of EU membership. The contestation of the United Kingdom's membership became clear, among other things, in the 1980s when Prime Minister Margaret Thatcher renegotiated the British contribution to the budget of the then European Community (EC) ("I want my money back"). The referendum in 2016 turned out to be a 52% majority favoring Leave and thus winning over the Remain voters (48%). The Brexit campaign deepened already existing opposed attitudes in the British electorate (Bulmer/Quaglia 2018; Hobolt 2016). Controversies focused on the costs of free trade and globalization, the restrictions on British sovereignty, the EU competencies over trade policy, and the fear of involvement in Eurozone bailouts and immigration. The following paragraphs will document, first, the material interests and ideational expectations on both sides and, second, explain how and why the material and ideational reasons for ending the EU membership prevailed over the ideas and interests that motivated the Remain voters. Third, the case study sheds light on the consequences of the development and institutionalization of globalization and Europeanization as a critical juncture that had repercussions on domestic politics, which in turn, led to a turning point for societal demands for NCP.

3.1 Societal material interests

The material interest side of the societal division centers on the (dis-) advantages of globalization and EU membership. The United Kingdom has been one of the drivers of the liberalization of trade since the 1960s and of finance since the 1980s. This process impacted the United Kingdom through a reduction of tariffs and non-tariff barriers for goods and services, first, through negotiations in the General Agreement on Tariffs and Trade and its successor WTO and, second, through the EC (EU since 1992), which Britain joined in 1973. Furthermore, the United Kingdom has experienced de-regulation since Prime Minister Margaret Thatcher in the 1980s and financial market liberalization, especially in the 1990s under Prime Minister Tony Blair. Stronger international economic integration that resulted from this experience increased imports of manufactured goods and led to a partial de-industrialization. Thus, while consumers benefited from cheap imports, the imports of manufactured goods, especially the "China shock" after China accedes to the WTO in 2001, contributed to the elimination of many industrial jobs (Colantone/Stanig 2018). Jobs were lost due to imports and automation, as well as technological development, which was also triggered by the stronger import competition. This crisis of de-industrialization since the 1980s and especially in the 2000s; led to a shift in societal demands, which in turn represents a turning point for policy change. Trade liberalization based on international rules led to a polarization of societal interests and strengthened opposition to the LIO.

On the one hand, transnational corporations, business consultants, and the financial services sector gained from economic openness through higher incomes, profits, and revenues. On the other hand, unemployment and economic degradation in the traditional industrial regions documented the downsides of international integration (McCorriston/Sheldon 2020). Regarding the material interests of economic sectors and their lobbying in relation to the government, the former businesses engaged in the Remain campaign, while sectors and voters in the latter regions endorsed the Leave campaign. The Confederation of British Industry feared for business opportunities and predominantly demanded a continuation of the United Kingdom's membership in the EU (James/Quaglia 2019; Kollewe 2016). The financial industry and other transnational firms largely favored Remain but miscalculated their strategy to threaten the EU with a referendum to achieve further de-regulation and exceptions for the United Kingdom: "The City alongside multinational corporations had wanted to see the EU reformed and for the United Kingdom to be granted a special deal that would give them a stronger say in issues relating to, for example, financial regulation. The best way of securing reform, they figured, was to back up negotiations with the EU with the threat of a referendum" (LobbyControl 2019). However, using the referendum as a negotiating chip backfired for the financial industry in the referendum.

The British Chambers of Commerce decided to officially stay neutral due to the split interests of their member firms, with companies that focused on the domestic market and less organized sectors, which thought to benefit from Brexit (BBC 2016). Jensen and Snaith (2016: 1308) conclude that most big business interest groups preferred to remain in the EU, but ultimately had limited influence on the political process. In the end, organized sectoral interests that predominantly supported Remain were not as influential as the *alignment* between general societal interests favoring Leave and societal ideas (see below).

Concerning *general* societal interests, evidence shows a clear correlation between the decline of industrial structure and the exposure to economic liberalization, as well as a statistically strong relationship between international economic integration and the vote for Brexit (McCorriston/Sheldon 2020: 81). The material dimension of the societal division induced by international economic openness did not only encompass the specific effects on the winners and losers of this development, but also included an increasingly unequal income distribution in the entire society. The Gini Index, which measures the distribution of income (0 = total equality, 1 = one person has all income) had risen from 0.284 (1979) to 0.348 (2016) (The World Bank 2020). Thus, rising income inequality materially shaped general societal interests. While the United Kingdom had become a more equal nation during the post-World War II decades, inequality has increased since the 1980s and reached a peak after the global financial crisis in 2009–2010.

The latter became possible because of the accelerated internationalization and liberalization of finance in the 1990s and 2000s and had magnified material divisions in society and ideational mistrust toward British elites. The financial crisis led to an economic downturn in most Western industrialized countries, rising unemployment, and large governmental rescue packages for the financial industry, which the taxpayers paid or guaranteed (Rodrik 2018). The latter management of the global financial crisis increased the perception of many voters also in the United Kingdom that the government would privilege the interests of the economic elite, while ordinary citizens had to bear the costs of this policy (Frieden 2017; Goodhart 2017). Pro-Brexit politicians took up and cultivated the anti-elite sentiment of many voters. The Equality Trust concludes: "Rising inequality has seen a dramatic increase in the share of income going to the top, a decline in the share of those at the bottom, and, more recently, a stagnation of incomes among those in the middle" (The Equality Trust 2020). This rise in socioeconomic inequality has three implications:

First, it indicates that the bottom and the middle strata of income receivers either did not benefit or gained only modestly from neoliberal policies and international economic openness, while the top earners became richer.

Second, it evidences that the losers and less advantaged of liberal economic policies were not compensated effectively by the winners. Apparently, re-distributive domestic institutional arrangements didn't suffice to prevent rising inequality. The post-war social contract, which acknowledged that socioeconomic hardship induced by liberalization had to be compensated to secure political support among voters, was no longer fulfilled (Colantone/Stanig 2018; Frieden 2017; Goodhart 2017; Owen and Walter 2017; The Economist 2020: 28). Compensation does not only refer to transfer payments but involves the maintenance or substitution of jobs with decent remuneration. In consequence of this institutional failure to cushion the impact of liberalization, the opposition to liberalization and unequal distribution increased and the demand for protection through nation-centered policy became attractive for a growing part of the electorate.

Third, these material conditions affected *ideational* expectations, since "fairness" of income distribution and economic opportunities is a widespread societal value in the United Kingdom (and other industrialized countries) (Rodrik 2018). Many voters identify with "the broad nation," which is characterized as capturing a society's aversion to inequality (Grossman/Helpman 2019). In other words, since both the economically disadvantaged and many of the economically well-off share an opposition to rising inequality, both groups felt discontent with this development. Thus, many voters became dissatisfied with the predominant economic course, even those who benefited from neoliberal policies (more on value-based ideas below). Hence, the liberalization of trade affects material interests and ideational expectations of equality and solidarity.

Although rising inequality triggered opposition toward international economic integration, especially concerning the EU (whose Commission is responsible for the common external trade policy), a part of the Brexit campaign and Boris Johnson did not argue in favor of isolationism. Rather, they advocated the idea of a "global Britain" that would gain by freeing itself from the restrictions of EU membership (Owen and Walter 2017: 6). These findings point to the conclusion that the motivation for some Brexiteers was not trade per se, but the impression that EU membership and unequal distribution of gains required correction through a stronger national control over trade and distribution. While the Leave campaign expected Brexit to benefit the United Kingdom economically, the Remain campaign feared economic losses. A YouGov (2016) poll conducted between June 20, 2016 and June 22, 2016, reported that when asked whether Britain would be worse or better off economically after Brexit, only 4% of Leave voters thought Britain would be worse off, while 78% of Remain voters thought Britain would be worse off. In addition to the trade and finance dimensions of societal interests, fears of losing a job, declining wage levels and public services induced by growing immigration also strengthened the Brexit camp (see below and Goodhart 2017; Schmidt 2017).

3.2 Societal value-based ideas

Besides the value-based ideas of equality, fairness, and solidarity of the domestic "social contract" mentioned above, the ideational dimension of the societal division relevant to the Brexit-vote centers on two issue areas: national sovereignty and culture. First, the process of the United Kingdom's international economic integration included its membership in multilateral organizations that had gained considerable competencies in the last decades. Particularly the EU Commission and the European Court of Justice obtained powers formerly exercised by the member states. Consequently, national power was restricted by international rules and partly by a transfer of state powers to European institutions, especially in the realm of foreign economic policy. This process of supranationalization of tasks that were formerly accomplished by elected governments was driven by the goal to enhance the efficiency of international economic integration. The institutions of international economic governance, however, do not possess the legitimacy and accountability of national parliaments and governments of democratic nation-states (Etzioni 2018: 33).

Thus, the intended increase in economic efficiency weakened sovereignty, accountability, and democracy. To many voters, the seemingly opaque and distant international organizations were exercising a growing influence without letting voters control them – a situation constituting a "failure of representation" according to Frieden (2017: 18). Consequently, one of the most important reasons for Leave voters was the wish to reduce this heteronomy and to "take back control" as formulated in one of the most visible slogans of the Leave campaign (Colantone/Stanig 2018: 207). The Economist (2018: 33) reports a poll among 12,000 Leave voters, which found that the main motive for voting Leave, mentioned by 49%, was democratic self-government and concludes: "By their own lights they were voting against a closed elite in favor of open and accountable government." On the other hand, those voters favoring the United Kingdom remaining in the EU shared the conviction that international organizations such as the EU were better suited to govern the globalized economy than the UK alone. The idea of multilateral governance and weaker national sovereignty appealed especially to voters who preferred a more cosmopolitan way of life that benefited from open borders, finance, and trade. In a nationwide YouGov poll, 72% of voters, who intended to vote for Remain thought of Brexit to be "bad for jobs" (13% responded it would "make no real difference"), while among the Leave voters 44%, thought it would be "good for jobs" (45% responded it would "make no real difference") (YouGov 2016). Hence, in the Leave campaign, the worry concerning material interests (jobs/income) *aligned* with ideational concerns regarding self-determination (accountability/heteronomy).

The second ideational issue of key relevance in the Brexit vote was cultural questions mixed with interests, especially relating to immigration. The latter involved the material interests of those voters who saw their jobs endangered by immigrants as well as ideational preferences concerning British culture and community and the wish to preserve a traditional British way of life (Goodhart 2017). The material and ideational parts of the rejection of large-scale immigration are difficult to disentangle. The influx of refugees during German chancellor Merkel's policy of unlimited immigration since 2015 contributed to concerns in the United Kingdom about immigration and thus to Brexit (Schmidt 2017: 262). Overall, immigration seems to have been an important reason for voting for Leave together with sovereignty and economic issues, while Remain voters mentioned the economy as their first motivation (Hobolt 2016; Owen and Walter 2017).

4 Conclusion

According to the polls and data mentioned above, ideas and interests can be analytically separated since they do possess *sui generis* characteristics, but need to be seen as interacting forces when shaping voters' demands. On both sides of the Brexit divide, material interests and ideational expectations *aligned* in informing politicians' preferences through public opinion polls and ultimately through the referendum in 2016 and the elections in 2019. Between 2016 and 2019, the government of Prime Minister Theresa May and Parliament struggled with the result of the referendum, but the 2019 election of Prime Minister Boris Johnson confirmed the electorate's wish. Johnson had promised to "get Brexit done," to revitalize neglected regions, and to create a "global Britain" that performs better on the world market without the EU. Johnson restated these campaign pledges as Prime Minister echoing the ideational and material demands for enhanced national self-determination, investing in neglected regions and groups as well as for free trade without EU rules (Schirm 2022: 254–255). Thus, Johnson's policy proposals did not aim at isolationism but rather at promoting the material interests and the desire for self-determination of many voters in a sovereign manner without the EU (McCorriston/Sheldon 2020). New *bilateral* free trade agreements, for instance, with Japan in 2020, as well as the trade deal with the EU in December 2020, follow this course.

In the Brexit process, both the Leave and Remain camps comprised ideational expectations as well as material interests that reinforced each other within the two camps. The camps competed in shaping politicians' preferences and in attempting to win the referendum in 2016 and the election in 2019, which ultimately led to the United Kingdom's withdrawal from the EU in 2020. The motives of the Leave voters included *ideational* expectations about democratic self-government, control, and accountability as well as greater equality (of the income distribution), a revitalization of the embedded liberalism social contract, and a more communitarian, traditionally British vision of society. Leavers' *material* interests in better economic participation of regions and voters disadvantaged by liberalization reinforced and politically *aligned* with ideational expectations. The smaller welfare provisions in the United Kingdom's LME (compared, for instance, with Germany's CME) did not prevent the erosion of the "social contract" and only modestly compensated for the negative consequences of the international institutionalization of liberalization. Thus, domestic institutions also impacted the societal foundations of Brexit. On the other hand, the Remainers' motives encompassed *ideational* expectations that favored supranational governance, and a more cosmopolitan vision of life. These ideas overlapped with the *material* interests of Remainers in the continuation of liberalization, European integration, and international governance, which had been beneficial materially to them. The Leave campaign narrowly prevailed in the referendum in 2016. The pro-Brexit *alignment* expressed itself again in the electoral success of Prime Minister Johnson in 2019. In both electoral cases, the winning *alignment* included, first, strongly supportive voters (resulting from high concern and issue salience) and, second, highly complementary material interests and societal ideas that informed governmental preferences in the same policy direction. Thus, the Brexit case plausibly confirms the argument concerning the conditions for the prevalence of one ideational-material *alignment* over the other stated in the theory section of this chapter.

The international institutionalization of globalization (as a critical juncture) such as the liberalization of trade conducted by the EU and WTO ("China shock") severely affected British industry and stimulated the perception of loss of control. Furthermore, the institutionalization of the liberalization and globalization of finance as an additional international critical juncture contributed to the magnitude of the global financial crisis that plausibly further increased material inequality and the perception of heteronomy and failure of representation. Thus, the domestic ideational and material turning points that led to societal demands for policy change represent a consequence of path-dependent repercussions of decisions anchored in the international institutionalization of liberalization. The latter had negatively affected the material interests and ideational expectations of many voters and strengthened the demands for re-distribution and for politically taking back control. Thus, domestic turning points occurred at the level of economic circumstances and their interpretation concerning incomes, jobs, and inequality as well as at the level of political circumstances and their interpretation regarding representation, control, and self-determination. In summary, the international institutionalization of economic liberalization (as a form of critical juncture) had domestic repercussions, which contributed to a shift in ideational and material societal demands (as a form of domestic turning point) that favored nation-centred economic policies (policy change).

References

BBC. 2016. EU referendum: BCC says businesses back Remain but gap narrows', 10 May, at: https://www.bbc.com/news/uk-politics-eu-referendum-36252315.

Bulmer, Simon and Lucia Quaglia. 2018. The politics and economics of Brexit. *Journal of European Public Policy* 25(8). 1089–1098.

Capoccia, Giovanni and Kelemen, Daniel R. 2007. The Study of Critical Junctures. Theory, narrative, and Counterfactuals in Historical Institutionalism. *World Politics* 59. 341–369.

Colantone, Italo and Piero Stanig. 2018. Global Competition and Brexit. *American Political Science Review* 112(2). 201–218.

Colgan, Jeff and Robert O Keohane. 2017. The liberal order is rigged. Fix it now or watch it wither. *Foreign Affairs* 96. 36–44.

Etzioni, Amitai. 2018. The rising (more) nation-centered system. *The Fletcher Forum of World Affairs* 42(2). 29–53.

Fioretos, Orfeo. 2011. Historical institutionalism in international relations. *International Organization* 65(2). 367–399.

Franke, Michael M. 2020. *Regierungspolitik in der Weltfinanzkrise. Der Einfluss von Interessen, Ideen und Institutionen in Deutschland und Großbritannien.* Baden-Baden: Nomos.

Frieden, Jeffrey. 2017. The politics of the globalization backlash: Sources and implications. WP Harvard University.

Goldstein, Judith andRobert O Keohane. 1993. Ideas and foreign policy: An analytical framework. In Goldstein and Keohane (eds.), *Ideas and Foreign Policy*, 3–30. Ithaca: Cornell UP.

Goodhart, David. 2017. *The Road to Somewhere. The New Tribes Shaping British Politics.* London: Penguin.

Grossman, Gene and Elhanan Helpman. 2019. Identity Politics and Trade Policy. Cambridge Mass: WP Princeton/Harvard University.

Hall, Peter A. 1997. The role of interests, institutions, and ideas in the comparative political economy of the industrialized nations. In M. Lichbach and A. Zuckerman (eds.), *Comparative Politics*, 174–207. Cambridge: Cambridge UP.

Hall, Peter A., and David Soskice. 2001. An introduction to varieties of capitalism. In P. A. Hall and D. Soskice (eds.), *Varieties of Capitalism. The Institutional Foundations of Comparative Advantages*, 1–68. Oxford: OUP.

Harnisch, Sebastian. 2018. Deutschlands Politik gegenüber der Belt and Road Initiative der Volksrepublik China 2013–2018. *ASIEN – German Journal on Contemporary Asia* 148. 26–50.

Hobolt, Sarah. 2016. The Brexit vote: a divided nation, a divided continent'. *Journal of European Public Policy* 23(9). 1259–1277.

Ikenberry, John G. 2018. The end of the liberal international order? *International Affairs* 94(1). 7–23.

James, Scott, and Lucia Quaglia. 2019. Brexit, the City and the Contingent Power of Finance. *New Political Economy* 24(2). 258–271.

Jensen, Mads Dagnis, and Holly Snaith. 2016. When politics prevails: the political economy of a Brexit. *Journal of European Public Policy* 23(9). 1302–1310.

Kassim, Hussein, Scott James, Thomas Warren and Shaun Hargreaves Heap. 2020. Preferences, Preference Formation and Position Taking in a Eurozone Out: Lessons from the United Kingdom. *Political Studies Review* 18(4). 525–541.

Kollewe, Julia. 2016. Brexit could cost L100bn and nearly 1m jobs, CBI warns. *The Guardian* 21 March.

Lake, David A. 2009. Open economy politics: A critical review. *Review of International Organizations* 4 (3). 219–244.

Mahrenbach, Laura C. 2019. The Domestic Foundations of Emerging and Established State Trade Cooperation. In Li Xing (ed.), *The International Political Economy of the BRICS*, 57–74. Abingdon: Routledge.

McCorriston, Steve, and Ian M. Sheldon. 2020. Economic Nationalism: US Trade Policy VS. Brexit. *Ohio State Business Law Journal* 14(1). 64–99.

Milner, Helen V. 1997. *Interests, Institutions, and Information: Domestic Politics and International Relations.* Princeton, NJ: Princeton UP.

Moravcsik, Andrew. 1997. Taking preferences seriously: A liberal theory of international politics. *International Organization* 51(4). 513–553.

Nölke, Andreas. 2017. Brexit: Towards a new global phase of organized capitalism? *Competition and Change* 21(3). 1–12.

Novak, Roman. 2020. Value-based ideas or material interests? An explanation of Polish governmental preference formation towards Eurozone accession. *Polish Political Science Review* 8(1). 100–115.

Owen, Erica, and Stefanie Walter. 2017. Open economy politics and Brexit: insights, puzzles and ways forward. *Review of International Political Economy* 24(2). 179–202.

Rodrik, Dani. 2018. Populism and the economics of globalization. *Journal of International Business Policy* 1. 12–33.

Schirm, Stefan A. 2011. Varieties of Strategies: Societal Influences on British and German Responses to the Global Economic Crisis. *Journal of Contemporary European Studies* 19(1). 47–62.

Schirm, Stefan A. 2013. Global politics are domestic politics. A societal approach to divergence in the G20. *Review of International Studies* 39(3). 685–706.

Schirm, Stefan A. 2016. Domestic ideas, institutions, or interests? Explaining governmental preferences towards global economic governance. *International Political Science Review* 37(1). 66–80.

Schirm, Stefan A. 2018. Societal foundations of governmental preference formation in the Eurozone crisis. *European Politics and Society* 19(1). 63–78.

Schirm, Stefan A. 2019a. In pursuit of self-determination and redistribution: emerging powers and Western anti-establishment voters in international politics. *Global Affairs* 5(2). 115–130.

Schirm, Stefan A. 2019b. Domestic Politics and the Societal Approach. In T. Shaw, L. Mahrenbach, R. Modi and X Yi-chong (eds.), *The Palgrave Handbook of Contemporary International Political Economy*, 103–117. London: Palgrave.

Schirm, Stefan A. 2020. Refining domestic politics theories of IPE: a societal approach to governmental preferences. *Politics* 40(4). 396–412.

Schirm, Stefan A. 2022. Globalisation, divided societies and nation-centred economic policies in America and Britain. *European Review of International Studies* 9(2). 240–269.

Schmidt, Vivian A. 2017. Britain-out and Trump-in: a discursive institutionalist analysis of the British referendum on the EU and the US Presidential Election. *Review of International Political Economy* 24(2). 248–269.

Sil, R., and P. Katzenstein. 2010. Analytic Eclecticism in the Study of World Politics: Reconfiguring Problems and Mechanisms across Research Traditions. *Perspectives on Politics* 8(2). 411–431.

Su, Fei. 2022. The Determinants of Leadership. China, Japan, and the United States in East Asia. Cham: Springer.

The Economist. 2020. 'Bagehot: The politics of somewhere', 25 January. 28.

The Economist. 2018. 'Bagehot: The politics of illusion', 23 March. 33.

The Equality Trust. 2020. *How Has Inequality Changed? Development of UK Income Inequality*, at: https://www.equalitytrust.org.uk/how-has-inequality-changed.

The World Bank. 2020. *Gini Coefficient UK*, at: https://data.worldbank.org/indicator/SI.POV.GINI?end=2016&locations=US-GB&start=1969&view=chart.

van Loon, Aukje. 2018. Diverging German and British governmental trade policy preferences in the Transatlantic Trade and Investment Partnership (TTIP) negotiations. *Journal of Contemporary European Studies* 26(2). 165–179.

van Loon, Aukje. 2021. Liberalism and Domestic Politics Approaches in IR. In Knud Erik Jørgensen (ed.), *The Liberal International Theory Tradition in Europe*, 45–58. Palgrave Pivot.

Widmaier, Wesley W., Mark Blyth and Leonard Seabrooke. 2007. Exogenous Shocks or Endogenous Constructions? The Meanings of Wars and Crises. *International Studies Quaterly* 51. 747–759.

YouGov. 2016. Poll on Brexit referendum, 20–22 June, at: https://d25d2506sfb94s.cloudfront.net/cumulus_uploads/document/atmwrgevvj/TimesResults_160622_EVEOFPOLL.pdf

Zimmermann, Hubert. 2019. Brexit and the External Trade Policy of the EU. *European Review of International Relations* 6(1). 27–46.

Oliver Schwarz
Brexit: From ever closer union to differentiated integration?

Abstract: The United Kingdom's withdrawal from the European Union (EU) has been widely recognized as a turning point. Brexit has fundamentally challenged the UK's global position, its relationship with the European Union (EU), and the entire European integration project – and these challenges continue. This chapter uses the theoretical approach of differentiated integration to better understand the crucial changes brought about by Brexit. Through the lens of three core dilemmas of differentiated integration, it shows that Brexit can be sequenced into three distinct phases, the last of which is still ongoing. Accordingly, EU–UK relations moved from a political dilemma to a legal dilemma and then to an institutional dilemma. With the continuation of the third phase, the entry into force of the Trade and Cooperation Agreement does not mean the end of the Brexit process, but flexibility will certainly be part of the evolving post-Brexit relationship.

Keywords: Brexit, differentiated integration, EU–UK relations, European integration, European Union, Trade and Cooperation Agreement

1 Introduction

In his ground-breaking book "The Choice for Europe", Andrew Moravcsik (1998: 1) argues that his liberal intergovernmentalism is best suited to explain the "major turning points" in the history of European integration. His analysis focuses exclusively on the major interstate accords up to and including the Treaty of Maastricht. This is a focus on what is usually called "deepening" in European integration theory (Jachtenfuchs 2002). In light of the Treaty establishing a Constitution for Europe, Moravcsik (2005) even argued that the EU had reached a stable constitutional equilibrium, a "European constitutional compromise." This compromise would make it unlikely to be undermined by substantive, institutional or ideological developments over the medium term because he regarded the constitutional arrangements as substantively effective, institutionally protected, and democratically legitimate. According to Moravcsik, the EU had reached "constitutional maturity" (Moravcsik 2005: 376). In retrospect, we know that Moravcsik's assumption was a miscalculation simi-

Oliver Schwarz, University of Duisburg-Essen

https://doi.org/10.1515/9783111272900-003

lar to Francis Fukuayama's (1992) *The End of History*. The following examples should illustrate this miscalculation: the attempt to establish a European constitution failed; the euro crisis followed, with severe economic and social disparities within the EU; the rule of law is eroding in some member states; European refugee policy has been raising humanitarian questions for years; the consequences of the Corona pandemic threaten to further intensify the negative effects still resulting from the euro crisis; lastly, the Ukraine war is currently calling into question the European, if not the global, security structure. The European Union seems to be in a permanent state of crisis. Former Commission President Jean-Claude Juncker even spoke of a "polycrisis" (European Commission 2016: 1).

It therefore seems appropriate to consider not only major treaty revisions as turning points in the history of European integration but also moments of crisis (Schwarz 2013: 204). In fact, many studies have attempted to interpret this crisis-induced momentum of EU history through old and new theories of European integration (Hooghe and Marks 2019; Moravcsik 2018; Niemann and Ioannou 2015; Puetter 2015; Schimmelfennig 2014, 2018b; Windwehr and Wäschle 2017; Zeitlin, Nicoli, and Laffan 2019). In their highly-acclaimed article "Failing Forward? Crises and Patterns of European Integration," Erik Jones, R. Daniel Kelemen, and Sophie Meunier (2021: 1533) therefore encourage the scientific community "to use existing theories to ask new questions about the patterns we see across different areas of integration, the strengths and limitations of diversity within the integration process, and the prospects for more formal differentiation in what constitutes Europe." In an attempt to respond to their call, this chapter aims to exploit the changes resulting from the withdrawal of the United Kingdom (UK) from the EU. It asks the following research question: How can we understand Brexit as a turning point in European integration? Theoretically rooted in historical institutionalism, a turning point is the point in time at which a significant change in the trajectory of a political system or society occurs (Capoccia & Kelemen 2007). As such, a turning point represents a new situation that is qualitatively different from the historical development that has prevailed up to that moment (for a further understanding of the concept, see Janusch et al. (this volume)). Indeed, Brexit can be considered one of the most fundamental changes in the history of European integration. It represents the first time that a member state has voted to leave the EU. However, it is difficult to reduce Brexit to a single point in time, such as the 2016 referendum or the actual exit of the UK in 2020. This event challenged the idea of an "ever closer union" and raised far-reaching questions about the viability of the entire European integration project. Brexit is a protracted crisis in the historical development of the EU and the UK. Instead, of a discrete moment, Brexit should therefore be understood as a process that began with the 2016 referendum, in which British voters decided whether to be part of the EU or not.

Consequently, this chapter approaches Brexit as a turning point in the ongoing process. Like every process, the UK's exit from the EU can be sequenced into different phases. In the specific case of Brexit, the first section of the chapter draws on the approach of differentiated integration. Here special focus is placed on three core dilemmas of differentiated integration. Making use of these three analytical dimensions, the third section identifies three phases of the UK's withdrawal from the EU, which helps to account for Brexit as a turning point in European integration. The empirical basis of this section consists of official documents, reports, speeches, and other secondary sources. The final section summarizes the main arguments of the chapter and points to further avenues of research.

2 Core dilemmas of differentiated integration

The debate on differentiated integration was initiated by the so-called "Tindemans Report," presented in 1975 (Stubb 1996: 284). In it, the then Belgian Prime Minister Leo Tindemans advocated the further development of the European integration project, particularly in the area of economic and monetary policy. According to his view, this development could take place at different speeds. His proposal sparked a debate that is not just a transitional phenomenon, but rather has become a structural feature of European integration (Deubner 2003). Frank Schimmelfennig, Dirk Leuffen, and Berthold Rittberger (2015) have even gone so far as to conceptualize the EU as a "system of differentiated integration." Generally, differentiated integration can be defined as "the possibility for different member states to have different rights and obligations with respect to certain common policy areas" (Kölliker 2001: 125). However, a clear distinction should be made here between internal and external differentiation (Pfetsch 2007: 22). Whereas internal differentiation involves the decision to move beyond uniform vertical integration in favor of different levels of vertical integration among member states, external differentiation entails the decision to move from no integration to selective, policy-specific integration of non-member states (Schimmelfennig, Leuffen, and Rittberger 2015: 765). In their 2012 overview article on the theoretical field, Katharina Holzinger and Frank Schimmelfennig (2012: 293) listed the Economic and Monetary Union and Schengen among the few important empirical cases of differentiated integration. However, in the recent past, scholars of differentiated integration theory have also turned their attention to Brexit (Holzinger and Tosun 2019; Leruth, Gänzle, and Trondal 2019; Peers 2017; Riedel 2018; Schimmelfennig 2018a; Schimmelfennig and Winzen 2014, 2020; Tekin 2016; Witte 2018). According to Schimmelfennig (2018a), Brexit is rather a test case of "differentiated disintegration." Disintegration can lead to internal differentiation if a member state remains in the EU but opts out of specific policies. It can also result in external differentiation if a member state exits the EU but continues to participate in selected EU policies.

According to Nicole Koenig (2015), both forms of differentiation raise important political, legal, and institutional dilemmas. First, there is a fundamental political dilemma between flexibility and unity. The Treaty establishing the European Economic Community already articulated the goal of "an ever closer union." Each subsequent treaty in the history of the EU, such as the Single European Act of 1986 or the Maastricht Treaty of 1992, continued the goal of deepening European integration. Against this background, the application of differentiated integration proves to be fundamentally problematic. "The fear," Koenig (2015: 7) points out, "is that differentiation can spur further heterogeneity, undermine the fragile sense of a common European identity, and trigger tendencies of disintegration." Second, there is a legal dilemma about organizing differentiated integration within or outside of the European treaties. An important trigger for differentiation within the treaties is, for example, EU enlargement. The accession of the Central and Eastern European states in 2004 alone was accompanied by almost 300 exceptions (Schwarz 2014: 311). In principle, however, these exceptions of so-called instrumental differentiation were all organized within EU legislation and strictly temporary in nature. However, when confronted with divergent member state preferences, limited EU competences or time pressure, differentiation may also occur outside the EU treaties. The Bologna Process is a prominent example of such so-called constitutional differentiation. Finally, there is an institutional dilemma over whether differentiated integration should take place in existing institutions, modify their composition or establish parallel governance structures. The economic governance of the EU can be seen as an example of all three modes of institutional differentiation. The European Central Bank is at the center of the Eurozone, the collective of the 19 EU member states that have already adopted the euro as their sole official currency. However, decisive cooperation takes place through the informal Eurogroup, which is composed of the finance ministers of Eurozone states. Finally, the events of the 2007–2008 financial crises led to institutional reforms within the Eurozone. Some of these reforms resulted in completely new governance structures outside the EU treaties. The Euro-Plus Pact may serve as an example. It was adopted in March 2011 under the EU's Open Method of Coordination as an intergovernmental agreement between all Eurozone members and other EU members.

As Brunazzo (2019: 4) highlights, these three dilemmas were always present in the history of European integration. However, they also reflect three different stages of the debate about differentiated integration. Since it seems appropriate to view Brexit as a case of differentiated integration, if not differentiated disintegration, the three dilemmas will now be analyzed as three different phases of the UK's process of withdrawal from the EU.

3 The political dilemma: UK renegotiation of EU membership (2015–2016)

While the idea of deciding on European issues via referendum was not an issue in the Conservative Party for decades, it began to gain traction with the emergence of the Referendum Party and the UK Independence Party. From the mid-1990s, all three of the main parties in British politics, Conservatives, Labour and Liberal Democrats, were committed to holding a referendum before any making decision to join the Euro (Smith 2016: 5). While David Cameron (2006) as the newly elected leader of the Conservatives initially urged his party to stop "banging on about Europe," EU membership became a defining issue in the first half of his term of office as Prime Minister. Finally, in his Bloomberg Speech in January 2013, Cameron announced that if he was reelected, he would hold an "in-out" referendum on EU membership (Cameron 2013). With this move, Cameron hoped to both resolve intra-party divisions and settle the question of the UK's place in the EU (Lynch 2015).

On November 10, 2015, Cameron set out in a letter to the President of the European Council, Donald Tusk, four key thematic areas in which he sought reforms as part of negotiations on the UK's membership in the EU: economic governance, competitiveness, sovereignty, and social benefits and free movement (Cameron 2015). On February 02, 2016, Tusk replied to the letter with his own proposal for "a new settlement of the United Kingdom within the EU" (Tusk 2016). EU leaders agreed to broadly follow Tusk's proposal at the European Council meeting on 18–19 February 2016. Following intense negotiations between the EU-27 and the UK, a deal was brokered at the European Council meeting from 18–19 February 2016. As Charles Grant (2016: 1) put it, this deal is "far from irrelevant." In fact, Cameron had considerable success in negotiations. With regard to economic governance, he won the guarantee that member states that do not use the euro as their currency, such as the UK, will not be required to fund crisis measures to ensure the financial stability of the Eurozone. As for competitiveness, the least controversial aspect of the British demands, the EU committed to lowering administrative burdens and costs for citizens and enterprises. In addition to the conclusions of the European Council, a Declaration on Competitiveness was released. With regard to social benefits and free movement, Cameron had to compromise in the face of strong opposition from Poland and three other Central European countries. While the EU allowed its member states to implement a safeguard mechanism to reduce the inflow of workers in exceptional situations, this emergency brake was not allowed to operate permanently and could be invoked only for seven years. However, the most important outcome concerns the issue of sovereignty, which was also the most contentious issue during the negotiations (Weiss and Blockmans 2016: 30). The section on sovereignty enhances the special status the UK already enjoyed within the EU. The UK had opted out of the euro and Schengen. It could choose whether to join justice and home affairs measures on a case-by-case basis. Finally, a protocol of the Lisbon treaty exempted the UK from the application of the Charter of Fundamental Rights. The final text of the new settlement for the UK within the EU reads as follows:

> It is recognised that the United Kingdom, in the light of the specific situation it has under the Treaties, is not committed to further political integration into the European Union. The substance of this will be incorporated into the Treaties at the time of their next revision in accordance with the relevant provisions of the Treaties and the respective constitutional requirements of the Member States, so as to make it clear that the references to ever closer union do not apply to the United Kingdom (European Council 2016: 16).

This phrase was important for Cameron. It allowed him to show his opponents that the UK was not being dragged into a "European superstate" (Weiss and Blockmans 2016: 7). The conclusions of the European Council even went beyond the special role of the UK and further elaborated:

> The references to an ever closer union among the peoples are . . . compatible with different paths of integration being available for different Member States and do not compel all Member States to aim for a common destination. The Treaties allow an evolution towards a deeper degree of integration among the Member States that share such a vision of their common future, without this applying to other Member StatesStates (European Council 2016: 17).

Given that the agreement not only acknowledged the integrationist exceptionalism of the UK but also called into question a fundamental part of the EU's *raison d'être* for all member states, this was nothing less than "a fundamental shift in both UK–EU relations and even in the legal order of the EU itself" (Cardwell 2016: 1291). Some observers of EU integration were irritated, to say the least, by the European Council's concessions to the UK. For example, Andrew Duff believed that, "relatively new to the EU in any case, Tusk failed to recognize the magnitude of the precedent he was braking" (Duff 2022: 74). In any event, he assumed that this arrangement never would have been accepted by the European Parliament or unchallenged at the Court of Justice. For the British side, the deal was "neither a crowd pleaser nor a vote winner" (Weiss and Blockmans 2016: 1). Nonetheless, "the final deal offered to the British public can be seen as the largest single shift in a member state's position in the EU" (Boer et al. 2019: 676). Not surprisingly, still during the meeting of the European Council, on 19 February, Cameron announced that his government was in favor of the UK's remaining in a reformed EU. However, 51.9% of the votes cast in the referendum which took place only four months later on June 23, 2016 favored leaving the EU (for more on voters' preferences of and the societal demands for

Brexit, see the contribution of Schirm (this volume)). Years later, Cameron admitted in an interview:

> I think the biggest mistake was letting expectations about what a renegotiation of Britain's position in the European Union could achieve. I mean, I still think the things that we did achieve were worthwhile. We got Britain carved out of ever-closer union. So, the other countries were going to go ahead and have more symbols of statehood, but Britain would stand aside from that. We managed to get agreement that when European Union citizens came to Britain, they could work, but they wouldn't get access to welfare for up to four years. We got protection for the pound because, you know, a lot of Europe's financial services are in the U.K., but we're not a member of the Euro currency, and so we wanted safeguards like that. But I think what I got wrong was that I allowed people to think there were much more fundamental changes – that we could almost have a sort of pick-and-choose aspect to which European laws we obeyed and which we didn't. And this, I think, was damaging (Martin and Bowman 2019).

Because of the negative outcome of the referendum, the European Council conclusions became null and void and never entered into force. It certainly would have been interesting to see how the Court of Justice transformed this intergovernmental interference into a cornerstone of community law. In any case, it is remarkable that the member states were willing not only to formally recognize the UK's special status once and for all, but also to accept the principle of differentiated integration as a new guiding principle for the entire EU. The aim was to allow maximum flexibility in order to preserve the unity of the EU as a whole, or:

> In a nutshell, the UK–EU negotiations of February 2016 were an attempt to accommodate British demands inside the EU institutional framework by reinforcing its internal differentiated integration and also moving towards an internal differentiated disintegration in some aspects, aiming to prevent an external differentiated disintegration demand, such as Brexit (Szucko 2020: 634–635).

4 The legal dilemma: Brexit negotiations (2017–2019)

Although the referendum was legally non-binding, Cameron promised to respect the outcome. He also ruled out the possibility of a second referendum. In July 2016, Cameron resigned as Prime Minister. His successor was Theresa May, who formally initiated withdrawal from the EU under Article 50 TEU by written notification to the European Council on March 29, 2017. With that done, the process then moved from internal to external differentiation (2018a: 1167). In its response to the British withdrawal letter, the European Council stated: "We regret that the United Kingdom will leave the European Union, but we are ready for the process that we now will have to follow" (Council of the European Union 2017: 1). The negotiation started on 19 June 2017, when Michel Barnier, the chief negotiator appointed by the European Commission, met his counterpart, David Davis, the UK Secretary of State for Exiting the EU. May had already presented her 12-point plan for negotiations in a keynote speech on 17 January 2017 (May 2017). Two main options had always been discussed beforehand: the "Norway model," which would keep the UK in the internal market or at least in a customs union with the EU, and the "Swiss model," which would result in a free trade and sectoral cooperation agreement (Pérez Crespo 2017). Unfortunately, the priorities presented by May were not fully compatible with either model. May rejected the idea of remaining in the internal market, which would have meant accepting EU legislation, the jurisdiction of the Court of Justice, freedom of movement, and British contributions to the European budget. She also spoke out against UK membership in the customs union, which would have prevented the conclusion of own trade agreements. Instead, May sought "the greatest possible access" to the internal market through a "new, comprehensive, bold and ambitious free trade arrangement" (May 2017). The EU's negotiating position stood firmly against this. In its guidelines, adopted on April 29, 2017, the European Council emphasized the "integrity of the Single Market" and excluded any possibility of "cherry picking." The document also highlighted the EU's ultimate goal "to effectively protect its autonomy and its legal order, including the role of the Court of Justice" and to "maintain its unity" (European Council 2017). Although the member states and European institutions had dialogued extensively on the guidelines in advance, the unity of the EU was surprising for many observers. After only a few minutes and without real discussions, the guidelines were approved (Ostry, Schramm, and Zenner 2017: 1). Indeed, with the UK's formal request to leave, the willingness of the EU-27 to show greater flexibility and allow for differentiated integration within the European treaties had diminished considerably. More than this, the EU was even unwilling to start negotiations about a future relationship without having made sufficient progress on an orderly withdrawal by the UK.

Under increasing pressure, May had to call for early elections. However, the general election on 8 June 2017 resulted in a hung parliament. May was forced to broker a deal with Northern Ireland's Democratic Unionist Party, which made the negotiations with the EU even more complicated. Nonetheless, on 14 November 2018, a 585-page withdrawal agreement and a 25-page political declaration on the future relation between the UK and the EU were reached. The basic point of the agreement was that the UK as a whole would stay in the EU customs union during a transitional period until December 2020 (and possibly beyond) in order to prevent a hard border between Northern Ireland and the Republic of Ireland – the so-called "backstop" clause (Schnapper 2021: 368). This was well short of what has been labeled May's "red lines" (Polak 2017). Schimmelfennig (2018a: 1169) sees the progression of a learning process which "resulted in the increasing readiness of the UK government to make concessions, but not in a change of its preference for 'hard Brexit.'" Accordingly, the vote on the agreement, scheduled for December 11, 2018 in the House of Commons, was postponed because of opposition, in particular over the backstop. Further negotiations with the EU were necessary. However, in three votes between January and March 2019, the House of Commons voted against the withdrawal agreement by a large majority on each occasion. To prevent a disorderly Brexit on 29 March 2019, the European Council and the UK twice agreed to postpone the exit date until October 31, 2019 at the latest. As the negotiations lagged, the UK even had to take part in the European Parliament elections on May 23, 2019, in which the newly founded Brexit Party won 30.5% and entered the EP as the election winner with 29 seats (Schwarz 2020b).

On July 24, 2019, May resigned from office and Boris Johnson succeeded her. The House of Commons passed legislation in early September 2019 requiring the new Prime Minister to apply to the EU for a further extension if no withdrawal agreement had been ratified by 19 October 2019. In response, on September 10, 2019, Johnson prorogued the House of Commons for an unprecedentedly long time, which was declared illegal by the Supreme Court on 24 September 2019. On 17 October 2019, the EU and the UK finally agreed on a renegotiated deal that no longer included the backstop. Nonetheless, even without the disputed backstop clause, the withdrawal agreement found no majority within the House of Commons. Johnson was forced to request a new postponement of the exit date to 31 January 2020. The European Council accepted this request on 28 October 2019. The very next day, the House of Commons agreed to an early election through a motion proposed by the Liberal Democrats and the Scottish National Party. In the general election that was held on 12 December 2019, the Conservative Party won an absolute majority of 80 seats in the House of Commons. In new composition, the House of Commons ratified the withdrawal agreement on 23 January 2020. Finally, the European Parliament gave its consent to the agreement on 29 January 2020. Accordingly, the UK left the EU on 31 January 2020, but remained part of the Single Market and Customs Union until the end of 2020. Halfway through the withdrawal process, the UK had to break with many of its original negotiating objectives. The EU was successful in maintaining its unity and resisted any special status for the UK that would have compromised the integrity of European law.

5 The institutional dilemma: The EU–UK relationship post-Brexit (since 2020)

EU Chief Negotiator Barnier had already made it clear in a speech to members of national parliaments in May 2017 that "whatever legal form this new partnership takes in all its dimensions, it will in any case be a so-called 'mixed' agreement" (European Commission 2017, translation by the author). Such a mixed agreement must be ratified in every single member state on the basis of its national constitutional provisions. The case of the Comprehensive Economic and Trade Agreement has shown that national parliaments and even some regional parliaments can act as serious veto players. Nonetheless, after eight months of negotiations under considerable time pressure and the real risk of failure, the final Trade and Cooperation Agreement (TCA) were concluded as an EU-only agreement. This means that the agreement was not examined by the Court of Justice before it entered into force, nor were national parliaments given the appropriate time to undertake a thorough legal analysis (Eckes and Leino-Sandberg 2022). The review process of the European Parliament also took place under considerable time pressure (Schwarz 2020a). Although the TCA, which went into effect on 1 January 2021, is over 1200 pages long including annexes and protocols, it has been criticized as a "shallow trade agreement" (Winters 2021: 147). As one critic has put it:

> To the uninitiated reader the TCA may come across as extensive and complex, but appearances are deceptive. It is really mainly an agreement that removes tariffs in EU–UK trade, and no other trade barriers. It is a WTO-plus agreement, with a small plus (Eeckhout 2021: 13).

Indeed, the agreement is basically limited to free trade in goods, which can move between the EU and the UK without tariffs or quotas. Thus, the TCA falls far short of a comprehensive vision for a future partnership envisaged by the EU and the UK (Kassim 2021: 149). The decision to go for a "small deal" (Usherwood 2021: 120) has left out many points that were previously addressed under the UK's EU membership. While the TCA entails a "close partnership on citizens' security," the scope of this part of the agreement is very limited. Ultimately, the biggest "missing piece" (Tonra 2021) appears to be in the areas of foreign policy, defense, and security. The agreement also did not include provisions on cooperation in the field of education, with the UK consequently exiting the Erasmus program (Fabbrini 2020: 13).

As the UK's aim was to avoid any reference to European law and in particular the Court of Justice within the agreement, it was necessary to set up a completely new governance structure. This necessity was even reinforced by the aim of the

EU to protect the autonomy of its legal system (Eeckhout 2021: 13). At the center of this new governance structure emerged the Partnership Council (Schomburg 2021: 208). It is co-chaired by European Commission Vice-President Maroš Šefčovič and UK Foreign Minister Liz Truss. The Council should meet at least once a year. It has the power to make amendments to the TCA, to adopt decisions, and to establish other specialized committees. Decisions by the Council are binding and should be made by consent. The TCA also provides a Parliamentary Partnership Assembly (PPA), comprised of members of the European Parliament and the House of Commons (Fella 2021). The power of the PPA is limited to the right to make recommendations to the Council. Finally, the TCA foresees the creation of a civil society forum to conduct a dialogue with actors and organizations from independent civil society. A number of specialized committees have been established to oversee specific areas of the TCA. Further working groups have been formed to assist these committees. All trade-related committees and working groups are supervised by the Trade Partnership Committee, which is co-chaired by senior EU and UK officials. Its main task is to supervise subordinate committees and establish, dissolve or change their tasks. All non-trade-related committees and working groups are supervised by the Council directly. Similarly to the trade-related bodies, each committee and working group has the power to adopt decisions and recommendations for the policy area of their responsibility. In each governance structure, the key provisions are those that apply in the event of non-compliance (Lydgate et al. 2021: 2). For the UK, it was politically unacceptable for jurisdiction to be given to the Court of Justice, so an independent arbitration tribunal was developed to handle disputes that the EU and the UK cannot resolve through consultation. However, it is unclear how a single member state or even an individual affected by a certain measure can challenge a committee decision (Schomburg 2021: 211). Annegret Engel (2021: 35) therefore skeptically concludes: "Any minor dispute in the future could have severe consequences and ultimately jeopardise jeopardize the entire agreement." Peter van Elsuwege (2021: 797), on the other hand, considers the TCA to be "a rather innovative and flexible structure for the further development of EU–UK bilateral relations." In a middle position, Nicolas Levrat (2021: 16) simply hopes that "the many flaws underlined above may, after all, create the conditions that will push this bilateral relations not to remain stuck in its current weak institutional and legal framework for too long, and then for a genuine and alternative framework for managing the future EU–UK bilateral relationship to emerge."

6 Conclusion

This chapter attempted to answer the following research question: How can we understand Brexit as a turning point in European integration? For this purpose, it made use of the theoretical approach of differentiated integration. Based on the three core dilemmas of differentiated integration, three phases of Brexit could be identified. In the first phase, which covers the period from 2015 to 2016, the renegotiation of EU membership under Cameron took place. Because of the Prime Minister's initiative, the EU granted the UK far-reaching flexibility to ensure the unity of the entire union. The political dilemma of differentiated integration has been solved in that the UK – had it decided to remain in the EU – would still be a full member with all rights, but assigned a special status that permits substantial opt-outs. The EU was even willing to abandon its mantra of an ever closer union, which would have had far-reaching consequences for the overall integration process. However, with the negative outcome of the referendum, those agreements became void. In the second phase, between 2017 and 2019, negotiations on the UK's withdrawal were held. The legal dilemma that now arose was solved in such a way that the new EU–UK relations were completely organized outside of the European treaties. This solution was driven by the UK's desire to break away from the EU as far as possible, and the EU was interested in preserving the unity of European law. Finally, in the third phase, which began in 2020, a new governance structure for future EU–UK relations was established. This phase was also determined by two mutually reinforcing logics: the EU wanted to protect the autonomy of its legal system, and the UK wanted to avoid any references to European law.

In conclusion, Brexit can be seen as a turning point. It is a turning point for the UK, its relations toward the EU, and the whole integration project. As the chapter has shown, Brexit cannot be reduced to a single event, such as the referendum on 23 June 2016. It is a process, and with the help of the three core dilemmas of differentiated integration, three different phases of Brexit can be identified. And although the TCA between the EU and the UK is now in force, the final phase of the institutional dilemma is still ongoing. However, whatever "post-Brexit contours" (Adam 2022) may emerge in the end, flexibility will certainly continue to be a decisive feature of future EU–UK relations and thus the focus of further research.

References

Adam, Christopher. 2022. The emerging contours of a post-Brexit Britain. *Oxford Review of Economic Policy* 38. https://academic.oup.com/oxrep/article/38/1/1/6514748.

Boer, Max de, Nathanael Hausmann, Miriam Mendelberg & Daniela Stammbach. 2019. Cameron's pre-Brexit settlement for the UK within the European Union: failure or missed opportunity. *European Journal of International Management* 13(5). 662–677.

Brunazzo, Bruno. 2019. The Evolution of EU Differentiated Integration between Crises and Dilemmas. https://www.iai.it/en/pubblicazioni/evolution-eu-differentiated-integration-between-crises-and-dilemmas. (8 January, 2022)

Cameron, David. 2006. Leader's Speech at the 2006 Conservative conference. http://www.britishpoliti calspeech.org/speech-archive.htm?speech=314. (7 March, 2022.)

Cameron, David. 2013. EU speech at Bloomberg. https://www.gov.uk/government/speeches/eu-speech-at-bloomberg. (7 March, 2022)

Cameron, David. 2015. EU reform: PM's letter to President of the European Council Donald Tusk. https://www.gov.uk/government/publications/eu-reform-pms-letter-to-president-of-the-european-council-donald-tusk. (7 March, 2022)

Capoccia, Giovanni & R. D. K. Kelemen. 2007. The Study of Critical Junctures: Theory, Narrative, and Counterfactuals in Historical Institutionalism. *World Politics* 59(3). 341–369.

Cardwell, Paul J. 2016. The 'hokey cokey' approach to EU membership: legal options for the UK and EU. *Journal of European Public Policy* 23(9). 1285–1293.

Council of the European Union. 2017. Statement by the European Council (Art. 50) on the UK notification. https://www.consilium.europa.eu/en/press/press-releases/2017/03/29/euco-50-statement-uk-notification/pdf. (8 March, 2022)

Deubner, Christian. 2003. Differenzierte Integration: Übergangserscheinung oder Strukturmerkmal der künftigen Europäischen Union? *Aus Politik und Zeitgeschichte* B53(1–2). 24–32.

Duff, Andrew. 2022. *Britain and the puzzle of European Union* (Routledge studies in modern British history). London, New York: Routledge.

Eckes, Christina & Päivi Leino-Sandberg. 2022. The EU-UK Trade and Cooperation Agreement–Exceptional Circumstances or a new Paradigm for EU External Relations? *The Modern Law Review* 85. https://onlinelibrary.wiley.com/doi/full/10.1111/1468-2230.12698.

Eeckhout, Piet. 2021. Brexit after the negotiation of the Trade and Cooperation Agreement: Who takes back control of what? *Revista de Derecho Comunitario Europeo*. https://doi.org/10.18042/cepc/rdce.68.01.

Elsuwege, Peter Van. 2021. A New Legal Framework for EU-UK Relations: Some Reflections from the Perspective of EU External Relations Law. *European Papers – A Journal on Law and Integration* 2021(6). https://www.europeanpapers.eu/en/e-journal/new-legal-framework-eu-uk-relations-from-eu-external-relations-perspective.

Engel, Annegret. 2021. The Long-Awaited Trade Deal Between the EU and the UK–Expectations and Realities. *Nordic Journal of European Law* 4. https://journals.lub.lu.se/njel/article/view/23443.

European Commission. 2016. Speech by President Jean-Claude Juncker at the Annual General Meeting of the Hellenic Federation of Enterprises (SEV). https://ec.europa.eu/commission/press corner/detail/de/SPEECH_16_2293. (15 March, 2022)

European Commission. 2017. Discours par Michel Barnier à la 57ème COSAC (Conférence des Organes Parlementaires Spécialisés dans les Affairs de l'Union des Parlements de l'Union Européenne) – Malte. https://ec.europa.eu/commission/presscorner/detail/en/SPEECH_17_1469. (9 March, 2022)

European Council. 2016. European Council meeting (18 and 19 February 2016)–Conclusions. https://www.consilium.europa.eu/media/21787/0216-euco-conclusions.pdf. (8 March, 2022)

European Council. 2017. Special meeting of the European Council (Art. 50) (29 April 2017)–Guidelines. https://www.consilium.europa.eu/media/21763/29-euco-art50-guidelinesen.pdf. (8 March, 2022)

Fabbrini, Federico. 2020. From the Withdrawal Agreement to the Trade & Cooperation Agreement: Reshaping EU-UK Relations. https://papers.ssrn.com/sol3/papers.cfm?abstract_id=3756331. (15 March, 2022)

Fella, Stefano. 2021. The UK-EU Parliamentary Partnership Assembly. https://commonslibrary.parliament.uk/the-uk-eu-parliamentary-partnership-assembly/. (15 March, 2022)

Fukuyama, Francis. 1992. *The end of history and the last man.* New York: Free Press.

Grant, Charles. 2016. Cameron's deal is more than it seems. https://www.cer.org.uk/publications/archive/bulletin-article/2016/camerons-deal-more-it-seems. (7 March, 2022)

Holzinger, Katharina & Frank Schimmelfennig. 2012. Differentiated Integration in the European Union: Many Concepts, Sparse Theory, Few Data. *Journal of European Public Policy* 19(2). 292–305.

Holzinger, Katharina & Jale Tosun. 2019. Why differentiated integration is such a common practice in Europe: A rational explanation. *Journal of Theoretical Politics* 31(4). 642–659.

Hooghe, Liesbet & Gary Marks. 2019. Grand theories of European integration in the twenty-first century. *Journal of European Public Policy* 26(8). 1113–1133.

Jachtenfuchs, Markus. 2002. Deepening and widening integration theory. *Journal of European Public Policy* 9(4). 650–657.

Janusch, Holger, Witold Mucha, Julia Schwanholz, Daniel Lorberg & Alexander Reichwein. 2024. Introduction: Turning Points, Typology, and Puzzles. In Holger Janusch, Witold Mucha, Julia Schwanholz, Alexander Reichwein & Daniel Lorberg (eds.), *Turning Points. Challenges for Western Democracies in the 21st Century*, 1–13. Berlin/Boston: De Gruyter.

Jones, Erik, R. Daniel Kelemen & Sophie Meunier. 2021. Failing forward? Crises and patterns of European integration. *Journal of European Public Policy* 28(10). 1519–1536.

Kassim, Hussein. 2021. Relations with the EU. In UK in a Changing World (ed.), *Brexit and Beyond: Government & Law and External Relations*, 149–150. London: King's College London.

Koenig, Nicole. 2015. A differentiated view of differentiated integration. https://institutdelors.eu/wp-content/uploads/2018/01/differenciatedintegrationjdibjuli2015.pdf. (15 March, 2022)

Kölliker, Alkuin. 2001. Bringing together or driving apart the union? Towards a theory of differentiated integration. *West European Politics* 24(4). 125–151.

Leruth, Benjamin, Stefan Gänzle & Jarle Trondal. 2019. Exploring Differentiated Disintegration in a Post-Brexit European Union. *Journal of Common Market Studies* 57. https://onlinelibrary.wiley.com/doi/full/10.1111/jcms.12869.

Levrat, Nicolas. 2021. Governance: Managing Bilateral Relations. https://ssrn.com/abstract=3811236. (15 March, 2022)

Lydgate, Emily, Erika Szyszcak, L. A. Winters & Chloe Anthony. 2021. Taking stock of the UK-EU Trade and Cooperation Agreement. https://blogs.sussex.ac.uk/uktpo/publications/taking-stock-of-the-uk-eu-trade-and-cooperation-agreement-governance-state-subsidies-and-the-level-playing-field/. (7 March, 2022)

Lynch, Philip. 2015. Conservative modernisation and European integration: From silence to salience and schism. *British Politics* 10. https://link.springer.com/article/10.1057/bp.2015.17.

Martin, Michel & Emma Bowman. 2019. David Cameron Talks Brexit And His 'Greatest Regret' In New Book 'For The Record'. https://www.npr.org/2019/09/29/764199387/david-cameron-calls-the-brexit-referendum-his-greatest-regret. (8 March, 2022)

May, Theresa. 2017. The government's negotiating objectives for exiting the EU: PM speech. https://www.gov.uk/government/speeches/the-governments-negotiating-objectives-for-exiting-the-eu-pm-speech. (1 March, 2022)

Moravcsik, Andrew. 1998. *The choice for Europe. Social purpose and state power from Messina to Maastricht*. London, New York: Routledge.

Moravcsik, Andrew. 2005. The European constitutional compromise and the neofunctionalist legacy. *Journal of European Public Policy* 12(2). 349–386.

Moravcsik, Andrew. 2018. Preferences, Power and Institutions in 21st-century Europe. *Journal of Common Market Studies* 56(7). 1648–1674.

Niemann, Arne & Demosthenes Ioannou. 2015. European economic integration in times of crisis: a case of neofunctionalism? *Journal of European Public Policy* 22(2). 196–218.

Ostry, Hardy, Lucas Schramm & Kai Zenner. 2017. Blueprint for the Brexit negotiations: A signal of unity by the EU-27. https://www.kas.de/en/web/bruessel/laenderberichte/detail/-/content/blau pause-fuer-die-brexit-verhandlungen. (8 March, 2022)

Peers, Steve. 2017. Differentiated integration and the brexit process in EU justice and home affairs. In Ariadna Ripoll Servent & Florian Trauner (eds.), *The Routledge Handbook of Justice and Home Affairs Research*, 253–263. London: Routledge.

Pérez Crespo, María J. 2017. After Brexit . . . The Best of Both Worlds? Rebutting the Norwegian and Swiss Models as Long-Term Options for the UK. *Yearbook of European Law* 36. https://academic.oup.com/yel/article/doi/10.1093/yel/yex021/4797568.

Pfetsch, Frank R. 2007. Die EU bedarf der Reformen. *Aus Politik und Zeitgeschichte*, https://www.bpb.de/shop/zeitschriften/apuz/30619/die-eu-bedarf-der-reformen/. (14 March, 2022)

Polak, Polly R. 2017. Brexit: Theresa May's Red Lines Get Tangled up in Her Red Tape. A Commentary on the White Paper. *European Papers – A Journal on Law and Integration* 2. https://www.european papers.eu/en/europeanforum/brexit-theresa-may-red-lines-get-tangled-up-in-her-red-tape. (8 March, 2022)

Puetter, Uwe. 2015. Deliberativer Intergouvernementalismus und institutioneller Wandel: die Europäische Union nach der Eurokrise. *Politische Vierteljahresschrift* 56. https://www.nomos-elibrary.de/10.5771/0032-3470-2015-3-406/deliberativer-intergouvernementalismus-und-institutioneller-wandel-die-europaeische-union-nach-der-eurokrise-jahrgang-56-2015-heft-3.

Riedel, Rafał. 2018. Great Britain and Differentiated Integration in Europe. In David Ramiro Troitiño, Tanel Kerikmäe & Archil Chochia (eds.), *Brexit: History, Reasoning and Perspectives*, 99–112. Cham: Springer International Publishing.

Schimmelfennig, Frank. 2014. European Integration in the Euro Crisis: The Limits of Postfunctionalism. *Journal of European Integration* 36(3). 321–337.

Schimmelfennig, Frank. 2018a. Brexit: differentiated disintegration in the European Union. *Journal of European Public Policy* 25(8). 1154–1173.

Schimmelfennig, Frank. 2018b. European integration (theory) in times of crisis. A comparison of the euro and Schengen crises. *Journal of European Public Policy* 25(7). 969–989.

Schimmelfennig, Frank, Dirk Leuffen & Berthold Rittberger. 2015. The European Union as a system of differentiated integration: interdependence, politicization and differentiation. *Journal of European Public Policy* 22(6). 764–782.

Schimmelfennig, Frank & Thomas Winzen. 2014. Instrumental and Constitutional Differentiation in the European Union. *Journal of Common Market Studies* 52. https://onlinelibrary.wiley.com/doi/full/10.1111/jcms.12103.

Schimmelfennig, Frank & Thomas Winzen. 2020. *Ever looser union?: Differentiated European integration*. Oxford: Oxford University Press.

Schirm, Stefan A. 2024. The impact of globalization and Europeanization on the societal foundations of Brexit. In Holger Janusch, Witold Mucha, Julia Schwanholz, Alexander Reichwein & Daniel Lorberg (eds.), *Turning Points. Challenges for Western Democracies in the 21st Century*, 17–34. Berlin/Boston: De Gruyter.

Schnapper, Pauline. 2021. Theresa May, the Brexit negotiations and the two-level game, 2017–2019. *Journal of Contemporary European Studies* 29(3). 368–379.

Schomburg, Sören. 2021. General provisions under the EU–UK Trade and Cooperation Agreement. *New Journal of European Criminal Law* 12(2). 202–212.

Schwarz, Oliver. 2013. Von der Krise zu den Vereinigten Staaten von Europa? Die Europäische Union zwischen Auflösung und Neugestaltung. In Wilfried Trillenberg (ed.), *Hürdenlauf zu den Vereinigten Staaten von Europa*, 204–217. Berlin: IWVWW.

Schwarz, Oliver. 2014. Die Erweiterung der Europäischen Union. Zum Wandel eines außenpolitischen Überinstruments. In Andrea Brait & Michael Gehler (eds.), *Grenzöffnung 1989. Innen- und Außenperspektiven und die Folgen für Österreich*, 305–330. Wien, Köln, Weimar: Böhlau.

Schwarz, Oliver. 2020a. Deal oder No-Deal: Das Europäische Parlament im Endspiel um den Brexit. *Regierungsforschung.de*. https://regierungsforschung.de/deal-oder-no-deal-das-europaeische-parlament-im-endspiel-um-den-brexit/. (9 March, 2022)

Schwarz, Oliver. 2020b. The 2019 European Parliament Elections and Brexit: Business as Usual? In Michael Kaeding, Manuel Müller & Julia Schmälter (eds.), *Die Europawahl 2019: Ringen um die Zukunft Europas*, 379–390. Wiesbaden: Springer VS.

Smith, Julie. 2016. David Cameron's EU renegotiation and referendum pledge: A case of déjà vu? *British Politics* 11. https://link.springer.com/article/10.1057/bp.2016.11.

Stubb, Alexander C.-G. 1996. A Categorization of Differentiated Integration. *Journal of Common Market Studies* 34(2). 283–295.

Szucko, Angélica. 2020. Brexit and the Differentiated European (Dis)Integration. *Contexto Internacional* 42. https://www.scielo.br/j/cint/a/Ls5NzPmX8xDcCTJCvfGV3dM/?lang=en.

Tekin, Funda. 2016. Was folgt aus dem Brexit? Mögliche Szenarien differenzierter (Des-) Integration. *integration* 39. http://www.jstor.org/stable/44076586.

Tonra, Ben. 2021. Defence and Security in the Trade and Cooperation Agreement: The Missing Piece. https://ssrn.com/abstract=3780021. (29.02.2022)

Tusk, Donald. 2016. Letter by President Donald Tusk to the Members of the European Council on his proposal for a new settlement for the United Kingdom within the European Union. https://www.consilium.europa.eu/en/press/press-releases/2016/02/02/letter-tusk-proposal-new-settlement-uk/. (7 March, 2022)

Usherwood, Simon. 2021. 'Our European Friends and Partners'? Negotiating the Trade and Cooperation Agreement. *Journal of Common Market Studies* 59. https://onlinelibrary.wiley.com/doi/10.1111/jcms.13238.

Weiss, Stefani & Steven Blockmans. 2016. The EU deal to avoid Brexit: Take it or leave. https://www.ceps.eu/ceps-publications/eu-deal-avoid-brexit-take-it-or-leave/. (7 March, 2022)

Windwehr, Jana & Manuel Wäschle. 2017. Mehr, weniger, anders? Europäisierung und Europäisierungsforschung im Zeichen von Dauerkrise und Neuem Intergouvernementalismus. *integration* 40. https://www.nomos-elibrary.de/10.5771/0720-5120-2017-4-295/mehr-weniger-anders-europaeisierung-und-europaeisierungsforschung-im-zeichen-von-dauerkrise-und-neuem-intergouvernementalismus-jahrgang-40-2017-heft-4.

Winters, L. A. 2021. Trade Policy. In UK in a Changing World (ed.), *Brexit and Beyond: Government & Law and External Relations*, 147–148. London: King's College London.

Witte, Bruno de. 2018. An undivided Union? Differentiated integration in post-Brexit times. *Common Market Law Review* 55. https://kluwerlawonline.com/journalarticle/Common+Market+Law+Review/55.2/COLA2018065.

Zeitlin, Jonathan, Francesco Nicoli & Brigid Laffan. 2019. Introduction: the European Union beyond the polycrisis? Integration and politicization in an age of shifting cleavages. *Journal of European Public Policy* 26(7). 963–976.

Holger Janusch and Daniel Lorberg
The American public and Trump's trade war with China
Critical junctures and uncertainties in liberal intergovernmentalism

Abstract: On the basis of liberal intergovernmentalism assumptions, particularly bounded rationality, we define a critical juncture as a period of great confusion about public and societal group interests, beliefs, and perceptions that enables policymakers to question and abandon existing path dependencies. The Trump presidency marks such a critical juncture for US trade policy, especially toward China. Confusion about trade among the American public contributed to Trump's election victory and enabled a shift away from previous liberal trade policies. As a result, the Trump administration launched a trade war with China. The trade war itself, in turn, affected public opinion on trade and China's image; led to national preference recalibration; and contributed to the so-called Phase One Agreement with China. The interaction among national preference formation, international bargaining, and (interim) policy outcome challenges the strict sequence in foreign policy stages as assumed in liberal intergovernmentalism. Although Trump's trade war with China is not the beginning of a protectionist path for US trade policy, it has initiated a radical shift from a belief in free trade to managed trade. The result is an increasing economic decoupling and a vicious cycle of intensifying hostilities that may trigger new path dependencies in US–China trade relations.

Keywords: Critical juncture, liberal intergovernmentalism, public opinion, uncertainty, US trade policy

1 Introduction

Since the end of World War II, the United States has been seen as a guarantor of free trade. Despite brief calls for protectionism, especially during economic crises, the United States has pursued a liberal trade policy. One part of this liberal trade policy was the US–China Relations Act of 2000, signed by President Clinton. It

Holger Janusch, Federal University of Applied Sciences for Public Administration, Faculty of Intelligence Services
Daniel Lorberg, Federal University of Applied Sciences for Public Administration, Faculty of Social Security Administration

https://doi.org/10.1515/9783111272900-004

guaranteed China permanent normal trade relations with the United States and paved the way for China's accession to the World Trade Organization (WTO). However, trade disputes intensified with China's accession to the WTO. Previous US administrations complained primarily of Chinese currency manipulations, intellectual property rights violations, state subsidies, and growing trade deficits. Despite the simmering conflicts, no radical change occurred in trade policy toward China under Presidents Bush and Obama (cf. Destler 2005; Siripurapu 2022).

Against this backdrop, President Trump's approach appears to be the turning point in US trade policy, especially toward China. The reckless and arbitrary tariff use in defiance of established norms of the world trade regime breaks with the previous liberal trade policy. The result was a trade war with tariffs on goods that account for approximately two thirds of both countries' imports. In the end, the Trump administration reached an agreement with China, called the Phase One Agreement. However, this deal should not be confused with a free trade agreement, but rather is only a ceasefire in the ongoing trade conflict. The tariffs imposed remain in place; the structural problems in US–China trade relations remain untouched (Janusch & Lorberg 2020). With the new Biden administration in office, the question now is whether Trump's trade war with China represents only a short-term disruption or a long-term shift in US trade policy toward China.

Drawing on liberal intergovernmentalism, we analyze the causes and extent to which Trump's trade policy marks a lasting turning point in US trade policy, particularly with respect to trade relations with China. Interestingly, the notions of critical junctures and turning points are rather underdeveloped and less noticed concepts in the field of international relations (except for historical institutionalism), although scholars often instinctively and implicitly focus on turning points in foreign policy analyses. This case makes sense, as turning points mark great shifts in foreign policy that attracts attention. This problem also applies to liberal intergovernmentalism and new liberalism in general (Moravcsik 1997). For example, in *The Choice for Europe*, Moravcsik (1998) analyzed five key treaties of European Integration as "major turning points," without defining and explaining what a turning point is.

Our study aims to address four conceptual gaps in liberal intergovernmentalism and to this end considers the US trade war with China as a theory-testing case study. First, the turning point concept remains largely undefined and unaddressed in new liberalism. However, its explicit formulation is crucial for identifying relevant cases, policy change causes, and ongoing trends. Second, uncertainty is also largely undefined in new liberalism but crucial for elaborating the turning point concept. Given that liberal intergovernmentalism assumes bounded rationality, we use this assumption to define uncertainty and, based on it, critical junctures and turning points. Third, we point to the importance of public opinion in explaining foreign policy. Although new liberalism studies and approaches often refer to interest group influences, public opinion is mostly neglected. However, the trade war with China demonstrates the relevance of public opinion, even in a policy area dominated by interest groups, such as trade policy. Fourth, we criticize the assumption of liberal approaches that national preferences are assumed to be fixed once international bargaining is considered. Although this assumption can be helpful in developing a parsimonious theory, it leads to a far-reaching explanatory gap. Instead of a one-way street from national preference formation to international bargaining to policies taken, Trump's trade war with China points to the interplay of all three stages.

In this study, we first develop a turning point concept for new liberalism, especially liberal intergovernmentalism, by referring to critical juncture definitions in historical institutionalism and considering notions of uncertainty, namely, confusion over interests, beliefs, and images. Thereafter, we take the US trade war with China as a theory-testing case to illustrate the explanatory advantage of the modified theoretical approach. In the case study, we analyze (1) how the shift in public opinion can explain Trump's election victory and thus new national preferences in US trade policy, (2) how the trade war with China itself changed public opinion again and pressured the Trump administration to sign the Phase One Agreement, and (3) whether the Biden administration continues Trump's trade policy. Finally, we discuss the extent to which Trump's trade war with China marks a short-term disruption or a lasting turning point that triggers new path dependencies.

2 Critical junctures, turning points, and uncertainties in liberal intergovernmentalism

Liberal intergovernmentalism (and new liberalism) explains state foreign policy from the bottom up, from society to government. To do so, it combines three distinct stages into a theoretical framework: national preference formation, international bargaining, and international institution choice. At all three stages, it draws on middle-range theories of economic interest, bargaining, and institutional choice to provide rationalist explanations (Moravcsik 1998; Moravcsik & Schimmelfennig 2009). Although liberal intergovernmentalism originally explains European integration, it can be applied to foreign policy analysis in general.

In the first stage, the influence of social actors (interest groups) are central for explaining national preference formation. For this purpose, scholars refer to collective action theory. According to this theory (Olson 1965), small groups can well organize themselves because their interests are homogeneous and they face small free-rider problems. As a result, small group interests are overrepresented in national preference formation. Moreover, domestic institutions play a crucial role in determining which interests prevail (Moravcsik 1997). In the second stage, national preferences are assumed to be fixed and the focus moves to interstate bargaining. The asymmetric interdependence concept (Hirschman 1945; Keohane & Nye 2001), for example, helps explain bargaining outcomes, especially gain and loss distributions. Following this argument, states that gain less from (existing or future) cooperation are less dependent. If an asymmetry exists in dependence, then less-dependent states have more bargaining power because they can more credibly threaten to end cooperations or break off negotiations. In the third stage, liberal intergovernmentalism explains certain international institution (and policy) choices. With regard to European integration, the focus is on explaining why states pool or delegate their competences at the supranational level (Moravcsik 1998). A key problem is incomplete and asymmetric information. According to an institutionalist explanation, states pool and delegate authority to signal credibility or to lock-in future decisions against domestic opposition. States can prevent behavioral uncertainties in the future by pooling and delegating. However, explanations can also be found for other forms of cooperation that do not necessarily lead to supranational solutions. For example, principal–agent theory (Jensen & Meckling 1976) explains institutional provisions in international agreements that are intended to prevent moral hazards by disclosing hidden intentions and monitoring hidden behaviors.

Even though liberal intergovernmentalism usually pays attention to decisive developments and transformations in institutions as starting points of its studies, it lacks definitions of turning point. By contrast, historical institutionalism, with its critical junction definitions, has one of the most well-defined turning point concepts in social science that can be integrated into liberal intergovernmentalism. Most famously, Capoccia and Keleman (2007: 348) defined "critical junctures as relatively short periods of time during which there is a substantially heightened probability that agents' choices will affect the outcome of interest." A critical juncture, then, is a short period of high contingency between two long path-dependent processes; a time during which a radical change is possible. Critical junctures thus mark the end and beginning of path-dependent processes (Pierson 2011). Path dependency describes a process according to which institutions once implemented constraint increasingly future agent choices. Reasons include increasing returns, network effects, and future lock-in. Path dependence, however, is not synonymous with determinism. Antecedent conditions and events can cause critical junctures and periods of uncertainty and contingency in which various choices for radical institutional changes are possible. Although antecedent conditions are the causes for critical junctures, they do not explain the outcome of interest (Mahoney et al. 2016: 78); rather, they define the range of possible paths available to key actors. Thus, at critical junctures, agents have additional choices and gain the ability to determine a new path.[1] In turn, the choices taken by agents during the critical juncture set in motion a new path-dependent process that constrains future choices (Mahoney 2000; Capoccia 2015).

Critical junctures do not necessarily lead to changes or (institutional) turning points; they are merely high probabilities of these changes. A turning point means the breaking of an old path dependency and the beginning of a new one that leads to a long-term institutional change. A critical juncture may still result in the previous path-dependent process remaining untouched (Capoccia & Kelemen 2007: 352). Analyzing such negative cases or "near misses" is important to avoid selection biases and flawed results (Capoccia 2015: 165–166).

Historical institutionalism captures turning points only in terms of institutional changes. By contrast, liberal intergovernmentalism seeks to explain three outcomes: national preferences, negotiation outcomes, and institutional choices. Although each of the three stages has its own independent explanations for its respective outcomes, they build on one another. National preferences serve as the basic interests that states seek to achieve in negotiations and the negotiated outcome raises the question of what institutional setting or provision may be best to safeguard the negotiated outcome. Based on this theoretical framework, institutional turning points should be sought at upstream levels. Changes in societal interests are reflected in new national preferences, which, in turn, lead to new negotiation outcomes and new institutional paths. Thus, critical junctures or institutional turning points trace back to major changes in societal preferences. Historical institutionalists capture this aspect only in a simplified form as antecedent conditions. Liberal intergovernmentalism can thus help further understand the societal causes of critical junctures that lead to institutional turning points.

In contrast to historical institutionalism, liberal intergovernmentalism has the weakness that it does not explore institutional path dependence, so appropriate institutional turning points are usually selected intuitively; as mentioned, it can lead to selection biases. Thus, the combination of both theories seems promising. On the one hand, historical institutionalism can help identify critical junctures, as it analyzes path dependencies. Liberal intergovernmentalism, on the other hand, promises an adequate explanatory approach for critical juncture

---

1 Mahoney et. al. (2016: 77) defined critical junctures as necessary conditions that are nearly sufficient conditions for outcomes. By contrast, antecedent conditions may be necessary but not sufficient conditions for outcomes. In contrast to such an agency-based account, Slater and Simmons (2010) emphasized that antecedent (structural) conditions, rather than decisions and events happening during critical junctures, trigger new paths taken after critical junctures.

analysis. It is better suited than historical institutionalism to explain what happens at critical junctures and why certain outcomes, including institutional turning points, come about.

We propose a specific approach for integrating critical juncture into new liberalism, especially liberal intergovernmentalism. Given that a critical juncture describes a period of heightened uncertainty, we first define uncertainty. Such a definition depends on the meta-theoretical assumption of a theory: rationalism, cognitivism (bounded rationalism), or social constructivism (Rathbun 2007). Considering that bounded rationality is a common assumption of liberal intergovernmentalism, we first look for a definition of uncertainty consistent with this assumption.

Iida (1993) distinguished between strategic and analytical uncertainties. The former fits into rational choice theories, whereas the latter is consistent with bounded rationality. Under strategic uncertainty, actors know their own characteristics but not those of others. Actors try to signal their own attributes or pretend to have attributes other than their own. Learning occurs by observing others' actions. Under analytical uncertainty, actors know others' attributes, but they do not know how the world works; for example, whether free trade causes job losses and low wages or the opposite. Actors do not only signal their attributes but also try to convince others of their beliefs. Learning not only happens by observing others' actions but also by considering previous outcomes; for instance, by considering what effect previous free trade agreements had on jobs and wages.

Iida's (1993) understanding of strategic and analytical uncertainties resembles Rathbun's (2007) definition of ignorance in rationalism and confusion in cognitivism. Ignorance implies a lack of information; the challenge is to judge others' intentions. Learning takes place by gathering additional information. By contrast, the problem with confusion is not a lack, but information overflow and ambiguity; the challenge is to reduce complexity. The definition of confusion is based on the bounded rationality assumption (Simon 1957). Actors still act rationally but have limited cognitive capacities to collect and process information. To cope with information excess, actors use cognitive shortcuts or heuristics for collecting and processing information. Cognitive shortcuts do not only include routines but also stereotypes, images, and beliefs about how things work.

Given that scholars often use interests, beliefs, and preferences synonymously, let us clarify these terms to avoid misunderstandings. Interests describe the basic goals, values, needs, or desires that actors strive for, whereas beliefs describe certain views about cause–effect relationships. For example, a trade union has the interest of high wages for its members who may believe that free trade leads to low wages.[2] Images are perceptions or stereotypes about others. They serve as mental models and shape how actors search and interpret information and fill in missing information. For example, when US decision makers hold an image of China being an enemy, they may interpret actions by the Chinese government hostile, regardless of their true intentions. Scholars often use preferences synonymously with interests. Although preferences and interests are related, they are different. Preferences are defined here as the order in which actors prefer different choices or action options. Preferences also depend on the interests, beliefs, and images actors hold (as well as the expectations about others' actions and expected pay offs). For example, whether a Congresswoman prefers a trade agreement over tariffs against China depends on her interests (or that of her constituency), her beliefs about free trade, and her image toward China.

Based on the uncertainty definition, we can now define a specific understanding of critical juncture for liberal intergovernmentalism. Such an understanding is still in accordance with Cappocia and Keleman's (2007: 348) definition of critical junctures as periods of "substantially heightened probability that agents' choices will affect the outcome of interest". Rather than providing an alternative definition, we argue that liberal intergovernmentalism can help explain the causes of such a period of high agency. Critical junctures represent a change in the agency-uncertainty nexus (see Introduction); increased uncertainty raises doubts about existing institutional constraints and opens up opportunities for agents to change them. A higher agency and uncertainty go hand in hand. Following the bottom-up approach of new liberalism, the starting point for a critical juncture is the changing preferences of societal actors. Changing societal preferences (including interests, beliefs, and images) point to periods of heightened uncertainty, especially confusion.

Two reasons explain such periods. (1) Social groups increasingly hold conflicting interests, beliefs, or ideas. Thus, an overarching consensus no longer exists as it previously did before the critical juncture, when path dependencies limited actor choices. (2) Social groups no longer have firm, stable interests, beliefs, or ideas. Instead, they are undecided, and their interests, beliefs, and ideas are volatile and constantly up for debate. To explain which path agents to take during critical junctures, we must identify how societal interests, beliefs, images, and preferences finally change. If societal interests, beliefs, or images change in a persistent way, then they

---

2 The advocacy coalition framework (e.g., Sabatier 1988) distinguishes between deep and policy core beliefs and secondary aspects. The former refers to the personal philosophy about (human) nature, whereas the latter describes the fundamental policy positions on specific issues and beliefs about policy implementations. All three types build together a belief system. Accordingly, a belief system in the advocacy coalition framework includes what we define as interests, beliefs, and images.

lead to new long-lasting national preferences, which then determine new bargaining outcomes and new institutional paths. New intuitional paths, in turn, mark turning points.

Following this critical juncture conceptualization, institutional and policy turning points are the results of persisting changes in societal preferences. Interestingly, such changes can also be termed as ideological turning points. To avoid confusion, however, we use the term "turning points" only to describe persistent intuitional or policy changes that constitute new path dependencies. Moreover, changes in social preferences are more likely to emerge over longer, diffuse periods than at specific points in time. The term "turning points" may then be misleading.

So far, we have followed Moravcsik's (1998) liberal intergovernmentalism. At this point, however, we deviate from basic assumptions of liberal intergovernmentalism in three respects. First, even though liberal intergovernmentalists acknowledge public impact on national preference formation, they focus on the influence of interest groups. Contrary to the Almond–Lippman consensus that the public plays no central role in shaping foreign policy (Almond 1960), we argue that public opinion can have a significant impact on state preference formation, especially during critical junctures. Certainly, public opinion plays only a role when domestic institutions (e.g., democratic elections or freedom of speech) provide the setting for it. Moreover, issue salience is of importance in democracies. When issue salience is low, issues do not receive much public attention and interest groups are central for decision making. However, the higher the issue salience, the more relevant the public or their interests, beliefs, and images become in political decision-making processes (Verdier 1994; Janusch 2021).

Second, Moravcsik (1998) assumed that societal groups form national preferences, with political decision makers becoming agents not before the second stage, the international bargaining. Societal interests, beliefs, and images are exogenously given. However, decision makers themselves can influence public opinion, including public interests, beliefs, and images and thus shape national preference formation. In this case, the abilities of decision makers to set agendas and frame issues become important. Decision makers can influence which issues attract media and public attentions by setting agendas and can influence public interests, beliefs, and images by framing issues. A common example is playing the security card. For example, a president can frame a trade agreement not only as an economic issue but also as a threat to national security. It not only makes a trade agreement further salient but also influences the public belief about free trade and its image about the trading partner (Janusch 2021).

Third, Moravcsik (1998) assumed that national preferences are fixed when international negotiations begin. However, international bargaining and institutional (interim) agreements can affect public opinion and thus national preference formation, which, in turn, affects ongoing international negotiations and institutional choices. We thus assume a constant interplay among the three stages.

As a result of the three proposed modifications, the theory loses parsimony, which is considered one of the major objectives of new liberalism (Moravcsik 1997). However, the theory gains decisively in explanatory power, without which at least the present case cannot be adequately explained. We argue for an approach that softens the assumption of the fixed sequence of the three stages but still identifies nomothetical explanations on the basis of mid-range theories within individual stages. Thus, we suggest an ideographical combination of nomothetical explanations based on mid-range theories. We do not rule out the possibilities of having valid hypotheses or scope conditions about the relationship between the three stages and their nomothetic explanations. However, finding such hypotheses or conditions is beyond the scope of this work.

3 Trump presidency as a critical juncture in US trade policy

On the basis of the proposed notion of critical juncture, we analyze the extent to which the Trump presidency led to a turning point in US trade policy, especially related to the trade relations with China. For us, the role of public opinion and the interplay among the three stages – national preference formation, international bargaining, and institutional choice – are crucial to explain the trade policy under President Trump and examine the extent to which it can cause a long-lasting turning point in trade policy. First, we show how public opinion can explain Trump's election and how it has led to new national preferences, albeit not stable ones (Section 3.1). Second, we demonstrate that the new national preferences initiated and escalated the trade war with China. However, the trade war led to changing beliefs of the US public about free trade, recalibrating national preferences again. As a result, the recalibrated national preferences and the upcoming presidential elections pressured the Trump administration to sign the Phase One Agreement with China (Section 3.2). Third, we show that the changing public opinion on free trade and alerting image about China are reflected in Biden's campaign and trade policy. The Biden administration does not continue Trump's trade policies one-to-one, but it nonetheless reflects a fundamental paradigm shift from liberal to managed trade (Section 3.3).

3.1 US public opinion, Trump election, and the "civil war" over trade

Similar to the US administration, the American public has traditionally been considered pro-free trade due to its basic libertarian attitudes. However, since China's accession to the WTO and during the financial market crisis, support for free trade among the public had steadily declined, compared with that in the 1990s. This shift in public opinion is not entirely unfounded; for example, studies (e.g., Autor et al. 2013) have shown that China's entry into the WTO led to massive job losses in the US manufacturing. Interestingly, public approval for free trade rebounded after the financial market crisis (Figure 1). During the 2016 presidential campaign, a clear majority of the US public saw free trade as an opportunity (58%), rather than a threat (34%) (Younis 2021), even though Trump's successful campaign gave a different impression. Nevertheless, Trump's anti-free trade rhetoric was still an advantage in the primaries and the general election because of the following reasons.

Although public approval for free trade rebounded after the financial market crisis, the disparity developed between Republican and Democratic voters grew. Republican voters had traditionally been more in favor of free trade; they (51%) were less supportive about free trade than Democratic voters (61%) in 2015 (Younis 2021). This trend in public opinion suggests a shift in beliefs, rather than in basic interests. Free trade is generally not a self-interest but is seen as a good or bad policy depending on whether it is believed to be beneficial or harmful to jobs, wages, or national prosperity as a whole. Interestingly, only a minority of all Americans believed that free trade creates jobs (20% in 2014) or increases wages (17% in 2014) (Stokes 2015), even though most Americans viewed free trade as good for the country. The shift in Republican voters' beliefs, among other reasons, gave Trump an advantage over other Republican candidates in the primaries. Emphasizing that previous trade agreements were bad for jobs and needed to be renegotiated, Trump was able to capitalize even on the concerns from voters who support free trade. His campaign even appeared to have fostered Republicans' unfavorable views on trade (Jones 2017). Trump's campaign, which successfully instrumentalized media, shows how the political elite can set agendas and frame issues to shape public beliefs.

Trump's criticism of past free trade agreements also scored points over Clinton with voters in the general election, with two aspects playing a central role. First, free trade opponents rank issues higher than free trade supporters (Hendrix 2016). As free trade opponents associate concentrated jobs and wealth losses with free trade, they put great effort in preventing such losses. Meanwhile, free trade supporters expect rather diffuse wealth gains that are less tangible. Behavioral economics, particularly prospect theory (Kahneman & Tversky 1979), explains such a behavior, as losses cause greater emotional impacts than the same amount of gains. In such a context, presidential candidates can gain votes by opposing free trade but do not risk losing many votes, as free trade supporters do not make their voting decisions dependent on it.

Second, under the US Constitution, a candidate needs a majority vote of the Electoral College to be elected president, and not the popular vote. The Electoral College comprises 538 electors, with each of the 50 states (plus the District of Columbia) providing electors in proportion to its population. Given the winner-takes -all principle, a presidential candidate with a relative majority in one state receives all electors of that state. In this institutional setting, a candidate winning battleground states, where a close outcome is expected, is crucial. For candidate Trump, this institutional setting was advantageous because voters who opposed to free trade were highly concentrated in decisive battleground states (Hendrix 2016). This case did not only include states of the so-called Rust Belt, such as Pennsylvania, Ohio, and Michigan, but also Florida.

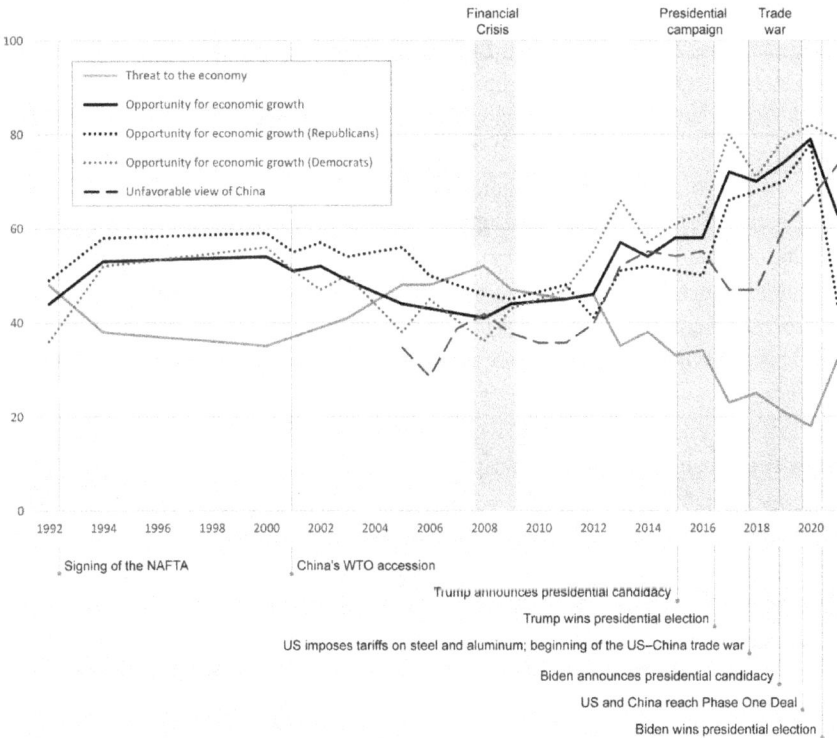

Figure 1: US public opinion on trade and China.
Sources: Silver et al. (2020), Younis (2021).

Trade policy, in general, is an issue that is less important than most domestic issues, but the fact that a presidential candidate who opposes free trade is likely to win voters without risking losing voters, especially in battleground states, gave Trump an advantage in the general election. By contrast, Clinton lacked credibility for her campaign critical of free trade, as she flip-flopped her position. Even though she rejected the Trans-Pacific Partnership (TPP) on the campaign trail, she supported it as Secretary of State. In the end, Trump's campaign on free trade contributed to his electoral victory (Hendrix 2016). The shift in public opinion, particularly among Republican voters, gave Trump an advantage in the primaries and general election and can be seen as a cause of the new national preferences that emerged during the Trump presidency (see below).

After his inauguration, Trump withdrew from the TPP that had been signed by President Obama but had to be approved by Congress, as one of the first official acts. Nevertheless, Trump's protectionist beliefs about trade and his confrontational negotiation style did not immediately cause a trade policy shift. National preferences still had to form in the White House. Here, small group conflicts (Mintz & Wayne 2016) played a central role.

In Trump's new cabinet, two factions with opposing beliefs clashed over the trade policy direction, resulting in a "civil war" over trade. On the one hand, US Trade Representative (USTR) Robert Lighthizer, Secretary of Commerce Wilbur Ross, the President's trade advisor Peter Navarro, and chief strategist Steve Bannon pushed for a new realignment, advocating for tariff imposition as an end in themselves or as bargaining leverage to achieve new trade deals that would protect domestic manufacturing and decrease trade deficit. On the other hand, Secretary of Treasure Steven Munchin and chief economic adviser Gary Cohn, while not pushing for a continuation of previous liberal trade policy, sought to prevent tariff hikes, fearing that doing so would hurt the economy (Smith 2017). In the end, after two years, the former faction prevailed, as Trump never changed his position and pushed forward his beliefs and approach on trade; backed by his belief that he must keep his campaign promise to voters. In March 2018, the Trump administration began imposing tariffs on steel and aluminum due to concerns about national security. As a result, Cohn resigned (Bown & Kolb 2021).

The White House "civil war" shows that national preference formation is a complex process. Even if voter and societal group interests processed by elections finally translate into new national preferences, nothing is certain at all times. In the present case, small group dynamics within the administration must be overcome. Nevertheless, it is not necessarily at odds with liberal intergovernmentalism. Approaches on groupthink (or polythink) and bureaucratic processes (Allison 1971; Mintz & Wayne 2016) can be integrated into liberal intergovernmentalism as mid-range theories because they share the same basic assumptions, such as bounded rationality.

After the White House "civil war" ended, national preferences were set for the trade negotiations with China. Republicans in Congress, usually known as free trade supporters, voiced criticism but did not crack down on Trump's new trade agenda (Pramuk 2018). From then on, Trump's beliefs and campaign promises became the new uncontested mantra of US trade policy, consisting of two key aspects (Navarro & Ross 2016). First, trade is a zero-sum game, with trade deficit a sign of losing. Second, tariff threat and imposition to exert "maximum pressure" on negotiating partners became the new bargaining approach. If a trade deficit is a loss anyway, then you can only gain from imposing tariffs. As Trump said, "trade wars are good and easy to win" (Hass & Denmark 2020). Trump did not reject free trade agreements in general, but only those he did not negotiate himself, as evidenced by Trump's later signing of the US–Mexico–Canada Agreement (USMCA), the follow-up deal of the North American Free Trade Agreement (NAFTA).

3.2 US–Sino trade war and changing public opinion

With the new national preference set, trade negotiations with China escalated. In January 2018, the Trump administration levied safeguard tariffs on $10 billion worth of Chinese imports, such as solar panels and washing machines. In March 2018, the Trump administration imposed additional tariffs on steel and aluminum against China (and US allies, such as the European Union [EU]) due to national security concerns. The tariffs targeted $2.8 billion worth of Chinese imports. In April 2018, China retaliated with tariffs on US imports worth $2.4 billion. From then on, the trade conflict escalated, leading to a vicious circle of retaliation. Over the next year till June 2019, the Trump administration and the Chinese government imposed tariffs in four rounds. In the end, the tariffs targeted Chinese imports worth $250 billion and US imports worth $100 billion. Both sides had already threatened further tariff increases (Bown & Kolb 2021).

The trade war, as a bargaining process and (interim) bargaining outcome, had a retroactive effect on national preference formation by influencing public opinion. Public opinion volatility suggests a period of heightened confusion and points to a critical juncture. Only few industries, such as steel and aluminum producers, profited from these tariffs, and many industries suffered; either the agriculture sector, which was targeted by China's tariff hikes, or the automobile sector, which had to pay high prices for steel and aluminum. US customers ended up paying high prices (Hass & Denmark 2020). As a result, US public opinion about free trade changed dramatically, regardless of party affiliation. In 2020, a vast majority (79%) saw trade as an opportunity for growth, whereas far less (18%) viewed it as a threat (Figure 1). Thus, the negative economic effects of the trade war led to changes in public beliefs about free trade. The US public largely shared the belief (at least for the moment) that free trade is good for the country. At the same time, China's image deteriorated during the trade war. It also suffered from the COVID-19 pandemic and alleged human rights violations in Hong Kong and Xinjiang. Meanwhile, only under one half of Americans (47%) had an unfavorable view of China at the beginning of the trade war in 2018; it reached an all-time high (73%) in 2020 (Silver et al. 2020), with most Americans increasingly supportive of a tough stance toward China (Silver et al. 2021).

Although the negative view of China reinforced a tough stance on the trade war, the dramatic shift of public opinion on trade put pressure on the Trump administration to find a deal. Moreover, the trade war with China attracted public attention; thus, issue salience rose, so public opinion became further important relative to interest group influence. The trade war itself and its negative economic consequences initiated national preference recalibration, which proves that national preference formation and interstate bargaining stages mutually influence each other. Public opinion gained additional weight due to the upcoming presidential election. As Trump had consistently presented himself as a dealmaker, he had to prove it as the election was approaching. The recalibrated national preferences pressured the Trump administration to present a deal before the presidential elections. In January 2020, the United States and China signed the Phase One Agreement (Bown & Kolb 2021). However, the deal should not be mixed up with a long-lasting free trade agreement.

On the one hand, the deal addresses some structural problems in the US–Sino trade relations, such as trade deficits and unfair trade practices. China pledged to buy additional US goods and services worth $200 billion above the 2017 levels for two years. China agreed to strengthen intellectual property protections to prevent piracy. It also promised to relax requirements for US companies to enter joint ventures and transfer technologies in return for having access to the Chinese market. China pledged to open its financial service sectors to US companies and reduce trade barriers related to sanitary and phytosanitary standards for agricultural goods. Furthermore, China reaffirmed its commitment under the International Monetary Fund not to devalue its currencies to boost its exports (USTR 2020).

On the other hand, whether the deal will solve the contentious US–Sino trade relations is questionable. First, the deal is not a free trade agreement; most imposed tariffs during the trade war remain in place. Second, the deal does not aim to balance trade by leveling the playing field but through managed trade (Hufbauer 2020). Instead of free markets, governmental commitments to purchase fixed quantities of goods determine the flow of goods and services. Apart from the diverting effects on global trade and inefficiencies, the deal provides an unstable basis for a conflict-free trade relation, as it sets unrealistic purchasing goals that can hardly be matched by China. Third, the deal leaves many major problems untouched, such as China's subsidies for state-owned companies or cyber theft. Fourth and finally, the dispute settlement prefers contract termination over conflict resolution (Bown 2020; Janusch & Lorberg 2020). In practical terms, it means that the United States and China agreed that after consultations between the USTR and China's vice premier, the complaining party can suspend obligations under the agreement or impose remedial measures, such as tariffs without counter responses. This situation applies as long as the action is taken in "good faith." Otherwise, it can simply withdraw from the agreement (USTR 2020).

To summarize, the imposed tariff maintenance, unrealistic purchasing target through managed trade, lacking solution for structural problem, and insufficient conflict resolution make the Phase One Agreement a "ceasefire," rather than the beginning of a conflict-free, stable trade relation.

3.3 Turning point or brief anomaly: Biden's campaign and trade policy

As previously mentioned, due to Trump's trade war with China (and trade conflicts with other countries), the US public had a significantly favorable attitude toward free trade, but a much less favorable view of China. Given this trend in public opinion, one might expect candidate Biden to take a tough stance on China but promise a return to pre-Trump liberal trade policies when it comes to other countries. Yet, it was not exactly the case.

On the one hand, Biden promised a tough stance on China in his campaign. For the polarization between Democrats and Republicans in Washington, a growing bipartisan consensus exists when it comes to attitudes toward China. The unanimous confirmation of Katherine Tai, the former USTR's head of China trade enforcement under President Obama and known critic of China's trade practices, and the new USTR confirms this bipartisan consensus (Nunley 2021). A U-turn in trade policy toward China is not to be expected from Biden or any other future president, Democrat or Republican. Thus, the Trump administration initiated a turning point in US trade policy toward China. However, this turning point was not a complete U-turn. Already before the Trump presidency, trade conflicts (and other issues such as human rights, Taiwan, and territorial disputes in the South China Sea) were coming to a head. The Bush and Obama administrations took confrontative approaches. Meanwhile, Trump chose a new form of escalation using far-reaching tariffs as a bargaining leverage, marking a turning point. Even though the trade war had economic and social costs (for an overview see Hass & Denmark 2020) and led to a shift in public opinion, Trump demonstrated that tariffs are a possible tool in negotiations with China. Trump's trade war has set a benchmark against which future presidents will be measured when it comes to taking a tough stance on China.

On the other hand, Biden did not promise in his campaign to return to the pre-Trump trade policy, for example, by joying the Comprehensive and Progressive Agreement for Trans-Pacific Partnership, the succession agreement of the TPP. Breaking the so-called "blue wall" in 2016 and winning in Pennsylvania, Michigan, and Wisconsin, former Democratic strongholds, Trump caused a structural shift in US trade policy. As trade attracted issue salience and public attention, public opinion gained importance over interest group influence. However, it does not mean that other issues, such as health care or immigration, were not important to many voters. Nevertheless, advocating for a continuation of trade policy before Trump would have been a risk. Biden's campaign aimed to win back the lost battleground states. Given that free trade opponents tend to live in important battleground states and count the issue to be more important than free trade supporters, a return to previous liberal trade policies would have risked losing votes in crucial battleground states. This circumstance may explain why Biden kept a critical stance toward free trade. Despite constantly changing public opinion on trade policy, Biden did not risk adhering to long-held beliefs about free trade advantages. Thus, with his 2016 campaign, Trump had already set the agenda and framed the issue for the 2020 presidential election.

Although Biden is neither returning to traditional liberal trade policies nor simply continuing Trump's trade policies, Biden's trade policy differs from Trump's in important ways. First, the Biden administration neither views trade as a zero-sum game nor is fixated on trade deficit. Second, the "maximum pressure" approach is not taken, meaning that the Biden administration does not use tariffs as a universal bargaining lever. Instead, the Biden administration attempts to resolve trade disputes without threatening or imposing tariffs, particularly with close trading partners and allies, such as the EU. For example, the Biden administration reached two agreements to resolve the 17-year-old Airbus–Boeing trade dispute (Birnbaum et al. 2021) and the trade conflict about Trump's tariffs on steel and aluminum (Bown & Russ 2021). In addition to improving the trade relations with its major partners, the Biden administration aims to create a united front against China (Ordoeñz 2021); although policies such as the Inflation Control Act alienate allies such as Germany, South Korea, and Japan because it subsidizes US electric vehicle and semiconductor manufacturing (Knox 2023).

Nonetheless, the Trump presidency led to a realignment of US trade policy that is evident in aspects that were unobserved in the trade policies of his predecessors but are now reflected in President Biden's. Free trade is no longer the guiding principle; similar to the Trump administration, the Biden administration adheres to the idea of a "managed trade." Free trade is no longer unequivocally seen as an appropriate means to improve US competitiveness and create good-paying jobs and national wealth. The idea of managed trade is reflected in the fact that unlike other policy issues, such as climate change, Biden has retained many of Trump's trade policies in place. The Biden administration promised to enforce strictly the Phase One Agreement (Bown 2021). It also did not lift the tariffs on steel and aluminum against allies, instead maintaining voluntary export restrictions the Trump administration had negotiated with countries such as Brazil and South Korea or negotiating a new agreement with the EU that lifts the tariffs, but only up to a certain quota (Bown & Russ 2021). Furthermore, the Biden administration has strengthened the "Buy American" rule, which requires federal agencies to procure domestic goods (Hoffman et al. 2021). Biden also signed industrial policy legislation aimed at strengthening the US chip industry to counter China's growing influence (Kanno-Youngs 2022). The Biden administration also tightened the ban on Chinese companies buying advanced semiconductors and chip-making equipment, escalating the tech war with China. Other countries such as Japan and the Netherlands have joined the export controls. The restrictions, thus, also include the Dutch company ASML, the leading producer of semiconductor manufacturing equipment (Toh 2023).

4 Path dependency and the Trump presidency as critical juncture in US trade policy

Since the end of the World War II, the United States has pursued a liberal trade policy. Although Presidents Clinton and Obama criticized previous trade agreements for neglecting labor and environmental standards, they pushed forward the same liberal policy, except for strengthening labor and environment provisions (Janusch 2015). Path dependencies may have contributed to this trend. First, with each new free trade agreement, business interests tied to liberal trade policies grow, whereas opposition steadily shrinks or even disappears. Second, given that trade agreements must be approved by Congress and are commitments to trading partners, they lock-in future administrations. Third, the more political elites and bureaucracies internalize beliefs that free trade is good for national wealth, the more unrealistic a departure from established liberal trade policies appears.

Assuming these path dependencies in trade policy, the Trump presidency marks a critical juncture. In line with liberal intergovernmentalism, we define critical junctures as periods of growing confusion (analytical uncertainty) over interests, beliefs, and images. As growing confusion leads to increasing questions about beliefs on existing institutions and policies, agents have additional new choices available to them to pursue different paths. Thus, agent choices become more important than path dependencies. As US public opinion on trade has been constantly shifting in the past years, this increased volatility of public opinion is a sign for a critical juncture in trade policy.

In these times, changes in beliefs are not only exogenous events but also are determined by the interplay of the three stages: national preference formation, international bargaining, and institutional choice. Initially, changing public opinion contributed to Trump's victory, as Republican voters became critical toward free trade. Voters who opposed free trade were also concentrated in decisive battleground states and gave more importance to the issue than those who held positive attitudes toward free trade. Public opinion on trade contributed to Trump's election victory and thus to new national preference formation, but no clear sequence of the foreign policy decision-making process exists, as usually assumed in liberal intergovernmentalism. Trump's campaign itself affected public opinion and led him to win the election. The trade war with China, as part of the international bargaining and as an interim bargaining outcome, in turn, resulted in a vast majority of Americans, including Republicans, to have more positive attitudes toward free trade. At the same time, unfavorable views on China hit an all-time high. With the presidential election looming, shifting public opinion put pressure on the Trump administration to reach a deal with China, leading to the Phase One Agreement.

The US trade policy toward China under President Trump marks a turning point. However, it was not as extreme as it appeared at first glance; it was not a U-turn. First, trade policy had not taken a clear protectionist path. Trump saw tariffs primarily as a bargaining leverage, rather than a remedy, as evidenced by the signing of the USMCA and the Phase One Agreement. Second, even before Trump took office, US–China trade relations were headed for conflictual times. Nevertheless, the Trump administration redirected US trade policy from its liberal course to one characterized by a belief in managed trade. The unfettered rule of the free market no longer serves as a US creed, as reflected in Biden's trade policy. Despite changing public opinion in the course of the trade war, Biden takes a critical stance on free trade, as he aims at winning back blue-collar workers in battleground states. This paradigm shift marks a turning point against the backdrop of the longstanding liberal US trade policy.

Although the shift in US trade policy initiated by Trump continued under his successor, whether this new path will persist over a long period remains to be seen. To become a lasting turning point, the emergence of a new path dependency is crucial. We point out two possible path dependencies when it comes to US–China trade relations.

First, public opinion has become further important in trade policy. The American public, regardless of party affiliation, had favorable attitudes toward trade before the 2020 presidential election, but Republican approval dropped precipitously after Biden took office (Figure 1). This volatility initially suggests a back-and-forth on trade policy, a clear trend exists in the perceptions about China. Americans have increasingly hostile attitudes toward China. In Congress, members of both parties share unfavorable views on trade and China, making the conflict with China further likely in the future and in turn will most likely lead to further unfavorable public attitudes toward China. Thus, public opinion and policy in Washington seem to be caught in a vicious circle, that is, a self-reinforcing mechanism that establishes a new path dependency.

Second, even though decoupling seemed almost impossible until 2018, Trump's trade policies changed views on US–China trade relations. However, this fact is not yet reflected in real trade. Although trade between the two economies has become less important than trade with many other countries, it has still grown in absolute terms in recent years (US Chamber of Commerce 2021). Nevertheless, the US administration and the Chinese Communist Party began implementing policies aimed at decoupling their economies to become less vulnerable to each other. In addition, transnational corporations began to diversify their value chains to make them more resilient than before. As decoupling increases, escalation becomes likely, which, in turn, fuels further decoupling. Given that existing interdependencies will continue to create vulnerabilities for a long time to come, an increasing escalation will come with high costs for both sides. In turn, enemy images among the public and among political decision-makers will reproduce, reinforcing the vicious circle.

Although the lasting impact of the Trump presidency on US trade policy remains to be seen, recent developments suggest that the Trump administration has embarked on a new path by making managed trade acceptable and setting in motion self-reinforcing economic decoupling toward China and a vicious circle of intensifying hostilities.

References

Allison, Graham T. 1971. *Essence of Decision: Explaining the Cuban Missile Crisis*. Boston: Little, Brown; Scott, Foresman and Company.

Almond, Gabriel A. 1960. *The American People and Foreign Policy*. New York: Praeger Publishers.

Autor, David H., David Dorn & Gordon H. Hanson. 2013. The China Syndrome: Local Labor Market Effects of Import Competition in the United States. *American Economic Review* 103(6). 2121–2168.

Birnbaum, Michael, Anne Gearan & David J. Lynch. 2021. Biden, E.U. end 17-year Airbus-Boeing trade dispute, seek to calm relations after Trump. *Washington Post*. https://www.washingtonpost.com/politics/biden-eu-tariffs/2021/06/15/88fcfe92-cd4c-11eb-a7f1-52b8870bef7c_story.html. (11 January, 2022)

Bown, Chad P. 2020. Unappreciated Hazards of the US-China Phase One Deal. https://www.piie.com/blogs/trade-and-investment-policy-watch/unappreciated-hazards-us-china-phase-one-deal. (12 February, 2020)

Bown, Chad P. 2021. Why Biden Will Try to Enforce Trump's Phase One Trade Deal with China. https://www.piie.com/blogs/trade-and-investment-policy-watch/why-biden-will-try-enforce-trumps-phase-one-trade-deal-china. (2 February, 2022)

Bown, Chad P. & Melina Kolb. 2021. Trump's Trade War Timeline: An Up-to-Date Guide. https://www.piie.com/blogs/trade-investment-policy-watch/trump-trade-war-china-date-guide. (6 January, 2021)

Bown, Chad P. & Katheryn Russ. 2021. Biden and Europe Remove Trump's Steel and Aluminum Tariffs, but It's not Free Trade. https://www.piie.com/blogs/trade-and-investment-policy-watch/biden-and-europe-remove-trumps-steel-and-aluminum-tariffs. (11 January, 2022)

Capoccia, Giovanni. 2015. Critical Junctures and Institutional Change. In James Mahoney & Kathleen A. Thelen (eds.), *Advances in Comparative-historical Analysis*, 147–179. Cambridge: Cambridge University Press.

Capoccia, Giovanni & R. D. Kelemen. 2007. The Study of Critical Junctures: Theory, Narrative, and Counterfactuals in Historical Institutionalism. *World Politics* 59(3). 341–369.

Destler, Irving M. 2005. *American Trade Politics*. Washington, DC: Institute for International Economics.

Hass, Ryan & Abraham Denmark. 2020. More Pain than Gain: How the US-China Trade War Hurt America. https://www.brookings.edu/blog/order-from-chaos/2020/08/07/more-pain-than-gain-how-the-us-china-trade-war-hurt-america/. (11 January, 2022)

Hendrix, Cullen S. 2016. Protectionism in the 2016 Elections: Causes and Consequences, Truths and Fictions. *Policy Brief* (16–20). https://piie.com/system/files/documents/pb16-20.pdf. (12 December, 2017)

Hirschman, Albert O. 1945. *National Power and the Structure of Foreign Trade* (Publications of the Bureau of Business and Economic Research University of California). Berkely: University of California Press.

Hoffman, Jason, Kate Sullivan & Maegan Vazquez. 2021. Biden Proposes Strengthening Buy American Rules to Boost US Manufacturing. https://edition.cnn.com/2021/07/28/politics/biden-buy-american/index.html. (2 February, 2022)

Hufbauer, Gary C. 2020. Managed Trade: Centerpiece of US-China Phase One Deal. https://www.piie.com/blogs/trade-and-investment-policy-watch/managed-trade-centerpiece-us-china-phase-one-deal. (16 January, 2020)

Iida, Keisuke. 1993. Analytic Uncertainty and International Cooperation: Theory and Application to International Economic Policy Coordination. *International Studies Quarterly* 37(4). 431–457.

Janusch, Holger. 2015. Labor Standards in U.S. Trade Politics. *Journal of World Trade* 49(6). 1047–1071.

Janusch, Holger. 2021. Audience, Agenda Setting, and Issue Salience in International Negotiations. *Cooperation and Conflict* 56(4). 472–490.

Janusch, Holger & Daniel Lorberg. 2020. Maximum Pressure, Minimum Deal: President Trump's Trade War with a Rising China. *Sicherheit & Frieden* 38(2). 94–99.

Jensen, Michael C. & William H. Meckling. 1976. Theory of the Firm: Managerial Behavior, Agency Costs and Ownership Structure. *Journal of Financial Economics* 3(4). 305–360.

Jones, Bradley. 2017. Support for free trade agreements rebounds modestly, but wide partisan differences remain. https://www.pewresearch.org/fact-tank/2017/04/25/support-for-free-trade-agreements-rebounds-modestly-but-wide-partisan-differences-remain/. (2 February, 2022)

Kahneman, Daniel & Amos Tversky. 1979. Prospect Theory: An Analysis of Decision under Risk. *Econometrica* 47(2). 263–291.

Kanno-Youngs, Zolan. 2022. Biden Signs Industrial Policy Bill Aimed at Bolstering Competition With China. *New York Times*. https://www.nytimes.com/2022/08/09/us/politics/biden-semiconductor-chips-china.html. (26 August, 2022)

Keohane, Robert O. & Joseph S. Nye. 2001. *Power and Interdependence*. New York: Longman Publishing Group.

Knox, Oliver. 2023. Europe's not Happy with Biden's Inflation Reduction Act. *Washington Post*. https://www.washingtonpost.com/politics/2023/01/17/europe-not-happy-with-bidens-inflation-reduction-act/. (13 March, 2023)

Mahoney, James. 2000. Path Dependence in Historical Sociology. *Theory and Society* 29(4). 507–548.

Mahoney, James, Khairunnisa Mohamedali & Christoph Nguyen. 2016. Causality and Time in Historical Institutionalism. In Karl-Orfeo Fioretos, Tulia G. Falleti & Adam D. Sheingate (eds.), *The Oxford Handbook of Historical Institutionalism*, 71–88. Oxford, New York: Oxford University Press.

Mintz, Alex & Carly Wayne. 2016. *The Polythink Syndrome: U.S. Foreign Policy Decisions on 9/11, Afghanistan, Iraq, Iran, Syria, and ISIS*. Stanford: Stanford University Press.

Moravcsik, Andrew. 1997. Taking Preferences Seriously: A Liberal Theory of International Politics. *International Organization* 51(4). 513–553.

Moravcsik, Andrew. 1998. *The Choice for Europe: Social Purpose and State Power from Messina to Maastricht*. Ithaca, N.Y.: Cornell University Press.

Moravcsik, Andrew & Frank Schimmelfennig. 2009. Liberal Intergovernmentalism. In Antje Wiener & Thomas Diez (eds.), *European Integration Theory*, 67–87. Oxford: Oxford University Press.

Navarro, Peter & Wilbur Ross. 2016. Scoring the Trump Economic Plan: Trade, Regulatory, & Energy Policy Impacts. (18 April, 2017)

Nunley, Christian. 2021. China critic Katherine Tai confirmed by Senate as Biden's U.S. Trade Representative. https://www.cnbc.com/2021/03/17/katherine-tai-us-trade-representative-confirmation.html. (2 February, 2022)

Olson, Mancur. 1965. *The Logic of Collective Action: Public Goods and the Theory of Groups*. Cambridge: Harvard University Press.

Ordoeñz, Franco. 2021. Biden And The EU Call A Truce In A 17-Year Trade Fight To Focus On Threats From China. https://www.npr.org/2021/06/15/1006445585/biden-worked-with-allies-to-speak-out-on-china-and-russia-now-the-hard-part-begi?t=1642416037308&t=1643836810614. (2 February, 2022)

Pierson, Paul. 2011. *Politics in Time: History, Institutions, and Social Analysis*. Princeton: Princeton University Press.

Pramuk, Jacob. 2018. Republican lawmakers hate Trump's trade war, but it's not clear if they'll try to stop it. *CNBC*. https://www.cnbc.com/2018/07/06/republicans-criticize-trump-tariff-trade-war-with-china.html. (2 February, 2022)

Rathbun, Brian C. 2007. Uncertain about Uncertainty: Understanding the Multiple Meanings of a Crucial Concept in International Relations Theory. *International Studies Quarterly* 51(3). 533–557.

Sabatier, Paul A. 1988. An Advocacy Coalition Framework of Policy Change and the Role of Policy-oriented Learning Therein. *Policy Sciences* 21(2–3). 129–168.

Silver, Laura, Kat Devlin & Christine Huang. 2020. Americans Fault China for Its Role in the Spread of COVID-19. https://www.pewresearch.org/global/2020/07/30/americans-fault-china-for-its-role-in-the-spread-of-covid-19/. (2 February, 2022)

Silver, Laura, Kat Devlin & Christine Huang. 2021. Most Americans Support Tough Stance Toward China on Human Rights, Economic Issues. https://www.pewresearch.org/global/2021/03/04/most-americans-support-tough-stance-toward-china-on-human-rights-economic-issues/. (6 January, 2021)

Simon, Herbert A. 1957. *Models of Man: Social and Rational*. New York: John Wiley & Sons.

Siripurapu, Anshu. 2022. The Contentious U.S.-China Trade Relationship. https://www.cfr.org/backgrounder/contentious-us-china-trade-relationship. (15 September, 2022)

Slater, Dan & Erica Simmons. 2010. Informative Regress: Critical Antecedents in Comparative Politics. *Comparative Political Studies* 43(7). 886–917.

Smith, Allen. 2017. Trump's allies see a 'civil war' on trade within his administration, and which side wins is anyone's guess. *Business Insider*. https://www.businessinsider.com/trump-trade-agenda-nafta-china-tpp-2017-4. (6 January, 2022)

Stokes, Bruce. 2015. Americans Agree on Trade: Good for the Country, but not Great for Jobs. https://www.pewresearch.org/fact-tank/2015/01/08/americans-agree-on-trade-good-for-the-country-but-not-great-for-jobs/. (2 February, 2022)

Toh, Michelle. 2023. ASML Says 'Rules are Being Finalized' on Chip Export Controls to China. *CNN*. https://edition.cnn.com/2023/01/30/tech/asml-chipmaking-export-controls-china-intl-hnk/index.html. (13 March, 2023)

US Chamber of Commerce. 2021. Understanding U.S.-China Decoupling: Macro Trends and Industry Impacts. https://www.uschamber.com/assets/archived/images/024001_us_china_decoupling_report_fin.pdf. (2 February, 2022)

USTR. 2020. Economic and Trade Agreement Between the United States of America and the People's Republic of China. https://ustr.gov/sites/default/files/files/agreements/phase%20one%20agreement/Economic_And_Trade_Agreement_Between_The_United_States_And_China_Text.pdf. (12 February, 2020)

Verdier, Daniel. 1994. *Democracy and International Trade: Britain, France, and the United States, 1860–1990*. Princeton: Princeton University Press.

Younis, Mohamed. 2021. Sharply Fewer in U.S. View Foreign Trade as Opportunity. https://news.gallup.com/poll/342419/sharply-fewer-view-foreign-trade-opportunity.aspx. (6 January, 2022)

Holger Janusch and Daniel Lorberg

Digitalization, Trumpismo, and the end of the liberal world order?

Turning points and Caesarism in neo-Gramscianism

Abstract: President Trump challenged American democracy and the liberal world order, raising the question of whether his presidency has contributed to a hegemonic crisis and a potential turning point in the prevailing state and world order. Since neo-Gramscianism addresses the radical change of world order, the conceptual turning points are at its very center. Surprisingly, a clear definition and conceptualization of turning points have been lacking. To address this gap, we propose a neo-Gramscian definition of turning points and structural breaking point to explain the growing crises of hegemony within the United States and the wider liberal world order. The digital revolution is leading to rapid transnationalization and increasing market concentration, making it an important source of change in the power relations between business, labor, and the state. The result is growing social inequality, which, in turn, has fostered political polarization within the United States and contributed to the current hegemonic crisis. Because a hegemonic crisis marks a time when the prevailing order and power relations are subjects for debate, it opens the door for a charismatic leader. Trump can be seen as such a leader who, invoking his charismatic authority, advances an alternative nostalgic image of the existing (world) order. Since US hegemony forms the basis for the expiring world order, the hegemonic crisis and Trumpismo are not limited to America but challenge the wider liberal world order.

Keywords: Breaking point, Caesarism, digitalization, neo-Gramscianism, US democracy

1 Introduction

On January 6, 2021, thousands of Trump supporters stormed the Capitol in Washington, DC intending to overturn the results of the 2020 presidential election. All this happened after President Trump called on his supporters to "fight like hell" at a

Holger Janusch, Federal University of Applied Sciences for Public Administration, Faculty of Intelligence Services
Daniel Lorberg, Federal University of Applied Sciences for Public Administration, Faculty of Social Security Administration

https://doi.org/10.1515/9783111272900-005

rally on the Ellipse in front of the White House (Phillips 2022). The insurrection on the Capitol marks a violent peak of political polarization between the two parties – Democrats and Republicans – and the wider society – liberals and conservatives – that began decades ago. Although the constitutional system has survived the insurrection, the current social and political order is far from stable. From a Gramscian perspective, the American divide is a sign of a crisis of domestic hegemony. Conflicting ideas about the social and political order struggle for national hegemony. By undermining the national consensus within the United States, the hegemonic struggle also erodes an important ideological pillar of the liberal world order. Since the hegemonic consensus within the United States de facto constituted the liberal world order, its decay undermines that very same order. This, in turn, enables social forces abroad to challenge world hegemony.

As one of the deeper causes of the hegemonic crisis in the United States, we identify the digital revolution, which has fundamentally changed and continues to transform social production relations. By contributing to transnationalization and market concentration, it affects power relations between corporations and the state, and between capital and labor. It acts as a catalyst for social inequality, which, in turn, undermines the material basis of the American ideological hegemony at home and abroad. In such a crisis of hegemony, when alternative ideas challenge the prevailing order, Gramsci recognized a time for charismatic leaders – a Caesar – who can end the hegemonic struggle between conflicting factions. This raises the question of whether Trump's leadership can be interpreted as a certain form of Caesarism, namely, Trumpismo?

Since neo-Gramscianism focuses on the radical changes of world orders, turning points of orders form the explanandum. Surprisingly, a clear definition and conceptualization of turning points have so far been lacking. This chapter aims to fill this gap, i.e., to define turning points within the neo-Gramscianist paradigm and to elaborate on the role of Caesarism in this context (section 2). To be clear, the aim is not to give the most accurate interpretation of Gramsci's understanding of turning points and Caesarism. Rather, we want to present an abstract interpretation that is consistent with neo-Gramscianism and its assumptions. Based on the definition of turning points, we then identify the digital revolution as one of the major reasons for the hegemonic crises (Section 3), which is expressed in a growing polarization between the parties and within society, paving the way for the Trump presidency (Section 4). This hegemonic crisis and Trumpismo, however, are not limited to America but challenge the wider liberal world order (Section 5).

2 Turning points and Caesarism in neo-Gramscianism

While Antonio Gramsci was concerned with national hegemony and order, neo-Gramscianism relocates the argument to world politics. It focuses on the stability and change of historical world orders. Such historical structures are specific configurations of three different forces: material capabilities, ideas, and institutions. Material capabilities are productive and destructive means such as natural resources, machines and weapons, as well as organizations and technologies. Ideas include intersubjective meanings about the nature of social relations. Such shared notions solidify habits and expectations of behavior. Ideas also comprise collective images of the social order, including the nature and legitimacy of existing power relations. While shared meanings usually exist across historical social orders and form the basis for social discourse, there are often multiple conflicting collective images at the same time. Institutions stabilize and maintain the existing order by providing mechanisms for conflict resolution to prevent the use of violence (Cox 1981).

Historical structures do not determine people's actions, but they do exert pressure on behavior. When people resist this pressure, they promote an alternative emerging configuration of forces. Historical structures can be hegemonic or nonhegemonic. In hegemonic structures, a dominant collective image exists. Power relations fade into the background of consciousness, and institutions stabilize the power relations. Material capabilities, especially destructive ones, are rarely used, as the order is accepted by the subaltern classes. In nonhegemonic structures, however, the discourse about power relations is in the foreground. Social classes, also called social forces, struggle for hegemony. Rival collective images offer alternative pathways for social orders. Such alternative images challenge the material and institutional basis of the dominant order (Cox 1981, 1983).

To better understand the difference between hegemonic and nonhegemonic structures, it is helpful to refer to Giddens' (1986) distinction between practical and discursive consciousness. Practical consciousness refers to tacit knowledge that actors reproduce in their routine practices without questioning or reflecting on it. While practically conscious actors know how to act, they cannot express discursively the reasons or conditions for their actions, although they are, in principle, able to explain their actions when prompted. In Marxism, "false consciousness" describes a situation in which a system of domination and exploitation is part of the practical consciousness of the working class, while in contrast, discursive consciousness implies that actors are discursively aware of the procedures, rules, and routines that condition their actions. They can reflect on them and express them.

Discursively conscious actors not only know what they are doing but can articulate their thoughts and reasons for their activities. Applied to hegemony in Gramscianism, collective images on which a hegemonic structure is based are part of the practical consciousness of the subaltern classes. In contrast, the power relations of a nonhegemonic structure are located in discursive consciousness.

Assuming a nonhegemonic structure, how does hegemony then arise? The ruling classes or social forces establish hegemony by making concessions to the subaltern classes and incorporating their interests into an ideology expressed in universal terms. In return, the subaltern classes accept the existing order (Cox 1981, 1983). Hegemony, thus, is a dominant shared idea about a social order that is part of the practical consciousness. Institutions consolidate hegemony by preventing the order from being questioned. Material incentives sustain hegemony by buying the acceptance of the ruled for the hegemonic order. Ideally, the use of force is a sign of lacking in hegemony. When a social order is accepted, it does not need force. Nevertheless, the possibility of using force is vital for hegemony to deter potential social forces that might challenge the existing order. "[T]he 'normal' exercise of hegemony [. . .] is characterized by a combination of force and consent which are balanced in varying proportions, without force prevailing too greatly over consent" (Gramsci 1975: 1638). Gramsci speaks of the "integral state" when there is a hegemonic balance between coercion and consent (Humphrys 2018). An alliance of social forces that organizes politically around a set of hegemonic ideas and establishes hegemony or advances a counter-hegemonic project is called a historic bloc (Gill 2002: 58).

While classical Gramscianism focuses on individual nation states, neo-Gramscianism considers three levels of historic structures: (1) the organization of production and the relationships between social forces that emerge through the production process, (2) the form of the state, and (3) the wider world order. All three levels are interrelated; they effectively constitute each other. Nevertheless, hegemony usually has to be established first at the level of social production relations and the state before it can take shape as a world order. World hegemony refers to an order within the world economy characterized by a dominant mode of production expressed in universal norms and stabilized by international institutions that co-opt the elites from other countries and absorb counter-hegemonic ideas (Cox 1981, 1983).

Turning points and uncertainty: Neo-Gramscianism does not refer explicitly to the concept of turning points, but turning points or their possibility are central to the theory. Neo-Gramscianism explains the change of world orders, i.e., times of hegemonic consent and hegemonic crises. With that focus in mind, we define historic turning points as radical changes in the existing (world) order. Changes can take the form of revolutions or evolutions (passive revolutions) of a prevailing order. A revolution here does not necessarily mean a violent overthrow, but an abrupt and radical change of the existing political and social structure. Evolution, on the other hand, means that an existing structure changes slowly and gradually so that despite the change, the old structure is always reflected in the new (cf. Gramsci 1973). As evolutions mark a change but also the continuation of a previous order, it appears to not qualify for being a turning point.

Turning points are possible only in times of hegemonic struggle. Only then do social forces challenge the existing order, and the prevailing order becomes part of discursive consciousness. Because of that, we recognize uncertainty as a central feature of the hegemonic crisis. Rathbun (2007) distinguishes four types of uncertainty. In rationalism, ignorance refers to uncertainty due to incomplete information. Learning occurs by gathering more information. In cognitivism, confusion describes an overabundance of information. It is resolved through cognitive shortcuts or heuristics. In realism, fear refers to uncertainty about the intentions of others. Fear cannot be addressed by gathering information, but by increasing power. In social constructivism, indeterminacy describes the uncertainty of a socially constructed world that lacks shared meanings and interpretation of norms. Uncertainty is reduced by the acquisition of a shared identity and shared norms through socialization and persuasion (Rathbun 2007). Uncertainty in neo-Gramscianism is best described as indeterminacy. To the extent that social forces produce rival collective images that offer alternative orders, indeterminacy grows. A hegemonic crisis, therefore, is a time of high indeterminacy, characterized by multiple rival collective images that challenge the existing order. A new hegemonic consensus requires a new dominant collective image, which, in turn, reduces indeterminacy.

However, new ideas alone are not enough. Material capabilities are also needed to make the subaltern classes accept the new ideas and prevent resistance, and new institutions are necessary to maintain the hegemonic consensus over time (cf. Cox 1981). In this sense, the transition from a hegemonic crisis to a new hegemonic structure can be described as a turning period rather than as a turning point. The turning point is then the specific moment when material capabilities, ideas, and institutions become congruent (again). Often, though not necessarily, this moment is when a historical bloc creates new institutions that fit the changed material capabilities and proposed new ideas.

Compared to historical institutionalism, periods of hegemonic crisis resemble the concept of a critical juncture. Capoccia and Keleman (2007: 348) define critical junctures as "relatively short periods during which there is a substantially heightened probability that agents' choices will affect the outcome of interest." A critical juncture thus is a short period of high contingency between two long path-dependent processes; a time during which radical change is possible. Critical junctures thus mark the end and beginning of path-dependent processes (Pierson 2011). A hegemonic crisis is a period between two hegemonic structures in which social forces have a substantially heightened influence on the formation of the historical structure. It is characterized by the incongruence of material capabilities, ideas, and institutions with each other. Unlike critical junctures, such periods do not have to be relatively short. Furthermore, institutional change is not of sole interest (unlike historical institutionalism) but is only one aspect of the changing order alongside material capabilities and ideas. While historical institutionalism may identify changes in material capabilities or ideas as reasons for institutional change, neo-Gramscianism sees all three aspects as intertwined and, therefore, aims to understand the reasons for changes in the whole structure, including material capabilities, ideas, and institutions (Cox 1981). As mentioned, turning points thus include not just a radical change in institutions but also in material capabilities and ideas.

Because the three forces – material capabilities, ideas, and institutions – are interrelated, neo-Gramscianism does not assume determinism in the same way as historical materialism does. Following historical materialism, history is rather a one-way street: the economic base shapes the superstructure. The superstructure, in turn, sustains the base. The base refers to the mode of production, consisting of the productive forces (e.g., machines, raw materials, and technology) and the relations of production (e.g., who owns the means of production and the product). The superstructure refers to ideology, norms, and identities, including law, politics, religion, education, and culture. In other words, historical materialism assumes that economic production and relations largely define the ideology, culture, and political system of a time. In contrast, neo-Gramscianism does not assume such strict determinism. Yet, it still stands to reason that times of hegemonic crises originate primarily in changes in material capabilities caused, for example, by technological innovations. As a result, social production relations are transformed and no longer fit the prevailing ideas and institutions. Subaltern classes start to question the prevailing order. The struggle for hegemony begins but again, all three forces are interrelated and constantly affect each other.

Breaking points and Caesarism: Turning points of (world) order are closely linked to what we call erosion and (structural) breaking points. Erosion describes a long-term, incremental process which undermines a prevailing hegemony. Major reasons for erosion are, for example, long-term trends such as technological innovations or demographic changes that slowly change social production relations. In contrast, breaking points are rather dramatic, short-term events such as an economic crisis, a war, or a violent revolution that mark the beginning of the hegemonic crisis. Often erosion and breaking points occur in combination. In both cases, the existing structure loses its constraining effect on the thinking and behavior of social forces. This gives social forces a new agency to redefine the structure. Decisive for being described as an erosion or breaking point is that the process or event leads to a questioning of the existing order and thus, ushers in a period of new indeterminacy; i.e., the agency-uncertainty nexus changes (see Introduction of this Edited Volume). The decisive difference between both is the pace: erosion is a slow and steady process; a breaking point is a quick and intensive event.

With the beginning of a hegemonic crisis due to erosion or a breaking point, two possibilities arise. On the one hand, a new hegemonic structure can emerge when a historical bloc establishes a new hegemony. The hegemonic crisis would then be only a brief period. When the hegemonic crisis leads to a radical change (and not just the evolution) of the previous order, it is classified as a turning point (period) in history. It comes close to what is called *Zeitenwende* in German, i.e., the end of an old epoch or era and the beginning of a new one. On the other hand, it is also conceivable that a hegemonic crisis becomes an enduring and defining feature of a period when no historical bloc can achieve dominance in the hegemonic struggle. It would make perfect sense to call it a turning point too, as it is the end of the prevailing hegemony, marked by a new and enduring period of indeterminacy. However, to avoid confusion, we refrain from calling it a turning point, which is defined here as a radical change of (world) order, implying the beginning of a new world hegemony and order.

As hopefully became clear above, we distinguish between a turning point and a structural breaking point (cf. Introduction of this Edited Volume). On the one hand, the turning point describes the beginning of a new order, i.e., the specific moment when material capabilities, ideas and institutions become congruent again. The breaking point, on the other hand, describes a historical event through which the structure loses its constraining effect and social forces gain the agency to define a new structure. Structural breaking points (or erosion processes) must occur before a turning point. They open the window of opportunity for a turning point; however, they do not necessarily lead to a turning point. Either the previous order can remain resilient and survive the hegemonic crisis, or the hegemonic crisis can lead to a permanent period of instability. In both cases, no new hegemonic structure emerges.

As agency becomes more important with growing erosion or after a breaking point, Gramsci recognized the particular importance of charismatic leaders (or Caesarism) in times of hegemonic crises. "At a certain point in their historical lives, social classes become detached from their traditional parties. In other words, the traditional parties in that particular organizational form, with the particular men who constitute, represent, and lead them, are no longer recognized by their class (or fraction of a class) as its expression. When such crises occur, the immediate situation becomes delicate and dangerous, because the field is open for violent solutions, for the activities of unknown forces, represented by charismatic 'men of destiny'" (Gramsci 1973: 210).[1] Caesarism "always expresses the particular solution in which a great personality is entrusted with the task of 'arbitration' over a historico-political situation characterized by an equilibrium of forces leading toward catastrophe" (Gramsci 1973: 219). Caesarism, thus, constitutes a third force that emerges only from the struggle between two conflicting factions.

Caesarism straddles hegemony (consent) and dictatorship (force) and, therefore, civil society and the state (Fontana 2004: 177). Force is a necessary, but not a sufficient element of Caesarism. Caesarism is connected both to the material base from which it emerges and its political and social ideology (Fontana 2004: 186). It does not necessarily lead to a new form of the state. Gramsci distinguishes between the qualitative and quantitative characteristics of Caesarism. Caesarism is qualitative when the form of the state changes to another. In this case, there would be a complete revolution. It is quantitative when there is no such transition to a new form of the state, but only an evolution of the existing one (Fontana 2004: 179–180). While a complete revolution is a turning point, as mentioned before, an evolution of an existing order does not qualify as a turning point.

Although Gramsci, echoing Weber, speaks of a "charismatic leader," he does not elaborate on the role of charisma. Following Weber (2002 [1921]: vol. 1, chap. 3), charismatic authority is the belief in a divine or heroic personality. In contrast, traditional authority draws its power from the long-standing traditions and practices within society and rational-legal authority derives from a belief in the legitimacy of a society's laws and rules. Considering Weber's typology, a hegemonic crisis refers to a situation in which traditional and legal authority are no longer able to maintain hegemony, i.e., to keep the collective images of the order in practical consciousness. Traditional and rational-legal authority feeds from existing ideas and institutions. When prevailing ideas and institutions erode, traditional and rational-legal authority lose their legitimizing effect, and vice versa. Charismatic authority can then act as a substitute. It empowers the charismatic leader to form or lead a historic bloc. If successful, a Caesar can establish a new hegemony, causing power relations to disappear again in practical consciousness.

In summary, turning points are the beginning of a radical new order. They become possible in times of hegemonic crises. Often (but not necessarily) a hege-

---

1 According to Gramsci (1973: 220), a Caesarist solution can exist even without a heroic personality, but through a parliamentary system.

monic crisis begins with a change of material capabilities, followed by a questioning of existing ideas and institutions. A hegemonic crisis is caused by protracted erosion or brief structural breaking points, and usually by both together. As a result, indeterminacy grows. The existing hegemonic structure loses its constraining effect on the thinking and behavior of the subaltern classes, while social forces gain new agency to redefine the existing order. As existing ideas and institutions erode, and with them, traditional and rational-legal authority as sources of legitimacy, charismatic authority can fill this void. If successful, a charismatic leader can lead a historical bloc to establish a new hegemony and order. A turning point occurs. If this does not succeed, the turning point fails to materialize for the time being, and the hegemonic crisis continues until a new hegemony emerges at some point. Since a world order usually originates in a national hegemonic project, a hegemonic crisis in the leading nation can take the form of an erosion or structural breaking point for the prevailing world hegemony.

3 Digitalization and the new mode of production

Based on the definitions of a turning point, uncertainty, and Caesarism, we next sketch a historic narrative that situates the crisis of US democracy, Trump, and the resulting consequences to the liberal world order in context. We identify the digital revolution as a major reason for changing material capabilities and changing social production relations, characterized by rising social inequality in the United States (Section 3). The new social production relations can help to understand the crisis of US democracy, as rising social inequality erodes existing ideas and institutions, leading to a period of indeterminacy. In this hegemonic crisis, the rational-legal authority stemming from democratic institutions loses its grip and opens up the space for charismatic leaders. The result is the Trump presidency, cumulating in a (structural) breaking point for US democracy: the January 6 insurrection at the Capitol (Section 4). The crisis of American democracy, however, is not limited to the United States but also undermines the liberal world order (Section 5). In these times of crisis, a window of opportunity is opening for a turning point – the radical change of the world order.

Although in the following we draw a strict line of argument from digitalization to social inequality and political instability, this should not be misunderstood as a determinism. We only want to highlight what we consider to be a central causal relationship, without denying that there are manifold interdependencies between various forces, as already assumed in neo-Gramscianism.

In the mid-1990s, the digital revolution began to go at full speed. Unlike previous industrial revolutions, digitalization is not about the extent and place at which physical power is available, but about the handling of information. It is a revolution in data storage, processing and transmission. In recent decades, the global capacity to store, process and transmit data has grown exponentially (Hilbert & Lopez 2011). Digital technologies enable businesses to store, process and transmit data at an unprecedented scale and speed, dramatically reducing transaction costs. Not only has data capacity increased, but digitalization permeates all businesses and economies, and is rapidly transforming more and more people into users. The digital revolution is fundamentally transforming social production relations in almost all areas of society and the economy. As far as companies are concerned, digitalization fundamentally changed management and production (OECD 2017; WTO 2018).

By reducing transaction costs, corporations can now easily bridge spatial distances that span no less than the entire globe. As a result, companies can trade goods and services more efficiently across borders, as reflected in a global increase in international trade since the onset of digitalization (World Bank n.d.). Of course, digitalization is not the only reason for the growth of global trade. The liberalization and opening of markets, especially in the fast-growing Chinese economy, or the reduction of transport costs through innovations such as ultra large container ships, have also boosted global trade (cf. OECD 2007; WTO 2018).

In addition to the growth in international trade, foreign direct investment, and with it the size of companies has also increased rapidly since the mid-1990s (World Bank n.d.). Here too, digitalization can be seen as one of the main reasons for this change. Drastically reduced transaction costs due to digitalization enable companies to handle increasingly complex business processes across borders. Digital innovation is what enables corporate management to coordinate complex global value chains in the first place. As a result, digitalization has enabled companies to become transnational on an unprecedented scale, steadily growing in size. As the size of transnational corporations grew, market concentration likewise increased both in the United States and globally (IMF 2019). Although digitalization is not the only factor that has contributed to the rapid increase in foreign direct investment (cf. Carril-Caccia & Pavlova 2018) – other factors include deregulation and economic growth – it is certainly a key factor.

While spatial distance became less relevant with the digital revolution as the rise of international trade and foreign direct investments proves, it, paradoxically, also became more important. The reason for this is that agglomeration areas and clusters such as Silicon Valley offer many location advantages for companies. The spatial concentration of similar corporate functions in different companies creates positive agglomeration effects such as labor pooling, positive knowledge externalities or investment in certain infrastructure (Porter 1996). As digitalization enables companies to manage increasingly complex business processes, they can increasingly exploit the location advantages of agglomeration areas and clusters. Space is, thus, becoming increasingly important. The result is the emergence of global value chains that increasingly take place between different clusters and simultaneously within transnational companies such as Apple, Nike or Volkswagen (UNCTAD 2013).

By contributing to transnationalization, clustering, and growing market concentration, the digital revolution transformed fundamental production relations in modern capitalist economies, especially in the United States, where digitalization started first. The new production relations, in turn, changed the power relations between capital, state, and labor. As transnationalization enabled firms to exploit the location advantages of different economies, regions, and clusters, it increased competition between states to create a business-friendly environment. As a result, states lost power vis-à-vis firms. Since labor is less mobile than capital, corporate transnationalization also put labor unions at a disadvantage. As corporations grew larger, they also gained more financial power, which also gave them more direct influence over the state and workers. At the same time, US labor unions have steadily lost members and thus, an important source of their bargaining power (OECD n.d.).

As capital gained international mobility and market power, while at the same time, the state came under pressure from growing competition and organized labor lost influence, it is not surprising that social inequality grew in the United States. In recent decades, inequality in income and wealth steadily grew (World Inequality Database o. J.). While productivity soared, real wages increased only marginally (Economic Policy Institute 2021). Social inequality has not only increased nationwide but has also become more spatially concentrated. Income, employment, and life expectancy grew more substantially in New England and the Mideast and remained high in the Far West and the Rocky Mountains, while decreasing in the Southwest and falling dramatically on the Great Lakes (Nunn et al. 2018). The spatial increase of social inequality reflects the structural transformation that began as early as the 1980s but has also been fueled by the growing cluster building caused by digitalization.

In addition to monopolization and declining unions, other factors such as the return on capital, tax rates, race or gender affected social inequality (Piketty 2014; Siripurapu 2022). Social inequality was already beginning to rise in the 1980s when digitalization was still in its infancy. The market-liberal policies and tax reforms of US administrations, beginning under President Reagan, paved the way for the transnationalization and market concentration that began in the wake of digitalization. By the time digitization took hold from the mid-1990s onward, market-liberal policies had already reached the point where the digital revolution could properly unleash its effect on the transnationalization of companies and transform social production relations. By changing social production relations and contributing to rising social inequality, the digital revolution facilitated the erosion of the hegemonic structure within the United States.

4 The end of the American dream and the rise of Trumpismo

As social inequality increased, hegemonic consent within American society began to crumble. After World War II, the United States established a world order based on its ideas about the American way of life, the liberal market economy, democracy, and a liberal (economic) world order: the beginning of *Pax Americana*. With the end of the Cold War, these ideas appeared to have gained universal acceptance, and the "end of history," when liberal democracy and capitalism were to prevail worldwide, was proclaimed (Fukuyama 1989). Beginning in the mid-1990s, as digitalization started to spread within the American economy and society, the economy grew rapidly, unemployment declined, and the Clinton administration ran a budget surplus. However, beneath the surface of a period of economic growth and technological innovation, the cracks in US hegemony were widening. From a neo-Gramscian perspective, technological innovation has transformed material capabilities and social production relations, leading to incongruence with prevailing institutions and ideas. Thus, digitalization may have contributed to the erosion of the hegemonic structure in the United States, but it was certainly not the only cause.

The growing hegemonic crises, characterized by the increasing indeterminacy and breakdown in hegemonic consent, manifested in three aspects: (1) the increasing polarization of political beliefs, including those regarding the role of the United States in world affairs, (2) the fading belief in the American dream, and (3) a declining trust in public institutions.

Polarization is not a new phenomenon but began in the 1960s with the civil rights movement and antiwar protests. Up until the 1990s, however, polarization can be seen more as a process of realignment. In the 1960s, the Democratic Party under President Lyndon B. Johnson took a step to the left with the passage of civil rights reforms. Since then, black voters have become a constituency of the Democratic Party. At the same time, this shift to the left alienated many white voters in Southern states from the Democratic Party. However, due to party loyalty, incumbency advantages, and a lack of institutional representation of the Republican

Party in the South, realignment occurred slowly over the next two and a half decades (Campbell 2016). Following realignment, beginning in the mid-1990s with the advent of digitalization, both the parties and the electorate became increasingly polarized in terms of their views on various issues such as health care, gun laws, abortion, immigration, climate change, and terrorism. Moreover, Democrats and Republicans increasingly hold negative views and feelings toward the other side (Finkel et al. 2020). This polarization was accompanied by an increasingly partisan media. The creation of Fox News in 1996 is emblematic of this trend. Later, echo chambers and filter bubbles in social media further intensified polarization (Barber & McCarty 2015). The polarization in the parties and the electorate reflects the growing indeterminacy characteristic of times of hegemonic crisis.

As social inequality grew, Americans also lost confidence in the American dream – the notion that everyone can achieve success with determination, regardless of their background, and that children will do better than their parents. When Trump took office, many Americans believed that today's children will be worse off than their parents (Stokes 2017). The costs of being poor not only manifest in material deprivation but also stress, insecurity, and lack of hope. Thus, social inequality includes not only an unequal distribution of income but also optimism. Lacking optimism, in turn, leads people not to invest in themselves, which further exacerbates inequality (Graham 2020). The loss of confidence in the American dream illustrates how a fundamental idea of the American hegemonic structure eroded. In addition to the American divide about the right policy and fading belief in the American dream, Americans lost trust in public (democratic) institutions. In recent decades, the trust in nearly all public institutions, from Congress to the church, schools, and news media, has declined. The only exception is the military (Gallup o.J.). Thus, institutions as one pillar of hegemony lose more and more of their stabilizing effect. Increasing indeterminacy thus undermines trust in institutions, which, in turn, fosters more indeterminacy.

Growing conflicting beliefs between liberals and conservatives about the right policies, paired with the diminished trust in public institutions, eroded hegemony. Many Americans, especially in rural areas, increasingly felt forgotten by Washington and not represented by the established parties. The erosion of the hegemonic structure and growing indeterminacy opened the door for a charismatic leader to break the stalemate between the Democratic and Republican parties and that is where Trump entered the stage. First, he had to take over the Republican Party in the primaries. At the 2016 Republican National Convention, when Trump became the Republican nominee, most Republicans of the establishment got behind Trump and his populist agenda. Finally, Trump won the general election (though not the popular vote), especially because he was able to win the votes of many blue-collar workers in the Rust Belt (McQuarrie 2017). That this constituency traditionally voted for Democrats illustrates that the parties had become alienated from their traditional members. Already since the 1990s, the Republican Party was gaining approval among the white working class (Carnes & Lupu 2021). Finally, Trump offered a populist alternative with "Make America Great Again." He drew a collective nostalgic picture of a past US world hegemony that many Americans yearned for.

During his presidency, Trump took over the leadership of the regressive historic bloc, composed of various social forces, for example, the Republican Party, conservative media outlets such as Fox News, and conservative billionaires such as the Koch brothers. On various occasions, the Trump administration then tested the boundaries of the public institutions or undermined them by, for example, attacking the free press as the "enemy of the people," pardoning political allies, breaking through the boundaries of the civil discourse, or attacking the independence of the judiciary. When public institutions resisted their subversion or investigated wrongdoing, Trump and associated social forces relied on conspiracy theories and claimed to be victims of a so-called "Deep State," i.e., a shadow government within the US bureaucracy (cf. Hetherington & Ladd 2020). This further discredited the public institutions that maintain the eroded but still prevailing hegemony. Under Trump's presidency, the regression of American democracy was facilitated. It became "dirtier," i.e., changing the rules of the game instead of winning public opinion became more important and violations of democratic norms became more frequent (Foa & Mounk 2021).

Most important was Trump's attack on the integrity of the presidential election. In doing so, he undermined a fundamental institution of American hegemony. The first impeachment trial exposed how Trump abused his power by asking the Ukrainian government for foreign interference to help his reelection and attempting to obstruct justice. In addition, he questioned the integrity of the election. After the election defeat, the Trump campaign accused Democrats of voter fraud, filed lawsuits in several states, and pressured states, legislators, and the vice president to nullify the election (Blake 2021). Not all of these attacks on the integrity of the election were without effect. Most Republican voters questioned whether the election was free and fair (Laughlin & Shelburne 2021). Moreover, many Republicans hold authoritarian beliefs (Dean & Altemeyer 2020; Easley 2021). The attacks by Trump and his allies on public institutions, particularly the integrity of elections, challenged the shared collective image of US democracy, reinforcing indeterminacy and exacerbating the hegemonic crisis.

In the end, the result was the attack on the Capitol on January 6, 2021, to prevent Congress from certifying the results of the Electoral College. Public institutions and civil opposition were strong enough to defend the attack on the state. Although Trump failed in his efforts to break the institutions of the prevailing hegemonic structure, Trump's attack on the integrity of elections and the following insurrection mark a structural breaking point, because of two aspects. First, the reliance on force by Capitol police to defend public institutions is a sign of the broken hegemony. Second, in addition to the erosion due to polarization, the "Big Lie" – the belief that Democrats had stolen the presidential election – became the ideological core of the wider Republican Party and Trump supporters.

Immediately after the insurrection, there was a space to counter Trump's populist agenda. Trump lost some of his charismatic leadership in the Republican Party and the electorate. Many Republicans condemned the attack on the Capitol. However, Trumpismo was here to stay. Trump is still a key player in the Republican Party. Even without Trump, his populist beliefs still drive the Republican Party. Many Republican members of Congress refused to certify the results of the presidential election. Trump's "Big Lie" has become a mantra of the Republican Party and his supporters over time. Conservative media outlets such as One America News or Fox News amplified the Big Lie. As a result, many Republicans distrust the elections, hold authoritarian beliefs, and would even support a coup (Lupu et al. 2022). The denial of the Big Lie leads to condemnation by the Republican Party and even death threats by Trump's supporters. Election workers face death threats and harassment nationwide. FBI agents became targets of increased death threats after the raid on Mar-a-Lago. Far-right terrorism has risen since the Trump presidency (cf. Kleinfeld 2021; Campbell et al. 2022). Without overdramatizing, because many Americans still believe in democratic institutions and share common values, the insurrection and its aftermath are signs of a counter-hegemonic project. Trump sowed a lasting distrust among his followers in the existing democratic institutions that increased a willingness to use violence and challenged the basic institutions of the previous hegemonic structure.

5 Trumpismo and the crises of the liberal world order

Over the past two decades, the liberal world order came under attack from various nations, most notably the two autocratic great powers, China and Russia. China's rapid economic, military, and technological rise led to dramatic shifts in international production and power relations. Since the opening up and reforms of the late 1980s, the Chinese Communist Party has integrated itself into the existing liberal economic world order while also challenging it. First, it frequently undermines existing norms and rules, whether by violating international trade rules such as antidumping and intellectual property rights or by violating international maritime law through actions such as building artificial islands in the South China Sea. In addition, the Chinese Communist Party has established regional organizations such as the Asian Infrastructure Investment Bank, which act as regional substitutes for international organizations such as the International Monetary Fund (IMF). While China challenges the ideas and institutions of the prevailing liberal world order, it has not yet proposed an alternative collective image to it (Economy 2018). Nevertheless, China's steady economic and military rise marks the slow erosion of the liberal world order. In contrast, Russia, while not an economic power, has directly attacked the liberal world order, at least in Europe. By invading Ukraine, Russia is undermining the European security architecture and international law. Putin presented an alternative collective image according to which Eastern Europe is part of Russia's sphere of influence (Hartnett 2022). Russia's war against Ukraine marks a structural breaking point in world hegemony as it directly questions the collective image of principles such as national sovereignty and peaceful conflict resolution on which the liberal world order is built. Both China's rise and Russian aggression indicate that world hegemony is in crisis.

Whether the rise of China or Russia's aggressions will eventually lead to a turning point of the world order remains to be seen, but most likely also depends on the state of the United States. The hegemonic crisis within the United States is a key event that continues to further undermine the liberal world order, the *Pax Americana*. For several reasons, national hegemony within the United States is still an important pillar of the liberal world order, whose institutions are still effective despite the crisis of world hegemony. First, new changes in social production relations on a global scale still originate in the United States. The United States remains the leading economy in most of the digital innovations that will continue to change the global economy in the near future (cf. European Patent Office n.d.). Second, the United States still leads in military capabilities and thus continues to possess the capacity to protect the ideas and institutions of the liberal world order (cf. SIPRI o. J.). Even without its direct involvement, military training and arms deliveries to Ukraine underscore this fact. Third, even if the United States has lost some of its ability to shape international ideas and collective images about the world order, it is still a role model for many countries (cf. BrandFinance o. J.). Many countries, especially in Eastern Europe and East and Southeast Asia, where Russia and China pose the greatest threat, yearn for US leadership.

Because American (national) hegemony originally shaped the post-World War II order and the United States has served as the guarantor of this liberal world order ever since, the American hegemonic crisis is contributing to the attendant erosion of world hegemony. Within the broader erosion process caused by the American hegemonic crisis, the question arises to what extent the Trump presidency marks a (structural) breaking point for the liberal world order, further contributing to the crisis in world hegemony. The Trump presidency – seen as one event – undermines the liberal world order in two ways.

First, the Trump administration directly attacked the prevailing international institutions, on which the liberal order is built, on numerous occasions. While US administrations before Trump's presidency have also violated international law – the Iraq War comes to mind – they have not challenged the existence of the liberal world order that the United States itself has shaped. Trump questioned the purpose of the World Trade Organization (WTO) and blocked the work of its Appellate Body, the central institution in the WTO's dispute settlement mechanism. He threatened North Korea with a nuclear attack. He questioned the US commitment to the North Atlantic Treaty Organization (NATO). He withdrew from the Paris Agreement to combat climate change. He submitted a formal US withdrawal from the World Health Organization. There are many more examples of how the Trump administration has blocked or undermined international law and regimes.

Despite Trump's assault on the ideas and institutions of the liberal world order, international institutions have so far proven resilient to subversion during the Trump presidency. Moreover, there is still more bipartisan consensus in Washington on foreign policy than on domestic issues. In particular, there is a strong bipartisan consensus on tackling the threat to the liberal world order posed by China and Russia. Bipartisan actions such as military and political support for Ukraine and Taiwan demonstrate this consensus (Galston 2022; Spegele 2022), although Republican right-wing populists in Congress cast doubt on such support (Caldwell & Meyer 2023).

Second, the Trump presidency indirectly favored a rising right-wing populism in many democracies. While Trump is not the origin point of the new right-wing extremism, his presidency contributed to making it more popular. Thus, the Trump presidency has helped undermine national hegemony in many democracies, simultaneously eroding another foundation of the world hegemony. Moreover, it may have contributed to the process that sees Russia and China challenging the liberal world order more aggressively, as Trump has signaled that he is not willing to share the burden of defending it.

While the Trump presidency, directly and indirectly, challenged the ideas and institutions of the liberal world order, it has not caused a turning point. It has not shaped a new hegemonic consensus and new world order. Nevertheless, along with other events such as the global financial crisis, the Trump presidency qualifies as a structural breaking point. By challenging the liberal world order, it increased indeterminacy, further undermining world hegemony. Even after the Trump presidency, the ongoing hegemonic crisis in the United States and the persistence of

Trumpismo continue to put pressure on the liberal world order. The growing incongruence between material capabilities, ideas, and institutions within the United States and at the global level, caused in part by the digital revolution, is increasingly undermining the stability of the world order; although the United States, because of its leadership, was able to preserve or even strengthen the unity of the Western democracies after the Russian invasion, thereby still protecting the world order. Trumpismo has contributed to the crisis of world hegemony and will continue to do so until a new hegemonic structure emerges based on a widely shared collective image.

6 Conclusions

Following neo-Gramscianism, we define turning points as radical changes in a dominant (world) order that become possible in times of hegemonic crises. Hegemonic crises are triggered by prolonged erosion processes and brief structural breaking points that increase uncertainty (indeterminacy) about shared ideas and norms. As a result, the dominant hegemonic structure loses its constraining effect on the thinking and behavior of the subaltern classes, while social forces gain influence to redefine the existing order. In times of hegemonic crises, social forces or historical blocs struggle for hegemony by propagating rival collective images of (world) order. As dominant ideas and institutions erode, traditional and rational-legal authority as a source of hegemonic consent dwindles. Charismatic authority can fill this gap. A charismatic leader can lead a historical bloc to establish a new hegemony and order. Therefore, Caesarism becomes crucial in times of hegemonic crisis.

While China's economic and military rise and Russia's military aggressions are usually cited as major threats to the liberal world order, the hegemonic crisis of American democracy may pose the greatest challenge to the liberal world order. Because the liberal world order emerged from the hegemonic structure of the United States after World War II and the United States has served as the guarantor ever since, a hegemonic crisis within the United States undermines an important pillar of the liberal world order. Thus, to understand the state of the liberal world order, we must look at the state of American democracy.

From a neo-Gramscian perspective, digitalization led to transnationalization and increasing market concentration of the US economy, transforming social production relations. This transformation, in turn, changed the power relations between capital and labor and between the state and business. The resulting social inequality and political polarization contributed to an erosion of the hegemonic structure within the United States. As indeterminacy grew, Americans lost confidence in public institutions. As a result, political leaders could no longer rely as much on legal-rational authority. During this period of hegemonic crisis, Trump's charisma served as a substitute for legitimizing authority. In addition to the erosion caused by ever-growing social inequality and political polarization, the January 6 insurrection at the Capitol and Trump's attacks on American democracy marked a structural breaking point for the American hegemonic structure. The "Big Lie" became a fundamental belief for the Republican Party and most Republican voters and because it calls into question the integrity of US elections, a core tenet of the prevailing national hegemonic structure is threatened. Although democratic institutions have proven resilient, Trumpismo (even without Trump) is here to stay. Since the United States is still a major economic, technological, and political anchor in world politics, Trumpismo will challenge not only the hegemonic structure of American democracy but also the liberal world order.

References

Barber, Michael J. & Nolan McCarty. 2015. Causes and Consequences of Polarization. In Nathaniel Persily (ed.), *Solutions to Political Polarization in America*, 15–58. New York: Cambridge University Press.

Blake, Aaron. 2021. Timeline: Trump's Pressure Campaign to Overturn the 2020 Election. *Washington Post*. https://www.washingtonpost.com/politics/2021/08/06/trumps-brazen-attempt-overturn-2020-election-timeline/. (22 August, 2022)

BrandFinance. o. J. Global Soft Power Index 2022: The World's Most Comprehensive Research Study on Perceptions of Nation Brands.https://brandirectory.com/softpower/nation?country=175&rRegion=1&rCountry=0. (24 August, 2022)

Caldwell, Leigh A. & Theodoric Meyer. 2023. Republican Divide on Ukraine Takes Center Stage. *Washington Post*. https://www.washingtonpost.com/politics/2023/02/28/republican-divide-ukraine-takes-center-stage/. (12 March, 2023)

Campbell, James E. 2016. *Polarized: Making Sense of a Divided America*. Princeton: Princeton University Press.

Campbell, Josh, Jessica Schneider, Donie O'Sullivan, Paul P. Murphy & Priscilla Alvarez. 2022. FBI investigating 'unprecedented' number of threats against bureau in wake of Mar-a-Lago search. *CNN*. https://edition.cnn.com/2022/08/12/politics/fbi-threats-maralago-trump-search/index.html. (14 September, 2022)

Capoccia, Giovanni & R. D. Kelemen. 2007. The Study of Critical Junctures: Theory, Narrative, and Counterfactuals in Historical Institutionalism. *World Politics* 59(3). 341–369.

Carnes, Nicholas & Noam Lupu. 2021. The White Working Class and the 2016 Election. *Perspectives on Politics* 19(1). 55–72.

Carril-Caccia, Federico & Elena Pavlova. 2018. Foreign Direct Investment and its Drivers: A global and EU Perspective. *ECB Economic Bulletin* (4). 60–78.

Cox, Robert W. 1981. Social Forces, States and World Orders: Beyond International Relations Theory. *Millennium – Journal of International Studies* 10(2). 126–155.

Cox, Robert W. 1983. Gramsci, Hegemony and International Relations: An Essay in Method. *Millennium – Journal of International Studies* 12(2). 162–175.

Dean, John W. & Bob Altemeyer. 2020. *Authoritarian Nightmare: Trump and His Followers*. New York: Melville House.

Easley, Cameron. 2021. U.S. Conservatives Are Uniquely Inclined Toward Right-Wing Authoritarianism Compared to Western Peers. https://morningconsult.com/2021/06/28/global-right-wing-authoritarian-test/. (14 March, 2022)

Economic Policy Institute. 2021. The Productivity–Pay Gap. https://www.epi.org/productivity-pay-gap/. (10 March, 2022)

Economy, Elizabeth C. 2018. *The Third Revolution: Xi Jinping and the New Chinese State*. Oxford: Oxford University Press.

European Patent Office. n.d. Patent Index 2021: European Patent Applications. https://www.epo.org/about-us/annual-reports-statistics/statistics/2021/statistics/patent-applications.html#tab2. (24 August, 2022)

Finkel, Eli J., Christopher A. Bail, Mina Cikara, Peter H. Ditto, Shanto Iyengar, Samara Klar, Lilliana Mason, Mary C. McGrath, Brendan Nyhan, David G. Rand, Linda J. Skitka, Joshua A. Tucker, Jay J. van Bavel, Cynthia S. Wang & James N. Druckman. 2020. Political Sectarianism in America. *Science* 370(6516). 533–536.

Foa, Roberto S. & Yascha Mounk. 2021. America after Trump: From "Clean" to "Dirty" Democracy? *Policy Studies* 42(5–6). 455–472.

Fontana, Benedetto. 2004. The Concept of Caesarism in Gramsci. In Peter Baehr & Melvin Richter (eds.), *Dictatorship in History and Theory: Bonapartism, Caesarism, and Totalitarianism*, 175–196. Cambridge, UK, New York, Washington, D.C: Cambridge University Press; German Historical Institute.

Fukuyama, Francis. 1989. The End of History? *The National Interest* (16). 3–18.

Gallup. o.J. Confidence in Institutions. https://news.gallup.com/poll/1597/confidence-institutions. aspx. (9 March, 2022)

Galston, William A. 2022. The invasion of Ukraine unites a divided America. https://www.brookings. edu/blog/fixgov/2022/03/03/the-invasion-of-ukraine-unites-a-divided-america/. (14 September, 2022)

Giddens, Anthony. 1986. *The Constitution of Society: Outline of the Theory of Structuration*. Berkeley: University of California Press.

Gill, Stephen. 2002. *Power and Resistance in the New World Order*. London: Palgrave Macmillan.

Graham, Carol. 2020. *Happiness for All?: Unequal Hopes and Lives in Pursuit of the American Dream*. Princeton: Princeton University Press.

Gramsci, Antonio. 1973. Selections from the Prison Notebooks. New York: International Publishers.

Gramsci, Antonio. 1975. Quaderni del carcere. Torino: G. Einaudi 3(13).

Hartnett, Lynne. 2022. The long history of Russian imperialism shaping Putin's war: Russia's imperial history is driving Putin, but today's global order may not reward him. *Washington Post*. https://www.washingtonpost.com/outlook/2022/03/02/long-history-russian-imperialism-shaping-putins-war/. (14 September, 2022)

Hetherington, Marc & Jonathan M. Ladd. 2020. Destroying Trust in the Media, Science, and Government Has Left America Vulnerable to Disaster. *Brookings Institution*. https://www.brook

ings.edu/blog/fixgov/2020/05/01/destroying-trust-in-the-media-science-and-government-has-left-america-vulnerable-to-disaster/. (12 March, 2023)

Hilbert, Martin & Priscila Lopez. 2011. The World's Technological Capacity to Store, Communicate, and Compute Information. *Science* 332(6025). 60–65.

Humphrys, Elizabeth. 2018. Anti-Politics, the Early Marx and Gramsci's 'Integral State'. *Thesis Eleven* 147(1). 29–44.

IMF. [2019]. *World Economic Outlook: Growth Slowdown, Precarious Recovery* (World economic and financial surveysApril 2019). Washington, D.C.: International Monetary Fund.

Kleinfeld, Rachel. 2021. The Rise of Political Violence in the United States. *Journal of Democracy* 32(4). 160–176.

Laughlin, Nick & Peyton Shelburne. 2021. How Voters' Trust in Elections Shifted in Response to Biden's Victory. https://morningconsult.com/form/tracking-voter-trust-in-elections/. (14 March, 2022)

Lupu, Noam, Luke Plutowski & Elizabeth J. Zechmeister. 2022. Would Americans ever support a coup?: 40 percent now say yes. *Washington Post*. https://www.washingtonpost.com/politics/2022/01/06/us-coup-republican-support/. (14 March, 2022)

McQuarrie, Michael. 2017. The Revolt of the Rust Belt: Place and Politics in the Age of Anger. *The British Journal of Sociology* 68(1). 120–152.

Nunn, Ryan, Jana Parsons & Jay Shambaugh. 2018. The Geography of Prosperity. The Hamilton Project. https://www.hamiltonproject.org/assets/files/PBP_FramingChapter_compressed_20190425.pdf. (10 March, 2022)

OECD. n.d. Trade Union Dataset: Trade Union Density. https://stats.oecd.org/Index.aspx?DataSetCode=TUD#. (22 August, 2022)

OECD. 2007. *OECD Economic Outlook*: *June No. 81 – Volume 2007 Issue 1*. Paris: Organisation for Economic Co-operation and Development.

OECD. 2017. Key Issues for Digital Transformation in the G20: Report Prepared for a Joint G20 German Presidency/OECD Conference. https://www.oecd.org/g20/key-issues-for-digital-transformation-in-the-g20.pdf. (14 September, 2022)

Phillips, Amber. 2022. What We Know – and Don't Know – about What Trump Did on Jan. 6. *Washington Post*. https://www.washingtonpost.com/national-security/2022/06/29/trump-january-6-timeline/. (14 September, 2022)

Pierson, Paul. 2011. *Politics in Time: History, Institutions, and Social Analysis*. Princeton: Princeton University Press.

Piketty, Thomas. 2014. *Capital in the Twenty-first Century*. Cambridge: The Belknap Press of Harvard University Press.

Porter, Michael E. 1996. *The Competitive Advantage of Nations*. Houndmills: Macmillan.

Rathbun, Brian C. 2007. Uncertain about Uncertainty: Understanding the Multiple Meanings of a Crucial Concept in International Relations Theory. *International Studies Quarterly* 51(3). 533–557.

SIPRI. o. J. SIPRI Military Expenditure Database, https://www.sipri.org/databases/milex. (6 September, 2021)

Siripurapu, Anshu. 2022. The U.S. Inequality Debate. https://www.cfr.org/backgrounder/us-inequality-debate. (14 September, 2022)

Spegele, Brian. 2022. Nancy Pelosi's Trip Reflects Growing U.S. Bipartisan Support for Taiwan. *Wall Street Journal*. https://www.wsj.com/livecoverage/nancy-pelosi-taiwan-visit-china-us-tensions/card/nancy-pelosi-s-visit-reflects-growing-u-s-bipartisan-support-for-taiwan-GgLl0Bo49Smj98pCVfux. (14 September, 2022)

Stokes, Bruce. 2017. Global Publics More Upbeat About the Economy: But many are pessimistic about children's future. https://www.pewresearch.org/global/2017/06/05/global-publics-more-upbeat-about-the-economy/. (9 March, 2017)

UNCTAD. 2013. *Global Value Chains: Investment and Trade for Development* (United Nations Publication 2013). New York: United Nations.

Weber, Max. 2002 [1921]. *Wirtschaft und Gesellschaft: Grundriss der verstehenden Soziologie*, 5th edn. Tübingen: Mohr Siebeck Verlag.

World Bank. n.d. World Bank Open Data, https://data.worldbank.org/. (19 October, 2021)

World Inequality Database. o. J. USA, https://wid.world/country/usa/. (10 March, 2022)

WTO. 2018. World Trade Report 2018: The Future of World Trade: How Digital Technologies are Transforming Global Commerce. Geneva: WTO Publications.

II Challenging the World Order? China, Russia, and Ukraine

Hubert Zimmermann
The end of the age of military intervention: Liberal interventionism and global order since the end of the Cold War

Abstract: Military interventions were among the most conspicuous and most contested phenomena of global politics in the decades following the end of the Cold War. These interventions were legitimized as missions to enhance collective security or to extend humanitarian protection. However, despite efforts to make intervention a formally accepted instrument at both global and regional levels, for example, in the context of the debate about the Responsibility to Protect, the so-called "age of liberal interventionism" ended during the 2010s. As the international community refused to intervene even in situations of conflict of the utmost gravity, both the emergence and the end of the "age of military intervention" signal particular turning points in this core practice of maintaining global order. Proceeding from a neoclassical realist perspective, this essay argues that shifts in constellations of global power create a permissive (or non-permissive) environment for international intervention. This influences domestic ideological divides that ultimately determine decisions about intervention. This study explains the turning points in debates over intervention as result of the interplay of domestic and international shifts.

Keywords: Collective Security Cosmopolitanism, Communitarianism, Liberal Interventionism, Multipolarity, Neoclassical Realism, Responsibility to Protect

The end of the Cold War, in many respects, was an indisputable turning point for the international system. It ended the bipolar superpower rivalry – a global conflict marked by nuclear stale-mate that made comprehensive global cooperation almost impossible. It also marked the beginning globalization that involved the continued expansion of liberal capitalist modes of organizing national economies and the spread of liberal global norms, particularly those associated with cosmopolitan and humanitarian values. The developments linked to the Second Gulf War, the multinational, UN-approved military campaign against Saddam Hussein's Iraq, were signature events in this respect. First, a global coalition applied the notion of collective security against Iraq's violation of Article 2.4 of the UN Charter, the non-intervention rule based on which the post-World War II (WWII)

Hubert Zimmermann, University of Marburg

https://doi.org/10.1515/9783111272900-006

international relations were formed. Second, the humanitarian interventions that followed endeavored to protect the Kurdish and Shiite populations in Iraq from the Iraqi dictator's violent oppression. These campaigns signaled the potential for a new global consensus for the protection of individual and group rights. The two fundamental goals of these events – the active pursuit of collective security and the protection of individuals and groups across borders – encompass the major justifications for military intervention, one of the most consequential practices of the global order since the emergence of the Westphalian state system. Interventions in this vein increased after the end of the Cold War, creating an "age of intervention" (or liberal intervention) that lasted more than twenty years and ended during the 2010s, as this study argues. Somewhat counterintuitively, the Russian invasion of Ukraine in February 2022 is another indicator that this period is now over. As a classic cross-border war against a sovereign country, Russia's invasion violates collective security and central humanitarian norms of global society, given the disregard for international law and civilian lives demonstrated by the Russian forces. However, the return of traditional war to Europe and the renewed focus on traditional security further limits the chances of effective military intervention in the interest of collective security or humanitarian causes.

What are the defining characteristics of military intervention as it is understood in this chapter (and more generally in the literature on this practice)? According to Anthony Lang (2002: 3), "Military intervention is the use of armed troops to effect a change in the political system of a sovereign state without prior permission and without declaring war" (see also: MacFarlane 2002: 7; Recchia and Welsh 2013: 5). It is pursued against the will of a significant part of the target society but supported by (most of) the relevant international community. Usually, therefore, it is conducted multilaterally, with the aim to forcefully change the government in the target country in order to pursue "altruistic objectives." These objectives encompass the provision or reconstruction of regional and global collective security or the security of groups and individuals in the case of humanitarian intervention. Evidently, the Russian war against Ukraine does not fit this definition, even though it was justified by Russian President Vladimir Putin with reference to international norms. The Russian war against Ukraine is a classic case of military action to expand or preserve spheres of influence. The action was taken for similar, nationalist reasons such as cross-border military campaigns undertaken for economic motives or the pursuit of national prestige, for instance, colonial conquest. This chapter addresses what I call "altruistic" intervention, although I know very well that pure examples of this phenomenon do not exist, and even the "purest" humanitarian interventions carry with them a host of other self-interested motives. For this reason, critical and postcolonial accounts of interventionism argue that the wave of armed interventions, undertaken mostly by Western states since the 1990s, was a series of actions taken to impose a Eurocentric vision of governance on so-called "peripheral countries," perpetuating colonial imbalances of power (Pison 2022; Quinton-Brown 2020). Such a widespread view is in fact quite similar to conventional realist accounts of military intervention that see them merely as the pursuit of national interests by the intervening powers. These views, I argue, are too simplistic. They fail to acknowledge that interventionism for the sake of "saving strangers" or "securing global stability" is not a propensity unique to Western states, nor do these interpretations do justice to the multifaceted roots of the phenomenon that make it distinctive. "Altruistic" interventions, I argue, were a core feature of international relations in the "age of intervention." As they are closely linked to the prevailing understandings of sovereignty and constructions of international responsibility, trends in their frequency and intensity must be explained.

Thus, the first part of this chapter deals with the rise and fall of liberal interventionism, identifies critical junctures in this respect, and discusses whether they can be viewed as indicators for turning points in the international order, as outlined in the introduction to this volume. I will first look at the "age of interventionism," clarifying what I mean by that and how it emerged and ended. The second part tries to explain the observed changes. My hypothesis is that the probability of intervention depends on an international system that creates a permissive or non-permissive environment that facilitates or impedes interventions (for a similar suggestion, see: Peak, Laderman, and Jacob 2022). Thus, the frequency of military intervention can be explained by shifts in the global order. Such a systemic argument is derived from a neorealist structural account of global politics. Debates about the "unipolar moment" after the end of the Cold War and the end of American hegemony after the disasters in Iraq and Afghanistan have shaped the research on the structure of the international system in the past few decades (Layne 2006; Krauthammer 1990/1; Fukuyama 2021; Lake, Martin, and Risse, eds., 2021). However, the intense debates about military intervention that occurred in this period, inattention to national interests proper, and frequent cases of non-intervention suggest that the explanation has to be supplemented with domestic variables – an argument forcefully made by neoclassical realists who posit that unit-level variables must complement systemic accounts to increase their explanatory power (Ripsman, Taliaferro, and Lobell 2016). As a result of a large comparative study of the legitimacy of military intervention (Zimmermann, 2023), I argue that domestic processes of identity construction and Othering that lead to the formulation of ideas of global and regional responsibility were decisive domestic variables in this respect.

1 Turning points? The age of intervention

In a March 2014 Chatham House talk on Channel 4 News, Michael Ignatieff discussed whether what he called the "age of intervention" was over (Ignatieff 2014; see also: Smith 1999).[1] Ignatieff was one of the authors of the report by the International Commission on Intervention and State Sovereignty (ICISS) that led to the proclamation of the Responsibility to Protect (R2P) norm by the United Nations in 2005. His focus was on humanitarian intervention in particular, arguing that, despite recent events, above all the occupation of Crimea by Russia and the ongoing humanitarian crisis in Syria, humanitarian interventions would remain a part of global politics. Ignatieff advocated a world wherein great powers or coalitions of great powers would join to protect vulnerable populations worldwide from gross human rights violations. In fact, the R2P represented exactly such a vision. It marked the rhetorical culmination of a cosmopolitan perspective on individual rights that gained traction in the 1990s and outlined crimes that required the international society to intervene if certain states were not able or willing to stop them (Bellamy/Dunne 2016; Bellamy and Luck 2018). The necessary authorization by the UN Security Council and the enormous diplomatic and economic cost of such an action implied that, in practice, the implementation of such a responsibility would be the onus of great powers. Proponents of the R2P imagined and hoped for a world wherein a convergence of norms toward certain basic fundamentals of acceptable state behavior would lead to an intersubjective understanding that the global community would no longer tolerate gross violations of the international order. This expectation and its manifestation in R2P emerged from a fundamental transformative process after the end of the bipolar superpower confrontation: the progressive weakening of the non-intervention doctrine that served as the central norm of the post-WWII international system.

The period of the two World Wars and especially the prior age of imperial colonialism, frequently under the banner of a paternalistic civilizing mission, had demonstrated the international system's primary vulnerability: insufficient protection of smaller states (and non-traditional states) against aggressive great powers. One result was the strict non-intervention rule that became enshrined in Chapter 2 (4) of the UN Charter. The exception to this rule was the pursuit of self-defense and fight against grave threats to international security, as outlined in Chapter VII of the Charter. This was basically a renewal of the collective security clauses of the

---

1 The following account is an extremely condensed version of a book on the global justification of military intervention by the author: Zimmermann, Hubert, Militärische Missionen, Hamburger Edition 2023.

League of Nations. However, with the exception of the Korean War, when the Soviet Union decided to boycott the vote, no intervention to Chapter VII took place until the end of the Cold War. The big powers embarked on proxy wars, such as the Vietnam War or the Soviet invasion of Afghanistan, whose main objective was to stabilize the aggressor's own sphere of influence, while the intervening countries claimed that the wars were being fought in the interest of humanity. Their motivation and consequences had little to do with either the protection of the population in the target countries or the stabilization of the region. Even interventions that resulted in a mass slaughter of civilians in target countries, such as Vietnam's invasion of Cambodia in 1979 or India's intervention in East Pakistan in 1971, were justified by the argument of self-defense, not by humanitarian or collective security goals (Wheeler 2000). In the 1980s, the non-intervention norm came under increasing critical scrutiny as the world was either forced to watch helplessly numerous humanitarian emergencies in the post-war decades, or, more frequently, was unwilling to do anything about them. It was the end of the Cold War that offered a critical juncture for the emergence of a new interventionism.

Using the definition established in the introduction to this volume, a critical juncture gives actors a much better chance to succeed in establishing a new path for a given policy owing to increasing contestation of the previous path. The developments in Eastern Europe and the Third Wave of Democratization seemed to vindicate the Western emphasis on liberal democracies and the rights of individuals and groups who live in oppressive states. As early as 1988, against the opposition of many governments, the UN General Assembly passed Resolution 43/131, which guaranteed international aid organizations access to scenes of humanitarian emergencies under international law (Weiss 2016). The potential that lay in the new global constellation was soon revealed in the worldwide reaction to the occupation of Kuwait by Iraqi troops in late 1990. The universal condemnation of this invasion resulted in "Operation Desert Storm," in which a coalition of 38 countries, under U.S. leadership and based on a unanimous Security Council mandate, liberated Kuwait, firmly implementing the international community's pledge to ensure collective security and protection of sovereignty as enshrined in the UN Charter. No regime change was undertaken after the successful conclusion of the campaign. However, its aftermath saw the revitalization of the other variant of altruistic military intervention, that is, humanitarian intervention. In response to the uprisings in the Shiite south and Kurdish north of the country, the weakened dictator Hussein used brutal force to crush these uprisings. Although this was explicitly an internal conflict and no approval from the Iraqi state for external intervention was to be expected, the international community acted after some hesitation. Security Council Resolution 688, introduced by France and Belgium in April 1991, provided for the establishment of military-monitored, so-called "safe areas" to protect the

Kurdish population in northern Iraq. The first application of Chapter VII of the UN Charter since the Korean War defined the actions of the Iraqi regime against domestic insurgents as a threat to international peace, a significant extension of the scope of the charter. Three non-permanent members of the Security Council (Yemen, Cuba, and Zimbabwe) voted against the resolution, while China and India abstained, demonstrating continued resistance against this new development.

Shortly afterward, the breakdown of order in Somalia that triggered a massive humanitarian crisis led to another intervention with the participation of ground troops provided by a multinational coalition. Once again, the motive was fundamentally humanitarian. Because Somalia had ceased to be considered a functioning state, even the more sovereigntist members of the Security Council approved of the measure. The situation there was also declared a "threat for international security" in UN Security Council Resolution 751 of April 1992, which passed in a unanimous vote. Thus, the interventions fused collective security and humanitarian protection – a fact that is often neglected by the literature on humanitarian intervention. In any case, the international consensus on both the Iraq and Somalia interventions, the acceptance of the leading role of the United States, and the approval of these interventions by the United Nations marked a clear change from the preceding decades: "Competitive, unilateral, self-interested intervention was common practice [in the Cold War era] . . . . In contrast, in the post-Cold War period, such intervention is rare (though hardly absent). Intervention increasingly occurs in a multilateral context, on the basis of authorisation by international organisations, above all the United Nations" (MacFarlane 2002: 11).

The debate, however, was not settled. For advocates of global human rights protection, the end of the Cold War raised hopes that the promise made in the founding documents of the United Nations to protect states and threatened groups and individuals from indiscriminate violence would finally be fulfilled in its entirety. If massive human rights violations were understood as a threat to international peace and collective security, they fell within the scope of Article VII of the UN Charter. Here was the decisive sticking point of the future debate: at what point did the international community deem events within state borders to be a threat to the security of its own collective? Only when there were fundamental threats to regional and national stability, or even when events gravely violated collectively shared moral concepts? In the case of delimiting morally acceptable behavior, effective military interventions to maintain collective security, including the management of catastrophic humanitarian emergencies, would have become possible under the leadership of the United Nations. The following two decades were shaped by heated controversies, usually catalyzed by instances of military intervention.

The tragic end of the Somalia intervention after the famous Black Hawk Down battle in Mogadishu put a temporary stop to interventionism in Africa.

However, the 1994 Rwandan genocide, where French troops arrived only after the mass killing had ended, served as another reminder of the necessity of humanitarian intervention in extreme emergencies. The same message resulted from the events in the disintegrating former Yugoslavia, with the Srebrenica massacre in Bosnia as the signature tragedy. Before this event, a sharp debate raged between those who saw the Balkans as a zone of atavistic ethnic conflict that one should stay clear of and those who saw it as part of a community of freedom-loving nations, or, more narrowly put, Europe (Hansen 2006). However, the fusion of both concerns for regional stability and an increasing mobilization of humanitarian discourses turned the tide toward intervention. A similar dynamic evolved in the case of Kosovo soon after the Bosnian conflict was momentarily contained following the 1995 Dayton Accords. In the case of the Serbian province, however, a clear separation of part of a sovereign state was at stake. Russia and China argued that events in Kosovo were internal affairs of the Federal Republic of Yugoslavia and that intervention without the consent of the sovereign government of this territory was a violation of the UN Charter. Nonetheless, most Security Council members accepted that the situation in Kosovo constituted a humanitarian disaster, as well as a threat to collective security. In a programmatic speech in 1999, Britain's Prime Minister Tony Blair laid out the following reasoning: "Acts of genocide can never be a purely internal matter. When oppression produces massive flows of refugees which unsettle neighbouring countries, then they can properly be described as 'threats to international peace and security'" (Blair 1999). The fusion of arguments concerning the responsibility of the European Union and the transatlantic alliance for regional collective security on the one hand and the outrage over the gross violation of humanitarian norms on the other hand provided pro-interventionist groups in domestic debates with sufficient clout to overcome the skeptics, for instance, in the United States and Germany (on the debates in these countries, see, for example, Daalder and O'Hanlon 2000; Ignatieff 2003).

The NATO intervention in Kosovo, however, revealed that the global interventionist consensus was still rather thin. Russia and China vehemently opposed the humanitarian rationale given by the Western alliance. In a statement dated September 24, 1999, the G77 states – an association of developing countries under the umbrella of the United Nations – sharply rejected the "so-called right to humanitarian intervention" as it had no basis in the UN Charter or in international law (G77 1999: §69). Nonetheless, a series of additional interventions followed, such as the 2001 NATO intervention in Macedonia, the U.K.'s intervention in Sierra Leone that same year, or the Australian-led UN mission in East Timor in 1999–2000.

The events of September 11, 2001, added another powerful motive to the arsenal of intervention: the fight against international terrorism under the pretext of collective security. Afghanistan and Iraq were the most visible results of this fight. However, the extremely controversial latter case, in particular, once more underlined the ambiguity of globally shared notions of threats to collective security. Meanwhile, regional organizations such as the African Union (Soares de Oliveira and Verhoeven 2018) and the European Union undertook their own interventions in the interest of regional security and human protection. What was remarkable in this period was that, to some extent, even clearly anti-interventionist states supported altruistic interventions. Russia and China, for example, supported UN missions in some African states and in East Timor. Russia participated in the Contact Groups in Bosnia and Kosovo, the United Nations Protection Force, and other multinational units deployed to stabilize the situation in the former Yugoslavia (Averre and Davies 2015).

Yet, the controversy over the Kosovo War demonstrated the essentially contested nature of these interventions. As a result, many policy entrepreneurs tried to reconcile persisting traditional notions of sovereignty with the new emphasis on individual protection across borders. Arguably, the most important of these entrepreneurs was UN General Secretary Kofi Annan, who, as a consequence of the interventions in the 1990s, argued for a new understanding of sovereignty, which would create a shared view among states of the conditions under which it was legitimate to violate the non-intervention principle. In a much-quoted opinion piece for the *Economist*, Annan wrote, "Just as we have learnt that the world cannot stand aside when gross and systematic violations of human rights are taking place, we have also learnt that, if it is to enjoy the sustained support of the world's peoples, intervention must be based on legitimate and universal principles" (Annan 1999). This call was taken up by the ICISS, which compiled the report leading up to the promulgation of the Responsibility to Protect at the 2005 UN World Summit. The decisive step in this report was the formulation of narrow constraints on military intervention and the framing of such a step as supporting the fragile sovereignty of the states concerned. This allowed even the states that were rather skeptical about such a responsibility to support the concept (Granville 2014).

Its application, however, turned out to be anything but smooth. Faced with mass atrocities in Darfur, the international community did not agree on decisive steps, and when it did so, in the case of Libya a few years later, the execution of the UN mandate proved to be extremely controversial (Kuperman 2015). The enforcement of a no-fly zone to protect the civilian population from atrocities threatened by the Libyan dictator Muammar Gaddafi effectively morphed into a regime change operation. Countries such as Russia, China, India, and Brazil voiced strong protests against what they saw as an unacceptable extension of the mandate. This critique would then also carry over to the Syrian civil war, which, after peaceful protests that started in 2011, soon descended into the most violent conflict of the 21st century to date. Even the use of chemical weapons there did not achieve a unified response. U.S. President Barak Obama's decision to not enforce a self-proclaimed red line regarding the use of weapons of mass destruction demonstrated that the United States, in the wake of Afghanistan and Iraq, would be focused on nation-building at home, a trend that was reinforced by Donald Trump's and Joe Biden's elections. One key element in the American decision against military intervention was the refusal of the British parliament to approve U.K.'s participation (Ralph, Holland, and Zhekova 2017) and the skepticism of other allies such as Germany. Furthermore, the precedent of the post-Libya debate had demonstrated that a similar mission in Syria would face fierce opposition outside of the West. Something fundamental had changed during the 2010s, making the response of the international community to the Syrian war a critical juncture in the global debate on collective security and humanitarian interventions. Not only in Syria but also in other hot spots of massive human rights violations and threats to collective security, such as Myanmar's Rohingya genocide and the War in Yemen, no international response was forthcoming (Peak, Laderman, and Jacob 2022). Large-scale interventions, for instance, in Afghanistan and Mali, were being wound down rapidly. In many countries, populist and nativist movements posited themselves against global governance and the notion of responsibilities beyond borders. The blatant disregard for international treaties and the UN Charter's norm of non-intervention on Russia's part in its invasion of Ukraine only underlines the failure of collective security and terminates the high hopes held at the outset of the "age of intervention." While it is not easy to identify a clear tipping point at which the trend toward "altruistic" intervention peaked and went into reverse, there are sufficient indications that the debate about Syria (linked with the aftermath of the Libya intervention) marked a critical juncture in this respect.

2 A systemic realist explanation

How can we explain the beginning and the end of the "age of intervention"? A systemic perspective suggests that the explanation might be related to the configuration of power in the international system. The start of the period of liberal interventionism coincided with the emergence of the United States as a unipolar power, and its end seemed to come at a time when this unipolar moment was clearly over, as contending powers, particularly China, rose in global influence while American politics turned inward with Trump's election as the U.S. President.

Looking back in history, we can also see that the first period of humanitarian interventions in Europe during the decades following the Napoleonic Wars was facilitated by a cooperative balance-of-power system, the so-called Concert of Europe (for an exhaustive study, see: Schulz 2009). This system disintegrated at the end of the 19th century and, thus, events such as the Armenian genocide evoked global indignation but no coordinated response, let alone military intervention (Laderman 2019). The lens of global power politics therefore indicates that systemic realist theories might yield useful hypotheses to understand this particular turning point. In what follows, I will look at realist predictions about the occurrence or non-occurrence of military intervention and assess whether changes in the constellation of the global balance of power might be a central factor in explaining this puzzle.

As is well known, the international system is structured by the logic of anarchy according to neorealist thought. This logic forces the central actors in the system – states that are seen as rationally calculating to secure their survival – to pursue a politics of power maximization relative to other actors. The core variable that explains the states' behavior is the "distribution of relative power capabilities" (Hyde-Price 2012: 18). Attempts of states to maximize their security lead to temporary equilibria, that is, a balance of power that becomes the major mechanism for preserving stability. Policies such as mutual deterrence, most notably by nuclear weapons, or, institutions of collective security, considered as less effective by the realists, which, in extremis, might authorize collective security interventions, serve the purpose of safeguarding this equilibrium. In 1955, in a classical realist treatise, Quincy Wright wrote, "Policies of balance of power naturally lead to policies of collective security which become institutionalized through common organs, procedures, and rules of law to assure that aggression will always be confronted by insuperable force. International organization to promote collective security is, therefore, only a planned development of the natural tendency of balance of power policies. It is the natural tendency of states, when faced by an emergency, to gang up on the aggressor who, if successful against his first victim, will eventually turn on the others" (Wright 1955: 163). In the realist world, therefore, collective security interventions make sense because they stabilize the existing system. The origins of this thinking in interpretations of the classic balance-of-power system of the 19th century are apparent.

However, how can it be explained that the first real humanitarian interventions also took place during this same period (Bass 2008; Klose 2016; Rodogno 2012)? Generally, realism is disdainful of humanitarian intervention as it does not see altruistic intervention as serving vital national interests (Ashley 1984; Fiott 2013). The godfather of classical realism, Hans Morgenthau, already argued against the idea of humanitarian intervention because he did not believe that the world could agree on the same standards of morality (Mason and Wheeler 1996: 101–2).

"Intervene we must," he wrote, "where our national interest requires it and where our power gives us a chance to succeed" (Morgenthau 1967). Later realists also clearly spoke out against humanitarian intervention, arguing that it would only result in entanglements in civil wars in far-off places and in a neglect of national interests (Hoffmann 2003: 23; Kissinger 2001: 234–82). Nonetheless, they had to grapple with the fact that humanitarian interventions did in fact occur and were even undertaken in times of unipolarity such as in "the age of intervention" outlined above. To explain this phenomenon, Michael Mandelbaum redefined humanitarian interventions basically as interventions in the interest of collective stability as they usually adjudicate border disputes and stabilize failed states that pose a threat to the system. While classic interventions for economic gain or the preservation of one's own sphere of influence were, according to him, no longer necessary after the Cold War, the end of systemic power competition opened the path for other kinds of intervention, which also served a systemic purpose (Mandelbaum 1994).

In fact, as we have seen in the short narrative on the liberal interventions, collective security arguments and humanitarian considerations were tightly interwoven in the justification of military intervention. The presence of a hegemonic power that takes some responsibility for the stability of the overall system might have helped, as suggested by hegemonic stability theory (Kindleberger 1973; Zimmermann 2020). In a wide-ranging overview of balance-of-power systems in history, Wohlforth et al. (2007) claimed that unipolar systems indeed tend toward stability rather than the counterbalancing dynamics expected by many realist authors. One example is the role of China in Asia from 1250 to 1850: "When China was stable, the international order in East Asia was stable. The dominant power had no need to fight, and the secondary powers had no desire to fight. The smaller states knew that China was more powerful and, if provoked, could fight a very costly war. For its part, China had no desire to attack lesser states, and intervened in them only to keep the system stable (p. 173)." It is this stability, then, which paves the way for military intervention that is not simply part of great power struggles but rather the result of more or less collective action. As Mandelbaum wrote, "The end of the Cold War . . . eliminated one of the main purposes of nonintervention: the prevention of conflict among great powers trying to impose their own models of legitimacy on other countries" (Mandelbaum 1994: 13). The existence of nuclear proliferation since the mid-20th century served as a further instrument to halt such potentially incalculable actions. As long as the American unipolar era lasted and the United States' image was not severely tainted by the wars in Iraq and Libya, cooperative collective security interventions were still possible.

In an unstable system, however, interventions beyond the confines of one's sphere of influence are risky undertakings and are easily seen as provocative, setting in motion a dynamic akin to the well-known security dilemma. This might have been the case in 18th-century Europe, when emerging states vied for power. It might also have been the reason for the absence of "altruistic" intervention from the late 19th century to WWII, when Germany's (and Japan's) ascendance and revanchism posed the major challenge, as well as during the Cold War and the bipolar rivalry. Finally, we find ourselves in a similar situation in today's order, wherein China becomes a credible challenger to U.S. preeminence while Russia seeks to maintain or rather regain its former status.

All in all, structural realism suggests that a stable system with a benevolent hegemon and a generally cooperative balance-of-power system might be a permissive condition for the occurrence of "altruistic" intervention. However, how do we explain that in some regions such as Europe and Africa, states used the instrument of intervention rather frequently, whereas in Asia, states such as China and India and regional organizations such as ASEAN adhere to a strict norm of non-intervention? Moreover, why do great powers intervene selectively? There are important empirical anomalies in any systemic realist account of intervention. Thus, in the final section, applying a neoclassical realist framework, I turn to an additional explanation, working with domestic normative struggles. The focus of neoclassical realism on unit-level variables makes it well suited to explain the phenomenon under research. It is particularly pertinent given that "altruistic interventions" have a high legitimacy threshold as leaders must convince domestic audiences to use military means despite the absence of direct attacks and obvious military threats (Zimmermann 2017). In addition, the (supposed) benefits accrue mostly to the target society or the international community.

3 A neoclassical realist perspective on turning points in the age of intervention

Neoclassical realism tries to remedy the limited explanatory power of structural realism for less-than-epochal trends. It does so through the inclusion of unit-level variables, in particular, the effects of domestic institutions, characteristics of leaders, and effects of strategic culture and perception (Ripsman, Taliaferro, and Lobell 2017). Numerous other domestic variables have been suggested and tested on diverse case studies (Meibauer et al. 2021: 2). The subject of military intervention is among them. As Jeffrey Taliaferro observed in 2004, states often engage and persist in costly interventions despite the absence of clear interests in the regions in which they intervene. He argued that leaders try to navigate between systemic constraints and domestic political imperatives (Taliaferro 2004). Electoral changes and shifts in popular opinion might be additional factors that explain decisions for or against interventions; however, these factors are indeterminate, considering how leaders from different sides of the political spectrum pursued and ended major interventions during the period under research and that public opinion polls provide no clear indicators. In a 2006 volume, Colin Dueck looked at American liberal interventionism and maintained that the choices made reflect dominant cultural preferences to maintain domestic support (Dueck 2006). In fact, a comparative study of intervention debates in liberal democracies by this author shows how competing factions operating with opposite identity constructions characterize the debates and how shifts in these coalitions explain periods of interventionism and anti-interventionism (Zimmerman 2023).

These coalitions line up along a cosmopolitan–communitarian axis that can be exemplified using Michael Walzer and Judith Shklar as exponents. Walzer, the author of the most frequently quoted work on the legitimacy of war, argues that the rights of individuals, their beliefs, and their loyalties are based on their membership in groups (Walzer 1977, 1983). Maintaining and not violating the autonomy and sovereignty of these groups is, therefore, a fundamental political requirement. This applies in particular to a community of states as long as one of its members does not commit capital crimes against humanity. Human societies of all kinds have a very deep basis of values they share among themselves, whereas the international community, according to Walzer, is characterized at most by a fairly thin layer of common values. This led Walzer to oppose liberal interventions, for example, in Libya. While he occupies a fairly moderate position with respect to intervention, more radical versions of group-based thinking on the left and right political spectrum are adamantly opposed to liberal interventionism. A lucid example is the case of Germany, where both the extreme left-wing party Die Linke and the extremist right-wing Alternative für Deutschland opposed all foreign military deployments of German forces during the age of intervention (Stengel 2020).

Liberal cosmopolitanism strongly disagrees with this position. Exemplary in this sense is the position of Walzer's friend and colleague at Harvard, Judith Shklar, who wrote in her famous essay "The Liberalism of Fear" that "it used to be the mark of liberalism that it was cosmopolitan, and that an insult to the life and liberty of a member of any race or group in any part of the world was of genuine concern" (Shklar 1989). In a rather influential article at the height of the German debate about NATO intervention in Kosovo, Jürgen Habermas spoke about an association of global citizens that would protect individuals against the excesses of abusive rulers (Habermas 1999). Such a cosmopolitan vision rests on a long pedigree of thought, for example, rulers' moral responsibility toward subjects beyond their jurisdiction, as proclaimed by many thinkers in the early modern age (Simms and Trim 2011), or the obligation to help coreligionists in danger, which is found in many religions (for Islam, see Hashmi 1993), in the Kofi Annan's Pan-Africanism ("suffering anywhere concerns people everywhere"),[2] and in liberal internationalist's democracy-promoting agenda (Ikenberry 2020). While these schools of thought appear as structural factors, as norms diffused across many societies, their fundamental validity depends on their acceptance in domestic debates that are shaped by contestation between cosmopolitan and communitarian ideologies in various guises. A comparative assessment of intervention debates in diverse countries shows that these debates can be classified into two dimensions: a communitarian–cosmopolitan divide and a left–right divide.

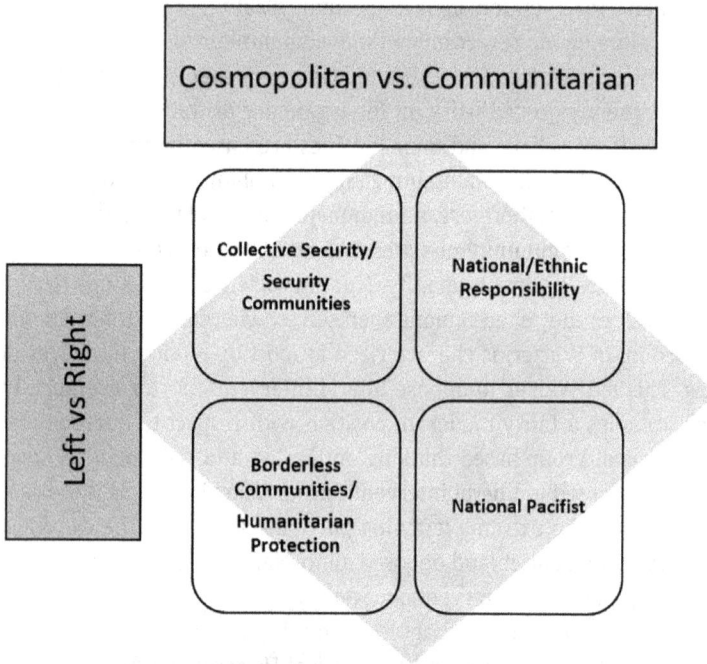

Figure 1: Domestic Coalitions in Intervention Debates.

Such a classification yields four discourse communities that interpret the lessons of history and responsibilities toward others quite differently. Depending on the strength of the different groups, the enabling or constraining space for interventions widens or narrows.

While right-wing cosmopolitans strongly emphasize alliances and collective security and support intervention for this reason, leftist cosmopolitans emphasize the

---

2 https://www.newworldencyclopedia.org/entry/Kofi_Annan.

importance of fundamental rights in a global community whose members have to be protected in extreme circumstances by military means. Communitarian or pacifist arguments on the left focus predominantly on the disadvantaged in their own societies, seeing military intervention as a threat to these parts of their societies and as useless anyway, as they primarily impact the underprivileged in other societies. Then, there are those who focus strictly on national interests, sometimes in ethnic terms, and reject any intervention that does not serve these goals. Such alignments can be seen, for example, in Germany, but also in the United States, as demonstrated by Walter Russell Mead's much-quoted four schools of American foreign policy (Mead 2001). Populist movements in the West, as well as in many other countries such as Brazil and India, operate with this exclusive notion of responsibility toward "Us" and not "Others." Thus, the return of a new communitarian view of global relations in many countries, compounded by the rise of traditional anti-interventionist powers such as China, Russia, and India, reinforced the anti-interventionist bias of the international order that emerged in the early 2010s when the limits of the power of the West became all too visible in the streets of Ghouta (Syria) or at the airport in Kabul in 2020. This double movement provides an explanation that can account for the beginning and the end of liberal interventionism.

4 Conclusion: Explaining turning points

This chapter seeks to explain a pattern in the rise and fall of "altruistic" military intervention, which it considers as marking important shifts in the global order. The end of superpower confrontation permitted the emergence and consolidation of a global norm of responsibility that was bolstered by domestic developments such as the so-called "third wave of democratization" (Haggard and Kaufman 2016) and led to a series of military interventions that were motivated to a considerable extent by humanitarian norms and norms of collective security. This period lasted until the 2010s, when shifts in the dynamics of global power distribution decisively limited the potential for cooperative, multilateral intervention. This was accompanied by a return to more nativist or communitarian policies in many countries that had contributed to multilateral interventions. The rise of right-wing populist parties, the election of populist leaders, and anti-globalist or anti-European movements that resulted, for example, in Brexit, signaled a turn inward. The end of large-scale military deployments in places such as Afghanistan, Iraq, or Mali are indicators that both the beginning and the end of the "age of intervention" can be characterized as turning points toward a new and enduring path.

This chapter used a neoclassical realist framework to explain these shifts and coupled a systemic argument with a theory of domestic identity formation. It argued that systemic explanations alone are insufficient in explaining decisive turning points: they must be accompanied with continuous shifts in domestic politics. This begs the question as to whether systemic incentives are the drivers in this process, or whether these are due to such persistent domestic transformations. In fact, it seems that these are co-constitutive processes: it would be absurd to claim at this point that one has precedence over the other. This article also makes a plea to consider the interrelation of domestic and international forces in bringing about fundamental change in the international system (see also Schirm in this volume). The mutual dynamics of domestic outcomes and systemic constraints in creating critical junctures that lead to real turning points must be specified further. In this sense, this chapter intends to contribute to a future research agenda that looks at the co-constitutive effects of domestic and international factors that give rise to turning points in international politics.

References

Andersen, Morten S. & William C. Wohlforth. 2021. The Balance of Power. In Benjamin de Carvalho, Julia Costa Lopez & Leira Halvard (eds.), *Routledge Handbook of Historical International Relations*, 289–301. London: Routledge.

Annan, Kofi. 1999. Sept. 8. Two Concepts of Sovereignty. *The Economist*. https://www.un.org/sg/en/content/sg/articles/1999-09-18/two-concepts-sovereignty (accessed 22.03.2023).

Ashley, Richard K. 1984. The Poverty of Neorealism. *International Organization* 38(2). 225–286.

Averre, Derek & Lance Davies. 2015. Russia, humanitarian intervention and the Responsibility to Protect: the case of Syria. *International Affairs* 91(4). 813–834.

Bass, Gary. 2008. *Freedom's Battle. The Origins of Humanitarian Intervention*, New York: Princeton UP.

Bellamy, Alex & Timothy Dunne (eds.). 2016. *The Oxford Handbook of the Responsibility to Protect.* Oxford: Oxford UP.

Bellamy, Alex & Edward C. Luck. 2018. *The Responsibility to Protect. From Promise to Practice.* Cambridge: Polity.

Blair, Tony. 1999. "The Blair Doctrine", 22. April. https://archive.globalpolicy.org/empire/humanint/1999/0422blair.htm (accessed 17 April 2023)

Daalder, Ivo & Michael E O'Hanlon. 2000. *Winning Ugly. NATO's War to Save the Kosovo*. Washington, DC: Brookings.

Dueck, Colin. 2006. *Reluctant Crusaders: Power, Culture and Change in American Grand Strategy.* Princeton: Princeton UP.

Fiott, Daniel. 2013. Realist Thought and Humanitarian Intervention. *The International History Review* 35(4). 766–782.

Fukuyama, Francis. 2021. The End of American Hegemony. *The Economist*, August 18. https://www.economist.com/by-invitation/2021/08/18/francis-fukuyama-on-the-end-of-american-hegemony (accessed 17 April 2023).

G77. 1999. "Ministerial Declaration", 24. Sept. https://www.g77.org/doc/Decl1999.html (accessed 26.02.2023).

Gilpin, Robert. 1981. *War and Change in World Politics*. Cambridge: Cambridge University Press.

Granville, Luke. 2014. *Sovereignty and the* Responsibility *to Protect: A New History*. Chicago: University of Chicago Press.

Habermas, Jürgen. 1999. Bestialität und Humanität. *Die ZEIT*, 29.4.

Haggard, Stephan & Robert R. Kaufman. 2016. Democratization During the Third Wave. *Annual Review of Political Science* 19(1). 125–144

Hansen, Lene. 2006. *Security as Practice. Discourse Analysis and the Bosnian War*. London: Routledge.

Hoffmann, Stanley. 2003. Intervention: Should it Go On, Can it Go On?" In Dean Chatterjee & Donald Scheid (eds.), *Ethics and Foreign Intervention*, 1–30. Cambridge: Cambridge UP.

Hyde-Price Adrien. 2012. Neorealism: Structural Approach to CSDP. In: Kurowska, Xymena & Fabien Breuer (eds.), *Explaining the EU's Common Security and Defence Policy*, 16–40. London: Palgrave Macmillan.

Ignatieff, Michael. 2003. *Empire Lite: Nation-Building in Bosnia, Kosovo, and Afghanistan*. London: Vintage.

Ignatieff, Michael. 2014. Is the Age of Intervention over? 2 March, Chatham House; https://www.files.ethz.ch/isn/178208/20140319AgeofIntervention.pdf (accessed 16 April 2023)

Ikenberry, G. John. 2020. *A World Safe for Democracy. Liberal Internationalism and the Crises of Global Order*. New Haven: Yale UP.

Kindleberger, Charles P. 1973. *The World in Depression 1929–1939*. London: Allen Lane.
The Penguin Press.

Kissinger, Henry. 2001. *Does America Need a Foreign Policy?Toward a Diplomacy for the 21st Century*. New York et.al.: Simon & Schuster.

Klose, Fabian (ed.). 2016. *The Emergence of Humanitarian Intervention. Ideas and Practice from the Nineteenth Century to the Present*. Cambridge: Cambridge UP.

Krauthammer, Charles. 1990/1991. The Unipolar Moment. *Foreign Affairs* 70(1). 23–33.

Kuperman, Alan J. 2015. Obama's Libya Debacle: How Well-Meaning Intervention Ended in Failure. *Foreign Affairs* 94(2). 66–77.

Laderman, Charlie. 2019. *Sharing the Burden: The Armenian Question, Humanitarian Intervention, and Anglo-American Visions of Global Order*. Oxford: Oxford UP.

Lake, David, Lisa Martin & Thomas Risse (eds.). 2021. Challenges to the Liberal International Order: International Organization at 75. *International Organization* 75 (Special Issue 2). 225–257.

Lang, Anthony F. 2002. *Agency and Ethics: The Politics of Military Intervention*. New York: SUNY Press.

Layne, Christopher. 2006. The Unipolar Illusion Revisited: The Coming End of the United States' Unipolar Moment. *International Security* 31(2). 7–41.

MacFarlane, N. 2002. *Intervention in Contemporary World Politics*. London: Routledge.

Mandelbaum, Michael. 1994. The Reluctance to Intervene, *Foreign Policy*, 95. 3–19.

Mason, A., Wheeler, N. 1996. Realist Objections to Humanitarian Intervention. In Holden, B. (ed.) *The Ethical Dimensions of Global Change*, 94–110. Palgrave Macmillan, London.

Mead, Walter R. 2001. *Special Providence*: American Foreign Policy and How It Changed the World. New York: Alfred A. Knopf.

Meibauer, Gustav, et.al. 2021. Forum: Rethinking Neoclassical Realism at Theory's End. *International Studies Review* 23(1). 268–295.

Morgenthau Hans J. 1967. To Intervene or not to Intervene. *Foreign Policy* 45(3). 425–436.

New World Encyclopedia. 2019. "Kofi Annan"; https://www.newworldencyclopedia.org/entry/Kofi_Annan. (accessed 17 April 2023)

Peak, Thomas, Charlie Laderman & Cecilia Jacob. 2022. Intervention and the Responsibility to Protect: Past, Present, and Futures. *Global Responsibility to Protect* 14(3). 261–268.

Pison, Hindawi C. 2022. Decolonizing the Responsibility to Protect: On pervasive Eurocentrism, Southern agency and struggles over universals. *Security Dialogue* 53(1). 38–56.

Quinton-Brown, Patrick. 2020. The South, the West and the Meanings of Humanitarian Intervention in History. *Review of International Studies* 46(4). 514–533

Ralph, J., J. Holland & K. Zhekova. 2017. Before the vote: UK foreign policy discourse on Syria 2011–13. *Review of International Studies* 43(5). 875–897.

Recchia, Stefano &Jennifer M. Welsh (eds.). 2013. *Just and Unjust Military Intervention. European Thinkers from Vitoria to Mill*. Cambridge: Cambridge UP.

Ripsman, Norrin M., Jeffrey W. Taliaferro & Steven E. Lobell. 2016. *Neoclassical Realist Theory of International Politics*. Oxford: Oxford University Press.

Rodogno, Davide. 2012. *Against Massacre. Humanitarian Interventions in the Ottoman Empire 1815–1914*. Princeton: Princeton UP.

Schulz, Matthias. 2009. *Normen und Praxis. Das Europäische Konzert der Großmächte als Sicherheitsrat 1815–1860*. München: Oldenbourg.

Shklar, Judith. 1989. The Liberalism of Fear. In: Nancy L. Rosenblum (ed.), *Liberalism and the Moral Life*, 21–38. Cambridge: Cambridge UP.

Smith, Dan. 1999. Sovereignty in the Age of Intervention. In McDermott A., *Sovereign Intervention*, PRIO-Report 2, Oslo: PRIO, 13–28.

Simms, Brendan & D. J. B. Trim (eds.). 2011. *Humanitarian Intervention. A History*. Cambridge: Cambridge University Press.

Soares de Oliveira, Ricardo & Harry Verhoeven. 2018. Taming Intervention: Sovereignty, Statehood and Political Order in Africa. *Survival* 60(2). 7–32.

Sohail, Hashmi. 1993. Is There an Islamic Ethic of Humanitarian Intervention? *Ethics & International Affairs* 7. 55–73.

Stengel, Frank A. 2020. *The Politics of Military Force: Antimilitarism, Ideational Change and Post-War German Security Discourse*. Ann Arbor: University of Michigan Press.

Taliaferro, Jeffrey W. 2004. Power Politics and the Balance of Risk: Hypotheses on Great Power Intervention in the Periphery. *Political Psychology* 25(2). 177–221.

Walzer, Michael. 1977. *Just and Unjust Wars*. New York: Basic Books.

Walzer, Michael. 1983. *Spheres of Justice. A Defence of Pluralism and Equality*. Oxford: Basic Books.

Weiss, Thomas G. 2016. The Turbulent 1990s: R2P Precedents and Prospects. In A. Bellamy & T. Dunne (eds.), *The Oxford Handbook of the Responsibility to Protect*, 57–73. Oxford: Oxford University Press.

Wheeler, Nicholas J. 2000. *Saving Strangers: Humanitarian Intervention in International Society*. Oxford: Oxford University Press.

Wohlforth, William C., et al. 2007. Testing Balance-of-Power Theory in World History. *European Journal of International Relations* 13(2). 155–185.

Wright, Quincy. 1955. *The Study of International Relations*. New York: Appleton-Century-Crofts.

Zimmermann, Hubert. 2017. Exporting Security: Success and Failure in the Securitization and Desecuritization of Foreign Military Interventions. *Journal of Intervention and Statebuilding* 11(2). 225–244.

Zimmermann, Hubert. 2020. Charles P. Kindleberger. In Holger Janusch (ed.),*Handelspolitik und Welthandel in der Internationalen Politischen Ökonomie*, 203–214. Springer: Wiesbaden.

Zimmermann, Hubert. 2023. *Militärische Missionen. Die Rechtfertigung bewaffneter Auslandseinsätze von ihren Ursprüngen bis zur Gegenwart* Hamburg: Hamburger Edition.

Witold Mucha

Crowding out the West? China's Belt and Road Initiative and the Asian infrastructure investment bank

Abstract: Governments in the US and the EU perceive China's Belt & Road Initiative and the Asian Infrastructure Investment Bank as powerful leverage for the propagation of Beijing's interests in the global (economic) system. Western decision-makers argue that China's ascendency coincides with a global economy that has been undergoing a fundamental phase of structural disorder and reorientation. While some economies such as China's greatly benefitted from those changes in terms of GDP growth rates, other countries suffered from the unequal distribution of welfare gains created by economic globalisation. Against the backdrop of Capoccia's critical juncture concept and Strange's (1994) understanding of structural power in International Political Economy, the article discusses the implications of BRI and AIIB from a US and EU governments' perspective: (a) to what extent do BRI and AIIB have the potential to contribute permanently to China's geoeconomic rise and thereby (b) to the alteration of global economic governance?

Keywords: China, USA, Europe, Structural Power, Critical Juncture, Asian Infrastructure Investment Bank, Belt and Road Initiative

1 Introduction

Governments in the US and the EU see China's Belt and Road Initiative (BRI) as powerful leverage for the propagation of that country's interests in the global economic system (Chen 2016; Casarini 2016; Feigenbaum 2017; Brown 2018; Layne 2018; Hameiri and Jones 2018; Zhou and Esteban 2018; Akcadag Alagoz 2019; Pascha 2020; Sarsenbayev and Véron 2020; Taube 2020; Henderson et al. 2021). Western decision-makers argue that China's ascendency coincides with a global economy that has been undergoing a fundamental phase of structural disorder and reorientation – at the latest since the Global Financial Crisis (GFC) between 2007 and 2008. While some economies such as China's benefited greatly from those changes in terms of GDP growth rates, other countries suffered from the unequal distribution of those wel-

Witold Mucha, Institute of Social Sciences, Heinrich-Heine University Düsseldorf, Germany

https://doi.org/10.1515/9783111272900-007

fare gains created by economic globalization (Taube 2020; Hung 2021; Brown et al. 2021). In contrast to the West's suspicions of the BRI, little heed has been taken of the creation of the Asian Infrastructure Investment Bank (AIIB). Established in 2013, its general purpose is to obtain funds to build infrastructure across Asia. The AIIB is open to participation by any country, but with the proviso that it would be kept under the leadership and control of Chinese authority (Dollar 2015; Bustillo and Andoni 2018; Wang 2019). Against the backdrop of a controversial public debate on the status of Sino-American relations, scholars in regional studies and/or economics have dealt with some of the issues related to the likelihood of the BRI and AIIB impacting the existing global economic governance architecture, known as the Bretton Woods system (Xiao 2016; Casarini 2016; Chen 2016; Wan 2016; Chan 2017; Feigenbaum 2017; Cai 2018; Hameiri and Jones 2018; Layne 2018; Loke 2018; Zhang et al. 2018; Zhou and Esteban 2018; Akcadag Alagoz 2019; Wang and Miao 2019; Biba and Wolf 2021; Chen 2020, 2021; Skålnes 2021). However, none of these studies has analyzed the path dependency dynamics of BRI and AIIB from a turning-point perspective.

In this chapter, the GFC between 2007 and 2008 will be understood as the beginning of an ongoing turning point of the global economic governance system. While the massive bailouts of financial institutions by governments in the West sparked worldwide recession and contributed to the European debt crisis, China was able to mitigate the housing bubble effects with the help of a large-scale economic stimulus package (Bottelier 2018: 86–87). In contrast to the over-indebted US, Beijing's massive infrastructure investments, government influence on banks, and the privatized housing market helped to restore full employment and economic growth quickly (Bottelier 2018: 88–90). This simultaneous occurrence of recession in the West and recovery in China sets up the turning-point moment of the GFC. Against this background, the launch of the BRI and AIIB in 2013 presents two significant case studies to understand the long-term implications of that moment. The goal of this chapter is to assess: (a) to what extent BRI and AIIB have the potential to contribute permanently to China's geoeconomic rise and thereby (b) to the alteration of global economic governance. These two questions can only be addressed by looking at both China's strategy and the US and the EU finding a way to respond to those changes.

The rationale of this chapter is based on the combination of two theoretical approaches. First, the GFC marks the starting point of an ongoing critical juncture in global economic governance (Capoccia/Kelemen 2007; Capoccia 2016). In International Relations (IR) Theory, the concept of a critical juncture has, traditionally, been understood as "events and developments in the distant past, generally concentrated in a relatively short period, that have a crucial impact on outcomes later in time" (Capoccia 2016: 89). In this regard, a broad understanding of historical institutionalism allows for defining the salient institutions as "organizations, formal rules, public policies, as well as larger configurations of connected institutional arrangements such as political regimes and political economies" (Capoccia 2016: 89). The latter in particular will be of interest in this chapter as the provision of BRI infrastructure development is only made possible by the establishment and management of industrial zones at those railway stations and ports located along the "New Silk Road". As a result of these zones (regardless of free trade status), a considerable part of the economic interaction will take place within the respective regions, thus significantly raising local income and wealth levels. Second, in addition to Giovanni Capoccia's (2016) notion of critical junctures, Susan Strange's (1994) understanding of structural power in the International Political Economy (IPE) theory will be used to assess China's leverage toward the US and EU countries based on the BRI and AIIB. Her differentiated approach to structural power (i.e., security, production, finance, knowledge) allows for a comprehensive understanding of the concept of leverage in the international system: "It is impossible to have political power without the power to purchase, to command production, to mobilize capital. And it is impossible to have economic power without the sanction of political authority, without the legal and physical security that can only be supplied by political authority" (Strange 1994: 25). In particular, an analysis of trade-related dimensions such as production and finance will shed light on the limited options the US administrations and EU governments have in that respect. Belt and Road Initiative projects and businesses are financed by the AIIB or Chinese banks which rely either on commercial terms or governmental subsidies (Gabusi 2017; Lairson 2018; Wang 2016). The influence of the US and EU on the AIIB is limited given Beijing's continuing control in that realm. The linking element between Capoccia's (2016) and Strange's (1994) concepts is the notion of temporality and agency. Turning points in the international system, be they critical junctures or the rise of hegemons, can only happen (or not) regarding other stakeholders such as the US and arenas such as Bretton Woods institutions. In other words, any process of structural change pushed by China is inevitably linked to Washington's, Brussels' or others' willingness or capability to let it unfold. Therefore, in this chapter, a turning point will be defined as 'an externally induced process recalibrating the governance modus operandi along with the range of outcomes in the long run (i.e., temporality) that can only be steered by powerful states and/or state actors in relation to each other (i.e., agency)'. To what extent, then, do the BRI and AIIB meet those turning-point criteria in the post-GFC scenario?

The analysis reveals two major results. First, Beijing has made use of both relational (e.g., diplomacy and infrastructure endowments) and structural power (i.e., institution-building) to alter the geo-economics 'rules of the game' in its favor. However, despite Western attempts to prevent the launch of the BRI and the AIIB, their overall impact on the global economic governance architecture has been limited from a turning-point perspective. On the one hand, there has been growing membership – even by G7 and EU member states – of both the BRI and AIIB. However, the BRI holds limited transformative power, given that 95% of total freight traffic is still being transported by sea on container ships. Also, Chinese banks have been struggling increasingly with granting bridge loans to prevent payment defaults in several BRI partner countries. Regarding the AIIB, it proved to have become a reform-minded multilateral financial institution that has made concessions to establish rules and has sought collaboration with its counterparts – similar to the ways other Multilateral Development Banks (MDBs) such as the World Bank have traditionally operated. In other words, against the backdrop of the GFC, the geo-economic hegemony of the US-based Bretton Woods system is being complemented but not supplanted. Despite its ongoing relative decline, the structural power of the US prevails for now. Second, the understanding of agency on turning points needs to be differentiated when it comes to global economic governance. In particular, the case of China shows that the rules-based international order is not shaped solely by Chinese leaders' intentions and their manifestation within the established rules of multilateral organizations. Far more decisive is the micro-level cumulative effect of the diverse activities of a variety of domestic actors involved in different projects, their goals, and ultimately, their power struggles. This chapter is divided into five parts. Following the introduction, the theoretical turning-point argument will be developed based on Capoccia's (2016) notion of critical junctures and Strange's (1994) understanding of structural power. An overview of the BRI and AIIB along with China's underlying foreign policy approach will be presented thereafter. The responses by the US administrations and EU governments will be analyzed in both cases. Finally, the findings will be summarized and the implications for further research on turning points will be discussed.

2 Critical juncture and structural power

Despite recurring fundamental changes in human history such as the French Revolution (1789–1795), the collapse of the postwar order (1925–1939), or the end of the Cold War (1989–1992), IR Theory has struggled to grasp turning points both conceptually and empirically (Katzenstein 1990; Ruggie 1993; Holsti 1998; Sindjoun 2001; Gunitsky 2013; Krause 2017; Sinha 2018). "[Since] no shared vocabulary exists in the literature to depict change and continuity, (. . .) we are not very good as a discipline at studying the possibility of fundamental discontinuity in the international system" (Ruggie 1993: 140). Meanwhile, realists' interest in change is limited to narrow criteria such as shifts in the balance of power, the poles of power, or the cast of great power characters. Liberalists and constructivists relate change to the variability of state interests, policymakers' capacity to learn, and the prospects for progress. The great debates among IR theorists have not been able to keep up with the observed facts of a constantly changing international system; be it the Arab Spring in 2011, the Brexit referendum in 2016, or the war in Ukraine in 2022. In terms of time and space, Strange (1996), therefore, argued that mainstream versions of IR theory "(. . .) cling to obsolete concepts and inappropriate theories (. . .) [that] belong to a more stable and orderly world than the one we live in" (Strange 1996: 3).

Strange's (1996) observation holds two implications that help to build a theory that applies to the international system of the twenty-first century. First, regarding the temporal dimension of change, there is a need for consensus not only on what has changed but also on how to distinguish minor changes from fundamental changes or turning points (Holsti 1998; Krause 2017). In other words, is it about temporary trends or structural transformations of the international system or parts thereof, such as global economic governance? Second, regarding the space dimension of change, IR theory has been deeply embedded in the Western canon of knowledge. Against this backdrop, IR theorists failed to understand changes, particularly in the so-called Global South where Westphalian statehood concepts do not apply to extant realities on local ground (Gruffydd Jones 2006; Castro Varela and Dhawan 2017). For instance, there is a need to go beyond classic IR theory to understand China's rise in the international system. In its attempt to become economically involved in Asian countries, Beijing has created Chinese-led institutional frameworks and thus, made the region suitable for Chinese existence (Suehiro 2017; Dolma 2020; Kim 2022), and this "sinicization" approach is also being applied in the BRI context. In this chapter, the conceptual lack in the temporal and spatial dimensions of turning points in IR theory will be addressed by Capoccia's (2016) notion of critical junctures and Strange's (1994) understanding of structural power.

The BRI is a long-term investment program which aims to develop infrastructure and accelerate the economic integration of the countries involved (BRI 2022). Given its transcontinental nature and its 147 participating states, it is likely to affect not only national but also global economic governance structures. Against this backdrop, there is a need to understand the implications of BRI (as well as the AIIB) for major global economic institutions such as the International Monetary Fund (IMF), the World Bank, and the World Trade Organization (WTO) which have, traditionally, been dominated by the US and European countries. Taking global economic governance as an institutional framework for analysis, the question needs to be addressed as to how and to what extent the BRI and the

AIIB affect its further development. The concept of path dependency as established in institutional economics is useful in this regard (North 1981; Berins Collier and Collier 1991; Pierson 2004). In times of critical junctures such as the GFC, different paths of development are logically possible. According to Berins Collier and Collier (1991), prior structural conditions do not necessarily determine the type and direction of subsequent institutional developments. While early works have been based on ex post analysis perspectives, more recent studies argue in favor of ex ante optics that take into account not only the institutional paths that were eventually taken but also those not taken, however plausible they were thought at that time (Berins Collier and Collier 1991; Mahoney 2002; Capoccia 2016). The merit of ex ante perspectives of path dependency is the focus on political agency and choice as determinants in selecting from the options available at the time of a critical juncture. Mahoney (2002) argues that "(. . .) critical junctures are moments of relative structural indeterminism when willful actors shape outcomes in a more voluntaristic fashion than normal circumstances permit (. . .)" (Mahoney 2002: 8). In other words, choices demonstrate the power of agency by revealing how long-term development patterns can be determined by the distant actor decisions of the past. Capoccia and Kelemen (2007) theorize that the decisions of some actors can be more influential than those of others in steering institutional development regardless of the fluctuating social and political contexts. For instance, the massive size of the monetary and fiscal policies of industrialized countries in the West was eventually able to prevent the collapse of the global financial system in the aftermath of the GFC in the 2010s. However, developing countries coped differently with the subsequent Great Recession and its effects, such as increased unemployment (León-Manríquez 2015). In contrast to merely looking at the cumulative effect of certain small events, the analysis of powerful actors is, thus, more appropriate to understand critical junctures (Capoccia and Kelemen 2007; Capoccia 2016).

In terms of time, the duration of a critical juncture is believed to be brief compared to the path-dependent processes that follow. The longer the period of juncture, the more likely that political decisions will be compromised by reemerging structural constraints: "[For] a brief period, agents face a *broader than normal* range of feasible options and (. . .) their choices among these options are *likely to have a significant impact* on the path-dependent development of an institution" (Capoccia 2016: 91–92) (author's emphasis), and with the more elevated role of agency in path dependency economics comes a more refined understanding of contingency (Mahoney 2000; Pierson 2000; David 2007). Contingency is understood as the analysis of "(. . .) what happened in the context [of] what could have happened" (Berlin 1974: 176). Taking that counterfactual rationale for granted, the implications for the analysis of critical junctures are twofold. First, actors could have opted for different decisions. Had they done so, those decisions would have had consequences for the institutional outcome of interest. Second, the salient range of plausible alternative options is not infinite. Rather, it is defined by prior conditions even though, within the limits of those conditions, actors still face real choices. In other words, randomness is ruled out in this understanding of contingency. To understand critical junctures, there is, therefore, a need to identify key decision-makers, the choices available at the time, the likelihood of actors to select alternative options, and what ramifications the choice of an alternative decision would have had for the institutional context of interest (Capoccia and Kelemen 2007: 355; Capoccia 2016: 92).

Capoccia's (2016) notion of timing and agency helps to understand the long-term impact of the BRI and the AIIB on global economic governance from a critical juncture perspective. The two initiatives were brought forward by China and officially presented in 2013, and ever since, both have been dominated by Chinese actors. The US, the EU and its member states have been the only relevant players on a global scale to influence the BRI and the AIIB in contrast to states such as Russia, Japan, and India (Moeller 2019; Gao 2019; Taube 2020). Strange's (1994) structural power approach in IPE is useful for assessing the interaction between China, the US, and the EU in both contexts. In contrast to relational power "(. . .) described in conventional realist textbooks as the power of A to get B to do something it would not otherwise do" (Strange 1987: 564), Strange (1984) favors the concept of structural power which is based on the rationale of indirect leverage by a hegemon in the international system: "[Structural power means] the ability of state A, through its domestic as well as foreign policies, to govern or influence the context or environment within which B also has to take domestic and foreign policy-making decisions" (Strange 1984: 191). Strange (1988) identifies four sources of structural power: national security, production and manufacturing, finance, and technology and network knowledge (Strange 1988: 135–139). In line with realist thinking, security is understood as the control of military capabilities and participation in alliances such as the North Atlantic Treaty Organization. Control over production and manufacturing refers to a country's raw materials and how these are processed to prevail on the global market (e.g., the share of global manufacturing output). The financing dimension of structural power means the ability to control and deny access to credit, thus affecting production and markets indirectly. Investments and technological advancements can only be financed by temporary debts. Lastly, control over knowledge is understood as the cultural and scientific dominance by state and non-state actors to influence or impose norms on institutions, networks, or the public (Strange 1989: 9–24; Rotte 2017: 473–474). In later works, Strange (1994) added into her framework secondary structures of power such as transportation, trade, energy supply, and welfare organizations. In contrast to realist understandings of power in the international system, Strange's (1994) approach allows for a dynamic look into a changing international system where the leverage of military power alone is limited when lacking complementary means in terms of production, finance, or knowledge.

Guzzini (1993) elaborates on Strange's concept by differentiating between agent power (i.e., agent referent to power phenomena) and impersonal governance (i.e., the capacity to effect intersubjective practices) that need to be brought together in a comprehensive power analysis: "Power lies both in the relational interaction of agents and in the systematic rule that results from the consequences of their actions" (Guzzini 1993: 474) This dyadic conceptualization allows for an analysis of the power to set rules and agendas in the international system. That being the case, states can prevent other states from changing existing privileges via their structural power. Bringing Strange's (1987) argument against the "persistent myth of lost [US] hegemony" together with Guzzini's (1993) rationale, illustrates their theoretical use in the present analysis of the BRI and the AIIB. According to Strange (1987, 1994), despite the relative decline in capabilities, the US was able to determine the rules of the international system in the 1980s and 1990s according to its interests (e.g., the Bretton Woods system). Once the US was no longer able to set rules, as seen, for instance, in the failed WTO Doha Round, this indicates the loss of structural power on the part of Washington (Viola 2020; Zangl et al. 2016). Critical junctures can, thus, be understood as phases where dominant states such as the US are no longer able to control the agenda or prevent the emergence of new 'rules of the game'. Furthermore, critical junctures are periods where there is no longer a monopoly on structural power but rather, a competitive (re-)balancing of structural power. Against this backdrop, phases of path dependency versus critical junctures correlate with phases of unipolar structural power versus multipolar structural power.

While historical institutionalism is capable of explaining phases of path dependency and identifying the moment of critical junctures, it fails to explain what happens within critical junctures. Therefore, there is a need to complement Capoccia's (2016) perspective with Strange's (1994). This conceptual link between critical juncture and structural power helps us to understand China's geo-economic ascendency in the international system. The first assumes a long-term effect on institutional development caused by a powerful actor (i.e., temporality). The latter shows how to assess whether that actor is more powerful in relation to others (i.e., agency). The figure below illustrates the analysis framework that will be used to analyze the turning point implications of the BRI and the AIIB (see Figure 1). A turning point will be defined as 'an externally induced process recalibrating the governance modus operandi along with the range of outcomes in the long run (i.e., temporality) that can only be steered by powerful states and/or state actors regarding each other (i.e., agency)'.

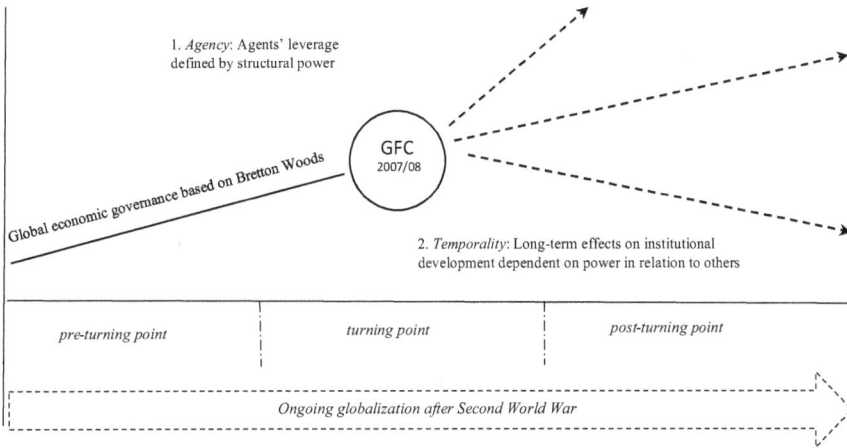

Figure 1: Turning Point Global Financial Crisis (GFC).

Figure 1 shows that the development of turning points is dependent on powerful actors steering long-term paths. The extent of that power is dependent on other powerful actors' means and interests in that context. The illustration does not imply that non-agent-related events such as exogenous shocks (e.g., natural disasters or pandemics) are not feasible for this analysis framework. Rather, the argument is about what capabilities in terms of structural power states have to respond to such events for the sake of their own interests. In other words, what makes states powerful enough to steer (or continue steering) institutional development in the case of turning point dynamics? As regards the two overarching research questions, the analysis will discuss to what extent the BRI and the AIIB contribute to the turning point scenario induced by the GFC between 2007 and 2008 in favor of China's geo-economic leverage. How do the BRI and the AIIB affect the institutional development of the global economic governance architecture that had traditionally been dominated by the Bretton Woods system? Given the focus of this chapter on global economics, the analysis will ignore Strange's likewise important structural power dimensions of security and knowledge and, instead, focus on trade and financing (Jones 2019; Vangeli 2018; Zhang 2017).

3 The BRI: Substantial investments, diffusion of institutions

Long before the COVID-19 pandemic (2020) and Russia's invasion of Ukraine (2022), globalization was still in full swing when the BRI was initiated in 2013. During that period "(. . .) [the] viability of a global economic welfare community based on global value chains and an ever more specialized international division of labor was not seriously put into doubt" (Taube 2020: 9). At that time, the BRI was presented by Beijing as an approach to invigorate comprehensive international collaboration and venture forth on joint growth and development based on interdependent national economic structures and transnational network-oriented business models (Yu 2017: 355; Schortgen 2018: 23–24). Stressing the mutual benefits of the BRI was in line with China's consistently stated commitment to "peaceful development" as related in Xi Jinping's speech at the "Meeting Marking the 60th Anniversary of the Initiation of the Five Principles of Peaceful Coexistence" in 2014: "China is guided by the principle of boosting amity, sincerity, mutual benefit, and inclusiveness in deepening mutually beneficial cooperation with its neighbors and strives to deliver greater gains to its neighbors through its own development" (Xi 2014). Indeed, ever since Xi Jinping's ascendency to leadership, China has emphasized its commitment to pushing for a comprehensive global engagement based on "amity, sincerity, mutual benefit, and inclusiveness". The extent to which China's economic statecraft – of which the BRI is the most ambitious manifestation – lends China geostrategic advantages is as much a response to US global retrenchment as it is a feature of twenty-first-century geostrategic economics (Schortgen 2018: 24). In light of this, China has been perceived as an ambivalent power in world politics. On the one hand, Beijing adheres to the principles of embedded multilateralism. This is reflected in the general commitment to a multipolar international system in which international mechanisms and domestic interests are regulated and institutionalization and legalization are advanced. On the other hand, China has also shown a *realpolitik* foreign policy approach based on national sovereignty, national interest, national power, and national wealth (Xuetong 2021; Dollar 2015; Layne 2018). Beijing's tacit overlooking of Russia's aggression against Ukraine, its self-confident presence in the South China Sea, and its uncompromising stance regarding Taiwan demonstrate China's current ambiguous foreign policy approach (Gabuev 2022; Zhang 2020; Lawrence et al. 2021).

As far as the BRI is concerned, China has been unrelenting in establishing a global network of multilateral economic and trade initiatives from the beginning of the twenty-first century: the Forum on China–Africa Cooperation (FOCAC) in 2000; the Forum for Economic and Trade Cooperation between China and Portuguese-speaking countries (Forum Macao) in 2003; the China–Arab States Cooperation Forum (CASCF) in 2004; the China–Caribbean Economic and Trade Cooperation Forum in 2005; and the Forum of China and the Community of Latin American and Caribbean States in 2014 (Schortgen 2018: 25). Against this backdrop, launching the BRI feeds into Beijing's general geo-economic strategy of promoting Chinese interests in the global arena (see Figure 2). Moreover, the economic motives and design underlying the initiative are grounded in a multitude of domestic challenges such as slowed economic growth, huge industrial overcapacity, and continued underdevelopment of hinterland provinces. The most important economic goals of the BRI have been based on establishing new impulses for growth and development in China by reducing the transaction costs of trade in newly opened-up markets. Furthermore, the initiative is intended to address the intra-China inequality by establishing new centers of economic activity in the Central and Western hinterland. The initiative is also intended to strengthen the Chinese state-owned enterprise sector, mostly by providing them with new business opportunities and sales outlets in state-directed international infrastructure and construction projects as well as development assistance programs. Given the sensitive Malacca Strait, yet another goal is to secure access to energy carriers and raw materials by establishing alternative shipping routes. Furthermore, the BRI rationale is to create a global network of business-driven bases predicated on the projection of Chinese soft power along with its geopolitical interests (Taube 2020: 9; Cai 2018). Taking Guzzini's (1993) understanding of structural power as the ability to set the agenda of the international governance system, the BRI (and the AIIB) have been perceived as Beijing's attempt to move from rule-taker to rule-maker against the backdrop of the Bretton Woods logic: "(. . .) China has tried to advance the establishment of new institutions outside the existing system to bypass the USA-dominated existing system and to increase Beijing's influence in the regional and global economic arena" (Cai 2018: 838).

Based on a variety of diplomatic initiatives and infrastructure endowments, China was indeed able to reduce red tape and ease the trade and investment administration of Belt and Road partner countries (Moeller 2019; Gao 2019). In particular, the diplomatic offensive was necessary to reduce transnational shipping times by using simplified border controls, customary procedures, and regulatory practices before starting the buildup of infrastructure facilities. In sum, the so-called "New Silk Road" has been realized in two features. First, as a set of multi-modal transport corridors between East and West (e.g., resulting in shipping time reductions). Second, by contributing to the formation of new centers of economic activity in regions beyond China that had previously been integrated into the global economy but only to a limited extent (Taube 2020: 10–11).

Regarding the temporal dimension of turning points, the new transport corridor has little potential to change practices in freight traffic (and thus, the global

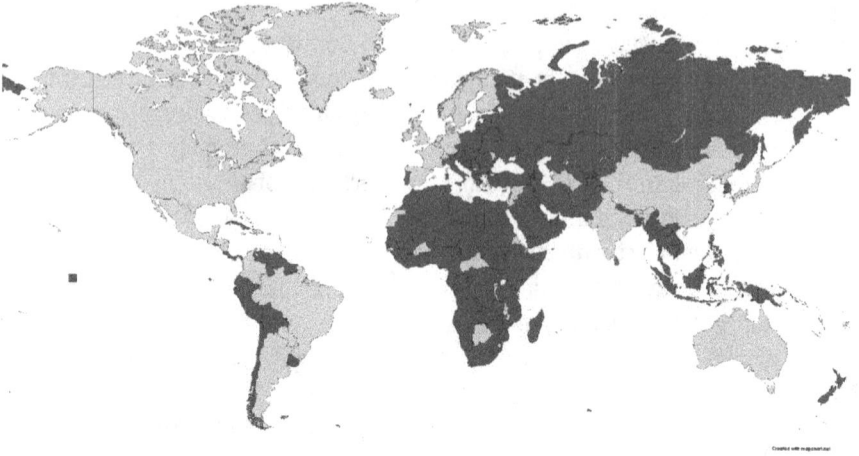

Figure 2: 147 BRI member states, 2013–2022.
Source: Author's own illustration based on the Green Finance & Development Center (2022).

economic system) because more than 95% is still transported by sea on container ships (Gao 2019: 167–168). However, the emergence of a network of industry hubs along the "New Silk Road" is different in that regard. It can potentially contribute to the redesigning of cross-border business models and thus, the structures of the global economy (Cai 2018; Gao 2019). The establishment, financing, and management of such industrial zones relies exclusively on Chinese initiatives. The long-term advantages for Beijing are substantial. First, China has effectively applied its own institutional solutions to those specific ordering problems caused by cross-border economic interactions. For instance, local economies have begun to adapt to Chinese business practices and customs, procedural norms, and technical standards. Second, it has set up technological and business path dependencies that favor Chinese technology owners and market participants (e.g., Huawei technology transfers). Third, it has accumulated political and social capital among decision-making elites in the BRI partner countries. One feature of that interdependency is the use of the renminbi as the billing currency for local companies, making it a reasonable reserve currency for local central banks. Yet another characteristic of the diffusion of Chinese institutions is the career paths of educational elites. For instance, after English, Mandarin has replaced German as the second-most popular foreign language in Belarus (Taube 2020: 10–11). Fourth, Beijing has established future holdup constellations as well as financial and technological path dependencies regarding asset specificities that favor Chinese interests by increasingly switching costs to non-Chinese business partners, technical solutions, or diplomatic initiatives (Taube 2020: 15). Fifth, overall debt owed to China has soared since 2013, surpassing 10 (e.g., Ethiopia, Kazakhstan, Turkmenistan) or up to 20% of GDP in some countries such as Mongolia, Cambodia, or Laos (Chatzky and McBride 2020). The latter in particular has turning-point implications given the long-term debt traps implicit in borrowing by developing countries.

Beijing's relational power in terms of diplomacy and infrastructure endowments led (and still leads) to the emergence of new norms and rules that business stakeholders need to adhere to on a national basis. This path dependency dynamic raises the theoretically and empirical-analytically unresolved question of to what extent relational power can be equated on a one-to-one basis with structural power. A close look at the AIIB below will shed additional light on the necessity of raising that question to assess the contours of turning points in the international system.

4 The AIIB: Disruptive, not revolutionary institution-building

On an institutional level, Beijing's initiatives have been no less ambitious and focus on deepening regional cooperation. The launch of the AIIB – along with the BRICS-led New Development Bank (NDB) – not only shows China's determination to secure a greater voice and input in global financial governance (Wang 2019; Xiao 2016) but is also a response to Washington's "pivot to Asia" policy, wherein the US expands its military presence by strengthening the existing alliance structure in the Asia-Pacific (Chan 2017: 570). Moreover, establishing the AIIB lays bare China's historic frustration with continued Western dominance of the World Bank and the IMF and Japanese dominance of the Asian Development Bank (ADB) (Schortgen 2018: 25). As far as reforms of the Bretton Woods system are concerned, China and other emerging economies have not been satisfied with the leadership, redistribution of quota shares, and voting rights that are still disproportionate to their GDP shares (Feigenbaum 2017; Xiao 2016). Creating the AIIB as a parallel financial institution alongside the World Bank and the IMF can, thus, be interpreted as a structural power attempt to thwart US geo-economic hegemony in the long run.

Established in June 2015, the new multilateral development bank, the AIIB, set out to "help fill a multi-trillion-dollar gap in financing for railways, roads, power plants, and other infrastructure in the world's fastest-growing region" (Feigenbaum 2017: 33). Proposed by China, membership grew rapidly from 57 founding partners to 86 members in March 2022 (Asian Infrastructure Investment Bank 2022). Membership of the AIIB is open to all members of the World Bank and the ADB. It is divided into 46 regional (i.e., Asia and Oceania), 27 non-regional members, and 18 EU member states. Regional members retain 75% of the total voting power while China, as largest contributor, holds a 28% stake, making it also the largest shareholder of the bank, followed by India (8%), Russia (6%), Germany (4%), South Korea (3%), Australia (3%), France (3%), Indonesia (3%), the United Kingdom (3%), and Turkey (3%) (Asian Infrastructure Investment Bank 2022). In terms of capital, the AIIB's initial subscribed capital is $100 billion, with 20% paid in and 80% callable. The total capital of the AIIB amounts to roughly two-thirds of the capital of the ADB and almost half that of the World Bank (Akcadag Alagoz 2019: 960; Chen 2021: 28–31).

Regardless of the official goals of the 2015 AIIB Agreement "to promote investment in the region of public and private capital for development purposes, in particular for the development of infrastructure and other productive sectors," decision-makers in Washington have perceived the new bank as a revisionist attempt to "create a Sino-centric financial system to rival Western dominated institutions" and thus, undermine US supremacy in global finance (Akcadag Alagoz 2019: 960). US-based observers feared that only three of 20 directorships would be allocated to non-Asian states; directors would, at best, have only limited oversight of the management board; environmental, social, and transparency safeguards would be largely neglected; loans would be issued mainly in renminbi; Chinese companies would be prioritized disproportionately in the awarding of contracts; and China would contribute 50% of the capital stock, thus giving Beijing exclusive veto power (Hameiri and Jones 2018: 574–575).

Eight years in, evidence suggests that the AIIB's design indeed distinguishes it from existing multilateral development banks (MDBs). The focus is exclusively on infrastructure development rather than poverty reduction. Also, loans are extended at commercial rates, and recipients are required to show repayment capacity as part of the business case for the projects funded. Nine out of twelve directorships are held by Asian members. The board of directors are nonresident, likely affording the bank's management more operational freedom than in other MDBs. Also, Beijing's 28% of the AIIB's vote share indeed gives it veto power over decisions that require a super-majority – even though this does not hold in most operational matters, including project approvals (Hameiri and Jones 2018: 575; Chen 2020: 721). In total, however, Western fears of the AIIB serving as a revisionist Trojan Horse to the Bretton Woods system have not proven true. Its structure, governance and operating procedures very much resemble those of other MDBs. Compared to the ADB and the World Bank, the AIIB has very similar power structure problems – the only structural difference being that Beijing is in the lead. For instance, it has the highest concentration of power among its top ten members. Also, China not only has stronger veto power in the AIIB but there are also more occasions when it is formally allowed to make use of it: "Even if Japan and the United States were to take up the unallocated shares as a regional member and a non-regional member, respectively, they would each only get a 1.58% and a 0.40% share of the votes, while China's voting power cannot fall below 25%." (Chen 2021: 97) In other words, even if European members of AIIB aligned with the US, Beijing would still retain its veto power. As far as loan competition is concerned, the AIIB does not seem to be the norm changer that observers in Washington suggested it would be. Indeed, the ADB reacted to the emergence of the AIIB by boosting its financial capacity in several aspects. The World Bank's reaction has remained unclear. On the one hand, its commitments to most AIIB members increased, while on the other hand, the growth in these commitments has been lower than for non-AIIB members (Chen 2021: 98).

Beijing's primary goal of improving its status deficit situation by establishing the AIIB has been achieved. China's status in the international financial system improved while developed countries joined the AIIB incrementally. Regarding the Bretton Woods system, Beijing seeks outside collaboration. The AIIB follows the lead of other major international financial institutions (IFIs) and is recognized as an important partner in the global economic governance architecture. Compared to the long-term implications of the BRI, at first glance, the AIIB appears to be less geopolitically sensitive (Chen 2020: 721; Hameiri and Jones 2018: 575; Xiao 2016). In terms of structural power, the AIIB is not used as a means to eliminate the prevalent global economic governance system, however, its creation is likely to alter the rules of that game to some extent in Beijing's favor. The growing number of AIIB members not only demonstrates the increased legitimacy of that IFI but also serve as additional creditors to third countries in need of loans. That parallelism of traditional IFIs such as the IMF or the World Bank on the one hand and the AIIB on the other, is an alteration of the pre-turning point global economic governance system that is likely to prevail in the long run. The AIIB does not replace the World Bank or the IMF; however, it accelerates the relative geo-economic decline of the US.

5 Responses by the West: Containment and connectivity

The analysis suggests that the AIIB appears to cooperate more with established international rules than was expected initially. In particular, decision-makers in the West had feared the bank might serve as the Chinese financing arm of the BRI. A closer comparative look at the fund distribution questions that assumption (see Table 1).

Table 1: Top countries and sectors receiving the most funds (US$ billions).

AIIB				BRI			
Country	Fund	Sector	Fund	Sector	Fund	Country	Fund
India	2.07	Energy	2.57	Energy	172.9	Pakistan	39.5
Indonesia	0.94	Transport	2.02	Transport	100.1	Malaysia	31.0
Turkey	0.80	Water	1.28	Real estate	44.3	Singapore	28.1
Azerbaijan	0.60	Multi-Sector	1.15	Metals	15.0	Indonesia	25.0
Egypt	0.50	Finance	0.20	Logistics	12.2	Russia	24.3
Pakistan	0.40			Utilities	10.7	Bangladesh	21.1
Oman	0.30			Agriculture	10.0	UAE	17.8
Bangladesh	0.29			Chemicals	8.4	Laos	17.8
China	0.25			Tourism	8.0	Egypt	17.2
Philippines	0.21			Technology	7.9	Iran	13.0
Total	7.22		7.22	Total	421.0	Total	421.0

Source: Author's own illustration based on Chen 2020: 720.

First, regarding the energy sector, the BRI concentrates 40% and the AIIB spends 36% of its total funds. In contrast to the BRI, the AIIB's selection of energy projects demonstrates its willingness to shy away from environmentally harmful energy projects. Second, concerning geostrategic bankrolling in borrowing countries, regardless of financial strength, the proportion of investment in the transportation sector in the AIIB is about 28%, comparable to the BRI's 24%. Third, while India, the long-term geopolitical foe, did not become a member of the BRI due to fears about Beijing's ambitions in the region, it has participated in the AIIB. New Delhi has secured about 31% of all AIIB funds so far. India's participation suggests that the AIIB does not act as a financial arm of the BRI. Fourth, while India received most of the funds from the AIIB, Beijing's strategic partner, Pakistan, received the largest share of funds of the BRI. The distribution of funds of the AIIB and BRI differ. "Unlike the AIIB's downplaying of China's political/strategic implications, the projects and countries the BRI has funded reflect more of China's interests" (Chen 2020: 720–721). The differences between the BRI and the AIIB also show when looking into non-regional membership by US and European participation, respectively. For instance, the top three biggest economies in Europe – Germany, the UK, and France – have not formally joined the BRI. However, they do belong to the top ten shareholders of the AIIB (Zanardi 2021; Skala-Kuhmann 2019). Washington has attempted to halt or at least marginalize the BRI and the AIIB (Feigenbaum 2017; Layne 2018). The ongoing parallel bilateral and multilateral collaboration with China sheds light on the lack of strategic unity between capitals in the West when it comes to the BRI and the AIIB. From a turning-point perspective, there is, therefore, a need to assess the responses by the US and European decision-makers in that regard. This will help to better understand the relational and structural leverage Beijing had, and still has, on the development of path dependencies in the global economic governance architecture.

As far as the establishment of the BRI is concerned, the Obama and Trump administrations pursued relational power based on a containment and in-capacitation approach. Washington did not become a partner in the BRI but rather, executed a variety of three broader sets of measures. First, successive US administrations have tried to strengthen alternative initiatives. For instance, after five years of intense negotiations, the Obama Administration tried to get the Trans-Pacific Partnership (TPP) agreement ratified in Congress. If realized, the TPP would have created the largest free trade zone in the world and thus, weakened China (as well as the EU) (Chen 2016). However, it was relinquished by the Trump Administration in January 2017 and not subsequently resumed by the Biden Administration (Kolmaš and Kolmašová 2019; Scherrer 2022). The revival of the Quadrilateral Security Dialogue (Quad) between Japan, India, Australia, and the US has been yet another alternative initiative. Responding to increased Chinese economic and military power as well as its maritime claims in the East and South China Seas, the Quad has evolved from security dialog only to regular actual joint naval exercises (Kliem 2020). Second, Washington has launched measures to undermine Beijing's activities along the "New Silk Road". Secondary sanctions have been made use of in an attempt to block companies from engaging with selected Chinese firms or exporting certain technologies to Chinese subjects blacklisted by the US government. Most prominently, the Blue Dot Network has been co-established by Washington, Canberra, and Tokyo. It has been tasked with assessing and certifying infrastructure projects in terms of their potential viability, sustainability, and transparency of procurement procedures. The rationale of the initiative has been to make potential infrastructure projects more attractive to non-Chinese backers and implicitly frame BRI projects as substandard (Ashbee 2021). Third, US governments have dissuaded third parties from joining or indirectly getting involved with BRI. For instance, in June 2020, former US Secretary of State Pompeo threatened Canberra to "simply disconnect" from Australia after its government had signed a non-binding agreement on infrastructure cooperation in the BRI framework that could, allegedly, harm US telecommunication security (Pan and Hagström 2021: 471).

Compared to its outward critique and undermining activities against the BRI, the US response to the AIIB has been less obvious. Again, mostly based on its relational power, there have been three ways in which Washington reacted to the AIIB. First, the US has refrained from stating its outright disapproval. Second, Washington has refused to join the bank despite losing leverage in the region and missing economic opportunities to partner with China. Third, it has launched a quiet diplomatic campaign to dissuade its traditional partners in Europe or (more successfully) in Japan from doing so (Feigenbaum 2017: 33; Chen 2021: 155, 162).

Despite several policy changes indicating an increasingly competitive and protectionist relationship (e.g., the tightening of regulations for foreign investors), the EU has sought a constructive response to the BRI (Menegazzi 2017). Based on the so-called "Connectivity Strategy", Brussels attempts to spread European values, ethical and technical standards, and economic interests as an alternative model to economies along the "New Silk Road" (Chen 2016; Taube 2020; Zanardi 2021). In terms of structural power, with a financial volume of around EUR 550 billion, the EU has reached out to partners in Eastern Europe and Asia using three modes of interaction. First, Brussels contributed to more efficient connections and networks between Europe and Asia based on priority transport corridors, digitalization, and energy cooperation. Second, the EU established new and revived prevalent partnerships for connectivity based on common standards to enable better governance of flows of goods, people, capital, and services. Third, Brussels addressed the investment gaps by improving the mobilization of resources and reinforcing the leverage of the EU's financial resources and thus, strengthening relations with partners in Eastern Europe and Asia (Taube 2020: 16–17). Despite the range of the Connectivity Strategy, that counterweight approach has not been successful yet because the corporate sector did not take up that capital. Fearing discrimination by the Chinese Belt and Road project tendering, many companies in Europe have been hesitant to get involved (Taube 2020: 17).

In general, the BRI has not seen a unified approach from geographical Europe or the EU or its member states. Long before launching the Connectivity Strategy, the EU member states and non-EU states, as well as European financial institutions such as the European Bank for Reconstruction and Development (EBRD) and the European Investment Bank (EIB) had already become engaged in the BRI. Indeed, half of EU member states had already signed BRI-related agreements, while many top European companies were also already participating in the BRI (Skala-Kuhmann 2019: 144–145; Zanardi 2021: 163; Casarini 2016). The lack of an EU–European unified response becomes even more evident in the case of the AIIB. Of the 57 founding members, 13 were from the EU, including four G7 countries (Germany, France, the UK, and Italy). Apart from the European memberships in the AIIB, the involvement in BRI also materialized via the engagement of European and other international financial institutions with European membership, such as the EBRD and the EIB. Both had already been involved in BRI projects at an early stage. For instance, in April 2019, the EBRD signed a Memorandum of Understanding with the People's Bank of China on strengthening cooperation in third-party markets within the BRI framework. Beginning in 2016, European commercial banks, especially in the UK and Germany, held conferences on the BRI and tried to enhance their roles in the initiative, setting up task forces to coordinate their approaches across different business activities (Skala-Kuhmann 2019: 148–149; Pacheco Pardo 2018). The case of Germany demonstrates the strategic and economic rationale of joining the AIIB independently of Washington's disagreement:

> [It] is no wonder that Germany saw, in membership of the AIIB, an opportunity to reap lucrative economic rewards, while at the same time helping to improve living standards in emerging economies, shaping a more multilateral global system and encouraging China to adopt global standards. In this way, China can be a responsible stakeholder rather than a potential challenger. (Chen 2021: 140).

The AIIB has faced less resistance from the West than the BRI (Cai 2018: 842; Skålnes 2021; Chen 2021). In light of the uncoordinated Western response, it is, therefore, not surprising that Beijing continued to pursue the BRI. In the aftermath of those responses, China moved the initiative further with even more political determination. Even before its announcement in 2013, the government had begun to invest a substantial amount of political and diplomatic effort in the BRI. Ranging from foreign policy to development aid and domestic planning, the successful rollout had turned into an all-encompassing national enterprise. Finally, in 2017, the successful implementation of the Belt and Road program in the constitutional status of China's Communist Party (CCP) has been the most straightforward message to any regional or global contenders and their undermining initiatives (Taube 2020: 17; Pu and Wang 2018). Enshrining the BRI in the CCP's Charter is perceived domestically as Xi's signature foreign policy initiative. A failure of the BRI could not only affect the legitimacy of the party itself but also, after spending billions of dollars abroad while China still faces many internal needs, failure to achieve the goals could lead the Chinese people to challenge Xi's authority (Deng 2021).

In sum, the analysis of the BRI and the AIIB shows that relational and structural power are interdependent. For instance, structural power depends on relational power when third countries are either threatened or rewarded financially by Beijing or the US. In this regard, two dimensions are particularly relevant in terms of different sources of power. First, how much resources (or relational power) are being invested, and second, how do these investments contribute to the emergence of new institutions or 'rules of the game'? Regarding the latter, there are two aspects to consider. On the one hand, there are the norms and rules of IFIs. On the other hand, there are the norms and rules for the business sector, which stakeholders are effectively forced to implement nationally because of the BRI and AIIB framework. The analysis, therefore, shows that relational power cannot simply be equated on a one-to-one basis with structural power.

6 Conclusion

By 2023, China's BRI and the AIIB have been fully operational. The analysis demonstrates that Western fears of Beijing rising as a revisionist hegemon and replacing the Bretton Woods system have not proved true. Although both Washington and European governments and EU decision-makers have not been able or willing to prevent the launching and joining of the BRI and AIIB projects, their overall impact on the global governance architecture has been limited from a turning-point perspective. On the one hand, the AIIB has become a reform-minded multilateral financial institution that has made concessions to establish rules and has sought collaboration with its counterparts (Chen 2020, 2021; Loke 2018; Chan 2017) – in similar ways to how other MDBs such as the World Bank or the ADB have been traditionally operating. For instance, 16 out of 21 infrastructure projects in Asia are being realized as joint ventures either with the World Bank or the ADB (Akcadag Alagoz 2019: 966; Hameiri and Jones 2018: 576–577). On the other hand, despite the BRI's massive scale in terms of investments and 'sinicization' on the ground (e.g., technology path dependencies), the new transport corridor holds limited transformative power given that 95% of total freight traffic is still being transported by sea on container ships (Gao 2019: 167–168; Taube 2020: 10–11). Moreover, Beijing has recently struggled with bridge loans that Chinese banks had to grant to prevent payment defaults in several countries such as Pakistan, Belarus, Mongolia, Argentina, and Sri Lanka. In the face of the pandemic and the war in Ukraine, loans have been used increasingly for natural gas or oil extraction instead of building railroads or roads (Fahrion et al. 2022). Against the backdrop of the GFC-induced turning-point moment, the geo-economic hegemony of the US-based Bretton Woods system is being complemented but not replaced. Despite its ongoing relative decline, the structural power of the US prevails for now. Regardless of their substantial impact on global geo-economics, the AIIB and the BRI (alone) do not recalibrate the governance modus operandi of the global economic governance system.

Regarding the conceptual difficulties of grasping turning points, the case studies hold three insights. First, the Western responses (or rather lack thereof) indeed reveal the crucial role of agency in turning-point dynamics. The prospect of likely economic gains, particularly the participation of the four European G7 countries in the AIIB makes an argument for agency as an analytical category. (Hypothetically) disregarding the economic costs, a more coherent approach on behalf of European governments such as those seen in Washington and Tokyo might have undermined the project. This is in line with Capoccia's (2016) range of plausible alternative options that might have had a different outcome. Second, in terms of temporality, the long-term impact of the simultaneous occurrence of the

GFC and China's rise on the global economic governance architecture is ongoing. It is, therefore, worth discussing whether the BRI and the AIIB serve as the most appropriate case study material to assess their turning-point potential. For instance, the AIIB is a rather marginal player in light of China's fragmented international development finance (IDF) domain. Even if AIIB-funded projects displayed the world's highest environmental, social, and technical protection standards, the huge majority of Chinese-funded projects will not be similarly regulated. The impact of China's rise on the prevalent rules-based, liberal international order will, thus, not be shaped solely by Chinese leaders' intentions and their manifestation within the rules of multilateral organizations. Far more decisive seems to be the cumulative effect of the diverse activities of a variety of actors involved in different projects, their goals, and ultimately their struggles for power and resources (Hameiri and Jones 2018, 592–593). In other words, a more differentiated perspective is needed when it comes to such micro-dynamics, rather than Xi's aspirations, which constitute China's turning-point potential for global economic governance. However, from an ontological social science point of view, such an idiosyncratic approach to the analysis of turning points might constrain its empirical feasibility altogether. Third, this need for differentiation challenges the theoretical use of Strange's (1994) and Guzzini's (1993) concepts of power for identifying turning-point thresholds. The analysis demonstrates the multitude of power dimensions that transcend not only transnational but also state and non-state agent levels on the ground. While the global dominance of freight traffic transport by sea constrains Beijing's power in terms of changing prevalent global trade practices, its 'sinicization' footprint on the business sector on the ground secures substantial structural power for local institution-building in the long run. The recent controversial debate in Germany and Brussels about China's Hamburg port investment illustrates those implications in terms of structural power (Kijewski 2022). In light of this, the analysis shows that relational power cannot be equated on a one-to-one basis with structural power, but rather, needs to be conceived of as a fluid interdependent process.

Going back to the definition of turning points introduced at the beginning of this chapter, future research will have to reflect on a more differentiated understanding of temporality and agency where (a) outcomes can manifest both 'turning' and 'un-turning' elements at the same time (e.g., international versus local institution-building) and where (b) actors largely detached from state authority can be powerful and steer institutional paths on their own (e.g., China's fragmented IDF). Taking these ontological imperatives for granted makes analyzing turning points in the international system even more challenging.

References

Akcadag Alagoz, Emine. 2019. Creation of the Asian Infrastructure Investment Bank as a part of China's smart power strategy. *The Pacific Review* 32(6). 951–971.

Asian Infrastructure Investment Bank. 2022. *Asian Infrastructure Investment Bank*. Accessed September 20, 2022. https://www.aiib.org/en/index.html

Ashbee, Edward. 2021. The Blue Dot Network, economic power, and China's Belt & Road Initiative. *Asian Affairs: An American Review* 48(2). 133–149.

Belt and Road Initiative. 2022. *Belt and Road Initiative*. Accessed September 19, 2022. https://www.belt road-initiative.com/.

Berins Collier, Ruth, and David Collier. 1991. *Shaping the Political Arena: Critical Junctures, the Labor Movement, and Regime Dynamics in Latin America*. Princeton, NJ: Princeton University Press.

Berlin, Isaiah. 1974. Historical Inevitability. In Patrick Gardiner (ed.), *The Philosophy of History*, 161–186. London: Oxford University Press.

Biba, Sebastian, and Reinhard Wolf. 2021. *Europe in an Era of Growing Sino-American Competition*. London/New York: Routledge.

Bottelier, Pieter. China after the international financial crisis. In Robert E. Looney (ed.), *Handbook of Emerging Economies*, 83–104. London: Routledge.

Brown, Alexander, Jacob Gunter, and Max. J. Zenglein. 2021. Course Correction: China's shifting approach to economic globalization. *MERICS China Monitor*, October 19. Accessed September 19, 2022. https://merics.org/sites/default/files/2021-10/MERICS-ChinaMonitor_Globalization_2021-10-13.pdf.

Brown, Scott A. W. 2018. *Power, Perception and Foreign Policymaking. US and EU Responses to the Rise of China*. London/New York: Routledge.

Bustillo, Richard, and Maiza Andoni. 2018. China, the EU and multilateralism: the Asian Infrastructure Investment Bank. *Revista Brasileira de Política Internacional* 61(1). 1–19.

Cai, Kevin G. 2018. The One Belt One Road and the Asian Infrastructure Investment Bank: Beijing's New Strategy of Geoeconomics and Geopolitics. *Journal of Contemporary China* 27(114). 831–847.

Capoccia, Giovanni. 2016. Critical Junctures. In Orfeo Fioretos, Tulia G. Falleti, and Adam Sheingate (eds.), *The Oxford Handbook of Historical Institutionalism*, 89–106. Oxford: Oxford University Press.

Capoccia, Giovanni, and R. D. Kelemen. 2007. The Study of Critical Junctures: Theory, Narrative, and Counterfactuals in Historical Institutionalism. *World Politics* 59(3). 341–369.

Casarini, Nicola. 2016. When All Roads Lead to Beijing. Assessing China's New Silk Road and its Implications for Europe. *The International Spectator* 51(4). 95–108.

Castro Varela, María do Mar, and Nikita Dhawan. 2017. Postkoloniale Studien in den Internationalen Beziehungen: Die IB dekolonisieren. In Frank Sauer and Carlo Masala (eds.), *Handbuch Internationale Beziehungen*, 233–256. Wiesbaden: Springer VS.

Chan, Lai-Ha. 2017. Soft balancing against the US 'pivot to Asia': China's geostrategic rationale for establishing the Asian Infrastructure Investment Bank. *Australian Journal of International Affairs* 7(6). 568–590.

Chatzky, Andrew, and James McBride. 2020. China's Massive Belt and Road Initiative. *Council on Foreign Relations*, January 28. Accessed December 6, 2022. https://www.cfr.org/backgrounder/chinas-massive-belt-and-road-initiative

Chen, Ian Tsung-yen. 2020. China's status deficit and the debut of the Asian Infrastructure Investment Bank. *The Pacific Review* 33(5). 697–727.

Chen, Ian Tsung-yen. 2021. *Configuring the Asian Infrastructure Investment Bank. Power, Interests and Status*. London/New York: Routledge.

Chen, Zhimin. 2016. China, the European Union and the Fragile World Order. *Journal of Common Market Studies* 54(4). 775–792.

David, Paul. 2007. Path Dependence: A Foundational Concept for Historical Social Science. *Cliometrica* 1(2). 91–114.

Deng, Yong. 2021. How China Builds the Credibility of the Belt and Road Initiative. *Journal of Contemporary China* 30(131). 734–750.

Dollar, David. 2015. China's Rise as a Regional and Global Power. The AIIB and the 'One Belt, One Road'. *Horizons: Journal of International Relations and Sustainable Development* 4. 162–173.

Dolma, Kelsang. 2020. Tibet Was China's First Laboratory of Repression. *Foreign Policy*, August 31. Accessed September 19, 2022. https://foreignpolicy.com/2020/08/31/tibet-china-repression-xinjiang-sinicization/.

Fahrion, Georg, Christoph Giesen, and Laura Höflinger. 2022. Road to Nowhere Debts Mount with China's Prestigious Silk Road Project. *Spiegel Online*, August, 24. Accessed September 20, 2022. https://www.spiegel.de/international/world/road-to-nowhere-debts-mount-with-china-s-prestigious-silk-road-project-a-74d6c558-34b2-4bd7-baa8-da8577d75feb

Feigenbaum, Evan A. 2017. China and the World: Dealing with a Reluctant Power. *Foreign Affairs* 96. 33–40.

Gabuev, Alexander. 2022. China's New Vassal. How the War in Ukraine Turned Moscow Into Beijing's Junior Partner. *Foreign Affairs*, August 9. Accessed September 20, 2022. https://www.foreignaffairs.com/china/chinas-new-vassal.

Gabusi, Giuseppe. 2017. "Crossing the River by Feeling the Gold": The Asian Infrastructure Investment Bank and the Financial Support to the Belt and Road Initiative. *China & World Economy* 25(5). 23–45.

Gao, Bai. 2019. China's Belt & Road Initiative: a counterforce to globalization reversal. In Huiyao Wang and Lu Miao (eds.), *Handbook on China and Globalization*, 156–176. Cheltenham: Edward Elgar.

Green Finance & Development Center. 2022. *The Green Finance & Development Center (GFDC)*. Accessed September 19, 2022. https://greenfdc.org/.

Gruffydd Jones, Branwen. 2006. *Decolonizing international relations*. Lanham: Rowman and Littlefield.

Gunitsky, Seva. 2013. Complexity and theories of change in international politics. *International Theory* 5(1). 35–63.

Guzzini, Stefano. 1993. Structural power: the limits of neorealist analysis. *International Organization* 47(3). 443–478.

Hameiri, Shahar, and Lee Jones. 2018. China challenges global governance? Chinese international development finance and the AIIB. *International Affairs* 94(3). 573–593.

Henderson, Jeffrey, Magnus Feldmann, and Nana de Graaff. 2021. The Wind from the East: China and European Economic. *Development and Change* 52(5). 1047–1065.

Holsti, K. J. 1998. *The Problem of Change in International Relations Theory*. Vancouver: University of British Columbia.

Hung, Ho-fung. 2021. Recent Trends in Global Economic Inequality. *Annual Review of Sociology* 47. 349–367.

Jones, Lee. 2019. Theorizing Foreign and Security Policy in an Era of State Transformation: A New Framework and Case Study of China. *Journal of Global Security Studies* 4(4). 579–597.

Katzenstein, Peter Joachim. 1990. *Analyzing change in international politics: The new institutionalism and the interpretative approach*. Köln: Max-Planck-Institut für Gesellschaftsforschung.

Kijewski, Leonie. 2022. Germany reaches compromise on China's Hamburg port investment, reports say. *Politico*, October 25. Accessed December 8, 2022. https://www.politico.eu/article/report-germany-deal-china-hamburg-port-investment-cosco/.

Kim, Young-Chan. 2022. From 'International Relations' to 'Global Foreign Policy' – Examining the New Framework of Chinese Strategic Relations Through the BRI. In Young-Chan Kim, *China and the Belt and Road Initiative Trade Relationships, Business Opportunities and Political Impacts*, 55–75. Basel: Springer Cham.

Kliem, Frederick. 2020. Why Quasi-Alliances Will Persist in the Indo-Pacific? The Fall and Rise of the Quad. *Journal of Asian Security and International Affairs* 7(3). 271–304.

Kolmaš, Michal, and Šárka Kolmašová. 2019. A 'pivot' that never existed: America's Asian strategy under Obama and Trump. *Cambridge Review of International Affairs* 32(1). 61–79.

Krause, Joachim. 2017. 'The Times They are a Changin' – Fundamental Structural Change in International Relations as a Challenge for Germany and Europe. *SIRIUS – Zeitschrift für Strategische Analysen* 1(1). 3–23.

Lairson, Thomas D. 2018. The Global Strategic Environment of the BRI: Deep Interdependence and Structural Power. In Wenxian Zhang, Ilan Alon, and Christoph Lattemann (eds.), *China's Belt and Road Initiative: Changing the Rules of Globalization*, 35–53. Basingstoke: Palgrave Macmillan.

Lawrence, Susan, Thomas Lum, Caitlin Campbell, Michael Martin, Rachel Fefer. 2021. U.S.-China Relations. *Current Politics and Economics of Northern and Western Asia* 30(1). 1–86.

Layne, Christopher. 2018. The US-Chinese power shift and the end of the Pax Americana. *International Affairs* 94(1). 89–111.

León-Manríquez, José Luis. 2015. The Global Financial and Economic Crisis: Origins, Effects and Responses in the Global South. An Overview. In José Luis León-Manríquez and Theresa Moyo, *The Global Financial and Economic Crisis in the South. Impact and Responses*, 3–20. Oxford: African Books Collective.

Li, Jiatao, Gongming Qian, Kevin Zheng Zhou, Jane Lu, and Bin Liu. 2022. Belt and Road Initiative, globalization and institutional changes: implications for firms in Asia. *Asia Pacific Journal of Management* 39. 843–856.

Loke, Beverley. 2018. China's economic slowdown: implications for Beijing's institutional power and global governance role. *The Pacific Review* 31(5). 673–691.

Mahoney, James. 2000. Path Dependence in Historical Sociology. *Theory and Society* 29(4). 507–548.

Mahoney, James. 2002. *Legacies of Liberalism*. Baltimore, MD: Johns Hopkins University Press.

Menegazzi, Silvia. 2017. Global Economic Governance between China and the EU: the case of the Asian Infrastructure Investment Bank. *Asia Europe Journal* 15(2). 229–242.

Moeller, Joergen Oerstroem. 2019. Global governance: how Asia shapes the world. In Huiyao Wang and Lu Miao, *Handbook on China and Globalization*, 140–155. Cheltenham: Edward Elgar.

North, Douglass Cecil. 1981. *Structure and change in economic history*. New York: W.W. Norton.

Pacheco Pardo, Ramon. 2018. Europe's financial security and Chinese economic statecraft: the case of the Belt and Road Initiative. *Asia Europe Journal* 16(1). 237–250.

Pan, Chengxin, and Linus Hagström. 2021. Ontological (In)Security and Neoliberal Governmentality: Explaining Australia's China Emergency. *Australian Journal of Politics & History* 67(3–4). 454–473.

Pascha, Werner. 2020. *Belts, roads, and regions: The dynamics of Chinese and Japanese infrastructure connectivity initiatives and Europe's responses*. Tokyo: Asian Development Bank Institute.

Pierson, Paul. 2000. Increasing Returns, Path Dependence, and the Study of Politics. *The American Political Science Review* 94(2). 251–268.

Pierson, Paul 2004: Politics in Time: History, Institutions, and Social Analysis. Princeton, NJ: Princeton University Press.

Pu, Xiaoyu, and Chengli Wang. 2018. Rethinking China's rise: Chinese scholars debate strategic overstretch. *International Affairs* 94(5). 1019–1035.

Rotte, Ralph. 2017. Internationale Politische Ökonomie in den Internationalen Beziehungen. In Frank Sauer and Carlo Masala, *Handbuch Internationale Beziehungen*, 465–492. Wiesbaden: Springer VS.

Ruggie, John. 1993. Territoriality and Beyond: Problematizing Modernity in International Relations. *International Organization* 47(4). 140–174.

Sarsenbayev, Madi, and Nicolas Véron. 2020. European versus American Perspectives on the Belt and Road Initiative. *China & World Economy* 28(2). 84–112.

Scherrer, Christoph. 2022. Biden's Foreign Economic Policy: Crossbreed of Obama and Trump? *International Review of Public Policy* 4(1). 1–11.

Schortgen, Francis. 2018. China and the Twenty-First-Century Silk Roads: A New Era of Global Economic Leadership? In Wenxian Zhang, Ilan Alon, and Christoph Lattemann, *China's Belt and Road Initiative: Changing the Rules of Globalization*, 17–33. Basingstoke: Palgrave Macmillan.

Sindjoun, Luc. 2001. Transformation of International Relations – between Change and Continuity: Introduction. *International Political Science Review* 22(3). 219–228.

Sinha, Aseema. 2018. Building a Theory of Change in International Relations: Pathways of Disruptive and Incremental Change in World Politics. *International Studies Review* 20(2). 195–203.

Skala-Kuhmann, Astrid. 2019. European Responses to BRI. *Horizons* 14. 144–155.

Skålnes, Lars S. 2021. Layering and Displacement in Development Finance: The Asian Infrastructure Investment Bank and the Belt and Road Initiative. *The Chinese Journal of International Politics* 14(2). 257–288.

Strange, Susan. 1984. What about international relations? In: Paths to international political economy, ed. Susan Strange, 183–197. London: Routledge.

Strange, Susan. 1987. The persistent myth of lost hegemony. *International Organization* 41(4). 551–574.

Strange, Susan. 1988. States and markets: An introduction to international political economy. London: Pinter.

Strange, Susan. 1994. *States and Markets*. London/New York: Pinter.

Strange, Susan (1996). The Retreat of the State: The Diffusion of Power in the World Economy. Cambridge: Cambridge University Press.

Suehiro, Akira. 2017. China's offensive in Southeast Asia: regional architecture and the process of Sinicization. *Journal of Contemporary East Asia Studies* 6(2). 107–131.

Taube, Markus. 2020. The Global Economic Regime at a Critical Juncture – The "Belt & Road Initiative" as a Means to Leverage Chinese Interests across Modern East Asia. In Nele Noesselt, *China's New Silk Dreams*, 7–20. Zürich: LIT Verlag.

Vangeli, Anastas. 2018. Global China and Symbolic Power: The Case of 16 + 1 Cooperation. *Journal of Contemporary China* 27(113). 674–687.

Viola, Lora Anne. 2020. US Strategies of Institutional Adaptation in the Face of Hegemonic Decline. *Global Policy* 11(S3). 28–39.

Wan, Ming. 2016. *The Asian Infrastructure Investment Bank: The Construction of Power and the Struggle for the East Asian International Order*. New York: Palgrave Macmillan.

Wang, Hongying. 2019. The New Development Bank and the Asian Infrastructure Investment Bank: China's Ambiguous Approach to Global Financial Governance. *Development and Change* 50(1). 221–244.

Wang, Huiyao, and Lu Miao. 2019. *Handbook on China and Globalization*. Cheltenham: Edward Elgar.

Xi, Jinping. 2014. *Carry Forward the Five Principles of Peaceful Coexistence to Build a Better World Through Win-Win Cooperation*. Speech delivered at the Meeting Marking the 60th Anniversary of the Initiation of the Five Principles of Peaceful Coexistence, June 28. Accessed September 20, 2022. http://www.china.org.cn/world/2014-07/07/content_32876905.htm

Xiao, Ren. 2016. China as an institution-builder: the case of the AIIB. *The Pacific Review* 29(3). 435–442.

Xuetong, Yan. 2021. Becoming Strong. The New Chinese Foreign Policy. *Foreign Affairs* 100(4). 40–47.

Yu, Hong. 2017. Motivation behind China's 'One Belt, One Road' Initiatives and Establishment of the Asian Infrastructure Investment Bank. *Journal of Contemporary China* 26(105). 353–368.

Zanardi, Claude. 2021. Europe and the Belt & Road Initiative (BRI). Infrastructure and connectivity. In Sebastian Biba und Reinhard Wolf (eds.), *Europe in an Era of Growing Sino-American Competition*, 155–169. London/New York: Routledge.

Zangl, Bernhard, Frederick Heußner, Andreas Kruck, and Xenia Lanzendörfer. 2016. Imperfect adaptation: how the WTO and the IMF adjust to shifting power distributions among their members. *The Review of International Organizations* 11. 171–196.

Zhang, Feng. 2017. Chinese Thinking on the South China Sea and the Future of Regional Security. *Political Science Quarterly* 132(3). 435–466.

Zhang, Feng. 2020. China's long march at sea: explaining Beijing's South China Sea strategy, 2009–2016. *The Pacific Review* 33(5). 757–787.

Zhang, Wenxian, Ilan Alon, and Christoph Lattemann. 2018. *China's Belt and Road Initiative: Changing the Rules of Globalization*. Basingstoke: Palgrave Macmillan.

Zhou, Weifeng, and Mario Esteban. 2018. Beyond Balancing: China's approach towards the Belt and Road Initiative. *Journal of Contemporary China* 27(112). 487–501.

John M. Callahan
American renewal or decline? The Biden administration, Europe, and the invasion of Ukraine

Abstract: This chapter looks to the Russian invasion of Ukraine to pose questions on turning points for the United States. The narrative sets a definition, based primarily on political science approaches, that a turning point is a time at which the cost of national security actions changes far beyond what it was before. It will then commence with discussion the state of play of the U.S. in 2021, particularly the series of seeming missteps by the Biden administration that may have constituted turning points of their own even if the war had not happened, especially the administration's media engagement strategy and its withdrawal from Afghanistan in 2021. It will then move on to the events which immediately preceded the Russian invasion, and those which came immediately after and are still ongoing. Given that many of the events discussed are ongoing, empirical evidence will primarily rely on media reporting, leaders' statements, and such scholarly articles as have been produced in recent months.

Keywords: Biden, Ukraine, Russia, Invasion, Media, Afghanistan, Communication, NATO

1 Introduction

A look at the content of the acclaimed journal Foreign Affairs from two points in time shows something startling. The two points in time in question are July/August 2019 and May/June 2022. The early edition was shockingly, but, at the time, appropriately titled "What Happened to the American Century?" while the second was titled "The World after the War." The 2019 edition featured titles such as "The Self-Destruction of American Power – How Washington Squandered the Unipolar Moment (Zakharia 2019), and "Globalization's" wrong turn – and How it Hurt America (Rodrik 2019)". The more recent edition led off with "The Price of Hegemony – Can America Learn to Use Its Power (Kagan 2022)?" and "The Outsiders – How the International System Can Still Check China (Goddard 2022)." While these are the author's

John M. Callahan, New England College

https://doi.org/10.1515/9783111272900-008

choices in terms of dates and topics, the mood change and the implied expectations for American and Western power between the two editions is palpable. The cause for the change is, simply, the Russian invasion of Ukraine in February 2022.

This chapter will examine a series of cases preceding and following Russia's invasion, with the objective of demonstrating that the supporting series of smaller turning points comprise a major turning point for the world in general and the U.S. in particular. The narrative will begin by setting a definition, based primarily on political science approaches, of what a turning point is. It will then commence with discussion the state of play of the U.S. in 2021, particularly the series of seeming missteps by the Biden administration that may have constituted turning points of their own if the war had not happened. It will then move on to the events which immediately preceded the Russian invasion, and those which came immediately after and are still ongoing. Given that many of the events discussed are ongoing, empirical evidence will primarily rely on media reporting, leaders' statements, and such scholarly articles as have been produced in recent months.

This section will focus on several events which are also easily definable as turning points. These include: The failure of the Russian invasion to achieve its stated and perceived objectives; the reinvigoration of the Atlantic Alliance and U.S. leadership, and the imposition of crippling sanctions by the west. Underlying this is the failure of institutions such as the United Nations Security Council (UNSC) to restrain Russia from aggressive action. A big question of this section will be an assessment of the role of the United States. The author asserts that the return, almost instantly, of the U.S. to the forefront of the anti-Russia coalition is a major turning point, not only for the U.S. but for those members of the Atlantic Alliance. This is especially important for Germany, which, though it has seen some turning points of its own in terms of its defense spending, military support for Ukraine, and acts against Russia, seems to openly refuse to take on the mantle of leadership for Europe. The third section of the chapter, and, by necessity, the most speculative, will focus on the bigger question of what the long-term impacts of the war will be on the global balance of power. It is impossible to know the future, but Russia's role as a great or even middle power is already changing as a result of its failures to date. This section will take as its core premise that Ukraine will either win the war outright or survive it in such a way that Russia will gain no benefit from the "victory". Sanctions, for example, will remain, as will Russia's increasing estrangement from the west. From this supposition, an argument will be made that the U.S. has the opportunity, should it wish to seize it, to arrest what many have identified as its decline, especially since 2001, as the hegemonic power. Such a return to the forefront of American power must come at the cost of the territorial ambitions, not only of Russia, but of other revanchist states, most notably the People's Republic of China.

2 Defining a turning point: Turns up or down the great power ladder

Before trying to identify events that may or may not be turning points, it is first necessary to come to an agreement on what constitutes a turning point where it might differ from the definitions designated in the introductory chapter of this work. Since the cases to be examined are political and historical in nature, it makes sense to look at political theories. Given the importance of perception and media in the perception of some of the cases, a literary or media-based definition of a turning point is also needed.

Two key discussions of turning points are offered by Paul Kennedy in *Rise and Fall of the Great Powers* and Jared Diamond. Diamond discusses turning points in many of his works, but the focus here is on *Upheaval: Turning Points for Nations in Crisis,* which specifically deals with the issue. Kennedy identifies a turning point in the history of a great power as "The point at which the cost of security becomes more than the great power can pay, given that other factors remain constant." (Kennedy 1987, XVI). This of course implies existential crises, at least viewed in retrospect. Diamond (2019) defines a turning point as a point in time after which the conditions in the test subject (in this case a country) are fundamentally different afterwards than they were before. They can mark a time when a response that worked to solve a crisis in the past no longer works to solve the same problem later on (Diamond 2019: 15). This implies some similarity to Kennedy's definition, although it does it in a more generalized way that is not implicitly linked with state power, or with great powers per se. For Nunning, who looked at how turning points are perceived in media and narrative, turning points are events that are constructed after the fact observers who use metaphors with which they are familiar to understand and explain them (Nunning 2012: 13). He adds that in the field of writing, turning points are used in order to help the reader better understand how events in the story unfold as they head toward the literary conclusion (Nunning 2012: 14), but he agrees with Diamond (2019) in that a turning point is a key "change of direction" for the story.

For Randall Collins (2007) there are a small number of types of turning points, all of which are approached after the fact in counterfactual fashion. These include military and political turning points, turning points of individual leadership, religious, and technological turning points as well as those based on human migration (Collins 2007: 248–249). In the cases to be presented, all fall within the first three turning point types, since none of them are of a religious or technological nature, or were caused by migrations. Writing after the Russian invasion, and drawing some lessons from it, Michael Mazarr focuses not on the individual actions of state actors, but rather on the resiliency of their societies (Mazarr 2022: 52). He posits that a "strong national ambition, a culture of learning and adaptation, and significant diversity and pluralism" are the ingredients of resiliency (Mazarr 2022: 52). Size also matters, so that the Netherlands or Singapore, for example, may rate highly in all of the relevant factors, but simply be too small for it to matter. Similarly, larger countries, like Sweden, do not seek global leadership (Mazarr 2022: 54). History and geography matter too, with the UK as an example, based on its long head start as a nation and its favorable geography (Mazarr 2022: 60).

A final insight is provided by Roger Launius, who wrote about the history of the U.S. space program, noting that "To a very real extent, turning points reflect the sea change that follows an event rather than the event itself (Launius 2015: 19)." He also noted that turning points do not have to be marked by a dramatic event, but can be a time period in which some attitude, thought process, or pattern can be agreed upon to have changed (Launius 2015: 19).

What, then, of a definition? For purposes of this study, a turning point will be described as a moment or brief period of time after which events take a course which is fundamentally different than things were before the triggering event or moment took place. This definition will be applied to national security and regime level events. The level of analysis for the cases presented triggers the Kennedy criteria of state security, but in almost all cases (The exception being that of Russia, which is clearly being degraded by its actions), it is too soon to assess the security impact of the decisions examined. That said, section three will attempt to use the cases to make some predictions about future actions, of course acknowledging the risk inherent in all predictions.

3 Setting the stage: The Biden administration's first year

Elections bring change in the foreign policy of any democracy, and the United States is no exception. New administrations make new promises and attempt to adhere to their own ideological views of the world in an attempt to address uncertainty. But, in many cases, the past maintains a grip on the future, and the dichotomy between the enacted worldview of the previous and current administrations can sometimes be difficult to reconcile with the political rhetoric of campaigns. Noteworthy examples of this are the transitions from the Eisenhower to Kennedy and Bush to Clinton administrations. Both cases saw departing presidents attempt, with some success, to bind their followers to their own policies. Bush, for example, bound Clinton to follow his lead by the intervention in Somalia. The Biden administration as it attempted to mark a foreign policy path that was ideologically unique from that of the preceding Trump administration, but did not lose ground unnecessarily. While the new administration did attempt to distance itself from the unilateral approaches favored by the Trump administration in favor of a return to multilateralism, it failed to articulate a vibrant, current doctrine that was also a demonstrable improvement over that of its predecessor. This resulted in a series of public relations disasters such as the badly mismanaged withdrawal from Afghanistan and the mishandling of the Russian threat through the fall and winter of 2021–2022. This chapter intends to analyze two political actions of the first year of the Biden administration. One, the administration's media relations, can now be seen as an ongoing inflection point rather than a turning point. The other, the Afghanistan withdrawal, would certainly have been seen as a major turning point in international relations and in the trajectory of the United States as a great power. In fact, if Russia manages to somehow succeed in Ukraine, historians will likely point to Afghanistan as the point after which America's decline was unstoppable.

4 Biden and the media

"... However, one year into the Biden administration, press freedom advocates remain concerned about issues like the president's limited availability to journalists, the administration's slow responses to requests for information, its planned extradition of Julian Assange, restrictions on media access at the U.S. southern border, and its limited assistance to Afghan journalists (Downie 2022)".

The media's relationship, and access to, the apparatus of American policy making has been waning for decades. That said, there is no question that the Trump administration significantly lowered the bar on media relations, going almost constantly on the attack, indiscriminately using terms like "Alternative facts" and "Fake News" to discredit all media that did not report favorably on its actions (Cilizza 2021). No outlet was safe, including Fox News. It may seem obvious that the Trump administration's actions should be considered as a turning point, however, there is significant evidence that key trends established by Trump, and even his predecessors, are being continued by the Biden administration, or made worse. The list of activities below constitutes a turning point in government-media relations which ultimately negatively impacts the ability of voters to get the information they need to hold the government accountable for its actions. This ultimately creates a turning point in the functioning of American democracy which in turn changes the diplomatic and security situations and send them on a new trajectory.

Reviewing the first year of the Biden Presidency in January 2022, the Center for the Protection of Journalism noted four concerning themes to date in the administration's Media relations:

- Freedom of Information Act [FOIA] experts have seen little improvement in the response of government agencies to journalists' FOIA requests for information, and the administration has not announced any FOIA response directives.
- Press freedom advocates are disappointed by the administration's reaction to requests to help Afghan journalists whose lives and work have been endangered by the Taliban's takeover of the country in mid-August.
- The Biden administration's efforts to extradite WikiLeaks founder Julian Assange from the U.K. have raised fears that the language of the espionage indictment against him could set a dangerous precedent for use against journalists trying to do their jobs.
- While political correspondents welcome the administration's return to daily press briefings, many are concerned about control by the White House and cabinet department press offices over access to administration officials – and restrictions on naming and quoting them in stories (Downie 2022: 4).

In short, the problem with the Biden administration's media relations is that the whole focus of them seems to be to keep the media away from Biden himself (Downie 2022: 5). Under the public facing leadership of Jen Psaki, the former White House Spokesperson, a commitment to a near daily press briefing, lacking under Trump, returned, and has continued under her successor, Karine Jean-Pierre. But the President himself is far less available to media than his predecessor, having done, in his first year, 22 press events, contrasting sharply with his predecessors Trump (92) and Obama (150) (Downie 2022: 6). Indeed, it appears as if there is a concerted effort to keep the media away from the President (Karem 2021). This has not changed significantly since the Russian invasion, and between January and May 2022, the President had only participated in a single media event (Karem 2021).

Of further concern is that that there is little back in forth in any press interaction with the President, and so no way to ascertain what he is really thinking on given issues. Although Biden does not vilify the media as a whole, in the manner of his predecessor, his limited interactions with them have frequently been abrasive and dismissive. This is combined with a reluctance for the administration to put its experts in front of the media for public comment. Instead of this, background interviews are offered. These are informative for journalists, but, since they cannot be directly attributed, are of limited value in their reporting. This all points to a general continuation of the policies of the Obama administration, and the objective is the same, an attempt to shape the media message (Downie: 13).

Of course, the big question is, does the Biden administration's stance toward the media mark a turning point, and, if so, why. The answer is, yes, it is a turning point because Biden had an opportunity to undo Trump's acrimonious relationship with the media and chose not to do so. This is because of where it puts the media. Under the Trump administration, the President chose to fight the media so bitterly at the beginning of their relationship that the relationship was irrevocably poisoned. For Biden, it cannot be said that any members of the media have much access. This is a turning point because the media should help to pierce the echo chamber that can form around a President. When the President is never pressured by the media, a critical forcing factor in his or her decision making is lost. If the overall history of the growth of presidential power is any precursor, there is no reason to expect that the media's access to, and ability to shape the thinking of decision makers will return.

5 Afghanistan withdrawal

The Afghanistan withdrawal was long looked for by American policy analysts. A long debate has raged for over a decade about when the U.S. should have gotten out, and it seems that everyone except for the generals whose careers rested on adequate service there and the constellation of contractors and other elements of the massive war support industry agree that the time of withdrawal should have been at least a decade ago, certainly after the killing of 9/11 mastermind Osama bin Laden in 2011 (Cronk 2021).

Ending the war in Afghanistan, America's longest, was a core pledge of the Biden administration, paired with Re-Engaging the Global Community (Hong Kong Post, January 2022). Then President Trump announced the eventual withdrawal of U.S. forces from Afghanistan in February 2020, in meetings with the Taliban at which representatives of the Kabul government were not present. This was followed by the announcement by the incoming Biden administration that the final withdrawal of the remaining 2,000 or so U.S. troops would begin in May and be completed by September 2021 (Cronk 2021). His announcement emphasized that the withdrawal would take place in full consultation of allies and the existing government of Afghanistan.

Unfortunately, in response to a summer offensive by the Taliban, and to criticism that the date for the final withdrawal would be on the highly symbolic date of September 11, the evacuation date was moved to the left, to August 31. But it was in the month of August that things completely fell apart. At the beginning of that month, only 650 troops remained in the country, protecting the main airport and the Embassy, but by the end of the month over 5,000 additional troops had been deployed in order to try to salvage some order from the chaos caused by embarking on renewed deployments without adequate time to plan or set mission objectives. This led to exactly what the Biden administration wanted to avoid, a repeat of the Saigon 1975 spectacle of desperate civilians hanging from helicopters and aircraft landing gear as they tried to escape the wreckage of the collapsing South Vietnamese capital and regime. So America was left with a second Vietnam disaster, along with enduring questions about the willingness of the country to engage in further wars, particularly those of long duration (Cohen 2021).

Amidst the firestorm of criticism levied on the administration over both the form and the function of the withdrawal, domestic concerns tended to fracture along predictable partisan lines. Liberal voices such as historian Clay Jenkinson adjusted a line from Macbeth when he said that "but for the United States of America, nothing reveals our national weakness like the way we leave our recent wars," noting that "it was not clear that we should leave Afghanistan just now (Governing.com 2021). He did add that "we have been diminished in the world arena," (Governing.com 2021) a prophecy that appears to have come true mere months later in the Ukraine crisis. In a similar vein, the Council on Foreign Relations's Richard Haass called the withdrawal an unnecessary "Withdrawal of Choice," and agreed that the results would raise questions about America's reliability both with allies and with enemies (Haass 2021).

In a rare move, U.S. military leaders did not withhold their feelings about the operation. The Pentagon had been against withdrawal in the first place, and Joint Chief's Chairman Gen. Mark Milley reminded Senators of that fact in testimony at the send of September 2021 (AP, Chairman Testifies 2021). International condemnation was also varied. One example of that condemnation came from Czech President Miloš Zeman, who called the withdrawal a "Manifestation of Cowardice," openly proclaiming that the U.S. had lost the "prestige of a global leader" for its botched efforts (TASS, August 17 2021).

Was the Afghanistan withdrawal a turning point? Presuming that Putin's Ukraine invasion plans (admittedly we cannot know this until after the war is over and the relevant actors speak about it) was given the go ahead after the Afghanistan failure, then the answer is yes. Ironically, the Russian invasion of Ukraine has allowed the Biden administration a second chance to address its role as alliance leader, as will be discussed below. Given the nature of turning points as "hindsight" affairs, the U.S. moral authority was significantly weakened by the withdrawal. It was noted as an indictment against U.S. global leadership by a cast of characters ranging from Vladimr Putin to the Chairman of the Joint Chiefs and prominent members of the foreign policy establishment. The most current, and attention grabbing, evidence of this is the Russian invasion of Ukraine, however, like the U.S. withdrawal from Vietnam a half a century earlier, this act will certainly be seen as a historical turning point.

6 Turning point – Biden statements on the opening of the Ukraine crisis

Although Russian military forces had been building up along the border with Ukraine since a military exercise in Spring 2021, the crisis which led up to the Russian invasion of Ukraine began in early December 2021, with a massive increase in the number and readiness of both those forces and in militant rhetoric from Moscow. By Christmas, nearly 100,000 troops had been assembled along Ukraine's borders with Belarus, Russia, and Transnistria, a number which nearly doubled by late February, when Russia renewed the invasion which it had begun with its 2014 occupation of Crimea and part of the Donbas. By mid-January, the U.S. adopted a strategy based on open sharing of intelligence data on the Russian buildup and Russian intentions, with the goal of deterring Russia from action (Barnes 2022).

The problem with this strategy is that the U.S. already had a trust deficit, particularly regarding intelligence releases, which traced its roots to the 2002–2003 claims, later proven to be inaccurate, that Iraq was much further along in its quest for nuclear weapons than was actually the case (van der Heide 2013: 288–289). U.S. credibility was also at a nadir following the withdrawal from Afghanistan. It was at this time that President Biden decided to give one of his rare press conferences, and the words that he said then form the root of this historical turning point. It was no problem, and, in hindsight, it was accurate for the President to predict that Russian forces would enter Ukraine (Liptak 2022). The problem came when he offered a characterization both of the form the invasion could take the potential U.S. response. Acknowledging the disunity existing in NATO and the European Union, Biden said "It's one thing if it's a minor incursion and we end up having to fight about what to do and what not to do".

Viewed from a perspective of twelve months into the Russian invasion it seems unlikely that Biden's statement contributed in any way to Russian planning, which appears to have been underway for months, if not years. What makes the Biden statement a turning point is how it fits into the problems noted in the discussion on Biden and the administrations interactions with the media. More Presidential exposure to the media would, in principle, lessen the chances of open mistakes such as this one, and to greater transparency of decision making, assuming of course that Biden was not attempting to offer the Russians terms by which he would react less severely to their actions. There was another possibility, that military and economic responses would have been prepared and publicized before the invasion. We know with certainty that the approaches used did not work.

7 The Russian invasion and its aftermath

"At the same time, there is considerable evidence that Putin's attack on international norms could ultimately strengthen the liberal world order. It has so far generated a unified and vigorous response from Western democracies, many of which have been suffering significant dysfunction and persistent authoritarian threats for more than a decade. (Way 2022: 5)".

Following a buildup of tensions through the winter, Russia attacked Ukraine on February 24, 2022. It was to be an attack on all fronts, utilizing the territory of Belarus and Transnistria to truly surround Ukraine. Although the latter front did not materialize, attacks did take place in a ring from the area north of Kyiv, around the entire eastern border, and from the south. Russia planned for the fall of Kyiv and the surrender of the Ukrainian government by day three of the invasion (Beauchamp 2022). At the time of writing, that has not occurred, and yet the war goes on, but, as noted by Way above, it is developing contrary to Russia's assumed desires in terms of the western response.

The invasion of Ukraine itself was the culmination of over a decade of Russian revanchism that had already victimized Georgia in 2008, and Ukraine, which had already been invaded in 2014, with Crimea and part of the Donbas illegally occupied. It is a watershed event, however, and a turning point in that major power conflict had returned to Europe for the first time since 1945. How pivotal a turning point it will be remains to be seen, and largely depends on how the war ends.

Russia's invasion of Ukraine was supposed to be over in 72 hours. An air assault on Kyiv, backed up by an armored thrust from the Chernobyl exclusion zone was to have eliminated the government, while other rapidly moving forces seized the major cities of Chernihiv, Sumy, Kharkiv, Kherson, and Odesa. Before there could be any international outrage, or response, it was all to be over. Beyond all expectations, the Ukrainian armed forces completely disrupted Russian timetables and repulsed most of the major Russian thrusts. This was exacerbated by unexpected (not only by the west, but also, seemingly, by the Russians themselves) near complete inability of the Russian armed forces to conduct combined arms mobile operations (Freedman 2022: 10). In late March 2022 Russia aban-

doned its early objectives in northern Ukraine (Freedman 2022: 20) and announced a new focus on the Donbas. By the end of April, Russia had abandoned
all of the territory that it had gained in the north and north-east of Ukraine (Ferris 2022), and by August was being pushed back from its most advanced lodg-
ments in the south, notwithstanding some gains in the Donbas. Daily videos,
managed by the Ukrainian armed forces and the Office of President Zelensky, emphasized two points: the first was that the Russian ground, air, and naval forces
were largely incompetent and incapable of mass maneuver warfare (Butler,
May 20, 2022). The second was that, when maneuver failed, Russia was more than
willing to engage in a campaign of indiscriminate attacks on civilian targets.
Putin has also threatened to use nuclear weapons in the conflict on numerous
occasions, attempting to simultaneously cow Ukraine, intimidate NATO out of a
supporting role for Ukraine, and to attempt to create an impression of parity with
the United States (Blank 2022: 4–5).

The early Ukrainian repulse, particularly of the thrust on Kyiv, bought time
for the west to formulate its responses to Russian aggression. In spite of Moscow's efforts to insulate itself from the effects of sanctions after those which
were imposed upon it after the invasion of Crimea and its tampering in the 2016
U.S. elections, the package of economic actions which was initially delivered,
and which has evolved in the months since February, is stunning in its breadth
and impact (Davidson 2022). Moscow clearly believed that its massive penetra-
tion of European markets, through petroleum exports, and of European society,
through investments and through the simple act of Russian travel to Europe
(Way 2022: 7) would impact European attitudes. Outside of Eastern Europe, the
most shocking turnaround has probably taken place in the UK. Britain had a
long way to go, given the purchase by Russians of over 2 billion USD in property
there between 2016 and 2022 (Austin 2022). Academic institutions across the
west have closed their doors to sanctioned individuals and their families, and
also reduced their involvement in research projects with Russian scholars and
institutions (Zubok 2022: 91). At the time of writing, a ban on non-humanitarian
visas from Russians wishing to visit Europe is under discussion. Essentially, it
would be a "Turn Back" to a Cold War level of minimal public relationships
with Russia if the visa decision is approved. Efforts by the Russian wealthy and
their oligarchs to hide their assets outside of the country have also proven to be
misguided. Italy, for example which relies on fuel from Russia, nevertheless has
joined the sanctions bandwagon, and directly seized Russian assets, mainly in
the forms of villas and yachts totaling over 143 million Euros (Way 2022: 11).

The sanction regime also exposes negative issues for the West. Westerners
(including Americans) have been operating for over two decades on the premise,
that the intertwinement of Russia (and the People's Republic of China (PRC), for

that matter) into the western and global economic systems would serve to moderate their behavior and slowly turn them, for lack of a better term, into us. Liberal Institutional theories of international relations, promulgated primarily by Robert Keohane, Joseph Grieco, and others, posit that "domestic and international institutions facilitate cooperation and peace among countries" (Johnson 2018). That has proven to be nearly the opposite of a reality in which Russia (and the PRC) have used access to the system repeatedly both to erode it and to generate support for their own actions (Way 2022: 8). In short, instead of them becoming more like us, the collective we (as this includes every country with a right-wing populist government elected in the last decades, or parties grown) have become more like them.

The implantation and evolution of the sanctions regime is a large enough issue to warrant a full, separate study. Some firms left Russia of their own accord, such as McDonald's. But, decoupling Russia from the financial grid, with actions such as the suspension of SWIFT access to Russians, quickly made forced decoupling Russian's western credit cards were no longer valid, and when western banks ceased to deal with the Russia Central Bank (Way 2022: 10). At the time of writing, Western mainstays such as BP, Disney, Goldman Sachs, Deutsche Bank, Western Union, UPS, and others (Chachko 2022: 20), have left or were forced out of Russia.

Western aid to Ukraine in response to the Russian invasion has lacked a unified drive, but it has been swift, and in rapidly increasing intensity, including humanitarian, financial, and military support. What began as an effort by those supporting countries which possessed them to offload old soviet equipment has turned into the free provision of an increasingly wide variety of top of the line weapons from around Europe. As of August 2022, the breakdown of support in terms of military aid, money, and humanitarian aid was as follows: 14.08 billion Euros in Military Aid; 12.44 billion in Humanitarian Aid, and 31.70 billion in Financial Support (Statista.com 2022). The U.S. has been the largest donor, with 2.5 billion, 9.21 billion, and 10.32 billion, not including the most recent aid package, approved on August 24, for 3 million more (Mongilio 2022).

8 Political impacts

"In contrast to the Russian Actions of 2008 and 2014, there has been nothing ambiguous or particularly "Hybrid" in about today's massive conventional assault on one of the largest countries in Europe (Way 2022: 10)."

In spite of the remarkable responses to the invasion, divisions have been highlighted in the western world. Unsurprisingly, the Baltic states and much of the Eastern tier of Central Europe have been outspokenly against the invasion from the moment it started. Prague and Warsaw have been at the forefront of the European response to the invasion in both political and military terms. Budapest, on the other hand, has, increasingly, although not completely, sided with Russia and against NATO, the EU, and Ukraine. Hungary's leader, Viktor Orban, leads one of the last populist governments in Europe, and is strongly politically aligned with Russia. A key issue for Hungary is the status of the Hungarian minority in far western Ukraine. Friction with Kyiv over the status of that minority is a factor in Hungary's support for Moscow. Strong dependence on Russian fuel supplies is another factor (Verseck 2022).

Unlike the case in Budapest, the war and responses to it have become the number one political issue in Poland. This is unsurprising given that Poland has hosted the highest number of refugees and is a part, along with the Baltic States, of the exposed eastern flank of the European Union. It also has significant religious and cultural ties to Western Ukraine. Finally, in stark contrast to others in the region, especially Hungary, Poland has historical ties to the UK and the U.S. which go back for centuries and which make Warsaw a natural ally for leaders and strategists in Washington and London. It is unclear whether this affinity and Poland's front line leadership in the crisis response will check its political slide to the right, and for the moment the ruling Law and Justice Party has been strengthened by the popularity of its response (Szczerbiak 2022).

Even beyond the three countries already mentioned, the rest of Eastern Europe has achieved increased prominence as a result of the invasion, for a variety of reasons. One is that, as the border line with an aggressive Russia, the eastern tier countries serve both as the conduit for Ukrainian refugees on one hand, and on the other, the path through which western assistance reaches Ukraine. The second aspect is that the main focus of the massive NATO deployment has been to the Baltic States and Poland. Third, and perhaps most identifiable as a turning point, is the new political importance of the eastern tier. As the most recent victims of Russian efforts to destabilize them, the eastern group have been outspokenly vocal both in their support for Ukraine and their increasing rhetorical attacks on the Putin regime. This is in strong contrast to the efforts of the big three EU members, France, Germany, and Italy, which have vacillated between showing their outrage and securing the benefits of their economic ties with Moscow. It remains to be seen whether and if the Eastern tier of the EU and NATO will gain increased political muscle from being proven right about Russia and for its strident response (Erlanger 2023).

For NATO, the Russian invasion has clearly been a major turning point in its fortunes. Between 2001 and 2017, the main NATO activities were in support of U.S. operations in Afghanistan. Its main member, the U.S. was increasingly questioning the utility of the alliance, especially and most notoriously during the Trump administration. Russia used NATO as a convenient excuse for its own aggression. As an aside, it is interesting that Putin specifically blamed NATO expansion, and the threat of its expansion to Ukraine, for his invasion. This in spite of the fact that member states are not supposed to have territorial conflicts underway, meaning that Russia's occupation of Crimea and the Donbas also meant that Ukraine could not join (Way 2022: 9). Vladislov Zubok went so far as to claim that "Russia's military setbacks have reinvigorated the Atlantic Alliance, and, for a moment, made Moscow look like a kleptocratic third rate power (Zubok, July/August 2022, 84)".

Almost overnight, the alliance was reinvigorated. The massive deployment of forces to the Baltic States, Poland, and Romania gave NATO the chance to show off its strength and demonstrate its resolve. Two countries, Sweden and Finland, were so shocked by the invasion, and by overt Russian posturing against them, that they have begun the process of joining the Alliance (NATO 2022). It is difficult to imagine more of a turnabout in fortune for an organization than what has been observed since February 2022. The ultimate test, managing a war with Russia, will hopefully not come about, but the alliance's reputation, especially in comparison with Russia's dismal performance in combat, is clearly being burnished every day that Ukrainian soldiers continue to hold off the Russians.

9 The case of Germany – Stumbling toward a "Zeitenwende?"

"In attacking Ukraine, Putin doesn't just want to eradicate a country from the world map, he is destroying the European security structure we have had in place since Helsinki. German Chancellor Olaf Scholz (DW.Com 2022)".

In a clear turning point in post-Cold War German foreign policy the Scholz administration announced on February 25, 2022, that Germany would increase its defense spending by 100 billion Euros (Kinkartz 2022). After decline to what can at best be called a hollow force since the end of the cold war, this announcement sent shockwaves around western defense departments. After the embarrassment of offering helmets to Ukraine shortly before the war began, the Bundeswehr has offered and delivered an increasing array of equipment, ranging from marginally useful legacy East German systems through increasingly modern mechanized artillery platforms (Bundeswehr 2023). By August 2022, Germany was one of the leading contributors to Ukrainian defense (Wild 2022). None of this has been without significant internal political debate within Germany, and almost every positive action takes place after a denial that it will do so. It cannot be overemphasized that these steps are a major turning point in German history, which has emphasized a pacifist approach to foreign policy since the end of the Second World War (Schläger 2022).

This is all the more surprising considering the close economic ties, particularly in the energy industry, that have formed between Berlin and Moscow in recent decades. Germany's economic choices, even those that were done begrudgingly, since February have also formed a turning point. In the weeks leading to, and immediately following the invasion, as the sanction regime was taking shape, spurred on by the UK and the Eastern tier countries of NATO and the EU, Germany made the momentous and potentially profoundly painful decision to cease certification of the nearly completed NORDSTREAM II Project, a series of pipelines that were designed to bypass Ukraine to get Russian petroleum products directly to Western Europe (Marsh, February 22, 2022).

Before its destruction in uncertain circumstances in September 2022, NORD-STREAM I, was impacted both by petroleum sanctions against Russia and by Russian tampering with the flow of gas in an effort to blackmail Europe into withdrawing its support for Ukraine. As early as March, Germany expanded coal extraction, and is considering ceasing the decommissioning of its three remaining active nuclear power stations (Pladson, December 29, 2022). This is a major turning point in the German economic and political realms, and the beginning of a signal that Berlin may truly decouple itself from Russian energy altogether.

10 The United States – No longer able to "Lead" from behind

"The West now faces a battle between democracy and autocracy, between liberty and repression, between a rules-based order and one governed by brute force (President Joe Biden, March 19, 2022)."

Departing from its role in the Afghanistan withdrawal, the U.S. took the leadership role in the Atlantic Alliance's responses to the Russian invasion, while also dealing with its other main threat, the People's Republic of China. In fact, Russia and the PRC are now the dominant issues in U.S. foreign policy and likely will be for the near future (Mazarr 2022: 52). Some experts predicted that Beijing would use the distraction of the invasion to press its claims against Taiwan (Way 2022: 5). A quick Russian victory may have even encouraged the PRC to act on its own, emboldened by Moscow's flaunting of international norms, just as Japan's aggression against Manchuria in the early 1930s emboldened the Fascist Italian and National Socialist German regimes to flaunt the authority of the League of Nations spurred the others on to ever bolder efforts.

Of course, that did not happen. But why did not it? A part of the answer is provided by Daalder and Lindsay (2022) who offer that one reason was the "speed, scale, and scope" of the U.S. response, which they claim surprised western leaders as much as they did Putin (and Xi). The U.S. role in supporting Ukraine has certainly evolved since December, essentially spurred on by Europe's inability to show political unity in responding to Russia. A significant event in the evolution of U.S. leadership came in March, when Poland offered to supply Ukraine with Soviet era MIG-29 fighters that would require no additional training for use by Ukrainian pilots. The issue was that there was significant fear that Moscow would see this as an escalation and act accordingly. With that in mind, Poland declined to directly deliver the aircraft to Ukraine, suggesting that they be sent to a U.S. Airforce base in Germany and flown from there back into Ukraine. Germany balked at this idea, and the U.S. did not press the matter. The point of the story, however, is that Poland was forcing the Biden administration not to "Lead from Behind," but to actually lead the alliance, to take the risks and to shield other alliance members (Stracqualursi 2022). From March onwards, Washington proved itself to be increasingly willing to do exactly that, through the provision of ever more advanced and lethal weapons systems, and through encouraging alliance partners to do the same.

President Biden's rhetoric has gone back and forth in its direction and vehemence. On the one hand, he has said repeatedly that Putin is a war criminal and should be removed from office. In a similar vein, the U.S. Secretary of State, Anthony Blinken, and the Secretary of Defense, Lloyd Austin have openly expressed that the U.S. wishes to see Russia weakened by the conflict (Phillips 2022). On the other hand, Biden consistently insists that the U.S. will not escalate the conflict (Nelson 2022). It is difficult to tell if these nearly contradictory statements, which are nevertheless backed by solid actions in terms of the provision of military support, indicate that the U.S. is seeking to restore its position of dominance and global leadership. An inference that at least part of the government apparatus may have this in mind can be found in the recent events on the other side of the world, in the Pacific region.

In a major turning point for that region, in August 2022 Speaker of the House Nancy Pelosi and a group of Democratic Congressional Leaders took the bold step of visiting Taiwan, a clear signal that the U.S. supports the Taipei government. Moving from implicit to explicit support of Taiwan in the event of PRC aggression is a tectonic event in international politics which may stand in importance with acts such as the recognition by the U.S. of Jerusalem as the capital of Israel in 2018. In spite of intense saber rattling by the People's Liberation Army (PLA) and its Navy (The PLAN), a second delegation visited Taipei two weeks later, openly pledging U.S. support. This is a change in U.S. policy, which heretofore focused on supporting Taiwan militarily without openly siding with it in against the PRC. It constitutes a definite turning point in U.S. Pacific and U.S. PRC relations, and, should Beijing back down, will have a ripple effect with other PRC-U.S. points of contention, such as the South China Sea and the issue of Chinese trade inequities and human rights abuses.

The administration's approach to the media, described earlier in this chapter, means that there is no way outside of partisan politics to press the administration to define its endgame with Russia. This is a pity, because the learning that could take place with such interactions may actually help the administration to find where it wants to be, and how to get there, through the simple expedient of having to share its thoughts with its people, and be forced to defend its decisions.

11 Conclusion: Are these turning points, and what next for the U.S.?

"The United States should wish to remain number one for as long as it proves feasible." (Gray 2004: 61).

This chapter aimed to settle on a set of definitions for turning points, and to then examine the U.S. withdrawal from Afghanistan and the Russian invasion of Ukraine to see which events could constitute turning points, either collectively or separately. Has the U.S. reached a turning point, and will it arrest its slow decline? The ingredients are there. Russia has certainly reached an inflection point beyond which there is no recovery without regime change. Europe's turning point revolves more around which part of Europe will take the lead and if Germany will firmly take the mantle of leadership as a complete (meaning military) power. Russia's ongoing failure certainly sets up the U.S. for a return to its dominant, hegemonic status. The question is more one of national will.

The issue of turning points was reviewed at levels ranging from the Great Power/Strategic level down to the role of individuals and single events. Bearing that review in mind, the definition used was that, in general, a turning point is a moment after which the perceived course of events pivots in an unexpected direction, and to which the responses which worked before the turning point no longer so. That pivot which follows can come with a security price, if old methods of problem solving are no longer effective or can no longer be afforded. A turning point is almost always something that is perceived in hindsight.

The new administration's actions, particularly with regard to the media, and to alliance relations, seem to be turning points. There is no question that they are the evolution of policies and actions of the previous administration. Many of the outcomes of the Trump administration, especially its vilification of the media and its "go it alone" attitude toward foreign affairs, were simultaneously strong adjustments in customary U.S. action and, it was thought at the time, aberrations. They only became turning points when they were continued, either in fact or in spirit, by the Biden administration. Clearly, there is something different about how the media is treated. It actually began in the Obama administration, but for sake of argument it can be said to be a Trump phenomenon, in that his administration went from controlling access to outright vilification. But under Biden we see the media's new diminished role enshrined.

The withdrawal from Afghanistan is, effectively, a re-run of the disastrous final evacuation from Saigon in 1975, and like its predecessor, will take some time to both assess and recover from. Coming as it did in the midst of a global pandemic and significant turmoil at home, it is inappropriate to assume that the negative impacts of the withdrawal will be as far reaching as the loss in Vietnam was, given the chance to recover given by the Russian invasion of Ukraine. One year out at the time of writing, the weight of the Afghanistan turning point is subsumed within the bigger question of the Russian invasion of Ukraine.

Time will tell, of course, but it looks as if the invasion is the greatest turning point in international relations since the September 11, 2001 attacks which sent America into a series of needless, strength dissipating wars. President Biden's misguided statement on what he was, in effect, willing to accept in terms of Russian aggression against Ukraine came shortly before the great turning point, when Russia tested Biden by launching a full invasion of Ukraine on February 24. So far, Europe, NATO and the U.S. are, to varying degrees, stepping up the plate in supporting Ukraine, with the U.S increasingly taking on the mantle of leadership.

Sometimes, we know a turning point when we see one, even as we live through the events and their consequences. The first year of the Biden administration, coming as it did thirty years after the end of the Cold War, and twenty after the last key turning point, occurred amidst a long and ongoing debate over the nature and endurance of American power. Whether the U.S. is rising, declining, or stagnating, the fact remains that knocking the U.S. out of a hegemonic role does not mean that a new hegemon rises, rather it means, not a multipolar world, but chaos (Gray 2004: 63). The Ukraine crisis is a turning point for Europe, for Asia, and for America's role in the world.

It is clear that two large powers, Russia and China, wish to disrupt or modify the norms-based world order that the West built through the 20th Century. Should the United States wish to undo almost two decades in which it squandered its power and place in the world, Ukrainian soldiers are giving it an opportunity to do so. Seldom has a great power been given such an opportunity to restore its fortunes, and it is to be hoped that, unlike in 1918, and 1991, the United States will not turn back from another opportunity to shape the future freedom of the world, and to stand as the guarantor of that freedom. To paraphrase Churchill, an American dominated world may be the worst thing ever except for all of the other possibilities. Of course, the U.S. has to want to do it, and also to clean up its own internal house, or, frankly, to earn it. Back in 2019, Fareed Zakharia was already positing that the U.S. had "lost interest" in leadership, and "lost faith" in itself, in spite of it being neither overextended nor bankrupt (Zakharia 2019). The biggest turning point of all will be the one in which a reinvigorated and confident United States reclaims its position as a "Shining City on a Hill" in a world that desperately needs it.

References

The Associated Press. 2021. Joint Chiefs chairman calls Afghan war a "Strategic Failure," In testimony to the Senate Armed Services Committee, Gen. Mark Milley offered a blunt assessment of the outcome to a war that cost 2,461 American lives. *The Associated Press*. September 28, 2021. https://apnews.com/article/joe-biden-bombings-kabul-taliban-terrorism-d1c939fc224a988dc6117ae4a70840e6. accessed on January 20, 2022.

Austin, Harry. 2022. U.K. crackdown on Russian oligarchs may spell the end for 'Londongrad'. *NBC News.com*, 5 March 2022. https://www.nbcnews.com/news/world/russia-ukraine-invasion-uk-london-londongrad-oligarchs-sanctions-rcna18762. Accessed on July 30, 2022.

Barnes, Julian. 2022. U.S. Battles Putin by Disclosing His Next Possible Moves. *The New York Times*, February 13, 2022. https://www.nytimes.com/2022/02/12/us/politics/russia-information-putin-biden.html. Accessed on February 20, 2023.

Beauchamp, Zack. 2022. Why the first few days of war in Ukraine went badly for Russia. Russia banked on Kyiv falling quickly. Here's why it hasn't. *VOX.com*, February 28, 2022. https://www.vox.com/22954833/russia-ukraine-invasion-strategy-putin-kyiv. Accessed on February 18, 2023.

Blank, Stephen. 2022. Nuclear Weapons in Russia's War Against Ukraine. *Naval War College Review*, Fall 2022. 61–83.

Bundeswehr. 2023. Military Support for Ukraine. www.bundeswehr.de, February 21, 2023. https://www.bundesregierung.de/breg-en/news/military-support-ukraine-205499. Accessed on February 21, 2023.

Butler, Michael. 2022. Ukraine's information war is winning hearts and minds in the West. *The Conversation*, May 12, 2022. https://theconversation.com/ukraines-information-war-is-winning-hearts-and-minds-in-the-west-181892. Accessed on August 24, 2022.

Chachko, E., & J. Heath. 2022. Watershed Moment for Sanctions? Russia, Ukraine, and the Economic Battlefield. *AJIL Unbound* 116. 135–139.

Cillizza, Chris. 2021. Here's Donald Trump's most lasting, damaging legacy. CNN.com, August 30, 2021. https://www.cnn.com/2021/08/30/politics/trump-legacy-fake-news/index.html. Accessed on 19 March 2023.

Cohen, Raphael S. 2021. The Big Unanswered Question of the Afghanistan War. Lawfare, October 23, 2021. https://www.lawfareblog.com/big-unanswered-question-afghanistan-war. accessed December 31, 2021.

Collins, Randall. 2007. Turning Points, Bottlenecks, and the Fallacies of Counterfactual History. *Sociological Forum* 22(3), September 2007. 247–269.

Coratella, Teresa. 2022. Italy's Challenging Divorce from Russia. European Council on Foreign Relations, 9 March 2022, https://ecfr.eu/article/italys-challenging-divorce-fromrussia. Accessed on July 20, 2022.

Cronk, Terri Moon. 2021. Biden Announces Full U.S. Troop Withdrawal from Afghanistan by Sept. 11. DOD News, April 14, 2021. https://www.defense.gov/News/News-Stories/Article/Article/2573268/biden-announces-full-us-troop-withdrawal-from-afghanistan-by-sept-11/. accessed on February 1, 2022.

Daalder, Ivo and James M. Linday. Last Best Hope: The West's Final Chance to Build a Better World Order. *Foreign Affairs* 101(4), July/August 2022. 120–130.

Davidson, Kate, and Aubrey Weaver. 2022. The West declares economic war on Russia. *Politico*, Washington DC, February 28, 2022.https://www.politico.com/newsletters/morning-money/2022/02/28/the-west-declares-economic-war-on-russia-00012208. Accessed on August 25, 2022.

Diamond, Jared. 2019. *Upheaval*. London: Allan Lane Publishing.

Downie, Leonard. 2022. Night and Day. Committee to Protect Journalists, January 13, 2022. https://cpj.org/reports/2022/01/night-and-day-the-biden-administration-and-the-press/. accessed on January 13, 2022.

Erlanger, Steven. 2023. Ukraine War Accelerates Shift of Power in Europe to the East. *The New York Times*, January 26, 2023. https://www.nytimes.com/2023/01/26/world/europe/eu-nato-power-ukraine-war.html. Accessed on February 20, 2023.

Ferris, Emily. 2022. Russia's Military Has a Railroad Problem. *Foreign Policy*, April 21, 2022. https://foreignpolicy.com/2022/04/21/russias-military-has-a-railroad-problem/ Accessed on August 19, 2022.

Freedman, Lawrence. 2022. Why War Fails: Russia's Invasion of Ukraine and the Limits of Military Power. *Foreign Affairs* 101(4), July/August 2022. 10–23.

Goddard, Stacie. 2022. The Outsiders: How the International System Can Still Check Russia and China. *Foreign Affairs* 101(3), May/June 2022. 28–39.

Gray, Colin S. 2004. *The Sheriff: America's Defense of the New World Order*. Lexington: The University Press of Kentucky.

Haass, Richard. 2021. America's Withdrawal of Choice. *Project Syndicate*, August 15, 2021. https://www.project-syndicate.org/commentary/americas-withdrawal-of-choice-by-richard-haass-2021-08. accessed on December 10, 2021.

Jenkinson, Clay S. 2021. Losing Faith: America's Standing in the World After 20 Years in Afghanistan. www.governing.com, August 29, 2021. https://www.governing.com/context/americas-standing-in-the-world-after-20-years-in-afghanistan. accessed on February 10, 2022.

Jessop, David. 2022. The invasion of Ukraine – a turning point in global history. *Stabroek News*, March 8, 2022. https://www.stabroeknews.com/2022/03/08/features/latin-view/the-invasion-of-ukraine-a-turning-point-in-global-history/. Accessed on August 1, 2022.

Johnson, Tana, and Andrew Heiss. 2018. Liberal Institutionalism – its threatened past, its threatened future. *The Brookings Institution*, Washington, D.C., July 18, 2018. https://www.brookings.edu/blog/future-development/2018/07/18/liberal-institutionalism-its-threatened-past-its-threatened-future/. Accessed on August 23, 2022.

Kagan, Robert. 2022. The Price of Hegemony: Can America Learn to Use Its Power. *Foreign Affairs* 101(3), May/June 2022. 10–19.

Kinkartz, Sabine. "German Chancellor Olaf Scholz announces paradigm change in response to Ukraine invasion." Deutsche Welle, Berlin, February 27, 2022. https://www.dw.com/en/german-chancellor-olaf-scholz-announces-paradigm-change-in-response-to-ukraine-invasion/a-60932652#:~:text=Boost%20in%20defense%20spending%20Scholz%20said%20the%20German,will%20be%20invested%20in%20our%20defense%2C%22%20Scholz%20said. Accessed on August 10, 2022.

Karem, Brian. 2021. Why is Biden failing? His tightly controlled relationship to the media might be worse than Trump's. Salon.com, October 14, 2021. https://www.salon.com/2021/10/14/why-is-biden-failing-his-tightly-controlled-relationship-to-the-media-might-be-worse-than/. accessed on March 1, 2022.

Kennedy, Paul. 1987. *The Rise and Fall of the Great Powers*. New York: First Vintage Books.

Kotkin, Stephen. 2022. The Cold War Never Ended: Ukraine, the China Challenge, and the Revival of the West. *Foreign Affairs* 101(3), May/June 2022. 64–78.

Launius, Roger D. 2015. What are the turning points in history, and what were they for the space age? from *The Societal Impact of Space Flight*. National Aeronautics and Space Administration, Washington DC, 2015.

Liptak, Kevin. 2022. Biden Predicts Russia 'will move in' to Ukraine, but says 'minor incursion' may prompt discussion over consequences. *CNN*, January 19, 2022. https://www.bing.com/search?q=Russia+%27will+move+in%27+to+Ukraine%2C+Biden+predicts%2C+but+%27minor+incursion%27+may+prompt+discussion+over+consequences+-+CNNPolitics.com&cvid=33b51532c2814da4a42116c6a7dc262c&aqs=edge..69i57j69i64.586j0j4&FORM=ANAB01&PC=DCTS. accessed on February 24, 2022.

Mazarr, Michael J. 2022. What Makes a Power Great? The Real Drivers of Rise and Fall. *Foreign Affairs* 101(4), July/August 2022. 52–63.

Marsh, Sarah. 2022. Germany freezes Nord Stream 2 gas project as Ukraine crisis deepens. *Reuters*, February 22, 2022. https://www.reuters.com/business/energy/germanys-scholz-halts-nord-stream-2-certification-2022-02-22/. Accessed on March 1, 2023.

McLaughlin, Daniel. 2022. Ukraine War is a turning point in history at which Moscow must be defeated – Zelensky. *The Irish Times*, March 24, 2022. https://www.irishtimes.com/news/world/europe/ukraine-war-a-turning-point-in-history-at-which-moscow-must-be-defeated-zelenskiy-1.4886378. Accessed on July 31, 2022.

Mongilio, Heather. 2022. U.S. announces nearly 3 Billion in aid for Ukraine. *U.S. Naval Institute Press*, Washington, August 25, 2022. https://news.usni.org/2022/08/24/u-s-announces-nearly-3-billion-in-aid-for-ukraine. Accessed on August 25, 2022.

Nelson, Steven. 2022. That's called World War III': Biden defends decision not to send jets to Ukraine. *The New York Post*, March 11, 2022. https://nypost.com/2022/03/11/thats-called-world-war-iii-biden-defends-decision-not-to-send-jets-to-ukraine/. Accessed on June 20, 2022.

North Atlantic Treaty Organization. 2022. Finland and Sweden submit applications to join NATO. *NATO.com*, May 18, 2022. https://www.nato.int/cps/en/natohq/news_195468.htm. Accessed on February 22, 2023.

Nunning, Ansgar, and Kai Marcel Sicks. 2012. *Turning Points: Concepts and Narratives of Change in Literature and Other Media*. Berlin: DeGruyter.

Phillips, Morgan.2022. "We want to see Russia weakened': Defense Secretary Lloyd Austin says he wants Putin's forces depleted so he cannot repeat what he has done in Ukraine during his Kyiv trip. *Mailonline*, April 25, 2022. https://www.dailymail.co.uk/news/article-10751233/We-want-Russia-weakened-Defense-Secretary-Lloyd-Austin-says.html. Accessed on June 20, 2022.

Pladson, Kristie. 2022. Lützerath: How Germany's energy crisis reignited coal. *Deutsche Welle*, December 29, 2022. https://www.dw.com/en/l%C3%BCtzerath-how-germanys-energy-crisis-reignited-coal/a-64203214. Accessed on January 10, 2023.

Rodrick, Dani. 2019. Globalization's Wrong Turn: And How It Hurt America. *Foreign Affairs* 98(4), July/August 2019. 26–33.

Schläger, Catrina. 2022. The Green transition – from pacifism to realpolitik. Foreign and Security Policy, *IPS Journal*, July 21, 2022. https://www.ips-journal.eu/topics/foreign-and-security-policy/the-green-transition-from-pacifism-to-realpolitik-6079/ Accessed on October 10, 2022.

Stracqualursi, Veronica. 2022. Why the US rejected Poland's plan to send fighter jets to Ukraine. *CNN*, March 9, 2022. https://www.cnn.com/2022/03/09/politics/ukraine-russia-poland-fighter-jets/index.html. Accessed on August 25, 2022.

Szczerbiak, Alex. 2022. Comment: How will the war in Ukraine affect Polish Politics? *BNE Intellinews*, March 3, 2022. https://bne.eu/comment-how-will-the-war-in-ukraine-affect-polish-politics-236845/?source=poland. Accessed on August 1, 2022.

Tharoor, Ishaan. 2022. The War in Ukraine and a 'Turning Point in History.'" *The Washington Post*, April 4, 2022. https://www.washingtonpost.com/world/2022/04/04/war-ukraine-turning-point-history/. Accessed on July 20, 2022.

van der Heide, Liesbeth. 2013. Cherry-Picked Intelligence. The Weapons of Mass Destruction Dispositive as a Legitimation for National Security in the Post 9/11 Age. *Historical Research* 38(1). 287–307.

Verseck, Keno. 2022. Hungary: What's Viktor Orban's problem with Ukraine? *DW.com*, December 22, 2022. https://www.dw.com/en/hungary-whats-viktor-orbans-problem-with-ukraine/a-64063750. Accessed on February 20, 2023.

Way, Lucan A. 2022. The Rebirth of the World Order? *Journal of Democracy* 33(2), April, 2022. 5–17.

Wild, Madeleine. 2022. Germany's Historic Defense Budget Growth Makes Them the Third Largest Global Military Spender with an Annual Budget of $83.5 Billion by 2024, Says GlobalData,. 28 February, www.globaldata.com/germanyshistoric-defense-budget-growth-makes-third-largest-global-military-spender-annualbudget-83-5-billion-2024-says-globaldata. Accessed on August 1, 2022.

Woods, Ngaire. 2022. What the Mighty Miss: The Blind Spots of Power. *Foreign Affairs* 101(4), July/August 2022. 24–33.

Ying, Zhu. 2022. Russia-Ukraine war: A turning point in Germany's Policy Towards China. *Think China*, May 31, 2022. https://www.thinkchina.sg/russia-ukraine-war-turning-point-germanys-policy-towards-china. Accessed on August 20, 2022.

Zakaria, Fareed. 2019. The Self Destruction of American Power: Washington Squandered the Unipolar Moment. *Foreign Affairs* 98(4), July/August 2019. 10–16.

Zubok, Vladislav. 2022. Can Putin Survive? The Lessons of the Soviet Collapse. *Foreign Affairs* 101(4), July/August 2022. 84–96.

Zubok, Vladislav. 2022. Foreign Aid to Ukraine from February through August 3, 2022. *Statista*, August 2022. https://www.statista.com/statistics/1303432/total-bilateral-aid-to-ukraine/ Accessed on August 10, 2022.

Zubok, Vladislav. 2022. US Foreign Policy in 2021: Key Moments in Biden's First Term. *The Hong Kong Post*, January 21, 2022. https://thehongkongpost.com/2022/01/21/us-foreign-policy-in-2021-key-moments-in-bidens-first-term/. accessed on February 10, 2022.

Zubok, Vladislav. 2021. US Lost prestige of global leader after withdrawing from Afghanistan. Czech President. *TASS*, August 17, 2021. https://tass.com/world/1327131?utm_source=bing.com&utm_medium=organic&utm_campaign=bing.com&utm_referrer=bing.com. accessed on January 30, 2022.

III Calling for Social Change? Norms and Practices

Julia Herrmann

A tipping point in feminist foreign policy in Europe? A constructivist analysis based on the norm life cycle model

Abstract: This article examines the phenomenon of feminist foreign policy (FFP) in Europe. Following the adoption of so-called "feminist" foreign policies in Europe (e.g., in France, Luxembourg, Spain, Germany, and Sweden until 2022), a growing debate has emerged regarding the extent to which this global trend presents a sustained normative shift. By applying norm life cycle models designed by constructivist scholars, this article systematically assesses the tipping point that a norm must exceed to diffuse successfully on the international stage. Steady path directions of FFP norms and the motion of gravitational forces are considered as potential key indicators for such a tipping point. Discourse analysis revealed a gap between rhetoric (promoting a progressive and structurally disruptive concept of FFP) and practice (revealing a narrow understanding of FFP comparable with gender mainstreaming). Nevertheless, FFP continues to raise awareness regarding gender issues in international politics, and it represents a new normative dimension that is seeking gradual acceptance.

Keywords: Feminist Foreign Policy, norm research, norm acceptance, turning point, social constructivism

1 Introduction

The macro-theoretical foundations of classic international relations theory – that is, realism and constructivism – are more appropriate for explaining continuity than change. When actors are assumed to behave according to the realist logic of consequentialism[1] or according to the constructivist logic of appropriateness[2] (Risse 2000), realist and constructivist approaches shed light on social order and stability rather than on how or when standards change (Finnemore and Sikkink 1998: 888;

---

1 action is driven by anticipated consequences in terms of material gain.
2 action is driven by what is believed to be appropriate based on norms and identity.

Julia Herrmann, researcher at the Friedrich-Alexander-Universität Erlangen-Nürnberg (FAU) in Germany

https://doi.org/10.1515/9783111272900-009

March and Olsen 1998: 947–949). Constructivism overcomes its lack of explanatory power regarding change through an extensive examination of norms, with a shift in norms being described as a main driver of structural change. This conception of an international ideational structure shows how reality is not fixed or objective but subject to change (Theys 2017: 41; Adler 2013: 113).

Concepts of change and turning points are essential to understanding the complexity of the current global transformation. Rapid shifts in global power relations – most significantly, the rise of China – challenge the existing international order and the sustainability of current foreign policy. Digitalization, the climate crisis, post-pandemic instability, growing authoritarianism, increasing numbers of refugees, and rising inequality have also exacerbated these disruptive dynamics and have undermined societal cohesion and liberal democracy.

Feminist foreign policy (FFP) has been implemented in various countries with the objective of tackling these challenges by "advancing ethics and gender equality in global politics" (Aggestam and Rosamond 2019). As of the end of 2023, several countries have adopted explicitly feminist foreign policy approaches, including Sweden (2014–2022), Canada (2017), France (2019), Mexico (2020), Spain (2021), Luxembourg (2019), and Germany (2023). Other countries, such as Chile, the Netherlands, and Belgium, have claimed to develop and implement feminist-informed foreign policy approaches under the banner of FFP in the future. Switzerland, Denmark, and Norway have strong gender equality-focused foreign policies, even if not labeled as "feminist". Libya announced its commitment to FFP in 2021 (however, it has taken no subsequent institutional or practical measures to implement this policy). In the United States House of Representatives, the Democrats brought an FFP resolution[3] to the floor, and three political parties in the United Kingdom have announced that if elected into power, they will pursue FFP (Bernarding und Lunz 2020:12; Gill-Atkinso et al. 2021: 7; Thompson et al. 2020, Thompson et al. 2021: 1; UN Women 2022). However, other developments have demonstrated the volatility of these endeavors and the gravitational forces involved. In January 2022, the Swedish Foreign Minister announced plans for in total 16 countries to cooperate on common policy action as part of the so-called Feminist Foreign Policy Plus Group. In this way, Sweden is seen as a pioneering force behind FFP efforts. However, at the end of 2022, a right-wing coalition consisting of Sweden Democrats, Moderates, Christian Democrats, and Liberals was elected in Sweden, and they officially revoked the country's FFP. Moreover, in the context of ongoing Russian aggression in Ukraine, and, more specifically, the Russian invasion of Ukraine in 2022, European

---

3 https://www.congress.gov/116/bills/hres1147/BILLS-116hres1147ih.pdf.

countries have increased their spending on military armament despite their FFP commitments (SIPRI 2023; UN Women 2022; The Guardian 2022).

On the one hand, FFP appears to be "gain[ing] momentum at a global level" (Gill-Atkinso et al. 2021: 7) and "clearly present[s] a growing global trend" (Thompson et al. 2021: 1). On the other hand, more skeptical voices anticipate that widespread adoption of FFP is unlikely given the rising trends of populism, nationalism, and traditionalism around the globe (Sundström and Elgström 2020: 419). Other skeptics question the novelty of this "feminist agenda" given that advancing gender equality has long been considered one of the key responsibilities of international organizations (Thomson 2020a and 2020b).

This article employs the norm life cycle models developed by constructivist scholars to assess whether FFP is reaching a turning point in Europe. More specifically, in the context of an empirical analysis of FFP, this article systematically examines the threshold (tipping point) that a norm must pass to diffuse successfully within society and cause structural change.

This article begins with a brief review of the constructivist approach to international relations as well as its definition of norms. Subsequently, it introduces the theoretical framework of the norm life cycle, focusing on the concept of a turning point – which, in this essay, is referred to as a "tipping point" – and the competing gravitational forces at play. The next section empirically assesses a potential tipping point for FFP in Europe; this section also defines FFP and differentiates between a transformative feminist approach and a less radical gender-informed approach. The concept of tipping point is then applied to current forms of FFP in Europe. Evidence demonstrating the steady path directions of FFP norms, and the motion of gravitational forces is collected as key indicators of an imminent (or improbable) tipping point.

2 The concept of turning points in social constructivism

The constructivist approach in international relations theory is derived from sociology and argues that international reality is socially constructed. That is, international relations theory asserts that the practices and objects of social life, which people usually take for granted as exogenously given, are "product of social construction by human agency" (Jung 2019: 3). As an example of the socially constructed nature of reality, Wendt (1995) describes how 500 British nuclear weapons are perceived as less threatening to the United States than five North Korean nuclear weapons. Indeed, social constructivism asserts that not only the distribution of material power and geographical conditions but also beliefs, identities, and norms determine world politics, and in this way, the theory established an approach that challenges rational choice theories, which heavily shaped international relations up until the 1990s (Krell and Schlotter 2018: 338–339; Adler 1997: 319). US scholars see conventional constructivism as an alternative to rationalist approaches (Locher and Prügl 2001: 112), whereas in Europe, it is commonly viewed as the "middle ground" between rationalist (liberals and realists) and interpretive approaches (postmodernists, poststructuralists, and critical theorists), incorporating elements from both theories (Gold and McGlinchey 2017: 50; Adler 1997: 319).

Constructivism does not describe a single, homogenous theoretical approach (see Jung 2019 for an overview of the variants of constructivism). Hopf (1998), for example, classifies constructivism into conventional, and critical variants, whereas Fearon and Wendt (2002) identified positivist, interpretivist, and postmodern strands that adhere to different epistemological foundations. However, all constructivist approaches (except perhaps variants of radical constructivism) share some key assumptions regarding the construction of social reality and the role of norms in international politics (Adler 2013: 113; Katzenstein 1996; Florini 1996; Towns 2012). The following theoretical framework is based on the work of conventional constructivists and incorporates aspects of sociological institutionalism. However, because the conceptualizations contained within this article are built on a common ground of shared basic assumptions, constructivists from a wide variety of theoretical traditions can apply the theoretical framework developed in this article to empirically assess turning points.

Definition of norms: Constructivism has a strong emphasis on the role of ideational factors, such as social norms, ideas, and values, in foreign policy. Political change and turning points occur when existing norms are challenged and new norms successfully emerge (Gold and McGlinchey 2017: 50f). Given the power of norms in international relations, a clear understanding of the term is crucial. According to Katzenstein (1996: 5), "norms," which commonly refer to beliefs, expectations, ideas, and social institutions, "set standards for the appropriate behavior of actors with a given identity." As such, norms are defined as common understandings that determine the interests and identities of actors. While rationalist scholars assume that agents comply with the norms embedded in regimes and international organizations due to cost-benefit calculations and material incentives, constructivists assert that individuals act in accordance with the social learning and behaviors that conform with their identities (Checkel 2001: 553; They 2017: 38).

Mechanism of change through norm shifts: Conventional constructivists assume that actors (in this case, states) act within environments that are material as well as social. Material structures, however, are given meaning by the social contexts within which they are interpreted. Consequently, actors shape reality based on how they perceive and interpret things (Krell and Schlotter 2018: 338; Adler 1997: 319; Checkel 1998: 325). Likewise, "shared ideas, expectations, and beliefs about appropriate behavior give the world structure, order, and stability" and at the same time, "norm shifts are the main vehicles for system transformation" (Finnemore and Sikkink 1998: 890, 894). Therefore, changes in norms are as influential for constructivists as shifts in the balance of power are for realist theorists. Above all, the focus on ideational factors and their intersubjectivity implies that reality is always under construction and subject to change. In summary, nearly all constructivists, regardless of their approach, have replaced "positional ontology" with "transformational ontology," meaning that they understand the world not as something that *is* but rather as something that *is in the process of becoming* (Locher and Prügl 2001: 114). Nevertheless, it is crucial to ask how structural change via norms occurs in the international system.

In line with our definition, norms have a regulative effect on behavior and a constitutive effect on identity (Finnemore and Sikkink 1998: 891). Most importantly, norms play a key role in shaping (collective) identities.

Following Hopf (1998: 175), identities perform essential functions in society: By telling individuals who they are, they establish interests and preferences with respect to choices of action in particular domains. In other words, norms shape identities, and identities determine the interests of actors. Thus, the state is supposed to shape its policies according to its identity and interests (see Figure 1, Cho 2009: 81). When accounting for the relations between norms and (state) identity, it can be seen that norms eventually affect the desires and actions of states.

Figure 1: Mechanism of norm influence in conventional constructivism.
Source: Personal illustration based on Cho 2009: 81–82.

By utilizing this mechanism, conventional constructivists can properly analyze state interests and the social structures of world politics (Cho 2009: 79; Checkel 1998: 324): If identities change, a perspective on a certain situation may also change, which, in turn, can lead to a redefinition of interests. These processes can explain structural changes within the international system (Ulbert 2010: 441f). Hopf (1998: 174f) even goes so far as to claim that a world without identities or with identities that change too rapidly would be a world of chaos and pervasive uncertainty. Within the constructivist framework used to carry out our empirical analysis of FFP, world politics is viewed as an intersubjective domain where actors' ideas of themselves and the world shape how they define their interests and, by extension, their foreign policies (Weldes 1996).

When analyzed from an agent-centric perspective, this same mechanism lies within constructivism's core assumption that international relations exist in the interactions between people. According to this perspective, it is not states themselves that interact but rather the agents of those states, such as diplomats, politicians, and activists (Gold and McGlinchey 2017: 50). Structures, such as norms, social institutions or culture constrain those agents, and define their identities. Thus, anarchy is what states make of it, and the qualities of anarchy may change over time if an influential group of individuals (and, by proxy, their respective states) adopt other norms (Gold and McGlinchey 2017: 50f; Towns 2010: 33; Wendt 1995). Constructivism offers an understanding of turning points and can explain the fundamental transformation of the international system (Koslowsky and Kratichwil 1994), which includes the almost worldwide acceptance of new norms (Ramirez et al. 1997: 743; They 2017: 2).

The explanation of structural mechanisms of change outlined above principally assumes normative stability in society, which is periodically interrupted by norm change. Consequently, as a point of departure for our analysis of turning points and FFP, our theoretical framework will further explain how and when norms are challenged and potentially replaced with new norms by employing the norm life cycle model.

The norm life cycle model: The norm life cycle models provide insight into the understanding of norm emergence and evolution. These models, which are based on (mostly) constructivist concepts, illustrate that new norms must pass through a "life cycle" before they can become successfully disseminated (e.g., in world politics). These models also describe how norms are contested, how they can fail along the diffusion processes, and how they become replaced. Finnemore and Sikkink (1998: 895–905) offer an extensive explanation of the norm life cycle, identifying its constituting stages as 1) norm emergence, 2) norm cascade, and 3) internalization. The first two stages are divided by a threshold – or rather, a "tipping point" – at which a critical mass of relevant state actors adopt the norm, the dynamic of norm imitation quickly progresses to an advanced level and norm acceptance rapidly accelerates (see Figure 2).

Additionally, other constructivist scholars have asked when a norm comes into existence (e.g., Checkel 1998, 1999, and 2001; Cortell and Davis 1996, Florini 1996, Klotz 1995, Legro 1997). Iommi (2020: 87) extended the model presented by Finnemore and Sikkink to include a fourth and final phase (norm regression) and suggested a more sophisticated reconceptualization of the norm internalization stage. Both of her adjustments highlight the role of norm contestation. Furthermore, Krook and True (2010), Sandholtz and Stiles (2009), and Wiener (2014, 2017) elaborated on norm life cycles, adding a contestation mechanism to norm change and describing norms as elusive and fluid rather than fixed (Iommi 2020: 79).

Although present-day norm research has developed significantly since the turn of the millennium and offers more complex and dynamic norm change scenarios, the model of Finnemore and Sikkink (1998) presents a suitable foundation to conceptualize a turning point in constructivist theory. Its straightforwardness allows us to specifically map out the momentum and mechanisms of norm tipping. Moreover, its simplicity and prominence enable researchers to most effectively apply the concepts of tipping points and momentum of inversion of gravitational forces to an analysis of the stages of other norm life cycle models. However, in order to offset the weaknesses of the model (e.g., privileging successful norms) and ensure a solid ground for our empirical analysis, we consider the dynamics of contestation and setbacks resulting from competition between state and nonstate actors to define these norms (Iommi 2020: 79f; Krook and True 2010: 106)

Next, the article offers a brief explanation of the three-stage norm life cycle of Finnemore and Sikkink (1998) to better understand the conceptualization of the tipping point. Within Finnemore and Sikkink's (1998: 895–905) explanation of a life cycle, each stage change is characterized by different actors, motives, and mechanisms of influence. During norm emergence, actors feel dissatisfied with a certain social context and spread their ideas about appropriate behavior. These so-called "norm entrepreneurs" attempt to persuade a critical mass of norm leaders (usually states) to adopt a new norm.

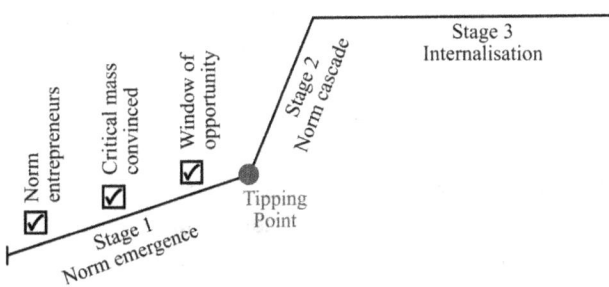

Figure 2: Norm life cycle and drivers for tipping points.
Source: Personal illustration based on Finnemore and Sikkink 1998: 895–905, and Brabandt et al. 2002: 22.

It can be concluded that a new norm has emerged when the number of relevant agents accepting the new norm exceeds a certain threshold (a critical mass). This moment is defined as a tipping point, and it is followed by a norm cascade (ibid.). Many emergent norms, however, fail to reach such a tipping point. At this stage, the norm acceptance dynamic rapidly accelerates. An imitation dynamic begins, by which agents outside the critical mass – who are so-called "norm followers" or "norm takers" – come to accept behaviors that conform with the new norm through socialization. At the end of the norm cascade, the norm is internalized. That is, once the norm becomes established, it induces self-reinforcing behaviors, and becomes taken for granted.

Finnemore and Sikkink argue that a turning point is more likely to be passed and that a norm is more likely to become diffused if certain requirements are met at the beginning of the life cycle. There are two essential conditions that must exist for a norm to reach a turning point: There must be norm entrepreneurs with novel visions who call attention to an alternative norm, and there must be a critical mass of relevant agents who have accepted the new norm as appropriate and ideal. Moreover, a so-called "window of opportunity" helps to set the agenda on the international stage (see Figure 2) (ibid. 896–902; Brabandt et al. 2002: 22).

Tipping points in norm change: It is difficult to define turning points within constructivism or norm research in general because norms do not emerge "fully formed" and because the intersubjective agreement necessary for a norm to survive does not arise automatically or at a predictable moment in time. That is, "[N]orms do not as a rule come into existence at a definite point in time, nor are they the result of a manageable number of identifiable acts. They are, rather, the results of complex patterns of behavior of many people over a protracted time" (Ullman-Margalit 1977: 8). Considering this prevailing vagueness, the norm life cycle is useful for narrowing down the moment a tipping point reaches critical momentum to a defined window of time between norm emergence and norm cascade (i.e., between Stage 1 and Stage 2 following the model of Finnemore and Sikkink 1998). As mentioned before, Finnemore and Sikkink (1998: 901) define this point in time as a norm passing a certain threshold, after which it is accepted as something that is appropriate and works well "compared with other principles that turned out to work poorly" and are discarded. After norm entrepreneurs have persuaded a "critical mass" of states to become norm leaders and adopt new norms, the norm can reach a tipping point, and a norm cascade ensues.

According to the explanation of tipping points presented in the introduction of this edited volume, the norm diffusion process describes a steady path or trend – that is, as a steadily increasing enforcement of a norm, standard, or way of thinking. However, at a certain point, the forces acting for, or against norm compliance reverse. Figure 3 shows one arrow pointing down during norm emergence and another pointing up during norm cascade and internalization following the tipping point.

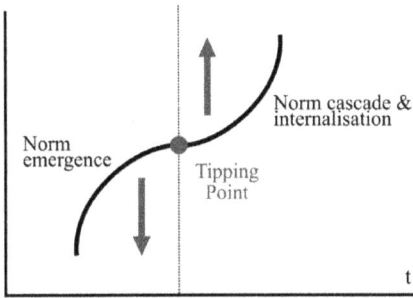

Figure 3: Tipping point of norm change as an inversion of gravitational forces.
Source: Personal illustration based on the introduction of this edited volume and Finnemore and Sikkink 1998.

This figure illustrates the changing dynamics and directions of these forces: Before the tipping point, norm entrepreneurs or agents who are in favor of the new norm must justify their actions, fighting societal pressures while propagating the new norm (e.g., feminist-informed, or gender-sensitive foreign policy). After the tipping point, however, people who do not agree with the new norm must justify their behaviors, and societal pressure begins to shift in favor of norm compliance (see the introduction of this edited volume). In contrast to a minor gradual change over time, this inversion in the momentum of gravitational forces, whereby societal pressure, and consensus begin to work in favor of a newly emerged norm, causes a tipping point in the norm diffusion processes. The following empirical analysis will identify norms related to the implementation of FFP and seek out examples or indications within rhetoric and policy praxis that indicate an (upcoming) inversion of such gravitational forces.

However, at this juncture, it is important to ask how a norm emerges in the first place. As mentioned before, norm entrepreneurs – whether individuals, NGOs, social movements, transnational networks, or states – play an essential role in setting agendas and identifying and spreading norms. Entrepreneurship is a well-established concept in political science, and it is used to explain the emergence of cooperation and norms (Schneider and Teske 1992; Moravcsik 1999; Rushton 2008; Towns 2010). A norm entrepreneur is committed to a certain norm and works to persuade other actors to alter their behavior in accordance with their ideas of appropriateness. Strategic framing and persuasion pressure norm leaders (usually states) into complying with the norm (Finnemore and Sikkink 1998: 897–900). Once a "critical mass" of states has been convinced to adopt the new norm, it reaches a tipping point, and dynamics reverse toward norm compliance (Finnemore and Sikkink 1998: 901). Furthermore, norm emergence benefits from incidents that change political structures or public opinion and opens a window of opportunity, which progressive political leaders are trained to exploit (Brabandt et al. 2002: 22). Empirical examples show that the success of norm diffusion is highly dependent on favorable institutional and political opportunity structures. Thus, windows of opportunity may also be an indicator of turning points (ibid.: 23; Gill-Atkinson et al. 2021: 3).

Our analysis involved gathering evidence demonstrating that a norm trend accompanied by an inversion of gravitational forces has occurred in the case of FFP in Europe, with an emphasis on predominant norm discourse and its agents.

Moreover, the above-described mechanism of international norm diffusion is neither automatic nor irreversible, regardless of whether it occurs before or after the tipping point. Despite the linear and progressive narrative suggested by the norm life cycle model, all norm dynamics are exposed to contestation "as state and nonstate actors compete to identify, define, and implement these norms" (Krook and True 2010: 106). Therefore, an empirical analysis of norms must recognize that the prevalence of contestation and conflict does not necessarily hinder norm tipping. Simultaneously, successful norm convergence does not inhibit future norm failure (Iommi 2020: 79).

3 Definition and forms of feminist foreign policy

The concept of turning (or rather tipping) points outlined above provides a better understanding of the origins and current state of FFP. This section briefly summarizes the characteristics and different forms of FFP currently in existence. Additionally, this section identifies the norms affiliated with FFP and applies the framework of tipping points to the case of FFP, particularly FFP in Europe.

Foreign policies determine how governments define peace and security, organize trade, provide humanitarian aid, and cooperate with other nations and nonstate actors (Thompson et al. 2020: 4). Following the introduction of Sustainability Development Goal 5 and the National Action Plans on Women, Peace, and Security (WPS), for example, gender equality has emerged as a self-evident component of foreign policy (Thomson 2020a). These concepts of gender have a narrow scope: They focus exclusively on women and their inclusion in the labor market. Such policies can be described as gender-informed, but not feminist, policies, as feminist policies imply a more rigorous policy shift. In contrast to traditional foreign policy thinking – which considered gender inequality as a part of soft diplomacy and as unconnected to hard topics like trade and national security – FFP aims to break out of this realist paradigm and promote a normative reorientation of foreign policy (Aggestam and Rosamond 2019; CFFP 2021). Thompson et al. (2020) comprehensively define FFP as "the policy of a state that defines its interactions with other states, as well as movements and other nonstate actors, in a manner that prioritizes peace, gender equality and environmental integrity; enshrines, promotes, and protects the human rights of all; seeks to disrupt colonial, racist, patriarchal and male-dominated power structures; and allocates significant resources, including research, to achieve that vision" (Thompson et al. 2020: 4). However, there are multiple competing definitions of FFP, and, in theory, they all entail a strong transformative claim questioning prevailing realist paradigms and their focus on military strength, repression, dominance, and armament.

Empirical studies often consider cases of foreign policies that have been explicitly labeled as "feminists" by the respective states; however, these studies do not evaluate whether such policies have been realized or whether they meet feminist standards in qualitative terms. It is clear from the policy documents published so far that feminism can mean different things to different states (Thomson 2020a: 2) and is prone to fail to meet their high standards in the pragmatics of foreign policy practices (Robinson 2021: 21f). Moreover, feminist scholars of international relations criticize existing FFP for not being as feminist as claimed. That is, existing FFP does not sufficiently interrogate the normative power wielded by Europe in relation to its past history as a colonial power. These policies also lack an intersectional approach and possess an obsolete understanding of gender as a sex binary (Thompson 2022).

Nevertheless, all definitions of FFP share a common political framework that aims to consider issues related to gender equality and marginalization in all relevant fields, such as international aid, trade, diplomacy, migration, defense, and security (CFFP 2021). Thompson et al. (2021) and Bernardino and Lunz (2020) present a comprehensive overview of forms of FFP that have been adopted by countries such as Sweden, Canada, Luxembourg, France, Mexico, and Spain, demonstrating that each country has adopted a different framework and policy approach. Some of these approaches are quite comprehensive, such as those of Sweden and Mexico. Other countries have introduced rather vague policies while taking few steps and making few institutional commitments after their announcement (e.g., Libya).

Norms promoted via FFP: In order to assess norm diffusion and norm tipping in the case of FFP, it is necessary to specify the normative principles affiliated with such a policy. The academic discourse presents different feminist perspectives with very heterogeneous demands, which is also reflected in practice (Thomson 2020b; Ansorg et al. 2021; Zilla 2022). Western liberal feminism, for example, highlights how the male dominance of patriarchal structures discriminates against the perspectives, ideas, and experiences of women. With respect to foreign policy, women are affected differently by war and poverty. Queer feminist currents criticize the assumptions related to the gender binary and heteronormativity, seeking a conception of FFP that is inclusive of LGBTQIA+ people. Intersectional approaches to FFP extend the one-dimensional focus on sex and gender by considering overlapping forms of discrimination. This comprehensive approach acknowledges unequal power structures that generate hierarchies based on sexual orientation, skin color, origin, disability, and religion, and challenges racist and colonial ideas within international relations. In addition, Marxist-feminist perspectives object to the economic growth paradigm and see the end of the capitalist system as a prerequisite for the abolishment of every form of domination (Zilla 2022: 2–3; Ansorg et al. 2021: 207f).

Regardless of the approach, the term "feminist" implies an emphasis on the transformative or even disruptive intention of the policy. This contrasts with policies that work toward gender equality without questioning the given system. However, the meaning of the FFP approach in theory and practice remains vague and controversial (Ansorg et al. 2021: 202f; Zilla 2022: 1). Because there is no common definition or joint political framework, it is unlikely that common norms, ideas, values, or strategies related to FFP will develop. Therefore, in order to measure the acceptance of FFP in international politics, the number of states that have adopted an explicit FFP can only be used as a very rough proxy. The label "feminist" does not consider how the respective FFP had been realized or how it meets feminist standards in qualitative terms.

Krook and True (2010: 104) observed that international norms are often vague, as this characteristic enables them to be filled with various content and to be appropriated for various purposes. This seems especially true in the case of normative policy approaches with a focus on gender equality. Gender equality is a commonly accepted value, for example, the UN Convention on the Elimination of All Forms of Discrimination against Women (CEDAW) is the most ratified human rights treaty. However, the definition of gender equality and its norm development remain highly contested, as the term can have different meanings depending on the national context, frequently causing inconsistent implementation (ibid: 104f; Lombardo et al. 2009).

4 Feminist foreign policy: Reaching a turning point?

In this section, the norm life cycle model (Finnemore and Sikkink 1998; see Figure 2), particularly the mechanism of norm tipping (see Figure 3), is applied to an analysis of international efforts to implement FFP. Subsequently, this section evaluates whether a tipping point is reached by tracing the path direction of FFP-related norms that have become diffused in international relations and by assessing the gravitational forces at play in Europe.

The first requirement for a norm to reach a tipping point and achieve (inter-national) norm diffusion is that the norm possesses a stable and persistent path while spreading with the support of norm leaders. FFP is a comparatively new phenomenon; however, it is the outcome of early feminist movements and an increasing awareness of gender in international politics. The focus on gender has expanded from development policy and human rights to security and foreign policy (Aggestam and True 2020; Bernarding and Lunz 2020).

Already at the beginning of the 20th century, women's rights movements across the globe began to promote progressive policy solutions to advance gender equality and the rights of women. A notable example is the 1915 International Congress of Women held at The Hague, which evolved into the Women's International League for Peace and Freedom, which demanded the dismantling of industries supporting the military. For decades, feminist civil society organizations acted as norm entrepreneurs and pressured states and international organizations to promote the participation of women in all aspects of peace and security policy. However, it was not until 2000 that the UN Security Council Resolution 1325 on Women, Peace, and Security (WPS) was passed, marking a shift whereby feminist initiatives – which had previously been topics only discussed in civil society and academia – became implemented in the international political sphere (Gill-Atkinson et al. 2021: 12). This landmark resolution transformed efforts to end gender-based violence in humanitarian conflicts and promote the participation of women in international peace and security processes into an integral part of the UN Security Council's mandate and convinced states to adopt gender-informed foreign policies. Due to a variety of resolutions, agreements, and policies meant to improve the empowerment and equality of women (and other minorities), these norms have become common sense in Europe and the Western hemisphere, as well as at international organizations (e.g., CEDAW, or the national plans on WPS). Since 2014, several European countries, such as Sweden (2014–2022), France (2019), Luxembourg (2019), Spain (2021), and Germany (2023), have introduced various forms of FFPs. The Netherlands, Belgium, Switzerland, Denmark, and Norway have strong gender equality-focused foreign policies (Bernarding and Lunz 2020: 12; Thompson et al. 2020; Thompson et al. 2021: 1; UN Women 2022). FFP is rooted in developments going back decades; it is the result of successful norm persuasion and demonstrates a clear and steady path direction toward gradual norm enforcement. The first prerequisite for a possible turning point has thus been fulfilled. Certainly, the comparatively recent label of a "feminist" policy implies a new transformative or even disruptive quality and sets a new standard.

The second requirement for a tipping point in the norm diffusion process is reversing gravitational forces. Before a norm "tips," states must explain or even justify their commitment to a feminist- or gender-informed approach; after the inversion of forces takes place, however, states must combat societal pressure and justify their action if they choose not to comply with the new norm. Our analysis then examined the momentum of gravitational forces at play in the context of FFP in Europe by assessing key policy documents and public discourse.

The EU addresses gender concerns, including women's rights, the WPS agenda, and LGBTIQ+ rights, in several aspects of its external relations. In 2018, the EU ratified its Women, Peace, and Security Agenda, which included an action plan for 2019 to 2024[4] and a strategic approach.[5] Two years later, the EU launched its Gender Action Plan III,[6] establishing gender equality as a priority in all EU foreign policy strategies and actions and establishing a set of quantitative targets to measure the achievement of these objectives (Schmidt 2021; Thomson 2022). All of these actions have contributed to gender mainstreaming in EU foreign policy, and they can cautiously be interpreted as conforming to the basic principles of a gender-informed foreign policy approach (even if this is not explicitly stated). However, these initiatives do not constitute a transformative feminist approach to policymaking. That is, existing policies do not rethink harmful trade patterns (e.g., the militarism–trade nexus) or question the traditional economic growth paradigm, including extractive industries and the concept of state security at the expense of human security. And with their mere focus on women, they also fail to adopt an intersectional perspective (Bernarding and Lunz 2020: 11; UN Women 2022; Thomson 2022: 121).

FFP is being developed by states rather than by the institutions of the EU. As a result, "[T]he focus of study within Europe on gender and foreign policy is shifting from a previous strong interest in the EU architecture to individual nation-states" (Thomson 2022: 120). However, even national FFPs barely go beyond gender mainstreaming when considering their policy frame, perspective, priorities, and tools. No existing FFP suggests a radical feminist norm change. Some states are showing more commitment toward a comprehensive approach that includes all dimensions of foreign policy (e.g., Sweden and Mexico), while others are not (e.g., France, Spain, and Germany). Overall, however, there has been no critical reflection regarding racialized and gendered inequalities on the domestic level and the power dynamics inherent within global politics (e.g., the legacies of colonialism). Indeed, national FFPs adopt an intersectional approach that considers other identity markers, but they do not offer possibilities to put an intersectional perspective into practice (Ansorg et al. 2021: 207).

There is an indisputable discrepancy between rhetoric and practice. On the one hand, progressive, and structurally transformative intentions are presented. On the other hand, a narrow, and uncontroversial understanding of FFP is exer-

---

4 https://data.consilium.europa.eu/doc/document/ST-11031-2019-INIT/en/pdf.

5 https://www.consilium.europa.eu/media/37412/st15086-en18.pdf.

6 https://ec.europa.eu/international-partnerships/system/files/join-2020-17-final_en.pdf.

cised, which displays a limited reformist commitment to gradual changes within existing power structures (Ansorg et al. 2021; UN Women 2022; Thompson et al. 2021; Zilla 2022).

However, although existing FFPs address feminist concerns only partially, they do introduce feminist approaches into the political discourse, supporting political acceptance, and the potential emergence of a tipping point in the future. Moreover, such policies still promote inclusiveness and more vigorous normative (or even ethical) standards in their political action (Ansorg et al. 2021: 209; Zilla 2022: 2).

The momentum of gravitational forces within FFP discourse is particularly evident during moments of intense change in global politics and security, such as ongoing Russian aggression and the war in Ukraine:

On the one hand, there is a growing militarization observable in EU foreign policy. This is, in part, a response to growing global uncertainty and the weight of the pressures on the EU's liberal institutionalism (SIPRI 2023; Thompson 2022: 126f). In addition, with the Russian invasion of Ukraine, the world is confronted with war in Europe and a hostile state. In its immediate reactions, the countries with official FFP in place fell back into old patterns of traditional foreign policy thinking, prioritizing the protection of material and state security over the safeguarding of human security and the lives of the most marginalized (Ergas 2021). For example, military expenses reached a new high in Europe, recording the most drastic year-on-year increase in the last three decades (SIPRI 2023). These circumstances do not seem conducive to the further dissemination of FFP, and they reveal that societal pressures and gravitational forces are working against the new norms implied by FFP.

Nevertheless, FFP, which originated in Europe, seems to be functioning as a rejoinder during these times of uncertainty, nationalism, and polarization (Thompson 2022: 127). In addition, Russian aggression stoked public distaste for Putin's male-dominated power structures and an awareness that every war resulting in a humanitarian crisis aggravates existing systemic inequalities (Santoire 2022). In contrast to the skeptical voices questioning how a feminist approach can counter current Russian aggression, an increasing number of scholars argue that such an approach has revealed and mainstreamed the need for a new understanding of foreign policy, even if "emergency care" in the form of hard-power politics is in the current moment (Adebahr 2022; Santoire 2022; Ergas 2022). The narrative of a "Zeitenwende" (meaning "historic turning point") and the newly elected German Chancellor Olaf Scholz embedding a new German security policy within a historical speech in March 2022 underline this new political environment (Adebahr 2022). In 2023, Germany launched its FFP guidelines under the guidance of German Foreign Minister Annalena Baerbock from the Green Party.

The clash of gravitational forces can also be observed at the domestic level, such as in the case of Sweden. Sweden, represented by the Minister of Foreign Affairs Margot Wallström, was a pioneer in promoting an explicit, comprehensive FFP that encompassed all dimensions of foreign policy, was backed with resources and research, and aligned with domestic policy. The country has been considered a committed state norm entrepreneur in the field because 2014. However, in 2022, with the election of a right-wing conservative government, Sweden officially revoked the country's FFP (The Guardian 2022). However, in spite of the repeal, the newly elected Minister of Foreign Affairs, Tobias Billström, fully supported gender equality as "a core value for Sweden" (Thomas 2022), and he criticized the feminist label as something that might distract from the content of the policy (ibid.). This presents an example of how feminist approaches are contested while approaches focusing on gender equality are taken for granted.

Similarly, NGOs can also influence gravitational forces and change their dynamics. In 2016, the Center for Feminist Foreign Policy (CFFP) was founded with a mandate to provide research, advocacy, and consulting services meant to promote FFP (CFFP 2021) while taking a holistic and truly feminist approach. International NGOs – such as the CFFP, the International Center of Research on Women (ICRW), and various members of the European Parliament (mostly of the Greens/EFO) – act as norm leaders and lobby in favor of FFPs with more structural depth (Bernarding und Lunz 2020; Schmidt 2021, Thompson et al. 2021)).

To conclude, evidence suggests that the tipping point of gender mainstreaming and a gender-focused foreign policy was reached approximately around the year 2000. Feminist approaches to foreign policy continue this trend, while gravitational forces are still working against this more drastic normative approach.

5 Conclusion

The constructivist concept of turning points helps explicate how FFP is currently discussed in international politics, particularly in Europe. By employing the norm life cycle model, this article analyzed the threshold (tipping point) a norm must pass to diffuse successfully on the international stage. The key indicator that a tipping point has been reached is an inversion of gravitational forces within the norm diffusion trend. Before norm tipping occurs, agents must explain why they support and comply with the emerging norm, whereas after norm tipping occurs, this societal pressure reverses, and people must justify why they do not accept the norm. Discourse analysis revealed a gap between rhetoric (promoting a progressive and structurally disruptive concept of FFP) and practice (revealing a narrow understanding of FFP comparable with gender mainstreaming, with only a reformist intention within the existing structures). Nevertheless, FFP convincingly continues the trend of increasing awareness around gender issues in international politics and represents a new normative dimension seeking acceptance.

References

Adebahr, Cornelius. 2022. What Germany's turning point means for its feminist foreign policy. *Deutsche Gesellschaft für Auswärtige Politik (DGAP)*, March 23, 2022. https://dgap.org/en/re search/publications/what-germanys-turning-point-means-its-feminist-foreign-policy.

Adler, Emanuel. 1997. Seizing the middle ground: Constructivism in world politics. *European Journal of International Relations* 3(3). 319–363.

Adler, Emanuel. 2013. Constructivism in International Relations: Sources, contributions, and debates. InWalter Carlsnaes, Thomas Risse, and Beth A. Simmons (eds.), *Handbook of international relations*, 112–144. London: Sage.

Aggestam, Karin, and Annika Bergman Rosamond. 2019. Feminist Foreign Policy 3.0: Advancing ethics and gender equality in global politics. *SAIS Review of International Affairs* 39(1). 37–48.

Aggestam, Karin and Jacqui True. 2020. Gendering Foreign Policy: A Comparative Framework for Analysis. *Foreign Policy Analysis* 16(2). 143–162.

Ansorg, Nadine, Toni Haastrup, and Katharine A. M. Wright. 2021. Foreign policy and diplomacy: Feminist interventions. InTarja Väyrynen, Swati Parashar, Élise Féron and Catia Cecilia Confortini (eds.), *Routledge Handbook of Feminist Peace Research*, 202–211. New York: Routledge.

Bernarding, Nina, and Christina Lunz. 2020. A Feminist Foreign Policy for the European Union. *CFFP*, June 2020. https://centreforfeministforeignpolicy.org/wordpress/wp-content/uploads/2023/01/Study-Feminist-Foreign-Policy-for-the-European-Union.pdf.

Brabandt, Heike, Birgit Locher, and Elisabeth Prügl. 2002. Normen, Gender und Politikwandel: Internationale Beziehungen aus der Geschlechterperspektive. *WeltTrends: Zeitschrift für internationale Politik und vergleichende Studien* 36. 11–26.

CFFP (Center of Feminist Foreign Policy). 2021. Feminist Foreign Policy. *CFFP*, March 26, 2022. https://centreforfeministforeignpolicy.org/feminist-foreign-policy.

Checkel, Jeffrey T. 1998. The constructive turn in international relations theory. *World Politics* 50(2). 324–348.

Checkel, Jeffrey T. 1999. Norms, institutions, and national identity in contemporary Europe. *International Studies Quarterly* 43(1). 83–114.

Checkel, Jeffrey T. 2001. Why comply? Social learning and European identity change. *International orqanization* 55(3). 553–588.

Cho, Young Chul. 2009. Conventional and critical constructivist approaches to national security. *The Korean Journal of International Studies* 49(3). 75–102.

Cortell, Andrew P., and James W. Davis Jr. 1996. How do international institutions matter? The domestic impact of international rules and norms. *International Studies Quarterly* 40(4). 451–478.

Ergas, Yasmine. 2021. Will Ukraine Bury Feminist Foreign Policies or Will It Reveal Their Power? *PassBlue. Independent Coverage of the UN*, March 9, 2022. https://www.passblue.com/2022/03/09/will-ukraine-bury-feminist-foreign-policies-or-will-it-reveal-their-power/.

Fearon, James, and Alexander Wendt. 2002. Rationalism v. Constructivism: A Skeptical View. In Walter Carlsnaes, Thomas Risse and Beth A. Simmons (eds.), *Handbook of International Relations*, 52–72. London: Sage.

Finnemore, Martha, and Kathryn Sikkink. 1998. International norm dynamics and political change. *International Organization* 52(4). 887–917.

Florini, Ann. 1996. The evolution of international norms. *International Studies Quarterly* 40(3). 363–389.

Gill-Atkinson, Lit, Alice Ridge, Joanna Pradela, Bronwyn Tilbury, Camille Warambourg, and Tamara Peña Porras. 2021. From Seeds to Roots: Trajectories towards Feminist Foreign Policy. *International Women's Development Agency (IWDA)*.

Gold, Dana, and Stephen McGlinchey. 2017. International relations theory. In Stephen McGlinchey (ed.), *International Relations*, 46–56. Bristol: E-International Relations Publishing.

Hopf, Ted. 1998. The promise of constructivism in international relations theory. *International security* 23(1). 171–200.

Iommi, Lucrecia García. 2020. Norm internalisation revisited: Norm contestation and the life of norms at the extreme of the norm cascade. *Global Constitutionalism* 9(1). 76–116.

Jung, Hoyoon. 2019. The evolution of Social Constructivism in Political Science: Past to present. *Sage Open* 9(1).

Katzenstein, Peter J. 1996. *The Culture of National Security: Norms and Identity in World Politics*. New York: Columbia University Press.

Keck, Margaret E., and Kathryn Sikkink. 1998. *Activists beyond borders: Activist networks in international politics*. Ithaca, NY: Cornell University Press.

Klotz, Audie. 1995. Norms reconstituting interests: Global racial equality and US sanctions against South Africa. *International Organization* 49(3). 451–478.

Koslowski, Rey, and Friedrich V. Kratochwil. 1994. Understanding Change in International Politics: The Soviet Empire's Demise and the International System. *International Organization* 48(2). 215–247.

Krell, Gert, and Peter Schlotter. 2018. *Weltbilder und Weltordnung: Einführung in die Theorie der internationalen Beziehungen*. Baden-Baden: Nomos.

Krook, Mona L., and Jacqui True. 2010. Rethinking the Life Cycles of International Norms: The United Nations and the Global Promotion of Gender Equality. *European Journal of International Relations* 18(1). 103–127.

Legro, Jeffrey W. 1997. Which norms matter? Revisiting the "failure" of internationalism. *International Organization* 51(1). 31–63.

Locher, Birgit, and Elisabeth Prügl. 2001. Feminism and Constructivism: Worlds apart or sharing the middle ground? *International Studies Quarterly* 45(1). 111–129.

Lombardo, Emanuela, Petra Meier, and Mieke Verloo (eds.). 2009. The discursive politics of gender equality: Stretching, bending and policy-making. New York: Routledge.

Manners, Ian. 2002. Normative Power Europe: A Contradiction in Terms? *Journal of Common Market Studies* 40(2). 235–258.

March, James G., and Johan P. Olsen. 1998. The institutional dynamics of international political orders. *International Organization* 52(4). 943–969.

Moravcsik, Andrew. 1999. Supranational Entrepreneurs and International Cooperation. *International Organization* 53(2). 267–306.

Ramirez, Francisco O., Yasemin Soysal, and Suzanne Shanahan. 1997. The changing logic of political citizenship: Cross-national acquisition of women's suffrage rights, 1890 to 1990. *American sociological review* 62(5). 735–745.

Risse, Thomas. 2000. „Let's argue!": Communicative action in world politics. 54(1). 1–39.

Robinson, Fiona. 2021. Feminist foreign policy as ethical foreign policy? A care ethics perspective. *Journal of International Political Theory* 17(1). 20–37.

Rushton, Simon. 2008. The UN Secretary-General and norm entrepreneurship: Boutros Boutros-Ghali and democracy promotion. Global governance: A Review of Multilateralism and International Organizations (14). 95–110.

Sandholtz, Wayne, and Kendall Stiles. 2009. *International Norms and Cycles of Change*. Oxford: Oxford University Press.

Santoire, Bénédicte. 2022. A Feminist Reality-Check on the Ukraine Crisis. *McGill*, February 14, 2022. https://www.mcgill.ca/rnwps/article/our-blog/feminist-reality-check-ukraine-crisis.

Schmidt, Juliane. 2021. A Green Feminist Foreign Policy for the EU. *Heinrich Böll Stiftung*, September 13, 2021. https://eu.boell.org/en/2021/09/13/green-feminist-foreign-policy-eu.

Schneider, Mark, and Paul Teske. 1992. Toward a Theory of the Political Entrepreneur: Evidence from Local Government. *American Political Science Review* 86(3). 737–747.

SIPRI (Stockholm International Peace Research Institute). 2023. World military expenditure reaches new record high as European spending surges. *SIPRI Military Expenditure Database*, April 24, 2023. https://www.sipri.org/media/press-release/2023/world-military-expenditure-reaches-new -record-high-european-spending-surges.

Sundström, Malena Rosén & Ole Elgström. 2020. Praise or critique? Sweden's feminist foreign policy in the eyes of its fellow EU members. *European Politics and Society* 21(4). 418–433.

The Guardian. 2022. Swedish government scraps country's pioneering 'feminist foreign policy'. *The Guardian*, October 18, 2022. https://www.theguardian.com/world/2022/oct/18/swedish-government-scraps-countrys-pioneering-feminist-foreign-policy.

Theys, Sarina. 2017. Constructivism. In Stephen McGlinchey, Rosie Walters, and Christian Scheinpflug (eds.), *International Relations Theory*. England: E-International Relations Publishing. https://www.e-ir.info/publication/international-relations-theory/.

Thomas, Merlyn. 2022. Sweden ditches 'feminist foreign policy'. *BBC News*, October 19, 2022.: https://www.bbc.com/news/world-europe-63311743.

Thompson, Lyric, Gayatri Patel, Gawain Kripke, and Megan O'Donnell. 2020. *Toward a Feminist Foreign Policy in the United States*. Washington, DC: International Center for Research on Women.

Thompson, Lyric, Spogmay Ahmed, and Tanya Khokhar. 2021. Defining Feminist Foreign Policy: A 2021 Update. *International Center of Research on Women (ICRW)*.

Thomson, Jennifer. 2020a. The growth of Feminist (?) Foreign Folicy. *E-International Relations*, February 10, 2020. https://www.e-ir.info/2020/02/10/the-growth-of-feminist-foreign-policy/.

Thomson, Jennifer. 2020b. What's Feminist about Feminist Foreign Policy? Sweden's and Canada's Foreign Policy Agendas. *International Studies Perspectives* 21(4). 424–437.

Thomson, Jennifer. 2022. Feminist Foreign Policy Studies in Europe. InMaria Stern and Ann E. Towns (eds.), *Feminist IR in Europe*, 115–132. London: Palgrave Macmillan.

Towns, Ann E. 2010. *Women and states: Norms and hierarchies in international society*. New York: Cambridge University Press.

Towns, Ann. E. 2012. Norms and social hierarchies: Understanding international policy diffusion "from below". *International Organization* 66. 179–209.

True, Jacqui, and Michael Mintrom. 2001. Transnational networks and policy diffusion: The case of gender mainstreaming. *International studies quarterly* 45(1). 27–57.

Ulbert, Cornelia. 2010. Sozialkonstruktivismus. InSiegried Schieder and Manuela Spindler (eds.), *Theorien der Internationalen Beziehungen*, 391–420. Leverkusen: Barbara Budrich.

Ullman-Margalit, Edna. 1977. *The Emergence of Norms*. Oxford: The Clarendon Press.

UN Women. 2022. Feminist Foreign Policies. An Introduction. *UN Women*, September 2022,
    https://www.unwomen.org/sites/default/files/2022-09/Brief-Feminist-foreign-policies-en_0.pdf.
Weldes, Jutta. 1996. Constructing national interests. *European Journal of International Relations* 2(3).
    275–318.
Wendt, Alexander. 1995. Anarchy is what states make of it: The social construction of power politics
    (1992). In James Der Derian (ed.), *International Theory*, 129–177. London: Palgrave Macmillan.
Wiener, Antje. 2014. *A Theory of Contestation*. Heidelberg: Springer.
Wiener, Antje. 2017. A theory of contestation – a concise summary of its arguments and concepts.
    Polity 49(1). 109–125.
Zilla, Claudia 2022. Feminist Foreign Policy. Concepts, core components and controversies. *SWP
    Comment* 48/2022.

Lars Berger

The turning point that was not: The Arab Spring, realism, and the circularity of Western policies toward the Arab world

Abstract: The Arab Spring marked a critical juncture in Western policies toward the Arab world. For a moment, it appeared as if a turning point was possible away from the long-term Western accommodation of entrenched authoritarianism in the region toward a recalibrated approach that respects the agency and dignity of people in the region. However, realist thinking and its fear-driven association of uncertainty with threat continued to provide a lens through which Western foreign policy elites viewed the wider region. Realist concerns about a new era of unpredictability and associated costs for Western policies as measured in irregular migration and transnational terrorism continued to reify sclerotic Arab state structures as, supposedly, the only guarantor of stability. The juxtaposition of "predictability" and "security" on the one hand with "unpredictability" and "insecurity" on the other not only led to policies that are at odds with US and European normative claims but also threaten Western long-term security interests. In the end, policies inspired by such realist thinking contribute to the circularity of authoritarianism and insecurity by creating self-fulfilling prophecies through the investment in the empty husk of the Arab state whose authoritarian nature is the source of the "unpredictable" security threats Western policymakers are concerned about.

Keywords: Arab Spring, Authoritarianism, Critical juncture, Realism, Turning point

1 Introduction

For a short while, it looked as if the Arab Spring in 2011 might constitute a critical juncture of world-historic proportions akin to the fall of the Iron Curtain in 1989, as hundreds of thousands of people across the Arab world demanded social justice and respect for their human rights and political freedoms (Boerzel, Dandashly, and Risse 2015). The frantic weeks of early 2011 with their unprecedented images of mass protests driven by transnational (social) media and the depar-

Lars Berger, Professor of International Politics and Terrorism Studies, Faculty of Intelligence, Federal University of Administrative Sciences, Berlin

https://doi.org/10.1515/9783111272900-010

tures of long-time autocratic leaders certainly fit Capoccia and Kelemen's (2007: 348) definition of critical junctures as "relatively short periods of time during which there is a substantially heightened probability that agents' choices will affect the outcome of interest." The quick succession of changes in leadership and political and socio-economic reform packages across so many countries was even more remarkable and surprising to Western academic observers and political and security elites alike, as the Arab world had represented up to this point "the largest bloc of countries under firmly and decidedly authoritarian rule" (Burnell and Schlumberger 2010: 2). Linkages and leverage – long seen as crucial aspects of the international dimension of democratization – were particularly weak compared to Central and Eastern Europe or Latin America (Ibid.: 6). In the end, however, only four out of fourteen countries saw a change in leadership, not to mention a genuine change in the form of government (Brownlee, Masoud, and Reynolds 2013). It is this failure of democratization and the resilience of authoritarianism that make it difficult for observers to speak of the Arab Spring as a critical juncture – or more precisely in this volume's understanding – a turning point in the region's political development (Bank and Busse 2021). However, as Capoccia and Kelemen remind us, we should not equate critical junctures with moments of change: "If change was possible and plausible, considered, and ultimately rejected in a situation of high uncertainty, then there is no reason to discard these cases as 'non-critical' junctures (2007: 352)."

The Arab Spring did, indeed, constitute such a moment when a fundamental repositioning of Western policies and thus relations with Arab countries was possible, but ultimately discarded. As this paper argues, the "space of uncertainty" inherent in such critical junctures sat uncomfortably with the realist preference for authoritarian stability and predictability typical of Western policies toward the region. Going beyond existing assessments of the degree of change and continuity in specific EU and US policies (Boogaerts, Portela, and Drieskens 2016; Lantis 2021; Quero and Dessi 2021), this paper critically interrogates Western ways of conceptualizing the region and its politics. In the process, this paper unearths how certain "truths" about the region that reflect realist assumptions about the drivers of insecurity and Orientalist essentialism regarding the impossibility of change made policies appear imprudent that could have responded to the sense of agency and dignity of the people, which the Arab Spring had highlighted. Instead, the policies of external actors are stuck in the circularity of policies, which, through their failure to address the root causes of instability in the region, help bring about the very problems which only realist thinking claims to be able to address. In the end, newly entrenched authoritarian regimes can instrumentalize their failures when seeking to extort Western governments into policy concessions on issues of political reform.

2 Realism and the foundations of authoritarianism in the Arab world

In historical institutionalism, a "critical juncture" denotes a moment in which, after extended periods of path dependency, dramatic change is possible (Capoccia and Kelemen 2007). Choices made in these moments have a lasting impact as they create new path dependencies since changing paths once again becomes increasingly costly the longer a path has, historically, been followed (see Boogaerts, Portela, and Drieskens 2016). In the case of relations of Western countries with regimes in the Arab world, such path dependency is closely shaped by a realist understanding of security and their association with notions of authoritarian "stability."

Realist vocabulary has long featured prominently in Western political commentary about the wider Middle East and North Africa (MENA) region whether it is via its depiction as the center of crosscutting "arcs of instability" (Kemp 2002: 62) or being part of the world's "wild zones" (Robert Kaplan quoted in Debrix 2003: 165). The region's extraordinary proclivity for conflict and war (Solingen 2007) makes (Neo-)realism appear an appropriate theoretical fit with its claim regarding the impact the anarchical nature of the international system has on uncertainty about the intentions and capabilities of other actors and fears over a state's national security or even its very survival (Gegout 2018; Rathbun 2007). From a structural realist perspective, "the weakness of the realist foundations for peace" (Miller 2010: 158) in the region could be addressed in two ways. One option would be the establishment of hegemony in which a predominant actor ensures the stability of regional order. This was a role that the US had played for some time (Miller 2010). Indeed, the region's peace processes of the 1990s reflected the recognition among regional actors that American hegemony would mean they can benefit from bandwagoning with the US and the associated closer ties with Israel (Miller 2010). This calculation, however, does not apply in a situation where the US pursues a reduction in its regional footprint (as has been the case since the Obama administration) and becomes increasingly unpredictable in terms of whether it supports the regional status quo or actively seeks to undermine it (as was the case during the first four years of the administration of George W. Bush) (Quero and Dessi 2021). Another option would be the establishment of bipolarity, which helps reduce uncertainties about the motivations and capabilities of relevant actors and thus, reduces the risk of war. In the Arab world, such bipolar configurations have long failed to materialize due to crosscutting cleavages like different political systems, national identities, and subnational identities (Gause 2014).

However, (Neo-)realism's focus on the systemic dimension of insecurity creates blind spots that are problematic from an analytical and a policy perspective. First, with its focus on the constraints imposed by the anarchical nature of the international system (Neo-)realism ignores the extent to which domestic politics plays a role in producing, maintaining, or overcoming conflict at the international level (David 1991). The assumption that states are rationally calculating actors reifies the state and ignores the extent to which attention to material power capabilities must be combined with attention to regime considerations and the impact of (trans-)national identities (Salloukh 2017).

Second, as a lens through which to guide policy, (Neo-)realism contributes to the problems it promises to address. Policies informed by the focus on systemic anarchy and interstate conflict drain resources away from the type of development that could bolster the domestic legitimacy of governments and thus build security in the region from the ground up. Western accommodation of such policies via the investment in close links with ruling elites not only produces considerable sunk costs, but such investments also exacerbate uncertainty, the very problem (Neo-)realism promises to address in the first instance. This is because, in such highly personalized authoritarian settings, political leaders see no need to develop robust institutions where the identity and personal interests of individuals are less relevant. Indeed, fear of potential rivals means that authoritarian regimes have no incentives in strengthening institutions that might serve as their domestic opponents' power bases. As leaders in authoritarian settings achieve "stability" via the dispersal of private goods among a small selectorate, little investment in public goods takes place (Escriba-Folch, Boehmelt, and Pilster 2020). Due to this lack of institution-building and public goods provision, the regime depends increasingly on a small set of supporters. The weak legitimacy of such regimes makes their hold on power tenuous and forces them to invest in ever more repressive measures. Weak institutions and weak legitimacy are causes of concern for external actors worried about maintaining "stability" and preventing "instability" and associated "uncertainty." However, the smaller a leader's winning coalition is, the less likely they are to initiate democratization as a way of bolstering their legitimacy. This is because rulers with large winning coalitions have, by definition, a greater chance of staying in power. In the end, Western policies appear stuck in their attachment to Arab regimes which, as "sinkholes of security" (Teti, Abbott, and Cavatorta 2018), are not stable, they just give the appearance of it.

Here, we see how authoritarianism with its claim to stability so cherished by realism's reification of the state exacerbates the problem of fear and uncertainty. While highly personalized regimes are less coup-prone than other types of authoritarian governments (and thus – considering Western obsession with supposed stability – offer greater predictability), once the leader departs from office, such types of regimes produce greater turmoil (Song 2022). Grundholm (2020) found that personalization increases the likelihood of outsider challenges as insider challenges are effectively prevented by personalist coup-proofing strategies. Irregular leader exits are particularly likely when highly personalized regimes meet mass mobilization (as happened during the Arab Spring). In the end, Western support for authoritarian regimes increases the chances of an anti-Western backlash once regime change occurs (Ratner 2009). The predicament of realist myopia is summed up in Ratner's (2009: 23) words:

> There is no doubt that the strategy of supporting current nondemocratic regimes in the likes of Saudi Arabia and Egypt provides vital short-term gains for the United States and must therefore be strongly considered. This research suggests, however, that such actions bring them considerable risk and lost opportunity.

The potential ramifications of political changes increase further via the various regimes' suppression of any type of moderate political opposition. As non-violent political transformations depend on the cooperation of moderates among the representatives of the old regime and moderates in the opposition, the targeting of opposition moderates reduces the chances of non-violent political transformations. Authoritarian political regimes in the region thus know that the suppression of moderate opposition increases their bargaining position vis-à-vis Western actors as violence and "chaos" emerge as the only alternatives to authoritarian "stability." Fareed Zakaria summed up the pre-Arab Spring conventional wisdom among Western political and security elites: "The Arab rulers of the Middle East are autocratic, corrupt, and heavy-handed. But they are still more liberal, tolerant, and pluralistic than those who would likely replace them" (Zakaria 2004: 9).

3 Roads not taken: Western policy postures during the critical juncture of the Arab Spring

With US interests in the region remaining rather constant (Berger 2007), questions arose at the onset of the Arab Spring over whether the Obama doctrine marked a critical juncture pointing toward the end of US regional or global hegemony (Gerges 2013) or whether it merely constituted an attempt to address the perceived over-extension of the Bush era (Brands 2017). Quero and Dessi (2021) saw a longer trend in the US withdrawal from the region, which had begun well before the Bush administration's disastrous decision to invade Iraq. For Quero and Dessi (2021), the Bush administration then added uncertainty over the (pro-

or anti-status quo) direction of involvement. This new unpredictability regarding the extent and direction of US involvement in the region might have created a "space of uncertainty" during the critical juncture of the Arab Spring, where regional actors could not have been confident in their assessment of US commitment to existing political structures and regimes. Thus, it might have looked as if the opportunity for a genuine turning point in US–Arab relations existed. However, such realist narratives centering on US behavior and interstate relations are problematic as far as they suggest variance where little variance exists. For instance, out of the nineteen cases that Quero and Dessi (2021) examine in their assessment of changes in the extent and direction of US policies toward the region, only six point in the direction of changes to the regional status quo. Out of these six cases, three cases relate to prominent Arab Spring countries such as Tunisia, Egypt, and Bahrain, where the US was mostly reacting to developments on the ground, rather than shaping them. Even in Libya, other countries such as the UK and France took the lead. The Joint Comprehensive Plan of Action with Iran did offer an example of US involvement and had the potential for a considerable long-term change in US policies and regional constellations but was short-lived. That leaves only the 2003 Iraq war as the sole direct involvement in pursuing change with the potential to be regarded as a critical juncture in the US posture. Problematically from the perspective of democratization in the region, it was this aberration that tarnished any effort at assisting political change as being part of a set of policies that were seen as "aggressive, paternalistic, neo-imperialist, or a combination of the three" (Burnell and Schlumberger 2010: 2).

The 2003 Iraq war offers an interesting case regarding the realist view of authoritarianism in the region. Leading neo-realists such as Mearsheimer and Walt (2003) strongly criticized the war as unnecessary and contrary to US security interests. Classical realists such as Hans Morgenthau had earlier warned in the context of the Vietnam War about the dangers of a moralizing foreign policy that ends up causing so much suffering that it becomes immoral itself and demanded that US democracy promotion should, therefore, be limited to the US representing an example of a successful democracy that offers genuine equal freedom to all (Reichwein 2021). However, from a liberal perspective, realist proclamations about liberal culpability for the US invasion of Iraq were misplaced as democracy promotion was never a seriously pursued goal (author conversations in Washington, D.C., January to July 2003; Deudney & Ikenberry 2017), and proponents of the war simply misrepresented liberal democratic peace theory in their arguments (Ish-Shalom 2008).

Either way, while the war in Iraq still looms large in public and political memory, the Obama administration's approach to the Arab Spring was the management of risk: "The goal was to avoid errors" (Schulhofer-Wohl 2021: 530). Or, in a more profane expression of the same sentiment: "Don't do stupid shit" (Rees 2021). Politically, there was little to be gained through increased involvement in the region. Obama had won the 2008 election on the promise of ending the US presence in Iraq as well as a leaner and meaner counterterrorism operation that addressed more effectively the threat posed by transnational terrorist groups such as al-Qaeda (Berger 2009). His positions were very much in line with US public opinion that favored reduced exposure to the region's conflicts but was quite willing to support military counterterrorism measures, when necessary, as in the case of al-Qaeda and later the so-called Islamic State of Iraq and Syria (ISIS) (Schulhofer-Wohl 2021). Obama's cautious approach also became evident in his reaction to Assad's brutal repression of the Syrian people. In August 2012, Obama warned the Syrian regime against the use of chemical weapons. One year later, Obama reacted to Assad's use of chemical weapons against civilians living in the Damascus suburb of Ghouta by calling for a Congressional authorization to use force that he expected not to receive (Schulhofer-Wohl 2021).

Lantis's (2021) analysis of advocacy coalitions helps us understand further the Obama administration's approach. Differentiating between foreign policy change, continuity, and "purposeful non-change," he seeks to explain how advocacy coalitions shape foreign policy behavior. With prospect theory teaching us that potential losses weigh more than potential gains, the losses from the status quo must be so evident that the argument in favor of prospective gains stands any chance of success. Change or non-change is thus also a reflection of the abovementioned successes and failures in framing and the distribution of interests in the legislative arena (see Berger 2012 for a discussion of the drivers of Congressional support for change and continuity in US policies toward Arab countries). By seeing the region as beyond redemption, risky endeavors, which would match the critical juncture at the people's level with corresponding changes at the policy level, appear futile and thus irrational. However, by behaving in this less risky manner, the Obama administration and the governments of other Western countries helped put forward the depiction of the region as stale and eternally conflict prone.

One case in point was the US approach to Egypt's short-lived experiment with democracy. As a heavily indebted country, Egypt was and is particularly vulnerable to foreign pressure (Brownlee 2012). The extent to which the West did have leverage, in this case, comes to light – quite ironically – in Stephen Walt's (2011) realist argument in favor of the Obama administration disassociating itself from the Mubarak regime. Walt did not put forth an argument based on the intrinsic value of democracy in Egypt, but rather, on the failure of the Mubarak regime to keep its side of the strategic bargain. For a long time, Egypt was a poster boy for how the perceived geopolitical importance of the region allowed regional actors to instrumentalize support from external actors to create and support (authoritarian) state structures (Brownlee 2012). By 2011, for Walt, the two main arguments in favor of close relations with the Egyptian regime could no longer survive closer scrutiny. Overflight rights appeared less valuable in times of a decrease in the US footprint in the region and in light of alternative routes. Israel's security does not depend on Egyptian cooperation anymore, if anything, the reverse is true. In addition, the close relationship with the Mubarak regime made the US a target of transnational terrorist groups like al-Qaeda (Walt 2011; on this last issue, see also Berger 2007 and Berger 2014a). In this regard, the opening of the political system and the increase in the number of beneficiaries of close relations with the US might have reduced the pool of anti-Western sentiment, which could be exploited by radical groups (Lake 2013: 108). While Mubarak was eventually forced from power, the Egyptian military re-established itself as the central political actor when it launched a coup in 2013 against the democratically elected government of Mohamed Morsi of the Muslim Brotherhood-affiliated Freedom and Justice Party. It is noteworthy that the brutal repression by the new regime, including the massacre of almost one thousand protesters at Rabaa Square in Cairo, was not seen more widely through the lens of the 1989 Tiananmen Square massacre in China. Instead, the US government went to great lengths to avoid the use of the term "coup" in 2013 as this would have triggered a law banning all foreign aid to the country. The new regime could get away with it because it cleverly instrumentalized the realist fear of the consequences of regime change. As Egypt's new ruler Abdel Fattah al-Sisi warned his Western audiences, "(if) this country fails, the whole region will slide into a cycle of anarchy that will present a grave danger to all countries in this region, including Israel, and would extend to Europe" (quoted in Weymouth 2015). Here we see how authoritarian Arab regimes cleverly play on what Debrix (2003: 180) had earlier described as "Orientalist melancholy" as a central part of what he labeled "tabloid realism."

The EU's policy posture was no more encouraging. The idea of the EU as a normative power has long been challenged by those who – in line with realist analysis – saw European foreign and security policies as determined by systemic factors highlighted by systemic realism (Hyde-Price 2006). For realist skeptics of the notion of the EU as a "normative power," the EU's policies toward its wider neighborhood thus did not constitute more than an attempt at "milieu shaping" by the EU's largest individual powers (Hyde-Price 2006: 222). This depiction fits with descriptions of the EU as pursuing a narrow set of security interests that are closely aligned with the stability of authoritarian governance in the Arab world (Cavatorta et al. 2008; Cavatorta and Rivetti 2014). Even before the Arab Spring, the EU's gradualist approach allowed local actors to derail reform initiatives via selection entry, the setting of conditions, and the simulation of reform (Malmvig

2014). Cavatorta et al. (2008) challenged the notion that the pre-Arab Spring's lack of success in EU democracy promotion was due to tensions between member countries, institutional inefficiencies, or robust resistance among target countries. Instead, they argue that the EU had never really been interested in promoting democracy in the first instance (ibid). While the depiction of security as a precondition for development in the 2003 EU security strategy does sound intuitive to many observers, it opened the door to exactly those realist-inspired, "security-first" approaches that have dominated EU strategies (Crawford and Karcaska 2019) – particular in light of such transnational challenges such as migration and terrorism.

In their reluctance to consider positive and negative conditionality seriously in dealing with authoritarian leaders who eliminate any non-violent political opposition aggressively in their countries, Western policies constitute a "missing link" in the region's ongoing political crisis (Berger 2011). A crude reading of the modernization school of democratization serves as an excuse for the lack of more proactive measures in support of the region's human rights activists and political reformers. Arab elites could then rely on their manipulation of the rules of the political game to silence political opposition in a manner that keeps Western criticism at a tolerable level. One such case in point is the ability of the Jordanian regime to make opposition parties appear either menacing or incompetent, with the only conclusion to be drawn for international donors to continue to support the regime (Martínez 2017).

In 2011, it appeared as if the EU and its representatives had suddenly understood the self-defeating nature of the realist recipe for stability. The EU commission, for instance, recognized the "importance of ensuring human rights, rule of law, and inclusive democracy to avoid alienating communities and creating conditions of insecurity" (quoted in Dandashly 2018: 64). Shortly after the fall of Ben Ali and Mubarak, Štefan Füle (2011), the European Commissioner for Enlargement and Neighbourhood Policy, admitted that

> Europe was not vocal enough in defending human rights and local democratic forces in the region. Too many of us fell prey to the assumption that authoritarian regimes were a guarantee of stability in the region. This was not even Realpolitik. It was, at best, short-termism – and the kind of short-termism that makes the long-term ever more difficult to build.

In critical junctures such as the Arab Spring, credible pro-democracy commitment from the US and EU can make a difference. It determines which options local actors can choose from and how attractive such options are (Freyburg and Richter 2015). Local actors will decide in favor of democratization if democracy promotion is "credible." Here, the perception of US and EU policies suffered from a long history of high levels of military and security aid compared with aid directly targeted at democracy promotion (Burness and Schlumberger 2010). Before the Arab Spring, less than 10% of assistance distributed via the Euro-Mediterranean Partnership (EMP) or the US Agency for International Development went to democracy programs (Huber 2013: 8). In addition, the benefits of democratization must be clear and outweigh the benefits offered by counter-democratic competitors. Bueno de Mesquita and Smith (2016) showed that the cost-effectiveness of foreign aid decreases, the larger the number of (potential) donors. In other words, a donor country must invest more foreign aid and expect less in return when other countries also offer aid to the receiving country. In the end, the payoffs for democratization which Western actors were willing to offer were too insignificant compared to alternative support from authoritarian regimes and to the threat of a fall from office for highly authoritarian rulers (Lake 2013).

Regime calculations are not only impacted by considerations about incentives and costs for compliance, costs of adjustment, and the credibility of prospective gains, but also by considerations about the perceived costs of non-compliance (Burnell and Schlumberger 2010: 7). The critical juncture index developed by Boogaerts, Portela, and Drieskens (2016) aims to consider the degree, speed, and origin of the change in Western policies. Differentiating between changes in the level and nature of policy instruments, they argue that the main change from an EU perspective came from the post-Arab Spring willingness to use sanctions in support of democracy. Previously, the EU only used sanctions in support of strategic considerations such as fighting terrorism or preventing the spread of weapons of mass destruction. Huber (2013) saw a slight change post-2011 toward different targets in terms of greater engagement with civil society and a greater focus on bilateral types of democracy assistance and conditionality. At the same time, the EU never utilized the "essential element" clause of the EMP, which stipulated that respect for democracy and human rights – which did not occur – was a precondition for any type of cooperation (Huber 2013: 7).

Contrary to the political conventional wisdom, targeted sanctions can be effective. While the threat of a sanction to further democracy is only successful in 10% of cases, imposed sanctions do increase levels of democracy in the targeted country on average (Von Soest and Wahmann 2015). The effect of positive conditionality heavily depends on the interest of the regime in question (Dandashly 2018). In the case of deeply entrenched authoritarian regimes, it is highly unlikely that such conditionality can somehow move the calculation toward a political opening that risks their fall from power. However, this calculation might be more relevant in situations such as post-2011 Tunisia, where representatives of the old order had been weakened significantly. In contexts where no genuine willingness to even contemplate political reform exists, the EU's "rhetorical bluff packages"

(Freyburg and Richter 2015) are easily instrumentalized by supporters of the authoritarian status quo.

The minimalist, narrowly civil liberties-focused democracy initiatives, which the EU championed, also did not match the aspirations of the citizens of Arab countries (Abbott and Teti 2022). They prefer instead a "thicker" social democracy, which addresses social inequality and the dramatically uneven distribution of life chances. Abbott and Teti (2022), thus, speak of the EU's policy blindness when it comes to (not) recognizing the root causes of the Arab Spring. Indeed, a considerable number of observers (Hollis 2012) saw the EU as having inadvertently brought about the Arab Spring protests by pursuing economic policies vis-à-vis North Africa that impoverished people and thus drove them to protest. Cavatorta and Rivetti (2014) similarly point out that the Arab Spring highlighted a link between economic liberalization and political reform, but not in the form Western policymakers had intended. Instead of economic liberalization creating a strong middle class that would then demand democracy and function as its main guardian once established, economic liberalization in an authoritarian context exacerbated social crises. While critics such as Abbott and Teti (2022) see the problem in too much market economy, the suffocation of private entrepreneurship in political and economic systems geared toward enriching the regime's core set of supporters could also mean that a genuine market economy does not even exist in the first instance (Roll and Batsi 2021).

4 Post-Arab Spring realist panic and Western policies toward a newly entrenched authoritarianism

While the non-violent demands for political reform of the early Arab Spring had the potential to produce a turning point in Western narratives about the region, the re-emergence of violent Islamism and escalating civil wars from Libya, to Yemen and Syria seemed to confirm Orientalist tropes about the supposedly never-changing nature of the region and the dangers which "tabloid realists" such as Kaplan, Mearsheimer, and Huntington (Debrix 2003: 161) had already warned about a decade earlier. Indeed, the seeming confirmation of Huntington's empirically and morally problematic claims about Islam's supposed "bloody borders" and "innards" in his prediction of a "clash of civilizations" gave new life to right-wing populism in much of the Western world (Haynes 2019).

It is quite telling that the Arab Spring ended up being discussed as a possible critical juncture not so much in the field of democratization studies as in the field of terrorism studies regarding the unprecedented surge in terrorist activity, the rise of ISIS as an unprecedented multifaceted terrorist actor, and the re-emergence of foreign fighters as a global concern (Schumacher 2021). Whether or not these developments are, indeed, without precedent and therefore, require a fundamental rethinking of terrorism studies is open for debate, but what this perspective does reveal is the tendency of Western analysis to understand the region in terms of disorder, upheaval, and associated threats to Western security interests. Brands (2017: 119) offers a take on Obama's presidency that combines realist myopia with Orientalist essentialism when he noted that "(s)imply put, 2016 was not 2009 anymore – the global scene had become considerably more disordered since Obama arrived. The Middle East was in chaos."

The aftermath of the Arab Spring was, thus, not dominated anymore by optimistic liberal references to 1989, but by pessimistic realist references to the possible end of the post-World War I regional system. A century ago, a critical juncture had become a turning point in the region's political development when the end of the Ottoman Empire gave rise to the states as we know them today (Fawcett 2017). With ISIS raising its banner across the region, the specter of the disappearance or a redrawing of borders loomed. In Europe, Nathalie Tocci, Special Advisor to EU High Representatives Federica Mogherini and Josep Borrell, even warned of the dangers of the "end of Sykes-Picot," the secret British–French agreement on post-World War I spheres of influence, which marked the beginning of the contours of the regional state system. While such concerns always appeared hysterically overblown given the regional state system's ability to fend off challengers to the status quo (Berger 2014b), they are relevant for this paper's overall argument in at least two dimensions. First, as mentioned above, critical junctures are moments where a range of future directions is, at least theoretically, feasible. In the case of the Arab Spring, we can witness how relevant actors strategically employed the most threatening scenario to close the discursive space so that major change becomes unthinkable. In other words, the very notion of living in or experiencing a critical juncture helps prevent the occurrence of a turning point. As Lake put it (2013: 107), "States loyal to the United States are preferred to regimes, however democratic, that are likely to resist its authority in the future. Plus ça change, plus c'est la même chose."

Second, we see a close link between Orientalism and realism and the associated preference for authoritarianism. Fear over the uncertainty associated with political change leads to a realist preference for the political status quo (Gegout 2018). Orientalist tropes about the "true" nature of regional politics exacerbate fear over the uncertainty associated with possible new pathways and thus tilt the scale even further toward the status quo. Fawcett (2017) rightly criticizes the notion of the "artificiality" of the MENA state system. In such narratives that leave little scope for imagining anything other than either "authoritarian stability" or "chaos," the iron lid of an "alien" state system must be preserved at all costs, even by "hard" or "fierce" (Ayubi 1995) human rights destroying states if necessary. As Jamal (2022: 17) summed it up:

> Unfortunately, normalized justifications for these policies continue to reinforce existing essentialist, orientalist, and racialized depictions of Arabs and Muslims as extremists and lacking the civilized norms that purportedly emerged only in Western civilizations. Keeping volatile Arabs under lock and key ensures long-term regional stability.

As was the case with the abovementioned US frames and policies, the EU also toned down the rhetoric of the early Arab Spring. The rise of ISIS and the failure of the Muslim Brotherhood to govern effectively and in line with minimum democratic standards pushed the EU toward favoring stability once again (Dandashly 2018). Koch (2019) describes the 2016 EU Global Strategy, for instance, as realist in the downgrading of the EU's ability to seek or even assist political transformations abroad and in its elevation of the need to deal with perceived security threats. Just as after 9/11, the EU pursued a set of foreign policy interests informed by a realist-themed, threat-based analysis. Here, perceptions of the Arab world's security environment suffered from the coincidence of the "failure" of the Arab Spring with Russia's occupation of parts of Ukraine and Brexit, which could both appear as constituting critical junctures in the EU's development and foreign policies in their own right. The EU's Global Strategy itself thus admitted in 2016 to "an existential crisis, within and beyond the EU" (quoted in Pishchikova and Piras 2017: 112). Quite tellingly, Nathalie Tocci (2014: 7), the strategy's main author, herself called for "down-to-earth realism" when dealing with an "arc of instability" in Europe's "turbulent backyard." While the critical juncture of the Arab Spring had offered Europe the chance to rethink its policies, the Tocci quote suggests that the EU became even less ambitious than before. The EU's return to the status quo of a security-first approach as opposed to a bolder, more transformative agenda is encapsulated here:

> What this suggests is that the EU may need to recalibrate its goals for the time being, setting objectives within its reach. Focusing on reducing ungoverned spaces, reducing polarization within and between states, reducing human suffering, and reducing extremism may appear unambitious when compared to the classic "promotion of democracy, human rights, and good governance" agenda. But it is probably a more realistic, and therefore more effective, route to reverse current trends and allow for the possibility of reverting to the classic "transformation agenda" in the future (Tocci 2014: 5).

Tocci represents the type of argument that says that the critical juncture is potentially so "critical" in terms of allowing a turning point toward a momentous change with implications so severe that the focus needs to be calibrated in such a way that new pathways that opened during the critical juncture should not be pursued. Interestingly, Tocci's (2014: 3) argument that the EU was too demanding of Ukraine in terms of political reform and thus, drove Ukraine "into the arms of Russia" has not aged well. It shows yet again the poverty of these types of realist thinking that consider promoting democracy abroad a normative luxury that might even interfere negatively with preferences for stability.

Regimes that have learned that their relevance to outside actors is linked to their ability to manage and survive "crises" can only hope that these perceived crises continue to exist. In that sense, realism becomes a self-serving ideology of conflict by helping to mask concern for regime security as concern for national security. However, in a region full of sclerotic regimes, the wellbeing of the nation and the wellbeing of the ruling elite are not the same. The image of an ever-threatening Arab world is something that authoritarian rulers know to exploit for their own benefit. The 2016 "migration crisis" demonstrated how, in the case of irregular migration in particular, the sending country has more power over the receiving country as compared to regular migration where the receiving country has more power over the sending country (Voelkel 2020). As part of their authoritarian adaptation to the challenges posed by the Arab Spring, these regimes revised their migration policies so that they could cater to Europe's emphasis on preventing irregular migration. This overall adaptation process received considerable support from the EU (Seeberg and Voelkel 2022). It also tied Europe to the authoritarian regimes' interest in effective security services. For Europe, these meant reduced migration, for the Arab regimes, these meant strengthening a central, if not the only (Bellin 2012) pillar of their rule. Migration, thus, offers another example of how the realist focus on external threats interlinks with the interests of authoritarian regimes in the region. Here again – as is the case with violent and non-violent Islamism – authoritarian regimes have honed their ability to shape narratives and perceptions of threat. Thus, they use the issue of irregular migration as a bargaining chip: "In consequence, the core interest of migration policies is not necessarily about the handling and wellbeing of migrants themselves, but more about image creation and international support" (Voelkel 2020: 4). The authoritarian instrumentalization of Orientalist racism is encapsulated in the infamous warning from Libya's previous dictator Gadhafi that if he were not to receive appropriate levels of funding from Europe for preventing migrants from crossing the Mediterranean, he would "turn Europe black" (quoted in Voelkel 2020: 5). Migration policies in line with European concerns help generate funds and other resources for authoritarian regimes, which they can then use to buy off the selectorate that keeps them in power (Voelkel 2020). The Egyptian military, for instance, uses its (un)willingness and (in)ability to effectively close the country's northern coast as a direct signal to Europe about how closely the Egyptian military's interests are tied to European political leaders' concerns about migration (Voelkel 2020: 14). Quite ironically, the policy area of migration, thus, does offer for some observers (Seeberg and Voelkel 2022) an example of a turning point when it comes to Western relations with North African governments from Morocco to Tunisia and Egypt, but not in the direction of greater Western pressure to democratize, but toward an ever-greater threat-based realist accommodation of upgraded authoritarian governance.

5 Conclusion

From today's perspective, the Arab Spring constituted a critical juncture not so much in terms of setting the region on a path toward democracy, but in helping bring about a new type of authoritarianism.

> The new forms of authoritarianism in countries such as Egypt, the renegotiation of constitutional terms in monarchies such as Morocco and Jordan, or the survival through extreme violence in countries such as Bahrain and Syria, produced very different regimes than those which existed in the late 2000s. Sisi's Egypt is not Mubarak's Egypt, just as Mohammad bin Salman's Saudi Arabia is not King Abdullah's Saudi Arabia. Minimizing the truly disruptive power of the 2011 protests does no more to advance political science understanding of regional politics than did exaggerating their transformative potential (Lynch 2021: 86).

It would be foolish, of course, to lay the lack of a turning point toward greater democracy in the region only at the feet of Western governments. Looking at the historic durability of a large share of dynastic systems in the region, Brownlee, Masoud, and Reynolds (2013: 43) point out that "(m)onarchies that have ruled for the better part of 250 years in Saudi Arabia, 400 in Morocco, or 100 in Jordan, and gathered into their hands all the threads of power and privilege, will not go quietly," yet there were many cases, such as Tunisia and Egypt, where the West did have leverage.

In many ways, realist-inspired Western policies during the Arab Spring showed a stark contrast between the EU's identity and self-perception as a normative power and the US as the "world's leading democracy" and their respective status quo actions. The absence of a turning point lies in the paths that external actors have not pursued and the Arab Spring, therefore, offers an example of a critical juncture where concerns about the specific nature of possible new pathways helped prevent a genuine turning point in policies from emerging. Through their support for authoritarian leaders and for economic policies that neither promote genuine development nor improve standards of living, external actors helped undermine the prospects of democracy. These low (and diminishing) prospects for democracy then reinforce the notion that democracy does not work in the region. The corresponding policies of Western actors, however, contribute directly to the underlying drivers of instability in the region and the possibility of further critical junctures occurring in the future. Demand for policies and polities that reflect dignity will continue to present considerable challenges to the legitimacy of authoritarian regimes (Fawcett 2017). The prospect for further critical junctures that open the path to a genuine change in the direction of political development across the Arab world is, thus, very real. The courage of Arab women and men in tackling decades of state terror and authoritarian manipulation of politics and society made their agency and dignity visible to each other and the outside world. In that sense, the turning point emerging out of the critical juncture of the Arab Spring lies not so much in the policies of Western democracies, but in the fact that women and men across the region had put ideas into action. The genie of freedom is out of the bottle.

References

Abbott, Pamela & Andrea Teti. 2022. Strangers in plain sight: conceptions of democracy in EU Neighbourhood Policy and public opinion across North Africa. *The Journal of North African Studies* 27(4). 691–713.

Ayubi, Nazih. 1995. *Overstating the Arab State: Politics and Society in the Middle East.* London: IB Tauris.

Bank, André & Jan Busse. 2021. MENA political science research a decade after the Arab uprisings: Facing the facts on tremulous grounds. *Mediterranean Politics* 26(5). 539–562.

Bellin, Eva. 2012. Reconsidering the Robustness of Authoritarianism in the Middle East: Lessons from the Arab Spring. *Comparative Politics* 44(2). 127–149.

Berger, Lars. 2014a. Foreign policies or culture: What shapes Muslim public opinion on political violence against the United States? *Journal of Peace Research* 51(6). 782–796.

Berger, Lars. 2014b. "Written evidence on situation in Iraq and Syria, submitted to UK House of Commons Committee on Defence." https://eprints.whiterose.ac.uk/81960/ (accessed 14 March 2023).

Berger, Lars. 2012. Guns, Butter, and Human Rights – The Congressional Politics of U.S. Aid to Egypt. *American Politics Research* 40(4). 603–635.

Berger, Lars. 2011. The Missing Link? US Policy and the International Dimensions of Failed Democratic Transitions in the Arab World. *Political Studies* 59(1). 38–55.

Berger, Lars. 2009. Between New Hopes and Old Realities – The Obama Administration and the Middle East. *Orient* 50(2). 22–35.

Berger, Lars. 2007. *Die USA und der islamistische Terrorismus. Herausforderungen im Nahen und Mittleren Osten.* Paderborn: Schoeningh.

Boerzel, Tanja A., Assem Dandashly & Thomas Risse. 2015. The EU, External Actors, and the Arabellions: Much Ado About (Almost) Nothing. *Journal of European Integration* 37(1). 135–153.

Boogaerts, Andreas, Portela, Clara & Edith Drieskens. 2016. One Swallow Does Not Make Spring: A Critical Juncture Perspective on the EU Sanctions in Response to the Arab Spring. *Mediterranean Politics* 21(2). 205–225.

Brands, Hal. 2017. Barack Obama and the Dilemmas of American Grand Strategy. *The Washington Quarterly* 39(4). 101–125.

Brownlee, Jason, Masoud, Tarek & Andrew Reynolds. 2013. Tracking the Arab Spring: Why the Modest Harvest? *Journal of Democracy* 24(4). 29–44.

Brownlee, Jason. 2012. *Democracy Prevention. The Politics of the U.S.-Egyptian alliance*. Cambridge: Cambridge University Press.

Burnell, Peter & Oliver Schlumberger. 2010. Promoting democracy – promoting autocracy? International politics and national political regimes. *Contemporary Politics* 16(1). 1–15.

Bueno de Mesquita, Bruce & Alastair Smith. 2016. Competition and Collaboration in Aid-for-Policy Deals, *International Studies Quarterly* 60(3). 413–426.

Capoccia, Giovanni & R. Daniel Kelemen. 2007. The Study of Critical Junctures: Theory, Narrative, and Counterfactuals in Historical Institutionalism. *World Politics* 59(3). 341–369.

Cavatorta, Francesco & Paola Rivetti. 2014. EU–MENA Relations from the Barcelona Process to the Arab Uprisings: A New Research Agenda. *Journal of European Integration* 36(6). 619–625.

Cavatorta, Francesco, Raj S. Chari, Sylvia Kritzinger, & Arantza Gomez Arana. 2008. EU External Policy-Making and The Case of Morocco: 'Realistically' Dealing with Authoritarianism? *European Foreign Affairs Review* 13(3). 357–376.

Crawford, Gordon & Simonida Kacarska. 2019. Aid sanctions and political conditionality: Continuity and change. *Journal of International Relations and Development* 22(1). 184–214.

Dandashly, Assem. 2018. EU democracy promotion and the dominance of the security–stability nexus. *Mediterranean Politics* 23(1). 62–82.

David, Steven R. 1991. Explaining Third World Alignment. *World Politics* 43(2). 233–256.

Debrix, François. 2003. Tabloid realism and the revival of American security culture. *Geopolitics* 8(3). 151–190.

Desch, Michael C. 2008. America's Liberal Illiberalism: The Ideological Origins of Overreaction in U.S. Foreign Policy. *International Security* 32(3). 7–43.

Deudney, Daniel & John Ikenberry. 2017. Realism, Liberalism, and the Iraq War. *Survival* 59(4). 7–26

Escriba-Folch, Abel, Boehmelt, Tobias & Ulrich Pilster. 2020. Authoritarian regimes and civil–military relations: Explaining counterbalancing in autocracies. *Conflict Management and Peace Science* 37(5). 559–579.

Fawcett, Louise. 2017. States and sovereignty in the Middle East: myths and realities, *International Affairs* 93(4). 789–807.

Freyburg, Tina & Solveig Richter. 2015. Local actors in the driver's seat: Transatlantic democracy promotion under regime competition in the Arab world. *Democratization* 22(3). 496–518.

Füle, Štefan. 2011. "Speech on the recent events in North Africa". Committee on Foreign Affairs (AFET), European Parliament Brussels 28 February. https://ec.europa.eu/commission/press corner/detail/en/SPEECH_11_130 (accessed 23 February 2023).

Gause, F. Gregory. 2014. "Beyond sectarianism: The new Middle East cold war". Brookings Doha Center Analysis Paper 11, July. https://www.brookings.edu/wp-content/uploads/2016/06/en glish-pdf-1.pdf (accessed 14 March 2023).

Gegout, Catherine. 2018. Realism, Neocolonialism and European Military Intervention in Africa. In Roberto Belloni, Paul Viotti & Vincent della Sala (eds.), *Fear and Uncertainty in Europe: The Return to Realism?*, 265–288. Cham: Palgrave Macmillan.

Gerges, Fawaz. 2013. The Obama approach to the Middle East: the end of America's moment? *International Affairs* 89(2). 299–323.

Grundholm, Alexander Taaning. 2020. Taking it personal? Investigating regime personalization as an autocratic survival strategy. *Democratization* 27(5). 797–815.

Haynes, Jeffrey. 2019. Introduction: The "Clash of Civilizations" and Relations between the West and the Muslim World. *The Review of Faith & International Affairs* 17(1). 1–10.

Hollis, Rosemary. 2012. No friend of democratization: Europe's role in the genesis of the Arab Spring. *International Affairs* 88(1). 81–94.

Huber, Daniela. 2013. US and EU Human Rights and Democracy Promotion since the Arab Spring. Rethinking its Content, Targets, and Instruments. *The International Spectator: Italian Journal of International Affairs* 48(3). 98–112.

Hyde-Price, Adrian. 2006. 'Normative' power Europe: a realist critique. *Journal of European Public Policy* 13(2). 217–234.

Ish-Shalom, Piki. 2008. Theorization, Harm, and the Democratic Imperative: Lessons from the Politicization of the Democratic-Peace Thesis. *International Studies Review* 10(4). 680–692.

Jamal, Amaney. 2022. Is there Room for "Bread, Dignity, and Freedom" in U.S. Foreign Policy towards the Arab World? New America Foundation, *Equity and Racial Justice: Where Do They Fit in a National Security Strategy?* 17–19. https://www.newamerica.org/political-reform/reports/equity-and-racial-justice-where-do-they-fit-in-a-national-security-strategy/is-there-room-for-bread-dignity-and-freedom-in-us-foreign-policy-towards-the-arab-world-by-amaney-jamal (accessed 14 March 2023).

Kemp, Geoffrey. 2002. Arcs of Instability. *Naval War College Review* 55(3). Article 1.

Koch, Christian. 2019. EU policy in the Middle East. Unfulfilled aspirations. In Shahram Akbarzadeh (ed.), *Routledge Handbook of International Relations in the Middle East*, 222–236. London: Routledge.

Lake, David A. 2013. Legitimating Power: The Domestic Politics of U.S. International Hierarchy. *International Security* 38(2). 74–111.

Lantis, Jeffrey S. 2021. Advocacy Coalitions and Foreign Policy Change: Understanding US Responses to the Syrian Civil War. *Journal of Global Security Studies* 6(1).

Lynch, Marc. 2021. Taking stock of MENA political science after the uprisings. *Mediterranean Politics* 26(5). 682–695.

Malmvig, Helle. 2014. Free Us from Power: Governmentality, Counter-conduct, and Simulation in European Democracy and Reform Promotion in the Arab World. *International Political Sociology* 8(3). 293–310.

Martínez, José Ciro. 2017. Jordan's self-fulfilling prophecy: the production of feeble political parties and the perceived perils of democracy. *British Journal of Middle Eastern Studies* 44(3). 356–372.

Mearsheimer, John & Stephen Walt. 2003. An Unnecessary War. *Foreign Policy* 134. 51–59.

Miller, Benjamin. 2010. Contrasting Explanations for Peace: Realism vs. Liberalism in Europe and the Middle East. *Contemporary Security Policy* 31(1). 134–164.

Pishchikova, Kateryna & Elisa Piras. 2017. The European Union Global Strategy: What Kind of Foreign Policy Identity? *The International Spectator* 52(3). 103–120.

Quero, Jordi & Andrea Dessi. 2021. Unpredictability in US Foreign Policy and the Regional Order in the Middle East: Reacting vis-à-vis a Volatile External Security-Provider. *British Journal of Middle Eastern Studies* 48(2). 311–30.

Rathbun, Brian C. 2007. Uncertain about Uncertainty: Understanding the Multiple Meanings of a Crucial Concept in International Relations Theory. *International Studies Quarterly* 51(3). 533–557.

Ratner, Ely. 2009. Reaping What You Sow: Democratic Transitions and Foreign Policy Realignment. *Journal of Conflict Resolution* 53(3). 390–418.

Rees, Morgan Thomas. 2021. Obama and the use of force: a discursive institutionalist analysis of Libya and Syria. *International Relations* 36(3). 382–402.

Reichwein, Alexander. 2021. Neoclassical Realism and Statecraft: Toward a Normative Foreign Policy Theory. *International Studies Review* 23(1). 284–287.

Roll, Stephan & Salima Batsi. 2021. More than Window-Dressing: On the Credibility of Public Statistics from Al-Sisi's Egypt. *Orient XXI*, 27 January. https://orientxxi.info/magazine/more-than-window-dressing-on-the-credibility-of-public-statistics-from-al-sisi,5330 (accessed 14 March 2023).

Salloukh, Bassel F. 2017. Overlapping Contests and Middle East International Relations: The Return of the Weak Arab State. *Political Science and Politics* 50(3). 660–663.

Schulhofer-Wohl, Jonah. 2021. The Obama Administration and Civil War in Syria, 2011–2016: US presidential foreign policy making as political risk management. *Journal of Transatlantic Studies* 19(4). 517–547.

Schumacher, Michael J. 2021. Critical junctures in terrorism studies: the Arab Spring and the new twenty-first century security environment. *Critical Terrorism Studies* 14(4). 470–473.

Seeberg, Peter & Jan Claudius Völkel. 2022. Introduction: Arab responses to EU foreign and security policy incentives: Perspectives on migration diplomacy and institutionalized flexibility in the Arab Mediterranean turned upside down. *Mediterranean Politics*. 27(2). 135–147.

Solingen, Etel. 2007. Pax Asiatica versus Bella Levantina: The Foundations of War and Peace in East Asia and the Middle East. *American Political Science Review* 101(4). 757–780.

Song, Wonjun. 2022. Dictators, personalized security forces, and coups. *International Interactions* 48(2). 204–232.

Teti, Andrea, Abbott, Pamela & Francesco Cavatorta. 2018. *The Arab Uprisings in Egypt, Jordan, and Tunisia: Social, Political and Economic Transformations. Reform and Transition in the Mediterranean.* Cham: Palgrave Macmillan.

Tocci, Nathalie. 2014. *The Neighbourhood Policy is Dead. What's Next for European Foreign Policy Along its Arc of Instability?* IAI Working Papers 14, 16 November.

Voelkel, Jan Claudius. 2020. Fanning fears, winning praise: Egypt's smart play on Europe's apprehension of more undocumented immigration. *Mediterranean Politics* 27(2). 170–191.

Von Soest, Christian & Michael Wahman. 2015. Are democratic sanctions really counterproductive? *Democratization* 22(6). 957–980.

Walt, Stephen. 2011. January 31. A realist policy for Egypt. *Foreign Policy*. https://foreignpolicy.com/2011/01/31/a-realist-policy-for-egypt/

Weymouth, Lally. 2015. March 12. Egyptian President Abdel Fatah al-Sissi, who talks to Netanyahu 'a lot,' says his country is in danger of collapse. *Washington Post*. https://www.washingtonpost.com/opinions/egypts-president-says-he-talks-to-netanyahu-a-lot/2015/03/12/770ef928-c827-11e4-aa1a-86135599fb0f_story.html

Zakaria, Fareed. 2004. Islam, Democracy, and Constitutional Liberalism. *Political Science Quarterly* 119(1). 1–20.

Susanne Fischer

Emerging and fading practices in the era of the internet: A reflexive approach to analysing intelligence professionals' changing practices of data collection

Abstract: Digitalisation is a global development that has penetrated virtually all levels and sectors of society. Drawing on Bourdieu, the chapter asks whether and how the evolution of the internet challenged intelligence professionals' routinised data collection practices in the field of signals intelligence (SIGINT). The chapter advances the continued low level of engagement of Bourdieu-inspired scholars with questions of changing practices and routines. To better grasp the "ebb and flow" of professionals' practices, this chapter distinguishes between fading and emerging practices and describes the moment at which a new practices is realised as breakthrough. Such a breakthrough can be understood as practice-theoretical contribution to scholarly discussion on turning points. This chapter illustrates these considerations empirically using statements data from professionals of the German intelligence service BND collected by the final report of the National Security Agency (NSA)-Investigation Committee. The empirical material indicates that the emergence of new practices in SIGINT challenged the practices of data collection among intelligence professionals in many ways, and it reveals that the BND, with the technical support of the NSA, implemented emerging practices of data collection, which qualifies as breakthrough.

Keywords: Bourdieu, Digitalisation, Intelligence, Intelligence Professionals, Practices

1 Digitalisation and intelligence: Existing practices challenged and disrupted?

Digitalisation refers a development of global extent that is penetrating virtually all levels and sectors of society.[1] To describe the increasing digitalisation, researchers

---

1 I thank the editors (especially Holger Janusch), the participants of the workshop in Wuppertal (2022) as well as Rüdiger Bergien and Ronja Kniep for their critical comments and helpful advice. Any errors in this contribution are my responsibility alone.

Susanne Fischer, Federal University of Public Adminstration.

https://doi.org/10.1515/9783111272900-011

refer to the amount of data generated per day worldwide. In 2020 the 64.2 zettabytes of data were generated, as against only 6.5 zettabytes in 2012 and against an expected increase to 181 zettabytes in 2025 (Statista 2023). These numbers are indeed impressive, but they tell us little about the implications that these developments have for states, especially democracies, including how they run their economies, labour markets, educational systems or international diplomacy and security politics. The latter are at the centre of this chapter, which investigates what the latest dynamics of the digital evolution mean for members of the field of security, or, as Bigo puts it: for the professionals of (in)security (Bigo 2013). Security professionals and security practices are situated at the epicentre of a state's security politics, as they (co)define what might be considered a risk or a (existential) threat (Bigo 2013: 119, 120).

Following the Snowden revelations in 2013, the practices of intelligence services have become interesting to researchers of International relations as those of the police or the armed forces.[2] Routinised practices of data collection and assessment form the nucleus of intelligence agencies' knowledge production. Therefore, it is important to understand the daily practices of security professionals in intelligence and to describe and analyse what takes place if their security practices and routines are confronted with the dynamics of the digital evolution. The phrases "information overload" (MacDonald & Oettinger 2002) and "drowning in data" (Chi 2017: 16) are commonly associated with the challenges that have arisen for intelligence analysts as a result of digital evolution. Within this context, this article seeks to examine what happens to intelligence professionals' routinised practices of data collection. By contrast with the notion that intelligence professionals anticipate, embrace and push developments such as the digital evolution, this article focuses on the questions (1) whether and how the digital evolution challenges intelligence professionals' routinised collection practices, (2) how security professionals interpret these challenges and (3) how these challenges were adressed.

---

[2] The Snowden disclosures of US-American and British programmes triggered an intensive public debate on methods of data collection by intelligence services and intensified academic research in International Relations (IR), International Political Sociology (IPS), Critical Security Studies (CSS) and Surveillance Studies (Baumann et al. 2014; Lahneman 2016; Lyon 2014; Lyon 2017) on the work of intelligence services. Snowden's documents made publicly accessible and visible that digitalisation was altering what has been described as a business that is "as old as history" (Warner 2014: 1). The programmes used by the NSA or the GCHQ (e.g. XKeyscore, Tempora etc.) functioned very differently with respect to the ways in which data were collected or filtered (Greenwald 2014: 140, 160, 221). From this material and the documents that followed parliamentary preoccupation, one could learn that digitalisation plays an important role not only for war fighting and the work of the police but also for the work of intelligence services, in this case, information collection through SIGINT in Western democracies in particular (Kniep 2017; Kniep 2021; Kniep 2022).

To describe and analyse intelligence professionals' data collection practices, this article draws on Bourdieu-inspired research by Bigo (2019), Ben Jaffel (2020a) and Kniep (2021, 2022). Those researchers have established the notion of intelligence as a field and have conducted case studies on, among others, counter-terrorism intelligence cooperation practices in the European context (Ben Jaffel 2020a; Ben Jaffel 2020b), practices of cooperation in the field of signals intelligence (Kniep 2021; Kniep 2022) and the structure of intelligence as transnational field (Bigo & Bonelli 2019). This study relies greatly on this research, but it tracks something different, namely, a conceptualisation of how intelligence professionals' daily practices transform in the context of the digital evolution. This chapter thereby aims to advance the still low level of engagement with the question of any change or transformation of (security) professionals' practices by Bourdieu-inspired scholars (Adler & Pouliot 2011; Schindler & Wille 2015).

Empirically, this study focuses on data collection practices called signals intelligence (SIGINT). SIGINT involves the collection of technical communication and could be characterised as an ideal type for the technical character of intelligence. This area seems best suited to investigating the nexus between digitalisation and intelligence professionals' data collection practices. Well-known SIGINT-intelligence services include the American National Security Agency (NSA), the British Government Communications Headquarters (GCHQ) and the German Bundesnachrichtendienst (BND). The latter is selected to illustrate the challenges that arise for intelligence professionals' data collection.

The empirical description and analysis of the practices of intelligence professionals is not easy, due to the secrecy that surrounds the field in general and operational methods in particular. Nevertheless, in recent decades, intelligence scholars have been able to make greater use of declassified material from the archives of intelligence services, interviews with contemporary witnesses and publicly available material (e.g. documents compiled and published in response to parliamentary oversight) to gain a better understanding of intelligence in general and SIGINT in particular (Aldrich 2010; Bamford 1982; Ferris 2020; Schmidt-Eenboom 2001). The scholarly literature has addressed the challenges for intelligence services that were posed by computerisation (during the 1960s and 1970s) or the rise of the internet (from the 1990s on) (e.g. Aldrich 2010: chapter 24, 488; Ferris 2020: 426–428, 689–691). Overall, however, scholars of intelligence history and intelligence studies have found that systematic research on the relationship between technology and intelligence services is still in its infancy (Warner 2012: 133; Wegener 2020; Bergien et al. 2022: 4; Agar 2016: 1).

This chapter relies on two main sources: the scholarly literature (Balzacq et al. 2010; Bigo 2013; Bigo 2019; Bigo 2020; Kniep 2017; Kniep 2021; Kniep 2022), in particular what could be described as sociological approach to intelligence, and the final report of the NSA-Investigation Committee (2014–2017) that was set up in Germany following the 2013 Snowden revelations. That committee addressed many issues, and it produced extensive documentation. This analysis focuses on statements made by BND employees during the NSA-Investigation Committee's questioning on the technological challenges, the cooperation between BND and the NSA in Bad Aibling, as well as Operation Eikonal (Memorandum of Agreement [MoA] of 2002). The latter cooperation was described and analysed from a Bourdieusian perspective in a detailed case study drawing on a range of empirical sources by Kniep (2022). This article, therefore, builds substantially on the theoretical and empirical findings of that publication. The article also refers to the findings of the MA thesis by Leixner (2021), which examines Operation Eikonal in a comparative case study.

Applying a Bourdieu-inspired perspective to the practices of intelligence professionals in the field of SIGINT produces three insights: First, Germany's foreign intelligence service was in the midst of a fundamental transformation aiming to adapt to the latest developments in the digital evolution, i.e. the shift to the internet that has grown since the 1990s. The empirical material illustrates the emergence of new practices and the fading of old ones as a kind of long-term transformation. Second, the emergence of new practices in the field of SIGINT disrupted intelligence professionals' practices of data collection and their existing know-how. As statements made in the final report of the NSA-Investigation Committee indicate, security professionals interpret their situation as difficult: statements provided describe their situation as "falling behind" (Deutscher Bundestag 2017: 666). Third, the technological transfer and knowledge transfer from NSA to BND through Operation Eikonal (2004–2008,[3] under the MoA of 2002) allowed BND to catch with developments to a certain extent, which finally led to the implementation of new practices of data collection. This could, speaking conceptually, qualify the operation as a breakthrough.

The next section (section 2) describes the theoretical concept and the conceptual extension being proposed to mark the emergence and disappearance of field practices, as well as the traceable moment of a breakthrough (as a conceptual alternative to a 'turning point'). Section 3 lays out the empirical illustration of intelligence professionals' practices in the context of the latest developments regarding the digital evolution. This section first lays out the selected case and reflects on the sources. Then, the challenges that arose from to the emergence of new practices and the fading of existing practices of data collection at the end of the 1990s and the beginning of the new millennium are illustrated. Having described the transfor-

---

3 Sources mention different years (2001/2002, 2004) for the beginning of the planning of Operation Eikonal (Deutscher Bundestag 2017: 663, 835, 1373).

mation of the practices of intelligence professionals and their perceived challenges during this period, the accomplishment of (new) data collection practices are illustrated with reference to intelligence professionals' statements on Operation Eikonal, implemented jointly by BND and NSA. Section 4 summarises the findings.

2 Conceptual approach to the study of (changing) practices

To reconstruct whether and how the practical routines of intelligence professionals are being challenged by the digital evolution, this article draws on the Bourdieu-inspired work of Bigo, Ben Jaffel and Kniep, among others. The approach is complex and multi-faceted. Nevertheless, some aspects, such as the notion of the field and practices stand out. To address the research question it is important to establish a solid understanding of the two terms. Additional conceptual elements, such as capital and habitus, are to be noted, as these seem to be important for following the general approach.

2.1 Studying the field of (signals) intelligence

Bigo's and Kniep's research formed the starting point for the analysis of the practices of intelligence services data collection in the digital age, as they established the understanding of SIGINT as a transnational field, applying the conceptual considerations of Bourdieu (Kniep 2017; Kniep 2021, 2022; Bigo & Bonelli 2019; Bigo 2020). Kniep showed that "digital technologies have contributed to the emergence of a transnational field within the world of intelligence: the field of Signals Intelligence" (Kniep 2017: 22). Use of the Bourdieusian notion of the field allowed Kniep to reconstruct the evolution of SIGINT as a field within the sphere of intelligence. What does field mean within practice theory? According to Balzacq et al., a field can be understood as

> a heuristic device that helps turn a not immediately apparent space of different positions (i.e. position of security agents/agencies) into a tangible social space determined by different forms and volume capital. (Balzacq et al. 2010: 3)

It should be noted that this concept of the field should not be thought of as fixed essence, and it remains permeable (C.A.S.E. Collective 2006: 458). Nevertheless use of the term allows us to describe a social context in which (similar) practices are realised, identified and described (Balzacq et al. 2010: 3) as Bigo and Kniep demonstrate in their research on the field of intelligence (Bigo 2019; Bigo & Bonelli 2019; Bigo 2020; Kniep 2017; Kniep 2021; Kniep 2022).

Thus, applying Bourdieu's notion of the field to the study of intelligence allows scholars to bring out at least two things. First, intelligence is more than a bureaucratic actor within the national security apparatus; that is, this perspective allows authors to escape the nation-state bias that is typical in political science and IR (Bigo 2019: 382; Bigo 2020: 59; Hoffmann et al. 2022: 2). Second, actors within a field maintain certain positions and compete with each other. A field can be described as "field of struggles" (C.A.S.E. Collective 2006: 458) meaning that actors within it are involved in offensive or defensive power struggles: that is, actors within a field are always (potential) competitors and (potential) partners with respect to each other. The outcomes of their power struggles are contingent, but the field nevertheless structures the possibilities and limitations of the actors involved in the power struggles (C.A.S.E. Collective 2006: 458). Thus, the field describes a more or less hierarchical structure, meaning that the position of an actor in it determines the actor's ability to (inter)act. The position in the field relates to the various forms of capital that an actor can dispose of. Kniep, who distinguishes for example between informational, economic, social and symbolic capital in SIGINT, considers the concept of capital as valuable to identify intelligence services' (relational) positions in the field (Kniep 2022: 146–147). Moreover, members of a field share a common understanding of what their business is all about (Kniep 2017: 22; Kniep 2021: 460, Kniep 2022: 144) such as the necessity to obtain strategic, tactical or operational knowledge about a perceived adversary or threat. Second, the members of a field share a common understanding of the rules of the game (Kniep 2021: 460; Kniep quotes Bourdieu & Wacquant 1996; Kniep 2022: 144). A typical example in this category is the so-called Third Party Rule, which says that information from an ally may not passed without approval (Kniep 2021: 467–469; Kniep quotes Gärditz 2015). However, the mechanism *do ut des* or *quid pro quo* (Clough 2004), which expresses the requirement for reciprocity in intelligence cooperation may also be subsumed under this concept. Members of the field of intelligence who have internalised those assumptions and rules consequently exhibit a specific habitus understood as "a system of (learned, SF) durable positions which governs the behavior and discourse of agents inside a field" (Balzacq et al. 2010: 3, Bourdieu 2020: 394).[4] The term is important for Bourdieu's thinking but will not be considered further in this chapter.

---

4 The concept of the habitus allows Bourdieu "to break with the paradigm of structuralism" (translation, SF) without falling back on the conceptions of classical economics (*homo oeconomicus*) or on methodological individualism (Bourdieu 2020: 394).

The introduction of Bourdieu's notion of the field and its application by Bigo and Kniep (Bigo 2019; Bigo & Bonelli 2019; Bigo 2020) and Kniep (2017, 2021; 2022) to SIGINT as sub-field of intelligence make it possible to conceptualise changes in data collection practices. This is all the more important, as fields are constantly being (re)produced through practices (Leander 2011: 298).

2.2 Studying emerging and fading practices

As noted, actors in a field perform a certain set of practices within it. To understand of what practices mean theoretically, this section draws on considerations of Adler and Pouliot, who were among the few scholars applying a Bourdieusian perspective to IR two decades ago.[5] According to Adler and Pouliot,

> Practices are competent performances. More precisely, practices are socially meaningful patterns of action which, in being performed more or less competently, simultaneously embody, act out, and possibly reify background knowledge and discourse in and on the material world. (Adler & Pouliot 2011 2011: 6)

The importance of the knowledge or know-how acquired in learning is also underlined by the definition of practices given by Reckwitz, who understands social practices as:

> expertise-dependent routines that are held together by a practical 'understanding', and whose knowledge on the one hand is 'incorporated' in the bodies of the acting subjects, and which on the other hand regularly takes the form of routinised relationships between subjects and material artefacts used by them. (Reckwitz 2003: 289, translation SF)

According to these definitions, four aspects that characterise practices should be highlighted. First, there is the aspect of (bodily) activity. Adler and Pouliot wrote of "a process of doing something" (Adler & Pouliot 2011: 7). Actors are involved in what they do, both bodily and mentally. Reckwitz refers to a phrase of Theodor Schatzki, who described practices as a "nexus of doing and sayings" (Reckwitz 2003: 290), which underscores the various forms that bodily activity take, in terms of the doing of something. In addition, such different forms of "doing" are embedded in fields and therefore carry field-specific struggles within them (Kniep 2022: 143, 156). Second, practice theory investigates the role of so-called artefacts in the course of action, namely, specific types of (supporting) technology. According to

---

5 Adler and Pouliot's perspective has been criticised by scholars for inconsistencies or insufficient theoretical rigor (Ben Jaffel 2020: 31). I share this critique to some extent, but I regard some suggestions as helpful for obtaining an (initial) understanding of Bourdieu's conceptual propositions.

Leander, "objects, technologies, and images (the props)" are "[. . .] at the heart of practices" (Leander 2011: 301). However, referring to Latour, she underlines that artefacts "are not allowed to escape the sociological context and the struggles they reflect" (Leander 2011: 302). Third, practices, understood as complex bodily activities, require regular training and knowledge, which lead to a certain degree of know-how; thus, a practical understanding of how to perform given practices must not be confounded with reasoned action (Ben Jaffel 2020a: 31). It should be noted that know-how, which is gained from practical experience, could also be unconscious. Fourth, according to the element of routine, the above-described doing is part of a (structured) routine and not one-time event. Only routinised doing allows the established field practices to be passed on and reproduced and only doing allows the development of know-how.

These aspects may help identify and investigate practices empirically. It is obvious that research inspired by Bourdieu tends to focus on the logic of reproduction and routine, leaving open the question of what happens if the modus of routine is challenged, such as by contextual developments. Interestingly, Bigo argues that the field approach understands social continuities as fragile moments and analyses "everyday practices and the emergence of new kinds of practices." (Bigo 2011: 241). Nevertheless, Bourdieu-inspired literature on change remains scarce (Schindler & Wille 2015) and several authors identify change as the theory's blind spot (Schindler & Wille 2015: 3, Büger & Gadinger 2014: 28). This article is tied in with preliminary work on this issue. Pouliot formulated some interesting suggestions that this article will take up. For instance, he proposed the idea of the lifecycle of a practice to clarify the idea of change in practice:

> The focus here is on a practice's lifecycle, which includes, in its ideal-typical form, the generation, the diffusion, the institutionalisation and the fading of a particular competent performance. To be sure, not all practices go through these four phases, it is an empirical matter to determine the ebb and flow of a specific practice in history [. . .]. (Adler & Pouliot 2011: 19)

Although the term lifecycle carries a conceptual burden through its use in other disciplines (e.g. product lifecycle in marketing and the lifecycle of norms in IR), the term is helpful in two ways. First, it signals that research on practices could also imply the description and analysis of changing field practices. Second, Adler's and Pouliot's ideal-typical distinction of different phases to clarify the "ebb and flow" (Adler & Pouliot 2011: 19) of practices is a helpful suggestion that can be used to further conceptualise dynamic aspects of field practices. This article adopts the idea of phases but distinguishes between emerging practices and fading practices to develop a balanced scheme. Practices that are increasingly realised can be characterised as emerging field practices, and practices that are less and less realised can qualify as fading field practices. This allows for the tracing of long-term, fundamental transformations of field practices. Because these fundamental developments seldom begin or end on a schedule, it would seem important to conceptualise phases as overlapping (see figure 1, gray marked zone).

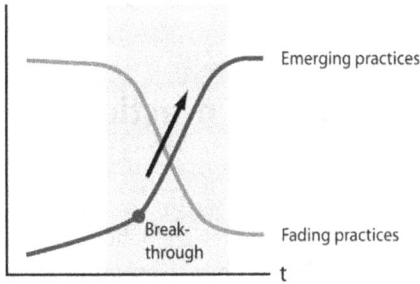

Figure 1: Emerging and Fading Practices Field Practices & Breakthrough.
Source: Own Production.

This article also investigates what happens to practices in situ when confronted by dynamics such as the digital evolution. As a second step, therefore, this article is tied in with the defining characteristics of practices noted earlier. Practices are described as a complex set of doings that are embedded in a field of struggle. A fundamental transformation challenges all of these dimensions, albeit in different forms: important knowledge is not available, and/or existing knowledge or knowhow loses its relevance, technological equipment (its artefacts) is not available or not (yet) interoperable, no practical doings have been established, or practical doing has become irregular or arguments discussing the necessity of fading / emerging practices arise. This article is especially interested in what happens to practices during a turbulent period of change. As described above, a period that marks the decline and/or the emergence of (new) practices. It can be assumed that professionals' doings could experience challenges and disruptions but also breakthroughs during these periods, meaning that it is possible to observe decisive moments or short periods of a particular effort and the realisation of a new form of doing for the first time (see figure 1). Having leapt over this hurdle, reproducing this practice and developing a kind or routine as well as extending these practices will be less challenging. This definition implies that a breakthrough forms a relatively short period, with decisive developments concerning practical doing, and the emergence and the fading of practices is to be described as long-term transformation. In addition, the notion of emerging and fading practices implies an analytical concentration on field dynamics, and the term breakthrough certainly allows the tracing of changing practices of (individual) intelligence professionals. Here, a breakthrough should not refer to a certain substantial shift in path direction, such as for example the term turning point suggests. This rather implies a moment of the successful realisation of something not hitherto realisable. The notion of a breakthrough seems, at first glance, similar to what historical institutionalists call a critical juncture (Capoccia und Kelemen 2007: 348), but it is important to note here that Bourdieu-inspired research makes a break with rationalist reading of actors' behaviour and proposes a reflexive perspective.

3 Emerging and fading (intelligence) practices: An empirical illustration

This section illustrates the "ebb and flow" of practices (Adler & Pouliot 2011: 19) and empirical breakthroughs in the realisation of (new) practices empirically. With reference to this, it is important to first reflect upon the case selection and the sources. The empirical material illustrates whether and how digitalisation challenges intelligence professionals' data collection practices, how they interpret this development as well as how the perceived capability gap was adressed.[6]

3.1 Reflection on empirical examples for illustration and sources

Intelligence studies propose several classifications for data collection. Gill and Pythian (2012: 78) distinguish OSINT (open source intelligence), HUMINT (human source intelligence) and various forms of technical collection (TECHINT) such as SIGINT (signal intelligence), IMINT (imagery intelligence) and MASINT (measurement intelligence). This article focuses on SIGINT practices for three reasons:

First, SIGINT refers to the collection of technical communication and therefore could be characterised as an ideal type for the technical character of intelligence. It thus seems best suited for investigating the nexus between digitalisation and intelligence professionals' data collection practices. Scholars distinguish three types of SIGINT: COMINT (interception of telephone, internet or radio communication), TELINT (intercepting telemetry) and ELINT (interception of electro-

---

6 This chapter contains testimony from the final report of the NSA-Investigation Committee in German, translated by this author. Moreover, names of witnesses are provided according to their use in the final report. Only the names of intelligence professionals of level 'head of department' (or higher) are fully spelled out there. The testimony of other intelligence professionals are abbreviated given with initials (Bundestag 2017: 118).

magnetic radiations) (Gill, Peter/Pythian, Mark 2012: 78). Since TELINT and ELINT primarily refer to military reconnaissance (Gill, Peter/Pythian, Mark 2012: 92), this article concentrates on COMINT within SIGINT. Second, Bourdieu's notion of the field was established especially by Bigo and Kniep (see section 3.1) as an analytical perspective to carve out the evolution of SIGINT as a sub-field of intelligence. In consequence, this article can build upon existing knowledge, allowing a deeper look into the issue of changing practical routines of intelligence agencies' SIGINT activities. Third, the Bundesnachrichtendienst (BND) is responsible for the provision of foreign and (strategic) military intelligence and therefore uses a broad spectrum of methods (SIGINT, HUMINT and OSINT, among others) to provide intelligence to its consumers. Various activities of German intelligence and security services, such as the BND, the Federal Office for the Protection of the Constitution (BfV) and the Federal Criminal Police Office (BKA), have been assessed and documented by the NSA-Investigation Committee (2004–2017). The establishment of the NSA-Investigation Committee was requested by the CDU and CSU, SPD, The Left and Alliance 90/The Greens following Edward Snowden's revelations.[7] The committee also investigated BND's SIGINT activities, including the cooperation between BND and NSA in Bad Aibling (MoA of 2002, including Operation Eikonal). This makes the activities a good case for empirical investigation.

The most important empirical source, which I will mainly refer to, refers to the second part of the final report of the so-called NSA-Investigation Committee (Deutscher Bundestag 2017). The approximately 1,800-page report has four parts. The mandate and additional administrative issues are laid out in the first part (Deutscher Bundestag 2017: 34–196), the conclusion of the NSA-Investigation Committee is given in the third, and dissents are in the fourth part (Deutscher Bundestag 2017: 1196–1822). The second part includes testimonies from service members, the services' oversight institutions and experts on the predefined topics (Deutscher Bundestag 2017: 197-1193). Because obtaining field access to intelligence work is difficult, the NSA-Investigation Committee's final report is extremely valuable, and it has been used by scholars before (Kniep 2017; Kniep 2022; Leixner 2021; Fischer 2018).

However, two things should be kept in mind (Fischer 2018: 11–12). First, it should be noted that the opinions of witnesses cited in the report were not obtained for the analysis of the everyday practices of intelligence professionals. Sec-

---

7 In November 2013, an Investigation Committee into the activities of the NSA was discussed for the first time (Deutscher Bundestag (2017): 36). In February, it was agreed that there should be a committee, but the mandate was still disputed. The committees' first meeting took place on 3 April 2013. The last committee meeting took place on 23 June 2017 and the committee report was made public.

ond, it must be emphasised that within the work of the NSA-Investigation Committee, concerns were raised regarding what information should be included in the report, and what should be redacted. In the end, two versions of the committee report were available to the public: an official variant (used here) in which parts of the dissenting opinion statements of the opposition parties were redacted and a second, publicly available and unredacted version from Netzpolitik.org. This indicates that the descriptions in the report are not only selected with regard to the intended purpose of the investigation but are also products of different political perspectives on the facts. This means that the empirical material must always be thought and critically reflected on in context.

3.2 Emerging and fading practices of data collection: An empirical illustration

In the following, testimony before the NSA-Investigation Committee is used to illustrate the challenges that BND's intelligence professionals faced as a result of developments in digital evolution on-going since the 1990s and through the beginning of the new millennium. It should be noted here that these statements were made in connection with the NSA-Investigation Committee's questions regarding the cooperation between BND and NSA in Bad Aibling. Initially, the so-called Bad Aibling Station (BAS) served the NSA by collecting data via satellite (Deutscher Bundestag 2017: 716). BND and NSA cooperated at Bad Aibling via Combined Group Germany (CGG) (Deutscher Bundestag 2017: 718). This arrangement was changed when NSA decided to give up BAS. A new modus of cooperation was established, the Joint Sigint Activity (JSA), with BND now acting as (leading) responsible partner (Deutscher Bundestag 2017: 728). Cooperation between BND and NSA in the context of JSA was agreed upon under a MoA in April 2002 (Deutscher Bundestag 2017: 722, 1260). This memorandum covered a broad spectrum of issues (including Operation Eikonal, section 4.3), but it seems to have focused strongly on collection via satellite (Deutscher Bundestag 2017: 663, 729; Graulich 2015: 78). The framework conditions of the cooperation were recorded in classified annexes (secret and top secret) (Deutscher Bundestag 2017: 722, 729). The memorandum was signed under the influence of the attacks of 9/11[8] and, as mentioned, the US decision to close BAS (Deutscher Bundestag 2017: 664, 727–729, 1249). It is impor-

---

8 Talks and decisions took place before 9/11 (Deutscher Bundestag (2017): 724).

tant to know that BND and NSA already had a long tradition of cooperation at that time (Schmidt-Eenboom 2001: 144–150).[9]

NSA-Investigation Committee hearings intensively discussed cooperation between BND and NSA in Bad Aibling, as documented in the final report (part 2: F I and II; part 3: C II; part 4: A V). The testimony of intelligence professionals during the NSA-Investigation Committee sessions illustrates the general context prevailing before the signing of the MoA, and it provides some initial impressions regarding how latest dynamics of digitalisation challenged intelligence professionals' practices of data collection in the field of SIGINT at the beginning of the new century:

> Witness W.K.: "At that time it [the internet, SF] gained increasing importance for us, because we recognised that a lot of communication moved, one could observe a general trend towards the internet and the applications that are being used by the internet-communication via telephone and other basic media assets lost importance." (Deutscher Bundestag 2017: 667, translation SF).

This testimony reports the trend towards communication via the internet, a development that began in the 1990s, as the 'new reality' that intelligence services had to deal with. Other statements within the final report appears to confirm the perception that the digital evolution altered the conditions of the intelligence agencies in the field of SIGINT. The following quotation describes conclusions drawn by intelligence professionals from the developments described above:

> Witness Dr Harald Fechner: "Bill Binney said clearly that data collection via short wave and satellite might still be helpful concerning countries in the eastern part [fading practices, SF], but he also argued that the internet will possibly become the dominating medium and that therefore the intelligence services need to apply new methods. Keyword metadata [emerging practices, SF]." (Deutscher Bundestag 2017: 667, translation SF)

This testimony, which refers to an expression of the former NSA director, illustrates the changing (material) conditions and the consequences of this development for practices in intelligence (with reference to this testimony see also Kniep 2022: 148–149). Practices such as data collection via satellite are perceived as fading practices,[10] and data collection via the interception of cable-based communications are considered as emerging practices. The paragraph containing this quotation has the heading "technical challenges due to the transition from satellite to cable-based communication" (Deutscher Bundestag 2017: 665). The chal-

---

9 I thank Ronja Kniep and Rüdiger Bergien for raising this point.
10 Interestingly, some practices that were considered 'fading practices' were nevertheless important for military intelligence gathered on the activities of Russian troops in Ukraine with the beginning of the war in February 2022. I thank Rüdiger Bergien for raising this point.

lenges that arise from a transformation of field practices are exceedingly diverse, as statements in the final report reveal:

> Witness Breitfelder: "The technical challenge was not only the sheer amount of data, but also making the data machine readable so that it could be further checked for its relevance to the intelligence services." (Deutscher Bundestag 2017: 668, translation SF)

> Witness Breitfelder: "The Internet has become very dominant as an intelligence target. And those who wanted to be successful had to have the technical penetration capability and at the same time the ability to control huge amounts of data and to analyse it in a way compliant with the law." (Deutscher Bundestag 2017: 665, translation SF)

These quotes indicate that not only did the latest dynamics of the digital evolution change the conditions for the practices of intelligence professionals, but also the emerging practices led to even-newer challenges (e.g. large amounts of data that are not machine-readable). As the following statement illustrates, technological expertise and know-how to tackle these challenges were rare and could not be made available at short notice:

> Witness Breitfelder: "So, now you have personnel who have grown up with short-waves-technology (fading practices, SF) and who are qualified. But you don't have staff that is able to process wired communication (emerging practices, SF). What are you doing now? You have two options now: Either you request new staff [. . .] or you have to manage with what you already have. I did that too, trying [. . .] to retrain people [. . .] from one task to another. You can't do that at a flick of a switch. That takes a lot of time. [. . .]." (Deutscher Bundestag 2017: 666, translation SF)

This indicates, that intelligence professionals' practices of data collection, SIGINT in this case, require highly specialised expertise. The handling of SIGINT technology can be described as a very complex, field-specific practice because it requires specific types of knowledge and technology, as well as the know-how for dealing with the technological artefacts. It also becomes clear here that the digital evolution and the resulting emergence of new practices of data collection severely challenged and ruptured existing but fading practices. Intelligence professionals needed answers to many questions that arose, such as: What kind of data is needed? How can data be obtained? How can it be made machine readable and then, in face of the sheer amount of data, how can the amount of data be reduced? (Kniep 2022: 150). To illustrate the complexity of these technical challenges: The so-called Graulich Report which dealt with the use of selectors by the BND and NSA comprises 262 pages (Graulich 2015).

Interestingly, similar questions were posed in the early 1970s, during the early phase of computerisation.[11] Obviously, some challenges were repeated

---

11 I owe this insight to Rüdiger Bergien.

through the digital evolution. Having illustrated the effects of digitalisation on intelligence professionals' field practices since the 1990s, the following question arises: How did intelligence professionals interpret these challenges? To illustrate this, reference is made again to selected testimonies from the final report of the NSA-Investigation Committee:

> Witness Breitfelder: "After the Cold War ended, the BND had to reinvent himself, shake up. Specific topics were abandoned etc. [. . .] But then a development got underway where we realised: The news technology in the world, i.e. the Internet, is changing so dramatically and so quickly that we will not be able to catch up if we cannot jump on the bandwagon somewhere now. That was actually the core of the whole. That was the idea [. . .]. To be at least partially involved in this worldwide telecommunications boom and not stand completely helpless in front of it and only deal with faxes or shortwave, and the rest is then lost. Of course we did not want that." (Deutscher Bundestag 2017: 665, translation SF)

> Witness Breitfelder: "The development capacities for new penetration capabilities were not sufficient from the back or from the front, and this was not due to the inability of our individual engineers and computer scientists, but to insufficient staffing numbers. Where we used one engineer, the NSA used 20 if it was important enough." (Deutscher Bundestag 2017: 666, translation SF)

This testimony is very important, as it presents two interrelated aspects. First, intelligence professionals appear to judge their position in the field and their performance in relation to other actors in the field, in this case, the NSA. This underlines the conclusion that everyday practices do not unfold within a vacuum but are necessarily embedded within a field that features competition and positional struggles between agents within as assumed by Bourdieu inspired research (Balzacq et al. 2010: 3). Second, the quotes indicates that (selected) intelligence professionals have the impression that the BND lagged behind with reference to the latest developments of the digital evolution. The final report also states the following: "According to the witness *J.F.*, head of BND-outpost Rheinhausen between 2002–2006, a technical capability gap had developed which has led to BND falling visibly behind by 2002" (Deutscher Bundestag 2017, translation SF). The following section recounts a development that gave a new spin to the perceived situation described above.

3.3 Breakthrough towards new practices: An empirical illustration

This section draws on selected witness statements and general information from the final report to illustrate the developments that arose for the BND in connection with Operation Eikonal. The NSA-Investigation Committee hearings intensively discussed Operation Eikonal (part 2: F IV II; part 3: C III; part 4: A V), and it also received academic (Leixner 2021: 56–67; Kniep 2022) and public attention (Krempl 2017, Mascolo 2014). The MoA of 2002 served as the formal basis for the Operation Eikonal (2004–2008), which (officially) evolved from the above described initiative shortly afterwards (for an critical perspective on this see Deutscher Bundestag 2017: 1368). Operation Eikonal tackled the challenges arising from the growing importance of (cable-based) internet for all types of communication (Leixner 2021: 60; Kniep 2022), although this was not laid down in the MoA expressis verbis (Deutscher Bundestag 2017: 729). Operation Eikonal primarily served the partners to access cable-based communications focusing on international communications from zones of conflict (Deutscher Bundestag 2017: 1260). The services therefore gained cable access near to Frankfurt am Main (Deutscher Bundestag 2017: 853, Kniep 2022: 149; Leixner 2021: 61). Filtered data were then sent to Bad Aibling (to JSA) for further analyses by the services' professionals (Leixner 2021: 62 [graphic]). It is important to note, from a technical point of view, that cable access meant two different things:

> Witness S. L.: "[. . .] So, we had in Operation 'Eikonal' both circuit-switched traffic, colloquially 'Telephony' – as well as packet-switched traffic; colloquially the 'Internet'." (Deutscher Bundestag 2017, translation SF)

Accordingly, the course of Operation Eikonal could be divided into two phases (Deutscher Bundestag 2017: 852–853, 1260, 1262): during the first phase, the partners established technological systems that allowed them to intercept circuit-switched communication (trial run 2004–2005 and operating mode 2005–2007). During the second phase, interception of package-switched communication was performed (Leixner 2021: 60). This indicates that Operation Eikonal incorporated technological support and knowledge transfer regarding emerging practices in the field of intelligence in which the BND had no capacity. The final report of the NSA-Investigation Committee indicates that the technical cooperation of the BND with the NSA in Bad Aibling had the goal of "technically upgrading" the BND (Deutscher Bundestag 2017: 549, translation SF), or, as the following statements illustrates:

> Witness Uhrlau (former president BND, SF): "It has been complicated, and there was no experience with circuit-switched traffic, and access to such a cable in Germany did not exist before. So that's why this was an upgrade for the BND with support also from the NSA." (Deutscher Bundestag 2017: 840, translation SF)

Accessing package-switched communication entails novel practical challenges for intelligence professionals, such as, for example in the selection of the data routes (to avoid G10-traffic), the necessary technology for data duplication and extraction, as well as the filtering of data (Deutscher Bundestag 2017: 673, 871, 866–867,

893–894, en detail also Kniep 2022: 150). The NSA, due to its heavy investments especially since 9/11, had the technical means and know-how regarding emerging practices at that time and was therefore regarded as a suitable strategic partner for dealing with emerging practices (Deutscher Bundestag 2017: 551).

Reviewing witnesses' statements and additional information gathered on Operation Eikonal by the NSA-Investigation Committee and case studies (Kniep 2022; Leixner 2021) ultimately produce a mixed picture: On the one hand, the NSA-Investigation Committee identified that several procedures and decisions that made the operation highly problematic from its inception until it was ended in 2008. It remains in question, *inter alia*, the legal basis for the operations and the deficits concerning the filtering of accessed data (Deutscher Bundestag 2017: 881, 1430). In hindsight, Operation Eikonal was regarded a problematic project from both a technical and particularly from a legal and political point of view (Deutscher Bundestag 2017: 1261). Moreover some indications showed that Operation Eikonal might have been part of a NSA programme called Rampart-A. Information on this programme was leaked by Edward Snowden (Deutscher Bundestag 2017: 1444). The parties Die Linke, Bündnis 90 and Die Grünen appear to reinforce this position in their dissenting vote in the final report of the NSA-Investigation Committee (Deutscher Bundestag 2017: 1442–1144). Kniep provides arguments for this position (Kniep 2022: 150–152). In addition, it should be noted that testimonies emphasising the technical aspects of Operation Eikonal articulate a slightly different assessment. The final report of the NSA-Investigation Committee indicates that Dr Dieter Urmann, former head of the department, testified that Operation Eikonal allowed the BND to collect package-switched communication via cable access for the first time (Deutscher Bundestag 2017: 838). This illustrates that Operation Eikonal, although it was only in effect for a few years and then closed down due to the impression that it lacks success (Deutscher Bundestag 2017: 1262), had a direct impact on the practical activity of intelligence professionals. The following testimony is also of interest:

> Witness W. K.: "One thing was of course, now purely from a technical point of view, what we have learned, what *made us capable* [italics, SF] for other, own operations and also for the G10 collection, for which we have a legal mandate, which we would not have done alone in this period of time. So, we *learned how to use this technology* [italics, SF], what problems you have to fight with. The other thing is certainly something that we did not foresee in this way [. . .]. So, something like that, we would now, with the current knowledge, no longer tackle. I think that would not be possible now, to carry out with a partner." (Deutscher Bundestag 2017: 908, translation SF)

The interpretation that Operation Eikonal, from a technical perspective and on a very practical level, allowed intelligence professionals to acquire emerging practices of data collection, namely the interception of cable-based (package-switched) communication, is given emphasis by a statement of a former BND president:

Witness Dr. Hanning (former BND president, SF): "The BND had huge problems with the interception of wired-based communication and operation 'EIKONAL' might be described as the door-opener for this technology." (Deutscher Bundestag 2017: 839, translation SF, reference to same quotation see Kniep 2022: 149)

Returning to the conceptual considerations of section 3.2 statements cited above suggest that Operation Eikonal enabled a breakthrough in the adoption of a new practice (Kniep 2022: 149). As noted, a short period of increased effort was described, which resulted in the first successful, albeit difficult and unglamorous realisation of a new practice. From this point on, it becomes possible to reproduce and extend newly acquired practices.

4 Conclusion

This chapter examined whether and how the digital evolution challenges or disrupts the routinised data collection practices of intelligence professionals. Moreover, it carved out an understanding of how security professionals could interpret these challenges and identifies what has changed in the perceived situation. The article is inspired by Bourdieu insofar as it uses his terms 'field' and 'practices' to describe and analyse the emergence and the fading of intelligence professionals' practices in the field of SIGINT and defines the term 'breakthrough' to represent the initial realisation of a new form of practical activity. This article thus breaks new conceptual ground, so to speak, as Bourdieu-inspired research on change remains in its infancy. As Bueger and Gadinger rightly put it: "[I]t is fair to say that the emphasis of Bourdieu's praxeology is on the stability, regularity and reproduction of practices and less on subversion and renewal" (Büger & Gadinger 2014: 28).

To answer the research questions and illustrate the value of the conceptual considerations, empirical illustration refers to testimony documented by the final report of the NSA-Investigation Committee (2014–2017) and the scholarly literature on the cooperation between BND and NSA in Bad Aibling (Kniep 2022; Leixner 2021). Statements selected from the final report of the NSA-Investigation Committee illustrate the ways in which the latest developments of the digital evolution, in particular, the emergence of the internet, challenged the existing routines and practices of intelligence professionals in the field of SIGINT (fading practices). Intelligence professionals' statements also show that the technological support, education and training through Operation Eikonal enabled a better understanding of the emerging practices of data collection and allowed them to be to realised (breakthrough).

Nonetheless, it must be said that the empirical illustrations used here rely on a small quantity of empirical material and a small selection of witness statements reproduced verbatim. The description of the challenges for the everyday practices of data collection in the field of SIGINT thus could contain misperceptions. At the same time, Kniep's (Kniep 2022) excellent case study is drawing on numerous sources. This article therefore builds on many findings from that publication to develop the argument of emerging and fading practices as well as the breakthrough.

Another important aspect that became evident through empirical analysis is that the transformation of field practices has had severe consequences for another field. As Leander notes: "Developments in one field may reshape other field logics. Technological innovations, financial crises, a war, the introduction of new public management or an educations reform are bound to impact fields far beyond those where they originate [. . .]." (Leander 2011: 298). Accordingly, implementing emerging data collection practices challenged the regulatory setting needed to effectively protect the basic rights of citizens in Germany and beyond, as the Federal Constitutional Court ruled in May 2020. This underlines the complex situatedness of intelligence professionals' work.

References

Adler, Emanuel &Vincent Pouliot. 2011. International Practices: Introduction and Framework. In Emanuel Adler & Vincent Pouliot (eds.), *Practices in International Relations and Social Theory*, 3–35. Cambridge: Cambridge University Press.

Agar, John. 2016. Putting the Spooks Back In? The UK Secret State and the History of Computing. *Information and Culture* 51(1). 102–124.

Aldrich, Richard J. 2010. *GCHQ*. London: Harper Press.

Balzacq, Thierry, Tugba Basaran, Didier Bigo, Emmanuel-Pierre Guittet & Christian Olsson. 2010. Security Practices. *International Studies Encyclopedia Online* 2010, http://www.open.ac.uk/re searchprojects/iccm/files/iccm/olsson-christian-publication7.pdf.

Bamford, James. 1982. *The Puzzle Palace: Inside the National Security Agency*. New York, NY: Penguin Books.

Baumann, Zygmunt, Didier Bigo, Paulo Esteves, Elspeth MGuild, Vivienne Jabri, David Lyon & R.B.J. Walker. 2014. After Snowden: Rethinking the Impact of Surveillance. *International Political Sociology* 2014(8). 121–144.

Ben Jaffel, Hager. 2020a. *Anglo-European Intelligence Cooperation. Britain in Europe, Europe in Britain*. London: Routledge.

Ben Jaffel, Hager. 2020b. Britain's European Connection in Counter-Terrorism Intelligence Cooperation: Everyday Practices of Police Liaison Officers. *Intelligence and National Security* 35(7). 1007–1025.

Bergien, Rüdiger, Debora Gerstenberger & Constantin Goschler. 2022. The Knowledge of Intelligence Agencies in the Cold War World. An Introduction. In Rüdiger Bergien, Debora Gerstenberger &

Constantin Goschler (eds.), *Intelligence Agencies, Technology and Knowledge Production: Data Processing and Information Transfer in Secret Services During the Cold War*, 1–17. Abingdon: Routledge.

Bigo, Didier. 2011. Pierre Bourdieu and International Relations: Power of Practices, Practices of Power. *International Political Sociology* 2011(5). 225–258.

Bigo, Didier. 2013. Security. In Rebecca Adler-Nissen (ed.), *Bourdieu in International Relations. Rethinking Key Concepts in IR*, 114–130. Abingdon: Routledge.

Bigo, Didier. 2019. Shared Secrecy in a Digital Age and a Transnational World. *Intelligence and National Security* 34(3). 379–394.

Bigo, Didier. 2020. Adjusting a Bourdieusian Approach to the Study of Transnational Fields: Transversal Practices and State (Trans)Formations Related to Intelligence and Surveillance. In Christian Schmidt-Wellenburg & Stefan Bernhard (eds.), *Chartering Transnational Fields. Methodology for a Political Sociology of Knowledge*, 55–78. Abingdon: Routledge.

Bigo, Didier &Laurent Bonelli. 2019. Digital Data and the Transnational Intelligence Space. In Didier Bigo, Engin Isin & Evelyn Ruppert (eds.), *Data Politics. Worlds, Subjects, Rights*, 100–122. Abingdon: Routledge.

Bigo, Didier & Elspeth Guild. 2005. *Controlling Frontiers: Free Movement Into and Within Europe.* Aldershot: Ashgate.

Bigo, Didier & Anastassia Tsoukala (eds.). 2008. *Terror, Insecurity and Liberty: Illiberal Practices of Liberal Regimes after 9/11.* Routledge: London.

Bourdieu, Pierre. 2020. *Habitus und Praxis: Schriften zur kollektiven Anthropologie 2.* Frankfurt am Main: Suhrkamp.

Bourdieu, Pierre & Loic Wacquant. 1996. *Reflexive Anthopology.* Frankfurt am Main: Suhrkamp.

Büger, Christian & Frank Gadinger. 2014. *International Practice Theory. New Perspectives.* Basingstoke: Palgrave.

Bunnik, Anno, Anthony Cawley, Michael Mulqueen & Andrej Zwitter (eds.). 2016. *Big Data Challenges. Society, Security, Innovation and Ethics.* London: Palgrave.

Capoccia, Giovanni & R. Daniel Kelemen. 2007. The Study of Critical Junctures: Theory, Narrative, and Counterfactuals in Historical Institutionalism. *World Politics* 59(3). 341–369.

C.A.S.E. Collective. 2006. Collective Critical Approaches to Security in Europe: A Networked Manifesto. *Security Dialogue* 37(4). 443–487.

Chi, Michael. 2017. Big Data in National Security (Australian Strategic Policy Institute). https://css. ethz.ch/content/dam/ethz/special-interest/gess/cis/center-for-securities-studies/resources/ docs/ASPI-Big%20data%20online%20resource.pdf.

Clough, Chris. 2004. Quid Pro Quo: The Challenges of international Strategic Intelligence Cooperation. *International Journal of Intelligence and CounterINtelligence* 17(4). o.S.

Deutscher Bundestag. 2017. *Beschlussfassung und Bericht des 1. Untersuchungsausschusses nach Artikel 44 des Grundgesetzes (Drucksache 18/12850, Vorabfassung 23.6.2017).* Berlin.

Ferris, John. 2020. *Behind the Enigma: The Authorized History of GCHQ.* London: Bloomsbury.

Fischer, Susanne. 2018. *Technology, Big Data and the Security Practices of Intelligence Services: Paper presented at the ECPR General Conference in Hamburg.* Unpublished Manuscript.

Gärditz, Klaus. 2015. Third Party Rule: Der Vertraulichkeitsvorbehalt als Grenze der Verwertung ausländischer nachrichtendienstlicher Informationen. *DVBI* 14(2015). 903–910.

Gill, Peter/Pythian, Mark. 2012. *Intelligence in an Insecure World.* Cambridge: Polity Press.

Graulich, Kurt. 2015. *Nachrichtendienstliche Fernmeldeaufklärung mit Selektoren in einer transnationalen Kooperation. Prüfung und Bewertung von NSA-Selektoren nach Beweisschlusses des BND-26 (Bericht im Rahmen des 1. Untersuchungsausschusses der 18. Wahlperiode des Deutschen Bundestages).* Berlin: Deutscher Bundestag.

Greenwald, Glenn. 2014. *Die globale Überwachung. Der Fall Snowden, die amerikanischen Geheimdienste und die Folgen.* München: Droemer.

Hoffmann, Sophia, Noura Chalati & Ali Dogan. 2022. Rethinking Practices and Processes: Three Sociological Concepts for the Study of Intelligence. *Intelligence and National Security* (September). 1–20.

Kniep, Ronja. 2017. Eine nicht mehr ganz so geheim Welt. Nachrichtendienste und Digitalisierung aus feldtheoretischer Perspektive. *WZB Mitteilungen* 155(März). 22–25.

Kniep, Ronja. 2021. "Herren der Information". Die transnationale Autonomie digitaler Überwachung. *Zeitschrift für Politikwissenschaft* 2021. o.S.

Kniep, Ronja. 2022. Praktiken und Rationalitäten Transnationaler Überwachung. Zeitschrift für Internationale Beziehungen (29)2, 140–161.

Krempl, Stefan. 2017. Geheimakte BND & NSA: Operation Eikonal – das Inland als "virtuelles Ausland". *Heise Online*, https://www.heise.de/meldung/Operation-Eikonal-BND-soll-jahrelang-Daten-detuscher-Buerger-an-NSA-uebermittelt-haben-2411680.html. (2 November, 2022)

Lahneman, William J. 2016. IC Data Mining in the Post-Snowden Era. *International Journal of Intelligence and CounterIntelligence* 29(4). 700–723.

Leander, Anna. 2011. The Promises, Problems, and Potentials of a Bourdieu-Inspired Staging of International Relations. *International Political Sociology* 2011(5). 294–313.

Leixner, Nicolas. 2021. *Clandestine Exchanges. Reciprocity in International Intelligence Cooperation between the United States and Germany.* München: Unpublished MA Thesis.

Lyon, David. 2014. Surveillance, Snowden, and Big Data: Capacities, Consequences, Critique. *Big Data & Society* 2014(July-September). 1–13.

Lyon, David. 2017. Big Data Surveillance. Snowden, Everyday Practices and Digital Futures. In Tugba Basaran, Didier Bigo, Emmanuel-Pierre Guittet & R. B. J. Walker (eds.), *International Political Sociology. Transversal Lines*, 254–271. London: Routledge.

MacDonald, Margret & Anthony G. Oettinger. 2002. Information Overload. Managing Intelligence Technologies. *Harvard International Review* Fall. 44–48.

Mascolo, Georg. 2014. Späh-Affäre: BND leitete Daten von Deutschen an NSA weiter. *Süddeutsche Zeitung*, www.sz.de/1.2157406. (2 November, 2022)

Reckwitz, Andreas. 2003. Grundelemente einer Theorie sozialer Praktiken. Eine sozialtheoretische Perspektive. *Zeitschrift für Soziologie* 32(4). 282–301.

Saetnan, Ann R., Ingrid Schneider & Nicola Green (eds.). 2018. *The Politics of Big Data. Big Data, Big Brother?* Abingdon: Routledge.

Schindler, Sebastian & Tobias Wille. 2015. Change In and Through Practice: Pierre Bourdieu, Vincent Pouliot, and the End of the Cold War. *International Theory* 7(2). 330–359.

Schmidt-Eenboom, Erich. 2001. The Bundesnachrichtendienst, the Bundeswehr and SIGINT in the Cold War and After. *Intelligence and National Security* 16(1). 129–176.

Statista. 2023. Volumen der jährlich generierten/replizierten digitalen Datenmenge weltweit in den Jahren 2012 und 2020 und Prognose für 2025 (in Zettabyte). https://statista.com/statistik/daten/studie/267974/umfrage/prognose-zum-weltweit-generierten-datenvolumen/. (17 May, 2023)

Warner, Michael. 2012. Reflections on Technology and Intelligence Systems. *Intelligence and National Security* 27(1). 133–153.

Warner, Michael. 2014. *The Rise and Fall of Intelligence. An International Security History.* Washington DC: Georgetown University Press.

Wegener, Jens. 2020. Order and Chaos: The CIA's HYDRA Database and the Dawn of the Information Age. *Journal of Intelligence History* 19(1). 77–91.

IV Changing Frozen Policies? Migration, Health, and Lobbying

Julia Rakers

The 2015 refugee situation as a turning point? Migration- and integration-related debates in the German Bundestag

Abstract: Migration politics in liberal democracies is often characterised by a gap between liberal elite discourse and the restrictive preferences of the electorate. As a result, migration politics exhibit an expansionist bias. However, ignoring public opinion could become costly for political parties: Especially after newsworthy events such as the refugee situation starting in 2015, parties may expect rewards for "riding the wave" as agenda takers and adjust to voter preferences to some extent. This chapter studies the effect of the 2015 refugee situation on the so-called policy–opinion gap. Surveys have revealed that public opinion became more negative after the start of the refugee situation. An analysis of plenary debates of the German Bundestag reveals that the number of speeches addressing migration increased at the same time. However, a sentiment analysis indicates a slight tendency towards positively connotated language during the entire 18th legislature before and after the start of the refugee situation. A qualitative analysis of concordances supports this finding and reveals that the tone of the debate is usually rather pragmatic and thorough.

Keywords: migration, parliamentary debate, issue attention, focusing event, text as data

1 Introduction

The 2015 refugee situation[1] posed an extraordinary challenge for Germany and attracted exceptional media attention with dramatic images from refugee routes

---

1 This paper uses the term 'refugee situation 2015' to refer to these events. At the same time, it avoids the use of terms such as crisis as such terms are dehumanising and depict migrants and refugees as threatening.

Note: The author would like to thank Christoph Leonhardt and Andreas Blätte for their constructive feedback and support.

Julia Rakers, NRW School of Governance, Institute of Political Science, University Duisburg-Essen

https://doi.org/10.1515/9783111272900-012

(Chouliaraki et al. 2017). As a focusing event[2] on the issue of migration, it had the potential to shift the agenda of parties in parliament as parties lost control over the political agenda and were forced to communicate a position (Mader and Schoen 2019: 70).

Migration politics in liberal democracies is characterised by an expansionist bias because policies and elite preferences are usually more liberal than restrictive preferences of the electorate (Freeman 1995). Departing from this, the refugee situation had the potential to shift the way migration is addressed. The resulting question is: To what extent does the refugee situation 2015 function as a turning point for parliamentary debates on migration and the policy–opinion gap in Germany? Theories of issue attention posit that parties face incentives to address existing issues in a way that is advantageous for the party and to show concern for issues the public cares about. Ignoring newsworthy, publicly salient events such as the refugee situation in 2015 may, in contrast, be costly for parties and democracy in two ways. In the short term, parties may lose voters as they do not seem convincing to the electorate. In the long term, parties may risk alienating voters who do not feel represented by *any* party in parliament and who, consequently, might abstain from voting altogether or cast a protest vote for a populist party in the future.

Based on previous findings that some parties follow the direction of changes in public opinion, this chapter investigates to what extent the refugee situation in 2015 marks a turning point in parliamentary debate based on the so-called policy–opinion gap. This chapter first provides an overview of focusing events, defines the policy–opinion gap and relates this characteristic of migration politics to theories of issue attention in politics and parliament. Another part sets out the methodology and data. Using the GermaParl corpus containing debates of the German Bundestag, a sentiment analysis is performed on liberal signalling words within speeches addressing migration-related topics to assess whether migration is labelled positive or negative. In addition, the word context of these signalling words is interpreted qualitatively. The third part presents the results: no significant changes in how parliamentarians discuss migration can be detected. At the same time, public opinion changes and more voters exhibit negative associations with migration. The discussion summarises the finding that migration politics in Germany from 2013 until 2017 may indeed be a special policy field characterised by a more positive parliamentary debate compared to a rather negative public opinion.

---

2 A focusing event is defined as an event that is "sudden, uncommon, harmful, concentrated on a particular geographical area or community of interest, and known to policymakers and the public simultaneously" (Walgrave and Varone 2008: 368).

2 The potential of focusing events as a turning point

Events such as the refugee situation in Germany can be categorised as new – meaning novel or near-novel events that faded from collective memory (Birkland 1997: 145) – focusing events. Previous research such as that of Mader and Schoen (2019) classifies the sudden increase of people seeking protection on humanitarian grounds in Germany from 2014 to 2016 as a focusing event (see Figure 1). Focusing events exhibit several characteristics. In general, they

1. are sudden and happen "with little or no warning" (Birkland 1997: 23)
2. are relatively rare, unplanned and "unpredictable with a reasonable degree of certainty" (Birkland 1997: 24)
3. affect many people in (a) the same geographic area or (b) a community of interest
4. are harmful or experienced as such
5. make planning a response impossible as the public and the policy community "learn of a potential focusing event virtually simultaneously" (Birkland 1997: 25)
6. are fixed in time and can, therefore, act as "a proximate cause for agenda change" (Birkland 1997: 26).

Events such as the refugee situation in Germany in 2015 were rarely seen before and became the most important issue for voters for almost the entire 18th legislature (see Figure 2). Furthermore, the influx of people concentrated on a smaller number of EU member states, especially Germany. Policymakers and the public became aware of the situation at the beginning of September 2015 at the latest. When approximately 3,000 of those refugees stuck at the Budapest main station decided to leave for Austria and Germany on foot, Hungarian Prime Minister Victor Orbán announced bus transports to the Austrian border to ensure safety. In the meantime, German Chancellor Angela Merkel and her Austrian colleague Werner Faymann agreed that stopping people at the border would require violence (Herbert and Schönhagen 2020). To avoid humanitarian catastrophes, Faymann announced that Austria and Germany enable protection seekers to cross borders on the evening of 4 September 2015.

Consequences of focusing events include the growth of the topic on the agenda (Birkland 1998: 60). However, the growth does not automatically imply a change in the substance of the discussion. This change in substance usually occurs in "reasonably well-organised policy domains" (Birkland 1998: 72). The scope of an event can provide a window of opportunity for a change in the problem perception due to the attention drawn to the topic. Focusing events are, thus, sim-

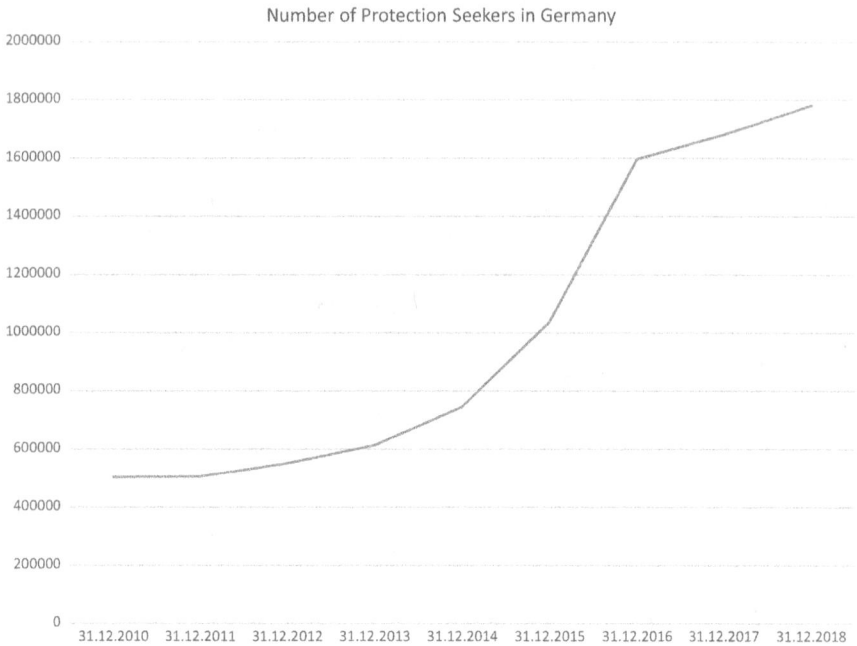

Figure 1: Number of protection seekers in Germany (Destatis 2022), own diagram.

ilar to critical junctures that there is a higher probability for a change in the direction of a path, development, or trend (Capoccia and Kelemen 2007). Based on the increased attention on a topic after a focusing event, these events can serve as turning points for the way a topic is addressed and can be utilised by societal groups to facilitate change in a different direction.

3 The policy–opinion gap and issue attention cycles

Scholars observe a gap between the restrictive preferences of voters and the more liberal perceptions of the political elite and, as a result, more liberal policies as a defining characteristic of migration politics in liberal democracies (Freeman 1995). Migration policies exhibit an expansionist bias as public opinion often is not well articulated and faces few incentives to organise based on the diffuse costs of migration. This bias is often referred to as the policy–opinion gap.

Czaika and de Haas flesh out this initial, vague observation by distinguishing three immigration policy gaps (2013): First, the discursive gap between actual policies and public opinion; second, the implementation gap between policies on paper and their implementation in practice; third, the efficacy gap between policies and their effect on migration. The discursive gap results from policy influences of various groups including, but not limited to, political parties with different ideological backgrounds and interest groups such as employers' associations and trade unions or civil society groups and NGOs. Furthermore, political, economic and legal constraints such as international law and the Geneva Convention restrict the room for manoeuvre of individual governments. Additionally, public discourses on migration are often broad, while policies are more specific, targeting subgroups of migrants instead of migration *as a whole*.

While this approach does not explicitly include the underlying mechanisms of how the discursive gap develops, other scholars take the democratic process into account. One strand of the literature focuses on the elite level of the democratic process and incorporates the partisan effects of refugee immigration, the manifesto–policy link and the fulfilment of the electoral mandate or claims-making by elites and the organised public (Gudbrandsen 2010; Lutz 2021; Statham and Geddes 2006). Another strand explores the connection between the elite and the public by looking at the congruence of citizens' policy recommendations with party positions and attitudes between elites and the public or the responsiveness of policies to public opinion (in different political systems) (Hobolt and Klemmensen 2005; Jennings 2009; Leruth and Taylor-Gooby 2019; Morales et al. 2015).

In doing so, most researchers focus on data such as elite surveys, manifestos and policies, whereas few include parliamentary speech in their work. Hobolt and Klemmensen, for example, extract governmental policy intentions from the annual opening speeches of the parliamentary year to investigate issue attention and policy priorities (2005: 386). In contrast to electoral programmes or party manifestos that capture party positions and issue attention at a specific point in time and may not respond to events immediately, parliamentary debates allow for a more dynamic understanding of political positioning and issue attention (Fernandes et al. 2021). They provide insights about elite positioning over time and are a "powerful tool to gauge parties' official positions during the inter-election period" (Ibid.: 1034).

More importantly, parliamentary speech functions as a tool for the communication of policy positions to fellow Members of Parliament and voters (Proksch and Slapin 2015: 1). Apart from using "agenda-setting rules strategically to shape policy outcomes" (Fernandes et al. 2021: 1033), parliamentary debate "creates a link between voters and their representatives" (Proksch and Slapin 2015: 2) and therefore, is an important part of signalling responsiveness to voters' concerns in public. According to this argumentation, policy outcomes are just one aspect of the political process; procedural fairness and the articulation of different positions during the debate are just as important and influence voters' satisfaction with democracy (Fernandes et al. 2021; Proksch and Slapin 2015). Some may argue that the electorate – if at all – infrequently follows plenary debates. Speeches and their content, however, reach voters through other channels, e.g. the media, after the debate (Proksch and Slapin 2015: 22).

These arguments of representation and the assumption that voters support a party based on its record have strategic implications for parties and legislators regarding plenary debates. Apart from serving constituents, floor time might serve the party agenda, policy goals, or individual career ambitions. In party-centred electoral systems such as Germany, parties act as gatekeepers to candidate selection and election. This creates two types of incentives (Proksch and Slapin 2015). First, legislators often focus on the party brand. Second, leaders of parliamentary groups control access to floor time during debates and emphasise party unity by selecting speakers closely aligned with the party line on a topic (Proksch and Slapin 2015: 64). Based on the role of plenary debates as a channel of representation and position-taking and on the incentives of the electoral system, one might expect that public opinion and its changes are reflected in parliamentary debates.

Remarkably, existing work on the policy–opinion gap rarely accounts explicitly for the effects of focusing events and shifts in issue attention in plenary debates that are one arena of elite discourse. Newsworthy and significant events such as the 2015 refugee situation may direct parties' attention, during plenary debates, towards a specific topic and shift the policy agenda based on an external shock (Bonafont et al. 2014). Parties may expect to feel rewarded for "riding the wave" by showing concern for a widely acknowledged problem and by addressing this existing topic in the most advantageous way for the party (Ansolabehere and Iygenar 1994: 337). This means framing the issue by "[selecting] *some aspects of a perceived reality and make them more salient in a communicating text, in such a way to promote a particular problem definition, causal interpretation, moral evaluation, and/or treatment recommendation* for the item described" (Entman 1993: 52; italics in original).

In contrast to that, ignoring the event possibly harms the party as voters perceive the party as "out of touch" (Sides 2007: 467). In addition, ignorance of the issue surrenders the issue itself and its framing to political opponents (Green-Pedersen and Mortensen 2010). This means that a party loses influence over the framing and perception of an issue. Parties, thus, face incentives to address even unfavourable issues when they appear on the agenda because voters expect them to formulate an opinion and might punish parties who do not address these issues (Green-Pedersen and Mortensen 2010; John et al. 2014).

Especially during times of crisis, "parties increase the weight given to public opinion on their calculus to determine which issues to prioritise in parliament" (Borghetto and Russo 2018: 74) and become more responsive to public opinion as Borghetto and Russo have demonstrated for the economic crisis in 2009. "When society comes up against overwhelming problems, parties have to restrain their role of agenda setters and, to some extent, become agenda takers" (Borghetto and Russo 2018: 67). In addition to that, "parties are generally responsive to voters' preferences" (Williams and Spoon 2015: 178), keeping vote- and office-seeking motives in mind. If public opinion moves to the right, party preferences do as well (Adams et al. 2004). In particular, if voter preferences move away from party positions, parties are more responsive to keep voters. These observations of party responsiveness to public opinion lead to the following expectations concerning parliamentary debates and the policy–opinion gap in light of the refugee situation 2015:

The focusing event of the refugee situation in 2015 closes the potential gap between public opinion and elite discourse, marking a turning point for parliamentary debate on migration in Germany.

The influence of incoming information on issue attention (for example Spoon and Klüver 2014) accordingly becomes more important. In contrast, some authors stress agenda-setting approaches and the motivation of parties to place issues they *own* or that are otherwise advantageous on the agenda (Brazeal and Benoit 2008; Green-Pedersen and Walgrave 2014; Walgrave and Swert 2007), while others mention electoral manifestos as one of many factors (Vliegenthart et al. 2013). As outlined above that parties increase the weight of public opinion as a reaction to focusing events, these motivations are expected to recede into the background in the immediate aftermath of a focusing event.

4 The GermaParl corpus of parliamentary protocols and sentiment analysis

Germany serves as an extreme case as a country that hosted a high number of asylum seekers during the 2015 refugee situation. As outlined above, German Chancellor Angela Merkel decided jointly with her Austrian counterpart to allow transfers from Hungary. This decision is often referred to as the starting point of the refugee situation 2015 (Herbert and Schönhagen 2020) and therefore, serves as a point of comparison between before and after.

Data to depict public opinion are obtained from surveys and include the question of the most important issues from the Politbarometer (Forschungsgruppe Wahlen 2022). Respondents are asked to name the policy problems they consider to be the most important ones for Germany. This item is used routinely in research to measure issue salience and the relative importance of policy issues (Hobolt and Klemmensen 2005: 386). Furthermore, items on negative and positive associations with migration and items on voluntary contributions are included to assess the direction of public opinion (Jacobsen et al. 2017; Bertelsmann Stiftung 2022). For these items, participants are confronted with several statements representing positive and negative attitudes towards migration and are asked whether they agree with these statements or not. Figures 3 and 4 provide an overview of these statements.

For plenary debates, the GermaParl corpus is used.[3] The updated corpus covers the parliamentary debate in the German Bundestag from 1949 to 2021 (Blätte and Leonhardt 2022). Structural attributes such as document-level metadata, including legislative period, date, year and speaker allow for extracting a subcorpus of the relevant legislature (Blätte et al. 2022). Following Blätte et al.'s approach, an extensive dictionary consisting of relevant terms for the policy field is employed to filter debates on migration and integration (Blätte et al. 2020).[4] To grasp the policy field in the broadest sense possible, this extensive approach is applied. A speech is considered to cover migration- and integration-related topics if at least two terms included in the dictionary appear in the speech to exclude speeches that cover the topic in a different setting such as animal migration. The period includes the 18th legislature of the German Bundestag from 22 October 2013 until 24 October 2017 and is divided at the point of comparison on 4 September 2015. Table 1 presents an overview of the subcorpora. The analysis focused on one legislature to include stable parliamentary groups and to rule out effects based on a changed composition of the Bundestag. These include, for example, possible contagion effects after the populist radical-right *Alternative for Germany* (AfD) entered parliament. Furthermore, including the entire legislative term accounts for peaks and breaks of parliamentary activity, for example, during summer recess.

---

3 For information on the compilation procedures of the corpus, see Blätte and Blessing (2018).
4 The dictionary includes 219 terms related to migration and integration. Blätte et al. (2020) developed this dictionary using query term relevance-techniques and fine-grained the dictionary using word embeddings and keyword extractions.

Table 1: Number of total speeches and migration- and integration-related speeches in the German Bundestag, 22 October 2013–24 October 2017 based on the GermaParl corpus (Blätte and Leonhardt 2022).

	22 October 2013–4 September 2015	5 September 2015–24 October 2017
Total number of speeches	14,927	16,780
Migration- and integration-related speeches	1,396	2,370
Shares in per cent	9.35	14.12

The analysis consisted of two steps. First, the sentiment analysis of plenary data was performed in R using the polmineR-package.[5] In short, "sentiment analysis or opinion mining aims to identify positive and negative opinions or sentiments expressed or implied in the text and also the targets of these opinions or sentiments" (Liu 2015: 3). It rests on the underlying assumption that the content of the text discloses information about attitudes and opinions. "To measure the sentiment of political messages then, the analysis resorts to predefined lists of terms supplying quantitative weights on positive and negative connotations, counts the presence of these terms in the texts of interest and finally aggregates their relative rate of occurrence to some sort of comparative measure, usually by normalizing it to the overall number of terms in the given text" (Rauh 2018b: 320).

Sentiment analyses have several advantages for political science research. First, the method can ensure transparency and replicability. Furthermore, its implementation is straightforward and does not demand numerous technical resources. In addition, "the assumption that the sentiment expressed in a piece of text is a function of the sentiment born by its individual terms seems pretty intuitive" (Rauh 2018b: 320). Finally, automated sentiment scoring allows for working with larger samples than manual coding. It provides advantages regarding reliability as human coders are often biased and may see sentiments where there are objectively none (Rauh 2018b: 326). Despite these advantages, automated sentiment analysis faces some challenges.

The first challenge relates to sentiment-scoring algorithms that often include a neutrality bias. This means that a score close to zero does not necessarily mean that the text message is neutral (Rauh 2018b: 326). The second challenge relates to the dictionary approach. General sentiment dictionaries may not lead to reliable results because researchers compiled them for a purpose other than political lan-

---

5 For more information on the Polmine-project and its different packages, see https://polmine. github.io. The R-script used for the analysis is available through the author's GitHub page (https://github.com/JuliaRakers).

guage, e.g., marketing, and therefore, the dictionary might be of limited use for other scenarios (Rauh 2018b: 321). To address this difficulty, this analysis utilises an optimised dictionary for the German political language (Rauh 2018a) that builds upon the established resources *SentiWS* (Remus et al. 2010) and *GermanPolarityClues* (Waltinger 2010).

To discover the parliamentary manifestation of the complex issues concerning migration, topic-specific word lists are included in the sentiment analysis to analyse the connotation of their context. Schmitz-Vardar and Leonhardt (2022) provide key terms to operationalise concepts concerning the support of diversity related to migration. Table 2 summarises these key terms that are clustered around four larger issues and presents their frequency for both periods within the 18th legislature. This operationalisation follows the assumption that a positive context of "liberal signalling words" implies support for liberal migration policies; similarly, a negative context suggests more restrictive policy preferences.

Table 2: Search terms for the sentiment analysis developed by Schmitz-Vardar and Leonhardt (2022: 161) using machine learning approaches and their frequency during the 18th legislature. Some terms are truncated to account for different grammatical functions in different contexts.

Issue	Terms	Frequency	
		22 October 2013– 4 September 2015	5 September 2015– 24 October 2017
Countering causes of refugee movements	"Fluchtursache*", "Entwicklungspolitik", "Entwicklungszusammenarbeit"	404	1,055
Distribution of asylum seekers in the EU	"Verteilmechanismus", "Verteilungsmechanismus", "Verteilungsschlüssel", "Resettlement", "europäisch.* Asylsystem", "Dublin", "GEAS"	129	160
Refugee migration to Germany	"Familiennachzug*", "*[Nn]achzug", "Schutzberechtigte*", "Familienzusammenführung", "subsidär.* Schutz"	87	364
Economic value of migration	"Fachkr(a|ä)ft.*", "Berufsanerkennung", "Punktesystem", "Arbeitsmigration", "Anerkennungsgesetz", "Bluecard", "Spurwechsel"	426	327

To account for the shortcomings of a quantitative approach, the second part focuses on the context in which a word is used to determine its semantic meaning as one "shall know a lot about a word by the company it keeps" (Firth 1957: 11). It is assumed that lexical units exhibit a relationship between their content and meaning if they appear together. To do so, a qualitative analysis of the concordances of the "signalling words" is performed. "A concordance is simply a list of all of the occurrences of a particular search term in a corpus, presented within the context that they occur in" (Baker 2006: 71).

Interpreting these contexts manually ensures capturing complex negations, references to numbers or metaphors implying a positive or negative connotation or referrals and quotes. Examples include describing refugees as victims but deriving the consequences of an action that refugees need help. Another example relates to metaphors that construct migrants as a natural catastrophe that is hard to control and dehumanises migrants and refugees as "something that requires control in order to prevent disaster to others" (Baker 2006: 81). Based on the material, several subcategories of the four issues (see table 2) were developed and refined. In addition to topic-based codes, an interpretative analysis takes restrictive and liberalising tendencies, language and wording into account. The analysis summarises and clusters the larger topics of the debates, condenses similar arguments and contrasts speeches that present opposing points of view. To account for the complexities of the German language, the context of twenty terms to the left and the right is interpreted.

5 Findings relating to public opinion

Soon after Merkel and Faymann's decision, pictures of the German society and its *Willkommenskultur* (welcoming culture) prevailed. Many citizens received refugees with highly visible posters stating *refugees welcome* and countless private initiatives, and volunteers assisted refugees upon arrival and thereafter. In 2016, about one-third of the respondents stated that they have made monetary donations or other material contributions to refugee assistance in the past twelve months (Jacobsen et al. 2017: 167). Almost ten per cent replied that they were engaged actively onsite through, for example, language courses (Jacobsen et al. 2017: 167).

The question of the most important issues underlines that many voters were concerned about foreigners, integration and refugees. While voters still considered pensions one of the most important issues during the first year of the 18th legislature, the perception changed during the second half of 2014. More and more voters observed migration as the most important issue reaching 88 per cent in October 2015 and followed by an uneven decline (see Figure 2).

Most Important Issues in Germany

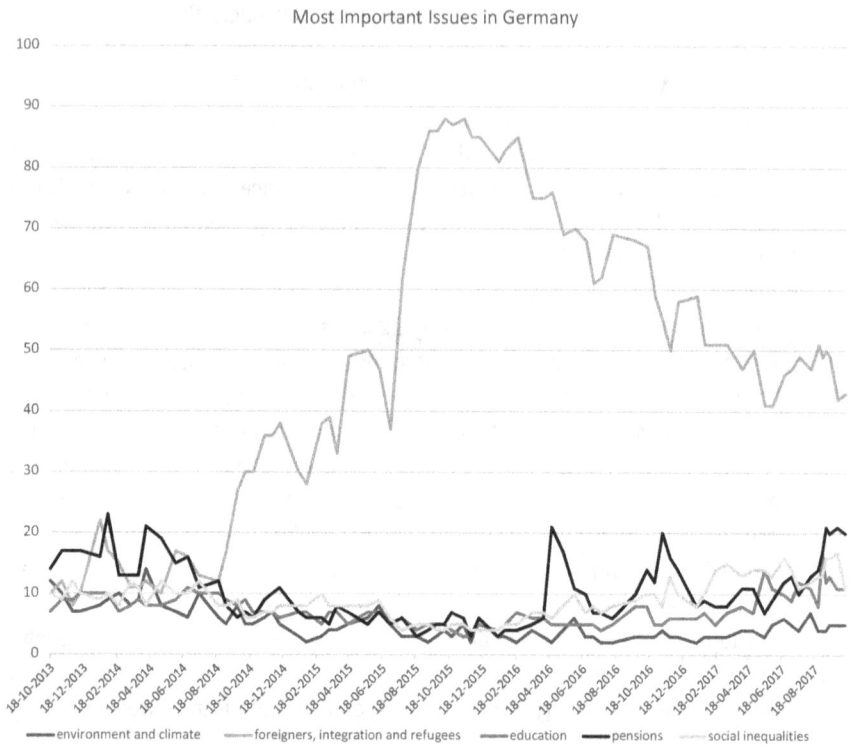

Figure 2: Perception of the most important issues in Germany, October 2013 until October 2017 (Forschungsgruppe Wahlen 2022), own diagram. Respondents were asked to answer the following question: What do you think is the most important problem in Germany at the moment? Participants could name two problems.

Voters' associations with migration provide a more fine-grained picture. Before the refugee situation, 64 per cent feared additional burdens for the welfare state, problems in schools and conflicts between natives and migrants (see Figure 3). While these numbers remained similar in 2015, negative associations increased up to 79 per cent regarding burdens for the welfare state, 72 per cent for conflicts between natives and migrants and 68 per cent for problems in schools in 2017 (Bertelsmann Stiftung 2022). Similarly, the number of respondents associating migration with housing difficulties in metropolitan areas increased from 52 per cent before the refugee situation to 65 per cent after.

In line with this, voters' positive associations with migration declined across the period (see Figure 4). While the number of respondents associating migration with a balance for shortages of skilled workers, an additional income for pension funds, an important factor for the settlement of international businesses and making

Negative Associations with Migration

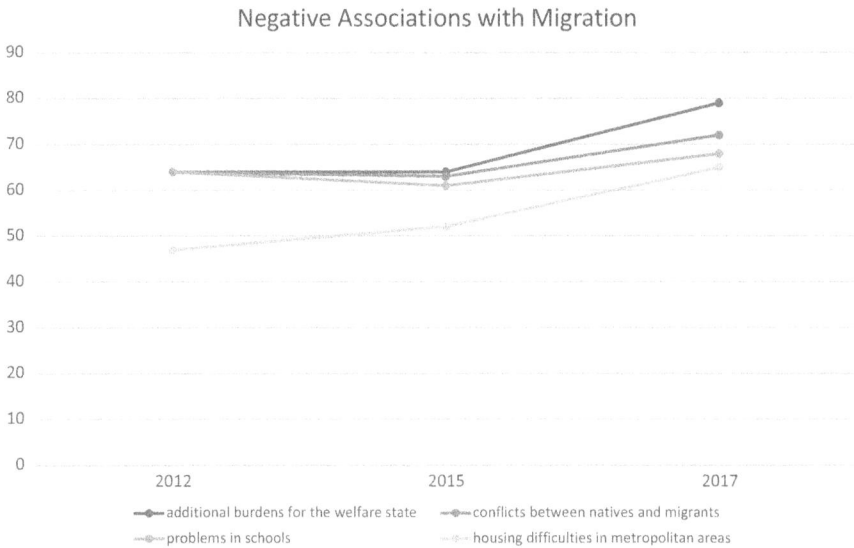

Figure 3: Negative associations of voters with migration from 2012 to 2017 (Bertelsmann Stiftung 2022: 14), own diagram. Respondents were presented with statements (see figure) and asked to tell the interviewer whether they think this applies or not. The figure depicts the share of respondents answering "applies" in per cent.

life in Germany more interesting remained similar from 2012 to 2015, the number decreased in 2017 (Bertelsmann Stiftung 2022). The decrease ranged between three and thirteen per cent. Only the mitigation of demographic change is an exception: After a slight decline from 63 per cent in 2012 to 60 per cent in 2015, the number of respondents associating migration with this increased to 64 per cent.

Overall, in 2015, 51 per cent stated that Germany can and should admit more refugees because of humanitarian reasons. On the contrary, 40 per cent stated that Germany reached its capacity and should not admit more refugees (Bertelsmann Stiftung 2022: 18). This initial optimism seemed to decrease quickly. In 2017, the picture was different: Just 37 per cent advocated admitting more refugees, while 54 per cent stated that capacities are exhausted (Bertelsmann Stiftung 2022). To summarise, public opinion seems to have become more negative and more restrictive in 2017 after the initial engagement of many volunteers who supported refugees in 2015.

Positive Associations with Migration

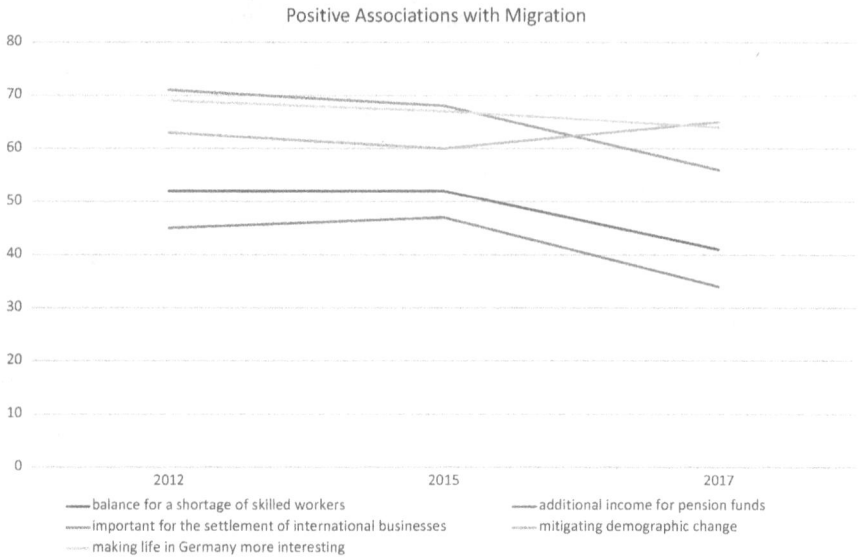

Figure 4: Positive associations of voters with migration from 2012 to 2017 (Bertelsmann Stiftung 2022: 14), own diagram. Respondents were presented with statements (see figure) and asked to tell the interviewer whether they think this applies or not. The figure depicts the share of respondents answering "applies" in per cent.

6 Findings from parliamentary debates

At first glance, the data reveal that parliamentarians did address the issue of migration slightly more often after the start of the refugee situation (see Table 1). Compared to 1,396 out of 14,927 speeches – 9.35 per cent – addressing the issue before September 2015, 2,370 out of 16,780 speeches dealt with migration after the event, which equals 14.12 per cent. Parliamentarians, thus, seem to be responsive to public opinion in prioritising the issue and discussing it more often. However, the number of speeches addressing migration does not provide information on *how* parliamentarians discuss the topic. A sentiment analysis provides more detailed insights on this.

The sentiment score for the period from 22 October 2013 until 4 September 2015 equals 0.025 (see Table 3). While 676 positive sentiments are found in the context of all liberal signalling terms, 417 negative sentiments can be counted. This points to a 2.5 per cent bias towards positive language in the speeches on migration during this period. In the period after Merkel's and Fayman's decision to allow transfers across borders, 947 negative sentiments and 1,178 positive senti-

Table 3: Sentiment scores of migration- and integration-related speeches in the German Bundestag, October 22nd, 2013–October 24th, 2017, using the GermaParl corpus (Blätte and Leonhardt 2022).

	22 October 2013–4 September 2015	5 September 2015–24 October 2017
Number of positive sentiments	676	1,178
Number of negative sentiments	417	947
Sentiment score	0.025	0.012

ments can be detected. This indicates a 1.2 per cent bias towards positive language. However, these averages might mask peaks in sentiment use, and a more fine-grained picture may provide additional insights.

To account for the peaks of sentiment use in speeches, positive and negative sentiments across the entire period are plotted per month (see Figure 5). The period of one month is chosen to consider differences in parliamentary activity that may

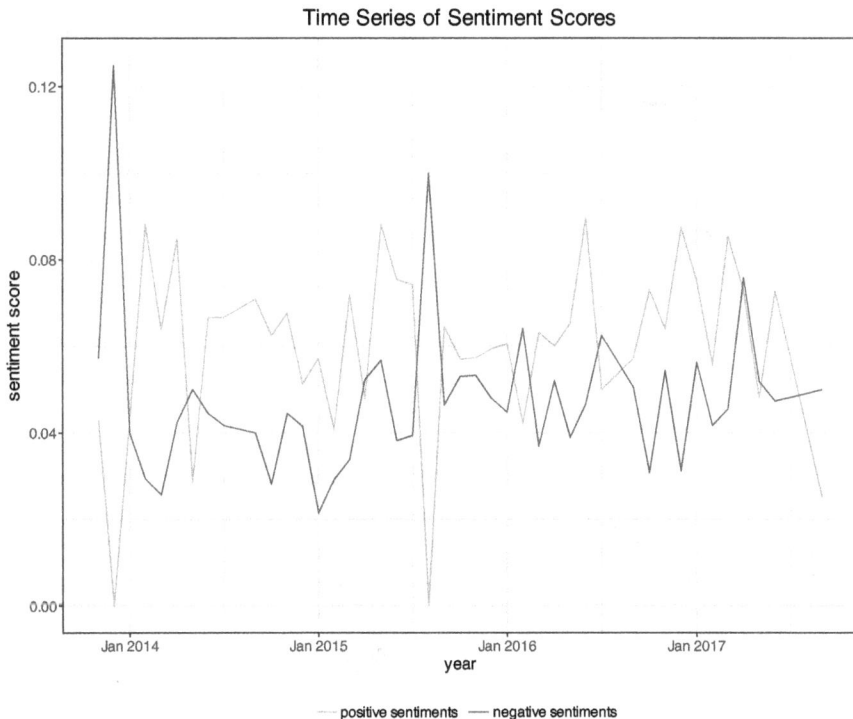

Figure 5: Time series of positive and negative sentiments regarding liberal signalling terms in migration- and integration-related speeches in the German Bundestag, 22 October 2013–24 October 2017, using the GermaParl corpus (Blätte and Leonhardt 2022).

change weekly. Two peaks can be detected across the legislature when looking at the negative sentiments accompanying signalling terms – one in December 2013 and one in August 2015. When taking a closer look at these months, it is striking that a low number of sentiments, in general, characterise the speech of these months compared to the few appearances of liberal signalling words, which exaggerates the influence of very few words. Across the rest of the legislative period, the use of sentiments remains relatively consistent.

The qualitative interpretation of the context of the signalling terms reveals a similar impression. Before September 2015, parliamentarians mostly present development aid and cooperation – the first cluster of liberal signalling terms – to create peace, deal with existing conflicts, or prevent conflicts from escalating in conflict-ridden regions. They name multiple goals such as democratisation, humanitarian aid, or ending poverty. Development aid is not questioned per se; parliamentarians, rather, disagree on priorities, the volume of funding for aid, or relating aid to political conditions. Occasionally, aid is linked to countering refugee movements. This link often includes thanking minister Müller for developing a strategy or questioning what root causes are referred to and how they can be countered.

After September 2015, the discourse shifted: references to conflict prevention and solution become sparse. Instead, parliamentarians describe development aid as a means to combat the causes of refugee movements on numerous occasions. In doing so, they demand a focus on countries of origin, especially in Africa and the Middle East. Moreover, many parliamentarians go on to state that the financial means of development aid need a stable fundament and some even refer to shares of the gross domestic product that are or should be devoted to aid. Criticism involves warnings that aid is an important building block but not a cure for refugee movements. In addition, some mention that a holistic approach – including, for example, human rights, stopping arms exports, sustainable and economic development, or education – is needed and aid should not be reduced to combatting refugee movements. Furthermore, few parliamentarians demand to question Germany's role in creating causes of refugee movements and to stop participating in globally unfair practices that cause people to flee their home countries. Despite this criticism, development aid in general is again not questioned.

The debates relating to the second cluster, namely, the distribution of asylum seekers in the EU, encompass multiple components before September 2015. One relates to the asylum system in general and another relates to more specific parts of the system such as the Dublin regulation and the distribution of responsibilities between EU member states. When discussing the asylum system in general, both the national level and the European level are addressed. Many parliamentarians express appreciation for European cooperation in asylum politics. At the same time, some highlight the need for clear rules, regulations and the return of rejected asylum seekers to use national capacities for those who "really" need protection. To avoid overusing these capacities, some emphasise the need to differentiate strictly between asylum and migration, among other motives. This would be necessary to secure public support for the system as well and hints at some restrictive tendencies. In contrast to that, a minority of parliamentarians criticise the asylum system and claim that its practices push humans into passiveness and neediness expressing opposition to current practices.

Apart from these more general aspects, specific components such as the Dublin regulation are part of the discussion. Many speakers push for a reform of the Dublin system and demand that all EU member states fulfil the common standards related to asylum. Reform ideas include a responsibility for all EU member states, solidarity, burden sharing and the elimination of inequalities between member states. Speakers agree on the necessity for reform; however, they disagree on what reforms should look like. While for some parliamentarians, solidarity means allocating asylum seekers based on distribution criteria across EU member states, others refer to equal financial burden sharing and material support as a solution and aim to restrict the influx into Germany. Despite this, the use of language does not contain strongly connotated vocabulary. A minority opt for abolishing the system altogether as it cannot be fixed.

Another aspect that comes up less frequently in speeches is related to the resettlement of refugees. While many parliamentarians express support for resettling refugees, some criticise that contingents are too small. One parliamentarian even describes the disagreement within Europe on resettlement contingents as shameful. This represents a rare moment of strongly connotated language use in parliament by condemning the current situation and expressing support for the liberalisation of contingents.

After the start of the refugee situation in September 2015, similar issues appear in the speeches in parliament. However, the emphasis shifts slightly. Concerning the asylum system in general, many still voice the necessity for reform in the direction of a common European system based on solidarity. Similar to the first period of interest, some argue that this needs to incorporate returns to protect people "really" in need of protection and thereby implicitly advocate for restrictions. In contrast to the period before, more parliamentarians raise concerns about an overburdened system at national and European levels. Reforms need to keep the system running, as some argue. What is new in this period of interest is the scepticism some exhibit as reforms at the EU level had failed already due to the opposition of some EU member states.

Likewise, the discussion about the Dublin regulation and distribution mechanisms involves criticism that a European solution to this challenge is not realistic due to opposition from, for example, Poland and Hungary, and therefore, other issues should be addressed first. Few parliamentarians point to the Dublin regulation as the current legislation that Germany should follow. Despite this critique, parliamentarians demand reforming the Dublin system on multiple occasions and point to the need to establish a long-term, solidary distribution mechanism for asylum seekers in the EU. Many reason that the existing system is suitable for few asylum seekers but stops functioning in the face of larger numbers. Furthermore, the temporary suspension of Dublin transfers would reveal that the regulation is dysfunctional and a failure.

The discussion concerning resettlement involves more concrete arguments compared with the previous period. One parliamentarian suggests binding quotas for Germany's participation in the UNHCR resettlement programme. Reasons that multiple parliamentarians name include resettlement as a regulation instrument and as a legal migration route. Furthermore, they mention that resettlement provides a unique opportunity for vulnerable groups such as children to find protection. Like the asylum system and the distribution of asylum seekers, parliamentarians bring in the EU level and maintain that a common solution is necessary and needs to ensure a fair distribution and burden sharing.

Little is said about the third cluster of liberal signalling words – refugee migration with Germany as a destination – before September 2015. Few parliamentarians mention family reunification for recognised asylum seekers and people with subsidiary protection. If they do so, they frame this type of migration as rather positive by deducting it from the basic right to family life and by supporting the possibility to expand and simplify this right. Reasons for this are the improvements in the integration of those affected because they do not need to worry about their loved ones. Criticism does not relate to the right to family unification in general but targets long waiting periods until one can welcome family members in Germany.

The events of September 2015 sparked an increase in this category (364 mentions compared to 87; see Table 2), and parliamentarians more often refer to this specific type of migration to Germany. One group of parliamentarians supports restrictive government policies to halt family reunification for people with subsidiary protection for two years. Reasons parliamentarians mention include the avoidance of the migration of people without perspectives and the prevention of overusing Germany's capacities to provide for family members on top of recognised protection seekers. Another group criticizes this decision harshly and argues that having one's family around facilitates the integration process; that family members might opt for a dangerous route when a legal one is non-existent, and that family life is a basic right that is protected by court verdicts. Debates on this topic present a rare occasion that restrictive and liberalising tendencies become explicit and strongly

connotated language such as *inhumane* or *not merciful* is used to critique government policies.

The final cluster of liberal signalling terms relates to the economic value of migration. Parliamentarians more often discuss the economic value of migration
before September 2015. Discussions revolve around the attraction of foreign skilled
labour. Some cite the so-called *Anerkennungsgesetz* that regulates the recognition
of foreign job qualifications as a useful instrument to tackle shortages of skilled labour and attract skilled workers. Other parliamentarians, however, criticise that
the law does not go far enough. Similarly, some argue based on figures that too few
migrants use the European blue card to migrate to Germany. In the same vein, a
group of parliamentarians signal openness for skilled workers from third countries
and demand to use the potential of refugees for the labour market more effectively.
Despite this optimism, many reject a points system for economic migration for
being too bureaucratic or too selective and elitist based on economic criteria. At
the same time, another group is more cautious regarding economic migration. Reasons include the separation of refugee migration and economic migration, the
warning of a brain drain in countries of origin and scepticism that migration can
compensate for existing shortages of skilled labour.

During the second period of interest, debates on these topics decrease in
number. Parliamentarians speak about the recognition of foreign qualifications
and the blue card similarly. The *Anerkennungsgesetz* and the blue card are still
evaluated as effective ways to attract and regulate skilled labour from third countries, and parliamentarians refer to numbers to make their point. The only criticism is that more financial support would make these procedures even more
effective. Contrary to these topics, labour migration and foreign skilled work, in
general, are discussed in relation to refugee migration. Some demand that legal
paths to labour migration are needed to alleviate the pressure on the asylum system and discourage illegal migration. This could involve a timely working permit
for refugees or allowing them to change the track from asylum procedures into
labour migration. Others oppose this change and demand a clear distinction between refugee migration and other forms of migration to avoid disincentives. At
the same time, others question whether refugees can solve labour shortages and
deny the potential in the short term, for example, due to refugees' lack of qualifications. Again, a points system is discussed briefly and supported by a minority;
most oppose a points system for similar reasons to those before September 2015.

Overall, the qualitative analysis confirms the results of the sentiment analysis
that the context of liberal signalling terms in speeches in the German Bundestag
did not become more negative after 4 September 2015. During both periods, parliamentarians voice both liberalising and restrictive tendencies in their speeches.
Strongly connotated terms or metaphors are an exception – especially in the case

of family reunification – and parliamentarians resort to pragmatic language most of the time.

7 Discussion and conclusion

All in all, the results support the claim that migration politics is characterised by a policy–opinion gap with a more negative public opinion preferring restrictive policies on the one hand and a more positive elite discourse favouring more liberal policies on the other hand. In line with previous research, parties in parliament are to some extent responsive to focusing events and issue salience in public opinion: When voters' perception of the issue's importance peaked shortly after the start of the refugee situation, parliamentarians indeed reacted to the event and speeches on migration and integration increased by 4.77 per cent post-September 2015. This increase concerns the number of speeches but does not provide information about their substance.

When including the content of speeches in the analysis, the findings do not support the hypothesis of gap closure. Contrary to previous findings of parties following voter preferences in other fields, this does not seem to be the case in the field of migration politics. After the refugee situation started, voters' negative associations with migration increased and positive associations decreased over time. At the same time, the sentiment of the context of liberal signalling words within speeches in the German Bundestag remained relatively stable and included a slight bias towards positively connotated vocabulary. This indicates that the refugee situation did not close the gap between public opinion and elite discourse in parliament. The qualitative analysis of the concordances of liberal signalling terms supports this finding and reveals that the tone of the debate is often rather pragmatic and thorough. Debates on family reunification form an exception to this. In addition, parliamentarians expressed both restrictive and liberal preferences both before and after September 2015.

This marks a different turning point for the policy–opinion gap from what was initially expected. Rather than closing the gap through an adjustment of language use, the lack of change concerning the sentiments of elite discourse in combination with the restrictive turn of public opinion points to a growing gap and a potential detachment of elite preferences and public opinions. The focusing event of the refugee situation starting in 2015 may, thus, not indicate a turning point for a weakening gap but mark the beginning of a widening gap.

One methodological explanation for these results might be the inbuilt neutrality bias of the scoring algorithms used for sentiment analyses. A seemingly neutral message might indeed not be neutral. The reason for this is that term-frequency distributions do not tend to be normally distributed. Furthermore, the "sentiment weights of individual terms might cancel each other out" (Rauh 2018b: 326). Context knowledge – for example, concerning the political affiliation of the speaker – might be needed to validate the results.

In addition to that, this chapter focuses on the parliamentary arena. Usually, formal and informal rules govern debates in the parliamentary arena and determine the allocation of time and what can and cannot be said in parliament (Proksch and Slapin 2015). These rules might bias the results as the speaker of the house may not allow certain negative expressions on the speaking floor and discipline speakers. Furthermore, parties might not allocate speaking time to certain parliamentarians due to dissenting views (Proksch and Slapin 2015). Accordingly, future research should include other arenas as well to assess the influence of focusing events on the policy–opinion gap. Maybe the "tough talk" on migration is not to be found in parliaments but rather in media outlets not governed by the rules of parliament. Future research could address the kind of debate content reaching voters through different types of media or the different messages that the same legislator sends in parliament compared to media.

Moreover, this chapter does not consider party differences but the Bundestag as a whole as the policy–opinion gap states a difference between "the elite" and "the public". However, parties and their electorate are not homogeneous. Parties may face different incentives to adjust their positions, and party responses are only "significant in situations where public opinion is clearly shifting away from the party policy positions" (Adams et al. 2004: 589). Further research should address this and investigate the need of individual parties to adjust their position after focusing events concerning migration politics, how these adjustments affect the policy–opinion gap and if the policy–opinion gap differs between individual parties and their respective electorates.

A final strand for future research includes the relationship between the policy–opinion gap and policy outcomes. Incremental changes or critical junctures changing these path dependencies influence the outcome of the political process. In some cases, these outcomes could be more visible than the policy process.

References

Adams, James, Michael Clark, Lawrence Ezrow & Garrett Glasgow. 2004. Understanding Change and Stability in Party Ideologies: Do Parties Respond to Public Opinion or to Past Election Results? *British Journal of Political Science* 34(4). 589–610. https://doi.org/10.1017/S0007123404000201.

Ansolabehere, Stephen & Shanto Iygenar. 1994. Riding the Wave and Claiming Ownership over Issues: The Joint Effects of Advertising and News Coverage in Campaigns. *Public Opinion Quarterly* 58(3). 335–357.

Baker, Paul. 2006. *Using Corpora in Discourse Analysis*. London: Continuum.

Bertelsmann Stiftung. 2022. *Willkommenskultur zwischen Stabilität und Aufbruch: Aktuelle Perspektiven der Bevölkerung auf Migration und Integration in Deutschland*. Gütersloh: Bertelsmann Stiftung. https://doi.org/10.11586/2022001.

Birkland, Thomas A. 1997. *After Disaster: Agenda Setting, Public Policy, and Focusing Events*. Washington, DC: Georgetown University Press.

Birkland, Thomas A. 1998. Focusing Events, Mobilization, and Agenda Setting. *Journal of Public Policy* 18(1). 53–74.

Blätte, Andreas &Andre Blessing. 2018. The GermaParl Corpus of Parliamentary Protocols. In Nicoletta Calzolari, Khalid Choukri, Christopher Cieri, Thierry Declerck, Sara Goggi, Koiti Hasida, Hitoshi Isahara, Bente Maegaard, Joseph Mariani, Hélène Mazo, Asuncion Moreno, Jan Odijk, Stelios Piperidis & Takenobu Tokunaga (eds.), *Proceedings of the Eleventh International Conference on Language Resources and Evaluation (LREC 2018)*. Miyazaki, Japan: European Language Resources Association (ELRA).

Blätte, Andreas & Christoph Leonhardt. 2022. GermaParl Corpus of Plenary Protocols (v2.0.0-beta.2). Zenodo. https://doi.org/10.5281/zenodo.6539967.

Blätte, Andreas, Julia Rakers & Christoph Leonhardt. 2022. How GermaParl Evolves: Improving Data Quality by Reproducible Corpus Preparation and User Involvement. In Darja Fišer, Maria Eskevich, Jakob Lenardič & Franciska de Jong (eds.), *Proceedings of the Workshop ParlaCLARIN III within the 13th Language Resources and Evaluation Conference*. Marseille, France: European Language Resources Association (ELRA).

Blätte, Andreas, Merve Schmitz-Vardar & Christoph Leonhardt. 2020. "MigPress. A Corpus of Migration and Integration Related Newspaper Coverage." https://polmine.github.io/MigPress/ (accessed 8 March 2022)

Bonafont, Laura Chaqués, Anna M. Palau & Luz M. Muñoz Marquez. 2014. Policy Promises and Governmental Activities in Spain. In Christoffer Green-Pedersen & Stefaan Walgrave (eds.), *Agenda Setting, Policies, and Political Systems: A Comparative Approach*, 183–200. Chicago: University of Chicago Press.

Borghetto, Enrico & Federico Russo. 2018. From agenda setters to agenda takers? The determinants of party issue attention in times of crisis. *Party Politics* 24(1). 65–77. https://doi.org/10.1177/1354068817740757.

Brazeal, LeAnn M. & William L. Benoit. 2008. Issue Ownership in Congressional Campaign Television Spots. *Communication Quarterly* 56(1). 17–28. https://doi.org/10.1080/01463370701839172.

Capoccia, Giovanni & R. Daniel Kelemen. 2007. The Study of Critical Junctures: Theory, Narrative, and Counterfactuals in Historical Institutionalism. *World Politics* 59(3). 341–369. https://doi.org/10.1017/S0043887100020852.

Chouliaraki, Lilie, Myria Georgiou & Rafal Zaborowski. 2017. *The European 'Migration Crisis' and the Media: A Cross-European Press Content Analysis*. London, UK: Department of Media and Communications, London School of Economics and Political Science.

Czaika, Mathias & Hein de Haas. 2013. The Effectiveness of Immigration Policies. *Population and Development Review* 39(3). 487–508.

Destatis. 2022. Statistik über Schutzsuchende in Deutschland. https://www-genesis.destatis.de/gene sis//online?operation=table&code=12531-0001&bypass=true&levelindex=0&levelid= 1646824316474#abreadcrumb (accessed 2 March 2022)

Entman, Robert M. 1993. Framing: Towards Clarification of a Fractured Paradigm. *Journal of Communication* 43(4). 51–58.

Fernandes, Jorge M., Marc Debus & Hanna Bäck. 2021. Unpacking the politics of legislative debates. *European Journal of Political Research* 60(4). 1032–1045. https://doi.org/10.1111/1475-6765.12454.

Firth, John Rupert. 1957. *Papers in Linguistics, 1934–1951*. London: Oxford University Press.

Forschungsgruppe Wahlen. 2022. Politbarometer. 2013–2017. https://www.forschungsgruppe.de/Um fragen/Politbarometer/Langzeitentwicklung_-_Themen_im_Ueberblick/Politik_II/#Probl1 (accessed 28 February 2022)

Freeman, Gary P. 1995. Modes of Immigration Politics in Liberal Democratic States. *The International Migration Review* 29(4). 881–902.

Green-Pedersen, Christoffer & Peter B. Mortensen. 2010. Who sets the agenda and who responds to it in the Danish parliament? A new model of issue competition and agenda-setting. *European Journal of Political Research* 49(2). 257–281. https://doi.org/10.1111/j.1475-6765.2009.01897.x.

Green-Pedersen, Christoffer & Stefaan Walgrave. 2014. Political Agenda Setting: An Approach to Studying Political Systems. In Christoffer Green-Pedersen & Stefaan Walgrave (eds.), *Agenda Setting, Policies, and Political Systems: A Comparative Approach*, 1–16. Chicago: Chicago University Press.

Gudbrandsen, Frøy. 2010. Partisan Influence on Immigration: The Case of Norway. *Scandinavian Political Studies* 33(3). 248–270. https://doi.org/10.1111/j.1467-9477.2010.00250.x.

Herbert, Ulrich & Jakob Schönhagen. 2020. Vor dem 5. September: Die "Flüchtlingskrise" 2015 im historischen Kontext. *Aus Politik und Zeitgeschichte* 70(30–32). 27–36.

Hobolt, Sara Binzer & Robert Klemmensen. 2005. Responsive Government? Public Opinion and Government Policy Preferences in Britain and Denmark. *Political Studies* 53(2). 379–402. https://doi.org/10.1111/j.1467-9248.2005.00534.x.

Jacobsen, Jannes, Philipp Eisnecker & Jürgen Schupp. 2017. In 2016, around one-third of people in Germany donated for refugees and ten percent helped out on site – yet concerns are mounting. *DIW Economic Bulletin* 16–17. 165–176.

Jennings, Will. 2009. The Public Thermostat, Political Responsiveness and Error Correction: Border Control and Asylum in Britain, 1994–2007. *British Journal of Political Science* 39(4). 847–870. https://doi.org/10.1017/S000712340900074X.

John, Peter,Shaun Bevan & Will Jennings. 2014. Party Politics and the Policy Agenda: The Case of the United Kingdom. In Christoffer Green-Pedersen & Stefaan Walgrave (eds.), *Agenda Setting, Policies, and Political Systems: A Comparative Approach*, 19–35. Chicago: Chicago University Press.

Leruth, Benjamin & Peter Taylor-Gooby. 2019. Does political discourse matter? Comparing party positions and public attitudes on immigration in England. *Politics* 39(2). 154–169. https://doi. org/10.1177/0263395718755566.

Liu, Bing. 2015. *Sentiment Analysis: Mining Opinions, Sentiments, and Emotions*. New York: Cambridge University Press.

Lutz, Philipp. 2021. Reassessing the gap-hypothesis: Tough talk and weak action in migration policy? *Party Politics* 27(1). 174–186. https://doi.org/10.1177/1354068819840776.

Mader, Matthias & Harald Schoen. 2019. The European refugee crisis, party competition, and voters' responses in Germany. *West European Politics* 42(1). 67–90. https://doi.org/10.1080/01402382. 2018.1490484.

Morales, Laura, Jean-Benoit Pilet & Didier Ruedin. 2015. The Gap between Public Preferences and Policies on Immigration: A Comparative Examination of the Effect of Politicisation on Policy Congruence. *Journal of Ethnic and Migration Studies* 41(9). 1495–1516. https://doi.org/10.1080/ 1369183X.2015.1021598.

Proksch, Sven-Oliver & Jonathan B. Slapin. 2015. *The Politics of Parliamentary Debate: Parties, Rebels and Representation*. Cambridge: Cambridge University Press.

Rauh, Christian. 2018a. Replication Data for: Validating a sentiment dictionary for German political language (V1). Harvard Dataverse. https://doi.org/10.7910/DVN/BKBXWD.

Rauh, Christian. 2018b. Validating a sentiment dictionary for German political language – a workbench note. *Journal of Information Technology & Politics* 15(4). 319–343. https://doi.org/10. 1080/19331681.2018.1485608.

Remus, Robert,Uwe Quasthoff & Gerhard Heyer. 2010. SentiWS – a publicly available German-language resource for sentiment analysis. In: Nicoletta Calzolari, Khalid Choukri, Bente Maegaard, Joseph Mariani, Jan Odijk, Stelios Piperidis, Mike Rosner & Daniel Tapias (eds.), *Proceedings of the 7th International Language Resources and Evaluation LREC*. Valetta, Malta: European Language Resources Association (ELRA).

Schmitz-Vardar, Merve & Christoph Leonhardt. 2022. Einstellungen und Sprachgebrauch politischer Repräsentant*innen zu Migrationspolitik, Eine triangulative Studie aus Umfragen und Plenarprotokollen. In Merve Schmitz-Vardar, Andrea Rumpel, Alexandra Graevskaia & Laura Dinnebier (eds.), *Migrationsforschung (inter)disziplinär, Eine anwendungsorientierte Einführung*, 149–180. Bielefeld: transcript.

Sides, John. 2007. The Consequences of Campaign Agendas. *American Politics Research* 35(4). 465–488. https://doi.org/10.1177/1532673X07300648.

Spoon, Jae-Jae & Heike Klüver. 2014. Do parties respond? How electoral context influences party responsiveness. *Electoral Studies* 35. 48–60. https://doi.org/10.1016/j.electstud.2014.04.014.

Statham, Paul & Andrew Geddes. 2006. Elites and the 'organised public': Who drives British immigration politics and in which direction? *West European Politics* 29(2). 248–269. https://doi. org/10.1080/01402380500512601.

Vliegenthart, Rens, Stefaan Walgrave & Brandon Zicha. 2013. How preferences, information and institutions interactively drive agenda-setting: Questions in the Belgian parliament, 1993–2000. *European Journal of Political Research* 52(3). 390–418. https://doi.org/10.1111/j.1475-6765.2012. 02070.x.

Walgrave, Stefaan & Knut de Swert. 2007. Where Does Issue Ownership Come From? From the Party or from the Media? Issue-party Identifications in Belgium, 1991–2005. *The International Journal of Press/Politics* 12(1). 37–67. https://doi.org/10.1177/1081180X06297572.

Waltinger, Ulli. 2010. GermanPolarityClues: A lexical resource for German sentiment analysis. In Nicoletta Calzolari, Khalid Choukri, Bente Maegaard, Joseph Mariani, Jan Odijk, Stelios Piperidis, Mike Rosner & Daniel Tapias (eds.), *International Conference on Language Resources and Evaluation (LREC)*. Valetta, Malta: European Language Resources Association (ELRA).

Williams, Christopher & Jae-Jae Spoon. 2015. Differentiated party response: The effect of Euroskeptic public opinion on party positions. *European Union Politics* 16(2). 176–193. https://doi.org/10.1177/ 1465116514564702.

Benjamin Ewert
COVID-19 as a potential turning point in German health policy

Abstract: This chapter sheds light on potential implications emanating from COVID-19 for the future outlook of German health policy. To investigate to what extent the pandemic will change health policymaking in Germany, two turning-point conceptions are applied: theoretical insights on 'critical junctures' and Peter Hall's (1993) approach to policy paradigms and social learning. Empirical findings reveal that COVID-19 does not represent an immediate turning point in German health policy. Instead, policymaking is in line with the rationales of a health system that is traditionally divided into the sectors of healthcare and public health. On the one hand, rather than exploiting the crisis for health policy renewal, policymakers pursue gradual reforms in well-known bottleneck areas (e.g. long-term care, digitalisation). On the other hand, the issue of public health has been re-established on the health policy agenda due to COVID-19. As concluded, this might spur paradigmatic policy change in the long run.

Keywords: health policy, COVID-19, critical juncture, paradigm change, path dependency

1 Introduction

At first glance, the upshot of the analysis of to what extent COVID-19 has been a turning point for health policy in Germany seems rather simple: regarding the healthcare sector, there has been no major policy change nor are there indications that significant change is underway. Instead, the systems' institutional setup has weathered the pandemic unscathed so far. Now and in the future, the healthcare sector could be regarded as a key pillar of the conservative, corporatist ('Bismarckian') system that is regulated by the self-government of service providers and payers in the 'shadow of the state'. Likewise, the financing and payment of healthcare services remain characterised by the unique dualism of Statutory Health Insurance (SHI) and private health insurance (Immergut and Wendt 2021). Hence, the German health system proves more general findings according to which the 'health sector is particularly noted for its resistance to change' (Bali

Benjamin Ewert, Department of Health Siences, Fulda University of Applied Sciences

https://doi.org/10.1515/9783111272900-013

et al. 2022: 84). However, if even a global health crisis such as COVID-19 is not able to spur change in the health sector, it is legitimate to ask: what event can do it at all? Therefore, policy science scholarship is challenged to search for the slightest indications announcing a revision of health policy's status due to COVID-19.

Indeed, there is reason to believe that the pandemic might eventually be considered a decisive turning point in German health policy. Not only in Germany, the virus outbreak has put an old issue back on the political agenda, i.e. the protection of public health and with it the balance between the health system's public health and healthcare sectors. In this vein, COVID-19 represents, first of all, a potential 'policy window for positive reforms' (Auener et al. 2020: 419). Following this logic, future health policy in Germany might become less healthcare-oriented by putting more emphasis on prevention, health promotion and population health than individual disease management and hospital care. Understood this way, a health policy renewal process bears hopes and potential to set off a paradigmatic policy change (Hall 1993) that essentially includes new efforts of strategic alignment between the German health systems' separated sectors.

Policy analysis scholarship provides a basket of theories such as path dependency, policy learning and the Multiple Streams Approach to explain why the health policy change happens or is absent (for an overview see: Capano et al. 2022: 2–3; Hogan et al. 2022: 41–42). While such theoretical concepts are accurate to identify institutional barriers towards current reform (e.g. medical professions' strong position within healthcare governance in Germany), they do not necessarily provide a fine-grained analysis of how change takes place procedurally, i.e. why, when and how policymaking within certain fields 'turns' in a different direction. This also includes the question of whether the accumulation of incremental reforms can be considered a turning point in health policymaking.

That said, this chapter asks whether turning-point conceptions help investigate German health policy's response to COVID-19 and to what kind of policy change this reaction might lead to in the long term. The analysis was structured into five parts. First, the historical separation of the German health system into public health and the healthcare sector will be reviewed and assessed concerning its present-day implications. Second, the term 'turning point' will be conceptualised concerning the German health system. Two theoretical strands are deemed crucial in this regard: on the one hand, the debate on critical junctures (Capoccia and Keleman 2007) in the evolution of institutional settings; on the other hand, an understanding of the turning point is derived from Peter Hall's (1993) theory on social learning and paradigmatic policy change. As suggested, comprehensive health system renewal that goes beyond incremental change requires the combined manifestation of both turning-point concepts. Third, empirical findings from the German health system will be presented in line with the conceptual definition of turning points. Fourth, the discussion refers back to the turning-point hypotheses and provides an outlook for a post-COVID-19 health policy in Germany. Finally, the conclusion summarises the chapter's key takeaways.

2 Germany's two-tier health system

The German health system consists of three *pillars* – outpatient care, hospital care and the public health service – formally governed by the Federal Ministry of Health (Busse and Blümel 2014). Speaking of pillars fuels the idea of sectoral alignment through more or less equally powerful policy actors within a coherent health system. However, research has shown that 'health care and public health in German coevolved in a decoupled way' (Trein 2019: 162), whereas 'public health remains to a large extent subordinate to health care' (Trein 2019: 167).

Curative treatment and disease management rather than prevention and health promotion are at the centre of the healthcare sector (Busse and Blümel 2014; Immergut and Wendt 2021). Hence, healthcare services address individuals (i.e. insured persons and patients) rather than groups and populations. Healthcare governance revolves mainly around the regulation, financing and provision of services. Recurrent policy topics are, among others, rising SHI contributions, healthcare benefit catalogues, hospital payment schemes and the level of individual healthcare consumption. Key healthcare actors are providers (i.e. the National Association of SHI Physicians or the German Hospital Federation) and payers (i.e. The National Association of SHI Funds) and – with much less influence – patient and self-help organisations. Following the principle of corporatist self-administration, healthcare actors broadly decide over their affairs within a state-controlled governance framework. Most significantly, within the highest self-governing body, the Federal Joint Committee, corporatist actors agree on the content of the SHI service catalogue and healthcare quality guidelines. Despite several competition- and market-based reforms within the last three decades (Immergut and Wendt 2021), key parameters of Germany's corporatist health governance system have remained stable. Overall, the system has shown an inherent tendency to protect medical professions' privileges and autonomy (Trein 2019: 169).

In contrast, the public health sector, institutionalised through the public health service (ÖGD), is not part of the corporatist self-governance system. Financed by taxpayers' money, the ÖGD is comprised of state and local health departments, certain institutions of veterinary and food inspection and health authorities at the national, state and municipality levels (Plümer 2018: 35). Key ÖGD agencies at the national level are the Federal Centre for Health Education

(BZgA) and state-owned research institutes (e.g. Robert Koch Institute, RKI). Although ÖGD's day-to-day business mostly takes place at the local level where public health departments are 'undertaking essential functions such as ensuring clean drinking water, monitoring hygiene in public facilities and restaurants, running immunisation programmes and developing strategies to counteract risky health behaviours (Plümer 2018: 45). Professional and political cooperation between healthcare and public health staff – in the sense of joint actions to improve health – barely exists (Trein 2019: 160).

The public health sector's aforementioned subordination to the healthcare sector becomes underscored by two major public health policies within the last two decades. First, the introduction of Disease Management Programmes for certain groups of chronically ill patients (e.g. asthma, breast cancer and diabetes) and second, the adoption of the Prevention Act in 2015. As a result of both policies, 'preventive services are now delivered within the same legal framework as curative services' (Busse and Blümel 2014: 181). Thus, despite some 'policy learning and policy integration between health care and public health' (Trein 2019: 170), both sectors remained principally separated in pre-pandemic times.

3 Turning points in health policy

Regarding COVID-19, this section seeks to apply two specific understandings of turning points to the realm of health policy. Emanating from institutional and policy theory, both concepts differ in terms of the speed, scope, and permanency of change. As argued, if combined, turning-point conceptions may lead to more analytical accuracy concerning the pandemic's implications on German health policy.

Characteristically, health systems are known for their 'slow and episodic nature of policy change' (Bali et al. 2022: 84). Given the plethora of powerful actors (e.g. state institutions, providers and payers) and conflicting interests (e.g. solidarity, efficiency, quality and growth) once-taken policy paths are very likely to be pursued continually. Even if comparative analysis revealed significant degrees of policy convergence 'between countries belonging to the same family' (Toth 2021: 69), such as Bismarckian health systems (Leiber et al. 2015), path dependency remains a key feature of health systems. So far, approaches that bridge sectors and responsibilities do not reflect realities on the ground.

In health policy analysis, the term 'turning point' has been used sporadically. In a comparative study on the German, Austrian and Dutch health systems, Leiber et al. (2015: 13) classified presumably 'groundbreaking' reforms such as the Healthcare Structure Act in 1992 (in Germany) or the Health Insurance Act in

2006 (in The Netherlands) as country-specific turning points. However, there is also reason to argue that, particularly in corporate health systems, 'changes are embedded in the existing institutions' (Hassenteufel and Palier 2007: 574). Such gradual reforms could be well explained by standard policy change theories such as Kingdon's (2014) Multiple Streams Approach or Baumgartner et al.'s (2018) Punctuated Equilibrium Framework that are driven by an 'underlying combinative causal logic' (Capano 2009: 27). However, in the face of a once-in-a-century event like a pandemic, it seems appropriate to question the explanatory power of medium-range theories that do not include the possibility of institutional change. First of all, we have to consider COVID-19 as a major 'crisis' that is more impactful than 'external' shocks or events (Capano 2009: 27).

As criticised, 'crisis' has become such 'a ubiquitous word that its discriminatory power is diminished across various disciplines' (Freeden 2017: 12). While this statement seems accurate in general, the occurrence of a pandemic, similar to the Spanish Flu (1918–1920), could be viewed as in 'a class of its own' (Boin et al. 2021: 6). Consequently, COVID-19 is well defined as 'a complex and multifaceted intersection of numerous crises' (Boin et al. 2021: 8) that have 'tested public institutions, crisis leadership and societal solidarity to the core' (Boin et al. 2021: 107). Others have classified the pandemic as a 'super wicked' problem by referring to its extraordinarily complex problem structure (Auld et al. 2021). As emphasised, pandemic management has provided unexpected 'opportunities to capture the limelight and shift policy agendas, claiming credit or navigating blame games and pushing for, or blocking, systemic reforms' (Boin et al. 2021: 6). Given this process, path dependency, perceived as institutional choices of the past that constrain policymaking in the present, has been identified as a key barrier (Auld et al. 2021). Nevertheless, policy change scholarship has hypothesised that the 'coronavirus disease can (. . .) be thought of as potentially a significant path disrupter' (Capano et al. 2022: 4). However, the verification of this hypothesis presupposes a more nuanced understanding of how policy paths do evolve in political systems. Therefore, it is useful to revisit theoretical insights on critical juncture.

Political theory revealed an imbalance in the study of critical junctures. While it is recurrently referred to as a way of explaining the existence of path dependencies, less is known about 'actions and decisions that occur during the critical juncture itself' (Capoccia and Keleman 2007: 342). Fixing this imbalance requires the term 'critical juncture' to be defined first. According to Capoccia and Keleman (2007: 348), critical junctures are '*relatively* short periods during which there is *a substantially* heightened probability that agents' choices will affect the outcome of interest'. The unprecedented outbreak of a pandemic fulfils this definition. Indeed, COVID-19 justifies assumptions concerning lasting institutional change in the field of health. If these assumptions come true, the pandemic could have been retrospectively considered 'the genetic moment' (Capoccia and Kele-man 2007: 369) that triggered transformational health policy reform. However, 'change is not a necessary element of a critical juncture' (Capoccia and Keleman 2007: 348). Despite occurring at certain points in time, critical junctures may also elapse as missed opportunities. With a view on the pandemic's impact on the Ger-man health system, we see contingent outcomes including 'wide-ranging change' and 're-equilibration of an institution' (Capoccia and Keleman 2007: 352). Thus, rather than merely identifying the existence of critical junctures, political science scholarship ought to investigate how 'decisions by influential actors (. . .) during a phase of institutional fluidity (. . .) steer [or do not steer, B.E.] outcomes towards a new equilibrium' (Capoccia and Keleman 2007: 354). Based on this theoretical understanding of critical junctures, the first hypothesis can be formulated:

H1: *Perceived as a critical juncture, COVID-19 has accelerated the realignment of the healthcare and public health sector in the German health system.*

Key indicators for the approval or rejection of H1 are the number and scope of (cross-sectoral) health policies that have been adopted since the start of the pan-demic and the allocation of new responsibilities for public health institutions.

Second, Peter Hall's (1993) framework to assess policy paradigm changes will be applied to investigate the extent to which COVID-19 has become a turning point in German health policy. The framework provides criteria to categorise and differ-entiate policy change by emphasising policymakers' social learning in relation to the policy process. Essentially, Hall distinguishes three levels of policy change:

First-order change: Drawing from new experiences and insights, policy-makers recalibrate the setting of (mixes of) policy instruments that are al-ready applied. For example, in many countries, it has been decided to increase taxes on tobacco products and to inform (potential) smokers about tobacco's health risks via deterrent pictures displayed on tobacco product packages. At this level, policy goals and the choice of applied policy instru-ments remain unchanged.

Second-order change: Policymakers stick to their initial policy goals but apply new instruments to reach them. The implementation of smoking bans (at least in restricted areas) fits this level of policy change.

Third-order change: At this level, the policy change is the most comprehensive. It comprises not only the setting and selection of policy instruments but also the revision of policy goals. In this regard, place-based public health policies that seek to improve the social determinants of health, affecting the socio-economic, structural and environmental causes of people's health conditions (rather than merely regulating 'undesired' individual behaviours), serve as an example.

In line with Hall's (1993) framework, policymaking is conceptualised 'as a process that is about making decisions about [these] three dimensions' (Knill and Tosun 2020: 210). However, policy paradigm changes – including the revision of instrument settings, instrument choices and policy goals – 'are associated with experimentation with new policies and lesson-drawing from policy failures' (Knill and Tosun 2020: 211).

Taking Hall's insights on the regulatory depth and scope of policy change into account, the second hypothesis reads as follows:

H2: *Turning to public health and prevention issues, policymaking in response to COVID-19 will lead to a lasting health policy paradigm change.*

Key indicators for the approval or rejection of H2 are (the sum of) changes in policy instrument settings, instrument choices and the revision of health policy goals.

By testing H1 and H2 empirically in the remainder of the paper, it is possible to investigate German health policy's response to COVID-19. This approach allows a better understanding of the specific turning-point character of the pandemic and its implications for the scope and degree of health policy change. Moreover, at best, hypotheses testing bring us closer to the answer to the pre-eminent question of whether a small change of degree in a persistent path that has not changed for a long time should be considered a turning point.

4 Empirical findings: Health policies in response to COVID-19

To what extent has COVID-19 been a turning point that 'fundamentally shaped the course of health policy development?' (Bali et al. 2022: 84). As hypothesised, with regard to the German case, this would mean a paradigm shift from individual healthcare towards public health. Thus, policies of interest are especially those that are likely to change German health policy permanently (e.g. a revision of the infection protection law) at the federal level, while short-term 'coronavirus politics' (Greer et al. 2021) such as temporary lockdowns are excluded from the analysis.

Since the outbreak of the pandemic, the German federal government[1] has passed 78 health policy laws and regulations (Table 1, see Appendix). Noticeably, regulations – which do not require approval by the parliament – were by far the

---

1 Consisting of a grand coalition between Christian Democrats, Christian Social Democrats and Social Democrats (until December 2021) and a traffic-light coalition between Social Democrats, the Green Party und Liberal Democrats (since December 2021). Under the new government, former Health Minister Jens Spahn (Christian Democrats) has been succeeded by Karl Lauterbach (Social Democrats).

government's preferred policy instrument (i.e. 53) to respond to the pandemic. The adopted regulations pursued two aims: to protect public health in a situation of national emergency and to safeguard the functioning of the health system. Thus, given the German case, one is inclined to confirm the assumption according to which '[e]emergency governance (. . .) is executive governance' (Ginsburg and Versteg 2021: 1498). However, throughout the pandemic, federal states *(Länder)* recurrently constrained regulations by the national government in controversial areas (e.g. COVID-19 testing strategies).

What learning emanates from health policymaking at the national level in response to the pandemic? Broadly speaking, there is evidence that more than half of all policies and regulations (40) between March 2020 and February 2022 are related to COVID-19, while a little less than half (38) are not. Among the latter, 33 policies and regulations exclusively belong to the healthcare sector, while only three policies and regulations belong to the public health sector. Eighteen policies and regulations are healthcare and COVID-19 related, while eight policies and regulations combine the categories of public health and COVID-19. Only two policies refer to the categories of healthcare and public health. Finally, 14 policies and regulations (most prominently: the federal law on infection protection) refer to each of the three categories (i.e. healthcare, public health and COVID-19).

Based on these numbers, one is tempted to conclude that despite ad hoc efforts of pandemic management (i.e. COVID-19 related policies and regulations), healthcare rather than public health issues have still dominated German health policy since February 2020. However, to qualitatively assess the degree to which health policymaking has changed in response to COVID-19, a closer examination is necessary. For that purpose, six policies,[2] standing out from the large number of small-scale regulations in response to COVID-19, are briefly introduced (starting with the most recent one):

(1) Federal law on infection protection (2020–22): before COVID-19, the crux of the law has been that the *Länder* 'have the right to impose restrictions on their populations in the event of specific risk situations' (Kuhlmann et al. 2021: 343). Hence, the power of the federal government, i.e. the Ministry of Health and the RKI, to protect public health in times of crisis had been rather limited. In this regard, COVID-19 has been a turning point since the law on infection protection 'pushed towards more centralisation and a strengthening of the federal level' (Kuhlmann

---

2 Policies were selected according to the following questions: Is the respective policy conceptual rather than merely responsive? Are healthcare and/or public health issues addressed in a novel way or cross-sectorally? Is there an expected impact with regard to the future trajectory of the German health system?.

et al. 2021: 345). The amendment empowers the federal parliament to declare an *epidemic emergency of national concern* and, therewith, centralised responsibilities in a politically charged area. The *Länder*, on the other hand, also benefitted from the amendment since it provided them with legal clarity concerning measures (e.g. obligation to wear a mask, social distancing rules, closing of schools and companies) they are allowed to take in response to the pandemic. Ironically, *Länder's* reluctance to take sufficient measures to protect public health led to another tightening of the infection protection law by the federal government: the enforcement of the *federal emergency brake* (i.e. a catalogue of protection measurements the federal government can take unanimously) if incidence rates rise above a certain limit. Even if the new government put an end to the epidemic emergency of national concern in March 2022, COVID-19 has fundamentally strengthened the weight of public health policy. The latter is proved by fierce political controversies over public health responsibilities and agencies that largely operated beyond the public radar before the pandemic.

(2) Vaccination prevention law (2021): Germany's post-war vaccination policy has been 'classical-voluntary' (Paul and Loer 2019: 173) characterised by 'a shift away from public health and towards the pre-eminence of individualised medicine' (Paul and Loer 2019: 172). Except for a recent law that stipulated vaccination against measles for kindergarten and school children, educators, teachers and medical staff, any form of compulsory vaccination has traditionally been rejected by German policymakers who preferred persuasive rather than coercive policy instruments. Thus, the legal introduction of compulsory vaccination against COVID-19 for healthcare professionals, effective since March 2022, could be considered groundbreaking. However, the implementation of the law has turned into a sluggish process since not only some *Länder* but also local authorities are reluctant to enforce employment bans for unvaccinated healthcare professionals. In April 2022, several proposals to make vaccination mandatory for the whole population did not win a majority in the *Bundestag*. If anything, the heated political debate on compulsory vaccination serves as a textbook example of how controversial public health issues can be effectively politicised and instrumentalised by policy entrepreneurs (e.g. Bavaria's prime minister, Markus Söder) for opportunistic reasons.

(3) Digital modernisation of health service provision and care law (2021): being part of a series of policy efforts that seek to accelerate the slow-moving digitalisation of the German healthcare sector (Bogumil-Uçan and Klenk 2021), the law allows the application of certified health apps for people in need of care, the expansion of telemedicine infrastructure and services and the improvement of electronic patient files. In particular, healthcare users' positive experiences with telemedicine were recurrently reported during the pandemic (Reitzle et al. 2021).

In addition, a coordination unit for the interoperability of health systems' digital services will be established.

(4) Healthcare and long-term care advancement law (2021): the law seeks to strengthen the financial situation and autonomy of care workers within the German health system. From September 2022 onwards, healthcare providers are obliged to pay healthcare and long-term care professionals according to collectively agreed wages. In addition, professional care workers have been enabled to select medical aids for people in need of care and have obtained more decision-making scope in home care settings. Also, nursing homes have to meet staffing ratios to be defined at the federal level.

(5) Healthcare and long-term care improvement law (2020): essentially, the law stipulated the provision of additional tax money (EUR five billion) for the SHI. It also included 20,000 new jobs for care workers in long-term care facilities and 600 new jobs for midwives in hospitals. Moreover, SHIs are provided with more leeway to move beyond the standard healthcare provision by concluding or joining integrated care contracts (i.e. selective tariffs).

(6) Pact for the public health service (2020): traditionally established as a health control and health education agency, the German public health service (ÖGD) has not accommodated itself yet to the status of a 'policy hub' inventing and facilitating cross-sectoral prevention and health promotion. In a first response to COVID-19, the federal government together with the prime minister of the *Länder*[3] passed the pact for the ÖGD to modernise the 377 public health departments in Germany. In total, the ad hoc policy includes EUR 4 billion for staffing, digitalisation and structural modernisation. Largely seen as a 'historic chance', the pact has increased public attention to the public health service in Germany. However, the pact's implementation is behind schedule due to unsolved financial responsibilities between the federal state and the *Länder*. There are also doubts about whether the pact will strengthen the ÖGD's voice and influence as a political actor in the health system (Ewert and Loer 2022).

---

3 Therefore, the Pact for the ÖGD is not listed in Table 1.

5 COVID-19 as a potential turning-point health policy in Germany

It should have become clear by now that the institutional framework of Germany's health system has not changed fundamentally in the course of the pandemic despite a series of policies adopted to advance reforms. In particular, there has been no considerable redistribution of responsibilities among healthcare and public health actors. Furthermore, in terms of budgeting, public health reforms are modest, if compared to the healthcare sector's (i.e. SHIs and hospitals) annual funds that have been further increased in response to COVID-19. While the pandemic has been a trigger for policymaking in longstanding reform areas (Ewert and Loer 2022) such as long-term care, the public health service, and digitalisation, the German health systems' division into two unequally strong sectors continues unaltered.

Despite this preliminary conclusion, turning-point concepts help us to analyse German health policy in response to COVID-19 in more detail. How do we assess the scope and degree of policy change we have seen in the German health system? Referring to policy science theory, the pandemic – by all accounts, an extraordinary event – represents a critical juncture (Capoccia and Keleman 2007). At least theoretically, the possibility exists that 'policy is assigned new objectives, new priorities are established, and new political and administrative coalitions [emerge]' (Peters et al. 2005: 1276). Thus, there were justified claims that policy, entrepreneurs (i.e. Health Ministers) or 'programmatic elites' (Hornung and Bandelow 2020) seize the crisis to impose groundbreaking policies. However, for the moment (i.e. July 2022), the German case largely confirms findings from international health policy research according to which 'the pandemic merely accelerated or advanced ongoing reforms that started well before the crisis' (Bali et al. 2022: 92). Therefore, the two hypotheses could not be verified based on the empirical investigation, even if the findings are more nuanced than expected.

H1: *Perceived as a critical juncture, COVID-19 has accelerated the realignment of the healthcare and public health sector in the German health system.*

As stated above, it is not a question of whether the pandemic could be defined as a crucial juncture but whether the latter has been seized or wasted by policymakers (Capoccia and Keleman 2007). By and large, the pandemic has yielded to the adjustment rather than the renewal of health policies. This is especially the case concerning neuralgic 'bottlenecks' of the German health system (Ewert et al. 2023) that have been well-known for decades but have only received full attention since the onset of the pandemic. COVID-19 has brutally exposed such bottlenecks from worse working conditions of professional care workers in terms of their workload, voice and payment, the considerable backlog in terms of digital health services to the underdevelopment of integrated care schemes. However, measured by this amount of problem pressure, the scope of the adopted policies such as the healthcare and long-term care advancement law from 2021 is relatively narrow. Small improvements for professional care workers that do not fundamentally change their standing or their political influence in the health system fit this category. We observe an incremental change that does not qualify for a disruption of the health system's path dependencies. Nevertheless, the federal government (together with the *Länder*) passed a series of policies that at least bear the potential to realign the healthcare and public health sector. Pandemic preparedness has become a matter of national concern, which is most prominently reflected in the federal government's plan, according to the coalition agreement, to establish a Federal Public Health Institute. In theory, such an institution may shake up the distribution of power among health sectors even if this seems unlikely in light of the institutional status quo. In addition, the pact for the public health service, if implemented successfully, may strengthen health departments considerably in terms of staff and budget. Nonetheless, since the pact does not provide health departments with additional responsibilities (e.g. to coordinate and conduct measures of prevention and population-oriented health promotion), they are unlikely to become powerful 'public health hubs' soon. Thus, despite public health's modest gains in importance, policymakers' decisions and actions during the crisis do not entail a revised vision of health policy nor do they boost cross- sectoral interaction. Consequently, COVID-19 has not been exploited as a critical juncture. So far, compelling evidence for major policy changes emanating from revised institutional structures is out of sight. Thus, H1 needs to be rejected.

H2: Turning to public health and prevention issues policymaking in response to COVID-19 will lead to a lasting health policy paradigm change.

Findings concerning the second hypothesis concern changes in instrument settings, instrument choices and the revision of health policy goals that, in total, may indicate an immediate paradigm shift in German health policy. All in all, the results for H2 are less clear than the ones for H1. Reasons for that are the continuation of the pandemic which is still characterised by ad hoc policymaking and the temporality of most COVID-19-related policies and regulations. In general, we see first-, second- and third-order change, albeit unevenly distributed. Unsurprisingly, the biggest share fits the category of first-order change, i.e. the revision of instrument settings. In terms of healthcare financing, primarily, the rise of SHI's tax portion (one-time from EUR 14.5 to EUR 28.5 billion in 2021 and permanently to EUR 19.5 billion as of 2023) fits this category. Other examples, predominantly stipulated by regulations, are legal possibilities to deviate from established laws due to extraordinary circumstances caused by COVID-19. For instance, the licensing procedure of doctors has become temporarily relaxed by a regulation in March 2020 to protect medical students who helped out in health departments from disadvantages concerning their study progress. A similar regulation was passed in June 2020 to safeguard the education of non-medical health professionals. Likewise, legal provisions for long-term care have been amended, allowing, among other things, remote consultations with patients. Hence, in the immediate response to the pandemic and for the sake of protecting public health, policy instruments became temporarily adjusted while their underlying rationales remained unchanged.

Policymakers also tested new (mixes of) policy instruments in the course of COVID-19 (second-order change). Most strikingly, the many amendments of the federal infection protection law amplified governments' opportunities to govern by directives (e.g. federal emergency brake) and decrees (e.g. obligation to wear masks). This also counts for regulations to restrict the transport of people travelling to Germany from countries where the virus has mutated. Consequently, the use of authority has become a key policy instrument to contain the virus in the short term. In addition, financial bonuses have been paid to incentivise long-term care workers' job maintenance. However, we rarely see instrument changes in health policy areas that do not refer to COVID-19. In this respect, a regulation (adopted in December 2020) that constrains advertising activities by health insurance (e.g. prohibiting advertising in combination with sporting events) represents an exception.

Finally, there are modest indicators for goal adjustments in health policy (third-order change) that may result in a paradigm shift in the long term. These adjustments concern policies and political appointments (1), political memorandums (2), symbolic decisions (2) and the involvement of experts (3). First, despite its shortcomings, the pact for the public health services increases political recognition for the institution's work, even if it does not automatically strengthen its political clout. The latter, however, may be the result of a recent appointment by the German health minister (Karl Lauterbach, Social Democrat): In February 2022, Ute Teichert, a former spokesperson for the federal association of physicians within the public health service, became the head of the federal health ministry's public health department. Second, the coalition agreement of the new federal government of Social Democrats, Greens and Liberal Democrats contains a strong commitment to the ÖGD by suggesting the adoption of a health security law and, as stated above, the establishment of a Federal Public Health Institute. The agreement also stipulates the adoption of a National Prevention Plan that includes public health issues such as climate and environmental risks. Third, to prepare the country for future public health crises, the previous government (in power till December 2021) has already established a National Reserve Health Protection stockpiling medical protection equipment (e.g. masks, ventilators, drugs) for six months in advance at 19 locations across Germany. Fourth, participants in the COVID-19 expert board, advising the new government, have a predominantly non-medical professional background. Even if the board is likely to be dissolved as soon as the virus becomes endemic, the expertise of not only epidemiologists, virologists and ÖGD representatives but also social scientists may have a lasting impact on the health ministry's strategic thinking and planning. At least one can conclude that public health and prevention issues will stay on the health policy agenda and may gain further relevance in light of global health challenges such as climate change. Thus, regarding H2, the future will tell whether the pandemic has provoked a paradigmatic policy shift (Hall 1993) towards public health. Right now, H2 can neither be confirmed nor denied.

6 Conclusion

German health policy is the epitome of institutional stability and path dependency (Immergut and Wendt 2021) and, hence, is not known for major turnarounds. However, if anything, a pandemic may unbalance this equilibrium and yield fundamental health policy change. By referring to two turning-point conceptions that emanated from political science, it has been argued that COVID-19 has not been exploited by policymakers yet, although the crisis meets the key criteria of a critical juncture. This juncture has not been used immediately by policymakers to steer transformational change. While empirical investigation demonstrates that regulatory density significantly increased in the course of the pandemic, adopted policies and regulations do not turn the underlying principles and premises of German health policy upside down. Above all, the healthcare sector maintains its dominant position, which may even be reinforced considering hospitals' key role in providing emergency care for COVID-19 patients. In contrast, the public health sector remains subordinated to the healthcare sector, despite some catch-up effects. Thus, at least for the moment, COVID-19 needs to be assessed as a missed opportunity that has not resulted in a realignment of healthcare and public health or in paradigmatic health policy change. However, by setting the issue of public health back on the political agenda policy pandemic spurs hopes for broader future change that may include the health system's institutional framework. If this will be the case, there may still be reasons to consider the current crisis as a decisive turning point in German health policy.

Appendix

Table 1: Health Policies in Germany (March 2020 – February 2022).

No.	Year	Law/Regulation	Healthcare	Public Health	COVID-19
1	2022	Coronavirus-Testverordnung	X	X	X
2	2022	Verordnung zur Änderung der COVID-19-Schutzmaßnahmen-Ausnahmenverordnung und der Coronavirus-Einreiseverordnung		X	X
3	2022	Coronavirus-Einreiseverordnung		X	X
4	2021	Verordnung über von den Approbationsordnungen für Ärzte, für Zahnärzte und Zahnärztinnen und für Apotheker abweichende Vorschriften im Rahmen der Bewältigung der Coronavirus-SARS-CoV-2-Pandemie oder ihrer Folgen	X		X
5	2021	Gesetz zur Stärkung der Impfprävention gegen COVID-19 und zur Änderung weiterer Vorschriften im Zusammenhang mit der COVID-19-Pandemie		X	X
6	2021	Gesetz zur Änderung des Infektionsschutzgesetzes und weiterer Gesetze anlässlich der Aufhebung der Feststellung der epidemischen Lage von nationaler Tragweite	X	X	X
7	2021	VO zur Änderung der Coronavirus-Testverordnung, der IntensivRegister-Verordnung und der Coronavirus-Surveillanceverordnung	X	X	X
8	2021	Hygienepauschaleverordnung	X		X
9	2021	DRG-Entgeltkatalogverordnung 2022	X		

(continued)

Table 1 (continued)

No.	Year	Law/Regulation	Healthcare	Public Health	COVID-19
10	2021	Gesundheits-IT Interoperabilitätsverordnung	X		
11	2021	Bundeszuschussverordnung 2022	X		
12	2021	Pandemiekosten-Erstattungsverordnung	X		X
13	2021	Verordnung zur Änderung der Approbationsordnungen für Zahnärzte und Zahnärztinnen, für Ärzte und für Psychotherapeutinnen und Psychotherapeuten	X		X
14	2021	EpiLage-Fortgeltungsgesetz	X	X	X
15	2021	Grippeimpfstoffrückerstattungsverordnung		X	
16	2021	Gesundheits-IT-Interoperabilitäts-Governance-Verordnung	X		
17	2021	Verordnung über die Erweiterung der Meldepflicht nach § 6 Absatz 1 Satz 1 Nummer 1 des Infektionsschutzgesetzes auf Hospitalisierungen in Bezug auf die Coronavirus-Krankheit-2019	X		X
18	2021	Fünfte Verordnung zur Änderung der Trinkwasserverordnung		X	
19	2021	Verordnung zur Verlängerung des Zeitraums für Vereinbarungen zur wirtschaftlichen Sicherung der Vorsorge- und Rehabilitationseinrichtungen	X		
20	2021	Zweite Verordnung zur Verlängerung von Maßnahmen zur Aufrechterhaltung der pflegerischen Versorgung während der durch das Coronavirus SARS-CoV-2 verursachten Pandemie	X		X
21	2021	Verordnung zur Verlängerung von Maßnahmen zur Aufrechterhaltung der pflegerischen Versorgung während der durch das Coronavirus SARS-CoV-2 verursachten Pandemie	X		X

#	Year	Title			
22	2021	Allgemeinverfügung zur Sicherstellung der flächendeckenden Verteilung von Impfstoffen gegen COVID-19 an Arztpraxen und Betriebsärztinnen und Betriebsärzte	X	X	X
23	2021	Zweites Gesetz zur Änderung des Infektionsschutzgesetzes und weiterer Gesetze	X	X	X
24	2021	Poliovirus-Verordnung – PolioV	X	X	X
25	2021	Zweiunddreißigste Verordnung zur Änderung betäubungsmittelrechtlicher Vorschriften	X		X
26	2021	Coronavirus-Schutzverordnung	X	X	X
27	2021	SARS-CoV-2-Arzneimittelversorgung	X		X
28	2021	Medizinischer Bedarf Versorgungssicherstellungsverordnung	X		X
29	2021	26. Verordnung zur Änderung der Risikostruktur-Ausgleichsverordnung	X		
30	2021	Viertes Gesetz zum Schutz der Bevölkerung bei einer epidemischen Lage von nationaler Tragweite	X	X	X
31	2021	Monoklonale-Antikörper-Verordnung	X		
32	2021	Verordnungen zur wirtschaftlichen Sicherung der Krankenhäuser	X		
33	2021	Verordnung zum Anspruch auf Schutzimpfung gegen Influenza und Masern		X	
34	2021	Gesundheitsversorgungsweiterentwicklungsgesetz (GVWG)	X		
35	2021	Coronavirus-Schutzmasken-Verordnung	X	X	X
36	2021	Änderung der Medizinprodukte-Abgabeverordnung	X		X
37	2021	Coronavirus-Surveillanceverordnung	X	X	X

(continued)

Table 1 (continued)

No.	Year	Law/Regulation	Healthcare	Public Health	COVID-19
38	2021	Gesetz zum Erlass eines Tierarzneimittelgesetzes und zur Anpassung arzneimittelrechtlicher und anderer Vorschriften	X		
39	2021	Digitalisierungsgesetz	X		
40	2021	Erste Verordnung zur Änderung der Coronavirus-Testverordnung	X	X	X
41	2021	Verordnung zur Aufhebung der Preisverordnung für SARS-CoV-2 Antigen-Tests zur patientennahen Anwendung	X	X	X
42	2021	Verordnung zur Anpassung des Betrags zur Finanzierung der Gesellschaft für Telematik für das Jahr 2021 (TeleFinV 2021)	X		
43	2020	Gesetzes zur Zusammenführung von Krebsregisterdaten	X		
44	2020	Preisverordnung für SARS-CoV-2 Antigen-Tests zur patientennahen Anwendung	X	X	X
45	2020	Digitale-Versorgung–und–Pflege–Modernisierungs–Gesetz	X		
46	2020	VO zum Anspruch auf Schutzimpfung in Bezug auf einen Influenza-Hochdosis-Impfstoff	X	X	
47	2020	Verordnung zur Testpflicht von Einreisenden aus Risikogebieten		X	X
48	2020	Gesetzes zur Änderung des Medizinprodukterecht-Durchführungsgesetzes	X		
49	2020	Drittes Gesetz zum Schutz der Bevölkerung bei einer epidemischen Lage von nationaler Tragweite	X	X	X
50	2020	Frischzellenverordnung	X		

No.	Year	Title			
51	2020	Gesundheitsversorgungs- und Pflegeverbesserungsgesetz			X
52	2020	Krankenhauszukunftsgesetz			X
53	2020	Online-Wahl-Verordnung			X
54	2020	Gesetz zur Reform der technischen Assistenzberufe in der Medizin			X
55	2020	Zweite Verordnung zur Änderung der Pflegepersonaluntergrenzen-Verordnung			X
56	2020	Einundzwanzigste Verordnung zur Änderung von Anlagen des Betäubungsmittelgesetzes			X
57	2020	Zwanzigste Verordnung zur Änderung von Anlagen des Betäubungsmittelgesetzes			X
58	2020	Verordnung zur Änderung der Anlage des Neue-psychoaktive-Stoffe-Gesetzes			X
59	2020	Arzneimittelbevorratungsverordnung			X
60	2020	Verordnung über von den Approbationsordnungen für Ärzte, Zahnärzte und Apotheker abweichende Vorschriften bei Vorliegen einer epidemischen Lage von nationaler Tragweite	X		X
61	2020	Verordnung zur Neufassung der Datentransparenzverordnung und zur Änderung der Datentransparenz-Gebührenverordnung		X	X
62	2020	25. Verordnung zur Änderung der Risikostruktur-Ausgleichsverordnung			X
63	2020	COVID-19-Ausgleichszahlungs-Anpassungs-Verordnung	X		X
64	2020	Verordnung zur Anpassung der Packungsgrößenverordnung und der Pflegepersonaluntergrenzen-Verordnung			X
65	2020	Methodenbewertungsverfahrensverordnung			X
66	2020	Verordnung zur Sicherung der Ausbildungen in den Gesundheitsfachberufen während einer epidemischen Lage von nationaler Tragweite	X		X

(continued)

Table 1 (continued)

No.	Year	Law/Regulation	Healthcare	Public Health	COVID-19
67	2020	COVID-19-Versorgungsstrukturen-Schutzverordnung	X		X
68	2020	Zweites Gesetz zum Schutz der Bevölkerung bei einer epidemischen Lage von nationaler Tragweite	X	X	X
69	2020	Gesetz zum Ausgleich COVID-19 bedingter finanzieller Belastungen der Krankenhäuser und weiterer Gesundheitseinrichtungen	X		X
70	2020	Gesetz zum Schutz der Bevölkerung bei einer epidemischen Lage von nationaler Tragweite	X	X	X
71	2020	Verordnung zur Beschaffung von Medizinprodukten und persönlicher Schutzausrüstung bei der durch das Coronavirus SARS-CoV-2 verursachten Epidemie	X	X	X
72	2020	Intensivregister-Verordnung	X	X	X
73	2020	IntensivRegister-Änderungs-Verordnung	X	X	X
74	2020	Verordnung zur Abweichung von der Approbationsordnung für Ärzte bei einer epidemischen Lage von nationaler Tragweite	X	X	X
75	2020	Anordnungen des BMG nach § 5 des Infektionsschutzgesetzes		X	X
76	2020	Intensivpflege- und Rehabilitationsstärkungsgesetz	X		
77	2020	Patientendaten-Schutz-Gesetz	X		
78	2020	Digitale-Gesundheitsanwendungen-Verordnung	X		

References

Auener, Stefan, Danielle Kroon, Erik Wackers, Simone van Dulmen & Patrick Jeurissen. 2020. COVID-19: a window of opportunity for positive healthcare reforms. *International Journal of Health Policy Management* 9(10). 419–422.

Auld, Graeme, Steven Bernstein, Benjamin Cashore & Kelly Levin. 2021. Managing pandemics as super wicked problems: lessons from, and for, COVID-19 and the climate crisis. *Policy sciences* 54(4). 707–728.

Bali, Azad S., Alex J. He & M. Ramesh. 2022. Health policy and COVID-19: path dependency and trajectory. *Policy and Society* 41(1). 83–95.

Bandelow, Nils C., Anja Hartmann & Johanna Hornung. 2019. Winter is coming–but not yet. German health policy under the third Merkel chancellorship. *German Politics* 28(3). 444–461.

Bandelow, Nils C., Colette S. Vogeler, Johanna Hornung, Johanna Kuhlmann & Sebastian Heidrich. 2019. Learning as a necessary but not sufficient condition for major health policy change: A qualitative comparative analysis combining ACF and MSF. *Journal of Comparative Policy Analysis: Research and Practice* 21(2). 167–182.

Baumgartner, Frank R., Bryan D. Jones & Peter B. Mortensen. 2018. Punctuated equilibrium theory: Explaining stability and change in public policymaking. In Christopher M. Weible & Paul A. Sabatier (eds.), *Theories of the policy process*, 55–101. New York: Routlegde.

Bogumil-Uçan, Simon & Tanja Klenk. 2021. Varieties of health care digitalization: Comparing advocacy coalitions in Austria and Germany. *Review of Policy Research* 38(4). 478–503.

Boin, Arjen,Allan McConnell & Paul ´t Hart. 2021. *Governing the Pandemic: The Politics of Navigating a Mega-Crisis*. Cham: Springer Nature.

Busse, Reinhard & Miriam Blümel. 2014. *Germany: health system review*. Geneva: World Health Organization.

Capano, Giliberto. 2009. Understanding policy change as an epistemological and theoretical problem. *Journal of Comparative Policy Analysis* 11(1). 7–31.

Capano, Giliberto, Howlett, Michael, Jarvis, Darryl S., and Ramesh, Michael. 2022. Long-term policy impacts of the coronavirus: normalization, adaptation, and acceleration in the post-COVID state. *Policy and Society* 41(1), 1–12. doi.org/10.1093/polsoc/puab018

Capoccia, Giovanni, & R. Daniel Kelemen. 2007. The Study of Critical Junctures: Theory, Narrative, and Counterfactuals in Historical Institutionalism. *World Politics* 59(3). 341–69.

Ewert, Benjamin & Kathrin Loer. 2022. COVID-19 as a Catalyst for Policy Change: The Role of Trigger Points and Spillover Effects. *German Politics*. 1–24.

Ewert, Benjamin, Iris Wallenburg, Ulrika Winblad & Roland Bal. 2023. Any lessons to learn? Pathways and impasses towards health system resilience in post-pandemic times. *Health Econ Policy Law* 18(1). 66–81.

Federal Ministry of Health 2022. Gesetze und Verordnungen. https://www.bundesgesundheitsministe rium.de/service/gesetze-und-verordnungen.html. (28 July, 2022).

Freeden, Michael. 2017. Crisis? How Is That a Crisis!? *Contributions to the History of Concepts* 12(2). 12–28.

Ginsburg, Tom & Mila Versteeg. 2021. The bound executive: Emergency powers during the pandemic. *International Journal of Constitutional Law* 19(5). 1498–1535.

Greer, Scott L., Elizabeth J. King, Elize Massard da Fonseca & André Peralta-Santos. 2021. *Coronavirus politics: The comparative politics and policy of COVID-19*. Michigan: University of Michigan Press.

Hall, Peter A. 1993. Policy paradigms, social learning, and the state: the case of economic policy-making in Britain. *Comparative politics* 25(3). 275–296.

Hassenteufel, Patrick & Bruno Palier. 2007. Towards neo-Bismarckian health care states? Comparing health insurance reforms in Bismarckian welfare systems. *Social Policy & Administration* 41(6). 574–596.

Hornung, Johanna & Nils C. Bandelow. 2020. The programmatic elite in German health policy: Collective action and sectoral history. *Public Policy and Administration* 35(3). 247–265.

Hogan, John, Howlett, Michael and Murphy, Mary. 2022. Re-thinking the coronavirus pandemic as a policy punctuation: COVID-19 as a path-clearing policy accelerator. *Policy and Society* 41(1): 40–52. doi.org/10.1093/polsoc/puab009

Immergut, Ellen M. & Claus Wendt. 2021. Germany. In Immergut, Ellen M., Karen M. Anderson, Camilla Devitt & Tamara Popic (eds.), *Health politics in Europe: A handbook*. 479–519. Oxford: Oxford University Press.

Kingdon, John W. 2014. *Agendas, Alternatives, and Public Policies*, 2nd edn. Essex: Pearson Education Limited.

Knill, Christoph & Jale Tosun. 2020. *Public policy: A new introduction*. London: Palgrave Macmillan.

Kuhlmann, Sabine, Mikael Hellström, Ulf Ramberg & Renate Reiter. 2021. Tracing divergence in crisis governance: responses to the COVID-19 pandemic in France, Germany and Sweden compared. *International Review of Administrative Sciences* 87(3). 556–575.

Leiber, Simone, Stefan Greß & Stephanie Heinemann. 2015. Explaining Different Paths in Social Health Insurance Countries–Health System Change and Cross-border Lesson-drawing between Germany, Austria and the Netherlands. *Social Policy & Administration* 49(1). 88–108.

Paul, Katharina T. & Kathrin Loer. 2019. Contemporary vaccination policy in the European Union: tensions and dilemmas. *Journal of public health policy* 40(2). 166–179.

Peters, B. Guy, Jon Pierre & Desmond S. King. 2005. The politics of path dependency: Political conflict in historical institutionalism. *The journal of politics* 67(4). 1275–1300.

Plümer, Klaus D. 2018. 'Germany'. In Bernd Rechel (ed.), *Organization and financing of public health services in Europe*, 35–48. Copenhagen: WHO Regional Office for Europe.

Reitzle, Lukas, Christian Schmidt, Francesca Färber, Lena Huebl, Lothar Heinz Wieler, Thomas Ziese & Christin Heidemann. 2021. Perceived access to health care services and relevance of telemedicine during the COVID-19 pandemic in Germany. *International journal of environmental research and public health* 18(14). 7661.

Toth, Federico. 2021. *Comparative Health Systems: A New Framework*. Cambridge: Cambridge University Press.

Trein, Philipp 2019. *Healthy or Sick? Coevolution of Health Care and Public Health in a Comparative Perspective*. Cambridge: Cambridge University Press.

Maximilian Schiffers and Sandra Plümer

Obstacles on the path to lobbying transparency in Europe: Assessing the German turning point at the end of the Merkel era

Abstract: Following 16 years of debate, Germany finally introduced a lobbying register in March 2021. This reform denotes an iteration of an unexpected policy change towards the end of the Merkel era, which stems from a turning point in Germany's transparency policy. For most of Angela Merkel's time in office, policymakers were set against stricter policy measures and very experienced political commentators did not expect any advance in the field. We ask, therefore, what mechanisms explain the introduction of the long-awaited German lobbying register.

Applying the Punctuated Equilibrium Theory, we examine a variety of policy documents using process tracing and qualitative content analysis. The results show that a breakthrough was only made possible through the combination of three mechanisms: a de-thematisation of the policy issue, a growing network favouring stricter transparency regulations, and increasing public validation of the issue through a build-up of scandals, leading to a waived refusal to put the issue on the parliamentary agenda. Thus, the turning point closely precedes the actual legislative policy change, enabling key political actors to carry through their proposal for stricter regulation successfully.

Keywords: lobbying register, transparency policy, policy change, turning point, Punctuated Equilibrium Theory

1 Introduction: Explaining unexpected policy change after 16 years of faced opposition

At the end of the Merkel era and after 16 years of faced opposition, Germany finally introduced a lobbying register in March 2021. The register is an example of an unexpected policy change resulting from a major turning point in Germany's transparency policy. With the introduction of the lobbying register and other reforms,

Maximilian Schiffers, Sandra Plümer, University of Duisburg-Essen, NRW School of Governance

https://doi.org/10.1515/9783111272900-014

such as a lobbyists' code of conduct, Germany reached the medium-regulated level after having had considerable deficits in relation to transparency and accountability measures.

From a theoretical perspective, the debate on stricter transparency measures is characterised by consecutive periods of policy stability with incremental and non-legislative changes, followed by substantial policy change. The concrete factors that led to the introduction of the lobbying register, however, are unknown. Therefore, we ask the research question: What mechanisms explain the final introduction of the German lobbying register?

Analytically, we divide our case into four temporal episodes (2008–2017, 2017, 2017–2020 and 2020–2021), showing numerous small peaks, a near breakthrough during a period of stability and substantial policy change at the end of the last episode. As the sequence of events corresponds to the main argument of the Punctuated Equilibrium Theory (PET), we use three core concepts of PET that relate to policy change and help to explain the introduction of the lobbying register: (1) policy images shared by issue networks, (2) policy venues, and (3) positive as well as negative feedback loops. With the help of these concepts, we analyse a variety of material, including election manifestos, position papers, legislation and media reports using process tracing and qualitative content analysis.

The empirical results show a combination of three mechanisms that made this historic breakthrough possible: a de-thematisation of the policy issue, a strong and growing issue-centred network that favoured stricter transparency regulations, and increasing public validation of the issue by previously accumulated scandals, leading to a waived refusal to put the issue on the parliamentary agenda. The major turning point closely precedes the actual legislative policy change and can be observed at the intersection of the third and fourth episode of the case, i.e. between late 2020 and early 2021. During this time, further attempts to oppose the policy failed, and key political actors were able to carry through their intended proposal for stricter regulation successfully.

In terms of governing style, the introduction of the lobbying register resembles many other reforms that have been implemented during Merkel's time in office. Sudden shifts against long-held beliefs also characterise other reforms, such as the end of conscription, the phasing-out of the nuclear energy programme and legalising marriage for same-sex couples, so-called 'Ehe für alle'. In these instances, the Chancellor was opposed to the reforms right until their eventual adoption.

This chapter proceeds as follows: Section 2 provides an overview of both the theoretical and empirical findings related to the study of turning points and policy change and presents our analytical framework. Section 3 outlines our case study design. Section 4 addresses Germany's structural deficits in its transparency policy in the context of European and wider international regulation levels. Section 5 presents our four temporal episodes from the debate on stricter policy measures addressing transparency and the lobbying register, followed by an illustration of the main policy networks in Section 6. Section 7 presents an overview of three mechanisms leading to the policy change derived from the empirical analysis, and Section 8 concludes the chapter.

2 About turning points and policy change: Theoretical and empirical insights

This chapter addresses turning points from a public policy perspective. Public policy is famously characterised by 'considerable continuity through and in spite of historical break points' (Streeck and Thelen 2005: 8–9). Policy theories, therefore, focus on explaining why we observe mostly policy stability and incremental change as opposed to rare instances of major policy change. Policy change, be it incremental or major change, can be caused by external shocks, focusing events and feedback loops that call attention to an issue, changed policy beliefs and other ideational factors (Capano 2009; Cairney and Heikkila 2018; Ewert and Loer 2022).

Unfortunately, there is no agreement on a common definition of policy change (for a conceptual overview, see Plümer and Schiffers 2022). Instead, we see a multitude of different definitions that are strategically applied to analyses (Capano 2009: 14). One of the most recognised definitions has been put forward by Peter Hall (1993), drawing a distinction between first-order change (routine adjustments), second-order change (changing policy instruments), and third-order change (a shift in goals and paradigms). Other scholars have echoed Hall's conceptualisation and differentiated between minor and major policy changes (Sabatier and Jenkins-Smith 1993) or incremental and substantial policy changes (Baumgartner and Jones 2009), slow or quick types of changes (Rüb 2014), proactive versus reactive actions and linear versus transformational changes (Plümer and Schiffers 2022). The following subsections expand our argument to employ both the concept of turning points and the theory of punctuated equilibria to analyse the dynamics of stability and change in policymaking.

2.1 Turning points as the translation of *possible* changes into *actual* changes

The concept of turning points helps to address the specific instances where frictions and triggers of *possible* policy changes translate into *actual* policy changes and mark a substantive shift away from traditional incrementalism (see Figure 1). Therefore, a turning point may be identified that leads to a final policy change. What, though, is a turning point? By our understanding, a turning point is a specific subtype of *critical juncture,* defined as 'relatively short periods of time during which there is a substantially heightened probability that agents' choices will affect the outcome of interest' (Capoccia and Kelemen 2007: 348). During this period, we see greater uncertainty and limited control of time (our case episodes), agency (key political actors in policy networks) and space (the cross-sectional policy field of transparency and lobbying regulation). However, critical junctures do not always automatically produce a turning point resulting in policy change (Capoccia and Kelemen 2007: 352). Due to the persistent forces of path dependency and policymakers' natural habit of maintaining the status quo, the outcome may also still result in continuing policy stability after the period of contingency and uncertainty has passed. Yet, if certain structural factors are surmounted, *a new policy path following a turning point* may allow for continuing reforms in the adjusted policy direction. Indeed, we do observe such changes on rare occasions, such as with the introduction of a German lobbying register in March 2021. The following figure summarises our conceptualisation of a *turning point as a specific subtype of critical juncture leading to policy changes.*

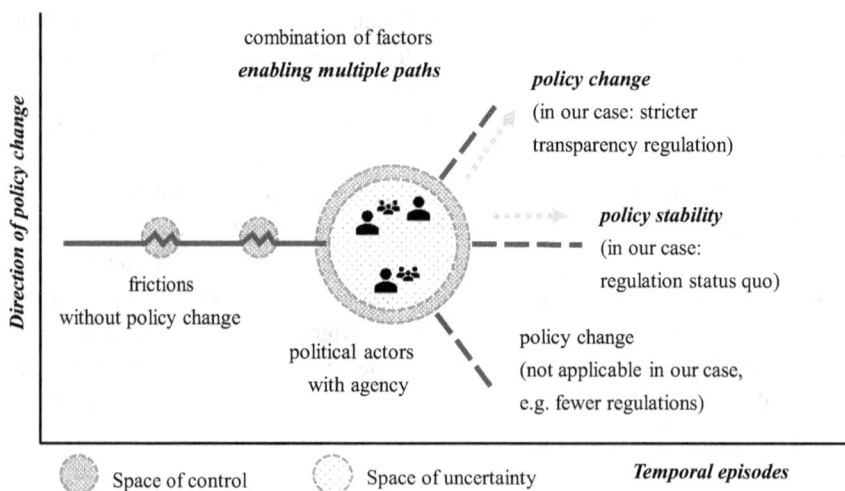

Figure 1: A turning point as a critical juncture in the PET framework for the case of German transparency policy.
Source: Authors' own compilation based on Janusch et al. 2023.

2.2 Three core concepts of PET as an analytical framework

Returning to policy change as our main analytical category, some policy theories offer alternative – and sometimes overlapping – explanations. Out of the five popular policy process frameworks either directly or indirectly referring to policy change,[1] PET seems the most promising when it comes to addressing and analysing the underlying processes of policy change. This is for two reasons: First, PET accounts for policy change *and* policy stability (Beyer, Boushey, and Breunig 2022), which is essential in explaining our case covering both dynamics. According to PET, the policymaking reality is characterised by long periods of stability with no or only incremental changes, and subsequent phases of sudden instability resulting in substantial policy changes (Baumgartner and Jones 1993, 2009; Jones and Baumgartner 2012). Second, PET not only mentions several driving forces for policy change (namely, focusing events and institutional or cultural friction) but also provides a mechanistic perspective that helps to open up the black box of how the policy changes come about (van der Heijden et al. 2021: 170; e.g. Baumgartner, Jones, and Mortensen 2018). As such, it goes beyond the simplistic perspective of identifying *reasons* for policy change and instead analyses the *pathway* from a starting point to an outcome.

Existing empirical analyses using PET, however, do not distinguish precisely between driving forces and mechanisms, but provide valuable insight into the processes accompanying policy changes. According to Worsham (2006), for instance, a venue change and an alteration of the dominant policy image are important factors leading to policy change. Robinson (2014) and Hong and Sohn (2014), however, identify cultural friction as being a trigger for policy change. While some studies solely identify internal and even local factors as having promoted policy change (Easterly 2015), other studies (Lowry and Josly 2014; Plümer and Schiffers 2023) argue for a combination of both internal and external factors.

This combination of factors is also stressed in the recent literature on the introduction of new lobbying laws. Thus far, empirical evidence identifies *scandals* as the main driver of policy change in the field of transparency policy (Bitonti and Hogan 2021: 4–5; Chari et al. 2019; Newmark 2017: 226–227; McKay and Wozniak 2020: 104). Although this simple link can be observed in some countries, comparative studies discover a more complex and nuanced multi-factored relationship. In his pioneering study, Michele Crepaz (2017) argues that scandals indeed lead to the discussion of stricter transparency rules, but that this rise in attention does not nec-

---

1 These include the PET, the Multiple Streams Framework (MSF), the Advocacy Coalition Framework (ACF), the Narrative Policy Framework (NPF) and the Institutional Analysis and Development Framework (IAD; Weible and Sabatier 2018).

essarily affect the adoption of new laws. Thus, scandals have an indirect rather than a direct effect on policymaking (see also Burkhardt 2018). In line with the PET literature, a combination with other factors may lead to stricter legislation. In transparency policy, these include, for example, processes of policy diffusion and learning (Greenwood and Dreger 2013; Crepaz and Chari 2014), a government's aim to increase the public's trust in political institutions (Keeling, Feeney, and Hogan 2017; Holman and Luneburg 2012), a political culture in favour of harsher transparency rules (Newmark 2005; Ozymy 2010), and increasing domestic pressure (Miller and Dinan 2008; McKay and Wozniak 2020).

Following these empirical analyses and adopting a meta-perspective, True, James, and Baumgartner (2007: 160–161) suggest that policy change is characterised by a mutually reinforcing process of increased attention, venue shifts, and changing policy images. Therefore, this chapter deploys these concepts as an analytical framework and adds the concept of feedback loops: (1) *policy images* that are shared by policy networks and vie for attention, (2) networks acting in *policy venues* and (3) *feedback loops* signalling a policy change (a positive feedback loop) or stability (a negative feedback loop).[2] Table 1 summarises the meaning of each concept, highlights empirical examples from earlier studies and illustrates empirical indicators for our analysis.

Table 1: Overview of the core concepts.

Concept	Meaning	Examples from existing studies	Empirical indicators/ examples for our analysis
Policy image shared by a policy network	Normative and empirical policy idea of a policy network	Tobacco policy as an economic issue or a health issue (Worsham 2006), nuclear energy as safe or dangerous energy source (Baumgartner and Jones 2009: 256–264)	Different views on the need for transparency of decision-making processes and the danger of (possible) illegitimate influence
Policy venue	Policy arena for policy discussion and decision	Committees and plenary debates in parliament (Schwanholz and Jakobi 2020), coalition negotiations after federal elections (Bandelow, Hartmann, and Hornung 2019)	Committee for the Scrutiny of Elections, Immunity and the Rules of Procedure, coalition negotiations after the 2017 German federal election

---

2 The concept of increased attention is indirectly used in this study, see Sections 5 and 7.

Table 1 (continued)

Concept	Meaning	Examples from existing studies	Empirical indicators/ examples for our analysis
Positive feedback loop	Policy change through amplified action	Policy change through events that shape public opinion (Crepaz 2017) or through scandals (Bitonti and Hogan 2021)	Triggered by increased attention for continuing structural problems of low-level regulation (Schiffers 2021a), series of scandals (Chari et al. 2019), a growing network in favour of stricter transparency rules
Negative feedback loop	Maintenance of the status quo through dampened action	No or incremental policy change due to balanced portfolio (Bandelow, Hartmann, and Hornung 2019), limited German revolving door regulation of 2015 ('*Abgeordnetengesetz*') as opposed to substantial transparency regulation (Schiffers 2021a)	Triggered by a powerful network against stricter transparency rules

Source: Authors' own compilation.

3 Case study design

This paper conducts a single case study (Gerring 2007) on the recent German debate on stricter transparency regulations, which eventually led to the introduction of a lobbying register in March 2021. With this decision, Germany advanced from being ranked as a lowly regulated country in terms of transparency measures (Chari et al. 2019; Bunea 2018) to a moderately regulated level. Despite some criticism of the legislation, experts value the lobbying register as a breakthrough in German transparency policy (LobbyControl 2021a: 10; see also Spitze 2022).

Therefore, we conceptualise the case as an example of an unexpected policy change at the end of the Merkel era, which resulted from a turning point in Germany's transparency policy. This policy change was prepared and implemented in the Merkel era. It must be recognised, however, that the breakthrough is not directly attached to Chancellor Angela Merkel as a person. Until the eventual decision, she opposed stricter transparency regulation (Bundeskanzleramt 2020), and the CDU can be seen as blocking stricter regulation. Thus, the introduction of the lobbying register is rather the achievement of the second Grand Coalition lasting from 2017 to 2021 (*'Große Koalition'*, Christian Democractic Party, CDU/Christian Social Party, CSU and Social Democratic Party, SPD).[3]

From a case selection perspective, the breakthrough constitutes a causal diagnostic pathway case (Gerring and Cojocaru 2016), as empirically, it serves to identify the mechanisms leading to the adoption of the lobbying register. Recent studies in the field of transparency policy have shown that the observation of a simple link between scandals and the introduction of lobby regulation is no longer salient and, therefore call for a more complex explanation. From a theoretical perspective, the case helps to refine our knowledge on turnings points and the mechanisms that lead to subsequent substantial policy change. As the literature review highlights, we have little knowledge of the detailed workings of the mechanisms of policy change, which go beyond examining the driving forces. For empirical explanation and theoretical refinement, we analytically divide the case into four temporal episodes (see Section 5). In line with PET, these episodes cover consecutive periods of policy stability with incremental and non-legislative change, followed by a substantial policy change. The succession of these episodes is, thus, the selection criterion for this case.

To analyse the case, we used explaining-outcome and theory-building process tracing (Beach and Pedersen 2019; Collier 2011) as well as qualitative content analysis (Schreier 2012). Process tracing aims to identify the mechanisms interceding between a cause and an outcome. In our analysis, however, the causes *and* the mechanisms are unknown, while the outcome is the introduction of the lobbying register (Lobbying Register Act, *'Lobbyregistergesetz'*) on 25 March 2021. To identify the mechanisms at work, we use qualitative content analysis combining value and process coding (Saldaña 2016: 131–132, 110–111). The data material includes election manifestos, position papers, legislation and media reports.

4 Germany's structural deficit in transparency policy in the context of European and wider international regulation levels

Lobbying registers are part of the cross-sectional field of transparency policy, which seeks to ensure the legitimacy of political decisions by making them both public and accountable. They address four key questions: *Who* is carrying out

---

3 The period is also labelled a 'legislative term of scandals' (*'Legislaturperiode der Skandale'*; LobbyControl 2021a: 6) due to the large number of scandals that were made public (see Section 5).

which lobbying activity towards *whom* on *which* issue? Its main building blocks are (1) (mandatory) registrations of lobbying actors, such as interest groups, businesses, NGOs and consultants, (2) documenting lobbying goals and activities, (3) listing contacts with officials in administration and parliament, (4) codes of conduct, (5) supervising compliance by independent entities, (6) legislative footprints and (7) regulations on conflicts of interest, anti-corruption and public financing (Bitonti and Hogan 2021: 2–3; Schiffers 2021a).

From a theoretical perspective, the goals of transparency and accountability rules are to secure the legitimacy of the democratic state in its input, throughput and output dimensions (Schmidt 2013) and to strengthen citizens' trust in political institutions. The principle of publicity in democracy, thus, takes effect by making information about political activities broadly accessible and by preventing covert influence. Transparency policy instruments document and regulate the ways and means of influencing the policymaking process by publicising administrative information. Further, they make it possible to trace the flow and use of funds and get information on the decision-making process. The policy instruments are located at the interplay of (a) transparency standards and the separation of powers, (b) the application of punitive measures and internal compliance, and (c) corruption prevention through organisational culture, economic incentives and knowledge transfer (Wolf 2014: 43–44, 68–70; Mugellini 2020: 7–8).

Regarding European and other countries belonging to the Organisation for Economic Co-operation and Development (OECD), current research identifies different levels of regulation. While the US has a highly robust system, medium levels are found in the EU's transparency register and in Canada. Before the introduction of the German lobbying register, Germany was ranked as being in the lowest regulated systems category (Chari et al. 2019; Bunea 2018). In the past decade, a new wave of stricter lobbying regulation in Europe saw reforms in several countries (Holman and Luneburg 2012); however, with different dynamics in regulated states, such as France, Ireland, Lithuania, Austria, Poland, Slovenia and the UK, and non-regulated states, such as the Scandinavian countries, Finland, the Netherlands and Belgium (Crepaz et al. 2019). Concerning the recently introduced lobbying register, Polk (2021) evaluated its aims and content and confirmed the initial expert assessment (Deutsche Welle 2021) that Germany now fulfils the criteria of a moderately regulated system. Despite this progress, however, the European Commission urged Germany to introduce stricter transparency and traceability rules, particularly when it comes to legislative footprints and the length of cooling-off periods for high-ranking officials before starting non-governmental jobs (e.g., 'revolving door' regulations, see Table 2; European Commission 2022).

In line with the cross-sectoral characteristics of transparency policy, Germany has a fragmented bundle of legislation covering not only the lobbying register but also aspects of party finances, conflicts of interest of members of parliament (MPs) and other government officials, codes of conduct for policymakers and lobbyists and procedural rules in parliament and administration (Schiffers 2021a: 471; for an overview see Table 2). Consequently, reforms following political scandals usually address only some of these aspects. As an example, conflicts of interest between high-level officials and cabinet members were regulated with the German revolving door regulation of 2015 ('*Bundesministergesetz*'). This law was passed after several high-profile politicians had left for industry jobs shortly after working on favourable regulations in the same sector. The following table presents an overview of Germany's fragmented transparency measures and the latest reforms.

Table 2: Overview of Germany's transparency measures and the latest reforms.

Reform (implemented and changed in)	Content	Additional information
Political Parties Law ['*Parteiengesetz*'] (1967, 1994, 2020)	Regulation on party funding, including party donations (since 2002 concealing origin is a criminal offence)	Reform on stricter limits for disclosure requirements for party donations was blocked in 2021
Members of the Bundestag Act ['*Abgeordnetengesetz*'] (1977, 1996, 2020, 2021)	Regulations on MPs' side jobs and disclosure requirements for income	Reform to ban mandate lobbying in October 2021 (Deutscher Bundestag 2021a)
UN Anti-Corruption Convention (2005)	Criminalising bribery of MPs, linked to the Criminal Code (Section 108e StGB) Bribery and Corruption of Mandate Holders (1994/2014)	Reform to partly increase penalty in Section 108e StGB in October 2021 (Deutscher Bundestag 2021a)
Freedom of Information Law ['*Informationsfreiheitsgesetz*'] (2006)	Regulation on access to official information	
Revolving Door Regulation in the Federal Ministers Law ['*Bundesministergesetz*'] (2015)	Regulation on personnel change from politics to business for ministers and state secretaries	
Rules of Procedure of Bundestag ['*Geschäftsordnung vom Bundestag*'], Joint Rules of Procedure of the Federal Ministries ['*Gemeinsame Geschäftsordnung der Bundesministerien*']	Rules of conduct for MPs, ministers and state secretaries.	Reform to introduce a code of conduct in June 2021 (Deutscher Bundestag 2021b)

Table 2 (continued)

Reform (implemented and changed in)	Content	Additional information
Lobbying Register Act ['*Lobbyregistergesetz*'] (2022)	Mandatory lobbying register at medium level of regulation in international comparison	Adopted in March 2021 (LobbyRG in April 2021), cabinet decision on reform of the lobbying register in June 2023
Code of Conduct for representatives of special interests in the framework of the Lobbying Register Act ['*Verhaltenskodex*'] (2022)	Principles and rules of conduct for lobbyists	Cabinet decision in June 2021

Source: Adapted and expanded from Schiffers 2021a; current legislation as of 22 August 2023.

A peculiarity of the German political debate on transparency and accountability rules is that hardly any reference is made to international and scientific benchmarks, commonly accepted standards or the practical experiences of German members of the European Parliament (Schiffers 2018). Rather, the discussion largely revolves around the same arguments in a continuous loop without recourse to empirical evidence, i.e. the limits of possible regulation through the free mandate of MPs (exemplified by several publications on the debate, see FES 2014; Abgeordnetenwatch 2016; Politik & Kommunikation 2018).

In addition, the term 'lobbying' has a deeply negative connotation among the German public and in the debate on lobbying regulation (ZEW 2019; Ron and Singer 2020: 38–39, 54). Traditionally, this negative image derives from an overly simplistic understanding of the common good in the public interest and the self-interest of businesses and interest groups. Two rival positions – that lobbying fundamentally undermines democracy, or that it is an essential element of the democratic process when certain rules of fairness are applied – still shape the public debate in Germany (see also our analysis).

5 Case episodes from the debate on stricter transparency measures and the lobbying register

Looking at the time frame, the Merkel era and the debate on a lobbying register run parallel. Before the Chancellor took office in the autumn of 2005, we observe limited efforts to introduce stricter transparency measures. The first milestone was set by de'ge'pol (Deutsche Gesellschaft für Politikberatung), an association of professional interest representatives in Germany whose members are directly affected by new transparency legislation. In 2003, five years before the Bundestag first debated the issue, the association established a code of conduct (de'ge'pol 2003).

A second milestone was the launch of two civic transparency organisations: Parliament Watch (Abgeordnetenwatch) in 2004 and LobbyControl in 2005. Both organisations managed to become central players in the German debate on the transparency and accountability of elected officials, voting behaviour, the second jobs of elected officials and other forms of influence perceived as illegitimate.

With these milestones as a prelude, we can observe a slight increase in political and public interest in the field of transparency policy. However, the issue remains largely latent. Starting from here, we divide our case into *four temporal episodes*, which are shown in Figure 2.

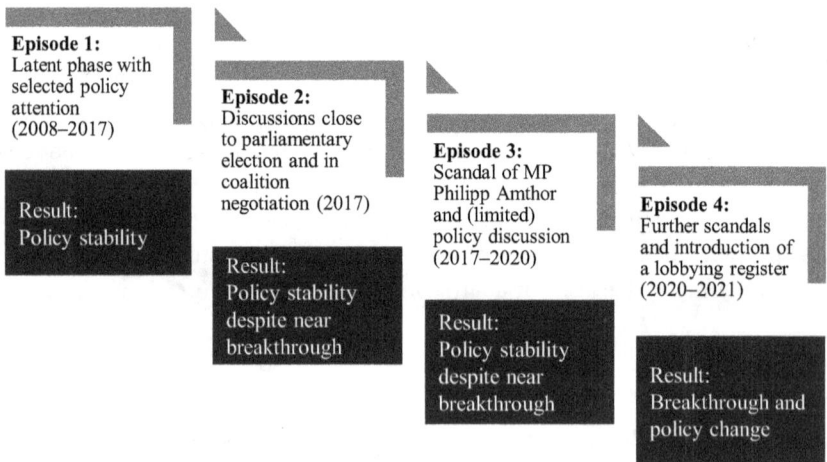

Episode 1:
Latent phase with selected policy attention (2008–2017)

Result:
Policy stability

Episode 2:
Discussions close to parliamentary election and in coalition negotiation (2017)

Result:
Policy stability despite near breakthrough

Episode 3:
Scandal of MP Philipp Amthor and (limited) policy discussion (2017–2020)

Result:
Policy stability despite near breakthrough

Episode 4:
Further scandals and introduction of a lobbying register (2020–2021)

Result:
Breakthrough and policy change

Figure 2: Four temporal episodes in our case.
Source: Authors' own compilation.

Episode 1 of our case analysis covers the period from 2008 to early 2017, and therefore includes half of the first term (2005–2009) of Chancellor Merkel's time in office, her second term (2009–2013) and most of her third term (2013–2017). During this time, we observe some selected policy attention regarding transparency issues. Nevertheless, the episode's result is one of policy stability and a reinforcement of the status quo.

In 2008, the German Bundestag first debated a proposal for lobbying regulation, when the Left Party (Die Linke) presented the first motion calling for a mandatory lobbying register. Earlier the same year, the EU Commission introduced its own lobbying register (Schmedes 2009). At the end of 2008, de'ge'pol positioned itself together with Transparency International Germany with a joint paper on lobbying. The following year, the de'ge'pol memorandum for a mandatory lobbying register was the first explicit demand from the lobbying industry itself for the regulation of its activities (LobbyControl 2009; de'ge'pol 2009).

During the 2010s, several expert hearings were held in the federal parliament (June 2009, May 2016) and in several state parliaments. Consequently, some federal states introduced lobbying registers with varying degrees of low-level regulation (see Schiffers 2018; Rasch 2020). During this time, other organisations and institutions commented on the need for stricter transparency regulation. In 2014, the OECD published a report on the key 'principles on transparency and integrity for lobbying' (OECD 2014) and even took retrospective stock of its 2010 recommendations in 2021 (OECD 2021). At the end of 2015, four civil society organisations (Transparency International, Access Info Europe, Sunlight Foundation and Open Knowledge International) jointly developed some 'international standards for lobby regulation' (Transparency International et al. 2015).

Several high-profile scandals overshadowed Chancellor Merkel's second term (2009–2013): As an example, the initiative to reduce the value-added tax on overnight hotel stays was seen as promoting clientelism in return for the tourism industry's election campaign donation to the Free Democratic Party (FDP). Another example was close contact between business and politics, which led to the resignation of German President Christian Wulff (CDU). Both instances contributed to an increased public awareness of the problem (Propach and Fuderholz 2012). Flanking regulations, such as the introduction of 'revolving door' legislation in 2015, addressed some areas of transparency policy.

Episode 2 covers a short timeframe around the German federal elections in the autumn of 2017. Thus, the episode covers the last months of Chancellor Merkel's third term (2013–2017) and again results in policy stability despite a near breakthrough in coalition negotiations. The election year was characterised by a series of lobbying scandals, such as *'Cum Ex'*, *'Dieselgate'* and *'Rent-a-Sozi'*, and high-profile cases of the revolving door operating between politics and business

(LobbyControl 2017a). Partly as a reaction to the recent scandals and partly as a continuation of earlier demands, the centre-to-left-wing parties – the Greens (Bündnis90/Die Grünen), the Left Party and the SPD – included the issue of lobbying regulation in their party manifestos (SPD 2017; Bündnis90/Die Grünen 2017; Die Linke 2017). In contrast, the CDU/CSU and the FDP opposed stricter lobbying regulations (CDU/CSU 2017; FDP 2017). The Alternative for Germany (Alternative für Deutschland, AfD) explicitly called for a lobbying law, but remained decidedly vague on the details and referred lobbying in particular to second jobs of MPs (see also the analysis of party manifestos by LobbyControl 2017b).

Furthermore, two NGO campaigns attracted great political attention in the run-up to the 2017 federal elections. First, LobbyControl and Abgeordnetenwatch presented a joint draft bill for a 'Lobby Transparency Act' in February 2017 (LobbyControl 2017a). Second, FragDenStaat and Abgeordnetenwatch explicitly demanded transparent laws ('*Gläserne Gesetze*') to track amendments and lobbying influences in the legislative process, publishing their research assessing the legislative footprint in legislation on the website stellungnah.me (FragDenStaat 2021).

The most prominent aspect of the episode covers the formation of the governing coalition after the 2017 federal election. The initial exploratory round on a 'Jamaica coalition' of CDU/CSU, FDP, and Greens agreed on stricter transparency measures by introducing a mandatory lobbying register with an emphasis on maintaining effective government action and the free exercise of the parliamentary mandate (Abgeordnetenwatch 2018). Accordingly, the negotiators from the CDU/CSU and the FDP abandoned their substantive reservations. However, the exploratory talks failed when the FDP withdrew from the negotiations. In the subsequent negotiations between the CDU/CSU and the SPD towards a renewed Grand Coalition, a similar proposal from the SPD was included in the draft. However, this proposal was marked as a contentious issue. The wording remained in the draft until the last day of negotiations when the issue was finally dropped due to the intervention of the CSU (Delhaes et al. 2018; Bank 2018). The exact course of the discussion and any quid pro quo for this deletion remain unclear. The episode illustrates how the lobbying register almost made it into the Grand Coalition's coalition agreement but failed late into the negotiation process.

Episode 3 starts with the formation of Chancellor Merkel's fourth governing coalition in 2017/2018 and lasts until late 2020. Therefore, it covers two-thirds of Merkel's fourth legislative term. This period is marked by limited legislative action, although the lobbying scandal in the summer of 2020 involving MP Philipp Amthor (CDU) increased support for stricter regulation. The coalition parties launched a proposal, but it ultimately became bogged down in committee. Even political commentators did not expect any change until the elections (LobbyControl 2020; 2021). The episode starts with observable frictions as a consequence of failed regulation efforts that arose amid continuing scandals; its conclusion, again, is a situation of continuing policy stability despite a near breakthrough.

The most prominent aspect of the episode follows the scandal and its aftermath of the 'Amthor case', where the debate was once again stirred up. In June 2020, it became public knowledge that MP Philipp Amthor provided a consulting firm with privileged contacts in ministries and the Chancellor's Office. In return, he received stock options and luxury travelling expenses (LobbyControl 2020). As a response, the government coalition announced a proposal for a lobbying register, but Merkel's CDU remained reluctant. The register was limited to parliament, excluding lobbyists' contact with the government and a legislative footprint. In her summer press conference in August 2021, Chancellor Merkel deemed these measures sufficiently transparent and underlined the supposedly high level of government transparency (Bundeskanzleramt 2020). Only after public demands by her vice chancellor and subsequent successor Olaf Scholz (SPD), the proposal was expanded to include top-level government contacts both in cabinet and the administration and ultimately proceeded to committee (Handelsblatt 2020). Although experts expected to see a quick adoption, the proposal was bogged down in committee shortly before the decisive second and third readings. While the SPD-led ministry of justice pushed for an 'executive footprint',[4] the CSU-led ministry of the interior blocked the proposal again. Failing to expand the scope of the lobbying register, the SPD took the proposal off the plenary's agenda in anticipation of further blockages by Horst Seehofer (CSU) (Politik & Kommunikation 2020; Dittrich et al. 2020). While this may have avoided a sizeable coalition dispute, the status quo seemed to hold up during this legislative period. This was particularly evident in LobbyControl's assessment in December 2020 and February 2021 (LobbyControl 2020; 2021) judging that the initiative for the introduction of a lobbying register was a failure.

Episode 4 starts at the beginning of the election year 2021. As Chancellor Merkel announced her intention not to seek re-election, the episode covers the end of the Merkel era and the last months of her fourth legislative term. The beginning of the second year of the COVID-19 pandemic was marked by a corruption scandal relating to the procurement of face masks by MPs, which subsequently dominated the debate about transparency regulation reforms. In addition, several Conservative MPs engaged in paid lobbying ('*Mandatslobbying*') commissioned by the government of Azerbaijan to improve its public image. This pairing of scandals added to the already agitated public mood following the Amthor lobbying scandal of the previous episode. Although the scandals dealt with different transparency

---

4 A legislative footprint that also includes the administration.

regulations – conflicts of interests and paid lobbying by MPs – they were framed through a lobbying lens and seen as part of the same structural issue.

The most prominent aspect of this episode was the agreement reached by the coalition parties on a legally binding lobbying register in March 2021 after many years of dispute and faced opposition. Further resolutions in the wake of the build-up of scandals concerned the parliamentary members' law ('*Abgeordneten-gesetz*') to focus on MPs' conflicts of interest and the existence of lucrative and dodgy dealings violating the code of conduct. The law was amended to 'improve transparency rules for members of the German Bundestag' (Deutscher Bundestag 2021a; for a critical appraisal of the content see Abgeordnetenwatch 2021). At the same time, the cabinet published the Code of Conduct for representatives of special interests, which was created as part of the Lobbying Register Act (Deutscher Bundestag 2021b). The episode concludes with the introduction of the lobbying register as a substantial policy change after a long period of policy stability.

6 Policy networks: Actor constellations and policy images

Before we identify the mechanisms in the episodes of the case, we structure the debate by illustrating two dominant policy networks and their policy images. Apart from the shared goal of ensuring the general transparency of policymaking processes, we find two opposing networks: a network favouring stricter regulation rules and a network opposing stricter regulation rules. While the former promotes an equal opportunities policy image (equal opportunity network), the latter promotes a freedom and efficiency policy image (freedom and efficiency network). The two networks with their actors and policy images are illustrated in Figure 3.

The *equal opportunity network* identifies the growing salience of issues and views lax transparency regulations as a structural problem of interest representation. Persistent asymmetries in terms of actors' resources and their access to policymaking venues are viewed as the reason for disparities in influence in favour of business interests (Schiffers 2021b: 8–9, 70; LobbyControl 2021a: 6). This development is considered a fundamental threat to basic democratic values and institutions (Allianz für Lobbytransparenz 2019).

The network consists of MPs and government officials from the Green Party, the SPD and the Left Party. They have been in favour of stricter transparency measures since the 2009 federal election (LobbyControl 2009; 2013; 2017b; for the 2017 federal election see SPD 2017; Bündnis90/Die Grünen 2017; Die Linke 2017). Therefore, these parties have been part of the network since the first case episode.

Equal opportunity network

- Network favouring stricter regulation rules
- Actors: Green Party, The Left, SPD, several NGOs and key intrerest groups from business and public interests, Alliance for Lobbying Transparency
- Policy image: Asymmetries of actors' ressources and their access to policymaking; regarded as a structural problem and a threat to democracy

Freedom and efficiency network

- Network opposing stricter regulation rules
- Actors: CDU/CSU, FDP, a variety of business interest groups and companies
- Policy image: Guarantee of a free mandate of MPs and a free flow of information, transparency problem because of a few outliers

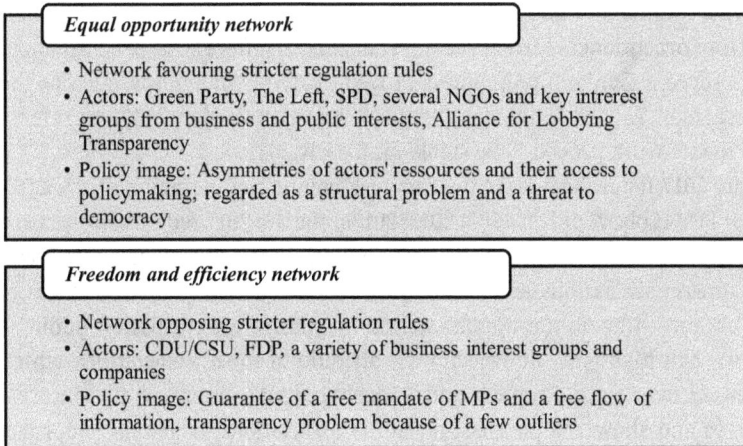

Figure 3: Two policy networks.
Source: Authors' own compilation.

Furthermore, this network includes several NGOs, such as LobbyControl, Abgeord-netenwatch, Transparency International Germany and FragDenStaat and some business associations, such as the Federation of German Industries (Bundesverband der Deutschen Industrie BDI), the German chemical industry association (Verband der Chemischen Industrie VCI), the industry association of family-owned businesses (Die Familienunternehmer), as well as public interests groups like the Federation of German Consumer Organisations (Verbraucherzentrale Bundesverband vzbv) and the Nature and Biodiversity Conservation Union (Naturschutzbund Deutsch-land (NABU). While Transparency International Germany has been a traditional member of the network since the first episode, the BDI joined the network during episode two (see also M2 below). Another central actor of the network is de'ge'pol who has advocated in favour of regulation since 2008 and even more actively since 2009 and is, therefore, a traditional member of the network. In addition, two prom-inent international players joined the network: the OECD and the Group of States against Corruption (GRECO) of the Council of Europe, which has been fighting cor-ruption since 1999.

The equal opportunity network is opposed by a *freedom and efficiency network*. This network's arguments are threefold. First, it argues that stricter transparency rules oppose the principle of the constitutionally guaranteed free mandate of MPs. Second, it warns of administrative hurdles that could restrict the flow of informa-tion in the legislative process, and the network's members criticise the very effec-tiveness of a lobbying register. Third, the network argues for the need to maintain lax transparency regulations, as only a few outliers do not adhere to the principles of publicity, accountability and legitimacy of political decisions ('*schwarze Schafe*', for voices from practitioners see PSCA 2018; Polk 2021; Schiffers 2018: 5–6). Although we could observe a (limited) willingness of some network members, such as the CDU spokesperson Patrick Schnieder (Politik & Kommunikation 2020), to reform legislation, the network proved to be stable until early 2021.

Until the 2017 federal election, the network comprised members of the CDU, CSU and the FDP (LobbyControl 2009; 2013; 2017b; for the 2017 federal election see CDU/CSU 2017; FDP 2017). Similar to the first network, this network also comprises several business associations and companies, which, however, cannot be easily identified because they do not oppose stricter transparency regulation publicly. However, we can highlight the rejectionist attitude of most associations which even increased over time. Propach and Fuderholz (2012) analysed two interest group surveys and showed a polarisation in the associations' landscape. Approval ratings in favour of a mandatory register and of no register at all were at 60 per cent (very good, good), while a voluntary register was mostly rejected (bad, very bad). Moreover, the number of associations rejecting a lobbying register *increased* by 41 per cent between 2009 and 2012. These results show that the rejection of a lobbying register was more widespread in the lobbying industry than many statements by the top associations suggest and that there was no mechanism for increasing the approval of the lobbying register over time. Furthermore, the great public and political astonishment regarding numerous statements by actors favouring stricter transparency rules shows how unexpected the idea of stricter legislation was for many policymakers in this field. The journalistic news value of this presumed deviation from former opinions shows that the resistance against stricter regulation was widespread.

7 Mechanisms of policy stability and change

Our analysis identifies three mechanisms (M1, M2, M3/M3*), which delineate our four case episodes leading to the introduction of a lobbying register in March 2021. Each mechanism reflects the three theoretical concepts of PET related to policy change (policy image and issue network, policy venue and feedback loop) in a different way. Furthermore, we identify a major turning point between the third and fourth episodes of our case. Table 3 summarises the key findings.

Table 3: Overview of the four episodes of policy stability and change.

No. of episode	Description of episode	Result of episode	Mechanism/ combination of mechanisms
1	Latent phase with selected policy attention (2008–2017)	Policy stability	M1
2	Discussion of policy initiatives in the run-up to the 2017 parliamentary election and in coalition negotiations (2017)	Policy stability despite near breakthrough (coalition negotiation)	M1, M2
3	Scandal of MP Philipp Amthor and (limited) policy discussion (2017–2020)	Policy stability despite near breakthrough (proposal bogged down in committee)	M1, M2, M3 Turning Point
4	Further scandals and decision on the introduction of a lobbying register (2020–2021)	Breakthrough and policy change	M2, M3*

M1: De-thematisation of the policy issue by the efficiency network
M2: Establishment of a dominant equal opportunity network and actor validation
M3: The beginning of issue validation/M3*: Dynamic issue validation through a build-up of scandals
Turning Point: M1 disappears and M3* emerges

Source: Authors' own compilation.

7.1 De-thematisation of the policy issue by the efficiency network (M1)

In this first mechanism, key actors manage to dampen the salience of the policy issue by using long-lasting formal procedures. Political and administrative actors opposing stricter transparency measures successfully kept the issue off the agenda in multiple *venues,* such as the German Bundestag. Therefore, the *policy image* of both networks is less prominent because there is no (or less) policy discussion. In terms of PET feedback, M1 is a specific example of *negative feedback.* The mechanism was identified as the only mechanism in the first episode but is part of a combination of mechanisms in the second and third episodes.

This mechanism shows the blocking attitude of the CDU and (partly) the FDP in the German Bundestag. During several policy debates, the lobbying register was taken off the agenda. The first example are the 2017 coalition negotiations in the second episode. The second example is the policy discussion in episode three in the autumn of 2020 (Dittrich et al. 2020; on micro-politics in parliamentary groups, see Schöne 2021). Surprisingly, this happened on the initiative of the SPD – a member of the network *favouring* stricter regulation. With this, the party reacted to the rejection of integrating an 'executive footprint' into the legislation by Germany's federal minister of the interior, Horst Seehofer (CSU). Failing to expand the scope of the lobbying register, the SPD took the proposal off the plenary's agenda. This was done in anticipation of further opposition by Seehofer and ongoing sizeable coalition disputes.

M1 is closely related to the turning point we identified in our case. Once M1 was absent from our case observations in the months following policy discussions in the autumn of 2020, we find a turning point as a subtype of a critical juncture with a space of uncertainty wherein political actors were able to lay out a path leading to the introduction of a lobbying register in early 2021 (see Figure 1). This substantial policy change was surprising to a variety of policy actors, including LobbyControl (2020; 2021b), which was still convinced of the register's failure in December 2020 and February 2021.

7.2 Establishment of a dominant equal opportunity network and actor validation (M2)

The second mechanism describes the growing prominence of the *network* promoting an equal opportunity *policy image* since 2017. A variety of new actors joined the issue network explicitly favouring stricter regulation, and traditional network members were increasingly perceived as experts in the field. As a result, the opposing network is, de facto, weakened, and its position is under increased pressure. From time to time, the network's default position of keeping the status quo dissolves and many lobbying actors become open to new regulations, without having any specific proposals (for examples see below). Furthermore, we observe several *venue changes*, e.g. from the German Bundestag in episode three, with a technical policy debate, to a wider public debate in episode four, focusing on scandals and normative arguments. In terms of PET feedback loops, M2 illustrates an example of *positive feedback*. The mechanism was observed in episodes two, three, and four together with other mechanisms.

Case observations show that from time to time, the equal opportunity network was joined by relevant associations and companies, such as BDI, VZBV, Die Familienunternehmer and NABU. These actors joined Transparency International Germany and VCI, which formed a transparency initiative in 2018. Together, they founded the Alliance for Lobbying Transparency (*'Allianz für Lobbytransparenz'*), serving as a subgroup of the network. After that, several other interest representatives joined the alliance, such as the Bundesverband deutscher Banken and the World Wide Fund for Nature (WWF).

In addition, Transparency International Germany and LobbyControl have increasingly been invited to comment on recent developments.[5] Consequently, they were no longer regarded as just one voice among many others but were now recognised as experts in the field. With this newly acquired expert status through actor validation (organisational validation, Berkhout 2013: 240; for an application on LobbyControl see Schiffers 2021b: 66, 91–92), both organisations occupy powerful positions in the network.

Meanwhile, the network promoting a freedom and an efficiency policy image has lost central members from its diffuse field of supporters. During the second episode, for instance, 15 out of 30 DAX companies declared in favour of stricter transparency regulations (Bewarder 2010). This led to the erosion of the network and its standing as a policy monopoly, as well as the emergence of a new policy monopoly comprising members of the equal opportunity network who now dominate the policy debate. In these discussions, this network slightly modified its policy image and emphasised scandals even more as structural deficits instead of seeing them as individual mistakes of politicians (see Schiffers 2021a).

7.3 The beginning of issue validation and dynamic issue validation through the build-up of scandals (M3 and M3*)

The third mechanism is twofold: it covers the beginning of the validation of the policy issue (M3) and its translation into dynamic issue validation through a series of corruption scandals (M3*). In terms of PET concepts, we observe discussions in the same *venue* – the German Bundestag – as in the other episodes. The uncovering of *external events*, such as scandals, however, did not lead to any open investigations in the existing venues, causing friction in the parliamentary and public arena. Both politicians and interest groups employed the outside strategy of 'going public', consequently accelerating the already scandalised public debate. Therefore, the equal rights policy image of the network favouring transparency measures received issue validation (Berkhout 2013: 240). Thus, political as well as media attention remained latent and could be activated easily. While the pressure in the third episode was not intense enough to push for the introduction of a lobbying register,

---

5 Transparency International Germany has almost quadrupled its expert comments in the media from 2018 (11) to 2021 (42), while LobbyControl has more than doubled its expert comments from 2018 (30) to 2021 (77). For an overview, see https://www.lobbycontrol.de/presse/press espiegel/ and https://www.transparency.de/aktuelles/pressespiegel.

issue validation was sufficiently potent after further scandals were made public. Therefore, M3 and M3* are examples of *positive feedback loops*. The mechanisms are attached to the third episode (M3) and the fourth episode (M3*).

Case observations show that the debate's momentum gained further attention when several scandals were made public at the same time. In addition to the face-mask scandal in early 2021, several MPs engaged in paid lobbying (*'Mandatslobby-ing'*) commissioned by the government of Azerbaijan to improve its public image (M3*). These scandals impacted the already agitated public mood following the Amthor lobbying scandal about privileged access to government members (M3). These scandals were framed through a lobbying lens, although they address different transparency regulations. Conflicts of interest of MPs as well as lucrative and dodgy dealings violating the code of conduct are part of the parliamentary members' law (*'Abgeordnetengesetz'*) that was subsequently reformed but had limited scope. The equal opportunity network finally benefited from this framing, leading to the increased issue validation of transparency policy in general.

In our case, the emergence of M3* together with the disappearance of M1 (de-thematisation of the policy issue by the efficiency network) created a turning point as a subtype of a critical juncture This turning point led to a substantial policy change, i.e. the introduction of the lobbying register in March 2021.

8 Conclusion: A combination of three mechanisms to enable policy change

This chapter analysed the introduction of the German lobbying register in March 2021 as an example of an unexpected policy change resulting from a major turning point in Germany's transparency policy. Applying three core concepts of the Punctuated Equilibrium Theory related to policy change (policy images, venues and feedback loops), empirical findings show that the introduction can be explained by a combination of three mechanisms: a de-thematisation of the policy issue, a strong and growing issue network that favoured stricter transparency regulations and, increasing public validation of the issue through a build-up of scandals. The major turning point becomes apparent when the issue was no longer blocked in the parliamentary procedure but was actively put on the political agenda, following increased issue validation through a build-up of scandals. In terms of time, the turning point can be observed between late 2020 and early 2021 and is, thus, located at the intersection of the third and fourth episodes of the case.

In line with a current shift in research, we find that scandals do indeed play an important role concerning issue validation but are not sufficient to induce a policy change in the field of transparency policy. Following Crepaz (2017), we argue that we need to look deeper into the complex mechanisms of policy change instead of assuming direct links between scandals per se and policy change. This speaks to recent PET literature and research on the introduction of new lobbying legislation which both emphasise the need for a combination of factors to explain policy change. Analysing the role of domestic pressure and a new political culture for policy change – in our case, favouring stricter transparency rules – go beyond a mere reaction to external shocks, such as lobbying scandals.

Our case corresponds in both time and style to Angela Merkel's reactive policymaking practices during her four legislative terms. In contrast, the successor government of the 'traffic light coalition' (SPD, Greens, Liberals) under chancellor Olaf Scholz (SPD) quickly announced the intention to further tighten legislation about transparency in the coalition agreement. Until early summer 2023, the issue has taken a back seat on the political agenda due to *'Zeitenwende'*, a major turning point in German foreign, global and energy policy following the Russian invasion of Ukraine in the spring of 2022. In June 2023, however, the cabinet passed a reform initiative on the lobbying register. On the one hand, it tightens lobbying rules (e.g. lobbyists will have to delcare contacts with department heads and heads of units in ministries), on the other hand, however, rules will be relaxed (e.g. public interest groups that are funded by donations will only be obliged to document larger sums they have received). The final decision will be made in autumn/winter where the legislation will be discussed in parliament (Deutscher Bundestag 2023). Based on our analysis, we do not expect new faced opposition, as the three coalition parties belong to the dominant issue network, and the policy image remains consistent within the ongoing policy debate. In line with the concept of turning points as a specific subtype of critical junctures, future initiatives addressing transparency can build upon the dominant pro-regulation policy image and the public validation of transparency and accountability issues as a whole.

References

Abgeordnetenwatch. 2016. 'Im Interview: Was Politiker, Lobbyisten und Zivilgesellschaft von einem Lobbyregister halten'. Available at: <https://www.abgeordnetenwatch.de/kampagnen/im-interview-was-politiker-lobbyisten-und-zivilgesellschaft-von-einem-lobbyregister-halten> (last accessed 11 April 2023).

Abgeordnetenwatch. 2018. GroKo streicht das Lobbyregister. Available at: <https://www.abgeordne tenwatch.de/blog/2018-02-07/groko-verhindert-lobbyregister> (last accessed 03 March 2023).

Abgeordnetenwatch. 2021. Augenwischerei statt Transparenz. Analyse des GroKo-Lobbyregisters. Available at: <https://www.abgeordnetenwatch.de/kampagnen/augenwischerei-statt-transparenz-update> (last accessed 04 March 2023).

Allianz für Lobbytransparenz. 2019. Allianz für Lobbytransparenz – Gemeinsam für eine transparente Interessenvertretung; von Transparency International Deutschland e. V. (Transparency Deutschland), Verband der Chemischen Industrie (VCI), Verbraucherzentrale Bundesverband (VZBV), Bundesverband der Deutschen Industrie (BDI), Naturschutzbund Deutschland (NABU) und Die Familienunternehmer. Available at: <https://www.transparency.de/aktuelles/detail/arti cle/allianz-fuer-lobbytransparenz-fordert-interessenvertretungsgesetz/> (last accessed 04 March 2023).

Bandelow, N. C., A. Hartmann and J. Hornung. 2019. Selbstbeschränkte Gesundheitspolitik im Vorfeld neuer Punktuierungen. In R. Zohlnhöfer and R. Saalfeld, R. (eds.), *Zwischen Stillstand, Politikwandel und Krisenmanagement*, 445–467. Wiesbaden: Springer VS.

Bank, H. 2018. Lobbyismus. Eine schlechte Entscheidung. *Frankfurter Rundschau*, 23 February. <https://www.fr.de/wirtschaft/eine-schlechte-entscheidung-10981522.html> (last accessed 11 April 2023).

Baumgartner, F. R., and B. D. Jones. 1993. *Agendas and instability in American politics*. Chicago, IL: University of Chicago Press.

Baumgartner, F. R., B. D. Jones. 2009. *Agendas and instability in American politics*. 2nd edn. Chicago, IL: University of Chicago Press.

Baumgartner, F. R., B. D. Jones and P. B. Mortensen. 2018. Punctuated Equilibrium Theory: Explaining stability and change in public policymaking' In C. M. Weible and P. A. Sabatier (eds.), *Theories of the Policy Process*, 55–101. New York: Routledge.

Beach, D., and R. Pedersen. 2019. *Process-Tracing Methods*. Ann Arbor, MI: University of Michigan Press.

Berkhout, J. 2013. Why interest organizations do what they do: Assessing the explanatory potential of 'exchange' approaches. *Interest Groups & Advocacy* 2(2). 227–250.

Beyer, D., G. Boushey and C. Breunig. 2022. Punctuated Equilibrium. In G. Wenzelburger and R. Zohlnhöfer (eds.), *Handbuch Policy-Forschung*. 2nd edn. Wiesbaden: Springer VS.

Bewarder, M. 2010. Ende des Versteckspiels. *Welt*. 24 June.

Bitonti, A., and J. Hogan. 2021. Lobbying Regulation. In P. Harris, A. Bitonti, C. S. Fleisher and A. S. Binderkrantz (eds.), *The Palgrave Encyclopedia of Interest Groups, Lobbying and Public Affairs*, 1–8. Cham: Palgrave Macmillan.

Bundeskanzleramt. 2020. Pressekonferenz von Bundeskanzlerin Merkel am 28. August 2020 in Berlin. Mitschrift Pressekonferenz. Available at: <https://www.bundeskanzler.de/bk-de/ak tuelles/pressekonferenz-von-bundeskanzlerin-merkel-am-28-august-2020-1781008> (last accessed 11 April 2023).

Bündnis90/Die Grünen. 2017. Zukunft wird aus Mut gemacht. Bundestagswahlprogramm 2017. Available at: <https://cms.gruene.de/uploads/documents/BUENDNIS_90_DIE_GRUENEN_Bun destagswahlprogramm_2017_barrierefrei.pdf> (last accessed 11 April 2023).

Bunea, A. 2018. Legitimacy through targeted transparency? Regulatory effectiveness and sustainability of lobbying regulation in the European Union. *European Journal of Political Research* 57(2). 378–403.

Burkhardt, S. 2018. Scandals in the network society. In A. Haller, H. Michael and M. Kraus (eds.), *Scandalogy: an interdisciplinary field*, 18–44. Köln: Herbert von Halem Verlag.

Cairney, P., and T. Heikkila. 2018. Comparison of Theory of the Policy Process. In C. M. Weible and P. A. Sabatier (eds.), *Theories of the Policy Process*, 301–328. New York: Routledge.

Capano, G. 2009. Understanding Policy Change As An Epistemological and Theoretical Problem. *Journal of Comparative Policy Analysis* 11(1). 7–31.

Capoccia, G., and D. Keleman. 2007. The Study of Critical Junctures: Theory, Narrative, and Counterfactuals in Historical Institutionalism. *World Politics* 59(3). 341–369.

CDU/CSU. 2017. Für ein Deutschland, in dem wir gut und gerne leben. Regierungsprogramm 2017–2021. Christlich Demokratische Union/Christlich-Soziale Union. Available at: <https://archiv. cdu.de/system/tdf/media/dokumente/170703regierungsprogramm2017.pdf?file=1> (last accessed 11 April 2023).

Chari, R., J. Hogan, G. Murphy and M. Crepaz. 2019. *Regulating lobbying. A global comparison.* 2nd edn. Manchester: Manchester University Press.

Collier, D. 2011. Understanding Process Tracing. *Political Science and Politics* 44(4). 823–830.

Crepaz, M. 2017. Why do we have lobbying rules? Investigating the introduction of lobbying laws in EU and OECD member states. *Interest Groups & Advocacy* 6. 231–252.

Crepaz, M., and R. Chari. 2014. The EU's initiatives to regulate lobbyists: Good or bad administration? *Cuadernos Europeos de Deusto* 51(1). 71–97.

Crepaz, M., R. Chari, J. Hogan and G. Murphy. 2019. International Dynamics in Lobbying Regulation. In D. Dialer and M. Richter (eds.), *Lobbying in the European Union*, 49–63. Basel: Springer.

de'ge'pol. 2003. Verhaltenskodex. Deutsche Gesellschaft für Politikberatung. Available at: <https://static1. squarespace.com/static/6017272360bac64bcb545bf9/t/607066ed8d60bd3ca162f4e5/1617979117950/ degepol_Verhaltenskodex%282%29.pdf> (last accessed 7 April 2023).

de'ge'pol. 2009. Eckpunktepapier der de'ge'pol – Deutsche Gesellschaft für Politikberatung zu einem Register für Interessenvertreter in Deutschland. Available at: <https://www.degepol.de/s/das_ eckpunktepapier_der_degepol_zu_einem_register_fuer_interessenvertreter_in_deutschland22. pdf> (last accessed 03 March 2023).

Delhaes, D., M. Greive, D. Heide and J. Hildebrand. 2018. Große Koalition. Was im Entwurf des Koalitionsvertrages fehlt. *Handelsblatt.*

Deutscher Bundestag. 2021. Gesetz zur Verbesserung der Transparenzregeln für die Mitglieder des Deutschen Bundestages und zur Anhebung des Strafrahmens des § 108e des Strafgesetzbuches. Available at <https://dip.bundestag.de/vorgang/gesetz-zur-verbesserung-der-transparenzregeln-f%C3%BCr-die-mitglieder-des-deutschen/276851>. (last accessed 15 June, 2023).

Deutscher Bundestag. 2021b. Änderung der Geschäftsordnung des Deutschen Bundestages – hier: Einführung einer Anlage 2a (Verhaltenskodex)'. Available at: <https://dserver.bundestag.de/btd/19/ 308/1930885.pdf> (last accessed 11 April 2023).

Deutscher Bundestag. 2023. Koalition will Lobbyregister aussagekräftiger machen. Ausschuss für Wahlprüfung, Immunität und Geschäftsordnung — Gesetzentwurf — hib 462/2023. Available at <https://www.bundestag.de/presse/hib/kurzmeldungen-954536> (last accessed 22 August 2023).

Deutsche Welle. 2021. Fighting corruption: Germany gets a "lobby register". Available at: <https://www. dw.com/en/fighting-corruption-germany-gets-a-lobby-register/a-56808321> (last accessed 11 April 2023).

Die Linke. 2017. Sozial. Gerecht. Frieden. Für Alle. Die Zukunft, für die wir stehen. Wahlprogramm zur Bundestagswahl 2017. Available at: <https://www.die-linke.de/fileadmin/download/wahlen2017/ wahlprogramm2017/die_linke_wahlprogramm_2017.pdf> (last accessed 11 April 2023).

Dittrich, B., K. Doering, J. Jordan and V. Rosigkeit. 2020. Lieferketten bis Lobbyregister: Welche SPD-Gesetze die Union blockiert. *Vorwärts.* Available at: <https://www.vorwaerts.de/artikel/lieferket ten-lobbyregister-welche-spd-gesetze-union-blockiert> (last accessed 11 April 2023).

Easterly, B. 2015. Playing Politics with Sex Offender Laws: An Event History Analysis of the Initial Community Notification Laws across American States. *Policy Studies Journal* 43(3). 355–378.

European Commission. 2022. Rechtsstaatlichkeit: Empfehlungen der Kommission, auch für Deutschland, Press release on 13 July 2022. Available at: <https://germany.representation.ec.eu ropa.eu/news/rechtsstaatlichkeit-empfehlungen-der-kommission-auch-fur-deutschland-2022-07-13_de> (last accessed 11 April 2023).

Ewert, B., and K. Loer. 2022. COVID-19 as a Catalyst for Policy Change: The Role of Trigger Points and Spillover Effects. *German Politics* 31.

FDP. 2017. Beschluss des 68. Ordentlichen Bundesparteitages. Schauen wir nicht länger zu. Freie Demokratische Partei. Available at: <https://www.fdp.de/beschluss/beschluss-des-68-ord-bundesparteitages-schauen-wir-nicht-laenger-zu> (last accessed 11 April 2023).

FES. 2014. Lobbyismus in der Kritik. Ansätze zu einer zeitgemäßen Regulierung von Interessenvertretung. Available at: <https://library.fes.de/pdf-files/dialog/10538-20140304.pdf.> (last accessed 11 April 2023).

FragDenStaat. 2021. Gläserne Gesetze. Welchen Einfluss haben Lobbyisten auf unsere Gesetze? Campaign website for the document archive 'stellungnah.me'. Available at <https://fragdenstaat. de/kampagnen/glaeserne-gesetze> (last accessed 03 March 2023).

Gerring, J. 2007. *Case Study Research. Principles and Practices*. Cambridge: Cambridge University Press.

Gerring, J., and L. Cojocaru. 2016. Selecting Cases for Intensive Analysis. *Sociological Methods & Research* 45(3). 392–423.

Greenwood, J., and J. Dreger. 2013. The transparency register: A European vanguard of strong lobby regulation? *Interest Groups & Advocacy* 2(2). 139–162.

Hall, P. 1993. Policy Paradigms, Social Learning, and the State: The Case of Economic Policymaking in Britain. *Comparative Politics* 25(3). 275–296.

Handelsblatt. 2020. Lobbyregister nun auch für Bundesregierung. 10. September.

Holman, C., and W. Luneburg. 2012. Lobbying and transparency: A comparative analysis of regulatory reform. *Interest Groups & Advocacy* 1. 75–104.

Hong, S., and H. Sohn. 2014. Informal institutional friction and punctuations: Evidence from multicultural policy in Korea. *Public Administration* 92(4). 1075–1089.

Janusch, H., Mucha, W., Schwanholz, J., Lorberg, D., Reichwein, A. 2024. Introduction: Turning Points, Typology, and Puzzles. In H. Janusch, W. Mucha, J. Schwanholz, A. Reichwein, and D. Lorberg (eds.), *Turning Points. Challenges for Western Democracies in the 21st Century*, 1–13. Berlin/Boston: De Gruyter.

Jones, B. D., and F. R. Baumgartner. 2012. From there to here: Punctuated equilibrium to the general punctuation thesis to a theory of government information processing. *Policy Studies Journal* 40(1). 1–19.

Keeling, S., S. Feeney and J. Hogan. 2017. Transparency! Transparency? Comparing the new lobbying legislation in Ireland and the UK. *Interest Groups & Advocacy* 6. 121–142.

LobbyControl. 2009. Wahlprüfsteine zur Bundestagswahl 2009. Available at: <https://www.lobbycon trol.de/wp-content/uploads/ubersicht-antworten-wahlprufsteine_02.pdf> (last accessed 11 April 2023).

LobbyControl. 2013. Wahlprüfsteine zur Bundestagswahl 2013. Available at: <https://www.lobbycon trol.de/wp-content/uploads/LobbyControl-Wahlpruefsteine-2013.pdf> (last accessed 11 April 2023).

LobbyControl. 2017a. Aussitzen statt anpacken: Eine Bilanz von vier Jahren Schwarz-Rot. Lobbyreport 2017. Available at: <https://www.lobbycontrol.de/wp-content/uploads/lobbyreport-lc-2017-web -1.pdf> (last accessed 11 April 2023).

LobbyControl. 2017b. Parteiencheck zur Bundestagswahl. Wie stehen die Parteien zum Thema Lobbykontrolle? Available at: <https://www.lobbycontrol.de/2017/09/parteiencheck-zur-bundestagswahl> (last accessed 11 April 2023).

LobbyControl. 2020. Ein halbes Jahr nach Amthor: Scheitert das Lobbyregister? Available at: <https://www.lobbycontrol.de/2020/12/ein-halbes-jahr-nach-amthor-scheitert-das-lobbyregister/> (last accessed 11 April 2023).

LobbyControl. 2021a. Lobbyreport 2021. Beispiellose Skandale – strengere Lobbyregeln: Eine Bilanz von vier Jahren Schwarz-Rot. Available at: <https://www.lobbycontrol.de/wp-content/uploads/Lobbyreport-2021_Beispiellose-Skandale-strengere-Lobbyregeln.pdf> (last accessed 11 April 2023).

LobbyControl. 2021b. Ist das Lobbyregister noch zu retten?. Available at: <https://www.lobbycontrol.de/2021/02/ist-das-lobbyregister-noch-zu-retten/> (last accessed 11 April 2023).

Lowry, W. R., and M. Joslyn. 2014. The determinants of salience of energy issues. *Review of Policy Research* 31(3). 153–172.

McKay, A. M., and A. Wozniak. 2020. Opaque: an empirical evaluation of lobbying transparency in the UK. *Interest Groups Advocacy* 9. 102–118.

Miller, D. and W. Dinan. 2008. Corridors of Power: Lobbying in the UK. *Observatoire de la société Britannique* 6. 25–45.

Mugellini, G. 2020. Corruption. In P. Harris, A. Bitonti, C. S. Fleisher and A. S. Binderkrantz (eds.), *The Palgrave Encyclopedia of Interest Groups, Lobbying and Public Affairs*, 1–9. Cham: Palgrave Macmillan.

Newmark, A. J. 2005. Measuring state legislative lobbying regulation, 1990–2003. *State Politics & Policy Quarterly* 5(2). 182–191.

Newmark, A. J. 2017. Lobbying regulation in the states revisited: What are we trying to measure, and how do we measure it? *Interest Groups Advocacy* 6. 215–230.

OECD. 2014. Lobbyists, Governments and Public Trust. Implementing the OECD Principles for Transparency and Integrity in Lobbying. Available at: <https://read.oecd-ilibrary.org/governance/lobbyists-governments-and-public-trust-volume-3_9789264214224-en#page1> (last accessed 11 April 2023).

OECD. 2021. Lobbying in OECD-Ländern: Es braucht mehr Regeln und mehr Klarheit. Available at: <https://www.oecd.org/berlin/presse/lobbying-in-oecd-laendern-es-braucht-mehr-regeln-und-mehr-klarheit.htm> (last accessed 11 April 2023).

Ozymy, J. 2010. Assessing the impact of legislative lobbying regulations on interest group influence in US state legislatures. *State Politics & Policy Quarterly* 10(4). 397–420.

Plümer, S., and M. Schiffers. 2022. Dynamics of policy change: Conceptualising policy change and stability in a transforming society. *dms – der moderne staat – Zeitschrift für Public Policy, Recht und Management* 15(2). 275–292.

Plümer, S., and M. Schiffers. 2023. Der unerwartete Durchbruch einer Blockade. Policy-Stabilität und -Wandel im Querschnittsbereich der Lobbyregulierung im Vorfeld der Bundestagswahl 2021. In K. R. Korte, M. Schiffers, A. von Schuckmann and S. Plümer (eds.), *Die Bundestagswahl 2021*. Wiesbaden: Springer VS.

Politik & Kommunikation. 2018. Wie steht es um die Transparenz? Available at: <https://www.politik-kommunikation.de/politik/wie-steht-es-um-die-transparenz/> (last accessed 11 April 2023).

Politik & Kommunikation. 2020. Lobbyregister. Ein Schritt zu weniger Anrüchigkeit. Available at: <https://www.politik-kommunikation.de/politik/ein-schritt-zu-weniger-anruechigkeit> (last accessed 11 April 2023).

Polk, A. 2021. Mehr Transparenz durch das Lobbyregister? *Wirtschaftsdienst* 101(2). 121–126.

Propach, U., and J. Fuderholz. 2012. Transparenz als Monstranz: Warum der lautstarken Debatte über ein Lobbyregister die Zuhörer fernbleiben. *Zeitschrift für Politikberatung (ZPB) / Policy Advice and Political Consulting* 5(1). 27–30.

PSCA. 2018. Sonderheft 2018. Interessenvertretung und Lobbyismus. Political Science Applied. Available at: <https://www.psca.eu/wp-content/uploads/2019/02/PSCA_Special_Issue_Lobbyis mus_Juni_2018.pdf> (last accessed 11 April 2023).

Rasch, D. 2020. Lobbying-Regulierung in den deutschen Bundesländern – ein Vergleich. *dms – der moderne staat – Zeitschrift für Public Policy, Recht und Management* 13(2). 1–19.

Robinson, R. 2014. Culture and legal policy punctuation in the Supreme Court' s gender discrimination cases. *Policy Studies Journal* 42(4). 555–589.

Ron, A., and A. A. Singer. 2020. Democracy, corruption, and the ethics of business lobbying. *Interest Groups & Advocacy* 9. 38–56.

Rüb, F. W. 2014. Rapide Politikwechsel in der Bundesrepublik. Eine konzeptionelle. Annäherung an ein unerforschtes Phänomen. In F. W. Rüb (ed.), *Rapide Politikwechsel in der Bundesrepublik. Theoretische und empirische Befunde*, 9–46. Baden-Baden: Nomos.

Sabatier, P. A., and H. C. Jenkins-Smith. 1993. *Policy Change and Learning: An Advocacy Coalition Approach*. Boulder, CO: Westview Press.

Saldaña, J. 2016. *The Coding Manual for Qualitative Researchers*. 3rd edn. Los Angeles: SAGE.

Schiffers, M. 2018. Schritte und Rückschritte der Debatte über gesetzliche Lobbyregulierung. Available at: <http://regierungsforschung.de/schritte-und-rueckschritte-der-debatte-ueber-gesetzliche-lobbyregulierung/> (last accessed 11 April 2023).

Schiffers, M. 2021a. Illegitime Geschäfte in der "Coronakratie" – ethische Perspektiven auf die Einflussnahme durch politische Entscheidungsträgerinnen und -träger. *Zeitschrift für Politikwissenschaft* 31(2). 469–477.

Schiffers, M. 2021b. *NGOs als besondere Akteure der Interessenvermittlung. Eine Analyse der politischen Rationalität von Nichtregierungsorganisationen*. Wiesbaden: Springer VS.

Schmedes, H. 2009. Mehr Transparenz wagen? Zur Diskussion um ein gesetzliches Lobbyregister beim Deutschen Bundestag. *Zeitschrift für Parlamentsfragen* (3). 543–560.

Schmidt, V. A. 2013. Democracy and Legitimacy in the European Union Revisited: Input, Output *and* 'Throughput'. *Political Studies* 61(1). 2–22.

Schöne, H. 2021. Die Mehrheit muss stehen. In K. R. Korte and M. Florack (eds.), *Handbuch Regierungsforschung*, 633–644. Wiesbaden: Springer VS.

Schreier, M. 2012. *Qualitative content analysis in practice*. London: SAGE.

Schwanholz, J., and T. Jakobi. 2020. There's a place for us? The Digital Agenda Committee and internet policy in the German Bundestag. *Internet Policy Review* 9(4). 1–24.

SPD. 2017. Zeit für mehr Gerechtigkeit. Unser Regierungsprogramm für Deutschland. Sozialdemokratische Partei Deutschlands. Available at: <https://www.spd.de/fileadmin/Doku mente/Regierungsprogramm/SPD_Regierungsprogramm_BTW_2017_A5_RZ_WEB.pdf> (last accessed 11 April 2023).

Spitze, J. 2022. Das Lobbyregister. Die Notwendige Entmystifizierung des Lobbyings. *Politik & Kommunikation*. Available at: <https://www.politik-kommunikation.de/das-lobbyregister-die-notwendige-entmystifizierung-des-lobbyings/> (last accessed 11 April 2023).

Streeck, W., and K. Thelen. 2005. Introduction: institutional change in advanced political economies. In W. Streeck and K. Thelen (eds.), *Beyond continuity: institutional change in advanced political economies*, 1–39. Oxford: Oxford University Press.

Transparency International, Access Info Europe, Sunlight Foundation and Open Knowledge. 2015. 'International standards for lobbying regulation. Towards greater transparency, integrity and participation'. Available at: <http://lobbyingtransparency.net/> (last accessed 11 April 2023).

True, J. L., B. D. Jones and F. R. Baumgartner. 2007. Punctuated equilibrium theory. In P. A. Sabatier, (ed.), *Theories of the Policy Process*. 2nd edn. 155–188. New York: Routledge.

Van der Heijden, J., J. Kuhlmann, E. Lindquist and A. Wellstead. 2021. Have policy process scholars embraced causal mechanisms? A review of five popular frameworks. *Public Policy and Administration* 36(2). 163–186.

Weible, C. M., and P. A. Sabatier (eds.). 2018. *Theories of the Policy Process*. 4th edn. New York: Routledge.

Wolf, S. 2014. *Korruption, Antikorruptionspolitik und öffentliche Verwaltung. Einführung und europapolitische Bezüge*. Wiesbaden: Springer VS.

Worsham, J. 2006. Up in smoke: Mapping subsystem dynamics in tobacco policy. *Policy Studies Journal* 34(3). 437–452.

ZEW. 2019. Majority of the German Population Views Lobbying in Europe in a Critical Light. Available at: <https://www.zew.de/en/press/latest-press-releases/majority-of-the-german-population-views-lobbying-in-europe-in-a-critical-light> (last accessed 11 April 2023).

V Dealing with Crises? Leadership and Market

Joscha Abels, Hans-Jürgen Bieling and Sarrah Kassem

Re-regulating the European high-tech capitalism? The EU's digitalization strategy at a turning point after the COVID-19 pandemic

Abstract: The European Union (EU) channeled a considerable amount of funds to digitalization and new technologies to counter the economic effect of the COVID-19 pandemic. This paper examines to what extent these measures represent a turning point in European economic governance and which structural conditions contribute to this development. From a theoretical perspective, it builds on regulation theory, extended by a neo-Gramscian crisis conception; and characterizes recent developments as "second-order change", not yet translated into a new paradigm but fundamentally altering policy instruments. The COVID-19 pandemic has opened the political and discursive space to break with the previous fiscal consolidation agenda and serves as a catalyst for a more interventionist high-tech agenda. Empirical evidence from the EU Chips Act and the Recovery and Resilience Plans reveals the enhanced focus the EU puts on the modernization and technological competitiveness of its economies. However, it also reveals that measures align with national development models rather than with shared strategic goals, which makes them relatively limited in scope.

Keywords: European Union, regulation theory, Recovery and Resilience Facility, digitalization, industrial policy

1 Introduction

The European Union (EU) has been undergoing a process of economic policy reorientation for some time now. During the realization of the internal market, the Economic and Monetary Union (EMU) and Eastern enlargement, market-liberal or even neoliberal concepts were in the foreground. However, due to overlapping crisis processes – uneven economic development, problems of political legitimacy, climate crisis, and the recent COVID-19 pandemic – i.e. phenomena of "mul-

Joscha Abels, Hans-Jürgen Bieling, Sarrah Kassem, Institute of Political Science, University of Tübingen

https://doi.org/10.1515/9783111272900-015

tiple crises" (Demirović et al. 2011), calls for state intervention and an active shaping of the common economic space have been increasing. This trend is reinforced by the changing global environment: the new triad of competition between the United States, China, and the EU (Bieling 2019) as well as the geopolitical "turn of an era" considering the Russian invasion of Ukraine. Therefore, at least incrementally, a policy shift is taking place that conceptualizes a higher degree of state intervention, meaning a stronger role of state institutions actively shaping capitalist development (Bergsen et al. 2020; Abels and Bieling 2022). Relevant indicators of this reorientation are: first, an interruption, or at least a weakening of austerity policy in European economic governance; second, an upgrading of industrial policy concepts and programs, including mobilization of resources required for these indicators; third, efforts to strengthen and modernize societal and transnational infrastructures considered as "critical" for the competitiveness and functioning of member states; lastly, a greater sense for the uneven development between EU member states and the employment and social security challenges associated with this – applying, for example, the Juncker Commission.

In the following, we will examine and discuss whether and to what extent these tendencies represent a "turning point" in the mode of regulation of the European economy and society, and then address this question from a perspective that extends regulation theory by a neo-Gramscian understanding of crises. This implies the assumption that ongoing struggles concerning appropriate ways of regulation are structured by and react to the contradictions and crisis dynamics of a transnational capitalist formation that can be described as "financialized European high-tech capitalism." We argue that there are indicators of a "turning point" in European economic governance, which can be classified as "second-order change" (Hall 1993) based on a reconfiguration of available political instruments without crystallizing in a comprehensive paradigm change yet. To provide substance to this argument, we first outline our analytical approach to the theory of regulation, which is extended by neo-Gramscian arguments, and how this approach conceptualizes crisis and turning points. After this, we turn toward the COVID-19 pandemic and its crisis management, which, from our perspective, have triggered a "state interventionist turn." We assess this "state interventionist turn" empirically by focusing on the project of a new European industrial policy and select processes of digitalization that accompany the project on a European and national level.

2 Crises and turning points in regulation-theoretical and neo-Gramscian thought

The mentioned crisis processes represent a series of "critical junctures." Their link toward a "state interventionist turn" is certainly not predetermined, but contingent. This is because crises are by definition phases of deep uncertainty, meaning critical periods of decision-making or potential turning points in which "the old is dying and the new cannot be born [yet]" (Gramsci 1971: 276). Previous parameters and routines are no longer applicable or rarely applied, but new paradigms for political action have not yet emerged or are at least disputed. Hence, from a neo-Gramscian perspective, crises often function as catalysts of social and political change. They act as reference points of public communication, yet they generally allow for different courses of crisis management. However, the nature of the course taken depends on social power relations and the efficacy of discourses whereby crisis actors articulate different perceptions of the root causes behind the crisis and their proposals to fix them. Consequently, crises are socially constructed and discursively contested, yet they also constitute a tool for reshaping social conditions (Koselleck 1988). Political actors, supported by think tanks, intellectuals, and media, view the crisis discourse as an opportunity to intervene publicly and influence the future course of societal development.

Therefore, crises are "open" constellations, which unfold against the background of historical structures. They represent a structured contingency because prevailing political-economic conditions, institutional settings, and solidified power relations significantly shape opposing discourses on crises (Jessop 2009). From a regulation-theoretical perspective (for a brief overview see Becker 2013), the interplay of these factors – and the relative stability of capitalism they provide despite its susceptibility to crises – is captured by adopting some specific analytical conceptions. The "regime of accumulation" refers to the macroeconomic regularities of an economy, which include the specific conditions of production – quantity and structure of capital, the relative importance of certain industries, technological know-how, productivity, and the consumption by different social groups or classes: workers, the bourgeoisie, middle classes, and state (Lipietz 1985: 120). These regularities are not simply given but are actively shaped and stabilized by the "mode of regulation", a broad network of institutional norms that shape the behavior of social and economic actors. Significant areas of regulation include wage relations (employment conditions, training, social security provision, and reproduction of labor), the form of business organizations (the legal form of companies, their competitive and cooperative relations), monetary and credit relations, as well as various forms of state intervention and international regimes. Regulation theory refers to a historically specific "model of development" or a "historical bloc" in which the regime of accumulation and the mode of regulation stabilize each other and balance internal contradictions and crisis processes (Lipietz 2013).

Consequently, it is no coincidence that the concept of the "historical bloc" was borrowed from Antonio Gramsci. Many regulation theorists of the early hour were guided by Gramscian reflections in their argument with Marxist structuralism – Lipietz (1987: 19) speaks of the "rebel sons of Althusser". This intellectual connection is expressed not just in the concept of the "historical bloc" and in the substitution of the static structuralist concept of "reproduction" (of power relations) by the more dynamic concept of "regulation", but also led regulation theorists to consider social struggles and the processes of political bloc formation – known as "hegemonic bloc" – that decisively mediate between the further development of the regime of accumulation and the mode of regulation. Part of these struggles are also discursive claims which, in times of crisis, aid in the creation of a widely shared crisis diagnosis that prompts specific projects and initiatives of crisis management. However, resolving the crises is not guaranteed because the success of such initiatives and projects depends on whether they have a hegemonic capacity, i.e., if they fix negotiated compromises in relatively broad consensual structures.

A theory of regulation expanded by neo-Gramscian arguments suggests an analytical heuristic (for the complementarity of both perspectives see Bieling 2014), which differentiates between three interrelated levels of analysis to capture the indicated relations and dynamics of structured contingency:

(1) The first level is the historical-structural dimensions of a specific capitalist social formation. This formation can be understood from a regulation theory perspective as a "historical bloc" or "model of development" (Cox 1983; Lipietz 2013). A "historical bloc" is characterized by a particular interplay of a "regime of accumulation", describing the key technological and material components of macroeconomic reproduction. Additionally, it builds on a specific "mode of regulation" whose formal and informal institutional and regulatory features may contribute to the stabilization of crisis-prone capitalist accumulation. Following the re-launch of integration in the 1980s, a transnational social formation emerged within the EU that reshaped, but did not overthrow pre-existing national formations of capitalism. The European social formation is based on regimes of accumulation that constitute dense networks of cross-border capitalist production and distribution through markets for goods and services, capital, and transnational value chains. Likewise, through the establishment of supranational organizations, mediated by European primary and secondary laws, new forms of European regulation and statehood have emerged. They are surrounded by private interest groups and civil society organizations, such as business associations, NGOs, think tanks, and transna-

tional social movements. The political-economic character of the European social formation has often been described as "transnational financial capitalism" (Bieling 2013). Yet, we argue that considering the increasing focus on (information) technological modernization, it is more appropriate to speak of an emerging financialized "European high-tech capitalism".

(2) The second level is the social power relations that shape the development of this formation. These power relations are conceptualized in both regulation theory and neo-Gramscian IPE as a "hegemonic bloc" that is composed of social and political alliances with the capacity to incorporate substantial parts of the subaltern social classes or groups materially and discursively. Since the 1980s, the power structure in the EU has become recognizably transnational (Bieling 2010). The transnational hegemonic bloc not only includes numerous political and civil society organizations, but also influential economic actors–transnational corporations, banks, and other financial market players – significantly shaping the course of European integration. However, the repeated crisis processes – the financial crisis, the sovereign debt crisis, the crisis of the European migration regime, political legitimacy crises, and the COVID-19 pandemic – showed that the transnational hegemonic bloc in the EU is characterized by internal contradictions and fissures, making the hegemonic bloc's organization difficult.

(3) The third level of analysis involves political or hegemonic projects that represent attempts to achieve exactly this organization. They capture the political processes through which strategic influence over political-economic development is exercised. Political projects and initiatives can be placed as the solution to severe problems or urgent crises. They are a programmatic crystallization of interests and discourses by which the alliances of the transnational hegemonic bloc attempt to actively influence the further course of the European model of development. The political projects and initiatives can be designed to stabilize or modify pre-existing socio-economic conditions, institutional arrangements, power relations, and political orientations. However, they sometimes work in the opposite direction, questioning past developments and pushing for a turnaround.

The regulation-theoretical discussion is mostly less interested in the "small" or "cyclical" crises that primarily have a function of cleansing or catharsis by destroying excess capital but leaving the patterns of capitalist development largely untouched. Instead, interest is placed on the ruptures in the process of capitalist development, which involves "major" or "organic" crises, where historical capitalist formations change and existing power structures are transformed. To express in terms of this edited volume: regulation theory extended by neo-Gramscianism is primarily concerned with turning and breaking points of those historical episodes in which established understandings of the order are challenged by crises and require a transformation. In the sense of a breaking point, crises can lead to phases of uncertainty whereby competing for social interests and discourses can lead to conflicts and a struggle for political power. However, we suggest that the current changes in the capitalist formation in the EU and related discourses and paradigms rather constitute a turning point. Since counter-initiatives to the prevailing political order have already been formed and a window of opportunity has been induced by crises, these counter-initiatives are being integrated into the existing order – Gramsci refers to this as a "passive revolution". This process does not lead to a rupture, but to a transformation whereby these counter-initiatives shift the agenda, political instruments, and goals.

The extent of these shifts is hard to determine in times of ongoing crisis, and classifying an ongoing crisis as a "major" or "minor" crisis might turn out to be somewhat premature. Thus, although the general interest of the regulation approach is on the development of a social formation, the analytical focus of this paper is more limited. This paper mainly focuses on the mode of regulation of European high-tech capitalism, particularly on the political projects, initiatives, and discourses that aim to promote and stabilize it. If we want to make sense of the current shifts in EU politics, we must consider not just the discursive processes but also the transformation of instrumental and material policy-making. According to Peter Hall (1993), both aspects interact as they transform political paradigms. In the first stage, the "first order change", available policy instruments – interest rate policies, labor market support programs, environmental standards – are used or applied differently than before, but without indicating a change of policy direction. In the second stage, known as "second-order change", the entire set of available instruments changes as it is partly reweighted, also by abolishing or creating new instruments. Although this reweighting of instruments is quite significant, it only condenses into a change of the guiding principle or paradigm ("third-order change") when the political goals are fundamentally redefined against the backdrop of altered crisis circumstances.

In line with this, we contend that the "state interventionist turn" in the EU following the COVID-19 pandemic can be classified as a "second-order change". Notably, crisis management goes beyond the readjustment of existing political instruments but remains below the level of a comprehensive paradigm shift signifying the transition toward a new capitalist formation. However, we observe the reorganization of the set of political instruments, particularly an enhancement of industrial and infrastructural policy tools that require more financial resources. They demonstrate a greater willingness to intervene politically if the promotion and stabilization of European high-tech capitalism require it.

3 The COVID-19 pandemic as a catalyst for state interventionism

The euro crisis after 2010 and the economic crisis following the COVID-19 pandemic make an intriguing case for comparative analyses. The euro crisis followed the global financial crisis and laid bare the structural problems of the Economic and Monetary Union (EMU): an uneven distribution of national economic conditions, a serious deindustrialization in its periphery, and a lack of a lender of last resort – to name some of the most pressing concerns (Aglietta 2012). However, politically and discursively, it was rebranded as a series of national debt crises and treated as such. Crisis management after 2010 consisted of a multitude of measures that reinforced the disciplinary mode of regulation and focused on consolidating national house-holds (Abels 2018). On a national level, austerity programs entailed cuts in wages, welfare benefits, and public spending while privatizations reduced the volume of publicly owned assets. On the European level, the euro countries reached an agree-ment on several institutional reform steps – including the Fiscal Compact, a tighten-ing of fiscal rules within the Stability and Growth Pact – which would commit states to fiscal discipline and a reduction of "excessive" debt levels. Together with the Euro-pean Central Bank's active monetary policy, these measures were enough to calm the markets and secure refinancing for the member states. Yet, they fell short in terms of bringing growth back across the eurozone. In 2016, when the entire euro-zone had already grown by 14% since 2008, major crisis countries like Spain and Italy had just returned to their pre-crisis output, while Greece was still at 72% of its initial gross domestic product. As the debt added during the crisis had offset their fiscal consolidation efforts, those countries' debt levels were also still at record highs.

There are two main reasons why euro crisis management took that path. First, northern countries like Germany, Netherlands, Finland, and Austria had an interest in redirecting reform pressure toward the periphery and the financial as well as political means to do so (Abels 2019). Second, fiscal restraint as a paradigm is deeply embedded in the European mode of regulation. Building the Single Market, the EU member states sought to create a level playing field for European businesses and economies through the implementation of competitive rules that would obstruct state subsidies and measures of industrial policy. The further integration path, which includes the establishment of the EMU by the Treaty of Maastricht in 1992, was strongly influenced by German ordoliberal ideology, which considers fiscal re-straint as a central building block of a competitive and stable economy (Dullien and Guérot 2012). Therefore, the handling of the euro crisis can be considered an intensification of the EU's traditional focus on fiscal discipline, its conception of competitiveness as attracting private capital as well as general hostility toward industrial policy. The fact that the Eurogroup called for a phasing out of "temporary crisis-related sectoral support measures" as early as March 2010 is evidence of that fact (Eurogroup 2010).

On a first look at the EU member states' negotiations over countering the recession after the COVID-19 pandemic, several factors were similar to the situation a decade earlier. Debt levels had risen across the eurozone during the outbreak of the COVID-19 pandemic; yet, the surge in public debt affected those countries with an already high debt ratio (Figure 1). Structural relations, even after the serious transformation that the EU's periphery underwent, were still lopsided in favor of the export-oriented north. Concerning the hegemonic bloc, while several changes in government had taken place since the euro crisis, conservative and liberal forces were still the dominant factions in European politics. The institutional provisions made during the crisis were still in place.

Against this backdrop, it is striking to note that the decisions made in 2020 differed substantially from those taken to counter after the euro crisis. In March 2020, the European Commission triggered the so-called "general escape clause" of the SGP, allowing member states to temporarily deviate from their budget and debt targets. By classifying the COVID-19 pandemic as a "generalized crisis", it was supposed to provide member states with fiscal leeway to support economic recovery.

Simultaneously, the EU has set up the €750 billion fund NextGenerationEU (NGEU), which consists of €390 billion in grants and €360 billion in loans. The instrument allocates funds to the member states in relation to their individual recession effects and levels of unemployment. By far, the largest component is made up of the Recovery and Resilience Facility (RRF), which member states can draw funds for their national investment plans if approved by the European Council. The main areas in which this money is supposed to be invested are green transition, i.e., climate protection and sustainable jobs, which must amount to at least 37% of spending in national programs, and digitalization, with a minimum of 20% of spending. Northern countries like the Netherlands, Austria, and Denmark have succeeded in shifting a large part of the NGEU's resources from grants to loans, effectively mitigating its impact (Rijksoverheid 2020). However, they failed to uphold one of their main red lines, which was no debt mutualization. To finance the NGEU, the member states issue bonds collectively through the European Commission, making use of the environment of low to negative interest rates. The NGEU is a temporary setup to operate until 2023 and is closely tied to the Multiannual Financial Framework (MFF), the EU's budget of over €1 trillion for the period from 2021 to 2027. Indicative of their aversion to jointly financed public stimuli, the aforementioned northern countries – plus Germany – have negotiated substantial national rebates in a total of €53 billion in exchange for their agreement to the NGEU and MFF.

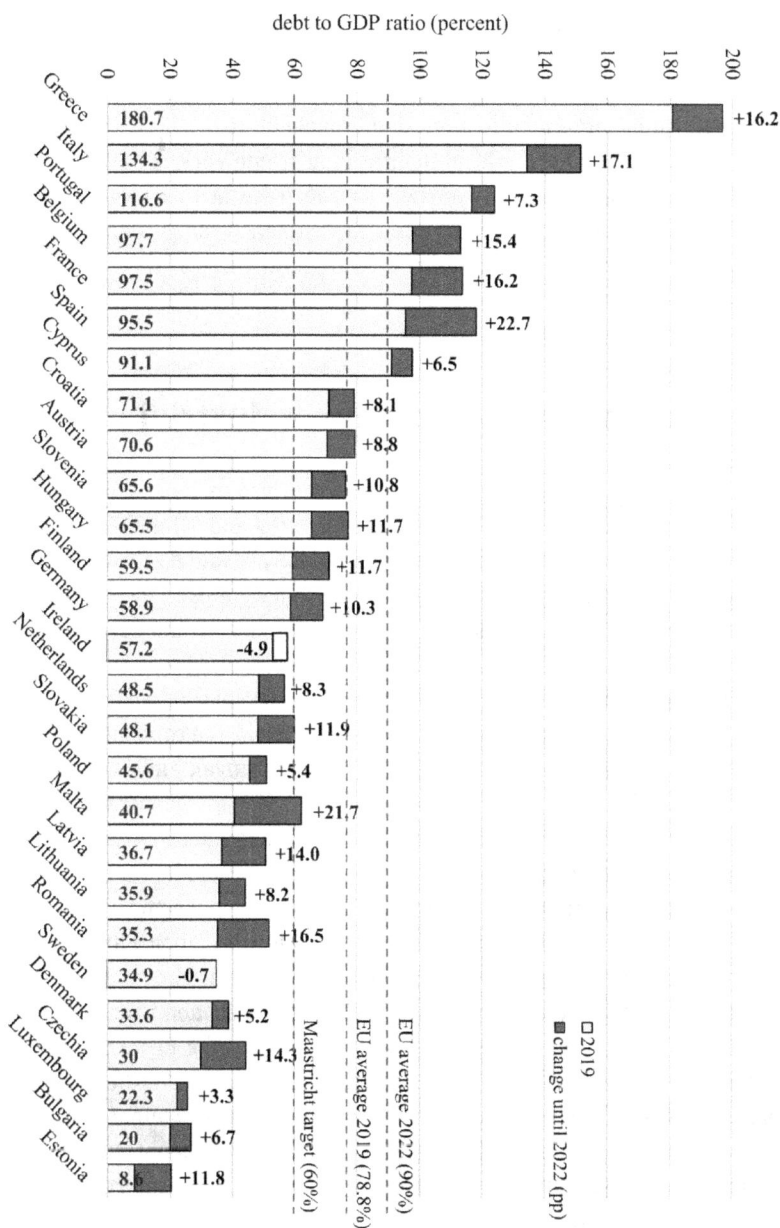

Figure 1: Government debt (in percent of GDP) for 2019 and percentage point changes from 2019 to 2022 (AMECO, own calculations).

Overall, the measures taken to counter the recessionary effects of the pandemic are breaking with the euro crisis style of regulation as they – at least in parts – replace fiscal consolidation with public investment and national liability for debts with joint funds. Additionally, they should make it possible for the state to intervene in conditions where a legal-institutional framework is adverse to it. This breach of economic norms did not come as a surprise, as there were already clear indications. A modest turn toward public investment strategies and state intervention has been imminent for quite a while, and the COVID-19 outbreak served as a catalyst for this gradual shift.

4 Steps toward a new European industrial policy

From a historical perspective, European integration is driven by inner-European dynamics and global shifts in production and power (Lavery and Schmid 2021). Thus, the reasons for the recent steps toward state intervention are found in both spheres. Internally, the euro crisis and its unsuccessful handling have eroded the support for the EU. Crisis management has fuelled Eurosceptic views across the eurozone and has undermined the political systems of the crisis countries (Bosco and Verney 2017). The recent recession has called into question the promise of economic prosperity after a decade of austerity and hardship. Again, it was the countries most affected by the euro crisis – particularly Greece, Italy, Portugal, and Spain – that suffered most from the economic contraction, among other things, because of the impairment of tourism. For the sake of political and economic cohesion, changes would need to be made to the previous course of economic regulation.

Externally, the EU has found that its limited understanding of competitiveness – one that is focused on liberalization and deregulation to strengthen European exports – has not improved its position in the global competition for market shares and geoeconomic control (Abels and Bieling 2023). China's economic and political expansion and the fragility of transatlantic ties are forcing the EU to rethink its globalization strategy and preserve its economic sovereignty (Leonard et al. 2019). This realization seems to have caused member states to consider amending their globalization strategies with a more state-interventionist component. In 2019, the economic minister of Germany, Peter Altmaier, and his French counterpart Bruno Le Maire published a common manifesto in which they argue that: in order to stay relevant in a digitalizing and carbon-neutral economy, the EU requires an investment agenda with strategic objectives. The manifesto states that "if Europe still wants to be a manufacturing powerhouse in 2030, we need a genuine European industrial policy" (Bundesministerium für Wirtschaft und Energie 2019).

Consequently, when Ursula von der Leyen took office in 2019, the European Commission had a reconsideration of its priorities (Renda 2021). The commission's European Green Deal, a policy initiative supported by all member states bar Poland, is meant to steer national policy in the direction of of climate protection and renewable energy. Its declared goal is to make the EU climate neutral by 2050. Although there are doubts as to whether this goal is sufficient or even achievable at the current pace of reform, the European Green Deal clearly shows that the EU is developing wider strategies to guide national economic policies and the targeted promotion of industrial sectors. While the European Green Deal stresses the urgency of climate issues in light of an impending disaster, a redefinition of European competitiveness has found its expression in the EU's New Industrial Strategy (COM(2020) 102 final). In this document, the Commission lays out the cornerstones of what a European industrial policy might look like in the near future. Also, the strategy again emphasizes the need for a "transition toward climate neutrality and digital leadership" to ensure "Europe's future progress and prosperity". It makes direct reference to the "new and ever-changing geopolitical realities", demanding that the EU defend its competitiveness and sovereignty by transforming its industries.

Concerning its digital agenda, which is strongly supported by a transnational hegemonic bloc, which is by a range of social forces, above all by transnational business (ERT 2021), the document explicitly addresses the fields of artificial intelligence, telecommunication, and data analytics. It outlines the need to "speed up investment in research and deployment of technology" in such areas, to retrain the workforce, and "enhance [. . .] critical digital infrastructure" (COM (2020) 102 final). Specifications on the EU's digital agenda are further made by the Strategy on Shaping Europe's Digital Future (COM (2020) 67 final), which illustrates the turn the EU's globalization strategy took in recent years. While there is still a major emphasis on free markets and private investments, the document puts the EU's "technological sovereignty" at the center. The EU would have to reinforce its industrial and technological capabilities and its ability to set global standards on technologies to stay competitive and "reduc[e] our dependency on other parts of the globe for the most crucial technologies". In 2021, the New Industrial Strategy has received an update that was supposed to reflect some of the lessons learned from implementing the strategy during the COVID-19 pandemic (COM(2021) 350 final). It stresses the need for the EU to decrease its dependence on vulnerable global value chains and unreliable partners in critical areas. Interestingly, the document also clarifies that the EU's industrial policy agenda should rest on public-private partnerships and the political support of "industrial alliances" of European businesses. Thus, while the general orientation in terms of defining seminal sectors and steering dependencies is subject to political control, the actual implementation in terms of allocation, production, and development is left to the private sector.

Consequently, we observe a political turn toward a more active, state-interventionist economic policy after 2019 in reaction to both internal economic troubles, and global power shifts. Climate protection and digitalization are the two main pillars of that strategy, redefining competitiveness in terms of sustainability and digital sovereignty. This turning point has gone beyond the rhetoric of member states and EU bodies and has also substantially influenced the distribution of public investment during the COVID-19 pandemic (Figure 2).

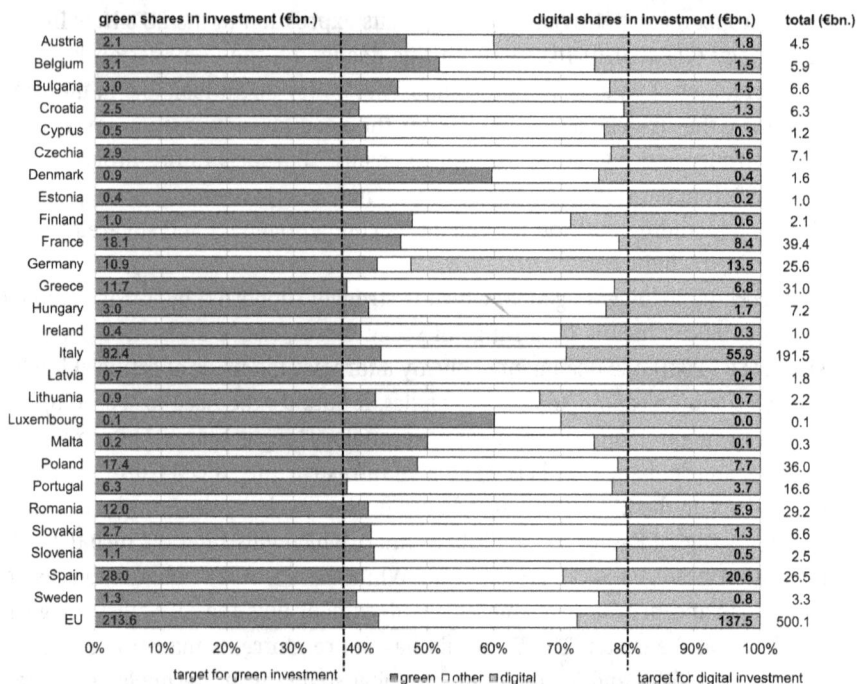

	green shares in investment (€bn.)	digital shares in investment (€bn.)	total (€bn.)
Austria	2.1	1.8	4.5
Belgium	3.1	1.5	5.9
Bulgaria	3.0	1.5	6.6
Croatia	2.5	1.3	6.3
Cyprus	0.5	0.3	1.2
Czechia	2.9	1.6	7.1
Denmark	0.9	0.4	1.6
Estonia	0.4	0.2	1.0
Finland	1.0	0.6	2.1
France	18.1	8.4	39.4
Germany	10.9	13.5	25.6
Greece	11.7	6.8	31.0
Hungary	3.0	1.7	7.2
Ireland	0.4	0.3	1.0
Italy	82.4	55.9	191.5
Latvia	0.7	0.4	1.8
Lithuania	0.9	0.7	2.2
Luxembourg	0.1	0.0	0.1
Malta	0.2	0.1	0.3
Poland	17.4	7.7	36.0
Portugal	6.3	3.7	16.6
Romania	12.0	5.9	29.2
Slovakia	2.7	1.3	6.6
Slovenia	1.1	0.5	2.5
Spain	28.0	20.6	26.5
Sweden	1.3	0.8	3.3
EU	213.6	137.5	500.1

0% 10% 20% 30% 40% 50% 60% 70% 80% 90% 100%

target for green investment   ■ green □ other ▨ digital   target for digital investment

Figure 2: Allocation of investments in national NGEU plans (Bruegel RRP dataset, own calculations).

One could certainly interpret the rhetorical and political shift toward stronger coordination of economic activities in the field of industrial policy as a fundamental reorientation of the EU's approach that comes close to Hall's idea of a third-order change: a redefinition of the underlying political goals. Nevertheless, we make the case (for now) for a more cautious assessment that views the recent steps rather as part of a process where the economic tools that are used are amended – and thus a "second-order change". We observe an enhancement of policy instruments by measures of industrial and infrastructural policy, in line with a political project we call "new European industrial policy". The hybrid financing used to support those measures through both national and European funds also constitutes a break with previous approaches and unlocks additional financial resources. Yet, these policy innovations continue to be embedded in a European mode of regulation, which looks to exploit an international market-liberal order for its export-dominated accumulation. Hence, the European bloc of financialized high-tech capitalism has further internationalized and deregulated its economies during the euro crisis. In an interesting process, this market-liberal component of European competitiveness is now amended by a more state-interventionist component that seeks to secure high-tech capacities through industrial and infrastructural measures. However, the latter remains subordinate to the market-liberal approach as strategic decisions are continually made on the basis of private profit interests that must fall in line with the rather modest public stimuli to cause effective shifts. Overall, the developments described in this section do not fundamentally alter economic paradigms in the EU, but they adjust its overall globalization strategy and have the potential to expand its ability to act. The following section further outlines this point through a closer investigation of specific policy measures.

5 Processes of digitalization

Focusing on digitalization as one of the two main pillars of the EU's industrial agenda, we investigate the recent empirical evidence to assess its real effect. The European digitalization strategy can be regarded as predating the COVID-19 pandemic (Vučić 2021), with initial efforts expressed in 2014, and again in 2019 as the von der Leyen Commission prioritized a green and digital transformation. The pandemic, which exposed economic, industrial, and technological vulnerabilities, has accelerated this transition toward Europe's digital sovereignty. In a general sense, the European Commission has identified different fields of action for its digital transition, ranging from artificial intelligence (AI), cybersecurity, and digital skills to regulations like the Digital Markets Act and Digital Services Act (European Commission 2022a). The EU's Digital Compass, published in March 2021, made the agenda more definite by grouping it into four cardinal points: digital skills (both basic and specialist), digital infrastructure that is both secure and sustainable, digital transformation of businesses, and digitalization of public services (COM (2022) 118 final).

The turning point in the regulation of European high-tech capitalism is exemplified by the EU Chips Act, a key component of the European industrial strategy and integral to the Digital Compass. Furthermore, the national recovery and resilience plans funded by the RRF have intensified previous efforts in the digitalization of sectors and services in member states and efforts to reduce the digital divide within societies. The plans of countries like France, Germany, Italy, and Spain provide information on how European strategies translate into national digitalization measures, against the background of newly established funding capacities.

5.1 The EU Chips Act

A day before WHO announced COVID-19 as a pandemic on 03/11/2020, the EU's New Industrial Strategy (COM (2020) 102 final) presented digital transformation as a central pillar to further increase the EU's global competitiveness and resilience. The pandemic can be regarded as a catalyst for the EU's industrial strategy of developing high-tech as it further exposed the EU's dependencies.

One such example is semiconductors, which rely on a complex global value chain – from initial research to production. Semiconductors are integral for the production of chips required in various fields, which ranges from the automobile industry and technological gadgets to automation, healthcare, the energy sector – and their respective infrastructures. Chips in turn are the "building blocks of current and future infrastructures and applications" (Hancké and Garcia Calvo 2022); in other words: "there is no 'digital' without chips" (COM (2022) 45 final). As a result, semiconductors constitute the fourth most traded product on a global scale, amounting to a total value of $550 billion in 2021 (Digital Europe 2022). Given the presence of a growing demand for semiconductors in Europe, Europe is leading in the area of research on semiconductors, their materials, and equipment needed for production – in which some like EUV lithography machines are indispensable to any chip production by the Dutch company ASML. However, the EU accounts for only a tenth of the market share of semiconductors, which has decreased by half over the past three decades due to declining manufacturing, processes of offshoring, and the emergence of leading manufacturing from East Asia, for example, Taiwanese firm TSMC (Taiwan Semiconductor Manufacturing Company) and South Korean Samsung (Hancké and Garcia Calvo 2022). It has limited production capacities and a low reserve in case of supply shortages. The dependency of European industries on semiconductors for more industrial production and infrastructure construction is a reflection of the integral role of semiconductors in (geo)economic interests and tensions (Bardt et al. 2022). This is *de facto* embodied in and accelerated through the "global technology race" where double to triple-digit billions of dollars of state funding are channeled into research and production of chips, as seen in the US CHIPS for America Act and

Beijing's Made in China 2025 initiative (COM (2022) 45 final). The centrality of semi-conductors in geoeconomic terms puts it among the "choke points in the global supply chain" constituting a target of state sanctions, as previously demonstrated by the US and China (Segal 2021). The EU's capacity to drive innovation and develop its industries strongly depends on the availability of semiconductors, access thereof, and Europe's autonomy amidst global rivalries (Bardt et al. 2022).

The demand for these chips increases with the digitalization of society and the economy, ranging from the rising importance of data centers and their infrastructure to technological developments like 5G infrastructure and the integration of AI, which are bound to have effects across sectors. This demand only increased during the COVID-19 pandemic, as work, education, and social relations were increasingly being pushed into the digital sphere, where digital platforms also played a crucial role in their mediation (Kassem 2022). The supply of semiconductor chips has been unable to match demand. It was further impacted by factory closures as well as shipment delays to Europe from countries in Eastern Asia, problematizing the global concentration of production lines. The shortage had constricting effects on certain industrial sectors like the automobile industry and public services; including healthcare, resulting in delayed deliveries of relevant devices. For example, car production plant closures due to shortages affect economic performance and employment of workforces. For the EU, this has demonstrated that "[r]einforcing Europe's leadership capacities in semiconductors is a requirement for its future competitiveness, and a case of technological sovereignty and security" (COM (2022) 45 final).

In September 2021, Commission president Ursula von der Leyen announced the EU Chips Act, whose central aim is to secure the union's supply and resilience, allowing it to amplify its competitiveness on a global scale. While previous EU funding had targeted research and development of semiconductors, the Chips Act aims to increase the current European semiconductor market share from 10% to 20% by 2030, which, considering the expected increase in demand until the stipulated year, would translate into quadrupling current outputs. Without the required investments within this time frame, it is predicted that Europe would not only be able to retain its 10% market share but will lose half of it (COM (2022) 45 final). Combining existing resources from the Digital Europe program and Horizon Europe with European and national funds dedicated to the Chips Act as well as equity support to private businesses, the Commission expects public investments and leveraged equity support in the semiconductor industry to rise above €43 billion by 2030. These funds are meant to support short- to long-term goal areas along the supply chain – from research to innovation, financing, and industrial production – essentially to "develop an in-depth understanding of global semiconductor supply chains" and the ability to identify and predict disruptions and risks to these through a "crisis toolbox" (COM (2022) 45 final). The European ambition is to not only develop the semiconductor ecosystem among and across its member states but also to navigate interdependent relations and "semiconductor partnerships with like-minded countries", which include "the United States, Japan, South Korea, Singapore, Taiwan and others" (COM(22) 45 final).

The Chips Act serves as an empirical example of a field in which the COVID-19 pandemic exposed a major vulnerability of the European industries and the EU pushed for a concerted and active approach to further its high-tech agenda, given chips' centrality and repercussions across the economy. However, there are obstacles – for instance that none of the largest global producers of chips are European (Hancké and Garcia Calvo 2022). Additionally, the EU depends on national funds to reach its targets, which are currently subject to rising bond yields and pressure for fiscal consolidation. Hence, it remains to be seen to which extent the EU will be able to translate its goals into industrial policy measures. For now, the EU Chips Act – and related policy measures – represent strategic guidelines for action at the member state level rather than a joint approach on how they are to be implemented in terms of regulation.

5.2 The national recovery and resilience plans

The EU's digital agenda relies on national action to advance the digitalization of its economies and combat the digital divide within its societies. In this context, the Digital Economy and Society Index (DESI) is a relevant tool for coordinative regulation. It monitors the member states' progress in the area of digitalization, based on indicators that measure internet coverage and usage, digital skills, and the digitalization of businesses and public services. It has also made evident the digital divide across Europe, which has proven to be a detrimental obstacle for private investments (European Commission 2021a). These problems predate the COVID-19 pandemic, but they underline the demand to further digitalize the EU's economies and societies.

The RRF funds provided financial boost that recalibrated these objectives. Out of the NGEU's €750 billion, €723.8 billion constitute RRF (€338 billion in grants, €385.8 in loans). As argued earlier, the RRF country plans surpassed the EU's targets for the shares of green and digital investments, demonstrating that they intensified their initial efforts. Taking a look at the EU's major economies – France, Germany, Italy, and Spain – it appears that not only does the proportion to which RRF funds are used for digitalization targets vary (Table 1), but also the purposes for which they are used. Generally, there is a shared focus on the digitalization of public services on local and national scales. The logic of this is that the EU expects simplified

Table 1: Comparison of EU major economies' level of digitalization and digital investments (Recovery and Resilience Scoreboard 2021; DESI 2021).

	RRF plan in € (% of GDP)	Contributions to digital objectives	Country ranking in Digital Economy and Society Index (DESI) 2021
France	€ 39.37bn (1.62%)	21%	15th of 27
Germany	€ 25.61bn (0.74%)	52%	11th of 27
Italy	€ 191.48bn (10.67%)	25.1%	20th of 27
Spain	€ 69.51bn (5.59%)	28%	9th of 27

administrative procedures to have a spill-over effect on businesses (European Commission 2021b). Yet, on a closer look, they are highly targeted and outweighed by large-scale investments in other areas.

In Germany, around €3 billion in funding are allocated to digitalizing public administrative processes, but these funds mostly fall under the label of implementing the *Onlinezugangsgesetz*, which makes administrative services and registers accessible online (Bundesfinanzministerium 2021). This rather specific investment plan in public administration is rivaled by a little over €3 billion dedicated to the digitalization of the economy. An insightful observation here is that almost €2 billion are meant to support the automobile industry, one of Germany's industrial strongholds and already the recipient of large amounts of RRF funds under the green pillar. As Rietzler and Watt (2021: 56) argue: "It is difficult, though, to see why this is really support for 'digitalisation' rather than sectoral investment support, focused on a strategically important sector". Also worth mentioning, there is a "digital education offensive" worth a total of about €1.5 billion that mainly consists of the procurement of end devices and the setup of a rather ominous "education platform". Thus, Germany as a case study illustrates how in a country with a strong digital investment share, dedicating around half of its funds to this area, it is used to finance singular projects instead of a comprehensive transformation and how investments generally align with national historical blocs or models of development.

For France, the funds dedicated to direct financing for companies are relatively low. However, a large share of the digital budget is aligned with EU strategies, focusing on high-tech investments, public administration, and digital skills (Gouvernement de la République française 2021). Interestingly, €3.2 billion are dedicated to "technological sovereignty and resilience", which is an umbrella term for public investments in high-tech sectors such as AI, cloud computing, quantum technologies, and cyber security. Under its *Programme d'investissements d'avenir* (PIA4), France is channeling investments in areas it considers strategically and technologically relevant. Thus, it uses RRF to buff up the funding. €2.1 billion are reserved for the digitalization of the central and regional government as well as "companies" and "culture" with the declared goal to improve competitiveness. Finally, a large share of France's funds is flowing into training and education. Given France's challenges in digital skills, it has centered its measures in this area. Overall, €7.5 billion are dedicated to work-linked and vocational training while €7.7 billion are invested in research and innovation, where €2.9 billion each is declared as "digital investments". Thus, in the case of France, we observe a high-tech agenda that is pursued through means of technology investments and training of the workforce, rather than the German combination of sectoral support for the automobile industry and acquiring hardware for education purposes.

When comparing country-specific plans, one must keep in mind that the expectations for the effects of the RRF significantly vary. While in Germany and France, investments are expected to be substantial but modest, in Italy and Spain the EU hopes for positive effects on the national GDP of up to 2.5% and the creation of a quarter million jobs each (European Commission 2022b; 2022c). Italy's staggering amount of funds amounting close to €200 billion, as well as its DESI ranking, highlight the challenges the country is facing. In practice, this translates into an RRF plan whose main expenditures target public administration, connectivity, and national business. Italy has dedicated €6 billion to the digitalization of public administration, including its cloud-based infrastructure *Polo Strategico Nazionale*. In contrast to the German and French plans, Italy plans to use almost €7 billion for setting up telecommunication networks and improving 5G coverage. Remarkably, another €13.4 billion will go toward the "digitalization, innovation and competition in the productive system", meaning that the country will give tax credits to businesses in exchange for digitalization efforts. Rested on the assumption that tax cuts incentivize investment, the Italian RRF plan foresees tax credits for Italian businesses that invest in high-tech capital goods, in research and development of high-tech products, or the training of staff on new technologies (Ministero dell'Economia e delle Finanze 2021).

For Spain, RRF investments are split over 30 components and thus harder to aggregate. Generally, spending on digital targets is also more diverse. However, it can be argued that most of these components imply support for businesses. €3.7 billion are dedicated to the financial support of various manufacturing industries, with special emphasis on digitalization and high-tech infrastructures. This is supposed to make Spain's comparably small industrial sector more competitive (Gobierno de España 2021). €4.9 are going to SMEs to support their recovery from the COVID-19 crisis and promote innovation and digitalization. €3.4 go to the tourism sector for similar purposes. However, contrary to other measures previously discussed, these components of the Spanish plan are only in parts targeting aspects of digitalization and new technologies and the exact proportion of digital investments is difficult to assess. Similar to Italy, Spain plans to invest a major sum of €4 billion in the setup of 5G networks and services, which will address coverage issues. Furthermore, the Spanish plan dedicates €4.2 billion to the digitalization of public administration, a common theme of the RRF plans we assessed. €3.6 billion are allocated to the *Plan Nacional de Competencias Digitales* which is meant to address the need for IT education and specialists, a measure comparable to France's training and education plans.

Despite some common emphasis on the digitalization of public administration and the public support of industries and services connected to high-tech, the RRF plans of the EU's four biggest economies vary substantially. It has become clear that national measures are far from comprehensive, but rather represent a targeted investment in particular infrastructure and businesses that align quite strongly with national regimes of accumulation. The general shift toward public investment in high-tech areas and the EU's joint financing of such schemes represents a turning point – not in economic paradigms, but in the composition of policy instruments. However, the funding for the EU's digital agenda will not suffice if institutions like the NGEU remain temporary. According to estimates from the think tank Bruegel, the funds allocated to the digital transformation over the next six years will barely cover the digital investment gap calculated for a single year, even if used effectively (Darvas et al. 2021). Concurrently, the resources of NGEU and MFF, despite their policy innovation character, stretch over several years and make up a little more than 1% of the EU's annual GDP. Both the national modulation of RRF plans and its limited size highlight that the NGEU in its recent form represents an addition to the previous economic instruments. It incentivizes and channels national spending in high-tech areas, but leaves the respective accumulation regimes and the underlying social relations largely untouched.

6 Conclusion

Having examined the recent developments in light of the COVID-19 pandemic, we conclude that efforts embodied in the NGEU and RRF demonstrate a "second-order change" characterized by a state interventionist turn. Focusing on digitalization and technology, the evidence we presented points toward a concrete effort to support and consolidate European high-tech capitalism in political, economic, and discursive terms. A key area of focus is the EU Chips Act, which aims to promote both the production of semiconductors and the training of the workforce to support transnational value chains and the connection of capitalist regimes of accumulation. Investment plans founded through the RRF allocation reflect the member states' ambition to not only undertake an information technological modernization of the economy and labor markets but also of administrations, indicating a comprehensive transformation of given modes of regulation. However, the member states' investments substantially vary in scope and are biased toward their respective national models of development.

The turning point has been supported by leading private and statist actors of the EU's transnational hegemonic bloc in reaction to a specific crisis interpretation, which emphasized information technological deficits and the EU falling behind in the global competition. In contrast to the euro crisis, the reactions to the COVID-19 outbreak have been embedded much more strongly in a modernization strategy that was accompanied by a "second-order change" or – more specifically – a state interventionist turn. As illustrated by the initiative of digital transformation, the political project of a new European industrial policy has created new instruments and mobilized additional resources to stabilize the deficient operations of European high-tech capitalism. Thus, the processes that this study covered empirically reflected a matter of fixing what is already there, stabilizing and furthering European high-tech capitalism by expanding its toolbox, rather than shifting its overall form. Accumulation in Europe remains nationally diversified, yet European regulation continues to promote an export-oriented agenda. For that purpose, market mechanisms and inner-European competition are maintained as underlying principles by the central statist actors and the relevant business factions.

Nevertheless, whether the European strategy will succeed is ultimately an open question. Hopes that the NGEU or SGP's escape clause could be more than temporary instruments, were dampened recently and it is still unclear how a fiscally restrictive EMU and the reinvention of industrial policy in Europe might go together. Thus, the second-order change has mainly resolved some contradictions of European high-tech capitalism by replacing them with new ones. Furthermore, the EU's reliance on the market-liberal paradigm implies substantial uncertainty about whether political guidelines and incentives translate into economic and technological development. Even if that is the case, many projects appear technologically very ambitious, which poses substantial risks of failure. We also have to keep in mind that information technological modernization occurs on a global scale and across important areas and sectors, where one cannot rule out leaps in development by competitors like the US and China that could quickly stifle European ambitions.

References

Abels, Joscha. 2018. Ein Europa Der Finanzministerien? Die Eurogruppe Im Projekt Der Austeritätspolitischen Restrukturierung Der Eurozone. *PROKLA. Zeitschrift für kritische Sozialwissenschaft* 48(3). 399–415.

Abels, Joscha. 2019. Power behind the curtain: The Eurogroup's role in the crisis and the value of informality in economic governance. *European Politics and Society* 20(5). 519–534.

Abels, Joscha & Hans-Jürgen Bieling. 2022a. Jenseits des Marktliberalismus? Europäische Industrie- und Infrastrukturpolitik im Zeichen neuer globaler Rivalitäten. *PROKLA. Zeitschrift für kritische Sozialwissenschaft* 52(3). 429–449.

Abels, Joscha & Hans-Jürgen Bieling. 2023. Infrastructures of globalisation: Shifts in global order and Europe's strategic choices. *Competition & Change* 27(3–4). 516–533.

Aglietta, Michel. 2012. The European vortex. *New Left Review* 75. 15–36.

Bardt, Hubertus, Klaus-Heiner Röhl & Christian Rusche. 2022. Subsidizing semiconductor production for a strategically autonomous European Union? *The Economists' Voice* 19(1). 37–58.

Becker, Joachim. 2013. Regulationstheorie: Ursprünge und Entwicklungstendenzen. In Roland Atzmüller, Joachim Becker, Ulrich Brand, Lukas Oberndorfer, Vanessa Redak & Thomas Sablowski (eds.), *Fit für die Krise? Perspektiven der Regulationstheorie*, 24–56. Münster: Westfälisches Dampfboot.

Bergsen, Pepijn, Alice Billon-Galland, Hans Kundnani, Vassilis Ntousas & Thomas Raines. 2020. "Europe after coronavirus. The EU and a new political economy". https://www.chathamhouse. org/sites/default/files/2020-06-08-europe-after-coronavirus-bergsen-et-al_0.pdf (accessed 27 March 2023)

Bieling, Hans-Jürgen. 2010. Konturen und Perspektiven einer europäischen Zivilgesellschaft. In Johannes Wienand & Christiane Wienand (eds.), *Die kulturelle Integration Europas*, 31–50. Wiesbaden: VS Verlag.

Bieling, Hans-Jürgen. 2013. European financial capitalism and the politics of (de)financialization. *Competition & Change* 17(3). 283–298.

Bieling, Hans-Jürgen. 2014. Comparative analysis of capitalism from a regulationist perspective extended by neo-Gramscian IPE. *Capital & Class* 38(1). 31–43.

Bieling, Hans-Jürgen. 2019. Globalisierungskonflikte: Die strategische Positionierung und Rolle der EU in der neuen Triade-Konkurrenz. *PROKLA. Zeitschrift für kritische Sozialwissenschaft* 49(1). 59–78.

Bundesfinanzministerium. 2021. Deutscher Aufbau- und Resilienzplan. https://www.bundesfinanzmi nisterium.de/Content/DE/Downloads/Broschueren_Bestellservice/2021-01-13-deutscher-aufbau- und-resilienzplan.pdf?__blob=publicationFile&v=6 (accessed 27 March 2023)

Bundesministerium für Wirtschaft und Energie. 2019. A Franco-German manifesto for a European industrial policy fit for the 21st Century. https://www.bmwk.de/Redaktion/DE/Downloads/F/ franco-german-manifesto-for-a-european-industrial-policy.pdf%3F__blob%3DpublicationFile% 26v%3D2 (accessed 27 March 2023)

Bosco, Anna, & Susannah Verney. 2017. From electoral epidemic to government epidemic: The next level of the crisis in Southern Europe. *South European Society and Politics* 21(4). 383–406.

Cox, Robert W. 1983. Gramsci, hegemony and international relations: An essay in method. *Millennium* 12(2). 162–175.

Darvas, Zsolt, J. Scott Marcus & and Alkiviadis Tzaras. 2021. 20 July. Will European Union recovery spending be enough to fill digital investment gaps? *Bruegel Blog*. https://www.bruegel.org/

blog-post/will-european-union-recovery-spending-be-enough-fill-digital-investment-gaps (accessed 27 March 2023)

Demirović, Alex, Julia Dück, Florian Becker, and Pauline Bader. 2011. *VielfachKrise. Im finanzmarktdominierten Kapitalismus*. Hamburg: VSA-Verlag.

Digital Europe. 2022. EU Chips Act. Promising ambition, but more clarity needed on how money will be sourced. https://www.digitaleurope.org/news/eu-chips-act-promising-ambition-but-more-clarity-needed-on-how-money-will-be-sourced/ (accessed 27 March 2023)

Dullien, Sebastian & Ulrike Guérot. 2012. The long shadow of ordoliberalism: Germany's approach to the Euro crisis. *ECFR Policy Brief* 49. https://www.files.ethz.ch/isn/173451/ECFR49_GERMANY_BRIEF.pdf (accessed 27 March 2023)

Eurogroup. 2010. Terms of reference on exit strategies and near-term policy priorities in the Europe 2020 strategy. Implications for the euro area. https://www.consilium.europa.eu/media/25672/20100315-2020_strategy_implications_for_the_euro_area.pdf (accessed 27 March 2023)

European Commission. 2021a. Digital Economy and Society Index (DESI): Thematic chapters. https://ec.europa.eu/newsroom/dae/redirection/document/80563 (accessed 27 March 2023)

European Commission. 2021b. Recovery and Resilience Scoreboard. https://ec.europa.eu/economy_finance/recovery-and-resilience-scoreboard/index.html (accessed 27 March 2023)

European Commission. 2022a. Europe's digital decade. Digital targets for 2030. https://ec.europa.eu/info/strategy/priorities-2019-2024/europe-fit-digital-age/europes-digital-decade-digital-targets-2030_en (accessed 27 March 2023)

European Commission. 2022b. Italy's recovery and resilience plan. https://ec.europa.eu/info/business-economy-euro/recovery-coronavirus/recovery-and-resilience-facility/italys-recovery-and-resilience-plan_en (accessed 27 March 2023)

European Commission. 2022c. Spain's recovery and resilience plan. https://ec.europa.eu/info/business-economy-euro/recovery-coronavirus/recovery-and-resilience-facility/spains-recovery-and-resilience-plan_en (accessed 27 March 2023)

ERT. 2021. Mapping a new world with the EU Digital Compass. Priorities for economic recovery. https://ert.eu/wp-content/uploads/2021/05/ERT-DigitalTransformation-Paper-May-2021_final-1.pdf (accessed 27 March 2023)

Gouvernement de la République française. 2021. National recovery and resilience Plan of France. https://www.economie.gouv.fr/files/files/PDF/2021/PNRR-SummaryEN.pdf (accessed 27 March 2023)

Gramsci, Antonio. 1971. *Selections from the prison notebooks*. New York: International Publishers.

Gobierno de España. 2021. Plan de recuperación, transformación y resiliencia. https://www.lamoncloa.gob.es/temas/fondos-recuperacion/Documents/160621-Plan_Recuperacion_Transformacion_Resiliencia.pdf (accessed 27 March 2023)

Hall, Peter. 1993. Policy paradigms, social learning and the state. *Comparative Politics* 25(3). 275–296.

Hancké, Bob & Angela Garcia Calvo. 2022. Mister chips goes to Brussels. On the pros and cons of a semiconductor policy in the EU. *Global Policy* (online first). https://doi.org/10.1111/1758-5899.13096

Jessop, Bob. 2009. Cultural political economy and critical policy studies. *Critical Policy Studies* 3(3–4). 336–356.

Kassem, Sarrah. 2022. Labour realities at Amazon and COVID-19: obstacles and collective possibilities for its warehouse workers and MTurk workers. *Global Political Economy* 1(1). 59–79.

Koselleck, Reinhart. 1988. *Critique and crisis. Enlightenment and the pathogenesis of modern society*. Oxford: Berg Publishers.

Lavery, Scott, & Davide Schmid. 2021. European integration and the new global disorder. *Journal of Common Market Studies* 59(5). 1322–1338.

Leonard, Mark, Jean Pisany-Ferry, Elina Ribakova, Jeremy Shapiro & Guntram Wolff. 2019. Securing Europe's economic sovereignty. *Survival* 61(5). 75–98.

Lipietz, Alain. 1985. Akkumulation, Krisen und Auswege aus der Krise: Einige methodische Anmerkungen zum Begriff der ,Regulation'. *PROKLA. Zeitschrift für kritische Sozialwissenschaft* 15(1). 109–137.

Lipietz, Alain. 1987. Rebel Sons: The regulation school. Interview with Jane Jenson. *French Politics and Society* 5(4). 17–25.

Lipietz, Alain. 2013. Fears and hopes. The crisis of the liberal-productivist model and its green alternative. *Capital & Class* 37(1). 127–141.

Ministero dell'Economia e delle Finanze. 2021. Recovery and resilience plan. https://www.mef.gov.it/en/focus/documents/PNRR-NEXT-GENERATION-ITALIA_ENG_FIN_08022021_17H00.pdf (accessed 27 March 2023)

Renda, Andrea. 2021. The EU industrial strategy: Towards a post-growth agenda? *Intereconomics* 56(3). 133–138.

Rietzler, Katja &Andrew Watt. 2021. Public investment in Germany: Much more needs to be done. In Floriana Cerniglia, Francesco Saraceno & Andrew Watt (eds.), *The Great Reset. 2021 European public investment outlook*, 47–62. Cambridge: Open Book Publishers.

Rijksoverheid. 2020. EU support for efficient and sustainable COVID-19 recovery. https://www.rijksoverheid.nl/documenten/publicaties/2020/05/26/non-paper-eu-support-for-efficient-and-sustainable-covid-19-recovery (accessed 27 March 2023)

Segal, Adam. 2021. Huawei, 5G, and weaponized interdependence. In Daniel W. Drezner, Henry Farrell & Abraham L. Newman (eds.), *The uses and abuses of weaponized interdependence*, 149–165. Washington: Brookings Institution Press.

Vučić, Mihajlo. 2021. European Union's Quest for Digital Sovereignty. Policy Continuations and Strategic Innovations. In Katarina Zakić & Birgül Demirtaş (eds.), *Europe in changes. The old continent at a new crossroads*, 99–115. Belgrad: NS Mala Knjiga.

Mark McAdam and Nils Goldschmidt

The Social Market Economy and institutional development: Change in times of crisis

Abstract: How does institutional change occur in complex societal settings? The spectrum ranging from stability via evolutionary or gradual change to radical change is one of the most important tensions in neo-institutionalist scholarship today. We employ the theoretical perspectives of historical institutionalism and punctuated equilibrium approaches as a backdrop, which take into account the mechanisms of stability and change in pronounced fashion. Our chapter examines the empirical case of the question of institutional change in light of the development of Germany's economic order: the Social Market Economy. We highlight that the historical success surrounding its implementation in Germany was tied up in agents' efforts to make a market-based economic order palatable to the public at large. Moreover, we argue that in its prospective development, reform proposals for the Social Market Economy must consider the role of democratic acceptance. That implies taking account of collectively-held thought patterns and ideational convictions in society, thereby acknowledging that discussions concerning institutional change ought to be discussed in relation to their respective societal environments.

Keywords: Neo-Institutionalism, Ideas and Institutions, Institutional Change, Social Market Economy, Reform, Embeddedness

1 Introduction

The past 15 years have exhibited a remarkably tumultuous period in European and global affairs, with policy makers navigating from crisis to crisis. The financial crisis of 2007–08 drove the global economy into a deep recession followed by a slow economic recovery. The European debt crisis ensued, casting light on the problem of public finances across much of Southern Europe with the imposition of austerity

Mark McAdam, Universität Siegen, Kohlbettstr. 17, 57068 Siegen, Germany,
E-Mail: mark.mcadam@uni-siegen.de
Nils Goldschmidt, Universität Siegen, Kohlbettstr. 17, 57068 Siegen, Germany,
E-Mail: goldschmidt@wiwi.uni-siegen.de

https://doi.org/10.1515/9783111272900-016

programs as a result (Hayes 2017; Cullinane 2018). In 2015, as a consequence of the ongoing conflict in the Syrian Civil War, large numbers of refugees fled to Europe, which culminated in "the long summer of migration," better known in popular terms as the "refugee crisis" (Hess et al. 2016; Otto 2020; Welsch 2021). A year later, in 2016, to the surprise of many, the United Kingdom voted in a referendum to leave the European Union, setting in motion an episode of political and economic disintegration in a political union which had only ever been familiar with adding new members (Clarke et al. 2017; Arnorsson and Zoega 2018). Five months later, defying pollsters' and betting markets' predictions, Donald Trump was elected President of the United States. A populist figure who on the campaign trail had raised doubts concerning his desire to support the liberal international order the United States was instrumental in shaping assumed office (Komlos 2017; Webb 2017; Ikenberry 2018; Mearsheimer 2019). A once-in-a-century style pandemic occurred in early 2020, catapulting the world into disarray. Two years later, as of the writing of this chapter, the degree to which further mutations may continue to pose a problem is still unclear, as is the question of how and when public health concerns related to COVID-19 will return to a pre-pandemic level (McAdam and Goldschmidt 2020; Wanka and Streinzer 2021). To top it all off, despite the annexation of Crimea by Russia and conflicts between Kremlin-backed separatists and Ukrainian security forces which had been ongoing since 2014, the Russian military launched an invasion of Ukraine in February 2022. Unprecedented economic sanctions by the West against Russia, military aid for the Ukrainian army, and millions of refugees fleeing conflict were some of the war's early consequences (Duszczyk and Kaczmarczyk 2022; van Bergeijk 2022). In its wake, as a result of pent-up demand following two years of the pandemic, supply chain crunches associated with sanctions against the Russian Federation, and prolonged periods of loose monetary policy, inflation soared to heights the Western world had not seen in four decades (Boungou and Yatié 2022; Orhan 2022; Yeoman 2022). With so many competing candidates, the climate crisis – arguably *the* challenge for an entire generation – only gets an honorable mention. What a decade and a half it has been.

Governing from crisis to crisis seems to have been in vogue during this time. But what impact have crises had on societal institutions? Certainly, a multi-faceted one. In some cases – consider the response to COVID-19 by the European Union and its decision, for the first time, to issue mutual debt at the EU level – changes in policy are pronounced, and the attendant shifts are likely to result in a sea change of the rules that govern our societies. In other cases – such as the regulation of migration and refugee management, especially in terms of EU negotiations with Turkey in 2016 – the previously prevailing institutions were largely resumed after the "refugee crisis." Institutional change was far less deep-reaching, even if the long-term number of refugees from the ongoing war in Ukraine will likely imply a new stress test. It is hardly surprising that crises do not have a uniform impact on the development of institutions.

The spectrum ranging from stability via evolutionary or gradual change to radical change is one of the most important tensions in neo-institutionalist scholarship today. Our chapter in this volume examines the question of institutional change in light of the development of Germany's economic order: the Social Market Economy. Institutional change is a metacategory which encapsulates different types of change which are present in this collected volume. Turning, tipping, and breaking points along with critical junctures are all important features which can contribute to institutional change, each with its own unique manifestation. We employ the theoretical perspective of historical institutionalism as a backdrop in our chapter, which takes into account the mechanisms of stability and change in pronounced fashion. While exogenous approaches that highlight the significance of crises have been important here, we note that crisis conditions at specific moments are often overemphasized in discussions in the literature (Capoccia and Kelemen 2007; Slater and Simmons 2010; Soifer 2012). What is happening in the surrounding societal environment, in contrast, receives significantly less attention (Widmaier et al. 2007; Béland 2010). Yet as scholars, we face difficulty assessing the degree of institutional stability or change of contemporary phenomena. Because of our cognitive limitations in grasping the essence of ongoing institutional development – and owing to the indeterminacy of events as they unfold – we focus on a historical case to make use of hindsight in contemplating institutional development. Our focus is on the *historical* introduction of the Social Market Economy in Germany to learn about important elements which can guide our understanding of its contemporary developments. In addition to the positive analysis we undertake here, we should also be transparent about our normative commitments: we find the concept of the Social Market Economy eminently desirable as an economic order, and we believe that it has much to offer in addressing the challenges we face in the 21st century. While we are primarily interested in processes of institutional change, the approach we undertake here is also motivated by the need to reform the Social Market Economy for its continued relevance in present-day societies.

2 Historical institutionalism: Institutional stability and change

Historical institutionalism (HI) is a branch of neoinstitutionalism which focuses specifically on how history shapes institutional development. HI scholars argue that history matters because 1) political events occur within a historical context (i.e., *what* occurs is strongly impacted by *when* it occurs); 2) political decisions are always dependent on previous choices and, simultaneously, also affect future choices at subsequent decision points; and 3) expectations are molded by the past (Steinmo 2008). Early accounts of HI assumed a deeply structuralist and materialist perspective, and the *explanandum* emerged of illustrating why institutional arrangements were stable and durable. Path dependence played – and continues to play – a pivotal role in HI theorizing on institutional stability, invoking what has been described as "history's heavy hand" (Ikenberry 1994). The emphasis on path dependence led to the criticism that theoretical accounts were excessively sticky – and hence stationary – focusing disproportionately on institutional stability in contrast to path-altering moments (Hay 2006; Mahoney and Thelen 2010).

Consequently, the question of institutional change came to the fore. A common approach to explaining institutional change emerged through the use of punctuated equilibrium approaches, in which an extended period of stasis could be interrupted and incur shifts leading to substantive change (Pierson 2004). Explaining change through exogenous means implied historical episodes of contention, instability, and uncertainty in which it was possible to challenge the status quo.[1] Revolutions, economic (and, indeed, public health) crises, and wars disrupted previously existing path dependencies and enabled transitions to new institutional forms. Highly contested, the window of opportunity for what was thought to be conceivable widened considerably. Once the dust settled, however, it was assumed that new path dependencies had been set in motion, locking in a new set of institutions.[2] Many of the specific concepts enumerated in the chapters collected here – turning points, tipping points, breaking points, and critical junctures which are the focus of this volume – also implicitly rely on a temporal moment during which decisive action occurs, even if the different concepts enable disparate outcomes to come into being. These descriptions and a reliance on punctuated equilibrium mechanisms at decisive moments also extend beyond narrow theorizing in HI as well, as is evident in the literature in the sciences more generally (Scheffler 2009; Lamberson and Page 2012), and also in Goldschmidt and Wolf's (2021) discussion of tipping points.

Relying exclusively on such a framework to explain institutional change is problematic. The following questions emerge: Do institutions change only when

---

1 Different terms have been employed to describe the same principle: Capoccia and Kelemen (2007) utilize the term "critical junctures"; Alston et al. (2016) refer to "critical transitions"; and Mukherji (2013) and Alston (2017) use the language of "windows of opportunity". For a view criticizing the perspective that institutions change from one equilibrium to another, see Zweynert (2018).

2 Several approaches require a version of "crisis" or necessitate some form of exogenous impact. See, for example, Capoccia and Kelemen (2007); Slater and Simmons (2010); Soifer (2012); Mukherji (2013); Widmaier (2016).

there is crisis? In other words, is "crisis" the *conditio sine qua non* of institutional change? And if we assume one path dependence to follow the next, does it imply that we only ever experience *radical* institutional change? Neither, of course, is the case. There is far more pluralism concerning the types and degrees of institutional change than is posited through punctuated equilibrium approaches. HI itself has acknowledged as much in its continued evolution, stressing how institutional change can be endogenous (Blyth 2002; Hay 2006; Peinert 2018), and also how it can be gradual and incremental (Streeck and Thelen 2005, chp. 1; Mahoney and Thelen 2010, chp. 1; Conran and Thelen 2016). It is difficult to assess the nature, depth, significance, and durability of institutional change for contemporary settings because of an abundance of interpretive issues. After all, how, amid the complexity and interpretive uncertainty that contemporaneous developments imply, do we adjudicate these matters and make dispositive statements about the ways in which institutions change? Resorting to historical cases and approaches to learning about (the mechanisms of) institutional change is particularly appealing, because it offers the benefit of hindsight and aids our understanding of contemporary developments through retrospective means. What the past teaches us about institutional change can have a bearing on what is occurring in the present.

It also brings elements of perception and cognition into focus. If crises are meaningful in grasping institutional change, it begs the question of which conditions are constitutive for it. Is a crisis an objective phenomenon which we can demarcate by specific criteria, or does it exist merely in the minds of perceiving agents? In other words, is it merely a social construction (cf. Mainwaring 2019) which becomes meaningful by our declaration and invocation of it as such? These questions are, ultimately, unanswerable in any definitive sense, yet they point to the tension that scholarship on crisis and institutional change entails. While we may not be able to define crisis according to specific criteria in an adequate manner, it nevertheless seems reasonable to acknowledge that forks in the road are indeed significant and may have the propensity to challenge hitherto-existing perceptions about institutional constraints. At the same time – and herein lies the insight for the question of institutional development – grasping the admission just made underscores the importance of cognition and ideational factors among citizenries. How we interpret our social environment collectively, what we consider to be approbative, and how we disapprove of specific ideas *is* meaningful for institutional change. Acknowledging HI's path from emphasizing structuralist and materialist elements to the importance of agents and their ideational commitments illustrates the long journey it has taken – and the progress it has made – in thinking about institutional change in moments of crisis and beyond.

3 Learning from history: The past and present of the Social Market Economy

To assess the viability of the continued success of the Social Market Economy as the economic order in Germany in the third decade of the 21st century, it is worthwhile reconsidering the conditions under which it arose in the aftermath of World War II. Our intention is not to illustrate the grander scheme of providing historical context concerning its implementation – irrespective of how valuable it is in and of itself (Goldschmidt and Wohlgemuth 2008) – but rather to argue that acknowledging the prerequisites of its coming into being can be instructive in thinking about institutional change today. The case of the introduction of the Social Market Economy thus demonstrates our conviction that examining the historical circumstances of institutional change can be insightful for our thinking on contemporary matters of public policy. Max Weber (1904; 1918) instructed academics to be transparent about their value judgments. Consequently, it is worth reiterating our claim from the introduction that the analysis of our case study also has the added benefit of considering what is necessary for the Social Market Economy – an economic order we find eminently desirable – to thrive in our time.

3.1 The introduction of the Social Market Economy: An episode of radical institutional change

The introduction and acceptance of the Social Market Economy as the predominant form of economic governance in Germany after World War II was itself improbable. It was unlikely because of the broadly anti-capitalist mindset present in Germany at the time, a reflection of the general skepticism about market-oriented economic processes among the populace (Zweynert 2008). The dominant ideational mentality had a long tradition in Germany: resulting from its relative economic backwardness and underdevelopment in the 19th century, the process of economic catch-up development at the end of the century elicited dramatic social change, stimulating doubts about the desirability of market-oriented processes among the population. Economic hardship after the Great War, hyperinflation in the early 1920s, and ultimately the Great Depression were seen in Germany, as in many other countries as well, to have exemplified the failure of capitalism (McAdam et al. 2018: 185–189). The attendant rise of National Socialism and the catastrophe of World War II cemented the belief among many Germans of the preceding years resulting as an outgrowth and the logical consequence of a failed capitalist system. The outlook was ascendant, viewing a socialist economic order to be preferable (Childs 1966).

Nonetheless, it was the idea of the market economy coupled with its concern for social questions which became public policy and served as the basis for the *Wirtschaftswunder* – the Economic Miracle – in postwar Germany. As a parallel to the theoretical perspective of ordoliberalism, which was emerging at the time in Freiburg and focused on the development and importance of an economic constitution (Vanberg 2015), the term "Social Market Economy" was coined by Alfred Müller-Armack, a professor of political economy in Germany who was particularly attentive to the sociological and cultural embeddedness of economic performance (Zweynert 2006: 466). The question Müller-Armack faced was how the acceptance of an economic order based on market logic might be improved by a population that harbored significant reservations about its desirability. Drawing on the four overarching worldviews present in Germany at the time – Protestantism, Catholicism, Liberalism, and Socialism – he discussed the prospect of the Social Market Economy as an irenic formula of reconciliation (Müller-Armack 1950).

It was the invocation of the term "social," however, which was particularly successful in raising positive associations and brought together complementary concepts – market logic *and* concern for social questions – previously viewed as unrelated or even antagonistic. As Zweynert notes:

> in accordance with the holistic patterns of thought prevailing in German culture, the adjective 'social' raised positive emotions in the German population. But what is more, for decades it had been the very battle cry of several protest movements against capitalism – and it surely is no accident that even the Nazis made use of it. 'Social' was, one may say, a killer word against capitalism in German political discourse. Müller-Armack's stroke of genius was to link it with a euphemism for its potential victim. This meant to transform the world 'social' [. . . to] serve a very alien master: capitalism. By promising a 'third way' between capitalism and socialism and by rhetorically linking an adjective that represented 'community' with a noun that stood for 'society,' the 'irenical formula' (*irenische Formel*) Social Market Economy played an important part in [. . .] achieving a wider acceptance of capitalism within the population (2006:469).

The shaping of the idea to make the emerging economic order amenable to the broader public was certainly also about framing the problem in a way which many found compelling in the early postwar years. But it was not merely a question of framing; indeed, it shaped the constitution of the idea – and its implementation in practice – in the first place.

3.2 Lessons learned

What can we learn from the introduction of the Social Market Economy in the postwar era about the importance of – and prerequisites for – successful institutional change? First, it should be noted that its implementation occurred at a moment of crisis. Unlike many other cases of institutional change that rely on punctuated equilibrium approaches in which a continuation of an institutional set is at least conceivable, the same cannot be said for the question of the economic order in Germany after the war. The continuation of National Socialist economic policy was *not* plausible after 1945. And yet the episode also reveals how crisis did indeed open a window of opportunity: it was a fork in the road in which different economic paradigms – different varieties of liberalism, socialism, and corporatism, to name but a few – would have been possible. "What follows next?" was a timely question, since *something* had to follow the untenability of what had preceded.

Second, it highlights, especially in democratic politics, how important the ideational component of a society is for the acceptance of societal institutions. Whichever institutions are introduced into society must, if they are to succeed, correspond to the *zeitgeist* of an era. Institutional implementation is never merely about an abstract set of institutional conditions which can be discussed in isolation; it must align with the prevailing ideas in society. Representative forms of government require public support for policy, so it is necessary for governments to ensure that the policies they enact can be appropriated in their society. It not only stresses the communicative act of introducing new policies and taking public sensibilities seriously, but also has an impact on the development of the institution in the first place. In the case of the Social Market Economy, it implied crafting an institutional arrangement with *complementary* elements, making it attractive to disparate groups in society (cf. Fritz et al. 2021). From its outset, the Social Market Economy was also about compromise between competing interests: between employer associations and trade unions, between rich and poor, and between liberal-conservative and social democratic forces. It bore in mind that establishing democratic support for its project was essential.

Third, the consolidation of an institution or a set of institutions after its implementation is also uncertain. Things – politics, the economy, society, culture – change. It is not clear *ex ante* how newly introduced institutions will respond to ongoing change, making institutional maintenance and adaptation important. The Social Market Economy in 2022 is not the same as it was at the time of the currency reform in June of 1948. It has had to reinvent itself – or, more accurately, agents have had to reinvent it – repeatedly over the past seven decades. Moreover, it is important that an institutional set adapts to these changing circumstances in a *successful* manner and succeed in establishing popular support. One of the strengths of the Social Market Economy is its *flexibility*, which has provided it with remarkable stability throughout its historical progression (Goldschmidt and Wolf 2021: 227). While not succumbing to institutional relativism in terms of the ability of *any* set of institutions to be subsumed under it – there are indeed certain delimiting factors – a multiplicity of different institutions may be contained within it. Perhaps the acknowledgment of the need for permanent reform is the clarion call of the Social Market Economy. As a "narrative of meaning, which has a bearing on its environment," (Goldschmidt and Wolf 2021: 220, own translation) it is more specifically an attitude or an approach than immutably concrete policy. Moreover, its ability to adapt to changing circumstances – in other words, its inherent flexibility – was recognized by advocates of the Social Market Economy who noted that it "is not a completed system; it is no recipe which can be employed in the same manner for all time. It is an evolutionary order in which it is continuously necessary to place new emphases according to the demands of changing times" (Müller-Armack 1974, our translation).

3.3 The future of the Social Market Economy

Which insights do we derive from such analysis for the future of our economic order? How stable is the Social Market Economy, and can we count on its continued functioning? Borrowing the logic of punctuated equilibrium approaches, is this the moment of contention at which prevailing institutions are called into question? Are we, given the abundance of crises outlined in our introduction, at decisive moments whose inexorable outcome is written in stone?

The future is not determinate. Indeed, to invoke the former German Chancellor Willy Brandt, the best way to predict the future is to create it. Myriad social and economic challenges do indeed raise questions concerning the ability of the Social Market Economy to address the problems of our age – the ecological question and the issue of climate change; the rise of digitalization and the impact it will have on labor markets; new geopolitical alliances and the questioning of hyper-globalization, from which Germany, as an exporting nation, has benefited tremendously. To a significant degree, addressing these issues in ways that yield positive results is a technical problem. Addressing these matters requires sensible public policy which deals with new problems in a targeted and purposeful manner. Yet we contend the development of efficient, feasible, market-oriented solutions to be only half of it. There must be, in addition to managing the problems we face as a society, a recognition of the necessity of public support as Alfred Müller-Armack sought in the postwar period. It is about generating workable economic solutions *and* concern for social questions. There are dangers lurking on the horizon. Germany does comparatively well in social mobility surveys (cf. World Economic Forum 2020), but the degree to which success in Germany is still largely dependent on the families children are born into and the upbringing they receive (Braun and Stuhler 2018) raises the question of whether citizens perceive their economic model to be fair and whether they deem it worthy of further support. The United States can serve as a warning: social mobility has dropped precipitously there, coinciding with the rise of extremist politics and societal polarization (Chetty et al. 2017; Alesina et al. 2018; *The Economist* 2021).

It is necessary to heed such caution. It should also provide an impetus to internalizing the need to view the Social Market Economy as a formula for reform. Merely relying on institutions which have worked well in the past and in *one* context says little about how they will fit under changed circumstances, in particular if their extension from the German case to the European level (Dörr et al. 2020) is considered. Economic and societal change requires our social economic order to be dynamic, which must not be a problem per se since flexibility can also confer stability. At the same time, it would be mistaken to view specific crises as the element which deserves our greatest attention in developing reform proposals. Parsing the inherent difficulties of the challenges of our time – of the ecological challenge and its associated transformation, of less robust supply chains, and of digital transformation – highlights an approach which elevates the crisis to the analytical foreground. We do not belittle the perspective of important inflection points for any set of institutions, but we believe that in cases of exogenous shocks, the crises themselves should not – at least not in isolation – generate analytical priority. The societal environment – the collective ideas which are present – deserves far more attention. If the Social Market Economy is to continue to be "a narrative of meaning," then it is incumbent upon us to translate it into practice, bearing in mind the specificities time and place require – including the beliefs, convictions, and ideas agents in society have and how they impact institutional development.

4 Conclusion

We acknowledge there are different (normative and positive) levels to considering the continued progression of the Social Market Economy. Stating openly that we find the approach of the Social Market Economy desirable nevertheless raises positive questions about how we anticipate it developing. Reluctance best marks our disposition in making predictions about its future, stemming from the open-endedness of our economic order despite the manifold challenges we face. What becomes of the Social Market Economy depends on how it evolves and how it is reformed to meet both the economic and social needs of our age. It is, ultimately, an approach to governing more than that it clings assertively to specific economic institutions (Goldschmidt and Rauchenschwandtner 2018).

We have outlined in our chapter under which conditions it displays robustness and what its implementation after World War II reveals about the importance of our time. For one, uncertainty and crisis are merely signals which issue an invitation to engage in the necessary reform to make our economic order suitable for contemporary problems. Second, we highlight the importance of non-materialist concerns. To generate democratic acceptance, it is essential that, in the grand scheme, policy corresponds to the ideational convictions and the dominant thought patterns present in society. It also means that agents who are seeking to entrench public policy positions in society must take account of and display sensitivity to what is in citizens' heads. Economic development has failed frequently enough because economic institutions diverged from the way in which societies thought about matters collectively. We overlook the ideational at our own peril. Third, taking the aforementioned together is important because acknowledging the importance of inflection points as well as the ideational level leads to a specific tension: whereas crisis can lead to abrupt institutional changes, many ideational underpinnings typically only ever change slowly and gradually. Practices which are not particularly important to identity-making among citizens may change more rapidly, but ideas about how the world is, or how it ought to be, can be remarkably stubborn and hence display pronounced durability. The specific consequences of such incongruent development raises important questions about the success of further institutional development in post-crisis settings.

Theoretically, we have illustrated how far HI has traversed: from predominantly materialist and structuralist accounts to taking the role agents play and the importance of ideas seriously. Yet the question of institutional change is not merely about collective ideas which anonymous agents embedded in society have; it is also about very concrete agents working to establish narratives of meaning, such as Müller-Armack in the postwar era. Moreover, the broad invocation of punctuated equilibrium approaches in historical institutionalism deserves some caution. Early proponents focused on the manner in which genuinely new, path-altering institutions could become entrenched in moments of historical crisis. That may also apply to the historical introduction of the Social Market Economy in Germany, yet it also suggests something misleading: moments of crisis do not *necessarily* require radical change. In part because agents' cognitive background is slow to adapt to new circumstances, radical change is not always the most likely. Nor is it frequently the most desirable. Here, too, the philosophy of the Social Market Economy is insightful, as the paradigm of reform implies that radical problems do not by necessity require radical solutions. Given the multitude of crises we face today that is worth bearing in mind.

References

Alesina, Alberto, Stefanie Stantcheva & Edoardo Teso. 2018. Intergenerational Mobility and Preferences for Redistribution. *American Economic Review* 108(2). 521–554.

Alston, Lee. 2017. Beyond Institutions: Beliefs and Leadership. *The Journal of Economic History* 77(2). 353–372.

Alston, Lee, Marcus A. Melo, Bernardo Mueller & Carlos Pereira. 2016. *Brazil in Transition: Beliefs, Leadership, and Institutional Change.* Princeton & Oxford: Princeton University Press.

Arnorsson, Agust & Gylfi Zoega. 2018. On the Causes of Brexit. *European Journal of Political Economy* 55. 301–323.

Béland, Daniel. 2010. The Idea of Power and the Role of Ideas. *Political Studies Review* 8. 145–154.

van Bergeijk, Peter A. G. 2022. Sanctions Against the Russian War on Ukraine: Lessons from History and Current Prospects. *Journal of World Trade* 56(4). 571–586.

Blyth, Mark. 2002. *Great Transformations: Economic Ideas and Institutional Change in the 20th Century.* New York: Cambridge University Press.

Boungou, Whelsy & Alhonita Yatié. 2022. The Impact of the Ukraine–Russia War on World Stock Market Returns. *Economics Letters* 215. 110516.

Braun, Sebastian T. & Jan Stuhler. 2018. The Transmission of Inequality and Across Multiple Generations: Testing Recent Theories with Evidence from Germany. *Economic Journal* 128(609). 576–611.

Capoccia, Giovanni & Daniel R. Kelemen. 2007. The Study of Critical Junctures: Theory, Narrative, and Counterfactuals in Historical Institutionalism. *World Politics* 59(3). 341–369.

Chetty, Raj, David Grusky, Maximilian Hell, Nathaniel Hendren, Robert Manduca, & Jimmy Narang. The Fading American Dream: Trends in Absolute Income Mobility Since 1940. *Science* 356(6336). 398–406.

Childs, David. 1966. *From Schumacher to Brandt: The Story of German Socialism, 1945–1965.* Oxford: Pergamon Press.

Clarke, Harold D., Matthew Goodwin & Paul Whiteley. 2017. *Brexit: Why Britain Voted to Leave the European Union.* Cambridge: Cambridge University Press.

Conran, James &Kathleen Thelen. 2016. Institutional Change. In Orfeo Fioretos, Tulia Faletti, & Adam Sheingate (eds.), *The Oxford Handbook of Historical Institutionalism,* 51–70. New York: Oxford University Press.

Cullinane, Mark. 2018. Public Service Austerity Broadcasts: Framing the Euro Debt Crisis. *International Journal of Communication* 12. 1350–1368.

Dörr, Julian,Nils Goldschmidt, & Alexander Lenger. 2020. Toward a European Social Market Economy? The Normative Legacy of Walter Eucken, Alexander Rüstow, and Beyond. In Malte Dold & Tim Krieger (eds.), *Ordoliberalism and European Economic Policy: Between Realpolitik and Economic Utopia,* 207–222. London & New York: Routledge.

Duszczyk, Maciej & Pawel Kaczmarczyk. 2022. The War in Ukraine and Migration to Poland: Outlook and Challenges. *Intereconomics* 57. 164–170.

Fritz, Roland, Nils Goldschmidt, & Matthias Störring. 2021. Contextual Liberalism: The Ordoliberal Approach to Private Vices and Public Benefits. *Public Choice.* DOI: 10.1007/s11127-021-00879-w.

Goldschmidt, Nils & Stephan Wolf. 2021. *Gekippt. Was wir tun können, wenn Systeme außer Kontrolle geraten.* Freiburg: Herder.

Goldschmidt, Nils & Hermann Rauchenschwandtner. 2018. The Philosophy of Social Market Economy: Michel Foucault's Analysis of Ordoliberalism. *Journal of Contextual Economics* 138(2). 157–184.

Goldschmidt, Nils & Michael Wohlgemuth. 2008. Social Market Economy: Origins, Meanings, and Interpretations. *Constitutional Political Economy* 19. 261–276.

Hay, Colin. 2006. Constructivist Institutionalism. In R. A. W. Rhodes, Sarah Binder, and Bert A. Rockman (eds.), *The Oxford Handbook of Political Institutions*, 56–74. New York: Oxford University Press.

Hayes, Graeme. 2017. "Regimes of Austerity." *Social Movement Studies*16 (1). 21–35.

Hess, Sabine, Bernd Kasparek, Stefanie Kron, Mathias Rodatz & Maria Schwertl (eds.). 2016. *Der lange Sommer der Migration. Grenzregime III*. Hamburg: Assoziation A.

Ikenberry, G. John. 1994. History's Heavy Hand: Institutions and the Politics of the State. Paper presented at the The New Institutionalism Conference, University of Maryland 14–15 October.

Ikenberry, G. John. 2018. The End of Liberal International Order? *International Affairs* 94(1). 7–23.

Komlos, John. 2017. The Triumph of Trumpism. *Journal of Contextual Economics* 137(4). 421–440.

Lamberson, P. J. & Scott E. Page. 2012. Tipping Points. *Quarterly Journal of Political Science* 7(2). 175–208.

Mahoney, James & Kathleen Thelen (eds.). 2010. *Explaining Institutional Change: Ambiguity, Agency and Power*. New York: Cambridge University Press.

Mainwaring, Cetta. 2019. *At Europe's Edge: Migration and Crisis in the Mediterranean*. Oxford: Oxford University Press.

McAdam, Mark, Stefan Kolev, & Erwin Dekker. 2018. Methods for Understanding Economic Change: Socio-Economics and German Political Economy, 1896–1938. *Journal of Contextual Economics* 138(3–4). 185–197.

McAdam, Mark & Nils Goldschmidt. 2020. Der Weg zur Knechtschaft reloaded. Autoritarismus inmitten der Krise. *Zeitschrift für Wirtschafts- und Unternehmensethik* 21(3). 81–90.

Mearsheimer, John J. 2019. Bound to Fail: The Rise and Fall of the Liberal International Order. *International Security* 43(4). 7–50.

Müller-Armack, Alfred. 1950. Soziale Irenik. *Weltwirtschaftliches Archiv* 64. 181–203.

Müller-Armack, Alfred. 1974. *Genealogie der Sozialen Marktwirtschaft: Frühschriften und weiterführende Konzepte*. Bern: Haupt.

Mukherji, Rahul. 2013. Ideas, Interests, and the Tipping Point: Economic Change in India. *Review of International Political Economy* 20(2). 363–389.

Orhan, Ebru. 2022. The Effects of the Russia-Ukraine War on Global Trade. *Journal of International Trade, Logistics and Law* 8(1). 141–146.

Otto, Laura. 2020. *Junge Geflüchtete an der Grenze. Eine Ethnografie zu Altersaushandlungen*. Frankfurt/ New York: Campus.

Peinert, Erik. 2018. Periodizing, paths and probabilities: why critical junctures and path dependence produce causal confusion. *Review of International Political Economy* 25(1). 122–143.

Pierson, Paul. 2004. *Politics in Time: History, Institutions, and Social Analysis*. Princeton: Princeton University Press.

Scheffler, Marten. 2009. *Critical Transitions in Nature and Society*. Princeton: Princeton University Press.

Slater, Dan & Erica Simmons. 2010. Informative Regress: Critical Antecedents in Comparative Politics. *Comparative Political Studies* 43(7). 886–917.

Soifer, David. 2012. The Causal Logic of Critical Junctures. *Comparative Political Studies* 45(12). 1572–1597.

Steinmo, Sven. 2008. Historical Institutionalism. In Donatella Della Porta and Michael Keating (eds.), *Approaches and Methodologies in the Social Sciences*, 118–138. Cambridge: Cambridge University Press.

Streeck, Wolfgang and Kathleen Thelen, eds. 2005. *Beyond Continuity: Institutional Change in Advanced Political Economies*. New York: Oxford University Press.

Vanberg, Viktor. 2015. Ordoliberalism, Ordnungspolitik, and the Reason of Rules. *European Review of International Studies* 2(3). 27–36.

Wanka, Anna & Andreas Streinzer. 2021. Die Arbeit der anderen. In Thomas Kaspar & Stephan Hebel (eds.), *Heile Welt. 32 Ideen für ein Leben nach Corona*, 87–91. Frankfurt am Main: Societäts-Verlag.

Webb, Steven. 2017. Populism: A Threat to Democracy? Or a Verification of It? *Journal of Contextual Economics* 137(4). 401–420.

Weber, Max. 1904. Die 'Objektivität' sozialwissenschaftlicher und sozialpolitischer Erkenntnis. *Archiv für Sozialwissenschaft und Sozialpolitik* 19. 22–87.

Weber, Max. 1918. Der Sinn der 'Wertfreiheit' der soziologischen und ökonomischen Wissenschaften. *Logos. Internationale Zeitschrift für Philosophie der Kultur* 7. 40–88.

Welsch, Heinz. 2021. Utilitarian and Ideological Determinants of Attitudes towards Immigration: Germany Before and After the 'Migration Crisis'. *Journal of Contextual Economics* 141(3). 215–242.

Widmaier, Wesley. 2016. *Economic Ideas in Political Time: The Rise and Fall of Economic Orders from the Progressive Era to the Global Financial Crisis*. Cambridge: Cambridge University Press.

Widmaier, Wesley, Mark Blyth, & Leonard Seabrooke. 2007. Exogenous Shocks or Endogenous Constructions? The Meanings of Wars and Crises. *International Studies Quarterly* 51(4). 747–759.

Yeoman, Ian. 2022. Ukraine, Price and Inflation. *Journal of Revenue and Pricing Management* 21(3). 253–254.

Zweynert, Joachim. 2006. Shared Mental Models, Catch-Up Development and Economic Policy-Making: The Case of Germany After World War II and Its Significance for Contemporary Russia. *Eastern Economic Journal* 32(3). 457–478.

Zweynert, Joachim. 2008. Die Soziale Marktwirtschaft als politische Integrationsformel. *Wirtschaftsdienst* 88(5). 334–337.

Zweynert, Joachim. 2018. Contextualizing Critical Junctures: What post-Soviet Russia Tells Us About Ideas and Institutions. *Theory and Society* 47(3). 409–435.

External Sources

The Economist. 6 November 2021. *The Democrats' Social-Spending Package Cannot Repair the American Dream*. https://www.economist.com/briefing/2021/11/06/the-democrats-social-spending-package-cannot-repair-the-american-dream.

World Economic Forum. *The Global Social Mobility Report 2020: Equality, Opportunity, and a New Economic Imperative*. https://www3.weforum.org/docs/Global_Social_Mobility_Report.pdf (accessed 26 March 2022).

Rogelio Madrueño

The emergent discourse on global threats and risks: An analysis of the contemporary empirical evidence extant in scientific journals

Abstract: The prominence of global megatrends and the emergent literature on threats, risks and vulnerabilities show that these two phenomena are arguably not mutually exclusive. This betrays, however, a lack of understanding about how these challenges are conceived by the scientific community from a more comprehensive perspective. This paper assumes that it is possible to identify the presence of turning points in world politics, focused on the analysis of threats and risks and the detection of citation bursts, which reflect new perspectives and emergent research fields using big data. I provide a systematic analysis based on bibliometric techniques, involving more than 6800 publications from the Web of Science over the last four decades. This paper addresses the following questions: what are the main areas of research on global threats and risks? What is the role of Western and emerging countries in this process? What are the most influential papers, countries and languages regarding the study of threats and risks? And how does this emergent literature connect to the understanding of discursive practices and turning points?

Keywords: Threats, risks, mega-trends, global development, development discourse

1 Introduction

The increasing prominence of global megatrends (e.g. technological breakthroughs, climate change and global inequality) and the emergent literature on specific challenges to people and the planet in terms of risks, vulnerabilities and potential threats, show that these two phenomena are not mutually exclusive. While researchers have looked carefully at specific global challenges from different somewhat narrow standpoints, there is a lack of consensus about how potential threats

Rogelio Madrueño, Center for Advanced Security, Strategic and Integration Studies (CASSIS), University of Bonn

https://doi.org/10.1515/9783111272900-017

to human security are conceived of by the scientific community from a more comprehensive perspective (Mitchel 2010; Kavalski 2015).

The increasing complexity of the global challenges facing us since the beginning of the twenty-first century has tested the capacity of the planet to operate without exceeding environmental and social limits (Meadows et al. 1972; Trüper et al. 2015). This ultimately indicates a broader controversy about the possibilities of the future, and the fundamental question of whether global challenges should be seen as a blueprint for progress, or as a universal threat to humanity (Bowler 2017). This leads to a point of contention within the understanding of progress between antagonised narratives at the two extremes of the political spectrum. On the one hand, there are those positions that emphasise the idea of progress and the forward direction and unity of history. These views use a specific vocabulary, assumptions, components of discourse, etc. to legitimise the goal of modernisation with a certain view of 'development', including a collection of policy interventions and recommendations (Ziai 2016). On the other hand, a constellation of approaches and emancipatory movements that pose as critics of modernisation theories, bringing a plurality to the understanding of history, such as in the case of post-colonialism and post-development theories (Ziai 2016). They provide a broad spectrum of critical analysis about the very concept and practice of development, highlighting the hegemony of the industrialised West over the rest of the world. While these offer a well-argued narrative on the process of development and underdevelopment, they are not without flaws in providing alternatives to overcome the problems associated with the modernity of capitalism, and its related development paradigms (Simon 2006), such as in the case of the counter-hegemonic approaches like the *Buen Vivir* in Latin America or *Degrowth* (Hickel 2021).

This antagonism, however, reaffirms intrinsically the paradigm made up of continuous conflicts, struggles and interdependencies between the various extant development models (Madrueño 2018, De Sousa Santos & Meneses 2020; O'Neill 2020). Accordingly, there is a strengthening of the role of asymmetries and heterogeneities across countries, including a source of recurrent socio-economic instability and continuing uncertainty about the future of the planet.

In this regard, turning points reflect both positive and negative aspects of progress, which may lead to a dualistic interpretation of human evolution. Turning points must be conceived within the framework of complexity thinking, where complexity and instability work together as essential parts of a system (Scheffran 2015). The process of adapting to movements in a changing environment is crucial in determining the emergence of the potential breaking points and turning points of a given system. This means that the emergence of a turning point, involving the transition of a system to a new context, can take on different forms depending on the quality of the system. Thus, for example, growing social movements or major natural disasters can lead to the possible emergence of cascading effects or tipping points into the unknown, that materialise in the form of conflict and instability (Scheffran 2015). These transitions are complex, but not necessarily, de facto, revolutionary. On the contrary, they are path-dependent and, therefore, arguably cumulative over time (Sovacool 2016; Fouquet 2016).

A positive reading of these points of transition within the major trends of the global economy would suggest that radical shifts are not necessarily the starting point of a new reality but rather, the destination of progress. Conversely, a negative view of a turning point would emphasise that simultaneous crises might lead to unprecedented changes, which could be disruptive and costly to human life (Capra 1982). This leads to the question of what criteria we should use to assess the direction of a turning point. The tentative answer lies essentially in the existing planetary boundaries and to what extent these decisive changes contribute to maintaining the planet's ecological and climatic balance while avoiding deterioration in the natural and human environment.

Not surprisingly, there is no consensus on this possible answer due to a wide variety of approaches, theories and methodologies deployed to understand the interrelationship between social and natural reality. This is partly a legacy of the different lenses (watertight compartments or silos) in which specialised scientific fields operate. While they share mutual concerns, their methodological differences slow down mutual communication and the required comprehensive treatment of complexity (Braudel and Immanuel Wallerstein 2009). This also arguably extends to the proper understanding of a turning point. For economists, it is directly linked to crises, structural changes and cycles (e.g. the dot-com bubble and the subprime crisis) (Piger 2020). For historians, it is shared widely through the notions of caesura and periodisation, such as *Sattelzeit* (Motzkin 2005), while for political scientists, it would be expressed in ideas of revolution, political transitions, or ideological shifts (Fairfax 2021), even though this characterisation is not as clear-cut as it might appear and it is possible to find overlaps.

What is more remarkable is the increasing use of buzzwords related to turning points with the expansion of the capitalist economic system. The excesses of the different variants of capitalism have enabled exposure to the negative side of global megatrends across geographic regions in the form of transformative global forces that have a major impact on global economies due to their increasing pace of change, including areas such as environmental degradation, rising inequalities and the rise in transnational organised crime (Singh 2012; UN 2020). Accordingly, these factors of instability are more likely to occur, including the rise of multiple threats and risks that can be either subject to securitisation, prescriptions of strategies with the promise of development, or both. This means shifting the focus from the traditional security concerns of nation-states to transnational security concerns, which include issues such as transnational terrorism, environmental risks and transnational organised crime (Robin & Melzar 2021).

The most striking instance is the issue of climate change. The identification of critical planetary boundaries suggests that humankind has already transgressed at least three of nine boundaries beyond which ecosystems become unstable. This implies that the earth can enter a zone of uncertainty and eventually, high-risk zones, in which the tipping points become irreversible (Rockström et al. 2009). Another example, following Keynes (1936), is the unprecedentedly high level of social inequality and the access to zones of uncertainty that can lead to social disruption and shifts in the balance of power in international relations, leading towards new wars and conflicts in the coming years.

More specifically, this paper sets out to answer the following questions: what causes a particular megatrend to become a challenge in the form of a global threat or interconnected risk? What are the main areas of research in these paradigms? What is the role of Western and emerging countries in this process? What are the most influential papers, countries and languages in the study of threats and risks? How does this emergent literature connect to the understanding of discursive practices and turning points?

Three main hypotheses could address these questions. The first suggests that it is perfectly possible to identify the presence of turning points and uncertainties in contemporary world politics focused on the analysis of global threats and risks through the detection of citation bursts from bibliometric analysis. This may indeed reflect new perspectives and emerging research fields related to big data. The second indicates that researchers play a supporting role in the creation of hegemonic discourses. Finally, the third hypothesis posits that the promotion of discursive practices relies upon the role of scholars located in the global North.

After this introduction, section two provides a theoretical contribution to the emergent discourse on global threats. It sheds light on the different theories and disciplines that have fostered the discourse on these new threats and risks. Section three uses bibliometric techniques and qualitative analysis to identify the main areas of research, the most influential articles, countries, authors and institutions that are largely behind the literature on threats and risks through the use of the Web of Science (WoS) database (Clarivate Analytics 2021) from the period 1975–2020. Section four concludes by providing a discussion about the implications of discourse formation and the empirical evidence surrounding global threats and risks.

2 Literature review

2.1 Dominant discourses, power and threats

The formation of scientific discourse involves a complex structure based on a combination of different discourse levels that highlight the interdependency and complementarity between linguistic components, rules that govern discourse formation, the channels and mechanisms of knowledge production and the set of institutions that enable the creation and momentum for dominant discourses (Ziai 2016; Madrueño & Tezanos 2018). The interrelationship between these elements becomes key to understanding the evolution of power structures behind this knowledge production, which involves a complex interaction and struggle for the appropriation and interpretation of reality and knowledge. This opens up the possibility to shape, codify and communicate wisdom for specific purposes that may include the use of knowledge for policymaking or even the construction of epistemic governance that allows the strengthening of structures of power and authority of hegemonic or dominant discourse (PoReSo 2020; Ozga 2020; Bisiada 2021).

For instance, Figure 1 illustrates the global setting in which the discourse on development and security takes place regardless of any specific interpretation of threats and risks that we will discuss in more detail below. Three main levels operate in the formation of a dominant discourse. The first level (a) emphasises linguistic components, its rules of formation and the field of continuous tensions between approaches, ideologies, beliefs, etc. that provide a framework in which the fight for supremacy in the production of knowledge is carried out. At the second level (b), a variety of institutions, organisations and networks are continuously interacting, either to convey information from scientific production, reproduce political, social and cultural narratives, or disseminate misleading, false or alternative political truths at the expense of scientific evidence (as in the case of the so-called post-truth era).

The third level (c) includes a set of factors that define discursive frames, through channels of dissemination from different communities and mechanisms of cooperation. This involves networks and groups of individuals that galvanise the formation of discourses, providing them with momentum.

At the same time, this framework provides the opportunity to reinforce so-called non-discursive practices. This includes a set of "institutions, political events, economic practices and processes", which give shape and context to discursive practices (Foucault 1972: 162). In other words, they are part of a close relationship with socioeconomic elements and play the role of external or hidden factors, which will emerge at critical junctures, such as in the emergence of turning points in history. Hence, the combination of those features provides the acceleration of long-term processes or existing trends (socioeconomic, political, etc.) that might spark

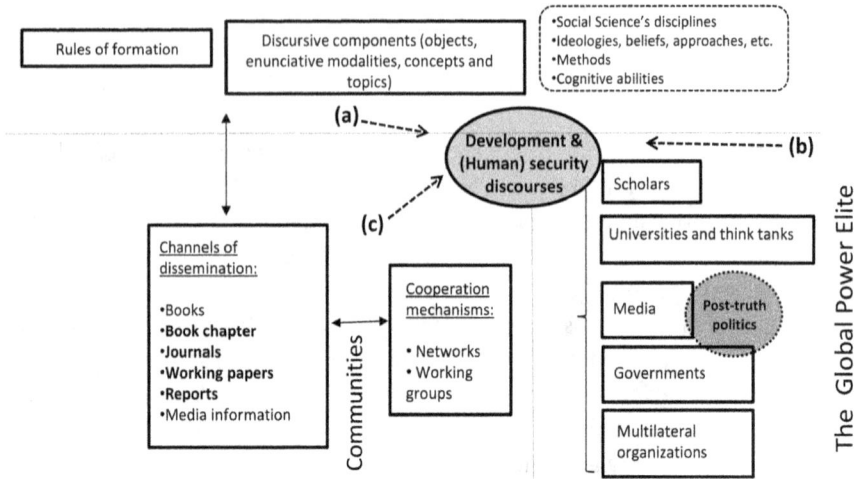

Figure 1: The formation of a dominant discourse.
Source: Author's own illustration based on Madrueño and Tezanos (2018).

new debates and narratives at a given point in time (e.g. the 9/11 terrorist attacks, the coronavirus pandemic), thus, creating a link with the emergence of turning points as seen above.

All in all, the connection between discursive practices (i.e. communicative practices that facilitate the formation of knowledge) and non-discursive practices (i.e. outstanding socio-economic or political events) in the formation of discourse echoes the importance of historical junctures and structural considerations, such as institutional changes. This reaffirms the role of context in the creation of "discursive shifts" (Biccum 2009; Ziai 2016).

Nonetheless, according to Foucauldian theory, the above also implies that some basic conditions would also need to be met to provide the "unity" of dominant discourse, as in the case of a group of rules of formation that give consistency to discursive practices (Ziai 2016). These rules involve components, such as objects, enunciative modalities, concepts and strategies of discourse, emphasising the importance of geographic and socioeconomic units (i.e. states or regions) that target the discourse and the sources of it, which includes the different concepts and theories that give substance to discourse (Foucault 1972). Interestingly, this implies that there can be contradictory components within the rules of formation that still create the conditions for a unique type of discourse, as is the case of the structure of the development discourse (Madrueño & Tezanos 2018).

2.2 The emergence of a discourse on global threats

While we are not yet at the point of having a dominant discourse on global threats, it now appears that we are moving in that direction. An expanding range of transnational threats would, in theory, make it possible to set up a "discourse on global threats", as it integrates a variety of elements that connects to the creation of a dominant discourse, which refers to a prevailing of thinking on any given topic. In the Foucauldian approach, four requirements are met: the existential, the normative, the practical and the methodological. The first suggests that threats exist as something that menaces the various dimensions of human life and it can be categorised, for example, in terms of societies that are more prone to or less likely to face threats. The normative assumption points out the negative side of a transnational threat. It is, in essence, a "public bad" due to its negative consequences affecting people and their communities. The practical assumption establishes that threats can be addressed and curbed. Finally, the methodological assumption provides the possibility to compare different levels of threats, for instance, either hierarchically or geographically, among possible modes of comparison.

From another angle, some features provide consistency to the creation of a 'hegemonic' discourse of human security relying on transnational threats. At this point, it is important to understand, as will be seen in more detail below, that threats are ultimately part of individual and social perception, which beyond their impact on people's lives, can be shaped in the collective imagination by other social agents with the capacity to influence others (big media, multinational companies, think tanks, governments, etc.) and thus, be placed at some point on the priority scale of people's perception of risk and threat.

Following Laclau's (2005) theory of hegemony, it can be shown that multiple threats emerging from the excesses of the capitalist system can be grouped without losing their specificity. Even more important is the fact that while threats grow individually, the broader socioeconomic and ecological basis of the system is affected. Therefore, these individual threats are potentially destructive to nature and human life on the planet. The perception of global threat would articulate all these individual demands of the system, providing the conditions for a hegemonic relationship. Moreover, the growing perception of global threats can lead to the emergence of a hegemonic discourse, which would convey contradictory messages on global development, without obstructing its discursive logic and its ability to endure over time. This means, on the one hand, that there are reasons to ensure a safer world for future generations based on the quest for a reduction in the severity of the dangers to humanity. On the other hand, there are concrete incentives that might divert the attention of the global community towards strategic objectives and security targets, and this is without necessarily prioritising human development goals (Madrueño 2016).

As shown in Figure 1, the factor that intersects and reinforces these discursive constructions is the role played by social and discursive practices, as has happened in recent years within the international system, especially after the end of the Cold War and particularly after the creation of the United Nations High-level Panel on Threats, Challenges and Change in 2003. This panel aimed to provide new forms of thinking about security approaches and collective security (Odello 2005). Since its first report in 2004, entitled *A more secure world: our shared responsibility* and following the precedent of the Human Development Report (1994), increased attention has been given to problems that affect collective security. These involve six clusters of threats that reflect new areas of human security within the UN system (UN 2004), including (i) economic and social threats, such as poverty; (ii) infectious disease and environmental degradation; (iii) inter-state conflict; internal conflict, including civil war, genocide and other large-scale atrocities; (iv) nuclear, radiological, chemical and biological weapons; (v) terrorism; and (vi) transnational organised crime.

It should be noted that these clusters mark an upward harmonisation of the notions of human security and human development over the last few years (Slotin & Elgin-Cossart 2013). Above all, this trend has been progressing as shown by the recent special report: *New threats to human security in the Anthropocene demanding greater solidarity* by the UN (UNDP 2022), which provides updated evidence about the new generation of interconnected threats, from which the concern about inequalities and the digital technology shift stand out.

2.3 Exploring discursive challenges: From theory to practice

It is broadly recognised that individual transnational threats are a fundamental problem at present; however, there is no unified understanding of these collective problems. There are various reasons for this, particularly in two very important areas: (i) the variety of buzzwords, concepts and indicators that relate to the notion of danger or menace and (ii) the different scope of analysis stemming from different disciplines, which includes the treatment of the issue of complexity.

On the first point, while clear differences of views remain between the concepts of threats, risks and vulnerabilities, they are often used interchangeably, leading to confusion of terms and inaccuracy. According to the Oxford English Dictionary (Simpson & Weiner 1989: 987 (vol. XIII) and 997 (vol. XVII)):

Threat is ['a declaration of hostile determination or of loss, pain, punishment, or damage to be inflicted in retribution for or conditionally upon some course, a menace. Also fig. an indication of impending evil']., while,

Risk is ['to hazard, endanger; to expose to the chance of injury or loss.']

Generally, these notions come within the framework of something that might happen against someone, or something due to a particular cause or action (threat) and through the identification of a weakness (vulnerability) and potential harm (risk). These distinctions are particularly relevant in the fields of risk management, threat assessment, strategy and security (Vellani 2021).

Moreover, these peculiarities are fundamental to understanding the bias in both perceptions from individual scholars and the treatment of a given threat by different scientific disciplines. An example of the former case is the issue of social and economic inequality (including wealth), which was ignored within the Millennium Development Goals (MDGs), markedly because of the greater focus on poverty reduction. However, its strong dynamics have led to a growing consensus that inequality marks a major threat to the global economy (Kabeer 2010). This involves recognition by social and group networks with the power to drive a global issue (see Figure 1 on discourse formation) as in the case of the global business community through the World Economic Forum, or the inclusion of inequality as a standalone goal (SDG 10) within the 17 Sustainable Development Goals (SDGS) of the 2030 Agenda for Sustainable Development, among others.

In this regard, I carried out a bibliometric analysis of publications within scientific journals between 1975 and 2020, which includes more than 2500 relevant papers on this topic obtained from the Web of Science (Clarivate Analytics 2021). The analysis shows that the most relevant areas of interest to scientific researchers involve the following items: wealth inequality, middle-income countries, health inequalities, historical inequality, economic inequality and inequality related to society and family. However, explicit reference was not made to the theme of threats of risks as shown in Figure 2. This chart shows the timeline view of these key topics, including the identification of years in which there was an exceptional interest in a topic by scholars as shown by tree-ring visualisations, which identify emergent trends of citations.

On the second aspect, regarding the treatment of threats and risks by different scientific disciplines, the specialised literature has provided different theoretical and empirical approaches to address distinctions in terms of different theories of risk, uncertainty and threats. First of all, unlike the Cold War which revolved around threats, mainly resulting from the action of a particular actor, there seems to be a shift in the interpretation of global challenges in the field of security. It is noted that the twenty-first century is permeated by the notion of risks, which by

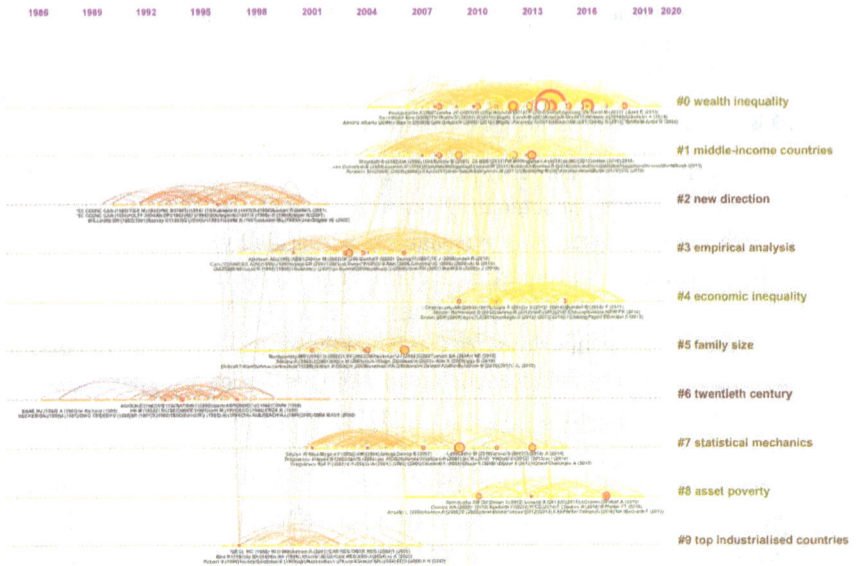

Figure 2: Timeline of key topics on economic and social inequality.
Source: Author's elaboration based on the software Citespace 6.1.R3 (Chen 2006).
Note: Tree-ring visualisations connect to the idea of emergent trends of citations (i.e the bigger the ring, the greater the number of citations in a specific year).

their variety become unpredictable or impossible to fully prevent. This means that precautionary work comes into play to reduce their occurrence.

This situation has given impetus to the topic of risk management through the idea of resilience (Dunn Cavelty & Giroux 2015). In this new framework, however, the complexity of the global challenges is conditioned by two fundamental aspects. That is, it can become both a threat and an opportunity simultaneously. In this sense, the wide range of global challenges is characterised by several elements, including (i) their high interdependence, (ii) being conceived of as a system of vulnerabilities, which depersonalises them from being a well-identified enemy as in the past and (iii) being embedded in the realm of technology. Consequently, threat representation is associated with a multidimensional perception of threat that is at once quasi-universal, multilevel, interconnected and increasingly unpredictable (Scheffran 2015; Dunn Cavelty & Giroux 2015). One example is the impact of climate change on rainfall, which accounts for recurrent extreme weather. Such new phenomena can take the form of unpredictable changes in rainfall patterns that can trigger torrential rainfall in a short time with devastating consequences in terms of flooding, landslides, destruction of infrastructure, loss of human life, human suffering, migration, etc. as in, for example, the extreme Monsoon rainfall in Pakistan in 2022 (Waqas 2022). In other words, it is possible to see cascading effects resulting from growing interdependencies.

Nonetheless, threats can be also an opportunity because they open the possibility to try to create risk prevention and mitigation mechanisms for social change (Scheffran 2015). In this context, threats, being part of a social perception, are part of a social construction, which will be shaped by key actors, such as experts, policymakers and the media, among others and, therefore, become an inherently political issue (Dunn Cavelty & Giroux 2015).

Despite this, we are still far from having a comprehensive theoretical framework for this subject as suggested by Battistelli and Galantino (2019). There exists a range of approaches and theories in various disciplines that underscore different positions on the emergence of a threat and risks, including those who try to connect the issue of security with the analysis of complex systems from a critical perspective (Masys 2013).

For instance, Table 1 highlights some of these views. Interestingly, while they emphasised the role of the state as a unit of analysis and its capacity to address security concerns, there is a clear dividing line between those approaches that seek to provide a macrostructural explanation for security issues, such as threats and risks, based on the struggle for power in the international system and other approaches that consider the behaviour of international actors as part of a social construct that needs to be explained. This is the case for political realism, wherein, despite its different versions, there is a strong preference for the imperatives of power as the main cause that enables proactive behaviour from states against threats. This contrasts with how liberalism faces special obstacles and dangers. Interestingly, while liberalism champions democracy, free trade and international cooperation as tools to reverse insecurity, neo-Marxism highlights the conflict and struggle between ruling classes and competing capitalist structures as the conditioning factors of threats, sharing in some sense similar concerns about power and conflict with classical realism and neorealism, although with specific features and particular flaws, such as arguably excessive confidence in social justice from leftist movements (Owen 2017; Brauch 2011).

This long-standing tradition of security studies has been enriched by recent approaches within constructivism. From this perspective, states' behaviour is the result of social construction that is shaped by the interrelationship of political elites and individuals, involving the interaction of ideas, beliefs, interests and social structures in the expansion and development of new threats (Jung 2019).

Of note are the various manifestations of the securitisation theory, developed by the Copenhagen School and the Paris School (Bigo & Tsoukala 2008; Stritzel 2014), the theory of the 'risk society' – and by extension to the 'world risk society' –

Table 1: Approaches to and features of the analysis of threats and risks.

Context	Classical approaches			Constructivism		
	Realism	Liberalism	(Neo) Marxism	Securitisation	World Risk Society	Hybrid Threats
Threats and Risks	States (unit of analysis)	States (unit of analysis)	States and ruling classes (unit of analysis)	States' behaviour is socially constructed and shaped by political elites and individuals, including ideas, beliefs, interests and social structures		
	Constant competition for power or security using economic, technology and military power, among other factors (assumption)	State behaviour is shaped by a normative commitment to liberal values and rational individuals and private groups (assumption)	Capitalist structures competing between highly and less-developed states, which may include alliances between ruling classes across states and conflict and struggle between the classes within countries	Security threats are socially constructed (securitisation) through speech acts of political elites. This includes the identification of existential threats, securitisation moves, emergency actions and the persuasion of the audience	Threats mutate over time. The set of social, political, ecological and individual risks (the risk society) is a consequence of the development of modern and industrial society (and its institutions) and the emergent technologies and innovation	Coordinated action by state or non-state actors in the form of hybrid threats to achieve specific political objectives and to destabilise other countries

Little emphasis on international changes (favours status quo)	Concerns for power and insecurity are to some extent overridden by the spread of cooperation based on the expansion of democracy, free markets and international institutions	Excessive reliance on strategies, tools, and actions implemented by left-wing movements and governments in their attempt to bring social justice	Over-emphasis on speech acts and under-analysis of the audience, non-discursive practices and macro-level decisions (external context), including its Eurocentric perspective	Critics emphasise the lack of nuance in treating risks, Beck's broad brushstrokes in his narrative of the development of capitalism and his West-centric perspective, among others	Excessive emphasis on the technological component and the use of conventional and unconventional, military and non-military practices (i.e. disinformation, cyberattacks, economic pressure, deployment of irregular armed groups and use of regular forces)

provided by Ulrich Beck (Beck 1992 2009 and 2016) and the most recent approach of hybrid threats (Atkinson & Chiozza 2020). All these views underlie the complexity of contemporary security challenges and the importance of state and non-state actors in triggering hazards and thus, becoming an emergent trend in the discourse about security policy.

The findings of this literature review suggest two key ideas: (i) The specialised literature provides interesting approaches to addressing the new landscape of threats for states in the twenty-first century. However, there is still a long way to go to integrate, from a comprehensive perspective, major challenges for nation-states that emerge from an increasingly complex world, including the rising importance of non-state actors, the power shift in the international system and the construction of emergent global threats; and (ii) only a few studies have analysed the construction of new threats and risks from an empirical perspective (Madrueño 2016; Cremer et al. 2022).

There is thus a need for further analysis that addresses the complexity of global threats, which can help provide global assessments of emerging global challenges and the capacity of states to offset these global "bads". This raises questions such as when and how does the emergence of contemporary global threats take place? Are we able to identify turning points of the different threats and risks over recent years? This piece of research aims to contribute to the latter point from the perspective of published research in academia.

3 Bibliometric analysis

The idea is to shed light on these previous questions by analysing the influence of academic journals in shaping contemporary discourse on global threats and risks. The sample comprises 6829 publications within the WoS database, which allow us to retrieve complete information from leading academic journals in relation to abstracts, keywords, authors, institutional affiliations and cited references, based on articles, book chapters, data papers, early access, proceedings papers and retracted publications. The WoS database as a key large platform includes other relevant databases such as the Science Citation Index Expanded (SCI-EXPANDED), the Social Science Citation Index and the Arts & Humanities Citation Index (AHCI).

I performed a bibliometric analysis using the software CiteSpace 6.1.R3, which detects and displays patterns and trends in the scientific literature. This technique aims to identify scientific trends and hot topics based on clusters or networks of research that can be visualised in different co-citation networks. These clusters follow a hierarchical order where the largest networks represent those references that are most highly cited in academic journals.

Table 2 shows the cluster network in the field of global threats and risks. The clusters are labelled by index terms based on cited references, thus indicating major areas of research in this literature. Figure 3 elaborates on this information by showing the largest clusters in this analysis. It is relevant to note that the size and relevance of each cluster are determined by different extraction methods, within which a silhouette value stands out that measures the homogeneity of a cluster and the Log-Likelihood Ratio (LLR) that provides the most likely words in each cluster. This also means that the higher the silhouette score (values closest to one), the better its consistency.

The empirical evidence suggests that the largest cluster #0 with 179 entries and a silhouette value of 0.863 is labelled as global change. The second largest cluster (#1) has 158 members, followed by Cluster #2 with 144 members. The first three clusters contain more than a hundred members in each network, which means that they are composed of at least 100 nodes of citations. Therefore, their overall citation hallmark is very positive.

Table 2: Summary of the five largest clusters in global threats and risk research.

ClusterID	Size (nodes)	Silhouette	Label (LLR)	Label (MI)	Average Year
0	179	0,863	**global change**	infectious agent	2009
1	158	0,857	**extinction risk**	infectious agent	2011
2	144	0,98	**coronavirus disease**	sample collection transport	2019
3	93	0,912	**predicting susceptibility**	comprehensive global mammal conservation strategy introduction	2003
4	68	0,985	**antibiotic resistance**	sustainable development goal	2014
5	56	0,934	**zoonotic viruses**	aedes aegypti	2011

Notes: The Silhouette index represents the homogeneity of a cluster. The higher the value, the more homogeneous the cluster and the more independent from other clusters. This value can range from −1 to +1. Additional extraction methods are the Log-Likelihood Ratio (LLR), the Mutual Information (MI) and the average year, which represent both the most salient aspects of the clusters and reflect the unique aspects of each cluster.

To summarise, there are six hot topics in the field of global threats and risks, which are ranked in order of importance: (i) global change; (ii) extinction risk; (iii) coronavirus disease; (iv) predicting susceptibility; (v) antibiotic resistance; and (vi) zoonotic viruses.

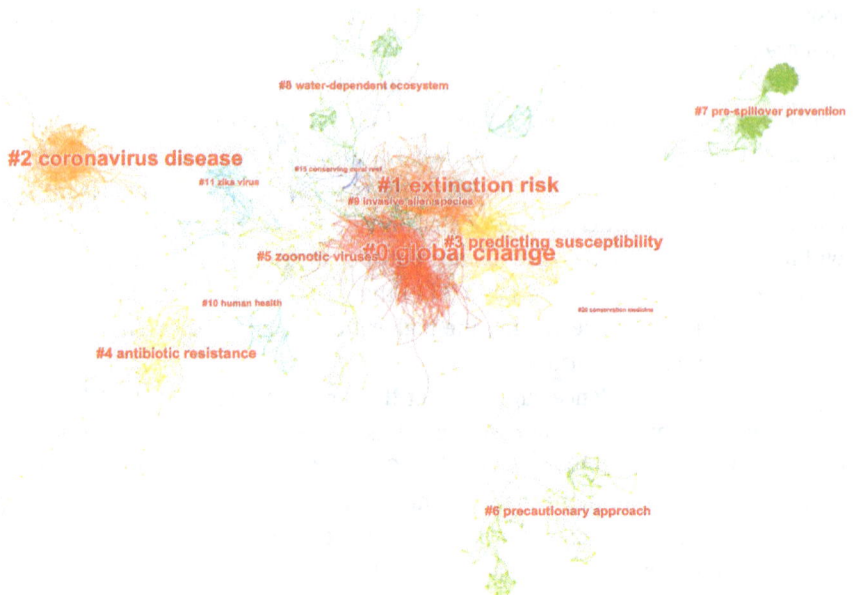

Figure 3: Research networks for threats and risks.

Most important is the analysis of "citation bursts" that comes from applying Kleinberg's burst detection algorithm (Chen 2006, 364). These bursts are an indicator of special events in the citation process where a publication receives outstanding attention from the scientific community in terms of extraordinarily large nodes. They can be seen graphically as the surge of citations in terms of concentric circles. Figure 4 illustrates this pattern of citations over a short period, which can be observable in a sustained manner (multiple years) or a single event (one year). It can be seen, for instance, that within Cluster #0 – about global change – there are multiple citation bursts between 2004 and 2019. Something similar happens with Cluster #1 related to extinction risk. The most recent example is Cluster #2 which provides evidence for the onset of the coronavirus disease impacting the emergence of a surge of citations in 2020.

Table 3 provides the same idea from a different perspective. It shows information about fast-growing topics in relation to the strongest citation bursts over more than four years. Graphically, it is important to note that the beginning of a red segment marks the beginning of the burst period, whereas its end is represented by the end of the red line. In this case, the detection of bursts is the first step in determining whether we are witnessing "active areas of research" or "emerging trends", as in the evidence provided by the first two largest clusters.

Here, it is possible to highlight two main findings. First, while this research has included the period between 1945 and 2021, the evidence in leading journals about threats and risks begins from 1990 onwards. Second, these publications focus on hot topics, such as climate change, global warming and its effects on biodiversity extinction and more recently, the other main topic has been the issue of the coronavirus pandemic.

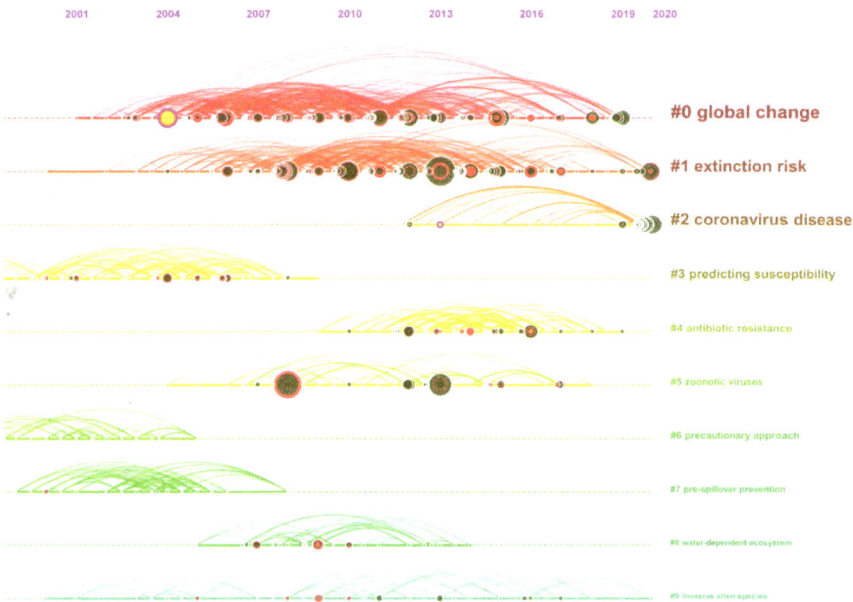

Figure 4: Research networks for threats and risks within a timeline view.

3.1 Most influential papers, disciplines, countries and languages

The analysis of citation bursts strengthens the idea of a clear pattern to new discourse formation on threats and risks. In this regard, Table 4 provides the top-ranked items by bursts. The largest emergent trends can be found in Cluster #0, based on the papers by Thomas et al., in 2004, and Elith, et al., in 2006, dealing with the topics of species, evolution and conservation. Then, three key papers in 2008 attracted the attention of scholars in the field of infectious diseases and extinction risk. These involved work by Jones, et al., in 2008 within Cluster #5, Mace, et al., and Schipper, et al., in 2008, corresponding to Cluster #1.

Table 3: Top references and topics with the strongest citation bursts (four years or more).

References	Topic	Year	Strength	Begin	End	1945 - 2021
Purves A, 2000, P ROY SOC B-BIOL SCI, V267, P1947	Extinction risk / declining species	2000	4.9	2002	2008	
Owens IPF, 2000, P NATL ACAD SCI USA, V97, P12144	Extinction risk / ecology		4.5	2002	2007	
WorldHealthOrganization, 2002, WORLD HLTH REP 2002	Human health	2002	4.5	2003	2007	
Parmesan C, 2003, NATURE, V421, P37	Climate change	2003	7.7	2006	2011	
Root TL, 2003, NATURE, V421, P57	Global warming		7.2	2009	2011	
Thomas CD, 2004, NATURE, V427, P145	Extinction risk / climate change	2004	21.4	2005	2012	
Stuart SN, 2004, SCIENCE, V306, P1783	Extinction / amphibian species		13.1	2008	2012	
Cardillo M, 2005, SCIENCE, V309, P1239	Mammal extinctions / climate change	2005	10.2	2007	2013	
Lockwood JL, 2005, TRENDS ECOL EVOL, V20, P223	Alien species and climate change		4.9	2008	2012	
Brooks TM, 2006, SCIENCE, V313, P58	Global Biodiversity Conservation		8.1	2008	2013	
Cardillo M, 2006, P NATL ACAD SCI USA, V103, P4157	Extinction risk / mammal conservation		6.0	2008	2012	
Pounds JA, 2006, NATURE, V439, P161	Extinctions / epidemic disease / global warming	2006	5.4	2008	2014	
Elith J, 2006, ECOGRAPHY, V29, P129	Conservation species / ecology		17.4	2009	2014	
Phillips SJ, 2006, ECOL MODEL, V190, P231	Species / environment		14.1	2009	2014	
Rodrigues ASL, 2006, TRENDS ECOL EVOL, V21, P71	Global conservation plants and animals		11.3	2009	2014	
Parmesan C, 2006, ANNU REV ECOL EVOL S, V37, P637	Ecology / Recent Climate Change		10.8	2010	2014	
Jetz W, 2007, PLOS BIOL, V5, P1211	Climate and Land-Use Change	2007	4.6	2008	2015	
Araujo MB, 2007, TRENDS ECOL EVOL, V22, P42	Species / climate change		10.2	2009	2015	
Jones KE, 2008, NATURE, V451, P990	Emerging infectious diseases		17.0	2009	2016	
Phillips SJ, 2008, ECOGRAPHY, V31, P161	Species distributions		9.9	2010	2015	
Brook BW, 2008, TRENDS ECOL EVOL, V23, P453	Extinction drivers / global change		9.4	2010	2016	
Carpenter KE, 2008, SCIENCE, V321, P560	Extinction risk / climate change		9.4	2010	2016	
Keith DA, 2008, BIOL LETTERS, V4, P560	Extinction risk / climate change	2008	8.4	2010	2014	
Maoc GM, 2008, CONSERV BIOL, V22, P1424	Extinction Risk / Threatened Species		16.3	2011	2016	
Schipper J, 2008, SCIENCE, V322, P225	World's Land and Marine Mammals		14.3	2011	2015	
Cardillo M, 2008, P ROY SOC B-BIOL SCI, V275, P1441	Extinction / decline in mammals		5.8	2011	2016	
Halpem BS, 2008, SCIENCE, V319, P948	Human activity / Marine Ecosystems		10.1	2012	2016	
Heller NE, 2009, BIOL CONSERV, V142, P14	Biodiversity management/ climate change	2009	7.9	2010	2016	
Davidson AD, 2009, P NATL ACAD SCI USA, V106	Ecological pathways/ extinction		7.7	2011	2017	
Hoffmann M, 2010, SCIENCE, V330, P1503	Conservation / World's Vertebrates		12.5	2011	2018	
Butchart SHM, 2010, SCIENCE, V328, P1164	Global Biodiversity	2010	11.7	2011	2018	
Elith J, 2010, METHODS ECOL EVOL, V1, P330	Shifting species / environmental change		7.4	2014	2018	
Godfray HCJ, 2010, SCIENCE, V327, P812	Food system / environment		4.7	2014	2018	
Elith J, 2011, DIVERS DISTRIB, V17, P43	Modelling species distributions		8.3	2012	2019	
Barnosky AD, 2011, NATURE, V471, P51	Earth / mass extinction	2011	7.1	2012	2019	
Dawson TP, 2011, SCIENCE, V332, P53	Predictions / biodiversity Conservation		5.9	2013	2018	
Chen IC, 2011, SCIENCE, V333, P1024	Shifts of Species / Climate Warming		6.3	2015	2019	
Mantyka-Pringle CS, 2012, GLOBAL CHANGE BIOL, V18, P1239	Climate and habitat loss / biodiversity		5.6	2013	2018	
Kriticos DJ, 2012, METHODS ECOL EVOL, V3, P53	Future climate scenarios		5.5	2014	2018	
IUCN, 2012, IUCN RED LIST CAT CR, V0, P0	Risk of global extinction	2012	5.4	2014	2019	
Taylor KE, 2012, B AM METEOROL SOC, V93, P485	Climate variability and climate change		5.4	2015	2019	
Magioranakos AP, 2012, CLIN MICROBIOL INFEC, V18, P268	Disease Control		6.9	2017	2021	
Bhat S, 2013, NATURE, V496, P504	Infection and disease		6.7	2014	2019	
Foden WB, 2013, PLOS ONE, V8, P0	Climate Change / Vulnerable Species	2013	8.0	2015	2019	
Bohm M, 2013, BIOL CONSERV, V157, P372	Global conservation / extinction risk		6.3	2015	2019	
IPCC, 2014, IMPACTS ADAPTATION V, V0, P0	Climate change, adaptation and vulnerability	2014	6.4	2016	2019	
Dirzo R, 2014, SCIENCE, V345, P401	Animal biodiversity loss / climate change		4.4	2017	2021	
Pacifici M, 2015, NAT CLIM CHANGE, V5, P215	Vulnerability to climate change	2015	10.3	2016	2019	
Ceballos G, 2015, SCI ADV, V1, P0	Mass extinction		5.1	2017	2021	
IUCN, 2016, RED LIST THREATENED, V0, P0	Risk of global extinction	2016	4.7	2016	2021	
Fick SE, 2017, INT J CLIMATOL, V37, P4302	Climate change	2017	4.4	2018	2021	

Source: Author's elaboration with data retrieved from Clarivate Analytics (2021).

Complementing this information, Table 5 shows the most cited articles. The top-ranked publications by citation counts belong to Cluster #2. These include Huang, et al., and Wang et al., in 2020, with hot topics about the clinical features of the coronavirus. The third is Hansen et al. (2013) in Cluster #1, regarding the issue of global forest change, with a citation count of 51. Then Bhatt et al. (2013) and Jones et al. (2008) in Cluster #5 follow in relation to the topic of infectious diseases, with similar citation counts of 50.

In terms of the institutional affiliation of these top scholars, their corresponding geographical locations and the journals where they published their work, there is a clear bias towards the Anglo-Saxon academic world. When we consider the analysis of citation bursts, there is a clear bias towards authors based in Western academic institutions in the UK, Australia, Switzerland and the US, where just a few universities and research centres have a leading role. This involves the University of Leeds, the University of Melbourne, the Institute of Zoology in London and Imperial College London. Regarding the main scientific journals, it is possible to highlight, in order of relevance, the following groups: Nature Ecography, Conservation Biology, Science and Ecological Modelling.

The fact that the concentration of academic work in high-impact journals is carried out by a relatively small group of academics working in countries of the global North and centres and institutes of recognised international prestige illustrates the de facto gap of epistemic inequality and marginalisation faced by researchers from the global South, who despite being drivers and promoters of innovative approaches, theories and categories in various disciplines, continue to face significant barriers to access, as stated by Acharya (2014) and Noda (2020).

Nonetheless, if the criterion is changed to emphasise publications by citation count, the image varies to underlie the emergence of Chinese scholars based in Wuhan, China and their work on the topic of coronavirus within two medical institutions. This contrasts with other key scholars within Cluster #1 and Cluster #5. These authors are based in the US and the UK, working at the Universities of Maryland and Oxford and the Institute of Zoology in London. Lastly, this group of authors have published their work in renowned journals, such as the Lancet, JAMA, Science and Nature.

Finally, it is also worth mentioning that there is a clear preponderance of disciplines from the natural sciences at the expense of disciplines from the social sciences as shown in Figure 5. For instance, according to the WoS categories and the topic under study, there is a significant concentration of the fields of environmental sciences and health sciences. They account for about 73 per cent of the 220 WoS categories, whereas social sciences, such as economics, sociology, political science, history, international relations, anthropology, development studies and philosophy, among others, account for around five per cent of the total categories.

Table 4: Citation Bursts.

Authors	Title	Journal	# Burst	Authors' countries of affiliation	Institutional Affiliation	Cluster ID
Thomas, Chris D. et al., 2004	Extinction risk from climate change	Nature	21.42	UK	University of Leeds	0
Elith J., et al., 2006,	Novel methods improve prediction of species' distributions from occurrence data	Ecography	17.44	Australia	Univesity of Melbourne	0
Jones KE, 2008	Global trends in emerging infectious diseases	Nature	17.04	UK	Institute of Zoology, Zoological Society of London	5
Mace GM, et, al. 2008,	Quantification of extinction risk: IUCN's system for classifying threatened species	Conservation Biology	16.29	UK	Imperial College London	1
Schipper J. et al., 2008	The Status of the World's Land and Marine Mammals	Science	14.28	Switzerland and US	International Union for Conservation of Nature / Center for Applied Biodiversity	1
Phillips SJ, et al., 2006	Maximum entropy modeling of species geographic distributions	Ecological Modelling	14.13	US	AT&T Labs-Research,	0
Stuart SN, et al., 2004	Status and Trends of Amphibian Declines and Extinctions Worldwide	Science	13.12	US	IUCN Species Survival Commission/ Conservation Intl. Center for A. Biodiversity	3

Hoffmann M. et al., 2010	The Impact of Conservation on the Status of the World's Vertebrates	Science	12.52	UK	IUCN SSC Species Survival Commission/UN Environment Programme World CMC	1
Butchart SHM. Et al, 2010	Global biodiversity: indicators of recent declines	Science	11.7	UK	United Nations Environment Programme World Conservation Monitoring Centre	1

Table 5: Citation COUNTS.

References	Title	Journal	Citation Counts	Authors' countries of affiliation	Institutional Affiliation	Cluster ID
Huang CL, et al., 2020	Clinical features of patients infected with 2019 novel coronavirus in Wuhan, China	The Lancet	87	China	Jin Yin-tan Hospital	2
Wang DW, et al., 2020	Clinical Characteristics of 138 Hospitalized Patients With 2019 Novel Coronavirus–Infected Pneumonia in Wuhan, China	JAMA	52	China	Department of Critical Care Medicine, Zhongnan Hospital of Wuhan University	2
Hansen MC, et al., 2013	High-resolution global maps of 21st-century forest cover change	Science	51	US	Department of Geographical Sciences, University of Maryland	1
Bhatt S, et al., 2013	The global distribution and burden of dengue	Nature	50	UK	Department of Zoology, University of Oxford,	5
Jones KE, 2008	Global trends in emerging infectious diseases	Nature	50	UK	Institute of Zoology, Zoological Society of London	5
Zhou F, et al, 2020	Clinical course & risk factors for mortality of adult inpatients w COVID-19 in Wuhan	The Lancet	48	China	Center of Respiratory Medicine	2
Mace GM. et al., 2008	Quantification of extinction risk: IUCN's system for classifying threatened species	Conservation Biology	47	UK	Centre for Population Biology and Division of Biology, Imperial College London	1

Hoffmann M. et al., 2010	The Impact of Conservation on the Status of the World's Vertebrates	Science	46	UK	IUCN SSC Species Survival Commission, c/o United Nations Environment Programme World Conservation Monitoring Centre	1
Butchart SHM. Et al, 2010	Globa biodiversity: indicators of recent declines	Science	43	UK	United Nations Environment Programme World Conservation Monitoring Centre	1
Thomas, Chris D. et al., 2004	Extinction risk from climate change	Nature	42	UK	University of Leeds	0

Source: Author's elaboration with data retrieved from Clarivate Analytics (2021).

Figure 5: Treemap chart of the most relevant disciplines in the field of threats and risks.
Source: Author's elaboration based on the Web of Science

4 Implications for discourse formation and turning points

The information from academic journals and the bibliometric analysis that I have collated provides an overview of the current status and the emerging trends about the new transnational threats and risks. As seen above, the discourse on global threats and risks is still in the process of formation. While this discourse contains distinctive features at a theoretical level to create a hegemonic discourse, there is a gap between a broad recognition of these threats and risks and a comprehensive approach which is arguably required to identify and deal with transnational harms. More important for this research purpose is the question of what makes a specific problem become a global threat.

The literature review has identified several discourse factors, which offer a complex constellation of relationships. It is assumed that, regardless of the approach, there is a combination of steps behind the emergence of new concerns in the form of threats and risks, including the interaction between key actors, individuals and political and socioeconomic circumstances. This means, as seen above, that global threats cannot be detached from their historical context nor the forces that shape their perception, where external agents and power structures play a key role. This is the case of academic publishing practices in top journals and also open-access publications, which not only are part of a highly concentrated market but also promote monopoly rents to large publishing companies, at the expense of academic institutions (Puehringer, et al. 2021). In particular, this affects the social sciences, which face a publication bias relative to the natural sciences as a result of their greater proclivity to produce null results or their lack of replicability, among other factors (Fanelli 2010; Peplow 2014). Finally, these elements come into play within the social construction of a discourse that is fuelled by the complexity of the planetary challenges.

This paper argues that to some extent at least, there is a link between the research interests of scholars and pundits and the formation of perceptions regarding new global threats and risks. More importantly, it seems to be possible to join the dots between theory and empirical evidence regarding discourse formation, although more research is needed in this area. This analysis shows that academic researchers seem to react to the external environment of threats and risks, thereby adding momentum to the process of discourse formation as will be shown below. The results obtained provide at least three relevant findings in the construction of discourse on threats and risks.

1. While a variety of topics can be identified directly as threats and risks over contemporary academic concerns in top journals, the academic literature ac-

knowledges this condition explicitly from the 1990s onwards. This is neither a coincidence nor a trivial matter. It is widely acknowledged that the fall of the Berlin Wall and the end of the Cold War opened the door to a new era of international order and the world-system (by way of a turning point), including a change in the logic of accumulation by increasing trade and financial integration, which redefined the role of the state in the economy and pro-market policies at the global level (Wallerstein 2000; Bagchi 2018). This also had an impact on the understanding of international relations and a shift in security paradigms as a result of the proliferation of global interdependencies and the emergence of new global threats in the twenty-first century.

2. Burst detection seems a plausible explanation for the identification of turning points as well, through the recognition of hot topics that receive particular attention from the academic community. Again, and without entering into a robust statistical analysis in describing causality, qualitative analysis suggests that there is a reaction on the part of academic publications to the emergence of global threats, with increasing threat perception having a cascading effect in subsequent years. This is the case of two global issues that are part of the discourse of global threats fostered by the UN since 2004: climate change (i.e. global warming, biodiversity extinction) and the COVID-19 pandemic. The former illustrates different concerns that started in 1990 but, interestingly, received particular attention in three relevant years: 2004, 2008 and 2013. These years underlie the effects of previous information provided, among others, by different reports from the third Intergovernmental Panel on Climate Change in 2000, 2001 and 2007 and a broad recognition of this global problem by public opinion since 2004 concerning the first major books, films and artworks on global warming appearing in that year.[1] The other example is the coronavirus outbreak in 2019, which triggered a turning point for foreign affairs due to its severe impact on a multilevel framework. It had an enormous influence on people and communities around the world and business activity, including the idea of the emergence of new threats to human security. The consequence has been a decline in the Human Development Index (HDI), on a global scale, which had never stopped growing from the 1990s until the outbreak of the pandemic. The HDI still has not recovered to its pre-pandemic level (UNDP 2022).

3. The focus on threats and risks by the academic community reflects a bias in the creation of knowledge and its repercussions on the formation of discourses. The most influential research, in terms of the production of several

---

1 See https://history.aip.org/climate/timeline.htm (Retrieved 10.03.2022).

highly cited papers, comes from Western scholars from the US and UK in the field of climate change, while a new feature highlights the relevance of authors from the global South, in particular from China, with the emergence of the coronavirus disease. This is not a minor issue because it could begin to show changes in the international political atmosphere and the ability of emergent powers to influence the formation of discourse, as in the case of China.

5 Conclusion

Over time, there has been a growing social perception in different geographical regions of the world that we are facing increasing global challenges which translate not only into social insecurity but also into threats and risks to the very sustainability of the planet and human life. This is remarkable on several fronts: social media, the negative effects of transnational problems in our everyday life (such as climate change, health threats and growing inequalities), the focus on urgent global challenges within the institutional agenda of international institutions, national governments and civil society organisations, among others. Accordingly, this has allowed for an emerging discourse on global threats and interconnected risks, which, however, still shows a lack of cohesion given the difficulty in understanding the complexity of the international system and its multiple challenges. In either case, the notoriety of these hazards and their discursive features do not prevent them from eventually becoming a dominant discourse on human security and global development.

It is true, however, that there are still obstacles to overcome as in the case of both the different treatment of interconnected and mutually reinforcing threats and risks by a variety of scientific disciplines and how scientific knowledge understands the issue of increasing complexity on a global scale.

This research has been able to prove partially our three main hypotheses. It seems that they can be grouped usefully into two. The first is that the bibliometric analysis carried out was able to identify the presence of turning points concerning joint transnational threats and risks and two individual threats: climate change and the COVID-19 pandemic. The evidence suggests, as shown above, that 1990 was the breakpoint for the analysis of multiple threats and risks in scholarly writing. The other two individual cases were the issue of climate change which became particularly relevant in 2004, and the most recent pandemic in 2020. Both are years that brought about a change in several areas of policy at international, national, regional and local levels.

The second and third hypotheses seem to work together under the idea that researchers play a supporting role in the creation of hegemonic discourses. At this point, it is undeniable that emergent discourses involve a variety of actors, structures and dimensions that are beyond the scope of the empirical analysis in this paper. However, the partial evidence provided indicates that publications of the academic community are not the main discursive element behind the new global threats, but part of a broader social construction, yet their influence helps to reinforce complex discursive practices. The evidence surrounding the third hypothesis supports the view that scholars located in the global North (in countries such as the UK, US, Australia and Switzerland) exert substantial dominance in the promotion of discursive practices upon threats and risks, specifically within the most influential literature on climate change. Nonetheless, it is also relevant to note that other actors can join in these hegemonic practices as shown by the leading role of Chinese scholars in the research connected to the coronavirus outbreak, which can account for the reality of a new multipolar and asymmetric world.

These results may be useful for specialists who are interested in understanding the evolution and relevance of drivers of change in world politics and global security, and those who seek a more accurate appreciation of the notion of turning points through the lens of empirical scientific research.

References

Acharya, A. 2014. Global International Relations (IR) and Regional Worlds: A New Agenda for International Studies. *International Studies Quarterly* 58(4). 647–659.

Atkinson, C., and Chiozza, G. 2021. Hybrid Threats and the Erosion of Democracy from Within: US Surveillance and European Security. *Chinese Political Science Review* 6. 119–142. https://doi.org/10.1007/s41111-020-00161-2

Bagchi, A. K. 2018. The 1990s: The Fall of the Berlin Wall, Globalization, and Crises. In J. A. Ocampo, A. Chowdhury, and D. Alarcón (eds.), *The World Economy through the Lens of the United Nations, Initiative for Policy Dialogue*, 148–169. Oxford: Oxford Academic.

Brauch, H. G. 2011. Concepts of Security Threats, Challenges, Vulnerabilities and Risks. In H. G. Brauch, Ú. Oswald Spring, C. Mesjasz, J. Grin, P. Kameri-Mbote, B. Chourou, P. Dunay and J. Birkmann (eds.), *Coping with Global Environmental Change, Disasters and Security*, 61–106. Hexagon Series on Human and Environmental Security and Peace, vol 5. Berlin, Heidelberg: Springer. https://doi.org/10.1007/978-3-642-17776-7_2

Bhatt S, et al. 2013. The global distribution and burden of dengue. *Nature* Apr 25;496(7446). 504–507.

Bisiada, M. 2021. Discursive structures and power relations in Covid-19 knowledge production. *Humanities and Social Science Communications* 8(s248). 1–10. https://doi.org/10.1057/s41599-021-00935-2

Biccum, A. 2009. Theorising Continuities between Empire & Development: Toward a New Theory of History. In M. Duffield and V. Hewitt (eds.), *Empire, Development and Colonialism: The Past in the Present*, 146–160. Cape Town: Boydell & Brewer.

Beck, U. 1992 [1986]. *The Risk Society*. London: Sage.

Beck, U. 2009 [2007]. *World at Risk*. Cambridge: Polity Press.

Beck, U. 2016. *The Metamorphosis of the World*. Cambridge: Polity Press.

Bigo, D., and A. Tsoukala. 2008. "Understanding (In)Security". In D. Bigo, and A. Tsoukala (eds.), *Terror, Insecurity and Liberty. Illiberal practices of liberal regimes after 9/11*, 1–9. New York: Routledge.

Battistelli, F., and M. G. Galantino. 2019. Dangers, risks and threats: An alternative conceptualization to the catch-all concept of risk. *Current Sociology* 67(1). 64–78. https://doi.org/10.1177/0011392118793675

Bowler, P. 2017. *A History of the Future. Prophets of Progress from H.G. Wells to Isaac Asimov*. Cambridge: Cambridge University Press.

Braudel, F., and I. Wallerstein. 2009. History and the Social Sciences: The Longue Durée. *Review* (Fernand Braudel Center) 32(2). 171–203.

Capra, F. 1982. *The Turning Point. Science, Society, and the Rising Culture*. Bantam Books: NY.

Chen, C. 2006. CiteSpace II: Detecting and visualizing emerging trends and transient patterns in scientific literatur". *Journal of the Association for Information Science and Technology*. 57(3). 359–377.

Clarivate Analytics. 2021. Web of Science, available at https://webofknowledge.com/

Cremer, F., B. Sheehan, M. Fortmann, A. N. Kia, M. Mullins, F. Murphy and S. Materne. 2022. Cyber risk and cybersecurity: a systematic review of data availability. *The Geneva Papers on Risk and Insurance – Issues and Practice* 47. 698–736. https://doi.org/10.1057/s41288-022-00266-6

De Sousa Santos, B., and M. Meneses. 2020. *Knowledges Born in the Struggle. Constructing the Epistemologies of the Global South*. Palgrave: NY.

Dunn Cavelty, M., and J. Giroux. 2015. The good, the bad, and the sometimes ugly: Complexity as both threat and opportunity in the vital systems security discourse. In Emilian Kavalski (ed.), *World Politics at the Edge of Chaos: Reflections on Complexity and Global Life*, 209–227. Albany, NY: SUNY Press.

Fairfax, D. 2021. *The Red Years of Cahiers du cinéma (1968–1973)*, Vol. I, Ideology and Politics. Amsterdam University Press.

Fanelli, D. 2010. "Positive" Results Increase Down the Hierarchy of the Sciences". *PloS ONE* 5(4). e10068–10

Foucault, M. 1972. *The Archaeology of knowledge and the discourse on language*. New York: Pantheon Books.

Fouquet, R. 2016. Historical energy transitions: Speed, prices and system transformation. *Energy Research & Social Science* 22. 7–12.

Geiß, R., and N. Melzer (eds.). 2021. *The Oxford Handbook of the International Law of Global Security*, Oxford Handbooks online edn. Oxford Academic. https://doi.org/10.1093/law/9780198827276.001.0001

Hansen, M. C. et al., 2013. High-Resolution Global Maps of 21st-Century Forest Cover Change. *Science* 342. 850–853. DOI:10.1126/science.1244693

Hickel, J. 2021. The anti-colonial politics of degrowth. *Political Geography* 88(2021). 102404. https://doi.org/10.1016/j.polgeo.2021.102404

Jones, K., Patel, N., Levy, M. et al. 2008. Global trends in emerging infectious diseases. *Nature* 451. 990–993.

Jung, H. 2019. The Evolution of Social Constructivism in Political Science: Past to Present. *SAGE Open* 9(1). https://doi.org/10.1177/2158244019832703

Kabeer, N. 2010. *Can the MDGs provide a pathway to social justice? The challenge of intersecting inequalities*. NY: IDS and MDG Achievement Fund.

Kavalski, E. (ed.). 2015. *World politics at the edge of chaos: reflections on complexity and global life*. New York: Suny Press.

Keynes, J. M. 1936. *The General Theory Of Employment, Interest And Money*. Cambridge: Cambridge University Press.

Laclau, E. 2005. *On Populist Reason*. London & New York, NY: Verso

Luhmann, N. 1993. *Risk: A Sociological Theory*. Berlin and New York: De Gruyter.

Madrueño, R. 2016. Human Security and the New Global Threats: Discourse, Taxonomy and Implications. *Global Policy* 7(2). 156–173. Doi: 10.1111/1758-5899.12290

Madrueño, R., and S. Tezanos. 2018. The contemporary development discourse: Analysing the influence of development studies' journals. *World Development* 109(September). 334–345. https://doi.org/10.1016/j.worlddev.2018.05.005

Noda, Orion. 2020. Replication Data for Epistemic Hegemony: The Western Straitjacket and Post-Colonial Scars in Academic Publishing. *Revista Brasileira de Política Internacional* 63(1). e007. http://dx.doi.org/10.1590/0034-7329202000107

Mitchell, M. 2010. *Complexity: A guided tour*. New York: Oxford University Press.

Masys, A. J. 2013. Human Security – A View Through the Lens of Complexity. In T. Gilbert, M. Kirkilionis, G. Nicolis (eds.), *Proceedings of the European Conference on Complex Systems* 2012, 325–335. Springer Proceedings in Complexity: Cham: Springer. https://doi.org/10.1007/978-3-319-00395-5_43

Meadows, Donella H., Dennis L. Meadows, J. Randers and W. Behrens III. 1972. *The Limits to Growth. A Report for the Club of Rome's Project on the Predicament of Mankind*. New York: Universe Books.

Motzkin, G. 2005. On the Notion of Historical (Dis) Continuity: Reinhart Koselleck's Construction of the Sattelzeit. *Contributions to the History of Concepts* 1(2). 145–158.

Piger, J. 2020. Turning Points and Classification. In P. Fuleky (eds.), *Macroeconomic Forecasting in the Era of Big Data*, 585–624. Advanced Studies in Theoretical and Applied Econometrics, vol 52. Cham: Springer.

Peplow, M. 2014. Social sciences suffer from severe publication bias. *Nature*. https://doi.org/10.1038/nature.2014.15787

PoReSo (The research group Power, Resistance and Social Change). 2020. Challenges to knowledge-making: the intricate interrelation of knowledge and resistance. *Journal of Political Power* 13(2). 169–178. doi: 10.1080/2158379X.2020.1764795

Puehringer, S., J. Rath and T. Griesebner. 2021. The political economy of academic publishing: On the commodification of a public good. *PLoS ONE* 16(6).e0253226. https://doi.org/10.1371/journal.pone.0253226

Odello, M. 2005. Commentary on the United Nations' High-Level Panel on Threats, Challenges and Change. *Journal of Conflict & Security Law* 10(2). 231–262.

O'Neill, D. W. 2020. Beyond green growth. *Nature Sustainability* 3. 260–261.

Owen IV, J. M. Liberalism and Security. *Oxford Research Encyclopedia of International Studies*. 30 Nov. 2017. Accessed 15 Nov. 2022.

Ozga, J. T. 2020. Elites and Expertise: The Changing Material Production of Knowledge for Policy. In G. Fan and T. Popkewitz (eds.), *Handbook of Education Policy Studies*, 63–69. Singapore: Springer. https://doi.org/10.1007/978-981-13-8347-2_3

Rockström, J., W. Steffen, K. Noone, A. Persson, F. S. Chapin III, E. Lambin, T. M. Lenton, M. Scheffer, C. Folke, H. Schellnhuber, B. Nykvist, C. A. De Wit, T. Hughes, S. van der Leeuw, H. Rodhe, S. Sörlin, P. K. Snyder, R. Costanza, U. Svedin, M. Falkenmark, L. Karlberg, R. W. Corell, V. J. Fabry, J. Hansen, B. Walker, D. Liverman, K. Richardson, P. Crutzen and J. Foley. 2009. Planetary boundaries: exploring the safe operating space for humanity. *Ecology and Society* 14(2). 32. http://www.ecologyandsociety.org/vol14/iss2/art32/

Scheffran, J. 2015. Complexity and Stability in Human-Environment Interaction The Transformation from Climate Risk Cascades to Viable Adaptive Networks. In *World Politics at the Edge of Chaos: Reflections on Complexity and Global*. New York: SUNY Press.

Simon, D. 2006. Separated by Common Ground? Bringing (Post)Development and (Post)Colonialism Together. *The Geographical Journal* 172(1). 10–21

Simpson, J. A., and E. S. C. Weiner. 1989. *The Oxford English Dictionary*, vol. XIII and XVII. Oxford: Clarendon Press.

Singh, S. 2012. *New Megatrends. Implications for our Future Lives*. Palgrave Macmillan: New York.

Slotin, J., and M. Elgin-Cossart, M. 2013. Why Would Peace Be Controversial at the United Nations? Negotiations Toward a Post 2015 Development Framework. New York University Center on International Cooperation: New York.

Sovacool, B. K. 2016. How long will it take? Conceptualizing the temporal dynamics of energy transitions. *Energy Research & Social Science* 13. 202–215.

Stritzel, H. 2014. Securitization Theory and the Copenhagen School. In *Security in Translation*, 11–37. New Security Challenges Series. London: Palgrave Macmillan. https://doi.org/10.1057/9781137307576_2

Trüper, H., D. Chakrabart and S. Subrahmanyam (eds.). 2015. *Historical Teleologies in the Modern World*. London: Bloomsbury.

UNDP. 1994. *Human Development Report*. New York: Oxford University Press.

UNDP. 2022. *Special Report. New threats to human security in the Anthropocene Demanding greater solidarity*. New York: United Nations.

United Nations. 2004. *Report of the High-level Panel on Threats, Challenges and Change. A More Secure World: Our Shared Responsibility*. New York: United Nations.

United Nations. 2020. *Report of the UN Economist Network for the UN 75th Anniversary Shaping the Trends of Our Time*. New York: UNDESA.

Vellani, K. 2021. *Unraveled: An Evidence-Based Approach to Understanding and Preventing Crime*. Texas: Threat Analysis Groups.

Wallerstein, I. 2000. Globalization or the Age of Transition? A Longterm view of the Trajectory of the World-System. *Asian Perspective* 24(2). 5–26

Waqas, A. M. 2022. Pakistan's floods flow from climate injustice. *Science* 378(6619). 482.

Ziai, A. 2016. *Development discourse and global history. From colonialism to the sustainable development goals*. London: Routledge.

Nora Schrader-Rashidkhan

On the precipice of the unknown: Discussing the paradigm of uncertainty as a political challenge to Western democracies

Abstract: From a peace and conflict perspective, it is a settled fact that "uncertainty is endemic" (Daase and Kessler 2007: 412). There is considerable body of research linking uncertainty – mostly understood as a perception of risk due to incomplete information about adversaries – to violent conflict and war, and being forced to act under tense conditions with limited knowledge is a well-known problem. This perspective is considered helpful for understanding "new", looming global threats that currently challenge Western policymakers. Drawing on the rich fount of knowledge of peace and conflict studies regarding uncertainty, this chapter focuses on the question of whether there is something qualitatively new about some of these vividly discussed challenges. The chapter adopts a systematisation of threats to develop an argument about core characteristics and distinguish emergent turning points, as appropriate. This interpretation is expected to identify qualitative differences within current political challenges and assess their inherent "turning point potential" in these uncertain times.

Keywords: uncertainty, risk, unknowns, turning points, conflict studies

1 When the "Unthinkable" becomes reality

In February 2022, after some months of military build-up, about 150,000 Russian troops were found to be deployed close to the Ukrainian border. Russian Armed Forces conducted large-scale military exercises with Belarus, and separatist leaders in Eastern Ukraine urged Russian-speaking people to evacuate, to prevent an alleged "genocide". The Western world was witnessing an arguably deliberate increase in tension during this period, and while "Putin sat observing the war

Nora Schrader-Rashidkhan, freelance political analyst

https://doi.org/10.1515/9783111272900-018

games on screens"[1] Russia declared stated Western fears of invasion as being "hysterical and dangerous".[2] For Europe and the US, the situation was difficult to assess: the antagonists' intentions were both obscure and blatant at the same time. Confronted with such a strategic limbo, the German Foreign Minister Annalena Baerbock went on to explain that "[we] must be prepared for all scenarios".[3] Less than a week later, Russia attacked Ukraine in full-scale unprovoked aggression. The uncertainty that had built before suddenly vanished confronted by the reality of force, and a dramatic shift in European history materialised. Not only political leaders but also the public stood in shock, the realisation taking hold that the *unthinkable* had happened. German chancellor Olaf Scholz announced a *Zeitenwende* (turning point) in the country's foreign policy towards Russia in response, and there is a strong consensus that these events constitute a turning point both for Germany and the whole of Europe. All the while, other challenges loomed as well, such as the COVID-19 pandemic, the climate crisis, and the digital revolution, which also confront Western societies with presumably unknown dynamics.

However, is there something qualitatively new about these developments? Do they all carry the potential to bring about substantial change characterised as turning points? These questions should be approached with a discussion focused on uncertainty as a conceptual cornerstone. The dramatic events in the spring of 2022 exemplify a prominent factor in politics, so this chapter concentrates on outlining uncertainty from a peace and conflict perspective, to approach a clearer notion of the term. It also aims to explore the conceptual relationship with turning points, which can be understood as "a point in time at which a substantial or radical change in direction from an old to a new persistent path happens" (see introduction to this volume). To enrich the debate about this very general concept and its possible applicability, the basic notion is developed by considering the role of anticipatory knowledge and indeterminacy to allow turning points to materialise, and by integrating a subjective dimension that touches upon the allocation of meaning. Specifically, it will be argued that turning points can be understood as an *interpretation* in retrospect, of unthinkable events, that bring about substantial change. Selected political challenges will then be assessed regarding the status of knowledge (or uncertainty) and their "turning point potential" before the chapter ends with a short conclusion.

From this viewpoint, uncertainty provides a precondition for understanding turning points in a stricter sense. It is important to be aware that with this ap-

---

1 https://www.aljazeera.com/news/2022/2/19/ukraine-crisis-president-putin-launches-nuclear-drills (accessed 20 Feburary 2022).

2 https://www.reuters.com/world/europe/ukraine-temporarily-closes-checkpoint-donbass-due-shelling-2022-02-20/ (accessed 20 Feburary 2022).

3 https://www.euronews.com/2022/02/13/uk-ukraine-crisis-baerbock (accessed 17 March 2022).

proach, the quality of turning points as rare events is – and should be – emphasised. To obtain a clear analytical function, it seems necessary to develop criteria for distinguishing historical turning points from more common political events because otherwise, nearly every decision by political elites could be, de facto, considered a turning point (if the direction of political developments is influenced). It depends, of course, on the analytical function within an argument to determine if such a broad meaning is appropriate, but for a more general discussion, a stricter meaning seems to be of greater appeal. Therefore, in an attempt to develop an idea about what the relative rarity of turning points could be established on, this chapter suggests a conceptual idea to restrict the term's validity and scope by linking given turning points to uncertain knowledge. As a caveat, this is an innovative and rather strict approach that follows a certain logic; being aware of the rigidity of this procedure and its explorative nature, one should keep in mind the limits and not take it at face value as an all-encompassing explanation. Instead, this chapter should be understood as a suggestion for substantiating the debate about turning points, by emphasising the latter's rarity (in contrast to other approaches that seem to "see turning points everywhere", maybe falling prey to a frequency illusion). This should be kept in mind in the following discussion.

2 Uncertainty and the limits of knowledge in peace and conflict research

From a peace and conflict perspective as a sub-discipline of international relations (IR), it is an established conviction that "uncertainty is endemic" (Daase and Kessler 2007: 412). It is "central to every major research tradition in the study of international relations" (Rathbun 2007: 533), and "arguably the most important factor in explaining the often unique dynamics of international as opposed to domestic politics".[4] Uncertainty is a prominent feature of a system of states characterised by (supposed) anarchy and produces strong effects on actors within this system, for example, by contributing to the emergence of security dilemmas and arms spirals (for an overview see e.g. Iida 1993a; Bas, McLean, and Whang 2017; Bas and Schub 2017). To explain the occurrence of war, uncertainty "has long been identified as an important cause" (Ramsay 2017: 506) due to imperfect information (Debs and Monteiro 2013) or bargaining failures (Fearon 1995; Walter

---

4 Cioffi-Revilla (1998) in contrast underlines that uncertainty is equally prevalent in domestic politics.

2009). Others, however, posit a "pacifying effect" (Bas and Schub 2016: 1099) that, in contrast, would structurally contribute to peace within the international system under certain a priori conditions (see also Singer, Bremer, and Stuckey 1972). Considering the ubiquity of uncertainty, it seemingly depends on its type in determining if "uncertainty can be a source of peace or conflict" (Bas, McLean, and Whang 2017: 166).

Substantially, uncertainty refers to a situation of *"non*knowledge" [sic] (Smithson 1989: 1). It is a state of missing information or knowledge that is perceived as being inaccessible and/or non-existent (cf. Smithson 1989; Cioffi-Revilla 1998; Bammer and Smithson 2008). Any decision touches on uncertainty (Bammer and Smithson 2008: 3), and it is often realised in interaction with an external counterpart whose intentions we could never fully decode. Smithson points to the fact that in this regard, uncertainty "does not simply impose itself on us from the natural world;[rather] it is socially constructed" (Smithson 2008: 15). Additionally, which might be evident, "uncertainty exists because in social life the future is indeterminate" (Mitzen and Schweller 2011: 25). This indeterminate element is a condition for agency as creating space and time for one's ability to take decisions; "No uncertainty, no freedom", as Smithson argues (2008: 18; see also Battistelli and Galantino 2019). It also builds the core of political action, "because all politics is behavior ultimately grounded on individual decisions made under uncertainty" (Cioffi-Revilla and Starr 1995: 449). In the end, politics just means decisions by those in power (to decide) and it, arguably, constitutes the essence of coping with a general contingency in modern societies, that is to choose a specific direction against other plausible alternatives (cf. Rüb 2012; Geis 2012).[5]

This power of human agency is, thus, grounded in uncertainty. In political science, the term is frequently used and relevant in various areas, but due to its diffuse nature, the notion carries very different implicit meanings (Cioffi-Revilla 1998; Rathbun 2007). An early account by Knight (1921) laid the conceptual foundation by claiming that "[uncertainty] must be taken in a sense radically distinct from the familiar notion of [risk]": while the latter only covers measurable risks, true uncertainty is of "the non-quantitive type" [sic] (Knight 1921: 19–20). Keynes similarly argued that by "'uncertain' knowledge [. . .], I do not mean merely to distinguish what is known for certain from what is only probable", but that "there is no scientific basis on which to form any calculable probability whatever" (Keynes 1937: 213–214). For that reason, uncertainty originally refers to essential "limits of knowl-

---

5 Contingency "describes something given [. . .] in the light of its possibly being otherwise; it describes objects within the horizon of possible variations" (Luhmann 2005: 106). This is also related to the concept of critical junctures (e.g. Capoccia 2016).

edge" (Aradau and van Munster 2007: 103). However, scholarship makes use of less far-reaching conceptualisations as well, for example, to account for "contexts where actors do not know the outcome or realization of a trait or event but do know the range of possible outcomes and their associated probabilities" (Bas and Schub 2017: 3).[6] Many applications in IR concentrate more tightly on being oblivious to "the attributes of opponents, such as resolve or power" (Iida 1993a: 433), or on "asymmetric information" (Iida 1993b: 410). Transferring these ideas to the explanation of war and peace then suggests itself, and scholars have developed a plethora of specifications of the term. These include, to name but a few, "decisional uncertainty" (Singer, Bremer, and Stuckey 1972: 19), "strategic uncertainty" (Meirowitz and Sartori 2008: 330; Iida 1993a), "structural uncertainty" (Mitzen and Schweller 2011: 8) and traditionally, uncertainty about war outcomes, capabilities, or intentions (Bas and Schub 2016, 2017). Others even argue that "misplaced certainty" (Mitzen and Schweller 2011) is the actual crux of the matter. After 9/11, the topic gained renewed interest from researchers and political actors, who widened the scope towards the "unknown unknowns" (Daase and Kessler 2007: 412; see below) and "fundamental uncertainty" (Mitzen and Schweller 2011: 25) which is much more profound. In this case, "information that is relevant to a decision today simply does not exist and as such is by definition unknowable. This is an ontological rather than epistemic claim – namely that there is not a state of the world about which one could be certain" (Mitzen and Schweller 2011: 25).

This multitude of terms and definitions illustrates that uncertainty comes in various guises (Bas, McLean, and Whang 2017: 166). Due to limited space, I will adopt a simple taxonomy for assessing the status of knowledge in an uncertain environment: the so-called *Rumsfeld matrix*. This should help discern current and future challenges that might be (or have been) surprising but not unknowable as distinct from those that are (or have been) unthinkable for the moment – or maybe ever. I will also suggest that especially those latter challenges, which originate as not-yet-knowable phenomena, have the power and potential to generate those turning points as conceptualised here. By referring to some examples at the end of this chapter, I will illustrate the basic idea and clarify the benefits (and the limits) of this approach. First, the concept of the systematisation of choice will be introduced below.

---

6 This would correspond to Knight's "risk"; cf. Bas and Schub (2017: 3).

3 Systematising uncertainty, discerning blind spots

In a press briefing on Iraq some 20 years ago, former US Secretary of Defence Donald Rumsfeld explained to the public:

Reports that say that something hasn't happened are always interesting to me, because as we know, there are known knowns; there are things we know we know. We also know there are known unknowns; that is to say we know there are some things we do not know. But there are also unknown unknowns – the ones we don't know we don't know. And if one looks throughout the history of our country and other free countries, it is the latter category that tend to be the difficult ones.[7]

Rumsfeld's systematisation of knowledge refers to a scheme developed by two psychologists in (1955) that they used to "illustrate relationships in terms of awareness" (Luft and Ingham 1961: 6). The scheme is based on a 2 × 2 matrix that combines knowledge and/or non-knowledge of others and the self into four fields: an open area of free activity, an avoided or hidden arena, the blind area or the unknown (the "Johari window"; Luft and Ingham 1961). While the approach itself was not new, it was to Rumsfeld's supposed credit that he popularised the expression to describe new kinds of dangers in debates on international security. Daase and Kessler (2007) elaborated the concept further concerning the creation of danger in the context of uncertainty. Their basic argumentation will be outlined in the following, as they provide a concise analytical tool for assessing new challenges for Western states in an international system that is perceived as somewhat increasingly uncertain (see Figure 1). To keep a straight line of focus, all categories will be discussed with an emphasis on their relevance for understanding the challenge of uncertainty and its potential contribution in laying the ground for turning points.

The first and least opaque form of knowledge alludes to the *known knowns*. These are dangers that have a clear anchor in the knowledge that is "in principle always available" (Daase and Kessler 2007: 420). The patterns of interactions are well-established, there is consensus about the salient terms, dynamics and relevant actors, and the mechanisms of international crisis management work as expected. This dimension refers to a constrained concept of uncertainty, one that is restricted to asymmetric information about opponents' resolve or military capabilities, for instance. Correspondingly, the authors illustrate the danger of known

---

7 Cited from http://archive.defense.gov/Transcripts/Transcript.aspx#selection-1053.10-1053.486 (accessed 9 March 2022).

Empirical knowledge

		knowns	unknowns
	knowns	**Known knowns** = threats	**Known unknowns** = risks
Methodological *knowledge*			
	unknowns	**Unknown knowns** = ignorance	**Unknown unknowns** = disasters

Figure 1: The Rumsfeld matrix as adapted from Daase and Kessler (2007: 415).

knowns with deterrence operating as a means of dealing with hostile intentions, that presuppose a common language among the adversaries. This category is the open arena where uncertainty is much reduced, as the basic parameters are shared, and there is "almost no doubt about the existence, the intentions and the military capacity of the opponent" (Daase and Kessler 2007: 422).

The second type of danger as conceptualised by Rumsfeld and Daase and Kessler (2007) refers to risk as *known unknowns*. This implies that "factual knowledge is partial, yet methods exist for reducing the uncertainty" (Daase and Kessler 2007: 414). Better intelligence and deeper political analyses are the tools required to discover the unknown, reveal hidden knowledge and "help to prevent policymakers from taking risks that they do not fully understand" (Friedman 2019: 2). There are some shared ideas of what is supposedly veiled, and this corresponds to "calculable uncertainty" (Daase and Kessler 2007: 423) and risks as distinguished by Knight (1921; see above). Known unknowns are the blind spots that could be nevertheless grasped by exposure and empirical exploration. Examples of this danger are the risks of clandestine terrorism (Daase and Kessler 2007; Amoore and Goede 2008), secret military investments (Debs and Monteiro 2014), or cyberattacks (Möller 2020: 35). These dangers can be properly subject to risk management and probabilistic calculation to measure their inherent uncertainty (Aven and Guikema 2015: 2166), and it could be argued that such a structured uncertainty gives birth to policy challenges that do not transcend the limits of knowledge.

The next section of the matrix describes a situation "in which factual knowledge is available in principle, but not used because it is ignored or repressed" (Daase and Kessler 2007: 413–414). These are *unknown knowns*, that avoided arena of knowledge, posing a danger due to ignorance. This may be "the most intriguing combination" (Rayner 2012: 108) as it touches on questions of hegemonic authority in the organisation of knowledge and much less on generic uncertainty. In this sphere of "not-to-be-wanted-to-be-known knowledge" (Daase and Kessler 2007: 428) information is systematically withheld on purpose, as "admitting it to the realm of what is 'known' may undermine the organizational principles of a society or organization" (Rayner 2012: 111). Jackson argues that unknown knowns constitute subjugated knowledge which is "masked or buried by more dominant forms of knowledge" (Jackson 2012: 13), to stabilise systems of meaning and rule (Jackson 2012: 19–20). This prioritisation of information often demands some effort to keep unwanted truths hidden behind a façade of ignorance, and it is under constant threat of disruption. Additionally, unknown knowns might be things "once known but now forgotten, things known but deliberately ignored, [or] things that are known but that people wish were not true" (Lin 2021). Being unaware is, thus, not a problem of lacking information, but of knowledge processing, perception and status allocation. Debates on terrorism and the "war on terror" in Iraq provide examples of this (Daase and Kessler 2007: 429; Jackson 2012), but it also applies to environmental policies (Rayner 2012; see below). It is an interesting side note that Rumsfeld himself left out this combination in his statement, considering the context: In the news briefing, Rumsfeld informed the public about the US "war on terror" in Afghanistan and Iraq. These operations produced several, sadly iconic "documents of barbarism" (Benjamin cited from Eisenman 2007: 44) about the systematic torture of Iraqi prisoners (Hersh 2004; Hansen 2015). The practices revealed were "neither exceptional nor singular" (Puar 2005: 13) and "seemed almost routine" (Hersh 2004; see also Gordon 2006), but at the same time, there was a consensual willingness to follow the government's framing of events as isolated, exceptional outliers of "abuse" – instead of questioning more deeply the blatant use of torture – and the issue "quickly faded from the headlines" (Bennett, Lawrence, and Livingston 2006: 9). Unknown knowns as "the disavowed beliefs, suppositions, and obscene practices we pretend not to know about" (Žižek 2006: 137) are, therefore, exemplified by this. Regarding uncertainty, it is noticeable that these processes are seemingly less subject to external indeterminacy. Instead, actors actively *pretend* to suffer from a higher level of uncertainty to obscure the scope of readily available knowledge.

This brings us to the fourth category, the *unknown unknowns*. They are the most enigmatic puzzles, and Rumsfeld's statement was perceived as "frightening" and "dramatic" (Ikenberry 2002: 50) in referring to these black holes of inaccessible information. Unknown unknowns are "things we do not even dream of and have no method of anticipating" (Daase and Kessler 2007: 413). It could be a rare event "outside the realm of regular expectations, because nothing in the past can convincingly point to its possibility" (Taleb 2007: xvii); an event that carries "extreme impact", but would be considered explainable afterwards. Taleb describes these events as *Black Swans* (Taleb 2007). In a contingent world, we must admit that some "things are simply unknowable" (Bammer and Smithson 2008: 5), and this applies also to decision-makers being "not aware of what they do not know"

(Bammer and Smithson 2008: 5). Unknown unknowns are, therefore, the true blind spots; they evade the standard risk management tools of control (Slayton 2020: 87) and remain unpredictable, as they are "unimaginable" (Daase and Kessler 2007: 424). They also evade being researched in advance, since there is "no measure to tame uncertainty" (Daase and Kessler 2007: 426) in this sphere. Striving for preparedness is a losing game, and for these reasons, dangerous events result in disasters if they stem from unknown unknowns (Daase and Kessler 2007: 427–428).[8] They happen without warning and bring about severe consequences for global politics (Boeckelmann and Mildner 2011: 3), and that being the case, the potential for unleashing seismic shifts is surely the most pronounced. The paradigmatic case is the use of civilian aircraft as weapons on 9/11 (cf. Gassert 2016). Daase and Kessler give the example of nuclear terrorism as a possible threat, highlighting the fact that unknown unknowns are "not only hard to identify, but also hard to refute" (Daase and Kessler 2007: 428). In terms of turning points, this arena of striking uncertainty is, arguably, the most relevant, as turning points in a strict sense might be understood as an interpretation in retrospect of unthinkable events that cause substantial change. Admittedly, this linking of uncertainty and turning points might be courageous and, in contrast to other approaches that identify turning points on many different occasions, lead to a neatly defined notion. It intentionally restricts the applicability to very few cases that have the force to shape a new era or epoch in certain regards (by enlarging the realm of thinkable developments, for instance). Consequently, I suggest a sparing use of the term, restricted to ground-breaking events and processes, and for this understanding, a higher level of uncertainty is considered a pivotal factor. This idea will be elaborated on shortly in the following.

4 Uncertainty and turning points in perspective

This definition of turning points as an interpretation in retrospect of unthinkable events that cause substantial change is based on three elements that will be worked out roughly below. This elaboration must remain cursory here. First and inspired by the above paragraph, I would like to bring up the idea that referring to turning points as watershed moments makes less sense if the future direction is, or has been, clear and expected. Far-reaching uncertainty could, thus, be considered a precondition for understanding turning points: if the process is predetermined or largely known in advance, changes of direction are normalised, like a train on a

---

8 One could hope for resilience, however. See Folkers (2018).

winding track. Consequently, it could be argued that only an uncertain direction of future developments gives room for turning points to materialise. Known known threats, risks based on known unknowns, and ignored unknown knowns in particular then have arguably little power to give rise to turning points, as they usually do not leave the common ground of existing political narratives and miss the fundamental moment of surprise. Climate change, as one of the most important political challenges at this time, illustrates the basic thought: it is indisputable that the processes of global warming and environmental degradation will cause massive changes in the future, but the prospects have been known for decades. Data on geophysical developments such as global temperatures, sea levels and ocean warming are readily available and pointing in a clear direction. Therefore, to identify a turning point, which point in time would be decisive in terms of climate change? Not surprisingly, Eva Horn describes climate change as a "catastrophe without event" (Horn 2018) that is not taking place "in spectacular disasters, but in creeping environmental destruction, inconspicuous changes to biotopes, gradual transformations of water cycles and climate patterns" (Horn 2021: 130). From my perspective as well, and notwithstanding its significance, the planet's continuous climate evolution of the Anthropocene is too incremental, too linear and too predictable to qualify as a turning point (as long there is no sudden meteor strike). For a stronger analytical benefit and discriminatory power, I suggest considering the limits of knowledge about an event or a phenomenon to identify turning points, and this is where the systematisation developed above contributes. (Formerly) unknown unknowns, thus, carry a high potential for causing turning points, as the surprise, unexpectedness and rarity of an event should be taken into account to avoid conceptual overuse. Taleb's *Black Swan* approach, as mentioned above (Taleb 2007), is surely a valuable source in this regard, as it combines an event's stark empirical rarity and magnitude with an allocation of extraordinary meaning, and these elements relate well to turning points in the stricter sense suggested here.

The second part of my approach integrates the basic understanding of turning points as bringing about substantial change. This is an important part as well, as a sustainable effect on developments also in the long term should be identified. Several authors have argued that (historical) turning points constitute starting points for new trends or developments and inspire the emergence of new structures and paths, in *la longue durée* (see e.g. Buzan 1995: 385; Endler et al. 2016; Gassert 2016: 37; Berg 2011: 467; Carlsson 2012: 3; see also Capoccia 2016 on critical junctures). As Buzan explains, "there is still a lot of continuity, but there are also changes significant enough to create expectations that the players and the rules of the game in the new era will be noticeably different from those which came before" (Buzan 1995: 385). Therefore, turning points not only arise from uncertain conditions but also produce disorientation and uncertainty regarding appropriate reactions after the event due to a lack of preparation. It is however important that a substantial change persists, and that the (attributed) effect is not neutralised shortly after. What, then, is a substantial change? As the debates in this volume illustrate, there is not necessarily consensus about which events and processes could or should qualify as a turning point, depending on the degree of substantiality allocated to a triggered change.

The subjective perspective is, therefore, considered constitutive as a third element, but as one that involves a loophole. There are, arguably, no clear-cut criteria, but crises are "[e]xperienced as 'turning points'" (Nelson and Katzenstein 2014: 362) and interpreted with the help of ex-post constructions (Berg 2011: 463) as being historical, influential events. These interpretations "elicit new narratives, signal the obsolescence of the status quo" (Nelson and Katzenstein 2014: 362), and enforce a reaction by synchronising heterogeneous perceptions (Gassert 2016: 48). Turning points, thus, seem to imply multilevel effects: such events also uncover what people take for granted regarding basic social structures, and by interpreting an event as a turning point, a statement is also made about what is assumed to be normal in the world – while the event itself constitutes the deviant, the rare, the exceptional, the historical caesura. This perspective underlines that turning points are a matter of inter-subjective, possibly collectively shared, perceptions, a way of describing events that are considered to have altered the pathways and trajectories of whole societies. It prioritises the interpretative dimension of the term with this constructivist element (for whom is it a turning point?). It seems a fitting side note that in psychological studies, people name "strangely trivial" events (Carlsson 2012: 4) if asked to describe turning points in their life so that some researchers even argue there would be "nothing inherent in a process or event that makes it a turning point" (Carlsson 2012: 4) in itself. For political science, and for the term to keep its purpose, however, the substantial side should not be neglected.

Bringing all three aspects together, it becomes clear that a turning point cannot be identified in isolation but only within its time-related and processual environment, and hardly in advance, but only in a retrospective interpretation of events. I, therefore, suggest that the criteria developed here – combining unexpectedness, momentousness, and perception – constitute turning points in a stricter sense. It could serve as a useful concept for identifying those events that have been unpredictable (resulting from limited knowledge and inherent uncertainty), cause substantial change, and are interpreted as a caesura in retrospect. To test the descriptive and analytical power of the term to some degree, the following section will discuss selected empirical challenges regarding their turning point potential. To maintain a rigorous argumentation, I will stick with the Rumsfeld matrix and focus on the status of knowledge at the start.

5 Categorising challenges to the West: Potential turning points or just conventional threats and risks?

To assess current and emerging challenges to Western democracies, the matrix is considered helpful for weighting the role of uncertain knowledge within these challenges. This short empirical section will, therefore, apply the given taxonomy in a first attempt to sort some selected challenges and to discern those areas where the potential for turning points can be expected to be most pronounced. It will be argued that most challenges that are discussed as dramatic follow rather common patterns in terms of (limited, structured) uncertainty, so from this perspective, the situation is not as unique as assumed. The matrix is used here as an analytical lens to highlight those aspects deemed important. Still, the interpretation in terms of (un)knowns is certainly open to discussion (particularly regarding politicised unknown knowns). Due to limited space, I am only able to refer to anecdotal evidence, and a deeper analysis is left to case experts to be conducted in future studies. The selection of examples is inspired by the topics covered in the present volume and other sources discussing the dynamics of *Zeitenwende* in international politics (e.g. Krause 2017) but remains admittedly eclectic. As a caveat, it must be noted that the categories are not clear-cut but come with blurred boundaries and that the status of knowledge assigned for the moment is certainly dynamic: if there is considerable progress (or regression), a change is always possible. Lastly, and as mentioned above, the concept applied here is certainly strict, it naturally highlights some aspects – mostly the continuities – at the expense of others. Its analytical contribution should, therefore, be seen in contrast to other, more generous approaches, by strongly restricting the term's validity, to see where it leads the argument. This may cause disagreement, which is legitimate. Despite all these stumbling blocks, I suggest the following:

5.1 Known knowns within structured patterns: US–China trade war, Brexit, Trump

Some of the new challenges confronting the US and European democracies arise from a realm of "secured knowledge" (Daase and Kessler 2007: 420). These threats of known knowns could be tensions or clashes of interest emerging from a fixed frame, and the actors compete, in principle, based on factual information. The *US–China trade war* seems to correspond well to this setting. Sparked by a dispute about Chinese trade surpluses, a struggle ensued between two actors that are on a par in many respects (Steinbock 2018: 518). In this conflict about economic imbalances, traditional instruments such as punitive tariffs, economic restrictions and subsidies are employed in a dynamic cycle of accusation and retaliation (Lukin 2019; Hughes 2005; Liu and Woo 2018). The "trade war" label evokes historical analogies, and the tensions are "now being driven less by economic realities and more by great power rivalry and nationalism" (Huang 2021) – very established parameters indeed. Uncertainty is, arguably, marginal within this challenge, as actors, instruments, and intentions are largely known and accessible (for the moment). The US–China trade war would, thus, not be considered a turning point if the model applies, as the rarity, unexpectedness, and meaning are not given.

Another example could be *Brexit*: interpreting this historical turn as a challenge originating from known knowns would underline that leaving the European Union (EU) after holding a popular referendum that prescribed exactly that was no unthinkable event (or unknowable). Although the European community and parts of British society could hardly believe that this accident was happening (cf. Welfens 2018), major facts concerning the decision were secured in available knowledge. The escalating process could be traced step by step (Clarke, Goodwin, and Whiteley 2017; Evans and Menon 2017; Arnorsson and Zoega 2018), and it respected the rules-based logic of EU integration treaties, even if the procedure set a precedent. Brexit was still not going beyond the scope of the known known, although, admittedly, it was a massive surprise. This classification diminishes Brexit's significance as a potential turning point.

The *Trump presidency* would be a third example. His election represented a culmination of structural condition effects in American politics in combination with individual chutzpa; this arguably led to a "new configuration" (Lieberman et al. 2019: 471), but one that remains to be explained as a symptom of "larger historical processes" (Lieberman et al. 2019: 476). This perception does not mean underestimating the depth of the named crises for the countries concerned, but it puts into perspective the claim about uncertainty, as knowledge and management methods were available and accessible. Political failures in this category cannot be apologised for by ostensible non-knowledge, and this interpretation emphasises the continuities, not disruptions, so they would constitute no turning points.

5.2 Known unknowns: Russian aggression, Iranian nuclear aspirations, and COVID-19

The second category is related to a partial knowledge of dangers. Known unknowns are not (yet) common knowledge, and in their evaluation, there is more "emphasis on the possible rather than the probable" (Daase and Kessler 2007:

426). Still, it is possible to carve out a bigger share of knowledge with better intelligence and related measures. Thus, current security issues such as the *Russian aggression* against Ukraine (as described above) would not necessarily constitute a turning point, as "this watershed moment has been in the making for a long time" (Bunde 2022: 519). It was, therefore, predictable in principle. For the moment, the pronounced subjective allocation of historical significance balances this to some degree, and the severe restrictions on economic ties it caused, together with the inducement of NATO enlargement and changes within energy supply chains etc., however, contribute to a higher turning point potential. A substantial change is noticeable, while at the same time, the reactions do not transgress any borders of knowledge. It remains to be seen in the longer run, if, viewed at a distance, the turning point quality of the Russian war in Ukraine can be maintained.

The tension about the *Iranian nuclear programme* is another example of a risk with a higher but still definable level of uncertainty. The Iranian aspirations to establish nuclear power facilities have sparked suspicion among Western governments about clandestine production of weapons-grade uranium and plutonium, despite the country's pledges to restrict itself to civilian activities (Bowen and Kidd 2004; Dunn 2007; Bowen and Brewer 2011; Fitzpatrick 2013). A seesaw of diplomatic efforts, sanctions, deals, threats and (impeded) controls increased the mutual uncertainty, and Europe in particular experienced painful dismay when the US quit the nuclear deal unilaterally in 2018 (Alcaro 2021). Despite its opaqueness, the basic conditions of the conflict remain largely knowable, so classification as a known unknown seems suitable.

A third challenge that could be interpreted in this light is the *COVID-19 pandemic*. Although there is no identifiable actor for states to oppose in this case and the virus was new in 2020 – which implies a high level of uncertainty – established tools and instruments of public health measures were quickly applied to gain back some degree of control (quarantine, social distancing, vaccination). "Coronavirus politics" (Greer et al. 2021) emerged as a politics of crisis (Lipscy 2020), and scientific methods constantly improve our understanding of the disease. A pandemic was certainly possible at any time (but not necessarily probable), and the tools for managing the health crisis were long approved, in a sense since the Spanish Flu (cf. Drezner 2020). The spread of a contagious disease is a risk related to structured uncertainty, although further development is not yet to be foreseen in detail (cf. Smith, Blastland, and Munafò 2020; McNamara and Newman 2020). Therefore, from this perspective, it seems that, on the one hand, the pandemic will not leave its footprint as a turning point if the stricter concept is applied, as it certainly was not an unthinkable event. Drezner similarly underlines that "despite its pronounced short-term impact, COVID-19 is unlikely to have the transformative effects on international relations that so many are confidently predicting"

(Drezner 2020: 2). On the other hand, and like the Ukrainian crisis, the subjective interpretation of the pandemic could add strong weight to its turning point qualities, although there seems to be little consensus about its long-term impact and meaning. In spring 2023, the pandemic is now declared to be over (e.g. Rinaldi 2023) – at least as a political challenge – and the potent "collective fantasy to 'go back to normal'" (Paul and Haddad 2023: 227) is uphold. It remains to be seen which assessment persists in the long run.

5.3 Unknown knowns: Ignoring the climate crisis against better judgement

As has been argued above, unknown knowns relate to "tacit knowledge" (Daase and Kessler 2007: 428) which is ignored for political reasons. The challenge of the *climate crisis* provides a perfect example of this handling.[9] Regarding uncertainty in this issue, it seems that there is a massive misconception: Facts are mostly readily available, and scientists all over the world produce ever better models for forecasting the planet's future. For decades, they have kept warning about irreversible tipping points soon to be reached, but the public still largely ignores the terrifying reports, hoping for a bigger uncertainty as there is, for a better ending, in defiance of all proof (see Schnellnhuber 2006; Rockström et al. 2009; Wijkman and Rockström 2012; Bradshaw et al. 2021 and others). Daase and Kessler's description of unknown knowns as "not-to-be-wanted-to-be-known knowledge" (Daase and Kessler 2007: 428) therefore certainly fits. Bazerman strongly supports this assessment, noting: "Accepted as fact by most experts, climate change became almost impossible to ignore – yet many politicians, and the voters who elect them, have done exactly that" (Bazerman 2006: 179; see also Ravetz 2008: xv). Consequentially, the process materialises as a "predictable surprise", defined as "an event or set of events that catch an organization off-guard, despite leaders' prior awareness of all of the information necessary to anticipate the events and their consequences" (Bazerman 2006: 180). His description seems paradigmatic for an unknown known. Although uncertainty is "a pervasive feature of climate change analysis" (Pizer 1999: 255), the actual political challenge is not caused by a lack of knowledge, but rather, stems from the strategies employed such as "denial, dismissal, diversion (or decoy) and displacement" (Rayner 2012: 113). To identify a turning point in this

---

9 The categorization is surely less neutral than the others and implies a judgement about climate change as a political challenge, and about the crisis management by political decision-makers. See e.g. Jamieson 2007 on the challenges related to climate change.

challenge, the surprise of general climate change is too predictable, according to Bazerman (2006). At the same time, it should be conceded that the consequences of climate change expressed as floods, droughts, or heat waves might carry turning point potential on local levels, as an exact forecast of the time and place of catastrophic events is not yet possible in detail. Therefore, while the general direction of climate change seems clear, the potential for natural disasters as turning points on the ground remains a given. Figure 2 depicts the systematisation of current political challenges developed so far:

| | | *Empirical knowledge* | |
		knowns	unknowns
Methodological knowledge	knowns	**Known knowns** • *US-China trade war* • *Brexit* • *Trump*	**Known unknowns** • *Russia-Ukraine war* • *Iran nuclear aspirations* • *Covid-19 pandemic*
	unknowns	**Unknown knowns** • *Climate change*	**Unknown unknowns** • *?*

Figure 2: Systematisation of current political challenges according to the Rumsfeld matrix based on Daase and Kessler (2007: 415).

5.4 Unknown unknowns: A blank space

It is not possible to discuss unknown unknowns definitively in advance, as they would then, de facto, not be unknown any longer. Yet, to fill the remaining pages, it is hopefully excusable to think about areas of limited knowledge, where effects are the most difficult to assess, and where the potential for turning points is high. These could be phenomena that carry the power to transcend the linearity of human history; those that come to mind are the unknown consequences of digitalisation, the Big Data revolution, and progress in machine learning. These developments lead to "posthuman forms of security" (Amoore and Raley 2017: 7) and to algorithmic governance (Katzenbach and Ulbricht 2019; Kalpokas 2019) that already interfere with human agency and decision-making (Amoore and Raley 2017; Cantero Gamito and Ebers 2021). Technological progress brings about a new interaction with the unknown. For instance, Agostinho et al. argue that the "tension between risk and uncertainty, and the presence of the two conflicting desires for control and uncertainty" (Agostinho et al. 2019: 425) are prevalent in Big Data archives. Kalpokas notes that with "both human persons and their environments being knowable to an unprecedented extent" (Kalpokas 2019: 1), agency "suddenly becomes debatable" (Kalpokas 2019: 3). Some authors warn about inherent dangers that touch upon the very basics of liberal democracies (cf. Feldstein 2019; Helbing 2019), as the self-determination and autonomy of citizens are at stake. At the same time, algorithms might be of use to protect societies from unknown unknowns, as they bear the potential to analyse digital noise and recognise patterns in many fields better than humans do (e.g. Grothe 2016). This enables "a horizon of security in which the detection of new events can reject traditional statistical risk criteria and embrace emergent futures" (Amoore and Raley 2017: 6). By using machines, having a lead over future disasters thus becomes a possibility; at the same time, others warn that "algorithmic anticipation of individual actions [. . .] can pre-emptively colonize the future" (Rona-Tas 2020: 2). In such a setting, the meaning of knowledge and non-knowledge might need profound reinterpretation (Aradau 2017). Digitalisation and related techniques bring about unprecedented challenges for Western democracies that are not yet knowable. If a true turning point – based on an unthinkable event, causing processes or developments with extreme impact and corresponding allocation of meaning – emerges, I suggest it starts here.

6 Concluding remarks

Peace and conflict research provides some helpful sources for a better understanding of current challenges for the US and Europe that have been interpreted as being rooted in growing uncertainty within the political realm. The insight that political trajectories are principally uncertain – even in established Western democracies – comes as no surprise from this perspective. In contrast, the rather stable and routinised settings in the West that for a long time were spared massive disruptions are exceptions in global comparison. These states now seem to rise from slumber to confront an ostensibly new reality of uncertainty. This chapter introduced a systematic perspective on past, current and upcoming threats to Western democracies that focuses on the role of knowledge/non-knowledge, as summarised in Figure 2. It showed that most trends are less caused by uncertain knowledge as claimed, and there is only limited evidence for determining unprecedented levels of uncertainty (keeping in mind the lack of clear-cut boundaries and the dynamic status of knowledge). From this point of view, the difficulty of acting and governing under tense conditions of limited knowledge is a well-known challenge. The only global challenge that arguably comes with a much different quality is the digital revolution

(AI/Big Data). Regarding turning points, this chapter suggests using the label sparingly: restricted to events that have been unthinkable before, have massive consequences, and are interpreted as being historically significant in retrospect. The chapter put a stricter concept up for discussion, to distinguish substantial turning points from more usual events. Integrating the role of uncertainty proved beneficial for putting into perspective most of the currently discussed challenges. Turning points in a substantiated form thus remain rare events.

References

Agostinho, Daniela, Catherine D'Ignazio, Annie Ring, N. Thylstrup & Kristin Veel. 2019. Uncertain Archives: Approaching the Unknowns, Errors and Vulnerabilities of Big Data through Cultural Theories of the Archive. *Surveillance and Society* 17(3/4). 422–441.

Alcaro, Riccardo. 2021. Europe's Defence of the Iran Nuclear Deal: Less than a Success, More than a Failure. *The International Spectator* 56(1). 55–72.

Amoore, Louise & Mareike d. Goede (eds.). 2008. *Risk and the war on terror*. London, New York: Routledge Taylor & Francis Group.

Amoore, Louise & Rita Raley. 2017. Securing with algorithms: Knowledge, decision, sovereignty. *Security Dialogue* 48(1). 3–10.

Aradau, Claudia. 2017. Assembling (non) knowledge: Security, law, and surveillance in a digital world. *International Political Sociology* 11(4). 327–342.

Aradau, Claudia & Rens van Munster. 2007. Governing Terrorism Through Risk: Taking Precautions, (un)Knowing the Future. *European Journal of International Relations* 13(1). 89–115.

Arnorsson, Agust & Gylfi Zoega. 2018. On the causes of Brexit. *European Journal of Political Economy* 55(4). 301–323.

Aven, Terje & Seth Guikema. 2015. On the Concept and Definition of Terrorism Risk. *Risk analysis: an official publication of the Society for Risk Analysis* 35(12). 2162–2171.

Bammer, Gabriele & Michael Smithson (eds.). 2008. *Uncertainty and risk: Multidisciplinary Perspectives*. London: Earthscan.

Bas, Muhammet, Elena McLean & Taehee Whang. 2017. Uncertainty in international crises. *The Korean Journal of International Studies* 15(2). 165–189.

Bas, Muhammet A. & Robert Schub. 2017. The Theoretical and Empirical Approaches to Uncertainty and Conflict in International Relations. *Oxford Research Encyclopedia of Politics*, https://oxfordre.com/politics/view/10.1093/acrefore/9780190228637.001.0001/acrefore-9780190228637-e-537.

Bas, Muhammet A. & Robert J. Schub. 2016. How Uncertainty about War Outcomes Affects War Onset. *Journal of Conflict Resolution* 60(6). 1099–1128.

Battistelli, Fabrizio & Maria G. Galantino. 2019. Dangers, risks and threats: An alternative conceptualization to the catch-all concept of risk. *Current Sociology* 67(1). 64–78.

Bazerman, Max H. 2006. Climate Change as a Predictable Surprise. *Climatic Change* 77(1–2). 179–193.

Berg, Manfred. 2011. Der 11. September 2001 – eine historische Zäsur? *Zeithistorische Forschungen* 8(3). 463–474.

Bennett, W. Lance, Regina G. Lawrence & Steven Livingston. 2006. None dare call it torture: Indexing and the limits of press independence in the Abu Ghraib scandal. *Journal of communication* 56(39). 467–485.

Boeckelmann, Lukas & Stormy-Annika Mildner. 2011. Unsicherheit, Ungewissheit, Risiko. *SWP-Zeitschriftenschau* (2).

Böschen, Stefan & Peter Wehling (eds.). 2004. *Wissenschaft zwischen Folgenverantwortung und Nichtwissen*. Wiesbaden: VS Verlag für Sozialwissenschaften.

Bowen, Wyn Q. & Jonathan Brewer. 2011. Iran's nuclear challenge: nine years and counting. *International Affairs* 87(4). 923–943.

Bowen, Wyn Q. & Joanna Kidd. 2004. The Iranian Nuclear Challenge. *International Affairs* 80(2). 257–276.

Bradshaw, Corey J. A., Paul R. Ehrlich, Andrew Beattie, Gerardo Ceballos, Eileen Crist, Joan Diamond, Rodolfo Dirzo, Anne H. Ehrlich, John Harte, Mary E. Harte, Graham Pyke, Peter H. Raven, William J. Ripple, Frédérik Saltré, Christine Turnbull, Mathis Wackernagel & Daniel T. Blumstein. 2021. Underestimating the Challenges of Avoiding a Ghastly Future. *Frontiers in Conservation Science* 1–10.

Bratianu, Constantin & Ruxandra Bejinaru. 2021. COVID-19 induced emergent knowledge strategies. *Knowledge and Process Management* 28(1). 11–17.

Bunde, Tobias. 2022. Lessons (to be) learned? Germany's Zeitenwende and European security after the Russian invasion of Ukraine. *Contemporary Security Policy* 43(3). 516–530.

Buzan, Barry. 1995. The present as a historic turning point. *Journal of Peace Research* 32(4). 385–398.

Cantero Gamito, Marta & Martin Ebers. 2021. Algorithmic Governance and Governance of Algorithms: An Introduction. In Martin Ebers & Marta Cantero Gamito (eds.), *Algorithmic governance and governance of algorithms: Legal and ethical challenges* (Data Science, Machine Intelligence, and Lawvolume 1), 1–22. Cham: Springer.

Capoccia, Giovanni. 2016. Critical Junctures. In Karl-Orfeo Fioretos, Tulia G. Falleti & Adam D. Sheingatethe (eds.), Oxford Handbook of Historical Institutionalism, 95–108. Oxford: Oxford University Press.

Carlsson, Christoffer. 2012. Using 'Turning Points' to Understand Processes of Change in Offending: Notes from a Swedish Study on Life Courses and Crime. *British Journal of Criminology* 52 (1). 1–16.

Cioffi-Revilla, Claudio & Harvey Starr. 1995. Opportunity, willingness and political uncertainty: Theoretical foundations of politics. *Journal of Theoretical Politics* 7(4). 447–476.

Cioffi-Revilla, Claudio A. 1998. *Politics and uncertainty: Theory, models, and applications*. Cambridge, New York: Cambridge University Press.

Clarke, Harold D., Matthew J. Goodwin & Paul Whiteley. 2017. *Brexit: Why Britain voted to leave the European Union*. Cambridge: Cambridge University Press.

Daase, Christopher & Oliver Kessler. 2007. Knowns and Unknowns in the 'War on Terror': Uncertainty and the Political Construction of Danger. *Security Dialogue* 38(4). 411–434.

Debs, Alexandre & Nuno P. Monteiro. 2014. Known Unknowns: Power Shifts, Uncertainty, and War. *International Organization* 68(1). 1–31.

Delanty, Gerard (ed.). 2021. *Pandemics, Politics, and Society: Critical Perspectives on the Covid-19 Crisis*. Berlin/Boston: De Gruyter.

Drezner, Daniel W. 2020. The Song Remains the Same: International Relations After COVID-19. *International Organization* 74(S1). E18–E35.

Dunn, David H. 2007. 'Real men want to go to Tehran': Bush, pre-emption and the Iranian nuclear challenge. *International Affairs* 83(1). 19–38.

Ebers, Martin & Marta Cantero Gamito (eds.). 2021. *Algorithmic governance and governance of algorithms: Legal and ethical challenges* (Data Science, Machine Intelligence, and Lawvolume 1). Cham: Springer.

Eisenman, Stephen F. 2007. *The Abu Ghraib Effect*. London: Reaktion Books.

Endler, Tobias, Till Karmann, Martin Thunert & Simon Wendt. 2016. Einleitung. In Till Karmann (ed.), *Zeitenwende 9/11? Eine transatlantische Bilanz*, 9–28. Leverkusen-Opladen: Budrich Barbara.

Evans, Geoffrey & Anand Menon. 2017. *Brexit and British politics*. Cambridge: Polity Press.

Fearon, James D. 1995. Rationalist Explanations for War. *International Organization* 49(3). 379–414.

Feldstein, Steven. 2019. How Artificial Intelligence is Reshaping Repression. *Journal of Democracy* 30(1). 40–52.

Fitzpatrick, Mark. 2013. *The Iranian Nuclear Crisis: Avoiding worst-case outcomes* (Adelphi Paper 398). London: Routledge.

Folkers, Andreas. 2018. *Das Sicherheitsdispositiv der Resilienz: Katastrophische Risiken und die Biopolitik vitaler Systeme*. Frankfurt: Campus Verlag.

Friedman, Jeffrey A. 2019. *War and Chance: Assessing Uncertainty in International Politics*. Oxford: Oxford University Press.

Geis, Anna. 2012. Komplexität, Kontingenz und Nichtwissen als Herausforderungen demokratischen Regierens. In Katrin Toens & Ulrich Willems (eds.), *Politik und Kontingenz*, 143–160. Wiesbaden: Srpinger Fachmedien.

Gassert, Philipp. 2016. Der 11. September 2001 – ein welthistorischer Wendepunkt?. In Till Karmann (ed.), *Zeitenwende 9/11? Eine transatlantische Bilanz*, 29–49. Leverkusen-Opladen: Budrich Barbara.

Greer, Scott L., Elizabeth King, Elize Massard da Fonseca & André Peralta-Santos (eds.). 2021. *Coronavirus Politics: The Comparative Politics and Policy of COVID-19*. Ann Arbor: University of Michigan Press.

Gross, Matthias & Linsey McGoey (eds.). 2023. *Routledge International Handbook of Ignorance Studies*, 2nd edn. London: Routledge.

Grothe, Martin. 2016. Früherkennung von Bedrohungen und Risiken im Internet. Unknown Unknowns in Echtzeit. https://www.risknet.de/themen/risknews/unknown-unknowns-in-echtzeit/.

Hansen, Lene. 2015. How images make world politics: International icons and the case of Abu Ghraib. *Review of International Studies* 41(2). 263–288.

Helbing, Dirk (ed.). 2019. *Towards digital enlightenment: Essays on the dark and light sides of the digital revolution*. Cham: Springer.

Hersh, Seymour M. 2004. *Torture at Abu Ghraib. American soldiers brutalized Iraqis. How far up does the responsibility go?* The New Yorker, Annals of National Security. https://www.newyorker.com/magazine/2004/05/10/torture-at-abu-ghraib.

Horn, Eva. 2018. *The Future as Catastrophe: Imagining Disaster in the Modern Age*. New York: Columbia University Press.

Horn, Eva. 2021. Tipping Points: The Anthropocene and Covid-19. In Gerard Delanty (ed.), *Pandemics, Politics, and Society: Critical Perspectives on the Covid-19 Crisis*, 123–137. Berlin/Boston: De Gruyter.

Huang, Yukon. 2021. The U.S.-China Trade War Has Become a Cold War. https://carnegieendowment.org/2021/09/16/u.s.-china-trade-war-has-become-cold-war-pub-85352.

Hughes, Neil C. 2005. A Trade War with China? *Foreign Affairs* 84(4). 94–106.

Iida, Keisuke. 1993a. Analytic Uncertainty and International Cooperation: Theory and Application to International Economic Policy Coordination. *International Studies Quarterly* 37(4). 431–457.

Iida, Keisuke. 1993b. When and how do domestic constraints matter? Two-level games with uncertainty. *Journal of Conflict Resolution* 37(3). 403–426.

Ikenberry, G. J. 2002. America's Imperial Ambition. *Foreign Affairs* 81(5). 44–60.

Jackson, Richard. 2012. Unknown knowns: the subjugated knowledge of terrorism studies. *Critical Studies on Terrorism* 5(1). 11–29.

Jamieson, Dale. 2007. The moral and political challenges of climate change. In Susanne C. Moser & Lisa Dilling (eds.), *Creating a Climate for Change: Communicating Climate Change and Facilitating Social Change*, 475–482. Cambridge: University Press.

Johnson, Chelsea. 2021. Power-sharing, conflict resolution, and the logic of pre-emptive defection. *Journal of Peace Research* 58(4). 734–748.

Kalpokas, Ignas. 2019. *Algorithmic Governance: Politics and Law in the Post-Human Era*. Cham: Springer.

Katzenbach, Christian & Lena Ulbricht. 2019. Algorithmic governance. *Internet Policy Review* 8(4). https://policyreview.info/concepts/algorithmic-governance.

Keynes, J. M. 1937. The General Theory of Employment. *The Quarterly Journal of Economics* 51(2). 209–223.

Kilgour, D. M. & Frank C. Zagare. 1991. Credibility, uncertainty, and deterrence. *American Journal of Political Science* 35(2). 305–334.

Knight, Frank H. 1921. *Risk, uncertainty and profit*. Boston: Houghton Mifflin.

Krause, Joachim. 2017. Die neue Zeitenwende in den Internationalen Beziehungen – Konsequenzen für deutsche und europäische Politik. *SIRIUS - Zeitschrift für Strategische Analysen* 1(1). 3–24.

Lieberman, Robert C., Suzanne Mettler, Thomas B. Pepinsky, Kenneth M. Roberts & Richard Valelly. 2019. The Trump Presidency and American Democracy: A Historical and Comparative Analysis. *Perspectives on Politics* 17(02). 470–479.

Lin, Herb. 2021. The Fourth Quadrant – the Unknown Knowns. https://www.lawfareblog.com/fourth-quadrant-unknown-knowns.

Lipscy, Phillip Y. 2020. COVID-19 and the Politics of Crisis. *International Organization* 74(S1). E98–E127.

Liu, Tao & Wing T. Woo. 2018. Understanding the U.S.-China Trade War. *China Economic Journal* 11(3). 319–340.

Luft, Joseph & Harry Ingham. 1961. The Johari Window: a graphic model of awareness in interpersonal relations. *Human relations training news* 5(9). 6–7.

Luhmann, Niklas. 2005. *Social Systems. Reprinted*. Stanford, Calif.: Stanford University Press.

Lukin, Alexander. 2019. The US–China Trade War and China's Strategic Future. *Survival* 61(1). 23–50.

McNamara, Kathleen R. & Abraham L. Newman. 2020. The Big Reveal: COVID-19 and Globalization's Great Transformations. *International Organization* 74(S1). E59–E77.

Meirowitz, Adam & Anne E. Sartori. 2008. Strategic Uncertainty as a Cause of War. *Quarterly Journal of Political Science* 3(4). 327–352.

Mesquita, Bruce B. de. 1981. Risk, Power Distributions, and the Likelihood of War. *International Studies Quarterly* 25(4). 541–568.

Mitzen, Jennifer & Randall L. Schweller. 2011. Knowing the Unknown Unknowns: Misplaced Certainty and the Onset of War. *Security Studies* 20(1). 2–35.

Möller, Dietmar P.F. 2020. *Cybersecurity in Digital Transformation: Scope and Applications*. Cham: Springer International Publishing.

Moser, Susanne C. & Lisa Dilling (eds.). 2007. *Creating a Climate for Change: Communicating Climate Change and Facilitating Social Change*. Cambridge: University Press.

Nelson, Stephen C. & Peter J. Katzenstein. 2014. Uncertainty, Risk, and the Financial Crisis of 2008. *International Organization* 68(2). 361–392.

Paul, Katharina T. & Christian Haddad. 2023. The Pandemic as we Know It: A policy studies perspective on ignorance and nonknowledge in COVID-19 governance. In Matthias Gross & Linsey McGoey (eds.), *Routledge International Handbook of Ignorance Studies*, 221–233. London: Routledge.

Pizer, William A. 1999. The optimal choice of climate change policy in the presence of uncertainty. *Resource and Energy Economics* 21(3–4). 255–287.

Puar, Jasbir K. 2005. On Torture: Abu Ghraib. *Radical History Review* 93. 13–38.

Ramsay, Kristopher W. 2017. Information, Uncertainty, and War. *Annual Review of Political Science* 20(1). 505–527.

Rathbun, Brian C. 2007. Uncertain about Uncertainty: Understanding the Multiple Meanings of a Crucial Concept in International Relations Theory. *International Studies Quarterly* 51(3). 533–557.

Ravetz, Jerome. 2008. Preface. In Gabriele Bammer & Michael Smithson (eds.), *Uncertainty and risk: Multidisciplinary Perspectives*, xiii–xvi. London: Earthscan.

Rayner, Steve. 2012. Uncomfortable knowledge: the social construction of ignorance in science and environmental policy discourses. *Economy and Society* 41(1). 107–125.

Rinaldi, Gabriel. 2023. The pandemic is over, says German health minister: Germany has overcome the COVID-19 pandemic successfully and with a good record, says Karl Lauterbach. https://www.politico.eu/article/coronavirus-pandemic-covid-19-germany-virus-lockdown/.

Rizzo, Rachel. 2022. Will the wake-up call last beyond this crisis? https://www.atlanticcouncil.org/blogs/new-atlanticist/experts-react-whats-behind-germanys-stunning-foreign-policy-shift/.

Rockström, Johan, Will Steffen, Kevin Noone, Åsa Persson, F. S. Chapin, Eric F. Lambin, Timothy M. Lenton, Marten Scheffer, Carl Folke, Hans J. Schellnhuber, Björn Nykvist, Cynthia A. de Wit, Terry Hughes, Sander van der Leeuw, Henning Rodhe, Sverker Sörlin, Peter K. Snyder, Robert Costanza, Uno Svedin, Malin Falkenmark, Louise Karlberg, Robert W. Corell, Victoria J. Fabry, James Hansen, Brian Walker, Diana Liverman, Katherine Richardson, Paul Crutzen & Jonathan A. Foley. 2009. A safe operating space for humanity. *Nature* 461. 472–475.

Rona-Tas, Akos. 2020. Predicting the Future: Art and Algorithms. *Socio-Economic Review* 18(3). 893–911.

Rüb, Friedbert. 2012. Politische Entscheidungsprozesse, Kontingenz und demokratischer Dezisionismus. Eine policy-analytische Perspektive. In Katrin Toens & Ulrich Willems (eds.), *Politik und Kontingenz*, 117–142. Wiesbaden: Springer Fachmedien.

Russett, Bruce (ed.). 1972. *Peace, War, and Numbers*. Beverly Hills: Sage Publications.

Sauer, Tom. 2007. Coercive diplomacy by the EU: the Iranian nuclear weapons crisis. *Third World Quarterly* 28(3). 613–633.

Schellnhuber, Hans Joachim. 2006. *Avoiding Dangerous Climate Change*. Cambridge: University Press.

Singer, J. David, Stuart Bremer & John Stuckey. 1972. Capability distribution, uncertainty, and major power war, 1820–1965. In Bruce Russett (ed.), *Peace, War, and Numbers*, 19–48. Beverly Hills: Sage Publications.

Slater, Dan & Erica Simmons. 2013. Coping by colluding: Political uncertainty and promiscuous powersharing in Indonesia and Bolivia. *Comparative Political Studies* 46(11). 1366–1393.

Slayton, Rebecca. 2021. Governing Uncertainty or Uncertain Governance? Information Security and the Challenge of Cutting Ties. *Science, Technology, & Human Values* 46(1). 81–111.

Smith, George D., Michael Blastland & Marcus Munafò. 2020. Covid-19's known unknowns: The more certain someone is about covid-19, the less you should trust them. *The BMJ (Clinical research ed.)* 371(m3979). 1–2.

Smithson, Michael. 1989. *Ignorance and Uncertainty: Emerging Paradigms*. New York: Springer New York.

Smithson, Michael. 2008. The Many Faces and Masks of Uncertainty. In Gabriele Bammer & Michael Smithson (eds.), *Uncertainty and risk: Multidisciplinary Perspectives*, 13–25. London: Earthscan.

Steinbock, Dan. 2018. U.S.-China Trade War and Its Global Impacts. *China Quarterly of International Strategic Studies* 04(04). 515–542.

Taleb, Nassim N. 2007. *The black swan: The impact of the highly improbable.* New York: Random House.

Vasquez, John A. 1993. *The War Puzzle.* Cambridge: University Press.

Walter, Barbara F. 2009. Bargaining Failures and Civil War. *Annual Review of Political Science* 12(1). 243–261.

Wehling, Peter. 2004. Weshalb weiß die Wissenschaft nicht, was sie nicht weiß? – Umrisse einer Soziologie des wissenschaftlichen Nichtwissens. In Stefan Böschen & Peter Wehling (eds.), *Wissenschaft zwischen Folgenverantwortung und Nichtwissen*, 35–102. Wiesbaden: VS Verlag für Sozialwissenschaften.

Welfens, Paul J. J. 2018. *BREXIT aus Versehen: Europäische Union zwischen Desintegration und neuer EU*, 2nd edn. Wiesbaden: Springer.

Widmaier, Wesley W., Mark Blyth & Leonard Seabrooke. 2007. Exogenous Shocks or Endogenous Constructions? The Meanings of Wars and Crises. *International Studies Quarterly* 51(4). 747–759.

Wijkman, Anders & Johan Rockström. 2012. *Bankrupting Nature: Denying Our Planetary Boundaries.* London: Routledge.

Žižek, Slavoj. 2006. Philosophy, the "unknown knowns," and the public use of reason. *Topoi* 25(1–2). 137–142.

Index

https://doi.org/10.1515/9783111272900-019

www.ingramcontent.com/pod-product-compliance
Lightning Source LLC
Chambersburg PA
CBHW071728270326
41928CB00013B/2597